PUBLISHER'S NOTE

MICRO-OFFSET BOOKS are published in editions of from 100 to 250 copies. The titles issued in this series consist largely of reprints of out of print and scarce books required by those doing research work, and for which only an extremely limited sale is possible. Copies of the original edition have become practically unobtainable at any price; the occasional one that might prove available generally is priced far beyond the means of most libraries or scholars.

It thus becomes necessary to employ some method of reproducing these books in very small editions and at a moderate price.

Our method of reprinting such volumes hence makes available again titles that might otherwise prove unobtainable, perhaps for all time.

Amos Kendall

AUTOBIOGRAPHY

OF

AMOS KENDALL.

EDITED BY HIS SON-IN-LAW,

WILLIAM STICKNEY.

NEW YORK
PETER SMITH
1949

Lithographed In The United States of America
N. Y. LITHOGRAPHING CORP., NEW YORK 3, N. Y.

INTRODUCTION.

THE present work has been prepared in compliance with the wish of him whose career it undertakes to describe. In his life Mr. Kendall shunned personal notoriety, with a sensitiveness remarkable in one so accustomed to public station and contact with the world. He was widely known, as much so perhaps as any American of his time; but it was in his public capacity as an editor, as a government official, as a politician, as the promoter of a great material enterprise. Of his private life the outside world knew but little. What a husband he was, what a father, friend, and Christian, the thousands who honored his great powers and admired his achievements were almost wholly ignorant.

It is not the object of the present work to expose to public scrutiny his inner private life. Its purpose is simply to set forth the leading facts in his career, to exhibit his intense patriotism, which was indeed his ruling passion, and to make such revelations of his purely personal history as are essential to the completeness and symmetry of the narrative. The means to that end, the materials for the work, have been almost wholly furnished by his own hand, and this memoir, though edited by another, is, in fact as in name, an autobiography.

It is often said that the history of every human life, even the humblest, furnishes some instructive pages, and it was a recognition of this truth, and a consciousness that his own experience had been rich, far beyond the average, in lessons especially fitted for the guidance of American youth, that prompted his desire that this record should be made. That his estimate of the exemplary value of his own career was just, it is believed the following pages will sufficiently prove. If they do not, — if there shall be found few instructive lessons, whose observance is a condition of our national welfare, in the life of Amos Kendall, — it may still be claimed that his was purely and distinctively an American life, and as such deserves careful study in these days when nationality is in danger of fading into a mere ideal sentiment.

The work of the editor in the preparation of this volume has been mainly that of selection and arrangement. The mere story of Mr. Kendall's career is, for the most part, told in his own words, — than which no words could tell it better. These writings represent and reflect with strict fidelity the nature of their author, and are themselves comprehensively and felicitously biographical.

The editor's chief difficulty has been in selecting from the great mass of Mr. Kendall's writings those best fitted for a place in the present work. This difficulty has been a serious one, and the necessity of confining the volume within reasonable limits has caused the omission of a large amount of matter which seemed, and still seems, essential to a satisfactory treatment of the subject. But it was necessary to draw the line somewhere, and this the editor has done according to his best judgment.

In offering this autobiography to the public, the editor has made no claim for it of literary merit or artistic and effective construction. Its preparation has been to him a labor of love, and if he has succeeded in giving a view not wholly unworthy and inadequate of the life and character of one whom it was his privilege to know intimately and love tenderly, — one of the very last of "the simple great ones gone," — he will consider his labor well bestowed, and his reward sufficient.

WM. STICKNEY.

WASHINGTON, D. C., February 1, 1872.

CONTENTS.

CHAPTER I.

CHAPTER II.

CHAPTER III.

CHAPTER IV.

CHAPTER V

CHAPTER VI.

CHAPTER VII.

CHAPTER VIII.

CHAPTER IX.

CHAPTER X.

Residence of Amos Kendall, Washington, D. C.

AUTOBIOGRAPHY OF AMOS KENDALL.

CHAPTER I.

THE Kendall family is one of the oldest in New England. The traditions of the family represent that two brothers, Thomas and Francis Kendall, came from England about 1640, and settled in Woburn, Massachusetts. Thomas had no sons.

Francis Kendall, the progenitor of the family, had four sons, Francis, Thomas, Ralph, and Jacob, — all born in America.

Jacob, born in 1686, was twice married, and had nine sons, Jacob, Daniel, Joseph, and Hezekiah by his first wife, and John, Ebenezer, David, Nathan, and Abraham by his second wife.

John, Ebenezer, and Abraham moved to Dunstable about the year 1726. There John had five sons, John, Jacob, Temple, Edward, and Zebedee.

John the second had two sons, John and Zebedee.

Zebedee, the father of Amos, had nine sons, six of whom grew to manhood; namely, Zebedee, Samuel, George-Minot, Amos, John, and Timothy. All these were living in 1858, presenting an array of old men not common in the same brotherhood.

Amos Kendall was born on Sunday, the 16th day of August, 1789. From early boyhood he was habituated to hard work on his father's farm. The farm was composed of bog meadow, pine plains, and oak hills. The meadows yielded the coarser kinds of grasses intermixed with various ferns, cranberry-vines, and small bushes; but they also supplied most of the hay on which the cattle subsisted during the long New England winters. Through these meadows meandered a sluggish stream called Salmon Brook, stocked with various kinds of fish. The pine plains rested on a bed of gravel, and, except along the foot of the hills, were almost barren. From these, however, the bread of the family was for the most part drawn. Next to the hills there were two four-acre fields cultivated alternately in corn and rye. The corn crop was always manured, and the rye was sown in the fall among the corn; so that these fields were manured alternately every other year. The plains between these fields and the meadows were generally used as sheep pastures, but once in five or six years they produced a very small crop of rye of excellent quality.

The oak hills were composed of clay soil, so full of rocks in many places as to preclude cultivation without removing them. With great labor small tracts were so far cleared as to become good upland meadow, furnishing excellent hay for horses and working oxen. These uplands supplied an abundance of stones, with which the whole farm, except the pine plains, was enclosed; the fences were of stone combined with posts and rails. The upland meadows were cultivated in potatoes or corn once in five or six years, but seldom in rye, on account of its inferior quality when produced on a clay soil. A patch of flax was generally a part of the annual crop, and this, with the wool from a small flock of sheep, manufactured and made up in the household, furnished almost the entire clothing of the family.

The rougher portions of the upland, much of which was never cultivated, furnished pasturage for the horses, oxen, and milch cows during the summer; but as much of the stock as was not used on the farm was generally driven in the spring to a pasture on Flat Mountain, in New Ipswich, N. H., twenty-five miles distant, whence it was brought back in the fall.

The father and mother of Amos Kendall were exemplary members of the Congregational Church, of which the former was a deacon. Grace before and thanks after meat, and morning and evening prayers, with the reading of a chapter in the Bible and the singing of a hymn on Sunday, accompanied by the bass-viol, played by their oldest son while he was at home, constituted the regular religious exercises of the family. The father and mother never failed to attend church on Sunday, except in case of sickness or when absent from home; and the entire family, one member only excepted, were required to maintain a like regularity in Sabbath observances. Except in special cases, all labor beyond the simplest preparation of food for man and beast and all recreation were strictly prohibited on Sunday. The evening was spent in learning and reciting the Westminster Catechism, in reading

religious books, and in practising sacred music. The whole family could sing, and when all were present, could carry all the four parts of ordinary tunes.

The family government was strict, and, so far as it bore upon their eldest children, severe. They were not only prohibited from dancing, playing cards, and all like amusements, but from going to places where they were practised. The consequence was, that the elder sons deceived their parents and indulged in those forbidden recreations clandestinely. But a change came over the father and mother before Amos grew up, and with him and the younger children advice and admonition took the place of prohibition.

The change which took place in the minds of this worthy pair with reference to domestic discipline is well illustrated by an example. When Amos was a little boy, a fiddle was an abomination to his father and mother. His eldest brother, who had quite a taste for music, having constructed a bass-viol or two, determined to try his hand upon a fiddle, and produced a very good instrument.

Not daring to bring it to the house, he kept it in a cooper's shop not far distant. His father, hunting there for something one day, mounted a bench, so that his head was raised above the beams of the shop, when his eyes fell upon the unlucky fiddle. He took it by the neck, and apostrophizing it, "*This is the first time I ever saw you*," dashed it into the fireplace.

Being on a visit to his parents about thirty years afterwards, Amos Kendall went to meeting in Dunstable on a Sunday, and there sat his father in the deacon's seat beneath the pulpit, as in former times, and *there was a fiddle in the choir!*

The early education of Amos was in the free schools of Massachusetts and New Hampshire. The boundary line between these States ran through his father's farm, who paid a school tax in both States, and had the privilege of sending his children to school in both. The summer schools were taught by women, and were in general attended only by children who were not old enough to assist their parents in their daily labors. They were generally kept from two to three months in each summer. The winter schools were usually kept by men, and lasted from six weeks to two months in each year. They were open to children of all ages from infancy to manhood.

These schools were from one to two miles distant from Deacon Kendall's, and having five children, of whom Amos was the youngest, and one niece to be taught, he hired a female teacher one winter and established a school at home. Here Amos won his first distinction. He had just begun to read and spell, and had no lessons to learn beyond the spelling-book. But he spelled in a class with the other children, and the teacher having promised a book to the one who should keep longest at the head, the prize was awarded to him, the youngest competitor.

At school he was obedient and studious, excelling in all branches except penmanship, in which he seemed to feel little interest. He was particularly fond of arithmetic, and by means of sums set by his elder brothers, and worked out in evenings by the light of the kitchen fire, he became master of the fundamental rules before he was allowed to cipher at school. He had just begun to read when he heard his father promise his elder brother George, that if he would read the Bible through in one year, he would give him a new one. He asked his father whether he could have a new one on the same condition, and was answered in the affirmative. The prize was easily won.

It was the custom of Deacon Kendall to allow his boys about two hours' nooning in the summer. A large portion of this time and of the winter evenings Amos devoted to reading, while the other boys were at play. There was a small township library in Dunstable, in which his father held two shares, entitling him to take out a book on each share and retain it two months. The use of one of these shares he gave to Amos, who in a very few years had read nearly every book in the library. On one occasion he brought home the second volume of Morse's large Geography, when his father smilingly asked, "Do you expect to read that through in two months?" Receiving an affirmative answer, he said, "Well, if you do, I will give you a pistareen." This was a Spanish coin then in circulation, worth about twenty cents. The pistareen was earned and paid.

This early reading was, perhaps, better remembered than the reading of subsequent years, since almost every sentence of it presented some new idea to the impressible and expanding mind. The value of it, especially in relation to geography and history, was fully appreciated by him in subsequent stages of his education.

In the free schools Amos had but one competitor for pre-eminence in spelling. This was a little girl of about his own age, named Sally Wright. For two or three years the competition was very keen, though Sally took the lead. At spelling-matches, then quite common, she was always the first chosen, and Amos Kendall was the first on the other side. Owing, however, to the superior advantages possessed by the latter, he finally took the lead of his fair rival. In this competition there was not a particle of envy or ill-will; on the contrary, the boy admired little Sally Wright for her smartness, and thought that when they grew up he would ask her to be his wife. But the Fates otherwise ordered. Sally married a worthless man. It was perhaps thirty years before she and her youthful competitor and admirer again met. He was then casually passing her residence, which bore all the outward signs of poverty, when it occurred to him to call, for the double purpose of seeing her once more and ascertaining whether she would recognize him. He knocked and was told to come in. On entering he beheld Sally Wright sitting in a plain but cleanly room, with several children around her, all clad in coarse clothing, but as neat as a good mother's labor could make them. "Do you not know me?" said he. "No, sir," was her reply. "Do you not recollect the boy, Amos Kendall, who used to go to school with you?" She sprang from her chair, and seized his hand, as if he had been a long-lost brother. The last he heard of her she was a widow, living with a brother.

So sober and thoughtful was Amos when a little boy, that he was generally called "the Deacon." Though often praised for his scholarship, he was as diffident and bashful as any girl. This peculiarity was, no doubt, natural; but in after life he attributed it chiefly to a singular incident which occurred when he was a little boy.

Though Dunstable was more than thirty miles from the sea, tales of money buried in that region by pirates, particularly by one Captain Kidd, were current among the population, and generally credited. This money was supposed to be in iron pots under the special charge of the Devil, who, though he could not harm those who might dig for it, would employ all sorts of noises and terrifying apparitions to scare them away, and not succeeding, would turn the money into something else. In this shift, however, his infernal majesty might be baffled by laying upon the transmuted money a Bible and an open penknife, under the influence of which it would, in the course of a few days, resume its original character.

One of Amos's elder brothers was a full believer in these tales, and the boys of the neighborhood entered into a conspiracy to test his courage.

They filled two small iron pots with blacksmith's cinders and buried them under a large white pine-tree in the midst of a dense wood. One of the boys was then commissioned to notify the destined victim that money was buried in that spot, and propose that they two should go in the night and dig for it. Arrangements were made, and in the middle of a dark night, rendered darker by the surrounding forests, the boys repaired with lanterns and tools to the designated spot, and began operations. They had not proceeded far before strange noises were heard in the bushes around them: dogs barked, cats mewed, sheep bleated, cows lowed, and horses neighed. The diggers came to a big root of the white pine, which they began to cut away. The noises redoubled, accompanied by the blowing of trumpets and other alarming sounds. Under the big root they came upon a large black snake lying upon a flat stone, which the companion of young Kendall pretended to kill. At this stage the noises became terrific: dogs howled, cats yelled, cattle bellowed, women screamed, and bang, bang, went guns over their heads in the pine-tree and among the surrounding bushes. Though his companion pretended to be much terrified, the brave boy, who believed it all the work of the Devil, nothing daunted hauled out the black snake, and, turning up the stone on which it was deposited, came upon the eagerly sought treasure; but the Devil had transmuted the gold and the silver into common blacksmith's cinders. As this was not unexpected, the boys lugged the pots home and deposited them in young Kendall's chamber, placing upon the cinders in each a Bible and an open penknife. There Deacon Kendall found them a few days afterwards and pitched them out of the window.

This incident led Amos to conclude that his father's children were not so smart as the neighbors' boys, and, enhancing his natural diffidence, produced a bashfulness and reserve which became habitual and invincible. Only once during boyhood was it thoroughly overcome in the presence of strangers. On a public occasion a larger boy began to insult and abuse his next older

brother, when young Amos, highly excited, opened upon and soon silenced him. The lookers-on thereupon insisted upon the vanquished blackguard's "treating" Amos and his brother, which he did, — with rum-toddy and gingerbread.

The mind of Amos Kendall always had a mechanical turn. When a boy, he constructed in a rude way the machinery of little wind and water mills and put them in operation. He thought much on means of using the air as a regular motive power, but with no result. He invented, however, a pump, on a principle not in use in this country, and never, so far as he knew, put into operation. His father had a cider-press operated by two large wooden screws. It occurred to him that if the threads had a water-tight covering, and one end of the screw was immersed at a suitable angle in water, and then made to revolve in the right direction, the water must necessarily follow the groove and be discharged at the top. With a jackknife he cut a groove around a stick of pine wood, tied over it a sheepskin, which made it nearly water-tight, and, turning it with the hand, one end being immersed in water, found it to answer his expectations.

Years afterwards he learnt that it was an old invention attributed to Archimedes, and had long been in use in Holland for draining marshes. Yet the conception was as original with Amos Kendall as it was with the first inventor.

It was a part of the parental teaching in the Kendall family never wantonly to take the life of any creature, snakes excepted. Birds and beasts which destroyed the farmers' crops, or were valuable for food, or on account of their skins, were fair game for his boys. In the neighboring streams and meadows were minks and muskrats, which were trapped by them, and the skins sold to raise "spending-money." Many an autumn morning Amos left his bed before daylight, and, walking or running two or three miles, visited his traps, and got home before sunrise. The boys were also allowed to cultivate a small patch of tobacco, which they manufactured into "pigtail" and sold to the chewers in the neighborhood. From these two sources were derived nearly all the funds they were able to control.

The amusements of Deacon Kendall's boys, other than such as are common to all youngsters, were fishing, both with the rod and spear, and hunting on a small scale. Salmon Brook, which ran through their father's farm, was stocked with a great variety of

fish, though none of them were large. Fishing with the spear was chiefly practised at night. The boys had a skiff, constructed by the oldest brother, in the centre of which was raised a jack, composed of iron ribs, upon a standard four or five feet high. On this were piled pine-knots, which, being set on fire, produced a brilliant light. The pickerel sleep in still water near the surface, and by careful rowing they may be closely approached. It was a beautiful sight to see them lying motionless near the surface of the water; but it was cruel sport to strike them dead in that condition.

An incident occurred while the boys were fishing with the rod which made a deep impression on the mind of Amos. They were joined by some neighboring boys, who suggested that fishes' eyes were excellent bait. The experiment was tried, and several fish just caught having been ruthlessly deprived of their eyes, the sport proceeded with gratifying results. One of the boys put back into the stream a sunperch, yet in full life, both of whose eyes had thus been extracted. This method of providing bait was new to the young Kendalls, but when they gleefully described it to their father, he gave them an impressive lecture upon its cruelty, and painted so vividly the condition of the poor blind fish returned to its native element to starve, that throughout his long life Amos Kendall, whenever he thought of it, seemed to see the mutilated creature, as he saw it then, making its dark way through the water among the bulrushes of Salmon Brook. It was thoughtlessness, and not cruelty, which furnished the occasion for this useful lecture.

The following instance of the motherly affection of a mouse, witnessed by Amos Kendall, and the impression it made upon him, are not unworthy of record.

He was passing in the fall through his father's cornfield, when he came upon a bundle of cornstalks lying between two rows, which had been overlooked when the rest were removed. He raised it up, when a mouse ran out of a nest which she had made under it. He sprang forward to kill her, when she suddenly stopped and turned back. Struck with this singular movement, he paused to await the result. The mouse came up to him, appearing to be perfectly tame. He stooped and put down his hand to her, when she crept into it and up his arm in the most confiding manner. On examining the nest, he found it full of young ones. It was evident that maternal affection had conquered fear; and her

movements were so much like an appeal for mercy to her offspring, that young Kendall gently replaced the bundle of stalks upon the nest, and left her to raise her family in peace.

The day on which the Governor of Massachusetts was inaugurated was formerly known as "'Lection Day." It was a holiday for the farmers' boys, who spent it in fishing, hunting, or such other amusements as they might fancy. It was in the latter part of May, a season at which the birds had hatched their young or laid their eggs, and the boys of the neighborhood were accustomed to have a hunt on that day for blackbirds' eggs, for the birds themselves, for crows and other feathered game. A blackbird's egg counted one, a blackbird two, a crow's egg or a young crow five, an old crow ten, etc. A meeting was held and sides chosen some days before "'Lection Day," and the woods were scoured for crows' nests. If any were found containing young ones, these were generally taken home and fed until the day of the hunt, for no bird not killed on that day was to be counted. The day was chiefly spent in exploring the bog meadows along Salmon Brook for blackbirds' eggs, and at first quarts of eggs were collected. In the afternoon the parties all came in, and the side which exhibited the most game was the victor. The day's amusement was closed by *threshing eggs*. In this game an egg was placed on the ground, and the thresher, taking his stand about two rods distant, with a large switch in his hand, advanced, with his eyes shut, and made a blow at the egg. The only reward of victory in the hunt or the game was the pride of success.

These hunts were encouraged by the farmers of the neighborhood as means of diminishing the number of mischievous birds, and they were eminently successful.

To that end young Amos contributed in another way. There was a large stake by the side of a causeway through his father's meadow, upon the top of which he observed a blackbird almost always standing. He set a small steel trap upon the top of this stake, and at first caught nearly a dozen birds a day. The survivors seemed finally to understand that there was danger at the stake, and captures soon became unfrequent. One morning the trap was missing, and not a trace of it could be found. Some time in the day a flock of crows in the edge of the woods, a few hundred yards distant, attracted attention by angry screams and violent plunges among the bushes. It proved that a large owl was there, with the lost trap hanging by the middle claw of one of his feet. He had carried it thus far, and being unable to alight in the trees, had fallen upon the ground. He could rise a few feet, but the weight of the trap dragged him down again. The owl was easily despatched, and thenceforward the trap was fastened.

One winter, when Amos was about fourteen years old, two or three neighboring men, after a deep snow, called at his father's to borrow tools for the purpose of digging out a fox which they had traced into a burrow in a neighboring wood. His brother George and himself accompanied them and witnessed the operation. After the next snow-storm they also went fox-hunting. Falling upon a track, they followed it to the burrow where the fox had sought shelter. With no great labor they opened it, and found therein two foxes, which they secured. Thus encouraged, they sallied out after the next storm, and soon caught a fox in the same way. They then took a wide circuit and came within a quarter of a mile from home, when they saw a fox at a distance wallowing through the snow, and gave chase. He, however, showed no disposition to burrow, but led them on a run about a mile and a half directly from home, when it becoming dark they gave up the pursuit. The snow was nearly knee-deep, and they were much heated and fatigued by the race. After stopping at a neighbor's and procuring a drink of cider they made towards home; but Amos complained of weariness in his limbs, which increased as he progressed, so that within half a mile of his father's house he gave out. He remembered having heard his grandfather speak of sleeping comfortably under the snow when out on a hunt, and proposed to his brother to cover him with the same bedding and go home for a horse. After attempting in vain to assist him to walk, his brother accordingly removed the snow with his feet, when Amos laid down on the ground, and, with the fox-skin over his face, was covered with several inches of snow. He fell asleep instantly and had a pleasant nap. Waking, he felt perfectly well, and thought he could walk home; but on getting up and making the attempt he found it impossible. The sinews of his legs seemed entirely unstrung, and he had no control over them. It was now night; but he was soon relieved by seeing his brother approaching through the darkness with a horse. Aided by his brother he mounted and rode home, but after his arrival could not walk without assistance. He felt entirely well, however, ate his supper

as usual, was assisted to bed, and the next morning was as strong as ever. But this was the last of Amos's fox-hunting.

For some three years, after Amos was eleven years old, he lived with his grandfather, who occupied a house about twenty rods from his father's. His duties were to cut the wood, make the fires, look after a few cattle, and do whatever jobs and errands his grandfather and grandmother might require of him. During this period, however, he labored with his brothers on his father's farm the most of the day, doing the "chores" at his grandfather's in the mornings and evenings.

During the year 1803 and 1804 nearly all the labors of the farm fell upon Amos and his brother George, who was nearly two years his senior, his elder brother having left home, and his father being disabled by rheumatism.

At this time he could do a man's work at mowing, reaping, chopping, and any other kind of ordinary farm labor. But the demands of the farm were so incessant and engrossing that he was unable to go to school more than two or three weeks in each of those years.

Deacon Kendall had become desirous to give his son Amos a liberal education; but his own means were not equal to such an expenditure. He, however, told his son that if he was disposed to go to college, and fit himself for a professional life, he would aid him to the extent of his ability. Having no predilection for any profession, and knowing that his life must be one of toil, Amos would have been content to be a farmer; but his love of knowledge induced him to avail himself of his father's kind offer.

His first object was to fit himself with all possible economy for teaching school, in order that he might, by his own earnings, eke out his father's scanty allowance. He had already made good progress in arithmetic and English grammar, when in the fall of 1804 his father closed a bargain with the preacher of the parish, according to which Amos was to live with the preacher during the winter, cut his fire-wood, take care of his horse and cattle, etc., and in return should receive instruction in the above-named branches. This turned out to be a most disagreeable and unprofitable arrangement. The preacher was morose, indolent, and thoroughly selfish. His sole study seemed to be to receive from Amos as much labor, and give in return as little instruction as possible. Much of the labor required of the boy was utterly unprofitable:

he was made to shovel paths from the house to the barn while snow was falling rapidly, filling them as fast as they were cleared.

But this was not all; the housework of the family was done by an orphan girl about Amos's own age, who had been intrusted to the care of the preacher's wife by her dying father. She was remarkably kind and amiable in her disposition, and, as far as he could judge, inoffensive in her conversation. Yet, upon the allegation that she had told falsehoods about family affairs to some of the neighbors, she was prohibited from visiting or speaking to any one out of the family, or holding any conversation with visitors except in the presence of the preacher or of his wife or his wife's mother. For the most trivial things she was incessantly scolded, and sometimes threatened even with horsewhipping. Amos sincerely pitied the girl, while he learned to hate and despise her tyrants, and he became the bearer of correspondence between her and her old associates in the outer world.

He was himself thoroughly homesick; but he was afraid to complain to his father, who was one of the deacons of the church, and appeared to have perfect confidence in his pastor. He therefore made the best of his uncomfortable situation, and endured it until he was called home in the spring of 1805.

Some time in the next summer his father asked him whether, while at the preacher's, he had been the bearer of any letters to his housemaid from the neighboring girls. He replied that he had; and not waiting for reproof, if any was intended, proceeded to tell his father how the girl was treated, and added that he had carried the letter in pure compassion, and would do the same again under like circumstances. His father was silent, but afterwards asked his son whether he would like to live with the preacher again the next winter. To this the son replied, that, if kept at work all day and furnished with a light at night, he could learn more at home than he could at the preacher's. The subject was never mentioned again.

Up to that time Amos looked upon preachers as almost perfect men, possessed of all those virtues and graces which belong to the Christian character, according to the New Testament, but he now found that they were no better than their neighbors.

In the fall of 1805 he became for about eleven weeks a pupil in the academy at New Ipswich, N. H. He boarded at the house of his brother Samuel, who lived a mile and a half from the academy, went thither to dinner every day, and paid for his board

by work on his brother's farm evening and morning. The expense to his father was twenty cents a week for tuition, and about six dollars in all for books.

This may be considered Amos Kendall's first entrance upon the theatre of the great world, and the opening scenes were by no means agreeable to him. Having been raised, thus far, among plain farmers, he had little knowledge of human nature, and none of the habits and humors of the more cultivated classes of society. Conscious of his own deficiencies, he looked upon every one as his superior, and was confused at the slightest incident or remark which could be construed as a disparaging reference to himself. Noting his sensitiveness, some of the boys took pleasure in annoying him by criticisms on his person and manners, against which his diffidence rendered him entirely defenceless. The discomforts of his situation were aggravated by the injudicious, or it may have been wanton, conduct of his preceptor. Before he had a chance to witness the performances of the other pupils, he was required to speak a piece of his own selection before the school. Receiving no instruction as to the length or character of the piece suited to the occasion, he committed to memory an oration, which occupied seven octavo pages in a school-book then in use, called "Webster's Third Part."

At the time of the performance he took his position, fixed his eyes upon the other side of the room, and repeated the whole oration, without moving hand or foot. His preceptor—who ought to have perceived, if he did not, that the selection of such a piece and the awkward performance were the result of ignorance and bashfulness, which demanded from a just and judicious teacher commiseration and encouragement— ridiculed him unmercifully, comparing him to an immovable hydrant pouring forth its steady stream of water. He carried his ridicule so far, that resentment took the place of mortification in the bosom of the young orator, and he resolved to show his persecutors that he could overcome the difficulties under which he labored.

The next winter he spent at home, except one month, during which he attended a free school in New Ipswich. His time at home was spent in labor, in reading, and in practising declamation. He committed to memory several pieces, and spoke them before a glass, studying emphasis and gesticulation, — performing himself the office of critic and instructor.

On the 15th of April, 1806, he resumed his studies at New Ipswich Academy, boarding at his brother's, and paying for his board by manual labor, morning and evening, as in the preceding season. The only addition to his expenses was the price of a dinner in the village, at twenty cents per day, during the hot summer weather.

Soon after his return to New Ipswich he was again called upon for an exercise in declamation. He selected one of the pieces he had practised during the preceding winter, and spoke it with a good degree of self-possession, and with appropriate action. His preceptor commended his performance, and his fellow-students said, " You have greatly improved since last year ; where have you been to school ? " They seemed more surprised when assured that he had not been to school at all. He soon became distinguished in his other exercises ; ridicule was succeeded by respect ; and before the season closed he had the sweet revenge of aiding in their lessons some of those who were most forward in ridiculing him on his first appearance at the academy. During all this time, however, though he wrote several pieces of composition, he could not be induced, by fear of any consequences, to read one of them before the school, — simply because of their want of merit, in his own estimation.

During haying-time, this summer, Amos left school to aid his brother on his farm, and spent two weeks in the severe labor of mowing. To him it was unusually severe, on account of his recent sedentary life.

In the fall of 1806 his studies were brought to a close by the unexpected disappearance of the preceptor of New Ipswich Academy. After remaining there a short time he returned to his father's house. He worked on the farm during most of the fall, but in December attended a free school, a few days, in the neighborhood.

Being now sufficiently advanced to become a teacher in the New England free schools, though but sixteen years of age, his father engaged a school for him, for two months, in the Lobb's Pond District, in Reading, Mass., at thirteen dollars per month and board. After closing his school in Reading he taught another for five weeks, on the same terms, in Dunstable, now Nashua, N. H. He was popular as a teacher, and was invited to teach both of these schools the next winter.

In April, 1807, he became a student in the academy at Groton, Mass., then, and for many years afterwards, under the charge of Caleb Butler. There he paid for his board, at one dollar and fifty cents per week, with the money obtained by teaching the preceding winter ; but close application to study, and neglect of physical exercise, impaired his health, never very robust, and it gave way to such an extent that he was compelled to return home and recruit his strength by hunting and moderate labor. On his return to the academy, after a fortnight thus spent, he adopted a regular system of exercise, walking and running, early in the morning and in the evening.

By the end of summer he had finished his preparation for college, and on the 10th of September, after examination and payment of four dollars as entrance-fee, was admitted as a member of the Freshman class, at Dartmouth College, by Professor Hubbard, who was on a visit to Groton. There were admitted, at the same time, Benjamin Prescott, Thomas C. Gardner, Moses Whitney, Josiah Danforth, Daniel Rockwood to the Freshman class, and Royal Bullard to the Sophomore class. The morning of the day was one of hope and fear ; the evening, one of congratulation and rejoicing.

His academic life, in fitting for college, was forty-seven weeks ; twenty-eight in New Ipswich, and nineteen in Groton. The expense of this preparatory course, exclusive of books, was eighty-five dollars and thirty-nine cents, of which forty-three dollars and twenty-five cents was earned by him in teaching school. The actual cost to his father, therefore, was forty-two dollars and eighty-four cents.

Having no means of paying the expenses of the fall term at college, Amos pursued the studies of the class at home ; at the same time participating, to a moderate degree, in the labors of the farm.

In September he visited his friends in Reading, where he was treated with the utmost kindness, and was strenuously urged to take charge of their school the next winter. This he declined to do, hoping to secure a larger school with higher wages.

Through his father, agreements were made that he should teach the schools of the two adjoining districts in Dunstable, now Nashua, N. H. One of them was the same which he had taught the preceding winter. His wages were to be the same, thirteen dollars

per month, and board, with the addition of one dollar should he go home, a distance of about a mile and a half, on Saturday evening, and return on Monday morning. The engagement was for four weeks only ; but by vote of a meeting of the district the school was continued a week longer. In consequence of this extension he lost the other engagement, but was soon employed to take charge of a school in his native town.

The custom, in many of the school districts in New England then, was to let out the board of the schoolmaster to the lowest bidder. It was the fortune of the master, in this case, to be bid off by a plain farmer, living more than a mile from the school-house in a direct line, and nearly two by an indifferent road. The food at this man's table was wholesome, but coarse, consisting almost entirely of rye-bread, salt beef and pork, with potatoes and cabbages, morning, noon, and night, varied only by various admixtures and variable cookery. The house was full of air-holes, and the fuel, green oak sticks. After wading through the snow several miles, to and from the school-house, young Kendall might be seen, late in the evening, sitting with his books on a table, — turning first one side and then the other to a fire which seemed itself to be freezing, with no sound around him but the wintry wind, — pursuing, by the light of a tallow-candle, the studies of his class in college. He found comfort, however, in an excellent feather-bed, furnished with an ample supply of home-made blankets and coverlets.

While Amos was teaching in this district the young people of Dunstable proposed getting up a sleigh-ride and ball, and he determined to join the party. There had been no snow for many days, and the roads were in beautiful condition. On the appointed morning the sky was overcast with ominous clouds, and by the time the company had collected it began to snow very gently. There were twenty-two sleighs, each containing a young man and his lady-companion. His was a farmer's daughter, of precisely his own age, having been born on the same day. The ride was to be from the rendezvous in Dunstable to a tavern in Chelmsford, about seven miles, where a ball was to be given at night. The snow fell faster and faster, and before they reached Chelmsford the wind began to blow from the northeast. During their stay there it increased to a gale, and the whole atmosphere appeared to be a mass of furiously driving snow. Their course in returning, for about three miles, was nearly north, along the banks of the Merrimack

River, the snow driving obliquely into their faces. It was impossible for the drivers to see their horses, except in glimpses, and they went helter-skelter in utter confusion, like a fleet of unmanageable shallops driven before the wind. It became intensely cold, and fingers, toes, ears, and cheeks were frozen. Umbrellas were no protection, and some were blown away. Kendall suffered none of these calamities, his right ear being protected by a sheet of ice. The snow blown among his hair, under the rim of his hat, melted there, and then running down from the hair, froze, and formed dangling icicles over the ear. At first he brushed them off as they formed, but finding that they did not adhere to the ear, which was not even cold, he suffered them to form anew, until they became a sheet of ice, constituting an effectual protection against the piercing wind.

The party all reached the rendezvous in scattered order, and though many casualties were recounted, none of them were very serious. Indeed, the disasters of the day added zest to the enjoyment of the night, and the merry dance was kept up for many hours with unflagging spirit. About midnight the storm abated, and a party went out to inspect the condition of the roads, which passed, almost uniformly, between stone fences. They reported them to be filled with driven snow to the tops of the fences, and wholly impassable. Of course the entire party, except three or four whose residences were just at hand, had to remain not only all night, but until the roads were broken out the next day. There being no beds for them, when tired of dancing they slept in chairs, or, gathering together in little clusters, amused each other as best they could.

Breaking the roads, after a violent snow-storm, is a sort of holiday sport in New England. The farmers with their boys and hired men, with their oxen and sleds, and with shovels of all sorts, from the capacious cider-mill shovel down to the common spade, turn out and make their way to the neighbors in every direction. Where drifts are so deep and solid that oxen and horses cannot get through, the snow is shovelled out until the road is made passable. Many a merry greeting between neighbors, as they meet, takes place on these occasions, ratified before extreme temperance days by a mug of flip. Flip is a very agreeable beverage, composed of sweetened beer put into a foam by the injection of a red-hot poker, or its equivalent, and finished by an infusion of rum.

It was but half a mile to the residence of Amos's lady-companion; yet it was not until eleven o'clock, the day after the ride, that he delivered her at her father's house, having made his way over fences and across fields. He had then over four miles to go to reach his lodgings, on about three of which the roads were broken out. On a part of the remaining distance the snow was drifted in so deep and hard that he was obliged to break the surface by stamping, before his horse could make his way through it, and the sun was setting when he reached the end of his journey.

There was much extreme poverty in this district, and some of the children could not attend school for want of shoes and decent clothing. Among the scholars was one negro-girl, who was entitled to all the privileges of the other children; but as public opinion would not allow her to be classed with the whites, she sat apart, and was taught by herself.

On the 19th January, 1808, Amos began to teach in his native town, and on the 10th February finished his engagement, which was not marked by any noteworthy events.

An occurrence happened in a neighboring school, however, illustrative of the troubles to which Yankee pedagogues are sometimes exposed. The master whipped one of his male pupils quite severely, though probably not more severely than the offence warranted. The boy was the pet of one of those fathers who can never be convinced that their children are in the wrong. A conspiracy was formed to seize the master, and ride him from the schoolhouse to his lodgings on a rail. The plot coming to the knowledge of young Kendall, he disclosed and defeated it. The outraged father then sued the master and held him to bail. The affair was subsequently disposed of by arbitration, which virtually justified the master and threw the costs upon the plaintiff. One of the arbitrators was Deacon Kendall, who was used to tell his own children that if they misbehaved at school, and being punished for it, came to him with complaints, he would punish them again.

On the 25th of March Amos took passage at Amherst, N. H., in the stage, for Dartmouth College. This was his first travel by stagecoach. The hill country between the Merrimack and Connecticut rivers was still covered with snow, which had almost entirely disappeared from the lowlands. The road over the hills having been much travelled after the last snow-storm, was worn into *cradleholes*. These are formed as follows. In every path of trodden

snow there are slight inequalities; the sleigh-runners in passing over these first acquire an upward tendency, and then, pitching suddenly down, dash up the snow and form another ridge, over which they pass and pitch in the same manner and with the same effect. Much-travelled roads, when the intervals between snow-storms are considerable, thus become a series of little ridges and hollows, over which the sleighs rise and fall like boats on the waves of the sea. Such was the condition of the road travelled by Amos on the 26th of March. The motion of the stage, then placed on runners, made him very sick.

Being transferred to a wheeled carriage near Connecticut River, he was much better on arrival at Windsor, Vt., about 4 P. M.; but he had no appetite for dinner, and immediately took the stage for the college, about eighteen miles distant. Here he met the young man with whom he had agreed to chum, and they went on together. The driver was a wild, drinking young fellow, careless and reckless, singing vulgar songs and shouting at passers-by. A cart appeared ahead attended by several persons, — some in the cart, some on horseback, and some on foot, — on whom the driver exercised his peculiar talent. As the stage drew alongside the cart the body of a drowned man was seen in it. The driver ejaculated, " I am very sorry," and was silent for a moment; but it was only for a moment; he soon burst out with a vulgar song. Owing to his frequent and long stops at taverns, his condition was becoming perceptibly worse. By collision with a cart he broke some portion of his running-gear, rendering it unsafe to ride down the steep hills, which were frequent. About 11 P. M., within three miles of the college, on a level plain, where there was a sled-track in the snow, which still appeared alongside of the carriage-track, the driver, too stupefied to recollect that his carriage-wheels were farther apart than the runners of a sled, wheeled suddenly into the sled-track, and the next moment, striking a stump, over went the stage. Slight bruises were the only injuries received by the passengers; but their strength, added to that of the driver, was not sufficient to right the stage, which was only effected after about an hour's delay, with the help of some of the neighbors, who had been called from their beds. It was then discovered that the vehicle, before badly damaged, was entirely disabled, and must be abandoned. The driver, now somewhat sobered, borrowed saddles, and placed his passengers on two of the horses, with their trunks

before them, and mounting the third with a bag of corn under him, started for the college, driving the fourth horse before him. They had gone but a few rods when his bag of corn became untied, emptying half its contents on the ground. Of course they must stop until he could gather up his grain. Again under way, his loose horse trotted off, upon a sled-path, into the woods, and it took half an hour to get him back. What with these incidents and slow travelling on a muddy road, it was near 2 A. M. when they reached the college. Having eaten nothing since breakfast the preceding day, Kendall was so exhausted and sick that he could take no supper, and went immediately to bed.

The next morning, Sunday, he rose about 10 A. M. in tolerable condition. The next day he was examined, re-entered his class, entered Commons for board at $1.50 per week, and became the occupant of a room with Thomas C. Gardner as his chum. On the 30th of March, 1808, he made his first recitation in college.

There were several societies at that time in Dartmouth College, two of which — the Social Friends, having about one hundred resident members, and the United Fraternity, with about two thirds of that number — embraced nearly all the students. On the 13th of April Amos became a member of the Social Friends.

During his preparation for college he had written several pieces of composition when that exercise was required, but could not be induced to read one of them in public, on account of their obvious imperfection, both in style and substance, according to his own taste. Knowing that no excuse was likely to be taken in college, he had, while keeping school, elaborated several pieces with all the thought and care which he could command. When called upon to read a piece of original composition in the class, he selected one of these; but so little confidence had he in its merits and in himself, that he had to lean against the wall of the room, and bring his elbows back against it, to enable him to hold the paper still enough to be read. His tutor praised the piece; his classmates said, " You must have practised much at composition," and were greatly surprised when told it was the first piece he had ever read in public. This success gave him considerable confidence; but never during his college life, and scarcely ever since, has he written an article which he did not think could be improved.

Many circumstances conspired to render his first term in college far from agreeable. His chum had been in college the preceding

fall term, and had formed his associations. He belonged to a club which spent part of the night in robbing hen-roosts, and cooking and eating the stolen poultry. They visited alternately the rooms of the members, each of whom in turn furnished table-furniture, salt, pepper, butter, and bread.

It was not long before his chum brought in his companions late at night, with a couple of stolen chickens which they proceeded to dress and cook. They insisted on his getting up and partaking of their cheer, and he reluctantly complied. On reflection, however, he made up his mind not to repeat this piece of complaisance, and to put a stop to the use of his room for such purposes.

Accordingly, the next time they came in with their game he declined getting up, without assigning any reason other than that he was not hungry and was very sleepy. When their poultry was cooked and on the table, they again invited him to get up, and, when he declined, began to pull the bedclothes off. This excited him, and he peremptorily demanded to be let alone, adding that if such habits suited them they did not suit him, and he begged not to be further molested then or thereafter. They dropped the bedclothes, ate their poultry in silence, and never came to the room again while he occupied it.

On another occasion, a party having procured a hand-cart, with ropes to haul by, proposed to supply each other with fuel from a pile of wood, cut and split for the fire, and deposited about half a mile from the college. Late one evening they called upon him and Gardner to join them. Gardner went, but Kendall declined. One of the party lingered behind, after the rest had gone, and inquired why he would not go? He answered, " If we were at home, and went to a neighbor's wood-pile in the night to supply ourselves with wood, we would feel like thieves, would we not? I do not perceive the difference." " You are right," the young man replied. " They have got me into this scrape, and I must go through with it; but they will not catch me in another."

Mr. Kendall, while teaching school, indulged in the common amusement of playing cards, and was familiar with a number of games. Though card-playing was prohibited at Dartmouth College, he was invited one evening into a room in the same building with his own, occupied by students of a higher class, and was induced by them to play for money, at a few cents a game. They played at loo until daylight the next morning, and when they quit, the balance of winnings and losses was about three dollars in Kendall's favor. He had felt an excited interest in the game, and therefore came to a firm resolution never again to play for money. Only once in after life was this resolution broken. On the 4th of July, 1814, a newly-made friend invited him to a picnic celebration of the day, near Lexington in Kentucky. There were several card-tables on the ground, and two of his companion's friends proposed that they should play a game of whist for their dinners. He plead his want of practice, when his friend insisted, and proposed to be his partner. They won the dinner, when the other side proposed to play on at a quarter each game. Having won the dinner, Kendall felt that he could not decline, and, contrary to his wish, continued to win. As in college, so here, he was in the end winner to a small amount; and having again felt an interest in the game, he renewed his resolution with more determination than before, and never after swerved from it. There is no difficulty in avoiding, without reproach, playing for money, if one will make it a a matter of principle, and so declare whenever invited to play.

On finishing the study of Homer, it was customary to sacrifice a copy of the book to the *manes* of the author; and the Freshman class, or some of them, determined to maintain the usage. A small altar of stones was erected in one of the college rooms, capped by a tin basin, into which was poured a quantity of rum. A copy of Homer was laid on the floor open at about the middle. The rum was set on fire, and the students marching around the altar stamped as they passed on the open book, uttering various ejaculations not at all complimentary to the ancient bard. As the leaves were broken loose from the doomed book, they were placed upon the altar and consumed in the blue flames of the burning rum. As in similar cases, a portion of the sacrifice went to the officiating priests, who became very noisy, locked the door and appointed a doorkeeper, declaring that no one should leave the room. Finding that affairs were taking a turn not at all to his taste, Kendall desired to be let out, but it was not until he had peremptorily declared that he would not remain, that the door was opened.

On the 9th of June there was a serious riot in town. The villagers suffered their cows to remain on the common in front of the college during the night, where they were a great nuisance. Under the main college building there was a large unused cellar,

easily accessible from without. In the night the cows, about twenty in number, were collected and driven into the cellar, and the entrance barricaded. In the morning, the owners coming for their cows, were told that they could not have them until they agreed to yard them during the night. In consequence of this refusal, excitement began to run high; an attack on the college was apprehended, and the students prepared to defend their prisoners. One of them, named Darling, picked up a boy who was very abusive and put him over a fence in the rear of the college. A short time after, the father of the lad, named Baldwin, approached with stones in his hands and dashed one of them through a window in the college building. A general rush was the consequence, and in an instant the villagers were flying before a shower of stones and brickbats. It was not long before a constable appeared and arrested Darling for assault and battery upon the boy. A crowd followed him into the presence of the magistrate who was to try him. Of the assault there was no question; but it was proved that the boy was very insulting and was not injured. The magistrate announced his decision to be a fine of two dollars. There were several hisses mingled with cries of "Appeal!" "Appeal!" The magistrate told the constable to arrest those who insulted the court; the constable replied, "I cannot distinguish them." The students then left the room, formed a procession, marched yelling by the complainant's house, and some of them threw stones at it. The cattle were released in the evening; but this was not the end of the affair, as far as Baldwin was concerned.

He kept a horse in a neighboring pasture. One morning the horse had changed his color, and the words "*Two dollars*" appeared in large letters on each of his sides. Baldwin was a goldsmith, and had a large bow-window in his shop, against which hung many watches. First his sign was stolen; then a large stone was dashed against his bow-window, scattering the watches all over his shop, and doing some of them serious injury.

About one hundred and thirty dollars had been subscribed by the students to enable Darling to prosecute his appeal, but both parties became anxious for a compromise, and it was finally effected. In this affair Kendall sympathized with the object of the students, and was one of those who attended Darling's trial and formed the procession; but he had nothing to do with shutting up the cows, and disapproved of the outrages committed upon Baldwin.

Another affair, more ridiculous in its origin, but more serious in its termination, soon after agitated the little community of Dartmouth College. Two of Kendall's classmates, Benjamin Prescott and John H. Slack, were bantering each other, at first in frolic, when Slack, becoming excited, said he would not take a banter. Thereupon Prescott challenged him to a fight with pistols on the morning of the 4th of July, at an hour and place which he named. Slack consulted some of his classmates, who told him his honor was concerned, and he must fight. On the evening of the 3d of July Slack invited Kendall to his room, and asked his advice. He was advised to see Prescott, in company with others, and bring about an explanation. This he declined, but was persuaded to write. Kendall and two others then went with the letter to Prescott's room, where they found him with his second. He declared that there must be a fight, and instructed his second to answer Slack that he expected to meet him the next morning at the hour and place appointed. He acted his part so well, that Kendall began to doubt whether he was not in earnest, and taking him aside asked him what he meant. He said he wished to test Slack's courage, but that nobody would be hurt. Having arrived at the true state of the case, Kendall returned to his room, not unwilling to see the game played out.

The next morning Prescott and Slack were summoned before the faculty, and Kendall and others called up as witnesses. Though it was proved that, so far as Prescott was concerned, the whole affair was a joke, the faculty sentenced both parties to six months' rustication, — Prescott, because he would not say that he thought duelling in all cases wrong, and Slack, because — though he thought it in all cases wrong — he would not say that he would in all cases refuse to fight. Prescott's second was condemned to read a public confession as a punishment for the part he had taken in the joke.

There was little sympathy for Slack, but much for Prescott. The three higher classes sent in a petition for a remission of the penalty; the Freshman class was divided, a part signing the petition and a part sending in a remonstrance. The result of this division in the class was much bitter feeling. It happened that Kendall was absent when these papers were drawn up and presented. On his return he found that both parties counted on his adhesion, but he sided with neither, because he considered petitioning useless and remonstrance unnecessary.

The justice of Prescott's punishment, however, as well as the expediency of Slack's, is very questionable. In effect, one was punished for not belying his opinions, and the other for admitting that he might be impelled by circumstances to do a wrong act. The plain duty of the teachers having charge of these young men was to reprimand their folly, and endeavor to instil better principles into the one and more correct views of moral duty into the other.

Prescott never returned to Dartmouth College; Slack returned and graduated with the class.

CHAPTER II.

The most interesting association formed by Mr. Kendall in college, resulted from his membership in a private club for mutual improvement, which had been organized in the autumn of 1807, and was unknown to him until he was invited to join it. It was composed exclusively of members of his class, not more than a dozen in all; it had no constitution or regulations, no officers, the members presiding in alphabetical order, and meeting weekly at their own rooms. Its exercises were composition, declamation, and forensic discussion; all participating in each, not by appointment, but in alphabetical order. It was the duty of all to observe and criticise the performances of each, and this function was uniformly exercised in a kindly spirit. Care was taken to invite none into the club who were not of irreproachable moral character and sincerely desirous of self-improvement. Though no injunction of secrecy was imposed on members, the understanding was that they should not speak of their club to outsiders, and its existence was apparently unknown out of their own circle during their whole college life. Never was a club more orderly, though without rules of order, and never were the objects of an association more steadily and faithfully pursued. It is with an affectionate remembrance that their names are here recorded: namely, Joseph Perry, Jonathan Curtis, Daniel Poor, Jonathan Fowle, Nathaniel H. Carter, Robert Crowell, Theophilus Wilson, Joseph Bailey, David Pierce, Daniel Rockwood, William Cogswell, Samuel Woodbury, and Caleb Chase.

In July of this year Kendall made a visit, in company with his classmate, Daniel Rockwood, to Windsor, Vt., West Parish, where lived a Mr. Cummings who married a sister of his father. They desired to ascend Ascutney Mountain, about three miles distant, and two young men, his cousins, consented to accompany them. The cousins proposed that the party should ride on horseback to the mountain, and up as far as practicable; but being full of life

and confidence the young students declined their offer. With a lunch and a bottle of rum, they started on foot early in the morning. The day was exceedingly warm, but they went forward with much spirit, though frequently checked by the cousins, until they were about half-way up the mountain, when they began to feel the effect of the heat and rapid walking. Resort was had to the rum-bottle to recruit their wasted strength. Around the top of the mountain the trees had been killed by fires, and decaying trunks had fallen across each other in every conceivable direction. Among them was a luxuriant growth of tall weeds. Rising above the whole, on the very summit, was a large rock. Up this they climbed, and were rewarded by one of the finest views in nature. On the west was the Green Mountain range; on the east were the mountains of New Hampshire; to the southward and northward the Connecticut River valley on both sides was skirted by a magnificent hill-country dotted with improvements. The river itself washing the foot of the mountain, and meandering through a narrow plain which formed the bottom of the valley, exhibited its silvery waters in many windings, like a succession of small lakes, giving a finish to the enchanting landscape. The isolated mountain on which they stood seemed like a tower raised in the midst of this magnificent scenery, merely to enable man to enjoy its beauties.

But alas! scarcely had the eye taken a general view of the scene, when a duskiness, like approaching night, seemed to be creeping over it. The cool air of the mountain-top, combined with the reaction of the unusual stimulant they had swallowed, closed the pores of the body and brought on a drowsiness which was perfectly overpowering. The young students, descending from the rock, made pallets of weeds, and had scarcely lain down upon them before they were fast asleep. The sun was low in the west when the cousins awoke them, saying it was time to go. On rising Kendall's sinews seemed to be unstrung, and his limbs refused to obey his will. He told his cousins that he was utterly unable to walk, and begged them to form the best shelter they could of the dead limbs and weeds, and leave him there until the next morning. They said he could go, and should; and taking him by the arms forced him forward. Becoming excited, he broke from them and ran some distance over logs and rocks with perfect recklessness, not caring whether he broke his neck or not. Becoming warm with exercise,

his indecision left him, and he kept on by himself, taking a ravine which led in the direction of his uncle's. Whether it had ever been explored before he knew not. Certain it is, that in some places it was flanked by solid rocks of great height which it was impossible to scale; its bottom was, in storms, the bed of a mountain torrent, and could be descended only by leaping from cliff to cliff, where a slip or false step would have plunged the leaper headlong among ragged rocks many feet below. Once he came to a huge rock, perhaps twenty feet high, which had fallen in from above and completely filled the channel. He could neither get around it nor over it, and there it seemed as if his journey would be ended for the night, and perhaps forever. Finally he discovered a hole under it, through which he crawled and reached the light of day on the lower side. At length he found himself at the mouth of the ravine, where there was a small house on a tract of land formed by the wash from the mountain. Entering, he found a young woman spinning, and telling her he was almost dead with fatigue, he begged leave to lie down on the bed in the same room. She consented, and he fell asleep immediately.

After perhaps half an hour he awoke, and going to the door saw Rockwood approaching, supported by the two young men, pale and bloody. It appeared that when Kendall broke loose upon the mountain, they supposed that he intended to hide and remain all night, and one of them followed until satisfied that such was not his purpose. He then returned to Rockwood, and they kept on down the same ravine. But Rockwood's nose began to bleed, and he gave out entirely, so that they had to carry him a considerable distance. As the cool of the evening came on he revived somewhat and became able to walk, supported on both sides. He was so exhausted it was deemed best to leave him in the farmer's cottage till the next day. Kendall, however, had so far recovered his strength as to be able to return home with his cousins. After a day's rest the young students returned to the college, satisfied that it is often bad policy in a hot day to walk six miles when one can ride four of them, and that rum is not always the safest restorative of exhausted strength.

On a subsequent visit to Windsor, with the same companion, they again visited Ascutney, but with a different object. One of the cousins claimed to be one of those fortunate mortals in whose hands the divining-rod would indicate unerringly the loca-

tion of valuable metals. He had a set of rods, composed of two hazel-bushes, of about eighteen inches long, flattened and tied together at the butts, around which was a small bulb composed of some unknown substance covered with leather. The operator held the small ends of the rods — one in each hand, back downwards — about a foot apart. The theory is, that the bulb is attracted by any metallic substance within its influence, and will incline the rods in that direction.

After witnessing the operation near watches and other articles composed in whole or in part of metals, they started for the mountain in which the operator said there were masses of ore. About half a mile distant he set his rods, which soon gave out a vibrating motion, with a gradual inclination towards the mountain. This increased as they approached and ascended, until they were more than half-way up the summit, when the inclination was downward. The operator then said they had passed the mine. Experiments were tried in different directions, and at length a spot was identified, where, apparently, the rods would not work at all. This was alleged to be directly over the mine. But the two students charged him with producing the action of the rods himself by an imperceptible action of his hands, which it was plain he might do from the manner in which he held them. This he denied, and offered to submit to any test they might require. Going a short distance from the alleged locality of the mine, they required him to set his rods and place the back of his hands on a log; each of them took hold of one of his hands with both of theirs, and watched with the utmost vigilance. Neither by the sense of sight nor feeling could they perceive the slightest movement of his hands, yet the rods bent downward and downward until they formed an angle of about forty-five degrees below a horizontal plane and made livid bruises on the sides of his hands. The spectators were confounded, but not convinced.

Their attention was now diverted by the discovery of a hedgehog, or porcupine, in a tree about thirty feet from the ground, which they determined to capture. One of the cousins climbed up another tree close by, and with a pole pushed the animal off. The rest stood below with clubs, and, as soon as he reached the ground, crossed them over his back and held him fast. They had no cord, but succeeded in tying a withe around one of his hind legs, though one of the cousins during the operation had several quills driven into his hands by a whisk of the creature's stumpy tail. He was as obstinate as any other hog, and it took them a long time to get him to the foot of the mountain, where, being out of patience, they gave him to some boys whom they met on the road.

Many suppose this animal can project its quills to a considerable distance. It is not so; they are merely a defensive weapon, and very effective against the brute creation. When threatened with an attack and unable to escape, the hedgehog crouches upon its belly, and erects the quills which cover its back and its sides to the end of its blunt tail. This it can vibrate a short distance and strike its quills into any object within reach. But woe to the man or beast that attempts to seize him with hands, paws, or jaws, while in its defensive position! A dog at the college once ventured on the perilous experiment. His mouth was stuck full of quills so that he could not shut it, and his master, deeming his case hopeless, thought it merciful to kill him.

In July, 1809, Mr. Kendall joined the Handel Society, one of several associations in New Hampshire and Massachusetts, organized for the purpose of cultivating sacred music, and expelling from the service of the churches the light and jangling airs then in general use. In this object they were entirely successful, though they carried the reform to an extreme from which there was afterwards a considerable reaction.

On the 19th of August the Freshman class was examined, and all its members admitted to regular standing in the Sophomore class. On Monday and Tuesday the various societies had exhibitions in the following order, viz.: on Monday, the *Religiosi*, on Tuesday the *Social Friends*, the *Phi Beta Kappa*, the *United Fraternity*, and the *Handel*. On the 24th was the annual commencement, with its usual performances. That evening, in company with his father, Kendall left for home, where they arrived on the 26th.

The want of funds to pay his expenses at college again compelled him to remain at home until he could replenish his exchequer by keeping school. After a few days spent in visiting relations and friends, he resumed his studies in order to qualify himself to re-enter his class the next spring.

In October he agreed to teach a school in New Ipswich three months, at $14.50 per month, beginning on the 21st of November. On going there he was informed by his uncle, with whom he was to board, that the school had heretofore been very

disorderly, and that as a prejudice had arisen against him from causes over which he had no control, it was feared that he would have trouble. Being thus forewarned, he began the school by imitating King Log. He announced no rules of order, took no notice of whispering, laughing, or leaving seats, and went through with all the duties of the day as listlessly as possible. The second day was passed like the first until near its close, and the children became so outrageous that he could stand it no longer. Suddenly he cried " Silence !" in a loud voice. Every eye was turned upon him, and there was silence profound.

He then stated that he had been informed there were disorderly persons in that school, and he had left them thus far to act out their natural dispositions without restraint, in order that he might find out who they were ; that he now had his eyes upon them, and knew how to meet their disorder. He then proceeded to announce his rules and dismissed school. The next morning his whole manner was changed. In everything he was prompt and decided, though kind and obliging, and the result was that this school was more orderly than any other he ever taught. The parents of the children were, generally, intelligent and kind, apparently exerting themselves to make his residence among them agreeable, and he was cordially invited to take charge of the school the next winter. Having by request continued the school a week beyond his original agreement, he finally dismissed it on the 18th of February, 1809. The amount received for this winter's labor was $ 47.12½.

Returning home he found that his grandfather had died a few days before at the age of eighty-five years, and a few days afterward he attended the funeral of his grandfather's brother, Jacob, aged also upwards of eighty years.

On the 6th of March he returned to Dartmouth College, and immediately thereafter was examined and re-entered his class.

The entire want of congeniality between him and T. C. Gardner induced him to look out for another chum, and soon after his return he found himself associated with Jonathan Fowle in a room in a private house.

Nothing out of the ordinary routine of college-life occurred until the 19th of April, when a series of transactions was inaugurated which afforded him a practical lesson not without its use in after life.

Each class except the Freshman had what was called its quar-

ter-day. It was distinguished by a public exhibition, which included the performance of certain orations and forensic discussions given out by the faculty, and called Appointments. By the order in which they were given out they indicated the relative estimation in which the recipients were held by the faculty for scholarship and general merit.

It had been a practice from time immemorial for those who received the higher appointments to "treat" the rest of the class on the evening of the day of announcement, and for the class to "treat" all the other classes on the day of performance. This custom was productive of intemperance and rowdyism disgraceful to the college, and a few members of Kendall's class determined to make an effort to break it up. They believed a majority of the class would sustain the movement, and one morning after recitation requested their classmates to stop for the purpose of ascertaining their views. Resolutions were presented denouncing the custom, and declaring that the class would neither encourage nor participate in it. They were opposed by those who preferred a frolic to the reputation of the college; but after discussion were adopted by a clear majority. Those who took an interest in the movement determined to meet at two o'clock the same day for the purpose of concerting further measures. The other party occupied the intermediate time in electioneering against the movement, and met the reformers at two o'clock with new recruits and in a most determined spirit. A resolution was offered rescinding the resolution of the morning and ratifying the time-disgraced custom. A violent discussion ensued, and the success of the rescinding motion became probable, when a few of the temperance party determined to change their tactics and make it an individual instead of a class affair. They retired and drew up a brief pledge to the effect that they would neither "treat" nor participate in a "treating" on the day when the appointments should be given out or on Sophomore quarter-day. Mr. Kendall returned into the meeting with this paper, signed by himself and five others, and calling the attention of his classmates, read it, and invited all those who were opposed to the custom of "treating" to sign it. This raised at once a storm of excitement. James Bradford, the son of a clergyman, and himself avowedly preparing for the pulpit, requested to see the paper. It was put into his hands, when he spit upon it, tore it in pieces, and stamped upon it. Kendall looked him in the face a

moment, and then said, " I can write another." Accordingly he retired, wrote another and signed it; but such a storm had been raised that a large portion of those who were disposed to act with the temperance party shrank from the responsibility, and only thirteen signatures could be procured to the pledge in the class of sixty members.

The next day the Sophomore appointments were given out. The first was assigned to Nathaniel H. Carter, the second to Joseph Perry, the third to Nathaniel Wright, the fourth to Daniel Poor, the fifth to Robert Crowell, the sixth to Amos Kendall, the seventh to Samuel Woodbury, the eighth to ———— Fairfield, and then followed several to whom were assigned dialogues and forensic discussions. Of the eight who received the principal appointments, six had signed the pledge against "treating." A tutor who had previously expressed his opinion against the practice, after reading off the appointments, in the name of the faculty prohibited it, and announced that any one who "treated," or allowed " treating " in his room, would be expelled.

Several of the students went from the recitation-room to Mr. Perry's room, which was on the lower floor of the main college building, for the purpose of congratulating him and talking over the incidents of the day. In the midst of their conversation the door was opened, and in came half a dozen classmates with a decanter of rum, which they set on the table of a study-chair ; they invited all present to drink, and set the example themselves. Kendall, who was present, immediately left for his own room, not knowing what might be going on there, and at the outer door met two of the " treating " party, whose faces confessed their guilt. He simply said " I see you," and passed on into his room, where he found the table standing in the middle of the floor, with every empty bottle and vessel in the room placed upon it in derision.

The next night several guns were fired into the windows of Mr. Perry's room, shattering them into a thousand pieces. The same night the windows of a room occupied by one of the tutors named Ayres were broken, and a large quantity of filth laid at his door.

On the 25th Mr. Perry was called before the faculty, on the charge of allowing " treating " in his room, and Kendall and Fowle were called upon as witnesses. They stated what they saw, and, among other things, that it was their classmate Folsom who brought the liquor into Perry's room. Folsom , when called up, denied it, when he was confronted with Fowle, Poor, and Kendall, who all confirmed their original statement to his face, and it was proved by Carter that the same party had thrust themselves with their liquor into his room.

On the 27th Bradford and several others were called to account for their conduct in this affair and various other misdemeanors. The next morning the "Temple of Cloacina," or the "Little College," so called by the students, was in ashes, the cushion of the chapel desk torn into shreds and scattered through the building and around the colleges, and the front and floor of the desk, together with the seats of the professors and tutors, were defiled with filth.

The President, however, though greatly agitated, made a feeling and excellent prayer, and then called on Tutor Ayres, who read the sentence of the faculty expelling Folsom , and also that depriving Bradford of all the privileges of the institution, and directing him to leave it without delay. The form of Bradford's sentence was occasioned by the fact that, in consequence of long absence, he was not at that time a member of the class. Folsom and Bradford immediately left the chapel, and as the faculty came out, the former accosted Tutor Brown, cursed him, and charged him with being the author of his disgrace. The Tutor, who was a most amiable man, though endowed with remarkable firmness and self-possession, took no notice of Folsom , but was seen to speak to Professor Hubbard, and laugh. Not content with this exploit, Folsom , the same day, threw a brickbat at Perry, insulted Fowle, hallooed at Kendall when passing at a distance, and said he had told a d—d lie, when his companions commenced singing a doggerel song about him which some of them had composed. Of all this none of the temperance party took any notice.

Mr. Perry was the only one of the obnoxious individuals whose room was easily accessible to the malcontents, and so strong were their apprehensions for his personal safety, that a few of his friends for several nights kept watch in his room. As long as the watch was continued, he was not molested; but twice, when it was suspended, his windows were dashed in, and once his door was battered open with a log of wood.

Twice as Kendall passed out of the main college building a stick of wood was thrown at him from a passage window in the third story, to the manifest danger of his life. Sitting near his class-

mate, Pillsbury, — who occupied one of the adjacent rooms, — at supper the evening after the second assault, Kendall asked in a good-humored tone, "Who keeps garrison in the passage between your room and Goodwin's ?" (The passage from which the missiles came.) Pillsbury replied, "That is our mode of salutation." Kendall rejoined, "I should like to be saluted in a situation where I could return the compliment." Pillsbury blushed, and was silent.

As quarter-day approached, all sorts of rumors were circulated, such as that the temperance party, and Kendall in particular, were to be hissed and driven from the stage; that the students in general would not attend in the chapel; that there would be disturbances, etc., etc. The evident object was to deter the public from attending; and such was the effect that the resident band of music declined to play. Upon the suggestion of one of the tutors and Professor Hubbard, application was made to the Handel Society to perform some pieces of sacred music. The panic had reached the society, and there was opposition, on the ground that the application was not made by the class. Being himself a member of the society, and also the committee to provide music, Mr. Kendall was called on for an explanation. Somewhat provoked at the hesitation of the society to aid the cause of right and virtue in such an emergency, he related all the circumstances, under some excitement, and concluded by telling them, "If you see fit to help us, well ; if not, we will help ourselves." As there was still an evident reluctance on the part of a large portion of the society, the application was pressed no further.

Being determined to have music, the temperance party sent a messenger to a neighboring town, where he engaged four performers. At their request the faculty had postponed the exhibition for one week, for the purpose of enabling them to complete their arrangements, and in the hope that the excitement would subside.

On the morning of the 24th of May, the day to which the performances had been adjourned, it was evident that active measures were on foot to prevent the attendance of an audience. About noon a party of negroes appeared and built a booth not twenty rods from the chapel, which was soon furnished with seats, tables, liquors, and eatables. Near by was mounted on a log an old iron cannon, which from time immemorial had been without an owner, and used by the students as a sort of plaything.

At 2 P. M. the faculty and performers entered the chapel. Not thirty students other than the performers came in, and the entire audience did not exceed eighty. A large portion of the other students, with a promiscuous crowd of people, surrounded the booth and the cannon. Simultaneously with those in the chapel began the exercises at the booth. They consisted of drinking, shouting, yelling, singing doggerel songs, and firing the old cannon.

Undismayed, however, the performers in the chapel went through with their exercises, removed their staging, retired to their rooms, and spent a pleasant evening in social intercourse. The party on the plain also dispersed, and all was quiet. Which party slept that night with the most easy consciences and with the best hopes for the future, it would not be difficult to determine. The performances were highly commended, and the little temperance party felt that they had achieved a great victory.

For several days all remained quiet, and the rioters, when questioned as to their reasons for absenting themselves from the chapel, generally gave some frivolous excuse. The faculty seemed undecided as to the course they should pursue. At length they determined to call up all those who had absented themselves from the chapel, and treat each according to the spirit he might evince on examination. The mildest punishment contemplated for those who had wilfully taken part in the disturbances, was a written acknowledgment of error and regret, in a form which the faculty had themselves prepared. They began with calling up the members of the Senior class, who generally signed the acknowledgment. Mr. Kendall's journal says, " Woodbury, however, who was deeply implicated in the affair, was excused, affirming that he was forced into the scrape." This was Levi Woodbury, afterwards distinguished in public life.

The Juniors engaged in the riot were next called up, only one of whom signed the acknowledgment. Several were excused and eight dismissed. All of those in the Sophomore and Freshman classes who were engaged signed the acknowledgment, when the refractory Juniors, finding themselves without support in the other classes, came forward and offered to sign. Their offer was accepted and they were restored.

Darling, of the Sophomore class, was dismissed, for the additional offence of singing a doggerel song, written to ridicule the attempt to

put down "treating," in which several names, including Kendall's, were freely used. Having much sympathy for him, in the belief that he had acted under the influence of worse young men, Kendall had a free conversation with him, during which Darling confessed his error and folly, exhibited the song, but disavowed all knowledge of the author, and said the disturbance did not originate in the Sophomore class, and tendered all the reparation in his power.

On account of the steady determination with which Kendall had acted in this affair he had become very odious to the "treating" party, some of whom vented their spite by writing his name on the college walls, in the chapel, and in the recitation-room, connected with curses, denunciations, and nicknames. Of this he made no complaint and took no notice.

Some time after Bradford left Kendall received an anonymous letter postmarked at Bradford's place of residence, containing nothing but a repetition of such vulgar insults as had been inscribed upon the college walls. Not doubting that Bradford was the author, Kendall concluded to lay it aside until Bradford became a preacher of the gospel, — that being the profession which it was known he intended to adopt. Hearing in 1818 that he had become a settled minister in an interior town in Massachusetts, Mr. Kendall wrote in Bradford's letter the following words, addressed it to him, paid the postage, and sent it by mail : —

"GROTON, November 16, 1813.

" REV. SIR, — I return to you the only memorial of your former folly and meanness in my possession. That I never injured you is known to my God, your God, and my own conscience. I am sufficiently revenged. That you are reformed, and that you may be useful and finally happy, is the sincere hope of   AMOS KENDALL."

It was believed that if Mr. Bradford had become a better man this note would elicit an apology from him; but no reply was ever received; nor did Bradford ever attend a class-meeting, though several were held while he was yet living.

The frolic of shutting up the cows in the college cellar had been frequently repeated with no incident worthy of note. On the night of the 14th of July, however, they were again shut up under circumstances which threatened serious consequences. It was given out that they should not be released until the people of the village would agree to yard them at night. This was not of itself an unreasonable demand, for their presence every night on the common was an intolerable nuisance. No attempt was made to release them during the day; but as night approached there were rumors that the inhabitants were preparing to take them out by force. Not much attention was paid to this rumor, until one of the students, in taking a walk, was assaulted by a half-drunken negro. Immediately all the college was in an uproar. Kendall had taken no part in the affair, as his room was at a distance; but hearing of the threatened attack, he repaired to the main college building, and prepared to join in the defence. It was soon ascertained that the inhabitants had collected in large numbers, that some of them were armed with muskets alleged to be charged with balls, and that an assault on the college was meditated for the purpose of compelling the students to let the cattle out. Nothing daunted by this information, the young men collected all the arms they could find in the college, consisting of one musket and a few pistols, some of which they, too, loaded with ball. They also collected in the passages of the main college building quantities of stones and brickbats, to be used in repelling the threatened attack. The excitement increased as the evening progressed, and several reports of firearms, discharged in defiance, took place both from the college and the crowd. These demonstrations alarmed the faculty and the peaceable citizens, who interfered and secured a parley. The students on the one hand, and the citizens on the other, appointed committees who met in conference. All the students demanded was, that the citizens should yard their cattle at night, and thus prevent a serious nuisance. This demand was acceded to, and a formal treaty concluded, which for a short time only was complied with by the citizens.

Among the amusements of this period was the institution of a new society, denominated *Ine Heber*, and also of a court to try offences against the rules of the class. The *Ine Heber* originated as follows: A large number of students met on a walk, when it was suddenly proposed that the ugliest man in the company should be designated by a vote of the majority, should "treat." The proposal was acceded to with alacrity and the victim selected. As it was rather unreasonable to require one to treat so large a company, the next ugliest and the next were selected until they numbered about half a dozen, including Kendall. When the cere-

mony of "treating" was over, the select few separated from the crowd, and, setting up claims to superior merit, organized themselves into a society with a Hebrew name, which was understood to mean the "Ugly Club." They had their officers, — whose superior merit consisted in superior ugliness, — their regulations and weekly meetings. Their exercises consisted of mock heroics and fun of all sorts. The meetings were not very orderly, and in the midst of the confusion one evening it was proposed to elect a despot to whom every member should yield implicit, prompt, and silent obedience, on pain of expulsion, — an admirable plan to preserve order, which has since been imitated by the French nation. But alas for the perversity of human nature! so numerous were the expulsions from the *Ine Heber* for questioning the wisdom of the despot that it soon ceased to exist.

The parents of Amos Kendall were conscientiously opposed to the amusement of dancing, and would not allow their older children to go to any ball or party where it was indulged in. As the younger ones grew up they became less intolerant on this subject, not from any change of opinion as to the sinfulness of the amusement, but evidently from a conviction that the severe restraint imposed on their older children was producing unhappy results. For prohibition, therefore, were substituted advice and admonition. Dancing had now become a general amusement at private parties in New England, and Kendall met with it constantly while engaged in keeping school. Though much disposed to participate, he was deterred by the fear of appearing ignorant or awkward to his pupils, many of whom were nearly of his own age. Having an opportunity at college in the summer of 1809, he determined to take lessons in dancing for a single quarter, without the knowledge of his parents. While practising one day in the dancing-hall, which was over a store, a messenger from below announced to him that a gentleman in the store wished to see him. It turned out to be a cousin of his father living about two miles distant. His visitor inquired what they were doing up stairs, and young Kendall, perceiving by the question that he did not understand the true state of the case, replied they were going through some of their college exercises. That quarter he practised the most rigid economy, and in the bill of expenses rendered to his father placed his dancing bills under the head of miscellaneous expenses, which, not being very heavy, passed without inquiry. Thus it was

that he escaped detection, and that his parents escaped the affliction of knowing that he had been to a dancing-school. It was the only time that Amos Kendall deceived his parents, and although he did it to save them unhappiness, and felt justified, he could not recommend the practice to others.

On the 16th of August, 1809, the members of the Sophomore class were examined and admitted to the Junior standing. On the 23d was Commencement, on which occasion Levi Woodbury delivered the salutatory oration, then considered the first appointment and the highest honor.

On the 25th Mr. Kendall travelled on foot to West Windsor, and spent several days at the residence of his uncles, Cummings and Wilkins, whose wives were his father's sisters, and in making sundry excursions therefrom. At a ball in West Windsor he committed a ludicrous blunder, which was a source of momentary mortification to him and of merriment to his cousins. During a long contra-dance he sat on a bench which ran along the side of the hall and fell into a "brown study," to which he was very little addicted. A part of the figure was a *chassée* from side to side, in which the partners joined hands with extended arms. Suddenly he was awakened from his revery by a pocket-handkerchief in the hand of a lady being thrust almost into his face, which he seized with a snatch. The lady stared at him as she *chasséed* away, and on her return he handed it back with a bow. She evidently did not understand the meaning of so strange an act, and her eyes were fixed upon him with a look of wonder during the rest of the evening.

On the 5th of September his father and mother joined him on a visit to his sisters, then living in Vermont. One of the sisters lived at Fairfax, on Lamoille River, about forty miles from the Canada line; and in an intermediate township called Underhill also lived their oldest son Zebedee and their only daughter Molly, who had married a man named Fletcher. The father and mother had come from home in a chaise, and Amos hired a horse to accompany them on the remainder of their journey. On the morning of the 9th they went over to Woodstock, where the father had some distant relations of his own name. It was Sunday, and in the evening they attended a meeting of a new religious sect calling themselves Christians (pronounced with the "i" long). They had no minister, and their services consisted of zealous conversa-

tion, singing, and praying, in which the women took a very active part.

On the next and three succeeding days the party pursued their journey through Randolph and Montpelier, etc., to Underhill. Here they saw how people live who settle on poor land upon a wooded frontier. Zebedee Kendall and Amos Fletcher had each purchased on credit a tract of wild land, built small log-cabins, and made clearings. Their accommodations and fare were of the rudest description, though the food was wholesome, and they appeared to be contented. Their mother, however, was much affected at the sight of their poverty and destitution of home comforts. In one respect the women presented a striking contrast with the ladies of polished society. One of them had an infant but a week old, and yet, without physician, nurse, or any other assistance than that of her husband, she had even during that week performed her household duties, and then appeared to be in her usual health.

This was a sad visit for Amos Kendall, not so much on account of the manner in which his brothers and their families lived, as of the conviction that they could never meet the payments for their land, and were making improvements upon it for the benefit of others. Such was the actual result. In the winter of 1813 his brother Zebedee abandoned his place, giving up all his improvements, and returned to his father's with little else than a wife and five children. In August of the same year his sister, having also five children, arrived at her father's under the following circumstances. Her husband, finding himself in painful pecuniary straits, enlisted in the army of the United States, and left her. She was destitute of the necessaries of life, and could not obtain them. A state of pregnancy added to the distress of her situation. She wrote to her father, and he was preparing to send for her when she arrived. She had sold her furniture, bought a horse and cart, taken in her five children, and, with no other companions, started on a journey of two hundred miles. Her oldest child was but twelve years old. Within forty miles of her father's she was taken in labor, but was received into a family and treated kindly. She lost her child, and in one fortnight thereafter reached her father's house.

After spending about three days at these log-cabins the party took an affectionate leave of their occupants, and went over to Fairfax on a visit to Mr. Wilkins and family, — Mrs. Wilkins being a sister of Amos Kendall's father. He owned valuable mills on

Lamoille River, and had several children living in the neighborhood. After spending about four days in visiting and various amusements, the party set out on their return to Windsor by way of Burlington, Vergennes, Middlebury, and Rutland. They were disappointed in the appearance of the college at Burlington, a portion of which was unpainted and the grounds very indifferently improved. The situation, however, was beautiful, commanding a fine view of Lake Champlain which was reached by a gradual descent from the building. The city of Burlington was then but a small village. The scenery from points along the eastern shore of Lake Champlain is exceeded in beauty by that of few places in America. The lake is but a few miles wide, and is studded with islands. The western shore exhibits a broken country, dotted with improvements, and rising as it recedes into hills and mountains.

Spending the night in Vergennes, the party passed on through Middlebury to Rutland, and the next day crossed the mountains to Cavendish. There they separated, the father and mother continuing their journey towards home, and the son returning to Windsor.

On the 25th of September Amos Kendall returned to Hanover, and remained with his class until about the 15th of November, when the necessity of replenishing his funds by keeping school compelled him to ask leave of absence. Three other students, Andrews and Wheeler of the Junior class, and Eastman of the Sophomore, were about leaving at the same time in the same direction, and the four determined to make the journey home on foot, more for a frolic than from any necessity. Early in the morning they started in fine spirits and travelled about six miles before breakfast. As they progressed, however, the unaccustomed use of their limbs in such long walks began to be sensibly felt, and falling in with an empty wagon travelling in the same direction they obtained permission to ride, and were thus carried forward about six miles. It was still a few miles to a tavern, which was reached with much difficulty. Eastman fairly gave out, and had to be assisted for the last mile or two. The whole distance made during the day was about thirty miles. Wheeler had left the party at Newport.

The good people of Goshen were holding a school-meeting at the tavern that evening, and the young students were not too much fatigued to be diverted by the speeches made by the plain countrymen on that interesting occasion.

On consulting their legs the next morning, the young men deemed it imprudent to trust them for another day's tramp, and hired horses to take them out to the stage-road, about ten miles distant. No stage was to pass until the evening, and they walked about three miles to the residence of Andrews, during which Eastman again required assistance. Having rested there until about sunset, they went down to Pierce's tavern, on the stage-road to Hillsborough. This house was kept by General Pierce of Revolutionary celebrity, one of whose sons was a late President of the United States. The evening passed agreeably in conversation with the General's daughters, to one of whom Mr. Kendall had been introduced at Hanover. The stage arrived about half past nine o'clock, when Kendall and Eastman bade adieu to Andrews, and reached Gibson's tavern, in Francestown, about midnight. Resuming their journey about 3 A. M., they arrived at their respective homes in Dunstable and Hollis in the afternoon.

Before Mr. Kendall left the college his father had engaged for him the school in New Ipswich which he had taught the preceding winter. After spending a few days at home and in visiting his friends in Groton, he repaired to the field of his winter's labors and commenced his school on the 4th of December. For him the winter was a remarkably happy one. His scholars were uniformly obedient and respectful, and most of them very studious. Their parents were, without exception, kind and confiding. The neighborhood was exceedingly social, and about half of the evenings there were small parties, to all of which the schoolmaster was invited.

On the 19th of January, 1810, occurred what was long remembered as the "Cold Friday." There had been a warm rain, and the snow, still perhaps eighteen inches deep, was saturated with water. Suddenly on Thursday night the wind changed to the northwest, and blew with the utmost fury. The snow on Friday morning was congealed into a hard mass. The school-house was about half a mile nearly west from Mr. Kendall's lodgings. Starting almost in the face of the wind on the hard snow, and walking rapidly, he soon found himself so exhausted from breathing the condensed atmosphere that he found it necessary to take shelter behind a high stump. He had on woollen mittens, but his ears were uncovered. He soon perceived that to remain there would be to freeze, and again started onward. By the constant use of his mit-

tened hands he saved his ears and reached the school-house without being frozen. But few children came, and some of these with frozen fingers and toes. One red-cheeked boy about twelve years old had, as he entered, a white spot on one cheek about as big as a half-dollar; but by the application of a rag wet with snow-water the frost was extracted without leaving even a soreness. The wind raged all through Friday and half of Saturday, and though there was scarcely a cloud to be seen, there was no sensible moderation of temperature. Many houses were wholly or partially unroofed, among which was the meeting-house at New Ipswich. Much timber was destroyed, and in some pieces of woodland few trees were left standing. They were not torn up by the roots, but broken off at different heights from the ground. The power of the wind may be appreciated from the fact that large trees, perfectly sound and destitute of foliage, were broken entirely off within a few feet from the ground.

On the 22d of February the school was inspected in the presence of a large portion of the people of the district, who expressed the highest satisfaction with the improvement of the children. On the 24th of February the school was closed for the season. While the members of a class of little girls from ten to thirteen years old were standing up to read, for the last time, some of them began to sob, when the whole class caught the infection, and being unable to proceed were remanded to their seats. The next older class were called on, and for the same reason were directed to resume their seats. There was a small class of girls and boys not much younger than their teacher, who were summoned to recite, but they also broke down. The teacher, therefore, with much emotion, made a short address to the children and dismissed them. In his journal he recorded that after he had dismissed the children he shed tears himself, and that he had never before been more attached to a circle of friends or parted from one with so much reluctance. But though pressed to say he would teach the school the next winter, he declined doing so, not knowing what might then be his interest or duty. For this winter's services he received forty-eight dollars.

After Mr. Kendall left college the preceding fall, great excitement had prevailed at the college and in the surrounding country, which had not entirely subsided on his return. A young man had been directed to go to Boston, it was said, to procure a subject for

the dissecting-room. Searching in the burial-ground of an adjacent town, he discovered a newly-made grave, and opening it, took out the body of a young boy and carried it to the college. The grave had been so imperfectly closed as to attract attention, and on examination a pocket-book was found near it, evidently dropped by the resurrectionist, which had his name in it. The grave was reopened. In what direction the missing body had been taken admitted of no doubt. The first knowledge of the discovery which the authorities of the college had, was the appearance at the door of the lecture-room of an officer and several stout attendants, armed with a search-warrant and demanding admittance. The room was searched, and nothing found; but as the party were about retiring, one of them discovered a loose plank in the floor among the seats. On removing it there were the remains of a boy so far dissected and so mangled as to leave nothing of face or form by which he could be recognized. From the size and other circumstances the father had no doubt that the remains were those of his son, and they were taken away for reinterment. This shocking development threw the surrounding country into a state of terror and excitement. People ceased for a time to bury their dead in the public burying-grounds. Town-meetings were held and violent resolutions adopted. Dr. Smith, the head of the anatomical department, rode out to attend one of the meetings, in the hope of allaying the excitement by timely explanations. But the people not only refused to hear him, but thrust him violently out of the meeting-house, and he mounted his horse and fled to escape further outrage. Threats to burn the college buildings were freely uttered, and indeed they were in imminent danger. The young man who had been the immediate cause of this outbreak fled upon its first demonstrations, and although vengeance was denounced against him if to be found on earth, and attempts were made to discover the place of his retreat, he escaped unpunished, though it is not known that he ever again appeared in that neighborhood. In process of time the excitement subsided; but it had the salutary effect of preventing for many years the indiscriminate violation of graves in that region of country for the purpose of procuring subjects for dissection.

On the night of the 19th of April the college and village were alarmed by the cry of fire. Suddenly aroused from sleep, Kendall saw a bright glow on the buildings in front of his window, and supposed the fire was in the roof of the large building in which his room was situated. In a few minutes he was dressed and had all his effects ready for removal. On further inspection, the fire was discovered to be in a barn belonging to Dr. Smith, which, with two adjacent houses, was entirely destroyed. Dr. Smith was that night in attendance upon a patient in the country. Alarmed at the serious face of the messenger sent to announce the disaster, who presented himself in the morning, he suddenly asked, " What is the matter ? Is anybody dead ? " The messenger answered " No ; but your barn is burned, with two of your horses." Relieved from his more serious apprehensions, Dr. Smith replied, " Well, it will make a good watermelon-patch." Dr. Smith was an amiable man, of strong sympathies, but much self-control. He had, perhaps, at that day, no superior as a skilful surgeon, and it was reported of him that he would perform the most agonizing operations with the utmost coolness, and when all was over go away and cry like a child.

In April of this year Mr. Kendall, on invitation, joined a literary society called the *Philoi Euphradias*, composed of students selected, on account of their supposed superior scholarship, from the societies of Social Friends and United Fraternity.

To the great disgust of those who had encountered so much odium in putting down the practice of " treating " on Sophomore quarter-day, it was resumed again this year without any interference of the authorities either before or after the fact. Another affair occurred not long afterwards, which further evinced the lack of discretion in the college faculty in the government of young men. A few wild fellows had amused themselves one night by collecting the cattle on the common and shutting them up in the college cellar. It was not an uncommon occurrence, and the faculty had not generally taken any notice of it. On this occasion they ordered the young men occupying the rooms above the entrance into the cellar to remove the obstructions and let the cattle out. They were among the most orderly students in college, some of them members of churches, and all young men who never participated in nightly frolics. They obeyed the order ; but their natural indignation at being required in open day to undo the nightly mischief of others was soon inflamed, as well by their own reflections as by the comments of their friends and the derision of their less orderly fellow-students. The result was a general deter-

mination to put the cattle into the cellar again, to come out as they might.

Kendall was not one of the young men on whom the indignity had been put ; but they were his associates, and he fully sympathized with their resentment. On the evening of the 19th of June he had gone to bed early, having an attack of sick-headache. Between nine and ten o'clock his chum came in, and told him they had resolved to turn out that night. He got up, dressed himself, and with his chum sallied out to take part in the fray. It was not ten o'clock, and the moon was shining brightly. Now, that even the church-members were engaged, the lovers of frolic turned out in force, and soon more than a hundred young men, most of them somewhat disguised, were perambulating in squads the common and roads adjacent, and driving cattle and horses towards the college. Some of the animals had been driven into the cellar, when President Wheelock, unobserved, approached the entrance. Seizing one of the young men by the arm, he spoke, and being recognized, was tripped up and fell upon the ground. He was not further molested, but deemed it prudent to make a hasty retreat. About a score of live stock had been driven into the cellar, and a party were engaged in carrying and rolling stones, taken from a fence just at hand, with which the entrance had been so far filled as to be impassable, when another party appeared with a horse and a number of cattle. The question was, Shall the obstructions be removed and this additional lot driven in ? It was known that the faculty had assembled at the President's house, and their appearance on the ground was momentarily expected. Nevertheless, it was determined that these new recruits should go in at all hazards. Probably more than sixty young men were on the spot ; and about half of them were assigned to prevent the interference of the faculty, while the residue removed the obstructions, drove in the cattle, and filled up the entrance. Amos Kendall was one of the party assigned to the duty of defending the working-party.

The cellar-way was under the rear of the main college building, and in full view of the rear of the President's house ; but a board-fence intervened, in which was a gate, and through that gate the faculty were expected to approach should they venture to interfere. The defensive party of students stationed themselves, armed with stones and brickbats, a few rods from this fence, with the under-

standing that in case the faculty made their appearance, advancing from the rear of the President's house, they should hurl their missiles against the board-fence, which demonstration it was believed would deter them from advancing.

The party at the cellar-way had removed the obstructions so that the entrance was passable, and were in the act of driving in the reinforcements of stock, when the two tutors made their appearance from the rear of the President's house, advancing toward the gate. Stones and brickbats rattled against the fence, but the brave men kept on, passed through the gate, and were rapidly approaching the array of students. At this crisis, more than half of the defensive party took to their heels, but the residue, knowing that the entire object of the movement would be defeated should they prove recreant, aimed their missiles directly at the tutors, who immediately ran behind the chapel, which was just at hand. No violence was offered them after they turned their backs, though Kendall and a few others followed them as a *corps* of observation. After a short consultation the tutors retired, evidently in despair of stopping the disturbance.

Kendall had been quite sick all the evening, and now, perhaps not altogether satisfied with the extremes to which the affair had been carried, retired to his room and went to bed. The next morning there was a mound of stones covered with earth near the cellar-way, and, near by a large stack of newly mown hay, brought from an adjacent meadow. Under the windows, at the end of the passage in the building above, were piles of small stones. These were significant indications not only that the students did not intend to let the cattle out themselves, but might resist their unconditional surrender by others.

The morning exercises and recitations passed off in customary quietude. About eleven o'clock there was a visible movement among the citizens of the village, and a rumor circulated that they were preparing to release their imprisoned live stock by force. Nearly all the students in college collected in the main building, and, barricading the doors, were ready for defence. The faculty appeared in a body, and, walking around the building, accosted the students standing in the windows, requesting some, and commanding others, to open the doors. The general answer from those addressed was, that it would not be safe for them to attempt it. At length all the faculty retired, and soon afterwards Professor

Hubbard, a most amiable man much beloved by the students, approached one of the end doors with an axe in his hand, and, unresisted, knocked out the panels. He then crawled in through the breach he had made, removed the fastening, and opened the door. The rest of the faculty then joined him, and, treating the students with the utmost courtesy, they took possession of the passages and sent word to the citizens that they might come and dig their cattle out. No aid was asked of the students in this operation.

The faculty were greatly excited by these events, and showed signs of a disposition to inflict condign punishment upon the leaders therein. But their tone soon changed. Calling up a young man of irregular habits who had been recognized on the ground by one of the faculty, they required him to state the names of others who were present. In the hope of saving himself, he named several of the most orderly young men in college, some of whom were brethren in the church with the President and professors. As soon as it was known that the inquisition was on foot, a meeting of students was held and a committee appointed, of whom Mr. Kendall was one, to prepare and send to the faculty a memorial setting forth the extenuating circumstances. This duty was performed. But the most effective step was, doubtless, the concerted determination of the orderly young men engaged in the affair to admit their participation and frankly state their reasons. The following is substantially the result of the examination of a church-member, one of those who had been required to undo the mischief of others, viz. : —

President. Your name has been furnished us as one of those who took part in the recent riot. Is the charge true ?

Student. It is.

Pres. What could have induced you to take part in such a scandalous affair ?

Stu. Your own injustice. I had always obeyed the regulations of the college, took no part in any of the mischievous frolics of other students, was punctual at recitation and studious to preserve the character of an upright and religious man. Notwithstanding all this, you put upon me and others like me the indignity of undoing the mischief of others, and subjected us to their taunts and sneers. Our friends sympathized with us in our natural indignation, and proposed, as the most appropriate mode of making known our resentment, to aid us in putting the cattle back again, and it was done.

Pres. What apology have you to make for your participation in this affair?

Stu. None whatever.

Having been answered in this style by three or four of their most worthy students, the faculty made no further inquiry. They dismissed the young man first called up, and another who was seen to carry into the college building a plank with which one of the doors had been barricaded, imposing upon the others summoned a fine to pay for damages done to some of the cattle and to a stone fence, a rod or two of which had been used for filling up the cellar-way. A general contribution of about twenty-five cents by each student paid the fine, and thus the affair ended. It was a lesson to the faculty by which they doubtless profited in their subsequent conduct towards their more orderly pupils.

About the same time a political excitement arose in the college, in which young Kendall participated. The party names of that day were Federal and Republican, the latter being then sometimes called Democratic. More than three fourths of the students belonged to the Federal party; but Kendall was a Republican. It was proposed to have a no-party celebration on the 4th of July, and a meeting was held to elect an orator and a poet. One of the most violent Federalists was chosen as orator, and Mr. Kendall as poet. The latter, satisfied that with such an orator it would not be a no-party celebration, declined to serve, and resolved to have nothing more to do with the matter. But some of the Republicans determined to get up a separate celebration, and finally made arrangements to have it in Norwich, Vt., a Republican town opposite Hanover on the west side of the Connecticut River. To furnish themselves with cannon for the occasion, a party from Norwich one night carried off the old iron gun which had long been a pet of the students, though they did not know to whom it belonged. The Federal students, as soon as they discovered the loss, became much excited, and determined to recover it, — not because they needed it, there being mounted pieces in the village at their service, but to deprive the other party of its use. They traced it into Vermont, and as they thought to a house not far from the village of Norwich. At their request the owner suffered them to search his house; but they found nothing, and returned to Hanover. Still believing that the gun was concealed in that

house, a large party the next day started for Norwich. Kendall had been bathing in the river, and on his way back to the college met the party near the bridge. Upon the invitation of their leader he turned and went with them to see the sport. As they approached the house in which the gun was supposed to be concealed, the owner met them and inquired what was their object. They replied that they desired to make further search in his house for the missing cannon. He said he had allowed them to search his house once, but could not have it ransacked by them every day, and he forbade them to enter or approach it. They then sent back to Hanover, and with the aid of a lawyer procured the issue of a search-warrant; but neither sheriff nor constable could be found in Norwich to execute it, — being Republicans, they had all disappeared. The day passed away with no other result than creating an excitement among the people of Norwich. In the evening they collected in considerable numbers, and finding that several students had been left behind as spies, they chased some of them over the bridge, and making prisoners of others, lodged them in the garret of the suspected house, and placed a guard over them. Before morning, however, they were suffered to escape.

The next day the excitement at Hanover was higher than ever, and more than a hundred men, including many citizens, gathered for the purpose of recovering the old gun. Their plan of action, by the advice of some considerate citizens, was changed. They sent a delegation to the Lieutenant-Governor of Vermont, living in Norwich, representing that the gun belonged to the State of New Hampshire, and asking him to interpose his influence to produce its peaceful surrender. Upon his declaring his readiness to comply with their request, if they would satisfy him of the justice of their claim, they submitted their evidence, which he deemed satisfactory. In a short speech he stated the case to the people of Norwich, and advised them no longer to insist on keeping a piece of property which belonged to the neighboring State.

The gun had been concealed in the house which had been searched by the students on the first day of the excitement, but on the night of the second day it had been removed, rammed full of rotten stone, and buried in a turnip-patch which had been sown and harrowed over early the next morning. In compliance with the advice of the Lieutenant-Governor, the Norwich people showed the Hanoverians the grave of the gun, but declined giving any aid in its disinterment.

While one party went to work in digging up the gun, another went back to Hanover and procured ropes with which to drag it home, and powder for the purpose of firing it by way of triumph as soon as they should get it across the State line. But they found it impracticable speedily to remove the rotten stone with which it was charged; and, not to be cheated out of their noisy triumph, they sent to the village for one of the mounted pieces. With their ropes they dragged the old gun along the ground and over the bridge, when they halted, fired several rounds, and shouted in the highest excitement. While every one at the college was listening to the distant uproar, the bell over their heads began to ring a merry peal. The Republicans said to each other, "Is it possible that our faculty are taking sides in this party row?" They immediately inquired by what authority the bell was ringing, and was told it was by order of the Treasurer of the Corporation. Most of them, including Kendall, had so far looked on with unconcern, having considered the theft of the cannon as a not very reputable transaction.

But this interference of the college authorities at once excited in every Republican bosom an universal feeling of indignant resentment. To show it in the only way obvious to them, they provided themselves with goose-quill squealers, reeds of wind instruments, and anything at hand with which they could make a disagreeable noise, and went out upon the common in squads for mutual protection.

It was now dark, and the Federalists were dragging their gun along the road from the bridge to the common, shouting as they marched. As soon as they entered upon the common they were saluted by a chorus of squeals and other noises as formidable as could well be made by thirty or forty young men whose hearts were in the cause. To drown their noise, the Federalists sent for a drum. Advancing to the centre of the common, they halted and gave out several toasts of a violent party character. Mr. Kendall has preserved one of them in his journal, with the name of the author. Let the name be forgotten; the toast is as follows: —

"May Democracy throughout the Union lurk in obscurity as on the Plain of Hanover."

All were silent to hear the toast; but as soon as each was given, one party shouted and drummed and the other squealed. Finally,

the Federalists moved across the common and deposited the gun in a cellar, shouting, yelling, and calling the Democrats opprobrious names, while the latter hung about with responsive squeals; and these noises, with the ringing of the bell and the beating of the drum were enough to rouse the echoes from the Granite Hills and the Green Mountains.

The more moderate Republican students had not intended to join the Norwich celebration; but the course pursued by the college authorities converted them into active supporters of the movement. A cannon was procured from a neighboring town, and the party had their oration, dinner, and toasts. Their hilarity, however, was suddenly changed to sadness by a serious accident to their gunner. The piece was fired before he had entirely withdrawn the ramrod, by which means he lost a finger and suffered serious laceration of his hand, arm, and face.

Mr. Kendall characterized the oration on this occasion as "not fit to be spoken by an American," being "too Frenchified"; but the toasts prepared by a committee consisting of Lieutenant-Governor Brigham and his classmates, Carter and Willard, he pronounced excellent.

Without any effort on his part, Kendall had now acquired a high degree of popularity among the students. It was exhibited in his selection to deliver a quarterly oration before the Social Friends, three fourths of whom were bitterly arrayed against him one year before. He was also one of the number selected from his class as members of the *Phi Beta Kappa*.

On the 11th of August died the Hon. John Hubbard, Professor of Mathematics and Natural Philosophy in Dartmouth College. Though not a man of brilliant talents, he was universally beloved and respected for his gentle disposition, his faithfulness as an instructor, and his unimpeachable integrity. He left a widow and four children, two of whom were then members of the Freshman class. The property left by him was insufficient to support his family, who were objects of universal sympathy. The Junior class presented a mourning suit to the widow, which she received with uncontrollable emotion.

On the 15th of August the members of the Junior class were examined and admitted to the Senior standing. On the 22d was Commencement, and on the same evening Kendall started for home on horseback in company with his classmates, Howe and

Ainsworth. The next day they reached Howe's residence in Jaffrey. Here, upon the invitation of his friend Howe, he intended to remain over the 24th for the purpose of ascending Monadnock mountain; but being deterred from that enterprise by clouds hanging around the head of the old monarch, he passed on to New Ipswich, where he was received by his friends with the most flattering cordiality. He was earnestly pressed to take charge of their school for the third season; but he declined committing himself, in the hope of obtaining a more lucrative situation. Having spent several days with his relatives and friends in New Ipswich and Mason, he reached home on the 31st of August, where he was pained to find his mother very low with dropsy, from which there were but faint hopes of her recovery.

On the 12th of September he attended a meeting of the Middlesex Musical Society, at Townsend, and joined in their performances. This society and the Handel Society of Dartmouth College were making a concerted effort to change the character of the music then used in the churches of New England, and to that end had arranged to have a public exhibition at Concord, N. H., on the 19th day of that month. The reform proposed, was to substitute the old-fashioned slow and solemn music for the light, jangling fugues which were in general use, and it was hoped to effect a change in the popular taste by the public performance of the best psalm-tunes and other pieces written by the most celebrated composers. At this meeting in Townsend information was received that a long-established Musical Society at Amherst, N. H., called the Handelian, had fallen into the ranks of the reformers.

Several days were spent by Kendall in visiting his friends in Groton and Dunstable, and in collecting money for his father, after which he started for the college by way of Concord, N. H., spending a day there to take part in the musical celebration. About forty performers were present, and though the day was rainy there was a large audience. An excellent oration on the object of the societies was delivered by the Rev. Samuel Worcester, of Salem, and his tribute to the memory of Professor Hubbard, who at the time of his death was President of the Handel Society and had projected that meeting, drew tears from a large portion of the audience. The music was of a very high order, though not so perfect as the separate performances of the Handel Society. Although the societies had practised the same tunes preparatory to this ex-

hibition, and each was very perfect in its way, yet, when they came to sing together, slight variances developed themselves, which, in a moderate degree, impaired the general effect. The exhibition, however, passed off with much applause. Of the male performers, Jonathan Curtis, and of the female, Miss Mary and Miss Annette Woodward, all members of the Handel Society, attracted particular attention and applause.

CHAPTER III.

On the 20th of October Mr. Kendall returned to college in company with his classmate, Jonathan Curtis, and the next day engaged a room and board in a private house kept by a widow lady named Davis.

On the 2d of November the appointments for Senior quarter-day were given out. According to custom, this was done by the class voting by ballot. Kendall was surprised to find himself elected to the first appointment, apparently by an unanimous vote. He was equally surprised at the elections to the second and some of the succeeding appointments, which fell upon young men deemed by him undeserving of the positions in the class thus assigned to them. Observing a cluster of students in a corner of the room, he approached and found them looking over an entire list of appointments already made out, and that the elections thus far were in accordance with the list. The thought at once flashed upon his mind, that there was a concerted scheme, well matured, to place certain young men in positions to which their merits did not entitle them, and that his name had, without consulting him, been placed at the head of the list as a cover of the meditated injustice to others. At his request the list was handed to him, and mounting a bench and inviting the attention of the assembly, he remarked, in a jocular manner, that somebody, it appeared, had already performed the service for which the class was called together, and as they had thus far ratified the arrangement prepared to their hands, it seemed unnecessary to waste time in voting upon each case separately. He therefore moved that the entire list be adopted just as arranged. Though the managers looked blank and raised a feeble opposition, the motion was carried by acclamation and a committee appointed to communicate the result to the faculty. Kendall immediately called on the President and informed him of the whole matter, stating that he did not consider it any honor to receive the appointment assigned to him by caucus

management and expressing the hope that the entire proceedings would be set aside and the class directed to go into a new election. The faculty, however, recognized as legitimate the appointments which had been assigned by separate votes, and directed the class to reassemble and fill up the list in the same way. But few attended the second meeting, and the caucus managers voted themselves, without exception, into the places which had been assigned them in the original list. Kendall had accomplished his object in satisfying every one that he had no hand in the caucus arrangement which placed him at the head of his class. But he exclaims in his journal: "Who, said I to myself, thought, Sophomore year, that these fellows would ever give the first appointment to 'Giles Scroggins'?" This was one of the nicknames applied to him during the "treating" excitement of 1809. He adds, "College popularity is variable as the wind."

On the 3d of November the father of Zerah Colburn, the celebrated boy mathematician, called with his son at Kendall's boarding-house. In his journal Mr. Kendall says of this prodigy: "His father gives the following account of him. He was born six years ago the first day of last September. He appeared to know even less than common children when one year old. Last spring he was observed to be talking of figures with the other children, when he appeared to answer questions in the multiplication-table much more readily than his elders. He, however, attracted no particular notice until last August, when his father observing his readiness in figures, began to question him, and soon found that he was better acquainted with the multiplication-table than himself. The affair soon spread, and the boy was taken to Montpelier and Burlington and examined. Being poor, the father had determined to take his child to some of the larger towns and cities of the country in the hope of raising money to give him an education.

"Professors Adams and Shurtleff examined the boy in private and afterwards in public. They were confounded. Professor Adams, himself an eminent mathematician, said he had never seen, heard, or read of anything like it. He could multiply together any two numbers under a hundred in less than a minute. He could tell, apparently without thought, how many days there are in any number of years less than thirty, and in any number over thirty and up to a hundred upon a minute's reflection. After being told the denominations of weights and measures, he would reduce one to another with the greatest readiness. He answered correctly the question, 'How many gills are there in three barrels?' The question, 'How many are $25 \times 25 + 35 \times 35 + 45 \times 45$?' he answered correctly with little hesitation. He readily multiplied any number over a hundred by any number less. In less than a minute he answered correctly the question, 'How many days are there in seventy-three years?' What rendered his performances more wonderful was, that he did not know a figure when written, and could not count more than fifty. How he knew the names of larger numbers was a mystery, and he was sometimes embarrassed in making his answers understood. After he had stated correctly the number of days in a given number of years, he was asked how many hours there were. He said he did not know the number of hours in a day. On being told it was twenty-four he immediately gave a correct answer.

"He was of the ordinary size, had a large head, red hair, blue eyes, a florid, healthy complexion, somewhat freckled, had five fingers (exclusive of thumbs) and was always in motion, even when calculating. On other subjects than numbers his remarks were sensible for a child of his age."

It was understood that the faculty offered to take the boy and give him an education gratuitously; but the father, without declining the proposition, wished to exhibit his son in the large cities.

On returning to college the next spring, Kendall fell in with Zerah Colburn and his father, in the stage between Windsor and Hanover, returning home from a very successful money-making tour to Boston and more southern cities. Zerah and his father (who was a very ignorant man) had become entirely spoilt by the attentions and money which had been bestowed upon them, and by their impertinence and vanity made themselves very obnoxious to the other passengers. The desire of the father to have his son educated had been superseded by "the cursed lust for gold," to be accumulated by the exhibition of his son's wonderful talent, and in furtherance of this object he was then meditating a trip to Europe. Mr. Kendall never again fell in with Zerah or his father. It was understood, however, that the contemplated trip to Europe was performed and was highly successful; but that Zerah's peculiar talent did not improve in proportion to his advance in years, and that when he became a man he was not pre-eminent for his mathematical genius.

It was the custom of the Society of Social Friends to select one of the Senior class to deliver an oration on the Monday or Tuesday preceding Commencement, and another to prepare a dialogue to be recited on the same occasion. The oration was considered the most honorable appointment. From indications hardly to be mistaken, Kendall believed he could have his choice of these appointments; but having at the time some poetical ambition, he preferred the second honor to the first, and though pressed to be a candidate for the oration with assurances of his election, he peremptorily declined. The second appointment was assigned to him with entire unanimity.

The 28th of November was Senior quarter-day, when Kendall performed the part which had been assigned to him by his class. Having undertaken to teach a school in Weston, Mass., which began on the 3d of December, he obtained leave of absence, and on the 30th of November left for home, which, after a rough stage-ride over frozen ground, he reached the next day. Resting one day, he rode to Weston on the 3d of December, and found that his school had met that day and dispersed.

This school he taught four months, commencing on the 4th of December. The entire number of children who attended during the winter was 85, and the average number in attendance exceeded 60. Of the 85, 63 were learning to write, 21 were studying arithmetic, 19 English grammar, 9 geography, 2 Latin, and 1 Greek. Often, also, little children were sent in who did not know their letters. It is very obvious that no man without an assistant could teach very thoroughly such a number of children in such diversified studies. The school had been very loosely governed, and at first was quite disorderly. At Mr. Kendall's request the school committee of the district visited the school, and in the presence of the children enjoined upon him the duty of exacting obedience and preserving order. Thus sustained, he soon succeeded, without the infliction of any severe punishments, in bringing the school under good discipline. A single instance of abstinence from punishment had a remarkable effect. A boy had committed some offence which excited his teacher, who called him up and reproved him in severe terms. He had taken hold of the boy's hand and raised his ruler for the purpose of ferruling him, when he suddenly threw the hand from him, saying: "Go to your seat, I am too angry to strike you." The children, most of

whom had probably never been corrected except in anger, stared in wonder.

It was only by classification that so large a number of children could be taught at all. There were four classes in reading and spelling, two in arithmetic, two in English grammar, and two in geography. The time allotted to teaching was six hours, three in the forenoon and three in the afternoon, with a short intermission at twelve o'clock. A recess of a few minutes, first of the girls and then of the boys, was allowed in the middle of the forenoon and again in the middle of the afternoon. To make and mend pens (steel pens being then unknown), set copies for the writers, and hear all these classes twice a day, was no small labor. The Latin and Greek scholars recited in the evening after the school was dismissed.

On the 29th of March, 1811, the school was examined by the clergyman of the town and the school committee, in the presence of a considerable number of the inhabitants. The teacher had kept in tabular form, and laid before them, a statement showing the names and ages of all the children who had attended the school during the winter, the number of days each was absent, the progress made by each in writing, arithmetic, geography, English grammar, and the languages; in the first class, the number of words missed in spelling, and in the second, third, and fourth classes, the number of times each had been at the head. The examination was highly satisfactory, and the committee solicited Mr. Kendall to take charge of their school the next winter; but having other views, he declined making any engagement. Though he fell ten days short of the stipulated time, the committee paid him for seventeen full weeks, — his wages amounting to eighty-five dollars.

Though the winter in other respects had passed very agreeably, there was not that cordiality between the teacher and the people which existed at New Ipswich, nor the same degree of affection between him and his scholars. Among his new acquaintances was the Rev. J. Kendall, D. D., the clergyman of the town, with whom he endeavored in vain to trace a relationship, though they did not doubt that they had descended from the same English ancestor. While Mr. Kendall was describing Zerah Colburn to Dr. Kendall, on mentioning his five fingers, — "Why," exclaimed the latter, "he is our cousin!" He proceeded to say that he had never met with a person favored with such a superfluity of digits, whose

kinship to the Kendall family could not be established, and he requested his young friend to inquire what was the fact in this case. When he, Kendall, met Zerah and his father in the stage on his return to college the next spring, he made the inquiry and was informed that Zerah's grandmother was a Kendall. She married a Green, her daughter married a Colburn, who was the grandfather of Zerah, and thence he derived his five fingers.

On the 30th of March Mr. Kendall returned home, and after spending about two weeks among his friends, reached Dartmouth College on the evening of the 13th of April.

On the 24th of May the Senior appointments were given out, and Mr. Kendall had the unexpected pleasure of finding himself placed at the head of his class. The second honor in rank was assigned to Joseph Perry, the third to Daniel Poor, the fourth to Nathaniel H. Carter, the fifth to —— Fairfield, the sixth to Nathaniel Wright, the seventh to Jonathan Curtis, the eighth to Joseph Curtis, the ninth (a dialogue) to Samuel Woodbury and —— Crowell, the tenth (a dialogue) to —— Bean and Ether Shepley, the eleventh (forensic) to Bezaleel Cushman and —— Whipple, the twelfth (poem) to —— Morse.

Had the duty of giving out the appointments devolved on Mr. Kendall himself, he would have assigned the first to Daniel Poor, and preferred several others to himself. It seemed to him impossible, that, laboring under so many disadvantages, he could entitle himself to the first rank in his class. Want of means had compelled him to be absent two whole terms and parts of several more. He had, indeed, entered college five times, four of them in consequence of forfeiting his connections by absence every year. Several branches of study he had pursued in winter evenings without a teacher, while keeping school. Though he thought he appeared well in every branch of study, he was yet conscious of superiority in none, and of inferiority in some. On the whole, he concluded that the faculty, in assigning the first rank to him, had made liberal allowances for the disadvantages under which he had labored. But his highest gratification arose from the congratulations of his classmates, all of whom seemed to concede that he merited the honor which he had received.

This year the faculty took efficient steps to prevent, and did prevent, the practice of "treating" on Sophomore quarter-day, and the "Temperance men" of that day had the satisfaction of reflecting that the indignities to which two years before they had been exposed in the cause, had not been encountered in vain.

There were two affairs in this portion of his college life from which Mr. Kendall deduced lessons for his future guidance in the outer world. One of them was a formidable conspiracy defeated by promptitude and firmness. The Society called the Philoi Euphradias was composed of young men selected from the Social Friends and United Fraternity, and was an object of envy and hatred to a majority of the members of those two societies, who had been passed over in making the selections. A conspiracy was formed, extending through both of those societies, whose object was the destruction of the Philoi Euphradias. The means by which it was proposed to accomplish this end was the adoption of a fundamental regulation prohibiting the members of the Friends and Fraternity from joining the Philoi, on the ground that the latter was incompatible with the interests of the former. The scheme was thoroughly matured, and preparations made to broach it in the Social Friends, which then embraced about two thirds of the students.

There was an unusually full meeting, and Mr. Kendall sat wondering what could have occasioned so general an attendance, many young men being present who seldom appeared, and who took little interest in the society or its exercises. At length his old chum, T. C. Gardner, arose, made a short speech, and submitted a proposition prohibiting members of the Friends from joining the Philoi. He had said but a few words when Mr. Kendall comprehended the cause of the full attendance, and perceived that there was a matured conspiracy, of which Gardner was the organ. He therefore promptly replied to Gardner's argument, denying the alleged incompatibility of interest and denouncing the proposition as an implied imputation upon the fidelity of those who were already members of the Philoi. He was followed by others of the Philoi and the conspirators ; but it was soon evident that the adoption of Gardner's proposition was a foregone conclusion. The vote was about to be taken, when Mr. Shepley, who was a Philoi, asked Mr. Kendall to step out with him. As soon as they were out of the room, Shepley asked, "What do you intend to do?" "Leave the society," was the prompt reply. "So will I," said Shepley. When they returned to the hall the vote had been taken, and Daniel Poor, the President of the society, and a Philoi, was making

a speech, which he concluded by asking a dismission. He was followed in the same request by Kendall, Shepley, and several others. Poor directed the Secretary to put the vote on his application for dismission. He did so, but there was no affirmative response. Poor then rose and said he would not remain in the society under the imputation which their proceedings cast upon him, and if they would not dismiss him he would dismiss himself, whereupon he left the chair, took his hat, and walked out of the hall. Much confusion ensued. The members generally were much attached to the society, and the decisive course adopted by the Philois had not entered into the calculation of the conspirators. Many members flocked around Kendall and his friends, some of them shedding tears, disavowing any intention to impeach their fidelity, and begging them to remain in the society. They were inflexible. Finally a President pro tem. was elected, and Kendall stated that the only thing which would induce him to remain in the society, — and he believed every Philoi felt as he did, — was the rescinding of the resolution they had adopted. A motion to that effect was made and carried almost unanimously. A committee was then appointed to invite Mr. Poor into the hall and resume the chair. The ceremony was duly performed, and there the affair ended.

In truth, the Philois were the flower of the society, embracing most of its officers, and most of those who infused talent into its performances and gave it character in the estimation of the community.

In pursuance of his appointment by the Social Friends, Mr. Kendall wrote a long tragedy, entitled "Palafox, or the Siege of Saragossa," the subject of which was the desperate defence of that city by the Spaniards against the armies of Napoleon. It was read to the society and approved.

Nathaniel Wright, who had been appointed for a similar purpose by the United Fraternity, had also written a long tragedy. As both could not be performed the same evening, a dispute arose between the two societies as to which should occupy the evening before Commencement, being Tuesday. That evening was greatly preferred to Monday, as many more strangers from abroad were likely to be in attendance. The Fraternity claimed Tuesday evening by right of prescription ; the Friends denied the claim, and urged the principle of alternation, the Fraternity having had Tues-

day evening on the last similar occasion. The dispute grew so warm that the faculty, fearing a disturbance, gave notice that unless the two societies could adjust the matter between themselves, both plays would be suppressed. With the consent of the authors, the societies agreed that only the best of the two should be performed, and appointed a joint committee to examine them and make the selection ; but the committee divided, each branch deciding in favor of the work which represented their own society. Each of the authors then submitted his production to the criticism of his competitor in the hope (not very reasonable, perhaps) that one might concede the superiority to the other ; but each very naturally preferred his own production. Wright's zealous defence of his own, and his extravagant criticism of Kendall's, suggested to the latter a mode of settling the controversy. Not doubting that his rival would sooner yield the point than have his play suppressed, he recommended to the Social Friends to pass, and send to the Fraternity, a resolution asserting their right to Tuesday evening, and their determination not to yield it, though the consequences should be the suppression of both plays ; his suggestion was adopted, and the result vindicated his sagacity.

This question being settled, Kendall proceeded to select performers for the different parts of his tragedy, and provide their costumes. He had never been in a theatre, and knew nothing about modern acting. His knowledge on the subject was derived altogether from books. His play, therefore, was on the ancient model, very long, with a prologue and epilogue. It was a work of much labor ; but at that period of his life he loved labor.

During the 26th and 27th of August the several societies had their annual performances, which were not marked by any unusual incidents, except that when the Philoi Euphradias entered the meeting-house they were saluted by the baffled conspirators with the blowing of horns, yells, and the ringing of the bell. On motion of Mr. Kendall, the members of the society wore their medals during the day and evening in token of defiance.

On the evening of the 25th the tragedy of the United Fraternity was performed. The manner in which it was received and the criticisms upon it had a depressing effect upon Kendall, filling him with apprehensions as to the fate of his own production.

The dreaded evening of the 26th arrived. Mr. Kendall's account of the performance, written at the time, is as follows : —

"The prologue was well spoken. The performance commenced ; but the performers spoke so low as not to be heard throughout the house. Intelligence soon came from different parts of the audience, and the performers raised their voices. The play proceeded, not without laughter and tears from many of the audience. The music was appropriate, having been previously selected. Then followed the epilogue. It was performed to admiration by Heywood and Miltimore, and received with repeated bursts of applause. I myself performed the third part, and had the vain momentary satisfaction of a general clapping when I left the stage. I soon likewise had the satisfaction to learn that the audience placed it much before the play of last evening. Fatigued, and I can likewise add satisfied, with the transactions of the day and evening, I speedily retired."

The next day was Commencement. The salutatory oration by Mr. Kendall, being in Latin, was unintelligible to most of the audience, and was not considered by himself as possessing any peculiar merit. With two or three exceptions, the other performances were very indifferent. Bean refused to make any preparation to perform the part assigned him, apparently thinking he had been underrated in the distribution of the appointments. Jonathan Fairfield, for the same reason, resolved to disgrace the Commencement by disgracing himself. He appeared on the stage with his stockings about his heels, and his whole dress in a most slovenly condition. He took no notice of the President or Trustees, and spoke so low as hardly to be heard ten feet from the stage. His oration was on the "Liberty of the Press," and was made up of extracts from Junius, awkwardly put together. Once he pulled a paper from his pocket, and for some time read from it in a most monotonous tone. The consequence of the conduct of Bean and Fairfield was, that both lost their degrees. As soon as the performances were over Mr. Kendall betook himself to his bed, being entirely exhausted by the business of the week.

Thus ended Amos Kendall's college life. It was one of disappointments ; but his disappointments were honors. His honors were not the result of management, but came upon him unsought. He performed no act and concealed no opinion with the view of gaining any personal advantage. Always truthful and punctual in every college duty, he became popular without seeking popularity. Never was he absent from recitation without a sufficient excuse, and never but once from the services in the chapel. On that occasion the tutor had seen him in company with some ladies after the hour for evening prayer had passed, and when asked what excuse he had, he replied, "None at all, sir." The tutor smiled, and passed to the next delinquent.

The following is a review of Mr. Kendall's college life, written by him in his journal at its close, and in it may be found the key to his entire subsequent career : —

"At this era the mind naturally reviews the incidents which have checkered my college course. I at first entered upon my collegiate studies with much diffidence in my own powers, but with an ambition to appear among the foremost. I soon found that popularity and excellence of scholarship are seldom connected, and that decision and firmness would best secure a person from the interruptions of the fools of dissipation. My first chamber-mate was too fond of company. I soon perceived that his associates were not suitable companions for one really desirous of acquiring knowledge. Though at first, from my ignorance of a college life, I had engaged in one or two trifling foolish adventures, I was soon freed from further vexation by a fixed and declared determination to take no part in these heroic achievements. The consequence was, that my popularity, which at first was great, began to decline, and I was looked upon with an eye of suspicion. About the same time I had an invitation to join a secret club, afterwards called the *Gymnasion Adelphon*, instituted for the promotion of friendship and mutual improvement. This society, which comprised the best part of the class both in morals and knowledge, had a wonderful effect in uniting all its members in all the succeeding difficulties. In fact, it formed a phalanx which not all the sons of dissipation were able to break or terrify. Notwithstanding it consisted of fifteen or more members, and met weekly, even its existence was never known in college. Its effects were seen, but the cause was hidden.

"At the beginning of Sophomore year my popularity had considerably declined. In the spring of that year commenced our attack upon the detestable habit of 'treating.' The open and decided part which I took in this quarrel gave a finishing blow to my popularity. I was stigmatized as an informer, nicknamed 'Giles Scroggins's ghost,' from my paleness of countenance, and had the mortification of seeing all these things written in fifty places on the college walls, and even in the chapel. But the effect was contrary to expectation. I affected to take no notice of it, and by treating every one with civility, soon had the satisfaction of seeing my enemies at my feet. Every one of them who had any sense of honor or propriety heartily detested the thing, and personally

ally conversed with me, acknowledging themselves in fault. To the inveteracy of my enemies I attributed my not being elected into the Philoi Euphradias at the first election, and I expected the same cause would close the avenues of the Phi Beta Kappa. But in the Junior year the tide changed, and I was elected into both of those societies. My friends or flatterers informed me that many considered me the first scholar in the class. This, I must confess, though contrary to my own opinion, somewhat raised my vanity. The truth is, that at a university of this kind, a few glowing pieces of composition, with one or two public declamations, written and spoken with spirit, have more effect in raising the reputation of a student than the reasoning of a Locke, the application of a Newton, or the wisdom of a Solomon. Upon this tinsel foundation was my reputation in a great degree established. Not that I had paid no attention to the classics ; I had always made them my first object. But I am conscious of being excelled in that kind of knowledge by more than one of my classmates. Yet the class first, and afterwards the government, have honored me with the first appointments. The society of Social Friends assigned to me the writing of a tragedy, which was my desire in preference to any other honor at the disposal of the society. The activity and versatility of my mind and the vivacity of my imagination have been mistaken for knowledge, and my reserve in not connecting myself with any of the officers of government has carried an appearance of independence, and these causes, combined with the good opinion of most of the students, have enabled me to bear the palm from those more studious and more knowing than myself. Besides the knowledge of books, I have gained much by my residence at college. I have seen the maxim, 'Self-love, the spring of action, moves the soul,' exemplified in almost innumerable instances. I have seen that man's opinion of right is generally founded upon his interest ; that to make a man your friend, you must promote his interest ; that difference of opinion, inflamed by continual dispute, begets coldness and suspicion ; that honors often depend on popularity, and popularity on accommodation and acquiescence ; but that the most stable kind of popularity — that which insures respect and lasting esteem — is founded upon decision of character. Yet this decision must be based on reason, and exercised with prudence. The man of decision is alone independent. It is remarkable to observe the effect of this quality. A word with him is as an action ; a promise, as a performance. The mass revere him, and never press beyond a denial. This I have seen completely exemplified in many of my classmates. Their characters are established, and their opinions, once expressed, are considered as deciding the course of their actions. They are never asked a second time, never urged. I have also seen the ill effects of the contrary disposition exemplified in numerous in-

stances. They refuse, are asked again ; begin to question, are urged ; waver, are besought for God's sake ; yield, and thus expose themselves to the importunities of every needy vagabond and cunning intriguer. Their reward is only contempt."

These were Mr. Kendall's opinions of himself and of mankind in general when he left college. He did not take a diploma, partly because he was indifferent to the bauble, and partly because he disliked the President of the college. On the 30th of August he left Hanover, and passing through Jaffrey, New Ipswich, and Groton, reached home on the 1st of September.

On a settlement with his father, it appeared that the entire cost of his education in fitting for, and going through college, exclusive of clothing, was a little over five hundred and seventy dollars, of which his father had advanced a little over three hundred. The residue was paid out of moneys received by him for keeping school.

The subject of a profession had occasionally occupied his thoughts during his college career. His parents were anxious that he should fit himself for the gospel ministry ; but he did not feel conscious of those inward qualifications deemed essential in that work. To medicine and surgery he had an invincible antipathy. The only remaining profession was the law, for which he had little inclination. His tastes would have led him to devote his life to philosophical studies and practical mechanics, embracing a wide field of experiments. But from that course he was deterred by the necessity of earning his bread by some productive occupation. His father had announced that he could render him no further aid ; and a return to teaching seemed to be the only practicable course, as a means of present support and to enable him to study law. Understanding that the preceptorship of the Academy in Groton, Massachusetts, was vacant, he had, before Commencement, visited that place with the view of securing the situation. To obtain his aid and influence, he called on William Merchant Richardson, Esq., then a practising lawyer in Groton, who had done business for his father, and broached the subject. Mr. Richardson advised him to enter upon the study of law at once, remarking that to teach, as a temporary expedient, was to throw away a portion of one's life. He said he had a student in his office and boarding in his family whom he had agreed to trust for his tuition and board until he should be able to pay him, and also allowed him certain perquisites

which enabled him to pay for his clothing ; that the time of this young man would be out in a few months ; that he would then receive Mr. Kendall into his office and family on the same terms ; and that if, in the mean time, Mr. Kendall could procure board elsewhere, he might enter his office at once. This generous offer Mr. Kendall decided to accept.

Having some money left of his last winter's earnings, and from the sale of a number of books for which he had no further use, he made an arrangement with his former preceptor, Caleb Butler, for board in his family, and on the 4th of September, 1811, entered Mr. Richardson's office as a student of law. On this occasion he says in his journal: "A new field now opens to my view, indeed boundless. Who can look upon so many volumes of commentaries, institutes, digests, and reports, without discouragement ?"

Mr. Kendall's classmate and friend, Samuel Woodbury, having taken charge of Groton Academy, became his fellow-boarder and bed-fellow at Mr. Butler's.

On the 25th of September there was an exhibition of the music-reform societies at Amherst, N. H., then consisting of the Middlesex, the Handel, the Handelian of Amherst, and another from Concord, N. H. The day was rainy ; but, nevertheless, the audience was numerous and brilliant. The principal pieces performed after a prayer and oration, were the anthem *O Lord God of Israel*, *Old Hundred*, *Wantage*, *Melton*, *Mowbray*, and the *Chorus of the Grand Hallelujah*. Though somewhat ill, from the effect of vaccination about ten days before, Mr. Kendall took part in this exhibition, which passed off with much *éclat*. His arm becoming much swollen and inflamed, producing frequent recurrence of violent sick-headache, he returned to his father's house three days after the exhibition, where he remained for two weeks. The time was spent chiefly in remodelling his tragedy and introducing female characters, none then being allowed upon the stage at Dartmouth College. His friends professed to think very highly of this tragedy, as well before it was remodelled as afterwards, and some of them advised him to offer it to the managers of the Boston Theatre. This excited a hope that he might, by that expedient, raise money enough to enable him to study law without accepting the perquisites offered him by Mr. Richardson, and he determined to try the experiment. Having digested his plan, he visited Boston, sent his play to one of the managers of the theatre by the hands of a servant, with an anonymous note requesting him, if the play was approved, to make proposals within a week in a manner pointed out, and if not, to hold it until called for. Nearly two weeks passed, and nothing came from the manager, when Mr. Kendall wrote to his old chum, Jonathan Fowle, who lived in Boston, requesting him to call and ascertain the fate of his play. The following is Mr. Kendall's account of the result : —

"*November 29th.* Received for answer from Fowle that he had obtained the copy ; that Mr. Powell (the manager) said they had a number of new plays for this season ; that mine was too long by one third ; that he objected to the too frequent repetition of pa, ma, grandpa, etc., as childish, and said that the whole character of ' Little Boy ' was too trifling for tragedy ; that a certain something was wanting to produce stage effect ; that he advised me to lay it before some judge of theatricals ; and he concluded by observing that, with such alterations as my judgment would suggest, it might be brought forward next winter. I was somewhat disappointed ; but soon took my resolution to do nothing more about it for the present. But if I should hereafter be disposed, I may once more attempt to please these gentlemen. From my inexperience, any attempt at first appeared like presumption, and though my friends were sanguine, I could never assure myself of final success. But I wanted money, and acted upon this proverb : ' Nothing venture, nothing have.' The result may be of advantage to me in confining my mind more to my studies."

Though Mr. Kendall afterwards wrote another tragedy, entitled " The Fall of Switzerland," he never again offered any production of his to a theatrical manager.

For want of money to pay for his board, Mr. Kendall spent the winter of 1811–12 at home, seeing very little company and devoting himself to his studies. The law books which engaged his attention were Blackstone's Commentaries, Coke on Littleton, and Bacon's Abridgment. He says in his journal: " My common lesson is eighty pages, thirty in the forenoon, thirty in the afternoon, and twenty in the evening. Too much, I am sensible ; but I have scarcely anything else to do. I cut wood about three quarters of an hour, read a few propositions of Euclid and a few pages of Stewart's Philosophy." He also amused himself with noting **down** projects of literary works and plays as they occurred to **him,** which he called his *Air-Castles.*

At this period political feeling ran very high. On receiving a letter from his friend Shepley, advising him to enter upon the business of an editor, Mr. Kendall noted down the following observations : —

" Though this business is not altogether agreeable to my ambition, his suggestions have led me to consider the practicability of a coalition between the reasonable men of both parties in the State. Party spirit has indeed arisen to a most alarming height. Nothing will satisfy our flaming demagogues but the prostitution of every establishment in which the opposite party have property or influence. I scarcely know how to choose. Although my principles as well as interests incline me to the Democratic or Republican side, I am not yet prepared to sacrifice my conscience and every principle of moral honesty to the unhallowed zeal of any party. Happily, I am not yet to enter on the theatre of public life, and though my ambition leads me to the active scenes of the legislature, my first design is to make myself a lawyer."

About this time were published the letters of John Henry, a British spy, who visited Boston in the time of the embargo of Jefferson's administration, for the purpose of promoting a dissolution of the Union and the establishment of a Northern Confederacy. Having read them, Mr. Kendall remarked in his journal, " They are a proof of the desperate designs which then actuated the leading Federalists."

It was not until the 25th of March, 1812, that Mr. Kendall resumed his residence in Groton, and he was enabled to do so then only by the liberality of Mr. Richardson, who lent him money without security to pay for his board.

Mr. Richardson was then a member of Congress from the Middlesex district of Massachusetts, elected by the Democratic party. He was an honest and upright man, and in talents above mediocrity. He was opposed to the embargo and other restrictive measures of Jefferson's administration, though they were supported by his party in general. His allegiance to his party, like that of many other democrats of that day, was secured by the violent and unpatriotic language and acts of the Federal leaders.

June 23d, 1812, Mr. Kendall records : —

" This day arrived in town the declaration of war by the United States against Great Britain. It was issued on the 18th inst. At length we are forced into the mighty conflict which has so long desolated Europe. The event, God only knows. Had it been consistent with our

honor and the preservation of our rights to have sided with Great Britain, it would have been much more consonant to the feelings of every friend of liberty. But her infatuated cabinet seem bent on destruction. May the God of peace avert from us civil commotion, lead our armies to victory, and soon restore our nation to honorable tranquillity."

On the 26th he writes : —

" The *Repertory* of this day (a Boston Federal newspaper) plainly advises Massachusetts to withdraw from the Union rather than engage in the war. The House of Representatives (of Massachusetts) have taken some measures which bear an appearance hostile to the general government, and are now debating an address to the people. It can hardly be conjectured to what lengths their madness will carry the Federal party, but I am inclined to think their rage will soon subside. Were their leaders sure of being seconded by the people, a separation of the Union would be but the work of a day. But cursed be the man who lifts his hand for this nefarious purpose."

On the 20th of July there was a National Fast, proclaimed by the President upon the recommendation of Congress. Mr. Kendall's anticipations as to the services of that day were recorded as follows : —

" One cannot reflect without pain on the mockery which must this day be offered to the Almighty by a large portion of the clergy of New England. These deluded men seem to have abandoned all the rules of common prudence, and seem to believe that on a man's politics depends not only his honesty, but the eternal salvation of his soul. They forget the maxims of charity inculcated by our religion, and treat a large part of their fellow-citizens as outcasts and ministers of Satan. Did the consequences extend no further than their political influence, their acrimony would be comparatively innocuous. But a man will not tamely be called a villain, even by his minister, nor will he ever put confidence in him, who he believes makes his discourse the vehicle of lies and sedition. The sacred desk should be unpolluted by party rage ; the mouth that pours forth the sweet promises of salvation and inculcates Christian charity and meekness, should never be defiled with the epithets of party scurrility or violent anathemas against national rulers. But this is not confined to one party. The delusion is general. The Federalists, to be sure, are most numerous, and at present most violent. The late State Fast has left many lasting specimens of their folly. If the people were united, it might be more excusable ; but as it is, a portion of the congregation first disbelieve, then hate, and at length desert their

religious instructor. It is a serious truth, that men's political prejudices are stronger than their religious opinions. Doubtless many of the clergy sincerely believe that while they are hurling anathemas on their fellow-citizens, they are engaged in the service of God. The event will probably try their sincerity. It cannot be supposed that the Democratic party, should they again hold the reins (in Massachusetts) will be disposed to patronize a body of men from whom they receive only execration."

Mr. Kendall's anticipations were fully realized. Denunciations of the President and Congress took the place, in many a New England pulpit, of humble petitions for the safety of the country and the success of its arms. The sermon in Groton was a rank specimen. Mr. Richardson, who had in Congress voted for the war, though not a member of the church, was a constant attendant upon public worship, and by presents, as well as by cheerful payment of his tax, contributed liberally towards the support of the clergyman. He was at meeting on the National Fast Day. The clergyman's text was, " Ye are of your father, the Devil ; and the works of your father ye will do." The theme of his discourse was a comparison of the President of the United States to Beelzebub, the Prince of Devils, and the members of Congress who voted for the war, to the subordinate devils who do his bidding. Mr. Richardson heard him through ; but when out of the meeting-house, though not a profane man, he turned and swore that he would never enter its doors again until the clergyman atoned for that discourse.

This clergyman and many others taught their families and friends to believe that all Democrats were irreligious profligates, and it was amusing for Mr. Kendall and Mr. Woodbury to hear from ladies whom they visited the cautions conveyed from that quarter about associating with them because they were Democrats, though Woodbury was a member of the church.

The result of the rabid interference of the Congregational clergy with politics, in Massachusetts, was the abolition of the constitutional and legal provision for their support by a general tax, and it was one of the principal agencies in building up societies of other denominations and sowing religious discord where all had been of one faith.

In October, 1812, Mr. Kendall, for the first time in his life, mustered twice with a militia company ; but on both occasions was so completely exhausted that he gave up all idea of encountering the fatigue of a regimental muster which was to follow. The incidents on that occasion, as far as he was concerned, he thus records:—

"Instead of doing military duty this day, I became gallant, and in the afternoon conducted two ladies to the field in a chaise. Soon after our arrival a sham-fight commenced, and was continued for some time with spirit. Suddenly the firing ceased, and there was a cry that a man had been shot. I had retired to a road in full view of the field, and was seated in the chaise with the young ladies. The wounded man was borne past us so near as to touch the chaise. The very idea had such an effect upon me, that though I turned my head when he came near, and did not even see him, I almost fainted. I endeavored to conceal my weakness, but believe it was observed by every one present. We were much shocked, and soon set out on our return. My sensations at the sight, or even the idea of blood, are altogether surprising. Even when a child I always ran and hid when a hog, a cow, or even a hen was killed. Since I became a man, although I am conscious of no dread, the sight of blood, and sometimes the idea of it, diffuses a mist over my eyes. I sweat profusely, and become helpless as an infant. The field of battle is no place for me. If I cannot carry a gun half a day, or see a wounded man without fainting, farewell to the tented field."

The wounded man on this occasion had the calf of one of his legs badly shattered by a ramrod, carelessly fired by one of the opposite party.

What active mind has not perplexed itself with the fascinating idea of "perpetual motion"? Amos Kendall's was not an exception. He invented and actually constructed a machine which he was quite sure would accomplish the great desideratum. It was based on the idea that if weights operating on a wheel could be made to ascend nearer the centre than they should descend, there would be a gain of power. By his machine, a weight was made to ascend within one inch of the centre and to descend six inches from that point. It was finished, and equal weights applied, one to ascend within an inch of the centre, and the other to descend on the opposite side six inches therefrom, which ought to have produced rapid motion,—ought it not? But it would not move at all! In a moment the fallacy of the device stood confessed. Though the weights were in fact at different distances from the centre, their bearings were practically at the same distance. He at once

threw away his machine, wondering that his mind could have been so easily deluded.

In January, 1813, Mr. Kendall spent several days in Boston on a visit to Jonathan Fowle, his college chum. The following are some of his recorded reminiscences of that visit:—

"January 27th. This day the Legislature met. There was a quorum, and the Governor's message was delivered. It was short, and that was perhaps its principal good quality. I could not see much majesty in the collected dignity of the State. They looked much as if some blind angel had thrust down his hand, and by the sense of feeling picked up a man here and another there, just as his hand happened to touch them, and, tossing all into the State House together, said to the people, Lo, your rulers! Above the Speaker stands the bust of Washington, which I could but look upon with reverential awe. Ah, thought I, how he would shake his head could he but hear many of the resolutions which have been adopted in this House. Opposite to him, on the other side, hangs a great codfish! I was generally pleased with the emblematical ornaments of the House; but this contrast of a codfish with Washington struck me as ludicrous in the extreme. The Senate Chamber is a beautiful room; but I could not help reflecting on the political villany by which many of the Senators have obtained their seats."

The "political villany" here alluded to was an act of Mr. Kendall's own party, by which they attempted to secure a majority in the Senate, though a large popular majority might be against them. Having had a majority in both houses of the Legislature, and apprehending that the power of the State, if wielded by Federal hands, would, in the impending war, be exerted to embarrass the general government, they rearranged the Senatorial districts, and by giving them most awkward shapes, and assigning to many towns the most unnatural connections, threw those having heavy Federal majorities into the same districts, and distributed those having Democratic majorities so as to make the latter most effective. In this manner they enabled about a third of the people to elect a majority of the Senate.

Mr. Kendall was one of the many Democrats who did not think the end justified the means, and utterly condemned this piece of management as not only wrong in itself, but calculated by its palpable injustice to alienate honest men and increase the bitterness and power of the party it was designed to hold in check. The Federal party made the most of this great Democratic error.

Among other means, they got up and inserted in their newspapers a cut containing a tolerably fair representation of one of the districts, somewhat in the shape of a crane, encircling with a narrow neck another district from the sea on one side to the sea on the other, and this they called a "Gerrymander," Gerry being the name of the Democratic governor. The result was, that at the next election the Federal party carried the election of the Governor and a large majority of the House of Representatives, and at the second election a majority of the Senate also. It was the intermediate session of the Legislature to which Mr. Kendall's journal has reference.

On a subsequent day Mr. Kendall listened with great interest to a debate in the Senate upon a question, whether officers in the army of the United States could rightfully hold seats in that body. Two of the Democratic Senators, Tuttle and Ripley, had been appointed colonels in the regular army, one of whom had taken his seat in the Senate. There was at that time nothing in the Constitution of Massachusetts or of the United States which rendered a seat in the Senate and an appointment in the United States army incompatible, and the argument rested entirely upon the incongruity of the two relations. The lobby of the Senate was crowded. The speech of Harrison Gray Otis was a superb display of eloquence, but full of bitterness and sarcasm. A plain Democratic member, named Stetson, alluding to the rumor then afloat, that Otis had been too intimate with John Henry, said in his reply, that he thought those who were ready to fight the battles of their country were quite as much entitled to seats in that body as those who had been closeted with British spies. Otis sprang to his feet and said that any man who charged him with having been closeted with a British spy was a scoundrel. He sat down amidst the applause of the spectators and cries of order. Of this debate Mr. Kendall says in his journal: "The speech of Mr. Otis was superior in manner to any I ever heard; but he displayed too much illiberality and contempt for his opponents. The young Mr. Lincoln made a truly Republican speech which did honor to his principles as a man and a patriot."

By the entire Federal and a portion of the Republican vote, led by Mr. Lincoln, the seats of Colonels Tuttle and Ripley were declared vacated.

For the first time in his life Amos Kendall, during this visit to Boston, saw the inside of a theatre. He says:—

"On entering the building I was for a moment lost. Everything was new and brilliant. But as soon as I listened to the actors the illusion vanished. I saw nothing but the fiction, and sank into disgust. The tragedy was 'Alexander, or the Rival Queens.' Mr. Holman in 'Alexander,' his daughter in 'Statira.' In judging of such things, I am the simple child of nature, and therefore should not perhaps be allowed to criticise. I cannot conceive what gives reputation to Mr. Holman as an actor. His voice is harsh, his articulation indistinct, and sometimes he speaks excessively loud. His gestures are not strikingly expressive, and he has a heaving of the bosom which, to me, appears unnatural and painful. He did tolerably well in a few instances; but I could not forget that it was Mr. Holman and not Alexander. Miss Holman, in one or two scenes, totally absorbed me. Perhaps my eyes were wet. The scenes were tender, and love was the subject. With these exceptions, my disgust was far greater than my pleasure. I was much better pleased with the afterpiece, 'Forty Thieves.' The scenery was brilliant and many of the characters well supported."

"In the intervals of the play I took some notice of the architecture and ornaments of the building. There is one thing which, though far different, put me in mind of the codfish at the State House. In front of the stage, on the arch above, is the motto, 'To hold the mirror up to nature.' This is well enough; but directly beneath it is a little angel sitting on a cloud, holding a looking-glass in one hand and pointing at it with the other. As the motto is a figurative expression, as broad in its significance as nature itself, this diminutive attempt to illustrate it struck me as very ludicrous."

The churches of Boston also commanded a share of Mr. Kendall's attention during this visit. He heard Mr. Kirkland, President of Harvard College, Mr. Channing, Dr. Griffin, Mr. Holley, and a Catholic bishop. In relation to the three latter he says:—

"In the forenoon I attended the Roman Catholic meeting. The house was ornamented as at Christmas. On entering, I felt a pleasing emotion; but there was nothing in it like devotion or reverence. Those evergreens, though they cast a pleasing gloom around, would better become a hall of revels than the church of God. The sermon was excellent; but the music was harsh and unintelligible, the ceremonies ridiculous, and to me almost a profanation. I should have no objection to their pictures; they appear to me to be well calculated to inspire devotion. I know that an ignorant people might degenerate into a worship of the pictures themselves; but of this I think there is at present little danger.

"In the afternoon I went to Mr Holley's church. Church! it might as well be called a forum; for it bears nothing of Christianity but the name. His subject was 'The Passions' and he made a very good *oration*. He appears to be a mere speculator, with much eloquence, considerable talents, and no religion. The young and dissipated attend his preaching because he preaches such *liberal* doctrines. In the evening I heard D. D. Griffin. What a contrast! Nearly equal in eloquence, their principles are as opposite as black and white. The latter would be my minister in preference to any other in Boston."

This D. D. Griffin was, in his day, the champion of the old Puritan faith against the inroads of Unitarianism, and Mr. Holley was one of the most latitudinarian professors of the latter creed. He afterwards figured awhile as President of the Transylvania University in Kentucky, where Mr. Kendall came in contact with him.

Mr. Fowle was a widower; his family consisted of himself, his son Jonathan, and three daughters. The latter's treatment of Mr. Kendall was most cordial, and the conversation on both sides most frank. He freely criticised their beaux, some of whom appeared to his plain country perceptions to be very deficient both in brains and in dignity of manners. They said two thirds of their beaux were of that character. Then said he, "I pity the ladies." "Truly," said they, "the ladies are to be pitied; for these fellows think themselves agreeable."

On the 5th of February Mr. Kendall returned to Groton. While in Boston, he had read a history of Switzerland, and conceived the idea of a tragedy, based on the conquest of that country by the French during their revolution. After his return from Boston he digested a plan and wrote a tragedy of three acts, which he called "The Fall of Switzerland"; but he was so little satisfied with it that he concluded his genius did not lie in that line, and never made another effort.

During the residue of the year 1813 Mr. Kendall's studies were much interrupted by the business of the office, which devolved on him as the oldest student. He had charge of the post-office; received, made up, and despatched the mails, delivered the letters and papers, and made out the accounts. He was frequently sent on business to the neighboring towns, and employed in collecting office dues.

His first vote was given in March, 1813, and it was an illegal

one. The election was for Governor. The Constitution of Massachusetts then contained a moderate property qualification for voters, and Mr. Kendall had no property whatever. There was a Federal student in the office who was equally poor. Both of their names had been entered on the list of voters, by what authority Mr. Kendall never knew. The Federal student went up to vote, when Mr. Richardson proposed to Mr. Kendall to go up and "kill his vote." He objected that he was not a voter. Said Mr. Richardson, "I will make you a voter," and handed him a sufficient sum of money, telling him to show it if his right should be questioned. He voted without being challenged, and returned the money. Of this transaction he says in his journal, "If I had had time for reflection, I know not what I should have done under the circumstances; but I am satisfied I ought to have declined."

In May an epidemic called the lung-fever prevailed extensively in Groton. Mr. Richardson was seized with it while making preparations for a journey to Washington. He was taken ill on the 10th, and on the 21st Mr. Kendall writes as follows:—

"Mr. Richardson continues dangerously sick. He is himself impressed with the idea that he shall never recover. Mr. Woodbury and I called on him to-day, when he faintly said he did not know that he could say anything that would do us any good, and was silent. He lay like a dying man. I have seldom experienced more painful emotions. He was a man whom I ardently esteemed. His wife leaned over him in tender compassion, her eyes glistening with the starting tear. I rose and left the room,—and left it, too, with the full conviction that he would soon be no more. His wife is one of the best of women. Not an angel could be more tenderly careful. She loves him as her own life, and should he die——

"To a feeling man, at such a time, it must afford a pleasure next to the joys of heaven to see one whom he tenderly loves so kind, so attentive, and so much interested in his safety. O, I would have a wife, if not to make my well hours more happy, at least to soothe me on the bed of sickness."

On the night of the 22d, however, Mr. Richardson's disease took a favorable turn, and he slowly recovered.

Mr. Kendall had for several nights watched with Mr. Richardson and others, and had been much in the atmosphere of the epidemic. On the evening of the 2d of June he felt an unusual depression and weakness, which he attributed to having taken cold. Simple

remedies were resorted to, but with no effect. The next morning, after putting the office in order, he was standing at a desk, with a book before him, when he began to feel faint. Supposing it was the effect of standing, after considerable exercise before breakfast, he sat down at a table. The faintness increased, and, repairing to Mr. Richardson's house, sent for a physician, who said he was threatened with the fever, and attempted to break it up by an emetic. Three doses were required to move his stomach, and then the violent retching caused the blood to gush from both his nostrils. He then felt better, but his strength was gone. That his bed might be made up, he rose, walked a few steps to a chair, and almost as soon as seated fainted away. He was soon restored by the efforts of Mrs. Richardson and her daughter, and helped to the bed. It was indeed the lung-fever, but not of the severest type. For a couple of days he had some headache, but after that, though as weak as an infant, he felt no pain. Any considerable noise, however, agitated him in a most extraordinary manner. The following are extracts from his journal, brought up from memory after he became able to write:—

"*June 7th.* Was this day visited by the Rev. Mr. Chaplin, minister of this place. He sat down in my chamber and conversed with Mr. Richardson, until I was very much exhausted by their noise. I called my mother, and told her I could not bear it. She spoke to Mr. Richardson, and he attempted to draw off the old gentleman. But he, not understanding my situation, sat down by the bedside and gave me much good advice, but much to the injury, at least, of my body. Nor can I think it did much good to my soul; for being in a quiver of nervous excitement, I could not help wishing every word the last. . . . .

"Here I cannot help remarking that incalculable injury is often done to sick persons by the mistaken kindness of friends. They sympathize in their friends' distress, and think they can be useful only in crowding around their bedside.

"That night and the next day were hardly sufficient to allay the disturbance caused in my nervous system by the mere noise of Mr. Chaplin's conversation.

"I could not help feeling gratified at the interest which the people of this place in general showed in my welfare. They suspended ringing the bell on my account, and if any noise happened to arise in the street, it was immediately stilled on information of its injurious effects. Many called to see me on the first days; but these calls were also suspended for my benefit."

Mr. Kendall's mother had been sent for on the second day of his illness, and nursed him most tenderly throughout. On the 13th he was able to sit up a few minutes, and thenceforward gained rapidly until the 19th, when, with his father and mother, he returned to the paternal roof. He was now well, though very weak, and his mouth was sore from excessive salivation. Though he returned to Groton after five days' rambling about in Dunstable in pursuit of renewed strength, it was not until the 4th of July that he felt himself competent to resume his ordinary studies and labors. The following is his hasty review of the incidents and reflections attendant upon his sickness and recovery:—

"I am under great obligations to Mr. and Mrs. Richardson, though the former started for Washington at the end of the second week of my sickness, and the latter was taken ill the third day, and continued almost as sick as myself until I left Groton. Her illness was probably brought on by her too careful attention to her husband and myself.

"Although I always believed I should recover, I often thought it not improbable that death was near, and contemplated it accordingly. It had no terrors, and sometimes I could almost have wished it. The affliction of my friends and the debts which I owe my benefactors were the principal things which gave me pain. Without any fixed, unwavering faith, I could have trusted myself to my Creator and calmly plunged into that eternity which generally appears so dreadful. I know nothing worth living for. No particular tie binds me to the world. My hopes of domestic happiness, which are the dearest pleasure of life, had left me; fame appeared too uncertain and too unsatisfactory to be worth my pursuit; and as for riches, I never thought of them. Yet was I unaccountably cheerful, especially when sickest, and sometimes even inclined to be merry. With reviving life my hopes revived, and I am now the same bustling animal as before.

"To my parents my obligations can never be requited. Never shall I forget the pleasure with which my father grasped my hand on finding me better. Joy sparkled beneath his gray locks; it showed his love and the concern he had felt. When leaving home on my return to Groton, I told my mother I did not know how I should repay her for the care she had taken of me; her eyes filled with tears, and she could only bid me adieu."

While convalescent Mr. Kendall indulged somewhat in his poetic vein. The "Port Folio" published at Philadelphia, had offered a premium of one hundred dollars for the two best naval songs. With little hope of success he determined to compete for this premium. He wrote several pieces which were much praised by his friends, Richardson and Woodbury, and sent two of them and some other scraps to the "Port Folio," but he never heard from them. When the prize poems made their appearance, Mr. Kendall wrote: "I am not disappointed, though I was not without hopes." Of the successful song, called "The Pillar of Glory," he said, "it has too much of that unintelligible swell so common in Paine's poetry, and is not so good as another song of the same author, also set to music and published in the same number." Of the other piece he said: "The ode to which the other prize is assigned, notwithstanding the very warm commendations of the editors, I must pronounce, in my opinion, a tissue of bombastic nonsense. Some parts of it are, indeed, tolerable; but as I am certain it will almost instantly fall into oblivion, I shall preserve four lines as a specimen, though hardly a fair one, as they are the worst in the whole piece.

'TO THE OCEAN.
'Power to whose hundred hands is given,
To toss their foam against the face of Heaven!
And ere insulted Heaven its wrath can show,
Retreats in safety to the abyss below.'

I have only to say that if poetry like this shall carry off the prize, I shall never have that honor."

In consequence of the state of his health, Mr. Kendall had been exonerated, by means of a surgeon's certificate, from militia duty; but having in a measure recovered, he consented to form one of a party of Indians in a sham-fight, to come off at a battalion muster on the 20th of October. This was his only military achievement, and it is described in his journal in the following words:—

"Arrived on the parade, three miles from Groton, about twelve o'clock. Only from twenty to thirty Indians collected. We went into the woods, made a fire, dressed, painted, and prepared for war. We were soon disturbed by unruly boys, who were fired upon and chased, when they began to throw stones into our encampment. We were holding a council, and sent a white man to tell them to desist, or the Indians would load with balls, and we were no more disturbed. An embassy, consisting of two chiefs and an attendant, was sent to the white men. While they were gone, a party, of which I was leader, reconnoitred the whole army of white men, and returned undiscovered, after having travelled nearly two miles.

"Our chiefs now returned, and announced war. We were directed to leave our encampment, and ambush a road about half a mile distant, where we were to act with a retreating party of whites, and fall upon the flanks and rear of their pursuers. Here we were again disturbed by boys,—left our coverts, made four or five prisoners, tied one of them to a tree, and the rest disappeared.

"We had strict orders not to fire until friends and foes had completely passed us. A company of old men, with the dress and arms of '75, appeared marching along the road through the Indian ambuscade. They wheeled, and had almost repassed us, when some one fired. The firing became general, until some one cried out 'Friends!' when it ceased. We afterwards discovered that they were really enemies.

"The contending parties of whites now approached, and passed part way through the ambuscade, when the enemy began to retreat. The war-whoop was given, and we sprang for the rear, now front, of the retreating party. I was about eight rods ahead of my comrades, and met a squad who had left the road, contrary to the order of the fight, and come into the woods to fight the Indians. I fired, and they fired; I ran, and seven or eight of them ran after me. Meeting several of my brothers, we turned upon them and had a smart skirmish, which ended in the defeat of the white men, with the loss of four or five taken prisoners. Two of them I helped take, and had my right hand slightly wounded by a bayonet.

"I now set out to gain the front of the retreating party. I was again prevented by the '75's, who pursued me a short distance and desisted. I now crossed over to the right flank, where most of my brothers were; was chased by a number of white men of our own party, escaped, flanked the enemy, fired several rounds and returned to the left. Soon came upon the flank of the enemy, shot one who had left the ranks to make water, and, being alone, retreated. Found an enemy behind the fence making cartridges, fired upon him, and, another Indian coming up, made him prisoner. At last, with several of my brothers, I gained the front of the enemy, and like a true Indian was attracted by the sight of a neighboring booth filled with all manner of good things, got as much *occupee* (rum) as I could drink *gratis*, and on returning with increased *spirit* found the enemy had surrendered. Joined heartily in a war-dance with my brothers, who were ordered to form with the battalion. This done, we gave a war-whoop and dance to Colonel Hastings, who commanded our friends, fired several rounds were marched in front of the tavern, fired again, and were dismissed. Retired to our camp, agreed to go home in Indian dress, and returned to the tavern. I was here standing, with my clothes in my left hand tied up in a pocket-handkerchief, in company with two others, when a soldier passed us,

turned, and fired. My bundle dropped from my hand on fire, and my hand was covered with blood. There was a charge in my gun, and I was on the point of discharging it at his head, but a whisper of prudence forbade me. I followed the soldier, whom I recognized, showed my hand, told him I had a charge in my gun which I could put into his face, but that I should speak to him another day. I went into the house, washed my hand, found it well peppered, gave my beads to a nymph I do not know, took a merry supper with six of my companions, and returned to Groton. I fired at the door, gave the war-whoop, and entered Mr. Richardson's house tomahawk in hand. The little girls screamed; the older people laughed. *Thus ends my bulletin.*"

At some points the *sham*-fight was a real battle. The soldiers could not apparently have been more vindictive if they had been fighting real Indians. Many of them left their ranks and went into the woods to fight the Indians, in violation of the order of battle. Without scruple, they fired their powder into the arms and faces of the red men, and in some instances attempted to use their bayonets. There were not half a dozen of the Indians who were not more or less hurt, though none of them seriously; but they contented themselves with capturing and disarming their disorderly adversaries, and in the course of the fight took probably more than a dozen prisoners by main force.

On the 21st Mr. Kendall wrote:—

"My hand has suppurated considerably, and the latter part of the night was very painful. This afternoon attempted to pick out the powder with a needle, grew faint, attempted to go to the house, got as far as Wheeler's store, growing fainter, stopped there, and had barely reached a chair when I fainted quite away. I was brought to life by the exertions of those present. When half alive, seeing a drunken man present, I could not help bidding them give the smelling-bottle to him, as he too seemed fainting.

"This made me weak and stupid the rest of the day, and though attempts were made by others to take out the powder, I grew faint again and could not endure it."

Most of it came off, however, with the lacerated skin; but his left hand never entirely lost the marks of that day's sport. The soldier who had done the mischief voluntarily called, apologized, paid damages, and was forgiven.

On the 29th of October Mr. Kendall wrote:—

"I have lately been examining my collegiate productions, and copying whatever I thought worthy of preservation into a book. Many

famous morsels have been committed to the flames, and many others preserved more for the sake of circumstances than on account of any merit of their own. I have nearly fifty pages of poetry and ninety of prose."

This fall Mr. Richardson, for reasons never fully explained, suddenly made up his mind to remove from Groton to Portsmouth, N. H. Of this resolution he informed Mr. Kendall, stating that by an understanding with Mr. Moore, to whom he had sold his house and business, his (Kendall's) position in the office was to remain unchanged, and that he had made an arrangement with James Brazer, Esq., for board, on the same conditions as theretofore in his own family. This was sad news to Mr. Kendall. He looked upon Mr. Moore as in all respects Mr. Richardson's inferior, and he had a positive dislike of Mr. Brazer. His opinion of that man's character stands thus recorded under date of December 9th, 1813:—

"Mr. Richardson has informed me that he has engaged me a boarding-place with James Brazer, Esq. He will let me board in his family, and wait for payment until I am able to make it from my practice. This is called a generous offer. It may be so; but I have contracted such a hearty contempt for that man that I can put no confidence in his generosity. He seems to be generous from no other motive than to have some meritorious action of which he may boast. There is a nephew of his whom he has assisted, and I have often sickened at hearing the old man recount the instances of his bounty. Ought I to curse the man and still make use of his bounty? I know not what else I can do. I can expect no other provision from Mr. Richardson; I ought not to expect it. It is probable I shall accept this offer. He is a man of property, a member of the church, does not get drunk, though he sometimes *staggers*, and, in his dealings, according to a modern expression, 'suits himself to the times.'"

Mr. Kendall boarded a few weeks with Mr. Brazer; owed him, on settlement, fourteen dollars; at his request procured a brother to sign with him a note for the money, and had been but a short time in the Western country when that brother was sued for the money! Yet, no doubt, Mr. Brazer never ceased to boast of his liberality to Mr. Kendall.

On the 19th of December Mr. Kendall had a settlement with Mr. Richardson, of which he wrote as follows:—

"He was generous to me beyond my expectations or even hopes. He charged me nothing for the expenses of my sickness, gave me several small sums in the course of the settlement, and I calculate his gratuities to me amount to about fifty dollars. But the instance of his generosity, of most importance, was discovered in his taking my note without the least security, not only for my board and tuition, but for one hundred and twenty-eight dollars which he has actually advanced in cash for me. My whole debt to him was three hundred and ninety-two dollars.

"After settlement, he gave me a certificate expressed in terms for which my gratitude was too strong for utterance. If ever a tear of acknowledgment was in my eye, it was then. I had been wrought up by the preceding instances of his bounty, and so warm a recommendation from such a man was too much. I could not thank him."

Of the note given on this occasion Mr. Richardson never even requested payment, nor was the whole of it, with interest, paid, until after Mr. Kendall's removal to Washington in 1829.

The depression of business in New England caused by the war with Great Britain, and the absence of any rich or influential family connections who could aid in his advancement, had already induced Mr. Kendall to think of emigrating to the South or West, where there was a wider and clearer field for individual exertion. The unpleasant change in his position occasioned by Mr. Richardson's withdrawal from the office, fixed his resolution, and the hope that his kind patron, having still one session to serve in Congress, might aid him with Southern and Western men, hastened its execution. He therefore determined to visit Washington at the next session of Congress, intending to be governed, in making a plan of settlement, by the information he might there obtain. But there was a serious obstacle in the want of funds. He could not ask Mr. Richardson for further assistance, though that gentleman approved of his resolution. His own father, though not rich, could, by his credit, always command money. To him an appeal was made, and though he did not approve of the movement, he consented to furnish, as a loan, two hundred dollars, which was the sum required.

A large portion of Mr. Kendall's time during the months of November and December, 1813, and January and February, 1814, was spent in journeys to adjacent towns, partly on the business of Messrs. Richardson and Moore, and partly in visiting connections and friends preparatory to his departure.

Not the least interesting incidents of Mr. Kendall's residence in Groton have thus far been touched upon in this biography. He

was, when he began the study of the law, twenty-two years old, and had never been in love, — perhaps because he had been too busy. There was in Groton a family of three very charming young ladies, with two of whom, the oldest and the youngest, the third being absent, Mr. Kendall and Mr. Woodbury became acquainted soon after their establishment there. Mr. Woodbury had engaged himself to a country girl before he entered college; but the superior beauty and education of the elder of his new acquaintances caused him to regret his early entanglement. Being an honest man, the conflict between his sense of duty and a new-born attachment was very painful to him. What might have been the issue, had it depended entirely upon himself, may be considered problematical; but he was most happily relieved by his rustic *fiancée*. Hearing that he was paying attention to another lady, she received the addresses of a new lover, and married him. Being now free, Mr. Woodbury offered himself to the present object of his admiration, and was accepted.

In the mean time Mr. Kendall had become much interested in the youngest of the three sisters. Her youth, and his poverty and prospects, forbade anything like a matrimonial engagement, and for some months he had no distinct purpose in his frequent visits with his friend Woodbury but to pass an agreeable hour with lovely and intelligent young ladies. But, as often happens in such cases, a warm friendship assumed a character somewhat warmer, and perhaps with a vanity by no means peculiar to himself, he imagined that the lady's passion was no less ardent than his own. In this conviction he finally made up his mind to address her. But at this stage of the affair she left home and was absent some weeks. On her return he met her with ardor and was marked in his attentions. Her manner was not so cordial as he expected; but whether her apparent reserve was the result of a change in her feelings towards him, or was the expression of female modesty natural under circumstances which indicated that affairs between them were speedily approaching a crisis, he was unable to determine. To satisfy his own mind he resolved to find or make an opportunity for an explanation. She evidently understood his object, and thwarted his intentions. Finally, without ever broaching the subject to her, he became satisfied that he had entirely mistaken her feelings; that the acts and language which he had accepted as evidences of attachment to him were but the ebullitions of an art-

less, romantic nature; and that the change in her manner was due to her discovery that they had produced an effect upon him which she had never contemplated.

It would not be true to say that this discovery gave Mr. Kendall no pain; but it pointed out the path of duty. He at once resolved to dismiss her from his heart, to treat her as he did other female friends, and never thereafter, by word or act, to indicate that he had ever entertained a partiality for her. Though there was occasionally a heart-rebellion against this resolution, it was faithfully kept, and in a short time her presence excited no peculiar emotion. For a time she maintained a studied reserve towards him; but this was soon overcome by his prudent conduct, and they remained as good friends as if Cupid had never maliciously amused himself with their mistakes.

In the mean time Mr. Kendall had become acquainted with the other sister, whom he found to be worthy of his highest regard. The incidents which had occurred did not break off his visits to the family, by whom he was always received with the utmost cordiality. It was perhaps natural that he should, under the circumstances, be inclined to transfer his affections from one sister, by whom they were not reciprocated, to another who might prove more appreciative. In this new attachment there was not that degree of romance which marked the former; but, perhaps for that very reason, it was more satisfactory. The object of it was older and better acquainted with the world, and possessed of all the qualities of head and heart necessary to make a man happy. Mr. Kendall had made up his mind to leave New England, and had no thought of marrying until he should be established in business, with an income adequate to the support of a family. Yet, having found that these affairs of the heart interfered very much with his studies and impaired his capacity for business, he became desirous to put an end to their distracting influence by an engagement which should settle the question of his future domestic relations, and leave his mind to pursue other objects undisturbed by restless passions. Entertaining these views, and satisfied that he should never find one better calculated to encourage and aid him in the rugged paths of life, he broached the subject to her, and was made quite happy by her reply. He told her frankly, that seeing no prospect of advancement in his profession in New England, he expected to settle somewhere in the South or West, and she

thought it would make no difference to her. Thus this interesting affair seemed to have reached a satisfactory adjustment.

But, alas! "the course of true love never did run smooth." While he was preparing for his journey to Washington the lady left home on a visit to her friends in Boston. He wrote to her there, and it seemed to him a long time before an answer came. And when it arrived at last, it announced her indisposition to engage herself to a young man who was about to leave for a distant land, where he must necessarily form new associations and perhaps new attachments. An animated correspondence ensued, in which both parties were equally inflexible. Avowing her partiality for him and her readiness to marry him if he would remain in New England, the lady firmly persisted in declining an engagement if he would not. On the other hand, he, as firmly refused, for her sake, to remain in New England, where he could have but the faintest hopes of advancement. The affair ended in the exchange of tokens of friendship and mutual promises of correspondence, the bargain being sealed with a kiss, which was the first and the last.

Romantic youngsters may think the love was not very ardent on either side, when neither would, for the sake of the other, give up the point of difficulty. Theirs was not an unreasoning love. The lady's decision was justified by prudence. Though his would doubtless have been the same had he known that the separation was final, he had a strong hope that when he had established himself in business, no matter where, she would, if still single, be willing to marry him. Nor did he give up this hope until after he had begun business, when, at his request, his friend Woodbury put the question as if to satisfy his own curiosity, whether in case Kendall returned and addressed her, she would go with him to Kentucky, and received in reply a decisive "No!"

Time passed, and Mr. Woodbury was on the point of being married to the eldest of the three sisters, when she sickened and died. To him the shock was terrible. After several months Mr. Kendall advised him to turn his thoughts to the second sister, as one well calculated to fill the void in his heart occasioned by the loss of the elder. Though in his reply Woodbury scouted the idea of his ever marrying any one, not a year passed before he had acted upon Kendall's advice. In a few years, however, he died of consumption.

Mr. Kendall also married, and after five years was left a widower.

His thoughts reverted to the girl he left behind him, now the widow of his friend Woodbury, and in a letter he indicated his disposition to renew the relations which once existed between them. Perceiving his drift, she at once put an end to all hope by replying that she would never leave her aged mother, then under her care, and hinting that she had no desire again to enter the matrimonial state. And she died a widow, at an advanced age.

Another singular incident may be mentioned in this connection. Mr. Kendall had an only son, and the third sister to whom he was once so enthusiastically attached had an only daughter. They casually met, contracted a mutual attachment for each other, and were married.

CHAPTER IV.

On the 7th of February, 1814, there was a family meeting at Deacon Kendall's. The following is Mr. Kendall's account of it: —

"This day, for the first and probably the last time, all my father's children dined together. The youngest was born since the oldest left home. Several incidents rendered the scene highly interesting. My three older brothers had their wives with them; my next younger, the girl whom he expects to marry; and, of all the near connections, my sister's husband alone was absent. While we were preparing drink, each for his partner, my mother observed to my sister, that as she had now no husband she must depend on me. My sister was so stung by the reflection, that she went away and wept bitterly. I, too, thought of another, but hushed my thoughts as well as I could.

"After dinner, our father addressed us. His voice was interrupted by the agitation of his feelings. Our mother attempted to speak; but tears choked her utterance. Our father continued. He advised us to cherish affection for one another, said we should probably never meet again in this world, and besought us to prepare for an interview in a better. Turning to me, he said they would probably see me no more, and bade me follow honesty in my profession, and, above all, seek for salvation through a Saviour.

"We were all drowned in tears. It was more like a scene of death than a meeting of joy. After some observations from my brother John, we sang together, and our father prayed with us. I was too much affected to be able to utter a word."

On the 18th he took leave of his father's family. On this occasion he says, "The parting was consecrated by abundance of tears; but we were too much affected to say anything more than 'farewell.'"

His mother was in such feeble health that there was little probability of his ever seeing her again. His father took him to Groton, and there they exchanged farewells. The same evening he

visited the family in which, during his residence in Groton, he had spent so many happy hours, and bade his friends there a painful adieu.

The next day he took leave of his other friends in Groton, and went to Boston, where he remained until the 21st, making parting calls and taking leave of his friends, among whom were Jonathan Fowle and his sisters, and the lady whom he still hoped to make his wife. The 20th was Sunday, in the record of which day he states that he attended church, and that "The young Mr. Everett was the clergyman, — a youth of great promise, lately ordained over the church in Brattle Square." This was Edward Everett, who afterwards became distinguished as a lecturer and statesman.

Extracts from Mr. Kendall's journal, with explanatory remarks, will best describe his journey.

"1814, February 21st. About nine o'clock set out from Boston. The stage was full, and I therefore took a seat with the driver. This I found the most pleasant seat. With the towns in the neighborhood of Boston, on the western road, I was disappointed. The soil generally is poor, with a mixed growth of hemlock, white-pine, and some hardwood. The effects of a late storm were apparent in the multitude of broken boughs strewed through the forests.

"On entering the stage I found my companions to be three speculating merchants, whose conversation related to their own business, two little girls lately from the West Indies, and one or two others.

"22d. It was one o'clock in the morning when we arrived at Ashford. I was sick with riding in the stage, and retired to bed. We were called about five o'clock, and, although not completely relieved, I set out with the rest. I had the precaution to take a seat with the driver, where I had a chance of viewing the country. The soil, as we advanced, grew better. We passed through Hartford, Wethersfield, etc., to New Haven, where we arrived about 11 P. M. No particular curiosity was observed to-day, excepting the rock down which the brave Putnam precipitated himself when pursued by the British. A road is now cut through the rock, a little to the left of the spot.

"After attempting in vain to get our baggage carried to the packet, we retired to bed.

"23d. Set out about six o'clock, and arrived at Rye, within twenty-six miles of New York. In consequence of horrible roads we could proceed no farther, and put up for the night. I was very much fatigued, and retired immediately to bed.

"24th. Started about seven o'clock, and with great exertion arrived

in New York about four. Entered my name on book for Philadelphia, in the Commercial, to-morrow at seven o'clock; put up at a villanous tavern near the stage-house, where I had dinner, which was served without a single vegetable except pickles; wrote a letter to Mr. Moore, and then roved out. New York has many beauties, but I have not seen enough of it to give a description.

"25th. Started from the tavern about seven o'clock, crossed the ferry to Paul's Hook in the steamboat. The wind was high, and the waves several times dashed over the deck of the boat. The prospect on this passage is very pleasant, and in the spring must be delightful. Great imposition is here practised by the servants who carry trunks, etc., to and from the boat. A York shilling is their price, however short the distance, and often they ask two. We were long detained before our team was ready, and about nine o'clock were under way. The face of the country in New Jersey is too level to be romantic, but it is very beautiful and productive. We passed through Newark and Elizabethtown, — two very fine places. In the latter we saw many soldiers of the United States, and were told that recruiting now progressed rapidly. The road this day was worse than I have ever before seen. I and others of the passengers walked many miles. We had seven passengers, most of whom were by birth Yankees, and, in principles, Democratic. We arrived at New Brunswick about 8 P. M., where we met passengers who had been nearly two days in coming from Philadelphia. They represent the road as indescribably dreadful.

"26th. Set out from New Brunswick soon after daylight, and in consequence of the badness of the roads several of us proceeded on foot. The mud was a little frozen, so that it would bear a man, but not a horse. Through the swamp, so called, every passenger walked twelve miles, except one, and he walked eight. So much faster than the horses did we get along, that we called for a breakfast and ate it before we were overtaken.

"Being considerably fatigued with our walk, the day passed rather gloomily, and we arrived in Philadelphia between 10 and 11 P. M. It was my inclination to take the packet from this place; but on learning that its course was very uncertain, I entered my name for to-morrow morning's stage.

"27th. Started from Philadelphia between five and six; but in consequence of bad roads and a poor driver, we made little progress. This day, for the first time, my stage companions excited peculiar interest. We had on board a Baltimore pilot, a citizen of Havre de Grace, a Philadelphia lawyer, turned horse-racer, and three medical students, two from Virginia and one from South Carolina.

"The Baltimore pilot was a clever, honest, moral fellow, who had, as he said, been somewhat dissipated in his youth, and caught a bad disease which induced him to reform. The racer was a man of no morals, who boasted of his profligacies, and was possessed of excessive vanity. He had beaten all America, and could beat all the world.

"The three medical students were very dissolute, told of their amours and irregularities with as little ceremony as a Northern man would tell a story. Yet they had agreeable manners and many of the qualities of gentlemen. When we arrived at Elkton, the opinion of the majority was that we should lodge there on account of the badness of the roads. Two of the students wished to go to Havre. A dispute arose, and the horse-racer swore we should not go, for he would prevent it. This was said at supper, and although my opinion was the same as his, I was vexed at his arrogance, and said that no *gentleman* ought to make his opinion the law of the company. One of the students thinking I meant him, dropped his knife and fork, and said he had as much pretensions to that character as others. I replied I did not refer to him, when he asked me a thousand pardons, and, after we rose, took my hand and again asked my pardon.

"*28th.* Started from Elkton about five o'clock, and travelled on foot considerable of the way to Havre de Grace. We passed the spot where the British burned a bridge and iron-works at the same time that they burned Havre.

"The iron-works are again in operation, but the bridge is not yet rebuilt. The day was extremely cold, and the Susquehanna, when we passed it, was full of thin ice. I did not find Havre, as I expected, all in ashes. Only a few of the best houses were burned, and there is yet a considerable village. This day's passage was not very agreeable, on account of the sourness among the passengers. But I had the good fortune to keep my temper with them all. As we approached Baltimore, I could hardly believe such a city so near, when the surrounding country was so dreary. Only once in several miles would we meet a decent house. The intervals had either no houses at all, or a few miserable huts, the habitations of slaves. The wood has been mostly cut off, and the soil is covered with a small growth. Arrived in Baltimore by moonlight, and was agreeably disappointed at finding the place so beautiful.

"*March 1st.* Started from Baltimore about 7 P. M. It is lamentable that a place of so much beauty should have been so disgraced by its inhabitants. The idea that it is so disorderly will intrude itself and mar every pleasant emotion.

"We here took in three more medical students on their way from Philadelphia to the South. Our time passed merrily away, excepting awhile which was spent in political dispute. Among the students were three Federalists, two from Virginia and one from South Carolina. In the

course of conversation one of them avowed himself an *atheist.* This raised a universal horror, and those who were proud to tell of their immoralities were loudest in protesting their abhorrence, and in applauding the doctrines of a Supreme Being and of Christianity. I was somewhat surprised, for I could not conceive how men avowedly so dissolute could believe in doctrines so diametrically opposed to the whole course and object of their lives.

"It was after dark when we arrived in Washington. The first object which presented itself was the Capitol, which, in the dusk of evening, made a very gloomy appearance. I could not get entertainment at the tavern, and therefore called at the boarding-house of Mr. Richardson. Here I met him and General Varnum, and engaged board with them while I remain in town.

"*2d.* This morning went to see a picture called the 'Dance of Wertmuller.' I never before saw anything which gave me any idea of the power of painting.

"I cannot describe the appearance of the picture; but the admiration which it excited I shall never forget. Passed from this to the Capitol. Its appearance was much better by day than by night. Only the two wings are built, and they are composed of huge piles of freestone.

"In the evening went with Mr. Varnum to the President's levee.

"I was introduced to Mr. and Mrs. Madison. I felt no awe, although Mrs. Madison is a noble, dignified person, apparently more able to manage the affairs of the nation than her husband. His personal appearance is very inferior. Many great men of the nation were present, and many fine ladies. I was, however, not much instructed, though considerably entertained. There were, I presume, nearly three hundred present, who did not form in clusters, but filled the whole drawing-room. In the course of the evening I obtained an introduction to Mr. Grundy, not with a design to converse with him on my own affairs, but to inquire of him concerning Henry Bullard, an officer of Toledo, according to the request of his father. I asked my questions, went away, and sat down. He soon came and sat down by my side, and asked if I was the gentleman who wrote him a letter. I answered 'yes'; when a conversation commenced which ended in his asking me to call on him as soon as convenient, which I promised. I saw few ladies with whom I was at all pleased. Indeed, I took very little notice of them. The elegance of the apartments or the dress and beauty of the ladies did not raise one emotion above the common course, and I had rather give the girl I love one kiss than attend a thousand such parties. A little past nine I retired, better pleased with the novelty of the scene than anything else.

"*3d.* This morning was taken into the Senate Chamber by General Varnum, where he introduced me to a Senator from Ohio, one from Louisiana, and Mr. Bledsoe of Lexington, Kentucky.

"Ohio, I am told, is already crowded with lawyers. Kentucky is not so full as Ohio, but even in that State there are enough. On my observing that I thought my best plan would be to introduce myself as an instructor in some family, Mr. Bledsoe said he thought it would, and that he wanted a man in his family in that capacity. I caught at the expression, but he was soon called away, observing as he went, that on further conversation we might probably make some arrangement. General Varnum promised to converse with him, and thus we left it.

"The Senate Chamber is much more elegant than that of the House, but I am not able to describe it. I should not think there was here so much talent as in the House, and the President is a satire on all legislation.

"General Varnum informs me that he has conversed with Bledsoe, who has four children, the youngest of whom is six years old; but he does not know on what terms he will receive me. He has referred him to Mr. Richardson.

"*4th.* Called on Mr. Grundy according to promise. His colleague was present, and several places were mentioned where prospects were good. If his house is finished, and he will know in a day or two, he will make an arrangement to admit me into his family.

"This forenoon I wandered to the Navy Yard and through the southern part of the city. It exhibits melancholy evidence of the folly of attempting to force a place beyond its natural growth. Whole blocks of brick buildings, which were never finished, are now in ruins. Yet the city increases rapidly, but the buildings are generally erected on the spots which nature has made most unpleasant. If the country flourish, this city must become great, for the site is beautiful.

"*5th.* This day Mr. Richardson conversed with Mr. Bledsoe, who will take me into his family; but the particular terms are not yet specified.

"*6th.* This day attended meeting in the Capitol. The preacher, it is said, is a Baptist, and is a chaplain in the army. His name is Jones. He told us he is seventy-seven years old, and has preached fifty-five years. His sermon might do for an army, but to an enlightened audience it was a piece of ridiculous rant. The burden of his discourse was, eternal hostility to England. His invectives against Federalists were severe, and such as by a preacher ought never to be used. In fine, I consider the whole scene a profanation of Christian worship, and should, had I not been ignorant of the preacher, not consider myself justified in attending his preaching. Many Federalists went out, and with just reason. The

President was present. In the afternoon heard a Presbyterian, who preached an excellent sermon.

"*7th.* This morning called on Mr. Bledsoe. He will admit me into his family, and if I will assist him in the instruction of his children, will give me the use of his books, my board, and $100 per year. I have closed with his proposal, and intend setting out day after tomorrow for Kentucky. I shall go to Pittsburg, thence down the river to Maysville (Limestone), thence by land to Lexington.

"Went into the Supreme Court to-day and heard an eloquent argument from Mr. Pinckney.

"*8th.* Went into the Patent-Office. There found a multitude of inventions, most of which are as unintelligible as they are useless.

"This evening bade adieu to my benefactor, Mr. Richardson, and Mr. Varnum's family, and rode in a hack to Georgetown. I had a melancholy ride; for the idea of bidding adieu to my *last* friend impressed me with sensations more enduring than I had before felt.

"*9th.* Started from Georgetown about seven o'clock. The day was rainy and very unpleasant. This was in some measure compensated by the agreeableness of my company. Those whose conversation was most interesting and instructive were Governor Cass and Major Trimble.

"Cass seems to be possessed of the genuine feelings of a Republican as to his politics, but has a contempt for religion and religious men. His opinion of Pinckney, the present Attorney-General, arose from a slight specimen of his vanity when he first saw him. It was at the levee, where Pinckney appeared with his hat under his arm. This raised Cass's contempt, and he cannot since see or hear him with the least patience. Though himself a Yankee, he has a great contempt for them, which is no great argument in favor of his heart or his judgment.

"Trimble is a native of Kentucky, and represents Bledsoe as one of the first lawyers in the State, and says his wife is an excellent woman. We arrived this night at Fredericktown, which, through the dusk of evening, seemed to be a considerable village.

"*10th.* Passed on through Hagerstown, and several other places called towns, to a considerable place called Chambersburg, beyond the Blue Mountains. We were informed that the land on the road, this day, sells generally from $100 to $120 per acre. By the appearance of the houses and villages compared with those in New England, one would not imagine there could be such a difference in the value of the land. In the latter country many farmers' houses may be seen scattered over the country, equal and even superior in elegance and size to almost any in these towns; yet land there will not average more than $ 20 per acre. The inference is, that the Northerners have much better taste than the Southerners. Their modes of living I am not yet able to compare.

"*11th.* Started from Chambersburg about three o'clock, A. M., and about nine arrived at the foot of the Cove Mountains, a branch of the Alleghanies. Here we had the misfortune to break our carriage. Consequently, all the passengers, except a lady, walked over the mountain about six miles to McConnell's town. It was eleven o'clock, and we had just arrived at our place for breakfast. But before we had proceeded a mile farther I became excessively sick, and found it absolutely necessary to stop and retire to bed.

"*12th.* Arose this morning nearly well, but very weak. As I found myself in a wagoner's tavern, without conveniences, I determined to return to McConnell's town, and wait there for Monday's stage. Accordingly I put my baggage into a wagon, and walked back to the house whence I last started. The roads in this country are extremely rough, and I am told much worse before than behind me. If I once get safely through, I doubt whether I will soon be caught on this road in the stage again. Wrote a letter to Woodbury, and afterward, being impatient, went in to the family, and found there three fine girls with whom I spent a pleasant evening.

"*13th.* By the aid of reading and writing, made shift to pass away this day. At night, about three hundred militia from Adams County, Pa., entered the place on their way to Erie. They were without order, and apparently without officers,—mean, dirty, ugly, and in every respect contemptible.

"*14th.* Started in the stage at four o'clock. My companions were a native of Ireland, naturalized, about fifty years of age, coarse, but very intelligent, and a native of Germany, amiable, polite, and merry. We passed over 'Scrub Ridge,' 'Sideling Hill,' and through the gaps of two other ridges of mountains which rise in huge broken cliffs on the sides of the Juniata River. Met several of this State's militia who had deserted, and it is said many more will follow their example, on account of scarcity of provisions. Near the last-mentioned hills is a brook called 'Bloody Run,' where a battle was once fought with the Indians.

"*15th.* We spent last night in a place called Bedford. Started about four o'clock, with the same companions as yesterday. For the young German I have conceived a considerable friendship. Passed the Alleghany Ridge to-day, where we found considerable quantities of snow. Put up at a place called Somerset.

"*16th.* We left our Irish companion at Somerset, and proceeded with only two passengers. My companion, whom I may now call my friend, gave me a sketch of some of the principal incidents of his life. I find it, in some respects, like my own, but checkered with much more

---

variety. In return, I gave him some of the most interesting incidents which have befallen myself, and, on condition of my staying in Pittsburg a week, he has promised to accompany me to Kentucky.

"We passed this day over Laurel Mountain and Chestnut Ridge, the last of the Alleghanies. Between these two ridges is a wide and dreary valley, almost in its native wildness. We stopped for the night at Greensburgh. I was again sick, and a gentleman named Smith offered to let me have his horse to-morrow, and, in exchange, take my seat in the stage.

"*17th.* Near 7 A. M., I arose and set out. I was tolerably well, but weak. Passed over a good, but hilly country, and at Turtle Creek had a delightful view. It is a small stream, which winds along through a very deep valley. The road on each side is bad, steep, and almost impassable. As I arrived on the top of the hill on one side, I saw a dozen wagons winding up the hill on the other, and heard the echo of bugle-horns. The creek was hid from me, but as I approached the bottom a meandering, romantic stream presented itself, with a house on its banks encompassed with five hundred fine soldiers.

"They were firing at a target, and just as I passed them the bugle sounded and they began their marching.

"Nothing else occurred worthy of notice until I arrived in the valley down which the Alleghany River winds to Pittsburg. Here a delightful scene struck my sight. The river runs between mountains, and at the end of the vale Pittsburg presents itself enveloped in smoke and dust. My sensations are not to be expressed. I said, 'Here is my country,' and almost resolved at any rate to go no farther. With these feelings I entered the place and found it a very blacksmith's shop, full of dust and noise. My friend did not enter it with the same pleasure as myself; for he came another road, and met the smoke at the distance of two miles. He was even rather disgusted, and became desirous of being away. We walked out together and took a hasty view of some part of the place, but, being much fatigued, returned to the tavern, and at an early hour retired to bed."

The portion of Mr. Kendall's journal which covered his stay at Pittsburg is unfortunately lost, and the incidents occurring there are narrated from memory.

The next morning after their arrival he and his friend rose early and ascended Grant's Hill, behind the city, for the purpose of enjoying the views. The hill had not then been occupied by buildings, and between it and the improvements of the city were small ponds of water, formed by excavations of clay for brick-making.

The city itself, then comparatively a mere village, was all within a half-mile of the junction of the Alleghany and Monongahela Rivers, chiefly skirting those streams. The present site of Alleghany City was in part covered by farms and in part thinly wooded. Beneath the cliffs on the east side of the Monongahela there were considerable improvements, including two glass-houses. The two rivers uniting below the city, the rivers beyond the Alleghany and the cliffs of the Monongahela constituted a display of natural scenery seldom equalled in beauty. The whole, however, was marred by coal-dust which filled the air. The glass-houses beyond the Monongahela, and numerous furnaces within the city, some of them burning night and day, sent up columns of black smoke, which settled upon and disfigured every terrestrial object.

Being in no haste to reach Kentucky before the arrival of Mr. Bledsoe, who had not yet reached Pittsburg, Mr. Kendall readily assented to the proposition of his friend to spend a few days in the city. He had a letter of introduction to the Hon. William Wilkins, who treated him with marked kindness.

The business of Pittsburg had been stimulated into unprecedented activity by the pending war with Great Britain. It was an *entrepôt* for military stores for both the Northwestern and Southwestern frontiers, many of which were manufactured there. While our travellers remained there, troops arrived on their way to Lake Erie, among whom was a fine company of volunteers from Petersburg, Va. They left in a snow-storm, and Mr. Kendall and his friend went out to see them cross the Alleghany River. The ferryboats had to make several turns, during which the men gathered in clusters on the bank and sang patriotic songs, while the snow fell thick and fast around them. Many of the Petersburg volunteers never returned, the company being terribly cut up in a subsequent battle on the Niagara frontier.

At his boarding-house Mr. Kendall became acquainted with a Frenchman who had begun the publication of a periodical at Pittsburg, called the "Western Gleaner." At the Frenchman's request he agreed to furnish him some of his poetic effusions for the young magazine, which, with the magazine itself, soon passed into oblivion.

The two emigrants were soon sated with their experience of Pittsburg, which seemed to them little better than a coal-hole for cleanliness. Steamboats had not then come into general use on

---

the Western rivers. Two had been built, of rude model, and not comparable in speed or comfort with the steamboats of the present day; but both of them were below on the Mississippi River. There was no stage or other public conveyance west of Pittsburg, and the ordinary route of travel westward was down the Ohio in flat-boats, keel-boats, or barges. But our young emigrants, being somewhat romantic and adventurous, determined to make the voyage from Pittsburg to Cincinnati in their own boat. So they bought a skiff, a buffalo-robe, and a quantity of such stores as they would not be likely to find along the river, intending to travel only by day, and put up with such lodgings at night as they might find near the banks.

Their preparations were complete, when they fell in at the landing with Major William T. Barry, of Lexington, Ky., who, with his wife, servants, horses, and carriage, was preparing to descend the river to Maysville, Ky. Informed of their plan, and having no skiff for the use of his boat, he proposed that they should put their stores into a common stock, come on board his boat, and tie their skiff alongside, to which they readily assented.

Major Barry's boat was over thirty feet long, and embraced three apartments. In the stern was a stable containing two horses. The centre apartment was occupied by Major Barry and his wife as a sitting-room and bed-room. In the bows was the kitchen, dining-room, and sleeping room (all in one) of the other passengers and servants. The stable, centre room, and half of the bow was covered by an arched roof of bent plank. Between Mrs. Barry's room and the bow was a chimney, with a small fireplace on each side. Turning on a pin upon the stern of the boat, there was a steering-oar about thirty feet long, and on each side, about a third of the way from the bow to the stern, was a side oar also turning on a pin. The body of the boat was a rectangular box, consisting of timbers, horizontal and perpendicular, mortised together and covered with plank made water-tight.

In this clumsy craft our travellers left Pittsburg on the 25th of March, 1814, and began the descent of the beautiful Ohio. Their motive power was the current of the river, the oars being used only to keep the boat in position and in the channel, as well as to effect landings. The bed of our emigrants was straw, in the bow of the boat, and their covering a buffalo-robe. The first night the straw did not suffice to protect their ribs against the ribs of the boat ; but this inconvenience was obviated thereafter by an increase in the quantity.

The subsequent portion of the journey is thus described in Mr. Kendall's journal : —

"*March 26th.* Started this morning half an hour before sunrise, and passed through a country affording at this season very little variety of scenery, about thirty-two miles to Faucettstown. This, with several other places which the legislatures of the different States have named towns, is a miserable village, consisting of a few houses built of logs and mortar. I am disappointed in the banks of this river ; for I supposed them to be covered with fields. Instead of that they are a hilly wilderness, much of which is not susceptible of cultivation. When clothed in the dress of spring, it must, however, afford much beautiful scenery, especially the small islands which fill the river. We hauled up about sundown, because we were unacquainted with the stream.

"*27th.* Pushed off about day. This morning I felt much better than yesterday, because I had much better sleep. Our bed is a little straw beneath and a buffalo-skin above, and our manner of eating, soldier-like. Our cooks are the black servants of Mr. Barry. In the forenoon, put off with my friend in our skiff, and visited a coal-mine lately opened on the bank. We found one of the two young men who had done the work. They bought as much as they could put in a boat for $ 10. The boat costs $100. Their labor may be that of a month. They will then descend to Cincinnati and sell their coal, 1500 bushels, for 37½ cents per bushel. Their freight will bring nearly the first cost of the boat ; so that the business must be profitable.

"About two o'clock passed Steubenville on the right bank, — a town containing some elegant buildings. Before we arrived at this place we saw a boat setting out for New Orleans. It was a beautiful day, and the whole neighborhood, male and female, were collected to bid their friends adieu. Some of them went on board and landed again at Steubenville. Opposite the town the bank rises in a high hill with frequent cliffs, around which were flying a number of black buzzards. We were told that they build their nests in these cliffs. Multitudes of ducks of a speckled and black color are seen along the river, and near by, in the swamps, are heard millions of peeping frogs.

"A little before night we passed Charlestown, a considerable village on the Virginia side. My friend having left us in the skiff, and not coming in sight before dark, we hauled to land to wait for him and collect wood. After his arrival, we passed on a little below Wheeling. Being very unwell, I had lain down, and did not see this place. With the exception of a few beautiful houses, the buildings which I have yet seen on the river look like the abodes of poverty.

"*28th.* When we arrived within five miles of Little Grave Creek, my friend and myself went forward in the skiff to view the curiosities in the neighborhood. The principal is a mound of earth evidently raised by human labor as a grave for heroes, or to perpetuate some great victory gained on the spot. It is an astonishing pile, and seems almost too great for human labor. There are many smaller ones in the neighborhood of the same construction, in which have been found human bones, and, our guide said, golden beads. About half a mile distant there is a regular fortification. Time would not permit us to view it, and our guide could give but a faint description. These things could not be the work of uncivilized Indians, and must, therefore, have risen under the hand of a more cultivated people. Our scenery this day was very much as yesterday, nor did we pass any considerable town. We observed one boat landing horses and cattle. It appeared to be a family boat, bound down with the owner's whole fortune on board. There are many of this kind annually carrying families to the different branches of the Ohio. A slave, whom we had on board, wondered what he (the poor emigrant) had done with all the property he had made, as he appeared to be an old man and had always been free, but observed, ' the devil a bit the better on't is he.'

"*29th.* Last night I guided the boat from eight till eleven. The evening was delightful. Several fires on the hills, the barking and howling of dogs, and the sound of violins which issued from the encampments of two boats' crews on the shore, made the evening singularly romantic. After this, I retired to my straw, and nothing occurred through the night except once running upon the point of an island, from which we easily swung. In the morning we passed Marietta, on the mouth of the Muskingum. It is a beautiful situation ; but the lowness of the bank so exposes it to inundation, that it can never become great. It is settled by New-Englanders, and contains many handsome houses. We now find ourselves in a more level country. When within a few miles of Blannerhasset's Island, three of us went forward in our skiff to take a view of it. We found this once beautiful spot covered with ruins. His house was reduced to ashes, soon after the owner left it, in consequence of his engagement in Burr's conspiracy. It was a crescent, the body in the centre, with piazzas continued to the wings, where were two small buildings thus connected with the main body. The chimneys are yet standing ; but every enclosure is destroyed, and barely a trace of them remains. His walks are obstructed by the trees which have been thrown down by the freshets of the Ohio, and the ruins of a summer-house are still seen among the uncultured shrubbery. Part of the garden-fence is still standing, and a young orchard shows the premature destruction of the owner's fortune. The

whole is a melancholy evidence of the folly of Blannerhasset, and I could not help wishing that the house of every man who would sell his country may become as desolate as the habitation of Blannerhasset.

"*30th.* Set out about day, and, as usual, I arose at that time and went on deck. The morning was cloudy, but the clouds soon blew over and presented us a fine sky. A Captain Swearingen, my friend, and myself, landed and walked about six miles to examine a place called the 'Devil's Hole.' It is a place in the side of a hill where a run descends, and the rocks have fallen from below in consequence of inundation by the descending water, and left the rocks overhanging above. There is nothing in it very curious or remarkable. At night the wind was so violent that we pulled ashore immediately, and there soon arose a thunder-storm. The thunder was not heavy, but the flash of the lightning and the echoes of the thunder from the hills and banks were romantic and sublime.

"*31st.* Started as soon as daylight would allow, and were soon at Letart's falls. I should not have known it but for the name, for the water is not so swift as in many other places. The river, however, is rather high, as it has risen rapidly for a few days past. Here I saw a floating mill. It is a small building built on a boat, which is moored to some immovable object in the current, the rapidity of which carries the wheel, which lies over on one side.

"This afternoon the wind was very high ahead. We made progress for a while, but were finally obliged to stop. Myself, with one other, went out in the skiff for amusement. We were sometimes a little spattered, but persevered until we were tired of the amusement. I had much delight in it, although it was dangerous sport. The wind becoming more mild, we resolved to ride through the night.

"*April 1st.* We passed Gallipolis and the Great Kanawha in my sleep. Soon after three I was called to the oar, where I remained until after daylight. This day we entered Kentucky.

"*2d.* Travelled again through the night, and I again held the oar from two till four. Soon after four we arrived at Portsmouth, where we landed Captain Swearingen, of Chillicothe, and a private soldier named Bruff, of Kentucky, who was taken sick while in Fort Niagara, and escaped from the British while his sentinels were drunk and asleep. The Captain was a very pleasant man, and very sociable. His only failing, which I observed, was a degree of that almost universal quality called egotism.

"*3d.* Although I found myself in a very good bed in Maysville last night, I slept very little. I was not half so easy as on my straw. We parted to-day with Mr. and Mrs. Barry, who set out for Lexington.

He appears to be a very good man, but not a great man. For our passage he charged nothing, and in every respect treated us like a gentleman. His lady seems to be a woman of a good disposition, but not well educated. They are, I think, a well-matched pair, and appear to be very happy. Different were their characters from that of a Captain Keshing, a passenger, who was affected in his language, and contracted in his disposition. Toward all the articles of provision which we purchased coming from Pittsburg he paid ninepence, and half of that he took from a negro fellow on board while making change, and as was thought, intentionally. We had one other companion, a Dr. Wilson, of Kentucky, whose physiognomy did not promise much ; but we were disappointed ; we found him pleasant and well educated. To all these we bid adieu, resolving to stay in Limestone till to-morrow.

"*At Limestone.* — We were surprised to see boys rowing our skiff away without ceremony, and we were told that it would certainly be stolen in the night unless we could put it in some boat or lock it. We, however, walked out to see the town, and came to a Methodist church, where a preacher was bawling, after the manner of his sect. Not being much edified, and having taken considerable alarm for the safety of our skiff, we returned to the shore. Here I watched it while my friend went and procured some articles of provision. Once three great women had loaded themselves into it, and a young fellow was just ready to row them off. I, however, spoiled their fun. After taking dinner, at two o'clock, we left the place. Limestone, or more properly Maysville, lies on a high bank on the left side of the river, and commands not an extensive, but a beautiful prospect. The town has some fine houses, but partakes much of the dirt and negligence which characterize all the towns I have seen on this river.

"We had proceeded but about six miles, in excellent spirits, when we were met by a violent wind, which was soon accompanied with rain. The river became so rough that our boat was in danger, and we landed at a house which the man called 'a kind of a tavern.' Observing a planter's house near, we walked towards it, and, although unwilling to satisfy my friend I consented to call. We found an old gentleman and lady named Mitchell, who, after some conversation, grew fond of us and invited us to take supper and spend the night. We took supper, but declined staying, under pretence that we must visit our skiff, but really because we did not wish to lay ourselves under the obligation. We returned to our tavern, and found it ' *a kind of a tavern*,' as the man had said. We were put into a bed the sheets of which were, I believe, bagging, or something as coarse.

"*4th.* We made shift to sleep badly, and rising about seven were surprised to find the ground covered with snow. Again the old planter sent his son and urged us to go and take breakfast with him and spend the day. We declined, and the young gentleman sat down and took breakfast with us. We, however, called as we passed, and made the planter drink a bottle of porter with us. He then gave us a hearty hand-shake, as did his wife, and invited us to call, should we again pass, which we promised to do. Peace be under his hospitable roof! We had just put off, when we observed two keel-boats floating together. My friend wished to go on board, but I said, ' No, they will only blackguard us.' I yielded, however; and as we approached we found on board a Mr. Lambert, who had boarded with us at Pittsburg. (I write while my friend is rowing, and he spatters so that I can write no more.) Towards night we again went on board the keels, which are two beautiful barges bound to New Orleans, named Mary and Eliza. The names brought to mind the tender scenes which had passed, and I sighed at the remembrance.

" We continued on board till ten o'clock, when we went ashore and took lodgings in the house of an Ohio squire. The family were all grannies.

" 5th. Set out after breakfast. This forenoon we tied for a while alongside of a flatboat which had overtaken us, but thinking our company not very acceptable, I rowed away, and arrived at Cincinnati before it. This place appeared the most beautiful of any I have seen on the Ohio.

" We took lodgings at Edson & Carlton's tavern, and wandered out to see the place. We went through all the principal streets, and visited the brewery. A gentleman interested had the politeness to lead us through the building and vaults. It was new to me and very gratifying. It has been in operation but three years, and, considering its age, is very extensive.

" The scenery around this town is beautiful, especially on the opposite bank, where stands Newport ; which contains many beautiful houses, an arsenal, fields and orchards now putting on their gayest attire. In the evening was introduced to a Yankee named Bayley, from Massachusetts, and had considerable conversation.

" 6th. This morning, walked again, and visited some of the most beautiful situations in the town, after which I went into the court, now sitting here. It is held in a small dwelling-house in consequence of the burning of the court-house, which happened a few weeks since. With my friend I then visited a stupendous building on the river-bank, prepared for a steam-mill and other machinery. It is six stories high toward the river, and I believe four towards the land. We then visited a cotton-factory, the machinery of which is moved by a horse.

" In the afternoon we crossed the river, rambled over Newport, took

a view of the beautiful plantation of General James Taylor, entered the arsenal yard, in a separate part of which are about six hundred British prisoners, part of Proctor's army, and then returned. I then called with my friend on two countrymen of his, and was introduced to them and another gentleman named Hopkins, with whom my friend had a prospect of getting employment.

" 7th. My friend will stay in Cincinnati with Mr. Hopkins, as clerk in a store soon to be opened by him. In consequence of this, I resolved to dispose of our joint property and set out immediately for Lexington. Accordingly, we sold our things for one half their value, and divided the money. In endeavoring to sell our skiff, we found a Spaniard who had fled from the ruins of Saragossa with a wife, two sisters, a grandfather, and I believe some other relatives. He wished to buy a skiff to descend the river and find a place to live. On his relating his misfortunes to my friend in Spanish, he proposed to me to give him our skiff, and I consented. Having adjusted everything, I took leave of my friend with mutual promises of correspondence, crossed the river, and left my trunk and great coat with a Mr. Kennedy, to be sent on by the first conveyance. I left Cincinnati with strong impressions in its favor ; for it is a beautiful and growing place, and the people appear civil and friendly. It is said now to contain about 600 houses, and the number is fast increasing. There is little doubt that it will be the first place in Ohio.

" I walked through a fertile country, but possessed by a people evidently poor, and living in miserable log habitations. A little after dark I rapped at a house and inquired how far to a tavern. A woman within answered about half a mile. I thanked her, but found in the event that I had little reason, for I went nearly seven miles through woods before I found a single house which was inhabited. The people were in bed, but I gained admittance, and permission to sleep on the floor. The man furnished me with a coverlet, with which I lay down upon a chair. I now inquired if there was any danger in passing through the woods in the night. The man said there was no danger, but that the woods were full of wolves. He believed there were few bears, and no panthers.

" 8th. My bed was so uncomfortable that I did not sleep much, and therefore rose early, thanked my host, and departed. In about three miles I found a very decent tavern, kept by a Mr. Gaines, where I took breakfast. I then walked on about twelve miles to a Mr. Brumback's, a queer old Jerseyman. In conversation with his wife, I understood her to say that she was one of the old Virginia w——s, but was told afterwards that she must have said hoes (Tankahoes). I do not know what the latter expression can mean, except by conjecture. When I said I came from Massachusetts, — ' Lord,' said she, ' how people does travel

about.' After having diverted myself thus awhile, I lay down and took a nap, and then walked nine miles farther to Mr. Arnold's.

" I am told the farms on this road are small, from four to forty acres, and was somewhat surprised to find very few slaves. Once to-day I overtook a number of children going home from school. I found at Mr. Arnold's two gentlemen travelling towards Lexington on horseback. After some conversation one of them informed me he lived in Springfield, Ohio, where is an excellent opening for a lawyer. From his description, I am much of the same opinion, and felt some inclination to turn my face thither. But I finally concluded it was best to go to Lexington and continue there for a time, where I shall again see this gentleman, whose name is Fisher. The other gentleman was from Massachusetts, named Hill, and knew many people who were known to me.

" It is very sickly in Lexington, with what I suppose was, in the North, called the spotted fever. It is said that from seven to fourteen are buried daily. The disease has likewise prevailed in some places in the country, and a son-in-law of our landlord is now sick within a few rods of this place.

" I am so lame in the knees this evening, that it is very doubtful whether I move to-morrow.

" 9th. Mr. Fisher had the goodness to offer me a horse, if I could procure a saddle. I attempted it, but was unable. He bid adieu to me, promising to see me in Lexington. Feeling restless, I set out past eight o'clock, and with considerable fatigue walked fifteen miles to Mr. Nelson's. The country was generally hilly, but the soil good. I was told that land sold in this part for $ 1.00 to $ 7.00 per acre, according to its situation and improvements. There are very few slaves on this road, except the white people, who are slaves to themselves and whiskey.

" 10th. In consequence of the unfavorable appearance of the day, the muddiness of the roads, and my own fatigue, I did not set out this day. I found the landlord and his lady pleasant company, and a daughter of theirs, who had been out, returned home in the afternoon, which added somewhat to the pleasure of the day. I also found the 'Journal of the Expedition of Captains Clarke and Lewis,' which I read to their arrival at the Pacific Ocean.

" 11th. Last night was rainy, and the morning cloudy. However, I set out about eight o'clock and went six miles to a Mr. Hunter's. As he was about to start for Georgetown with a lead-horse, he offered her to me if I would ride on a blanket. I accepted, and rode so about three miles, when I got a saddle, and we arrived in Georgetown about sunset. The old gentleman gave me some advice with regard to my behavior here, and, among the rest, to be sure and keep my finances under my own control.

" At Georgetown he introduced me to a house which was not the best. The man appeared as if he loved whiskey, and the woman her ease. In the evening I went to hear a Methodist preacher, and found him a well-informed but noisy man. He had much flower, and some bombast. On the whole I was well entertained.

" 12th. Bid adieu to my friend Mr. Hunter, and set out for Lexington, through a fine country covered with beautiful plantations. About twelve I arrived in sight of Lexington. The neighborhood is one of the most beautiful spots I ever beheld. It is not hilly nor level, but gently waving, with an exuberance of verdure, many orchards in bloom, and many gardens laid out with taste.

" The town appeared pleasant, but of that I cannot now give a description. I am excessively lame in my left knee, and fear it will continue some days."

Thus it will be seen that Mr. Kendall left Boston on the 21st of February, and after spending eight days in Washington, eight in Pittsburg, and three in Cincinnati, he reached Lexington, Ky., on the 12th of April.

Four days were occupied in travelling from Boston to New York, a journey which now (in 1871) occupies about eight hours.

From New York to Philadelphia was then two days ; now about four hours. And there is the same difference between Philadelphia and Baltimore. From Baltimore to Washington was one day's hard travel ; now it is an easy journey of an hour and a half.

Washington was then nine days distant from Pittsburg ; now the journey is made in about as many hours.

Then there was no public conveyance beyond Pittsburg. The only modes of travel, west of that point, were riding on horseback or boating on the rivers. Though two steamboats had been built, they were slow and unsafe. The travel from West to East was on foot or on horseback, and from East to West by flatboats down the river, and from the river to the end left on horseback or on foot. Now rapid steamers traverse all the navigable Western rivers, railroads intersect vast regions then a howling wilderness, and the railroad-cars run to the Pacific Ocean.

Then the ordinary mail from Washington to Lexington occupied about twelve days in its transit, while an express mail carrying only letters made the trip in eight days. Now railroads convey letters and newspapers in less than three days, and the telegraph flashes intelligence ahead of time.

Then all transportation of merchandise and baggage other than such as could be conveyed on horseback from the Eastern cities to the Ohio river, and thence into the interior, was by means of slow-moving covered wagons. Now the swift railroad engine, with its train of heavily laden cars, ascends the mountains, threads the valleys, and darts across the prairies.

But why should we attempt here to depict the wonderful advancement of our country between 1814 and 1871 ?

When Mr. Kendall passed through New York, the frigate "John Adams," with John Quincy Adams, Henry Clay, and the other commissioners who afterward negotiated the treaty of peace with Great Britain, was lying below waiting for a fair wind. Little did he then think of living in Mr. Clay's family, or of the political relations which should afterwards exist between him and Mr. Clay.

Mr. Grundy, to whom, at Mr. Richardson's instance, he had written before he left Groton, he many years afterwards met at Washington, a Senator in Congress, and was finally with him in Mr. Van Buren's cabinet.

Governor Cass, who was a fellow-passenger in the stage from Georgetown, he long afterwards met in public life at Washington, and was associated with him in General Jackson's cabinet.

Mr. Wilkins, to whom he delivered a letter of introduction, and by whom he was most kindly treated at Pittsburg, he encountered as a member of the United States Senate in General Jackson's administration, and knew him afterwards as Secretary of War under John Tyler.

Major Barry, with whom he descended the Ohio River, became for years his personal and political friend and associate in Kentucky, and in 1829 was at the same time with himself appointed by General Jackson to an office in Washington.

And, subsequently, he received from Mr. Flügel, the German friend whom he had first met in the stage at McConnellstown, and with whom he crossed the mountains and descended the Ohio River, a letter dated in Leipsic, Germany, where the writer then resided, soliciting the appointment of United States Consul at that place, which, at Mr. Kendall's instance, was bestowed upon him.

At Maysville, Ky., Mr. Flügel, while Mr. Kendall watched their skiff to prevent its being stolen, went up into the town to procure some change, and came back with a handful of *cut money.* Never having before seen or heard of that kind of currency, Mr. Kendall

at first thought an imposition had been practised upon his friend; but he was mistaken. The banks of the West were then in a state of suspension, and the small change of the country consisted of the fragments of silver coins cut into two or more parts. Thus, a dollar cut into four parts made four quarter dollars, and cut into eight parts, so many twelve and a half cent pieces. Halves and quarters were also cut to make smaller change; but anything less than six and a quarter cents was wholly unknown. The cut money, however, was nearly all fraudulent. Five quarters, or nine twelve and a half cent pieces were sometimes made out of a dollar; but the more general practice was to cut a slip out of the centre of the dollar, and make halves and quarters out of the balance. The smaller coins were treated in the same way, and doubtless some parties made considerable sums out of these clippings. They did not, however, at all interfere with the currency of these mutilated fragments, which constituted the small change of the country until, clipped as they were, they became more valuable than the bank-notes, when they disappeared, and their place was supplied by small tickets, issued by corporations and individuals, called "*shinplasters*." Of these Mr. Kendall afterwards devised a form for the corporation of Georgetown, Ky., where he resided, having in the centre, stamped with leaden dies set with ordinary type, the form of the cut half and quarter dollar, etc., enabling the negroes and others who could not read to recognize their value upon inspection.

These tickets obtained a very wide circulation. When the banks resumed specie payments, the change tickets disappeared; but the cut money never returned.

As Mr. Kendall and his friend floated down the river between Maysville and Cincinnati, they observed that the heavy drift-wood progressed faster than their skiff. They therefore tied their skiff to the roots of a large floating tree nearly buried in the water, and were thus towed many miles. The solution of this problem is, that the current of the river is more rapid beneath than at the surface. A loaded boat will, consequently, float faster than an empty one.

On Mr. Kendall's arrival in Lexington he found that Mr. Bledsoe, instead of living in Lexington as he supposed, resided about thirty miles distant; but that he had rented a house in town, and was expected to move into it soon after his return from Washing-

ton, then daily expected. He therefore remained quietly at Postlethwaite's tavern, where he had no acquaintances, not even having registered his name, and waited for Mr. Bledsoe. The lameness in his knee, produced by his journey on foot from Cincinnati, kept him very much confined for some days; but as soon as he could move with comfort he spent a large portion of his time in roaming about the town and neighborhood, exhilarated by the purity of the atmosphere and the luxuriance of the vegetation. The wood pastures, so called, were particularly novel and interesting. Originally, the site of Lexington and the surrounding country were covered with heavy timber, under which was a thick growth of cane so intertwined with pea-vine as to be almost impenetrable to man and beast. The leaf of the cane very much resembled that of Indian-corn, and constituted the favorite food as well of the buffalo as of domestic cattle. As soon as the latter became numerous, they fed the cane so closely as to kill it as well as the pea-vine, leaving the forests without any undergrowth. The cane and vine were soon replaced by a thick and luxuriant growth of blue-grass; affording, perhaps, the richest pastures in the world, — as beautiful to look upon and wander over as pleasure-grounds kept in order by incessant labor in other regions. But the thought would intrude, that even the beauties of these natural parks are transitory, for there is no young growth to take the place of the trees that are destroyed by the axe or by time, and that at no distant day the forest must entirely disappear.

On the 18th of April Mr. Kendall met Mr. Bledsoe in the street, who said his family would be settled in town in about a week, when he would be ready to carry into effect the arrangement made in Washington. But he suggested at the same time that Mr. Kendall might do better by becoming an assistant teacher in a neighboring academy. Connected with other circumstances, this suggestion raised a doubt as to Mr. Bledsoe's desire to fulfil the agreement. This doubt was strengthened by his failure to call, for further conversation, as he had promised, and leaving town without any explanation. Mr. Kendall's pride was touched, and he needed only to be satisfied that Mr. Bledsoe did not want him, to banish at once the thought of ever residing in his family.

Thus far, he was without other acquaintances in Lexington than Major Barry and his lady, who were very polite, but neither they nor Mr. Bledsoe had introduced him to any other person.

A short distance from Lexington, in a beautiful piece of woods, was a ropewalk, then used as barracks for soldiers recruited in that region. Some of the officers stationed there boarded at Postlethwaite's hotel, where Mr. Kendall had formed a speaking acquaintance with them. In one of his walks, on the 27th of April, while passing through the grove near the barracks, he observed a number of gentlemen sitting on the grass in the shade of the trees, enjoying themselves with conversation and liquor. Among them were some of his tavern acquaintances, whose names he did not know. As he was passing within a few rods, some of them beckoned to him, and he approached. After inviting him to drink, one of them took him aside and asked his name, and then introduced him to the rest of the company.

Among them were several young men of Lexington, with whom he had considerable conversation. One of them, named Watkins, a half-brother of Henry Clay, then a law student, invited him to call at his room.

The following is Mr. Kendall's record for the 30th day of April, 1814: —

"This day I have suffered more mortification than ever at any period of my life. While walking the street, I saw Mr. Bledsoe in a crowd, and he appeared to see me, but turned his head away. I crossed the street, and went to make my observations upon a company of troops which was parading at the market-house. When I returned, I passed him again, but, as he was reading a letter, I suppose he did not observe me. I went to the tavern, and after some time, on entering the bar-room, I saw him sitting in conversation with several gentlemen, and as I approached he put on his hat and pulled it down as if to avoid seeing me. I advanced, however, and, as I thought, catching his eye, went up with the intention of shaking hands and called him by name. The other gentlemen looked towards me, but he kept his head down as if he neither saw nor heard. Mortified and provoked, I turned aside to a window, stood a minute, and then, with no very pleasant emotions, went into another room and sat down alone. In a few minutes Mr. Bledsoe came into the room with Colonel Owens for some private conversation. On entering the room he stepped behind the Colonel, and seemed studiously to maintain that position until they finished their conversation, when they left the room. That he saw me, both now and before, I had no doubt. What were my feelings! There was intentional neglect and unnecessary mortification. To be thus treated by the man on whose promise I had come to this country is too much."

Mr. Kendall at once resolved that he would have nothing more to do with Mr. Bledsoe if he could avoid it, and began to inquire after employment in other directions. He saw nothing more of Bledsoe, who in fact never removed his family to Lexington. He was afterwards assured that he was mistaken in supposing that Mr. Bledsoe intentionally neglected and slighted him; that he was so short-sighted that he could not recognize any one across the room; that he was very eccentric, and that he had spoken in high terms of him (Kendall) among his friends, suggesting plans for his advantage. When they met months afterwards, Mr. Bledsoe expressed his regret that the arrangement between them had not been carried out, and remained very friendly to him in after years.

Mr. Bledsoe was a man *sui generis*. He was endowed with splendid talents, and, with the exception of Henry Clay, was the most eloquent man in Kentucky. His manner was slow and deliberate, his language beautiful, his gestures graceful, and his thoughts communicated with the utmost clearness. But his talents were marred by excessive vanity, and finally destroyed by drink.

In consequence of Mr. Bledsoe's treatment, Mr. Kendall made known to his new acquaintances his desire to find employment as a teacher. As invited, he called on young Watkins, who informed him that Mrs. Hart, with whom he boarded, desired to obtain a teacher for her two daughters, and afterwards, at her request, Mr. Kendall called and took tea with her. She seemed at once to take a lively interest in him, and of her own accord proposed to get up a school composed of the children of the first families in Lexington, which would give him an income of a thousand dollars. She asked no testimonials from him of character or qualifications; but he felt it due to her generous confidence to put into her hands the certificate voluntarily furnished him by Mr. Richardson, and another from the Treasurer of Dartmouth College, showing that he had graduated at that institution. These papers were never asked for or returned, and Mr. Kendall was left without any written evidence in relation to his character and education.

Mrs. Hart failed to get up the proposed school, for various reasons, — one of which was, that Mrs. Clay, who had five children of a teachable age, lived so far from town that it would be inconvenient for them to attend. She then said that if Mr. Kendall would live with her and teach her daughters, she would give him his board,

two hundred dollars a year, and the use of her late husband's library; but she continued, "Mrs. Clay will do more for you, and wishes to see you at my house, between ten and eleven o'clock to-morrow."

Mrs. Hart was the widow of one of Mrs. Clay's brothers. Mrs. Clay had recently returned from Washington, after a residence there of two or three years, and had collected her children around her, two of the eldest, Theodore and Thomas, having, during her absence, been at a very ill-regulated school in Jessamine County.

The next day, the 5th of May, Mr. Kendall met Mrs. Clay at Mrs. Hart's. She offered to give him his board, the use of Mr. Clay's library, and three hundred dollars a year, if he would teach her five children. Her offer was accepted, with the condition that he should be at liberty after six months to surrender his trust on furnishing a substitute as well qualified to teach as himself. The same day his trunk, which had been left at Cincinnati to be forwarded by a wagon, and which, he feared, had been lost, came safely to hand.

One of the principal inducements for accepting Mrs. Clay's offer was the hope of profiting by Mr. Clay's friendship and advice on his return from Europe, then expected within a few months.

On the 10th of May Mr. Kendall left Postlethwaite's tavern, and became an inmate of Mr. Clay's family. He then had, of $216 with which he left home, $17.75. He had sent back to his father a ten-dollar note pronounced counterfeit, and had expended about $30 for clothing. His expenses were much increased by taking an indirect route, and stopping unnecessarily at Washington and Pittsburg. His estimate was that he could have made the journey by the direct route, without stopping, for $100.

The family at Ashland then consisted of Mrs. Clay and seven children, the oldest of whom was about thirteen years. Five of these, two boys and three girls, constituted Mr. Kendall's charge. The two boys, respectively about twelve and thirteen years old, had, in the absence of their father and mother, been left at a school in a neighboring county, where there was no regular government, either in school or at their lodgings. The consequence was that they profited very little by their lessons, and became ungovernable in their tempers. All the children, except the oldest, were endowed with fine minds, and in that respect, the younger boy had few equals. At first Mr. Kendall was much discouraged at the

prospect before him; but by a mild firmness, and the countenance and support of Mrs. Clay, he by degrees reduced his refractory pupils to order and secured their respect. The boys would listen to him attentively, and he took every proper occasion to represent to them how essential it was, if they desired to acquire the character of gentlemen, that they should not only be attentive to their studies, but learn to govern their tempers. It was not long before the improvement of the children, especially in their temper and manners, was very marked and most gratifying. Through Mrs. Clay, Mr. Kendall became acquainted with her relatives and friends, who treated him with the utmost kindness, and his time passed pleasantly, not only in his little school, but in the social circle.

Mr. Kendall's manner of life, his observations, speculations, and troubles, during his residence in the family of Henry Clay, and for some time afterwards, are best illustrated by extracts from his journal: —

"*1814, May 13th.* My two boys, I perceive, have not been very well taught, and know almost nothing either of Latin or English grammar. They have begun in Cæsar's Commentaries, and after having recited, I make them write out a translation of the whole, which I intend they shall copy into a book. This is with the design, not only of impressing it more strongly upon the memory, but of improving them in writing and in English grammar.

"The oldest little girl reads and writes, and bids fair to make an excellent scholar. The second knows little of reading, and seems to be an idle, although a fine little girl. The third is yet in her Abs. The whole of them are passionate, and have never been governed at all. But they are by no means unmanageable.

"*14th.* Thomas refused this forenoon to go to his lesson; but, on being carried into the room, he yielded.

"*17th.* This evening a number of ladies called, and, for the first time in Lexington, I was merry with them.

"*20th.* I find the children, especially the boys under my care, have been indulged till they are almost ungovernable. The oldest, Theodore, has the most amiable disposition, but Thomas is the smartest boy. They have been accustomed to fight each other, so that, at the school which they lately attended, they could not be boarded at the same place. Their father is almost always absent, and their mother has been so for nearly two years past, and they have been left to their own management. Their mother attempts to assert her authority over

them; but it is not supported with a steady hand. This evening Thomas began to whine and growl after his usual manner, when I looked towards him with an eye which, no doubt, expressed my feelings. Mrs. Clay, observing me, said to him, that he must take care, for Mr. Kendall was just ready to speak. And then said to me with perfect good-nature, that she had many times seen me nearly out of patience; for she could tell. I blushed at perceiving my feelings were known, and made some indirect answer, which no doubt confirmed her opinion. However, I was not in reality ashamed of it; for often have I been provoked to ask her to deliver the boys over to me. Thomas, however, grew worse and worse, until she was obliged to take him into a room, and, giving him a severe whipping, she actually conquered him. I congratulated her with real pleasure.

"*25th.* In conversation this evening, Mrs. Clay bade me ask her if I wanted money. I told her I would, and said I had short of twenty dollars, when she told me she would give me one hundred to-morrow; I was affected by her generosity, and begged to be excused from taking it, for I was in no need at present. The true reason is, I cannot think of making myself so dependent.

"*27th.* In the evening I had a long contest with three ladies on the impropriety of sending word to visitors that you are not at home. I sturdily maintained an adherence to truth, and was opposed on the plea of necessity. I often have such contests with Mrs. Clay, who is of the polite world. But I have as yet found no difficulty in adhering to my principles, and think I shall not yet quit them.

"*28th.* We have news to-day that Paris is in possession of the allies. I lament it, as I would anything which would tend to *destroy* the power of France.

"*29th.* Yesterday, Mrs. Clay being absent, Thomas got into a mighty rage with some of the negroes, and threatened and exerted all his little power to kill them. I took him into the office and held him until he was cool, and then let him go. Notwithstanding Mrs. Clay had told me to do this on such occasions, I perceived by her conversation to-day that she did not feel exactly right about it. I was surprised, but am resolved to interfere no more unless it be to save life.

"*June 9th.* This evening there was a large party of ladies with several gentlemen at Mrs. Clay's. I was not very sociable, but silently made my observations. I find the company already have a butt, so if I am rather unsocial for a while, I shall have a good chance to escape unobserved. This evening Thomas got into a great rage after the departure of the company, and at Mrs. Clay's request I dragged him, not very tenderly, into the office. He fought me like a tiger, and cursed me with all his might. 'You damned Yankee rascal,' cried he, 'you have been trying to make yourself of great consequence among the ladies this evening.' This he kept up for some time. At first I was provoked, and cuffed him once or twice, but not feeling myself authorized to whip him, I let him bawl. Finally, I went out and asked his mother what I should do. She ordered him to bed, and he readily, though unexpectedly, complied.

"10th. The sequel of last night's adventure exhibits a striking characteristic of that singular boy. He would not get up until I had gone to breakfast, nor even show himself at the table. Afterwards, when alone with his mother, he burst into tears. On being asked what was the matter, he said it was because he treated me so ill last night. He then mentioned an anecdote which is told of General Washington,—how that good man having in anger abused an officer, afterwards asked his pardon. He wished to ask pardon of me, but feared the other children would laugh at him. He, however, came up with his mother, who asked pardon for him, which I readily and heartily granted. Notwithstanding his foibles, he is an admirable boy.

"13th. Mrs. Clay this day once more offered me fifty dollars, but I declined accepting it.

"15th. This day I lent to Mrs. Anne Hart, widow of Captain Hart, who is living here, a selection from my poetry containing all my best pieces. I will not deny that a wish to have my talent known was my strongest motive, and at first I intended to give it her, hoping she would show it to others. In this I was restrained by a diffidence which is eternally at war with my pride. After school, I offered to read my last play to her and Mrs. Clay. This same diffidence again rose upon me, and I thought for a while I should be obliged to desist, for want of a voice. But I was finally victorious.

"17th. Arrived the news of the dethronement and abdication of Bonaparte. If this news be correct it is the greatest act in that *great man's life*. I call him a great man because his talents are great, not that I have any respect for his character. The most important view of this subject is as it respects ourselves. We are now left to contend single-handed against the whole power of Great Britain. I have lost every expectation of peace, for I do not believe that haughty nation will lose so good an opportunity to humble the rival of her commerce.

"Destroy everything which floats in our waters she certainly can, and if she does not lay waste our sea-coast, it will be because such would not be her interest. But we must breast the shock, and pray God to unite us and bring us off with honor. Young men are already talking here of going into the army, but it will be my last resort.

"19th. After this I returned home, and was obliged to listen to a

long talk in ridicule of religion or religious men. The parties concerned were Mr. and Mrs. Mentelle, professed deists, Mrs. ——, and Mrs. ——, who is, I believe, a deist in heart. To attempt reasoning, I find, does no good, and therefore I generally find it best to preserve a prudent silence.

"21st. I was surprised to-day by a call from Mr. James Dana, with whom I had a partial acquaintance in Boston and Groton. He has been to New Orleans, and returned through the wilderness. He will stay a few days in town, and then return to Boston. I shall load him with letters.

"25th. This day I went with others to give in an invoice of my *rateable property*, and attend a Kentucky training. One rateable poll is the amount of my whole fortune, and even that not without *encumbrances*. I suppose about two thirds of the company appeared, some without muskets, some with muskets without locks, and some with useless pieces,—all without bayonets, uniform, or cartridge-boxes. The business seemed to be electioneering as much as training. After calling the roll, the captain drew up his men in a hollow square, for the accommodation of a Mr. McKinley, who addressed them, offering himself as a candidate for election to the next General Assembly.

"He gave a considerable dissertation on the subject of banking, and drew some conclusions which to me seemed incorrect. He was in favor of an extension of the system to an unlimited degree. He then took notice of the Kentucky revenue law, which it seems is rather unpopular, and promised to attempt its repeal. National politics he carefully kept out of view, for it seems he is a Federalist. After he had finished, the company resumed their order, and marched to the whiskey-table under a tree, where, several more candidates arriving, they were dismissed for a short time. I expected more public harangues; but as there were now five or six candidates present, I suppose they had some reluctance to speak in the presence of each other.

"Private talk was the only means now used, and after some time most of them departed. The company again paraded and manœuvred till about six o'clock, when they were dismissed. It was dull business, for they had neither fife, drum, nor whistling. This was the first stump oration I had ever heard. I was not so unpleasantly impressed as I expected. Although a good orator may often mislead the people, the system certainly has a tendency to give them much useful information. It seems to be a sort of primary assembly, where future subjects of legislation are discussed, which are afterwards, in a measure, decided by the choice which the people shall make of their representative. But there seemed to be an indelicacy in a man's saying all this to promote his own election that I could not forgive. It seemed to me that I could

have spoken there for a friend, but never for myself. Time may reconcile me to it.

"July 1st. Received a letter from my old friend Fowle. He seems to labor under a great barrenness of ideas, if that can be called a burden. Though an excellent fellow, he is not blessed with a very capacious intellect, and, I am afraid, is too indolent to give it the artificial aid of extensive knowledge. There was a postscript from Rockwood, in so cold a style that I fear he thinks I have neglected him. I am sensible that in his situation I should have expected more; but I am equally sensible that much more is expected from a friend, when in a distant place, than he is able to perform. We seem to think the whole country where he is spread beneath his eye, so that he has nothing to do but look and write us the result. However, I hope my last letter will set everything right. Fowle informed me that a Mr. Hunt was coming out from Boston, and Mr. J. Prentiss, of this town, told me that Hunt would come into his family, and that D. Rockwood was coming with him.

"4th. Heard a common oration from a Mr. Breckenridge. The day was excessively rainy from about ten o'clock till the afternoon. Consequently I did not go to the dinner.

"10th. Received a letter from Woodbury. He informs me that his Susan has made a profession of religion, and that Mary and Eliza are much engaged. Mary is teaching school in Shirley. This short article interested me more than all the rest of the letter. I am sure that my *reason* at least will *never* cease to prefer her to all with whom I am yet acquainted.

"17th. This morning, Miss E. P. and some others being at Mr. Clay's, Mrs. Clay rallied her upon marrying a certain gentleman in town, when I blushed excessively. I know not whether any one observed it, but I know I felt like a fool. And a fool I am to let that lady so much interest me, when I know her so ill qualified to make a poor man happy. Except in beauty and amiableness of disposition, she will not bear a comparison with Mary.

"20th. Went to the circus. It is temporary, and supplied by an itinerant company. I was considerably diverted, but there was too much buffoonery intermingled. It appears little business to see *men* so employed, but there is much more satisfaction in seeing the arts which have been taught their horses.

"22d. A requisition is made on this State for 5,500 militia, to be held in readiness to march at a moment's warning. It is said they are destined for New Orleans. If they have enrolled me, as was their duty, I shall be liable to a draft, and I care but little if the lot should fall upon me. If I should manage well and return safe, it would give me a reputation which would be useful.

"26th. I had long been desirous to hear a more particular account of Mrs. Price and her daughters,—for what reason I could hardly satisfy myself. In conversing of the family, I took occasion to ask if Mr. Price had left his wife any property. The answer led to a history of the family, which concluded with the remark that the girls would not probably be married, as gentlemen did not like to marry where there is no fortune. I derived considerable satisfaction from this conversation, and I believe, because it seemed to destroy the difference between E. and myself!

"30th. I was at Mrs. Hart's, Sr., this evening, when John and N. Watkins coming from the circus, the former proposed going to the theatre, where it was advertised there would be a concert by an Italian. For fifty cents each, we were admitted. He sang two or three Italian songs, accompanied by his Italian guitar, as he called it, and after giving one in French, he apologized, saying that he was so unwell he could play no more. After much urging, however, he played part of a tune on a clarionet, and broke off crying 'Hurra, America,' to make the spirits of his audience. He is no doubt an impostor, who thus imposes on the public to pay his expenses. After leaving him, my companions proposed that I should celebrate the performance in poetry, which I promised to do.

"31st. John Hart, with E. and A. P., called at Mrs. Clay's this evening, and when I had read the rough draft of my *Pauvre Italien* to him, he insisted that I should read it to the ladies. I declined, but he took it from me and carried it into the room, and as it was so much interlined that he could not read it, they all insisted that I should do it. I was never more embarrassed. I hesitated, declined, felt and looked and acted like a fool, and at last read it.

"August 1st. Had a letter two days ago from my long-lost friend, E. Shipley, and one this day from ——, Esq., both of whom have become Democrats. The former is practising law in Saco, Me. For ——'s reasons we need not look beyond interest, but Shipley's is because the Federalists are attempting to divide the Union.

"5th. Mrs. Clay had a small party this evening, and I must needs be again requested to show my silly poetry. I put it into John Hart's hands, and went out. Having, as I thought, given time sufficient for the reading, I returned, and found a young man murdering it at a mournful rate. So provoked was I, that I took and finished it myself. Of the poetry I am actually ashamed, it is so silly.

"12th. Spent some time this evening with the Misses Price and Miss Hart, more to my satisfaction than at any time since I have been in Lexington. J. Hart returned to me a manuscript of my poetry which I had lent him some days since.

"*13th*. I have read of law, since I have been here, most of the general laws of Kentucky and the first volume of Blackstone. A multitude of miscellaneous books I have read, and have now begun the 'History of Russia,' by Tooke.

"*14th*. Attended church in the forenoon, and spent the afternoon at home, where were Mrs. Shelby, daughter of Doctor Pindell, an amiable woman, and Doctor Pindell himself. Inquiries rose where Ghent was situated. I took the Atlas, and in tumbling it over, found a piece of paper written in my hand. I crushed it up and was securing it. This raised the curiosity of Mrs. Clay, who said it was some of my love-letters. I told her no, and that she might see. She took it, but as it was carelessly written, she could make no progress, so I took it from her hand, saying that I would read it. It purported to be from an Indian to his brother, giving an account of the persons and manners of the Kentuckians. It raised some laughter, and Mrs. Clay took it from my hands, and said she would keep it to bear witness against me, as I had made very free with some of their notions. Now, the fact was, I was desirous to have it seen, and had put it there for that purpose, but had entirely forgotten it, and should then have destroyed it had she let me alone. However, in this thing I was actuated more by vanity than any honorable motive.

"*15th*. Wrote to my old classmate, J. Danforth, and half an hour before sunset went to the post-office. I returned, and passing through my room, sat with Mrs. Clay till about nine o'clock. I' had left my watch hanging on a nail, as usual, and, as I entered the room, looked to see the time, and lo, it was gone. A counterpane was likewise taken from the boy's bed. A negro girl in the house was seen in the room, and therefore suspected. She had stolen before, and on being severely whipped, said she had taken them, and named several places, one after another, where she had put them, but they were not to be found. Although she at the outset denied having been in the room, I was finally convinced that she had not taken the things, and desired she might be whipped no more on my account. Indeed, I could hardly justify myself for permitting her to be whipped at all, for it is more like torture than justice.

"*16th*. (*His birthday.*) This year of my life is ushered in with several attentions from the good people here not at all to my taste, — my watch stolen, notice this morning to attend a company of militia to-morrow to stand a draft, and in the afternoon a warrant to one regimental and two company musters. No news of the watch. I went this evening and left descriptions of it at all the silversmiths; but I have no expectations of ever finding it. All these things have very little effect on my spirits, although Mrs. Clay says it is otherwise. Indeed,

I had almost as lief be drafted as not. I want to see what soldiers suffer.

"*17th*. When I came upon the muster-ground to-day, and saw by what men I was surrounded, and heard all speaking of the draft with so much dread, my heart failed, and I earnestly wished myself clear of it. Our company consisted of fifty-eight men fit for duty, out of which twelve were to be taken. I drew into the third class, which, of course, contained five. I offered twenty or even thirty dollars, to enable the one who should be drafted to hire a substitute, but none of the class would give more than ten, and two nothing at all. I now gave up, and determined to go if drafted ; for I had not money to hire a substitute, and I would not borrow. Three of us finally agreed to give to either of us who should be drafted five dollars each, but it fell upon one of those who would give nothing. I was considerably relieved, and we went away and drank together. I was astonished at so great an aversion to the service in the patriotic State of Kentucky. $150 is given for substitutes, and they do not know that they will be obliged to march.

"About three o'clock I set out for home, after having drank considerable whiskey, eaten watermelons, etc., and was stupid as a dunce through the evening.

"*18th*. Read Lord Byron's 'Corsair.' The measure does not flow so easy as the eight syllable, and sometimes his lines appear stretched. Where words may be left out without injury to the sense, the language is weaker than it should be.

"*19th*. One of those mortifying little incidents, which may be called the miseries of human life, happened to me. There was a dialogue in the Boston ' Patriot,' which now comes to me, in which Mr. Clay is introduced with King George, and the Emperors, Kings, etc., etc., now in England. The object is to ridicule their Majesties, and bring to view their real motives. I was about to read it to Mrs. Clay, and reading over the names, observed that they had put Mr. Clay into bad company. At this she took such dislike, that I had scarcely begun when she interrupted me by ' That 's silly, that 's silly.' I got off as well as I could by reading detached pieces of it, but could hardly conceal my mortification.

"*22d*. Received a letter from my friend Flügel. Either he is an arrant, flattering hypocrite, or his heart is much warmer than mine. The affection which he *expresses* I am sure I can never *feel* except for a woman.

"*23d*. Mrs. Clay being gone, the care of the boys devolved in a great measure upon me. Hearing a great noise in the kitchen, I went in, and found Theodore swearing in great rage, with a knife drawn in attitude to stab one of the big negroes. I did not wait to inquire the

cause, but seized him by the collar, took the knife away, and very expeditiously had him in the house. If he were my boy I would break him of such tricks if it cost blood.

"*27th*. Attended a temporary muster. The soldiers are under no more restraint than a herd of swine. Reasoning, remonstrating, threatening, and ridiculing their officers show their sense of equality and their total want of subordination. The officers are, I presume, clever men, but ignorant and without energy. An attempt is here making to raise a rifle company, and I consented that my name should be put to it, but as my stay here will be temporary, declared I could not equip. From this they promised to excuse me. The day being rainy, I returned home, wet, muddy, and disgusted.

"*28th*. This day I received a letter from my friend Carter, who previous to the receipt of my letter had engaged himself for another year in his academy. The consequence is that he will not be able to take my place next winter, and I must either find another to do it, or remain a year myself. I am inclined to think I shall do the latter, however contrary to my inclination. The forenoon previous to the receipt of this I had written to Mr. Richardson, giving a statement of circumstances, and asking his advice whether I should remain in Lexington. Carter strongly advises me to stay. I have finished reading a new novel by Miss Edgeworth, entitled, ' Patronage.' Good, but too long.

"*September 2d*. It is reported to-day that the city of Washington is taken and burnt. I shall not be surprised to hear the news confirmed. Finished the History of Russia, by Tooke. A wretched performance without thought or arrangement.

"*3d*. Set out with a view of calling at Mr. James Prentiss's, but met Thomas at the gate, who informed me they were just going to the circus. He told me that he had conversed with two gentlemen of Russelville, that the place is well supplied with lawyers, but that there is a school in the place for which they want an instructor, and will give any price. If I should have any inclination to engage, he bid me call on Mr. Crittenden, of Lexington, who had a brother there. The idea of engaging in a school at any price is not agreeable to me, but I think I shall call and converse with Mr. Crittenden. Afterwards I called on the Misses Price. I am not at home there. Ease in conversation is the greatest charm in a family, but here it seems to be far otherwise. It is by continual exertion only, and suggesting every new idea myself, that anything is said. I have heard them complain of unsociable gentlemen, but I am sure the fault is more their own.

"*4th*. In the morning had a conversation with Mr. Crittenden, and learned that the salary of the school at Russelville has been about $750,

and that their wish is probably to obtain a permanent preceptor. I told him $ 1,000 would induce me to engage for one year, but as I learned that there was little chance of the terms being acceptable, and even less that I could then settle there with any prospect of success, I bade him trouble himself no more about it. I think it very likely if one would engage for several years, they would give $1,000, and I may repent that I did not pursue the matter further. But the business of teaching is so inconsistent with my ambition and inclination, that I cannot think of it.

"*5th*. The loss of Washington and destruction of public buildings is confirmed. It seems to have been taken on the evening of the 24th ult., after considerable fighting, in which American militia could not stand against British regulars. We have not yet received authentic particulars. The impression on the resources of the country will not be materially felt, but I fear the final consequence will be a change of the seat of government. Personal, and in some respects, public convenience, has long since called it to Philadelphia ; but thus to make the United States Congress dependent on any particular State would be, in my opinion, a most unfortunate event.

"*6th*. A sort of air-castle came into my head. John Hart, brother to Mrs. Clay, has lost nearly half his fortune by a partner in business, and although it becomes necessary to go into business himself, he has an unconquerable aversion to its drudgery. My air-castle was this, — to propose to him to vest a given capital and commit the drudgery to me, under conditions. Afterwards, Mrs. Clay told me that she had almost persuaded John to adopt the very plan which my fancy had laid, excepting what regards myself. This put me upon thinking seriously on the subject. The question for my decision is, whether I shall make such a proposal ? The changing one's whole course of life requires too much thought for one day.

"*7th*. This day I have been one hour a liberal-minded merchant calculating gains, promoting science and literature, and extending my connections for trade and knowledge to every part of the country ; the next, an eloquent lawyer defending the cause of innocence, basking in the sunshine of popularity, getting rich, and then thundering with Ciceronian eloquence in the Congress of the United States. On the whole, I think the latter course most brilliant, and best adapted to my knowledge, talents, and ambition. Not that I shall ever realize all the enchanting prospects of fancy, but they will keep my mind alive, and give a spring to every exertion. With these thoughts is connected a half-formed resolution to settle in Lexington. However, I shall not form the other half at present. Still, I may introduce the subject of turning merchant to John Hart, should a proper opportunity offer in conversation.

"*10th.* John Watkins, half-brother to Mr. Clay, had been attempting to raise a rifle company, and this was the day appointed for a choice of officers, etc. But it appeared that they had all mistaken the law, which requires every company to consist of sixty-four privates, and forbids any militia company being reduced below that number by the raising of independent companies. I had consented that my name should go with the rest, more to promote a thing which I should consider useful, than expecting to derive any benefit. But we concluded to quit on the spot, for the foregoing very good reason, as we had but about thirty men. So the afternoon was spent in drinking whiskey and pitching dollars, till I was entirely out of patience. I stayed more than two hours longer than I wished, for the sake of my company, who seemed to think I was too soon tired with them.

"I have, I think, learnt the way to be popular in Kentucky, but do not as yet put it in practice. Drink whiskey and talk loud, with the fullest confidence, and you will hardly fail of being called a clever fellow.

"*15th.* This evening I received a useful check from Mrs. Clay, although given in severer terms than the occasion required. N. Watkins was present, and in conversation I observed that I believed there was very little literary taste in Lexington. She bid me take care, I must not say that, and went on to compare Western men with Northern men, to the disadvantage of the latter. I defended my countrymen. My principal points were, that the people were not only better, but better informed. She said I was too much prejudiced in favor of my own country, and knew very little of this. I observed, I believed I knew as much of this as the Kentuckians did of that. Her eyes sparkled, but the remark was as just as it was cutting. However, she quite the argument, and said I ought not to say so much; that it was disgusting to hear one always praising their own country. I told her I knew precisely to what feeling my observations were addressed. She said I ought not to say all I thought. Said I, with a smile, I do not say all I think, which, although it did not mend the matter, caused a pause in the dispute. Watkins had supported her, but after a short silence, whether she thought she had gone too far, or thought my feelings injured, she said to Watkins that she should like to become acquainted with the literary men of Lexington, and went on to support almost precisely the same opinions I had advanced. After he was gone, she resumed her remarks, but I neither seconded nor disputed. Thus I have often found it the case, that she will dispute with me at the time, and afterwards adopt my opinion. However, although I think I was perfectly correct in all I said, it taught me in practice what I before knew in theory, and will put me on my guard for the future.

"*21st.* Did duty in the militia. We had a barbecue in the field, of which I partook, not because I was pleased with the principle on which it was provided, but because I was hungry. It seems it was a proposal of the Captain to remunerate Mr. Picket, who had been fined for selling whiskey to his company without license.

"*26th.* I have finished a little story of Kotzebue's, called 'Zaida,' with a short dramatic piece called the 'Beautiful Unknown.' Also, this evening finished the History of Massachusetts. I have gained some knowledge from it; but it has been tedious to me and my hearers.

"*30th.* This morning was awakened by a firing of musketry, at first scattered, then frequent and continued. It was a little after day, and going to the door, I distinctly saw the flashes of the muskets a little more than half a mile distant. The morning was clear and still, and the echo sounded like a roll of thunder. I supposed it a sham-fight of the soldiers, but learnt that it was a drill-muster of militia officers.

"About seven o'clock the mail arrived with the news of McDonough's victory on Lake Champlain, and the repulse of the enemy at Plattsburg. A firing of cannon and small arms commenced, and continued about an hour. In the evening a large part of the town was illuminated.

"*October 1st.* This day I wrote to Hon. J. B. Varnum, according to his request. I was almost resolved to apply for a commission in the army, should more troops be raised, but have deferred it for the present.

"This day arrived the news of Jackson's victory at Mobile. Twenty guns announced it to the public, and in the evening almost every house in town was filled with lights. I had been to town, and returned, not knowing of the intended illumination; but on seeing the white cloud of light slowly brightening over the houses, I resolved to be present. I started, but on my way was arrested by the appearance of a thousand lights in the woods on my left. I turned aside and found the barracks most romantically illuminated by rows of candles on the tops of the buildings, and others perched among the boughs and in the tops of the trees. With feelings highly electrified, I proceeded to the town. Many a hovel, which had scarce a pane of glass to admit the light of heaven, was lined in front with candles. Through the glaring windows, as I passed along, many faces of wrinkled age and blooming youth appeared beaming with joy. The pleasure of the ignorant laborer, whose bosom is, notwithstanding, warmed by patriotism, is perhaps, on such occasions, greater than that of a more cultivated mind. However, I passed into the town, and was highly delighted, until a procession, headed by drum and fife, paraded the street with a thousand candles, and began to break dark windows. Strongly as any one, do I despise the man who would not light a candle to participate in his fellow-citizens' joy; but I would leave him to the darkness of his own bosom. Few were broken, except

in shops. The procession was often saluted by muskets, to which they responded by continual cheers. Pictures and emblems were displayed in different places, and the streets were filled with men and ladies. I walked almost over the town alone, though I had called at Mrs. Hart's with hopes of finding the young ladies; but they were already gone. About nine o'clock I returned home fatigued, but much pleased with the evening.

"*4th.* This evening was at a party at Mrs. Nelly Hart's, given by Thomas to Colonel Croghan, the hero of Sandusky. Before breakfast I wrote an ode, before dinner copied it, and it was handed round in the evening. I thought myself it was not contemptible, and my vanity was gratified by the praises bestowed upon it. It was shown to the Colonel, immediately after which he was introduced to me; but from a diffidence not very common between the flatterer and flattered, not a word more was said. This conduct very much raised my opinion of the man, although a conversation would have been very agreeable. His countenance pleased me much better than when I saw him on Sunday, and on the whole, he is an intelligent, pleasant-looking man.

"Of the gentlemen at this party little can be said. They were generally unsocial, and paid little attention to the ladies, excepting the Colonel and one or two other officers. I was told that wine was not put on the side-board, lest some of the young men should get tipsy. Of ladies, I suppose there were about forty, of all sorts of faces. The most beautiful I saw was Eliza P. There are very few who are beautiful. With their dress, especially that of the more fashionable class, I find the same fault as with the ladies of Washington, — they have monstrous bosoms behind. The shoulders are so bound back with corsets, that the skin is wrinkled, and a huge valley appears between them, far from lovely or agreeable.

"*7th.* Had a letter from Mr. Richardson. It contains some excellent advice, which, if I will follow, he bets his life that I will succeed in Lexington. I shall preserve it as my practical creed."

CHAPTER V.

"*1814, October 10th.* I have determined to go to Frankfort day after to-morrow, and apply for license to the Court of Appeals, — the highest court in the State. My object is to have a license which will carry the greatest weight with it, should I leave the State.

"*12th.* Having waited in town from past seven to nine for Major Barry, on whom I relied to introduce me to the judges at Frankfort, I set out for that place alone. I found the country similar to that around Lexington, until I approached the capital, where it becomes hilly. On all the road, but a small part of the land is cleared.

"All at once the capital of Kentucky opens upon the view on the right, on a little spot of flat ground almost under you, and surrounded by hills. The Kentucky River, now a small and dirty stream, winds along among these, and so deep and crooked is its channel, that it scarcely makes an opening. The town is not at all pleasant, except to those who look down upon it from the hills.

"It was about two o'clock, and Barry had not arrived. I dined, and wandered over the town and banks of the river until about four, when, learning that he had not yet arrived, I began to think of some other method of being introduced.

"Understanding that Mr. Wickliffe, a lawyer of Lexington, to whom I had been introduced, was in town, I sought for him, but in vain. I then adopted the only remaining alternative; inquired the names of the judges, and introduced myself. They asked me some questions relative to my education, and bade me call after supper. I called, and was questioned for about an hour, and made several blunders. The questions were more particular than I had been led to expect. Some person came in to do business, and I was told to call again after breakfast, to-morrow, and they would consider my case. I went away with the idea that their impressions were favorable.

"*13th.* I called again, and, contrary to my expectation, they proceeded to examine me further. This continued for nearly half an hour, and though for most of the questions an answer was on my tongue, I blundered in one, and in another I could not answer at all. The Chief Justice asked the others if they had any questions to ask, to which they answered, 'no.' He then asked what they thought of it. One of them, a suspicious-looking fellow, who seemed thoughtful, asked me if Mr. Barry had arrived. I answered them in the negative, when another of them said that he had. I rejoined that I would ask him in, if they wished to ask him any questions concerning me. 'No, no,' they said, and the suspicious-looking man asked if an answer before noon would do. I said 'yes,' and retired, not with the most pleasant feelings. In answer to what had been my course of reading, I had enumerated most of the books that I had read. I had blundered on some questions which one who has read so much ought to answer. I had told them I had depended on Major Barry to introduce me, and no Barry appeared, and when he did come I did not know it; these circumstances led me to suspect they doubted my whole story. Nothing opposed this impression except my certificate from the county court. I now trembled for the event. What must be my mortification! Can I return to Lexington? With these feelings, I called on Barry and told him the judges seemed desirous of seeing some person who was acquainted with me. He promised to call. At ten o'clock I went into the court. Barry was there; I asked him if he had seen the judges, — 'no'; but he would at dinner. Here I sat listening in torment to the proceedings till half past one. I often caught the judge's eyes, and fancied they gave me a look of respect. Here conversation with Wickliffe and Barry showed them that I was not a stranger. The former showed me much attention, and when the court adjourned, invited me to his room. I remained in this suspense till after dinner, contriving expedients in case of a refusal. I thought one moment I would give a true statement of my education, and beg another examination; the next, that I would apply to the next circuit court, and, by my exertions, make their honors blush for their refusal. I could not, however, for a moment hesitate to admit the justice of their apparent suspicions.

"After dinner I again called, and was told by the Chief Justice that they had concluded to give me a license, but I must procure the form. I attributed much in this decision to Mr. Barry; but what was my surprise when, soon after, Barry passing by, asked if the judges were now in their room, saying that he would now call and see them! Thus I learned that my license was procured without a word from any mortal who had been before acquainted with me! Although I could not help severely blaming him for negligence in a matter in which I was so deeply interested, I was heartily glad he had not called, — there is something so pleasant in owing everything to ourselves.

"I could not now help feeling that my fears had far underrated my appearance on examination, and I am still convinced that such was the fact. I was told I must procure a form of license, and having done this,

I called, but the judges were gone out. I waited nearly an hour, and then, as it was near four o'clock, left it with Major Barry, and set out for Lexington.

"I know not whether I shall stay in Lexington, but every week makes it more likely. The advice of Mr. Richardson and my other friends, with the character of all the young lawyers here, afford me strong hopes of success. My friends have become more and more interested in my favor, and this, joined with my own inclination, will very likely decide me.

"17th. This day I received my license, — so, as J. Hart told me, I want nothing but clients to make me a lawyer.

"18th. This day attended a regimental muster. The militia here are but an ill-armed, undisciplined rabble. There were many without guns, and I do not recollect to have seen a cartouch-box or bayonet in the whole regiment. We formed, marched half a mile to a field, after one drum and fife, our only music, formed in échelon three times, marched back again, and were dismissed. I was much fatigued, for we were a great while performing these manœuvres, as both officers and men had to learn them.

"30th. In conversation with Mrs. Clay, an observation was made characteristic of herself, and as it regarded myself, not without foundation. The conversation was on bows, and I said I did not know what sort of a bow I was accustomed to make, for it was a long time since I had thought on the subject. She answered she knew, and imitated it, continuing, that I always looked as if I was ashamed when I came into a room. I blushed at the remark, and the more as I was conscious it was just. But I am glad it was made, for it will be a stimulus to make me attempt assuming a little more confidence and dignity. I feel that it is possible, and it shall be done.

"November 1st. John Hart, with some of the ladies, walked out. He informed me that he was about to vest five or six thousand dollars in the grocery business, and wished to know if I could recommend any person who would come out and manage it for him. I recommended my friend Brazer, Jr., but observed, that, were I five years younger, I would engage in it myself. He said he wished he could make it an object for me, and observed he would gladly put all his property under my care. I thanked him, and little more was said, but I concluded to write to Brazer. However, this set me thinking, and attempting to contrive ways in which it should be mutually advantageous.

"2d. With several plans in my head I called on J. Hart, but before I had time to divulge them he made me a proposal. It was to vest in business five or six thousand dollars, of which I should take the care, and receive one third of the profits, or should that fall short of $500

per annum, he would insure me that sum. He wished me to vest what money I could obtain, from time to time, in the business, and finally make the business my own; but he was averse to every plan like partnership.

"To change the whole object of one's life I thought too serious a matter to decide hastily, and therefore resolved to take a day or two to consider it. The inducements to accept are the certainty of an immediate support, the prospect of riches, the doubtful nature and bad prospects of my profession, which are daily darkened by the clouds of war, and the swarms of New-Englanders flocking to this country.

"On the other hand, my ignorance of the business, the long term spent in the study of law, my ambition, and the supposed opinion of my absent friends, throw me into a state of doubt and perplexity. I returned to the tavern, walked out to Mr. Wickliffe's with R., spent a social hour, and again returned to the tavern, where were four of us Yankee emigrant lawyers, and we made ourselves merry with brandy and our ill prospects. I proposed my case, and asked their opinion, and found them unanimous that I should accept Mr. Hart's offer. My own inclination is to the same opinion, although I am not perfectly pleased with the arrangement. Should I do it, Breck will probably take my place at Mr. Clay's. Would to God that Mr. Clay was at home! for I should probably be decided by his opinion.

"3d. Thought made me restless. I dreamed that I had resolved to pursue the business of law, and was likely to be successful. When awake I returned to the same state of doubt, from which I was relieved in the afternoon by a call from Mr. Hart, who informed me the goods were not to be procured, and he had concluded to abandon or defer the business to a more favorable opportunity. Thus are all my mercantile hopes blasted, and I am again a lawyer. I am almost resolved to make a solemn promise that I will follow the profession through thick and thin, betide me weal, betide me woe. At the present time I need such a resolution.

"5th. Breck dined with me and spent the afternoon. I am sometimes almost resolved to quit my place, and go immediately into practice; but I cannot but have hopes that by delaying I shall derive advantage from the friendship of Mr. Clay.

"6th. Two more law students arrived in town from Worcester County, Massachusetts. They come with strong hopes, and will therefore be more disappointed. Yesterday I had a letter from Fowle, who says he must quit Boston, for business is at a dead stand. He has joined an infantry company, and done duty one week in the forts.

"13th. Wrote to Fowle. I now recollect an anecdote of last evening, which serves to illustrate what is the impression of the slaves here

concerning the British. It was after dark, when I was walking from town, when two negro boys passed me on the other side of the road, driving some cattle. There was a large fire of shavings in town. 'There,' said one, 'that looks like the fire of a house.' 'Yes; what if we should find the British in town when we get back!' 'They would n't hurt us, would they?' 'No.' 'Then I would have this horse, would n't you have that?' Thus they spoke until they had passed out of hearing.

"14th. Called on the Misses P. Mary H. was present. I confess I could not help blushing for my friend who was with me; although, perhaps, I had more reason to blush for myself. Even with ladies, I cannot use any conversation which I myself think silly. Nor can I think that a gentlemen can ever in that way recommend himself to the esteem of those with whom he converses. I had rather be esteemed unsocial than silly. Received a letter from Hough, at Louisville. Like the rest of the Yankees he does not know where to put himself.

"18th. I was this evening in company with a young gentleman, named Guilford, from Massachusetts, with whom I have been much pleased. The conversation now confirmed my good opinion. It turned on matrimony, when he said he should never marry. On my appearing surprised, he said he had always been the dupe of love. I then told him he was a foolish dupe if he had taken such a resolution. He blushed; and said we did not know his reasons. As we did not seem satisfied, he proceeded to say that he had a mother, and several brothers and sisters, who had been in affluent circumstances, but that his father had died insolvent, and left them to labor for a sustenance. That he believed it would give him more pleasure to relieve them, should it ever be in his power, than to marry. We could not help approving his principles and admiring his resolution. I resolved on the spot to solicit his correspondence, for his is the heart which I love.

"21st. By my Boston paper I find something like an account of the designs of the Federalists there, which has for the first time given me a desire to return. If I am eligible, and the people of my native town would choose me to the next legislature, I would fly back in a moment.

"22d. Wrote a long letter to Parson Heywood, intimating what were yesterday my thoughts, so that if my friends there have any such inclination, and find the objections surmountable, they may know my sentiments. But I do not expect anything.

"23d. After school I walked into town, and took from the post-office a letter from Woodbury. He had not received my last, and by his expressions I am left to suppose that he had written me, but that the letter has miscarried. He gives me quite a sermon, which I am afraid, is wasted ; but I must do justice to his good intentions. He spent the evening at the Deacon's, and Mary sends me something, — he does not remember what. That girl is, after all, the best in the world ! And this evening, too, I have called on the amiable, the beautiful——. Did I think she loved me, perhaps I should think her the best in the world. What a labyrinth is the human heart ?

"27th. In the fluctuations of my mind with regard to settling, I have nearly come to the conclusion to quit Lexington, and go into some of the neighboring counties, where I can try my talents, and if I find them equal to the competition, return, and finally settle in Lexington. But the distracted situation in which the country is likely to be placed precludes the possibility of calculating upon any plan with certainty. Should revolution prevail in the North, it will not be very likely to stop until these Western States will be separated, not only from the Northern, but the Southern. If they cannot all remain united, this will doubtless be the interest of the West, which, under a strong but liberal government, may increase with an unparalleled rapidity. But God forbid the necessity of resorting to this dilemma. Better sacrifice one hundred thousand men and preserve the Union.

"28th. Went to a party this morning at Mr. Thomas Pindell's. The evening passed pleasantly. Out of patience at sitting as a mere spectator, I undertook to dance, and blundering several times in the figures of cotillons, with which I was unacquainted, I sat down quite satisfied, and thought I should dance no more. But while they were dancing reels, I took a partner, but when I came upon the floor the party wished to turn it to a cotillon. As they were nearly unanimous against me, I yielded, and succeeded admirably. By another evening I shall be able to dance almost any of their figures.

"29th. Having returned home about one o'clock, I was very dull to-day, and especially in the evening. Yet was my imagination on the wing, and I began a piece of poetry on an incident which happened last evening.

"December 2d. Called at Thomas Prentiss's with Rockwood and others, and getting into a game of cards, it was two o'clock before we departed. It was not my fault, but that of my companions, for I had never been there before. At any rate, I am resolved to avoid such a shameful hour in future.

"From a Boston 'Patriot,' received to-day, I learn the death of the Rev. J. Heywood, of Dunstable, to whom I had lately written. It likewise announces the unanimous resolve of the Vermont legislature that it is inexpedient to choose delegates to meet the New England convention.

"12th. To-day further news was received from our commissioners at Ghent, by which it appears there are still some hopes of peace. But

such delays are interposed by the British that the business will not be concluded in time to allow the commissioners to return before spring. Thus I shall probably be disappointed in all the advantages which I had hoped from an acquaintance with Mr. Clay.

"This evening my friend Rockwood came out, and I spent with him and the young ladies the most merry hours I have seen in Kentucky. I said many foolish things, and some for which I was sorry ; but this is the natural consequence of much talking. Messrs. Hart and Watkins went out to hunt opossums, but returned without success.

"1815, January 1st. The New Year finds me at Winchester, Ky., ready to bid a long adieu to a friend. During the last year I have seen much, and felt much. It has indeed been an eventful year to me and the world. What the present may have in store, God only knows. It is ushered in by doubt, fear, and dismay. Heaven grant that its evening may be as propitious to me and my country as the beginning is gloomy and portentous !

"February 13th. Things have gone forward in a uniform train with me for some days, excepting that I received a letter from Shipley. But this day an incident occurred which bids fair to change the whole color of my life. Mr. Sawyer, Mr. Hunt, and Mr. Whiting, three New-Englanders, called on me and proposed a scheme which had been suggested to them, by which they think we may make our fortunes. The plan is to take up a considerable tract in the Indiana Territory, and form on it a settlement exclusively of New-Englanders. It is contemplated to petition Congress for some indulgences in the payment for public lands, and if they should be granted, to commence on a grand scale. But should the application be unsuccessful, there are several moneyed men who will assist us to take up perhaps 50,000 acres on the usual terms. The young men of the company, from five to ten in number, are to do all the business, settle on the land themselves, and procure emigrants. It is contemplated to take up some central place, with such conveniences and communications as to render it the seat of government for the future State of Indiana. The plan struck me as a feasible one, and I said I would think of it. I accordingly thought of it, and resolved to join the company, although I perceive some obstacles which may defeat the scheme. In the first place, Congress will not grant the petition. In the next, the place must be near the frontiers, and liable to be harassed by the Indians. But, on the whole, I can lose nothing by it, except time, and wear and tear of body and clothing. On the other hand, should the plan be successful I shall, in ten years, make a fortune.

"14th. This day was spent in preparing a petition to Congress, and writing letters. We petition for leave to take up 150,000 acres of land

in the Indiana or Mississippi Territory, and pray that each payment may be delayed five years from its usual time, and engage in six years to have on the ground fifteen inhabitants for every thousand acres, provided the three last years be clear from all Indian hostilities. But it will arrive at so late a day of the session, that it is doubtful whether Congress receives it. It was signed by Benjamin Sawyer, G. W. Hunt, Amos Kendall, Amos Whiting, for themselves and associates, — for we intend to associate a considerable number more. In the mean time, it is intended that several of us shall set out immediately to investigate the country. But we were all, but one, engaged in business which we could not leave. I offered to go if some person could be found to take my place. It was mentioned that there was a young man at Cincinnati ; and Mr. Whiting, who was acquainted with him, wrote to him on the spot. If he can come, in little more than a week I shall be on my way to Indiana. I fear I shall suffer from fatigue, but I will make the attempt. It was past twelve o'clock when our papers were completed, and I took lodging again in town.

"15th. Mentioned my probable journey to Mrs. Clay. She will accept my substitute, and even tells me to go if he does not come, if I find it for my advantage. But I am not resolved on that.

"18th. Wishing to engage Mr. Thorn as one of the active men in our speculation, we sent Mr. Whiting for him, who made him come with him on his return. We called on Mr. J. Prentiss in the evening, in order to determine on the principles and means of executing our projected scheme. We were a long time provoked with the whiffling, prevaricating temper of the man, and at length surmised that his intention was to use us more as servants than partners. It was a long while before he could be brought to anything definite, and he finally thought we ought to be satisfied with one twentieth of the profits. To this he endeavored to reconcile us by extravagant calculations of gain, which had no effect but to show his own duplicity. Unluckily for him, he had told us that since he had been in this country it has been his practice to make use of men according to his own views, without regard to their character or principles. Were no petition sent, we should probably have abandoned the business on the spot, but we remembered his own confession, and determined to await the event of that. Should it be granted, we shall have the staff in our own hands, and our terms must be accepted, or we shall apply elsewhere. Our terms are, that the inactive partners shall advance $10,000 each, which, with interest, shall be refunded from the first profits, and the remainder shall be equally divided among the whole, after deducting all the expenses. On the whole, it was agreed that Mr. Thorn, Mr. Whiting, and myself should set out as soon as practicable to explore the country, and that our ex-

penses should be borne by the rest of the associates, provided the scheme shall not succeed.

"But unless the young gentleman from Cincinnati should consent to take my place I shall not go. Indeed, I grow very indifferent about it ; for I believe the scheme can never be effected with Mr. P. for a leader. I could not help feeling a sovereign contempt, and never had a stronger inclination to quiz a man in my life.

"22d. This being Washington's birthday, was set apart by the trustees of the town for thanksgiving for the boon of such a hero, and more particularly for the late success of our arms under General Jackson.

"Services were held at the Methodist, Episcopalian, and Presbyterian churches. About 4 P. M. was a discourse at the court-house by Mr. Shannon, which was attended by a crowd of both sexes. In the evening there was a general illumination, but the heavens were lighted up with such a plump and brilliant moon, that the little candles' beams were lost in her mellow flood of light. The people did not enter into the business with the spirit which the importance of the occasion would seem to demand. It is so long since they received the news, that the enthusiasm has had time to cool, and it seemed more like constrained approbation than animated joy.

"23d. This day the news of the signing of preliminaries of peace between this country and Great Britain, arrived at Lexington. To many it was a messenger of joy, but others shook their heads. They say it would be dishonorable to make a peace on the terms offered by our own government. For myself, I was elevated with a sober, heartfelt joy, which I cannot describe. In the continuance of the war I see no advantage to be gained, except a possibility of glory, — a glory stained with the blood of our citizens, and half obscured by the flames of our towns and villages.

"There was no illumination at Lexington, nor do I believe there will be in case of a full confirmation. What ! Shall a people light their windows at the prospect of blood, and not put each pane in a blaze at the news of that which saves their country ? But they fear it is dishonorable.

"24th. Called at Mr. J. Prentiss's to see him with regard to my intended expedition to Indiana. He had company, and asked me to walk in and spend the evening.

"After the company retired, I asked Mr. Prentiss to furnish me with a horse, money, and instructions, for the intended expedition, — all of which he promised.

"26th. Mr. Hunt having forgotten to send the billet which I wrote to Mr. Hough, I took a horse and rode out. I wished him to promise decisively that he would come if K. should fail, but that he would not do. He feels under no obligations to remain where he is, and some circumstances make his situation rather unpleasant; but he, notwithstanding, feels a delicacy at leaving and going again into the same business. On telling the result to Mrs. Clay, she strongly intimated an unwillingness to have me go, and, alluding to Mr. Hough, said she should be very angry if any person were to induce a teacher to leave her house, or were so ungenerous as to attempt it. I felt injured, but repressed my feelings, for it never entered my heart that I was acting an ungenerous part by accepting the services of Mr. Hough, in compliance with his own inclination first expressed to me. I was, however, afraid to say I would remain here if it was her desire, for I had resolved to go. I went to town in expectation of meeting Mr. Thorn, but was disappointed. Our departure must of course be delayed till Tuesday.

"This day an express brought an account of the ratification of the treaty of peace with Great Britain, which took place on the 15th inst. The transaction has been so sudden, prompt, and unexpected, that people can hardly realize the transition. English papers find great fault with the treaty, which predisposes the people of this country to be satisfied. It seems that something has transpired at the Congress at Vienna which has given a spur to the British government. On this occasion I cannot help feeling grateful to God, and congratulating my country. My reflections on the prospect before us were, a few days ago, extremely gloomy. Civil war and the destruction of our government were by no means improbable events. Credit was gone, our army was weak, the States were assuming their own defence, and instead of a hydra who should turn its heads on an external enemy, we were likely to become a nest of serpents, equally fatal to ourselves and others. But now the prospect changes. Our government will rise more strong from the contest, opportunity will be afforded for necessary improvements of the Federal system, and, under the fostering influences of freedom and a liberal policy, the North and the South, the East and the West, will rejoice together. Perhaps I am too sanguine; but it appears to me the war has cured us of those fatal mistakes which have hitherto rendered our government so weak. Our navy has burst into favor in a blaze of glory, commerce is felt to be necessary for a revenue, all parts of the Union have learned that they are mutually dependent, and will draw closer the bond which unites them.

"27th. My expedition to Indiana is deferred. We have received information that many murders have lately been committed in that territory by the Indians, and it will not be safe to proceed. Peace has likewise somewhat changed our prospects, and, unless Congress grant us some facilities, it is doubtful whether our plan can succeed.

"28th. I went in town this morning, and it was agreed to wait the

event of our petition before we proceed. Should there be a prospect of obtaining it by the next Congress, we shall wait; but should no such hopes be entertained, the event will depend on the moneyed men who can be induced to engage.

"Lexington men will not illuminate for the peace! I believe the majority sincerely rejoice, but a few discontented men throw a damp on every ardent feeling. They say the peace is dishonorable. It must arise from ignorance in the assertors, or this is to be made a hobby on which other men are to ride into office. He who understands the situation of the country, and would prefer the continuance of war to such a peace, must be a madman.

"March 1st. A recommendation was this morning issued in a handbill for an illumination this evening. In the afternoon appeared a counter handbill, and some violent young men threatened to break every window which should be lighted. However, about a third part of the houses were illuminated, some of them brilliantly, and no outrage was committed. Many were glad of peace, but would not illuminate because nothing has been gained by the war.

"5th. According to previous agreement, or rather on an invitation from Mr. Farnham, who lives in the family, I rode with Mr. Hunt to the house of Mr. Alexander, thirteen miles from Lexington, towards Frankfort. That family had been represented to me as one of the most pleasant in the country, and I was not disappointed.

"6th. Rode with Mr. F., Mr. H., and two Mr. Alexanders to see some young ladies named Lee, but finding they were gone to church we followed. Here we were put out of patience by wretched music and a tedious sermon, left the house, and before service was over started for Mr. Alexander's. After dinner we bade adieu to this hospitable family and returned to Lexington.

"12th. A storm prevented Mr. Hunt and myself from going to visit Mr. Hough yesterday, as we had previously agreed. This day I wrote to my friend Flügel, and gave him a short piece of poetry in congratulation of his late marriage. I likewise desired him to write me immediately and inform me what prospect that neighborhood offers for a lawyer.

"13th. Attended court this day in order to observe the manner of doing business here, but was greatly fatigued, with very little profit. Their manner of conducting business is extremely dilatory. When they are ready to try a cause, a jury must be picked up in the highways and hedges; for there is nobody summoned beforehand, as in Massachusetts, because that would make expense. Of course much time is lost, and the juries often consist of men as little fitted for jurors as they are for governors. This causes a delay of nearly an hour. Well, this is not

all. The witnesses are now to be called and hunted out, which takes up almost an hour more. Thus by delays and foolish speeches the day is frittered away and very little is done. At least that was the case to-day, for but one case was tried.

"15th. This day was assigned for the trial of Mr. Payne for the murder of his wife; but on the request of his counsel, Mr. Pope, time was given till to-morrow for him to make preparation for contesting the point whether he ought to be tried or not in his present state of health. I had gone to court to hear the trial, but on this delay to consider the question of postponement I returned home in disgust.

"16th. Monday the 27th inst. is assigned for the trial of Payne. On our petition to Congress nothing has been done, and we presume it has not been presented.

"21st. Went into court, and on motion of Mr. Wickliffe took the oath required by law to practise as an attorney. According to the best of my recollection, it amounted to an oath that I would observe and support the Constitution of the State, demean myself honestly in my practice, and that I had not given, accepted, or been the bearer of a challenge for a duel since April, 1812, and that I would not give, accept, or bear one hereafter, in this State or elsewhere.

"27th. This day being assigned for the trial of young Payne for the murder of his wife, I went to the court-house after school, and saw the prisoner arraigned. On being asked whether he was guilty, he answered, "I am not guilty, but I wish I was, and I would tell you so." The whole conduct of the man was made up of impudence and indifference. Nearly sixty were called before a jury was obtained, and then the evidence was as conclusive to his guilt as circumstances could make it. The court adjourned a little after dark.

"28th. This day was spent in the examination of testimony.

"29th. The testimony was closed, and the arguments were opened by Mr. Breckenridge, appointed by the court to assist Mr. Shannon, on the part of the commonwealth. The beginning of his argument was good and eloquent, but it became more feeble as he proceeded, and was continued to the unreasonable length of four hours. Mr. Pope, in behalf of the prisoner, then commenced in a very eloquent strain, addressed to the feelings of the jury. He summed up the evidence very handsomely, but was led from his subject by many irrelevant ideas which seemed to strike him on the occasion, and at length made his discourse tedious. I left the court just at night, but was told he continued his argument till nearly ten, and, though he had spoken six hours, did not finish! He seems to have no doubt of the fact, but hopes to save him on the plea of insanity; but he is no madman, and if he should be saved justice will mourn.

"30th. Through darkness, mud, and torrents of rain I rode into town, and attended a ball at Postlethwait's. I did not dance, but spent the evening very pleasantly in conversation with the ladies and gentlemen.

"April 1st. This afternoon I attended court, and heard sentence pronounced on Payne. A motion was made for a new trial, but overruled by the court. I sat at some distance, but had a fair view of his face, and could not discover the least change. The second Tuesday in April is appointed for his execution.

"5th. —— made a proposal to me last evening, at which I was somewhat surprised. He expects to deliver a 4th of July oration, and he wishes me to write it, because, he says, I can write much better than he. I sincerely doubt the fact; but though I am sure I would never depend for my reputation on the talents or exertions of another, I consented to write, with this proviso, — that I should deliver it myself if opportunity offers.

"I attended the ball this evening again, but not without qualms. From the arrangement of the parties, or from some other cause, they would not let me pay last week. They are, I believe, subscription balls, and those only pay who have subscribed for the whole number, which was eight, if I rightly remember; but not having any wish to amuse myself at the expense of others, I should not have gone at all had not Mrs. Clay and her daughters been there.

"6th. We had a considerable party of ladies and gentlemen, and nothing would satisfy them but the reading of my poem. It is the last time I will read it when any of the same persons shall be present.

"9th. It being Sunday, and Mrs. Clay being absent, I spent the day at home in writing an argument from my recollection of the evidence in the case of Commonwealth vs. Payne. It was against the prisoner, and I found the subject a prolific one. I spent the day in writing and did not finish.

"10th. Concluded my argument, and I found I had written about sixteen quarto pages of common writing-paper. To-day I proposed to Mrs. Clay to hear the boys recite separately, on account of the striking superiority of Thomas, the younger. The difference was conspicuous this afternoon, for Thomas recited sixty lines, and Theodore only twenty.

"15th. Mr. J. Hart and Mr. Smith came out this morning and spent most of the afternoon. On speaking of the Tammany Society in Lexington, I observed I believed I would join it, and write a poem or something for their celebration, on the 4th of July, when Hart said I had better, and bid me write a petition to the Grand Sachem. This was a formality I was unacquainted with, but nevertheless wrote it, and despatched it by him.

"My principal object is to make myself known, and get an opportunity of displaying such talents as I may possess.

"*18th.* Went this afternoon to Mr. Alexander's, in Woodford, to a party. To me the fore part of the day was full of little vexations: I suspected Mrs. Clay did not wish me to go; the gardener went away with my horse and did not return until, being out of patience, I walked into town and hired a horse from a stable. Here I met with more vexations: I found myself on a miserable, hard-trotting animal, and withal had on a new pair of shoes, so tight that they actually blistered my feet. However, the party was small, and the evening passed pleasantly in dancing, wherein I also took part. It was just two o'clock when the ladies retired.

"*19th.* Rose a little after sunrise. After breakfast the party recommenced dancing, but Mr. Hunt and myself took 'French leave' and returned to Lexington. I was pinched and shaken almost to a mummy. However, as I had petitioned the Tammany Society for admission as a member, and hoped to be admitted this evening, I walked into town. Finding Mrs. A. Hart and the Misses P.'s at Mrs. T. Hart's, I had a pleasant walk and very agreeable conversation with them, and was afterwards ushered into the Society. The principles of the Society are liberal, and its object noble.

"*25th.* This day arrived Mr. Kilpatrick from Cincinnati. I am very much pleased with his appearance, and shall next week resign. My first steps will be to visit a number of the counties, and learn, if possible, which promises most.

"*29th.* Resigned my sceptre to Mr. Kilpatrick. Though the behavior of Mr. Clay's children out of school has not been very agreeable, yet their attention to study and their good hearts, and uniformly respectful conduct towards me, have attached me considerably to them, and I cannot leave them without regret. Yet, I cannot but feel a glow of joy that my pedagogical labors are closed, and ardently hope I shall never be under the necessity of resuming them.

"In the afternoon I went to town, and there met Mr. Farnham, who invited me to ride to Richmond with him. On a moment's thought I resolved to go, if possible, and return to Nicholasville. I accordingly procured a letter to Mr. Woodson, clerk of the court in the latter place, from Major Barry, and invited Mr. Farnham home with me to spend the night.

"*30th.* Set out after breakfast, and had a pleasant, though moderate ride, to Jack's Creek Ferry, on the Kentucky. The contrast is so striking between the uniformly uneven ground near Lexington, and the stupendous cliffs and hills on the river, that I was filled with delight. The soft tints of spring added much to their beauty. After taking dinner,

and being entertained by our host with many anecdotes not at all to the credit of his neighbor, General Green Clay, we crossed the river. We had not proceeded a mile before a cloud arose, thunder rolled, and threatened instant rain. We accordingly took shelter in the first house that offered, which was Clay's, and, for myself, I was glad of the shower, as I hoped it would afford me an opportunity of seeing his daughter. Unfortunately she was not at home. The father treated us with great complaisance, gave us peach-brandy, invited us to dinner, and pressed us to remain through the night. All, excepting the first, we declined. This old man is said to be worth a million; but there is no happiness in his look, which beams a cold hospitality. We had not proceeded far when it again began raining, and we called at a tavern. Again it ceased, and we started, and had proceeded a few rods when my companion's horse slipped down and threw him into the mud, but with no other injury than daubing his clothes. But it soon began to rain once more, and, resolving not to stop, we arrived in Richmond, well drenched, about dark. We found our friends, Wheelwright and Breck, in good business, and contented.

May 1st. It was county court day, and a very great multitude of people were collected, apparently with no other motive but curiosity. They were, generally, decently dressed, and had agreeable, intelligent countenances. Having said all we had to say, and seen all we could see, we set out directly after dinner for Nicholasville. Before we arrived at the Kentucky our road was bad, being for miles nothing else than the bed of a creek. The scenery about its mouth compensated for every difficulty, for it was remarkably grand and beautiful. After passing the river, we once missed our road for a few rods, and, meeting with a woman, we inquired the way to Nicholasville. 'Why,' said she, 'I never was there.' This was within three miles. But the woman, who had a charming air of benevolence and simplicity in her countenance, said she had come from Virginia a year ago. However, she knew enough to put us right, and we arrived at Nicholasville after dark. We found this a small village, though larger than I expected.

"*2d.* Presented my letter to Mr. Woodson, and procured such information as led me to believe that Nicholasville is not a place for me to settle. About nine o'clock I set out for Lexington. Here my companion, Mr. Farnham, left me for Woodford. He seems a young gentleman of merit, and I am much more pleased with him than on first acquaintance. He gives me a description of the family he is in, which makes it almost angelic, and much increases my esteem of his fair pupil Mary Ann. Again I had proceeded not more than two miles when it began to rain. Having been somewhat wetted before I arrived at a tavern, I concluded not to stop. But I repented my determination, not

in sackcloth and ashes, but in gusts of wind and torrents of rain. At length I was obliged to stop, for even my horse could scarcely face the storm. But it soon abated, and taking a hearty draught of whiskey, I proceeded, dripping, through mud and water to Lexington. I arrived at Mr. Clay's about twelve. I have returned with a resolution, unless something more promising shall offer, to try my fortune in Lexington.

"*4th.* Visited Georgetown, in Scott County. I took a letter to Mr. Herndon, a trader, who was very polite, said he would do anything for me he could, and offered to board me until I could suit myself better, if I would come to that place. The representations which I derived from him and others led me to believe that county the most favorable in the neighborhood. There are five lawyers living in the county, but only one lives in town, and he talks of removing. I went thence to Mr. Alexander's. Mr. Farnham expected soon to go to Natchez, but I brought him a letter, which determined him not to go. He was glad of the disappointment, and is almost resolved to settle in Versailles. I spent the evening very agreeably in this charming family, — a considerable part of it in playing at checkers, or draughts, with Miss Alexander.

"*5th.* Mr. Alexander showed me a piece of poetry written by Miss Alexander, which does honor to her talents, her heart, and her education. Mr. Farnham set out with me this morning for Versailles. We called at Mr. N. Hart's to see Mr. Ruggles. There I was introduced to several young ladies, and among the rest to one named Preston, twelve years old, whom from her size and appearance I judged to be eighteen. I saw here a number of little negroes almost naked, — a disgusting spectacle, which at once prepossessed me against their master. Porter Clay, on whom I depended for an introduction to the clerk of the court, was not at home. We saw several of his children at the door of a miserable cabin, which at present forms his house. We therefore rode out to Mr. Watkins's, two miles and a half from town. Here we took dinner, and Nathaniel W. had the politeness to accompany us to town, and introduce us to persons in the clerk's office, from whom we derived the necessary information. This place does not, I think, offer advantages equal to Georgetown. Besides, as F. has nearly formed a resolution to settle here, I would not willingly interfere with his plans. After a short conversation, bade adieu to my friend and rode to Lexington.

"*6th.* As I considered myself deficient in the legal forms necessary for practice, I this day put myself on inquiries to obtain them. But I find the practice here is almost without form. Every writing, if understood, is equivalent to a bond duly executed.

"*8th.* Purchased what books were absolutely necessary for practice, and made other preparations.

"*9th.* Was not able to go to Georgetown to-day for want of a horse, but shall go to-morrow.

"*10th.* It was almost eleven o'clock when I started. Called at several places in town, and, among the rest, at Mrs. Hart's. I arrived in Georgetown about two o'clock; despatched a boy, who came with me, back with the horses, and took up my abode in the family of Mr. Herndon. His house is small and crowded, so that I repented having accepted his offer, but knew no remedy.

"*11th.* Made some inquiries for a room, but was unable to procure one. Went fishing in Elkhorn Creek, but found it miserable sport. The fish of this country are small and mean.

"*12th.* Made further inquiries for a room, and found a fine one, which I shall probably be able to obtain next week. I shall be glad when the time arrives, for accommodations in this family are extremely bad. Was to-day introduced to Mr. Henry, the only lawyer here; who seems to be a very pleasant man, and gives me much encouragement. I have likewise been introduced to a few others, but Mr. Herndon, though a clever man, is not one who will take much pains to introduce me, a stranger. He is not a man of the world, or as some would say, not extremely polite.

"*13th.* Began reading the Statutes of Kentucky, particularly such as regard the county courts and their jurisdiction. This evening a party played cards till nearly midnight. I had previously told Mr. H. and others that it was my principle never to bet. Of course I am not troubled on that score. Mr. H. and Mr. Craig bet only ninepence on the game.

"*14th.* Attended preaching in the court-house, forenoon and afternoon. The preachers were Baptists. But after the exercises closed in the afternoon, a man without education, but with excellent natural talents, gave us a long discourse in explanation of a new principle, which he pretends to derive from Scripture. The principal tenet is, that the wicked shall be destroyed, soul and body, after the judgment, but the spirit, which he says is not the soul, will survive and be reunited to God. The details were long and not wholly intelligible, but generally he explained himself very lucidly.

"*16th.* Engaged board at Mr. Theobald's tavern, and, as I can there have a room in which but one other man sleeps, I shall not rent an office at all. In the evening had my things moved, and took up my abode in this house.

"Mr. Herndon would have nothing for the time I have spent in his family. Mrs. Herndon had the numbers of the 'Western Gleaner' which contain the pieces of poetry written by me; I pointed them out to her, and she thought some of them pretty.

"I should not mention these trifles, were it not my intention to relate everything, now that I have started in the world, which may give a color to my reputation. In conformity to this resolution, I mention the following trifle which took place, I believe, this day. Mr. Craig put to me this mathematical question : 'Two men were travelling and stopped to take dinner ; one produced five loaves, the other three. A third man came up and took dinner with them, for which he paid eight pieces of money ; how should those eight pieces be divided?' After a little thought I answered, 'Seven and one.' He said he never heard anybody answer it aright before ; that it had been proposed to the whole bar here in time of court, not one of whom could answer it. Trifling as this is, it will leave an impression, and of such impressions on the minds of others are our reputations made up.

"17th. Set about reading statute law, and as I find the judiciary system of Kentucky very complicated as it stands in the statute-books, on account of numerous alterations, I determined to write it out. I accordingly began with justices of the peace.

"18th. Continued my labors, but find the business more difficult, and likely to take more time than I expected.

"19th. This day being cold and wet, I could not sit in my room, and consequently did nothing. Towards night my spirits fell into such a state of depression, and I felt so strongly the want of a friend, that I resolved to set off as soon as convenient and visit my friend Flügel. I thought I should be much more happy, and perhaps succeed much better in my profession if I could live with him. I made some attempts to obtain a horse ; but one I would not take because the owner would charge nothing, and another because he charged too much.

"20th. After a night's consideration, I resolved not to go until after July court, when I could better judge whether I should succeed in this place. Accordingly I again sat down to my books. I feel that I must resist this desponding inclination, as well as this desire for change, or I shall not only be always poor, but also unhappy.

"On an invitation from Mr. Thomas Theobald, who seems very friendly to me, I rode a short distance. This neighborhood is much more pleasant than that of Lexington, on account of the variety of water prospects.

"23d. On the invitation of Mr. G. Miller, rode out ten miles to a battalion muster. I was in much better spirits than yesterday, and made considerable talk with the people. I was made acquainted with several gentlemen, and the time passed merrily away. When we set out for home, the company consisted of from fifteen to thirty, half of whom were a little tipsy. We came on in high spirits, and stopped at almost every tavern ; but I had kept myself perfectly sober, and came home as

cool and almost as lively as when I started. All the candidates made speeches, and old Captain Hunter, the man who was so good to me when I was on my way to Lexington, appeared among the number.

"24th. Spent the day in writing a piece of composition for a club, to which I have a promise of being introduced on Saturday next. It contains many of the most respectable men of the county, and its only object is composition.

"25th. It came into my head again to go and see my friend Flügel after the next county court. I am hardly satisfied to settle myself down here in a place made to my hand, but not made such as I would wish it. My ambition leads me to some new country, where I can have a part in forming new societies and institutions. Many are the visions of my fancy, but alas ! the realities would probably be but a series of disappointments. I made some inquiries for a horse, and found I could hire one at almost any time at seventy-five cents per day.

"June 3d. Went out to the Great Crossings, was introduced to the club, and read a piece of composition prepared for the purpose. Many pieces were read, which were purely political, and of the most violent kind. I was not much delighted, but console myself with the idea that I am able to out-write, if not out-speak, all of them.

"8th. This forenoon Mr. Henderson sent for me, and when I came to his store I found Colonel R. M. Johnson and Mr. Chambers present. They proposed to me to buy the printing establishment here, and undertake the editorial part of the 'Minerva.' They said they doubted not I would find it profitable, and if I would purchase, I should have it on such terms that, on a reasonable calculation, I might pay for it from the proceeds. The proposal was new to me, and I resolved to take time for thought and inquiry. In the evening I mentioned it to my friend, Mr. Rankins, who seemed to recommend the purchase. Afterwards I mentioned it to my friend, Mr. T. Theobald, who bid me at once to wash my hands of it. He said it had ruined two men, and one of two things was certain, I must either become the tool of the Johnsons, or suffer for my independence. He had no doubt it was a trick of the Johnson family to lay me under some obligations, that I might be hereafter bound to support them. At any rate he advised me to inquire, and think well before I engaged. I thanked him for his freedom, and was much inclined to be of his opinion. I shall, however, inform myself perfectly on the subject, and shall, at least, avoid any obligation. Could I do it with independence, I should be pleased with editing the paper for a while, but not with owning the property. The reputation of the paper is now very low, for its management is contemptible.

"9th. From representations made to me, and an aversion to own

any property of the kind, I have almost determined not to purchase the printing establishment, but will perhaps offer the paper for a fixed price. I had a long talk with Mr. H. to-day, wherein I suggested the idea, which seemed not disagreeable. But neither of us made any fixed proposal. There were races in this vicinity to-day, which I attended. But disputes arose, which deferred them for so long a time that, before the principal race, I had retired sick and disgusted. The field is a scene of iniquity. Gamesters and prostitutes walk in open day, nor seem to excite one emotion of public indignation.

"10th. I had retired to bed before dark last night, but here new afflictions awaited me. A party of gamblers kept the house in an uproar all night, and prevented my getting but a few short naps. I felt some indignation, but to no useful purpose. There were races again to-day, and I walked down, but did not enter the field. The race was a fine one, except that one of the horses flew the track, jumped a fence, and threw his rider. This evening there was a play in the court-house by a strolling company of players. With the play I was rather disgusted than pleased.

"11th. Rode to Lexington. Attended the Episcopalian Church, dined at Mr. Clay's, attended church in the afternoon, and commenced boarding at Mr. Allen's.

"12th. Attended court to-day, but very little was done.

"July 15th. This day I returned to Georgetown, after a violent sickness, which has to this time detained me in Lexington. I have no recollection of many things that passed during the first two weeks, but so far as I do recollect I will proceed to minute them.

"June 13th. I ate a little breakfast, but soon found myself getting sick, and sent for Dr. Pindell.

"For several days continued to take medicine, suffered excruciating pain a considerable part of the time, and finally was relieved by a blister. I received very little attention from Mr. Allen's family, was in a very hot room, and, on the whole, very uncomfortably situated. Mrs. Clay had invited me to come out to her house, and this day sent in her carriage for me. I was as glad as if I had escaped from prison. There is nothing more painful to a sick man than to see those around him look on with indifference. To Messrs. Dana and Hunt I am under great obligations. Had they not been boarding in the house, I believe I should have suffered for want of attendance.

"July 1st. I gained strength very slowly, and this day was able to sit up very little. Soon after I came here I sent in town, by the carriage-driver, for some wine, but Mrs. Clay finding it out from him, forbade him to buy it, and ordered him to return the money to me, saying that she had wine enough in the house to which I was quite welcome. A

few days after this, a circumstance happened, which mortified me very much. I had no appetite, and ate very little. Beef was the only kind of meat that I pretended to eat. Though I had requested that it might be left very rare, it invariably came to me too much cooked. I wished the Doctor to speak to them about it, and mentioned it to Mr. Dana, in the presence of a servant, who reported it to his mistress. Contrary to my knowledge or even suspicion, she had attended to the cooking of the beef herself. She was angry. She came into the chamber with a very angry look, and said she was sorry she could not please me, and seemed to think me very ungrateful. I was extremely agitated, but said that nothing was further from my heart than ingratitude, acknowledged my obligations to her, told her I might have spoken imprudently, but meant no ill, and asked her if she had ever seen anything like ingratitude in my character. She said 'No,' and was appeased in a moment. I said I would be more prudent in future, and hoped she would forget what was passed. She answered, 'It is all over now ; I shall remember nothing,' and turned the conversation upon my medicine. What made her most angry was the servant's report that I said to Dana they did not know how to cook a beefsteak. It is possible I might have said so ; but according to the best of my remembrance, I simply said my beef was cooked too much, and he made answer that they did not know how to cook a beefsteak in Kentucky, for he has not met with one at the boarding-house fit to be eaten. After this, no more beef came for two or three days, when a piece came with other meat, cooked as I wished. I ate it all without tasting the other meat, and after that had beef very well cooked. It is very likely, however, that my squeamishness before arose principally from want of appetite. There were celebrations of the 4th of July in Lexington, but I was unable to sit up more than a few minutes at a time. Mrs. Clay has her carriage brought out for me to ride every fine day.

"15th. I have thought myself able for two or three days to ride to Georgetown, but was prevented by rain, which has fallen every day, more or less, for about ten days past. As this day was fair, I determined to improve it. In bidding adieu to Mrs. Clay, a sense of the obligation under which I have been laid by her so affected me, that I could not make those acknowledgments which I intended. She has done everything for me in her power, and I reflect on it with gratitude. Yet, I could not help remembering the difference between her best endeavors and those of my mother, — that good, affectionate woman and excellent nurse.

"I was received with great cordiality at Georgetown, where it was not known for three weeks that I was sick. There has been considerable merriment here since I have been gone, but that I do not regret. I regret the term of the circuit court, which I have entirely missed. But we must submit with resignation to the will of Providence.

"When at Lexington, Mr. Woosely offered me my board and a room for an office, if I would select and write for the 'Reporter' when he could not attend to it. But I know very well if I were to undertake on these conditions, the whole management of the paper would fall on me. For this the compensation is not adequate. If he had added $100, I think I would have accepted it. But, as it is, I think I could do better with the paper at Georgetown.

"16th. I am still stronger to-day, and walked out in the evening to Mr. Ward's, more than a mile. Dr. Henry was my companion.

"18th. My strength continues daily to mend, and I have a voracious appetite. I have been again bantering concerning the editing of this paper. This day Mr. Miller, the postmaster, wished me to become his deputy, and offered half the profits, which would amount to $200 per year. I had calculated that they would give me $400 for editing the paper, and by undertaking both these I thought I should obtain a handsome income. I applied to Mr. Henderson and made my offer, but having sold one half of the office to Mr. Reid during my absence, he was obliged to consult him. Reid was unwilling to hire me. Here, then, the business ends. Yet many here are anxious to have me undertake the paper, and Mr. Henderson wishes much to have me buy the other half of the office. On consideration, I resolved to have nothing to do with the post-office. So I am again left to sink or swim by my profession.

"19th. A man called on me for advice, which is the first business I have had in Georgetown.

"21st. So much is said to me of buying the half of the printing-office, that I think I shall offer to buy, on condition that I may, if not satisfied, return it within a year.

"23d. This day was again applied to in the business of my profession, so I have obtained the privilege of charging two fees, $2.50 each, during this week.

"27th. Being extremely weak, and unable to attend to any business, I rode to Sander's Well, — a medicinal well, about twelve miles from Georgetown. There was a dance at the house of entertainment this evening, and being invited into the hall, I spent a short time in looking at the company and chatting with some girls of my acquaintance. There were present people of all descriptions, — from those very respectable to gamblers and prostitutes, or something little better. About ten o'clock I retired, but found myself in a room adjoining the ball, with an open doorway, which could not be entered without stooping, and so many holes between the timbers that every wind of heaven could pass

over me. On examining my bed, I found on it but one sheet and one counterpane. I lay down without undressing, but got little sleep until the party broke up, which was about 1 A. M.

"28th. The day passed in rather a dull manner, as I had not yet formed acquaintances. I drank plentifully of the water, which produced a slight medicinal effect.

"August 2d. After breakfast started for Georgetown. I think I have derived much benefit from the waters, for my appetite and strength have increased astonishingly within a week. I attended a ball this evening and danced three times, but found my strength unequal to much exertion. I made some blunders in dancing Kentucky reels, and on the whole was rather sober during the evening.

"4th. Yesterday Mr. Henderson was again bantering me on undertaking the paper here, and at length I offered to take one half the office, and give him twenty per cent on the net profits by way of rent. This day he said he would accept my offer, and wished me to draw up articles of agreement. But as I have not yet heard whether we shall be able to prosecute the Indiana speculation, I declined closing until I should have time to hear from Lexington.

"6th. Having learned some circumstances concerning the office, of which Mr. Henderson did not inform me, I became dissatisfied and resolved not to fulfil my agreement. In this I considered myself perfectly justifiable, on account of the concealment of material circumstances. Borrowed a horse and rode out to the Great Crossings to meeting, principally with an intent to have a conversation with Colonel Johnson. Had an invitation to dine with Colonel J. Johnson, which I accepted. Colonel R. M. Johnson seemed very desirous that I should undertake the paper, and was sure some agreement might be made.

"8th. Colonel R. M. Johnson brought Mr. Henderson and myself together, and by his intervention we came to an agreement, which was sketched in writing, but not completed.

"I agree to undertake the editorial duties of the paper, the reading of proof-sheets, keeping a copy of accounts and drafting them for collection, collecting such of them as should come within the range of my business or travels, and laboring in the office one hour each day, unless otherwise engaged or absent, in folding papers, etc.

"As I mentioned that I could, if I pleased, have the post-office in my hands, I was advised to take it. I therefore applied to Mr. Miller, postmaster, and inquired if he still wanted a deputy. After some bantering, he offered to make me postmaster, on condition that I should resign in his favor at any time when he wished it, and pay him a certain sum yearly for five years. Now I should like the office, but do not like the conditions.

"Nothing has been completed, and from my observation of Mr. Henderson I conclude he has some inclination to be off from the bargain. I have no wish to bind him as it is contrary to his inclination.

"Last evening Mr. Arnold, the schoolmaster here, offered me my board if I would come and help him when he should find difficulties in his studies.

"10th. Agreed to board with Mr. Arnold. He gives me my board in consideration of some little instruction. I have the promise of six weeks certain, and more if we shall be mutually pleased. This evening had a letter from my friend, G. W. Hunt, informing me of the return of Mr. J. Prentiss, but not giving me any definite information with regard to our Indiana business. Resolved to go to Lexington to-morrow.

"11th. Went to Lexington, but could not obtain any correct information in the above business. Called on Thomas Prentiss to see if he had transmitted money due to Mr. Williams of Boston. For this business I shall probably obtain a fee of two dollars.

"12th. This morning a man by the name of Brashears was brought to town for examination before a magistrate for killing his father-in-law, a Mr. Joseph Snell. I went to the court-house, and for ten dollars, and the probability of being employed in the final trial, I appeared in his behalf. But he is poor and without money, so that my present fee as well as my final appearance in his behalf depend upon his father, who was not in town. My only object was that the prisoner might be admitted to bail, but this indulgence I was unable to obtain. The magistrates could not at first agree, but, finally, mutually consented that he be committed for murder according to the information.

"A little while after this determination the father of the prisoner arrived, and went to make an application to Judge Johnson, the event of which I have not yet learned. The circumstances of the killing seem to be these: The parties had been together during the day on some business. All was good humor. They drank cider together in company with two others, until the whole of them were somewhat inebriated, when they all came to town and there completed their intoxication by drinking whiskey. A quarrel arose between Brashear and Snell, in which the former made use of harsh expressions. They went to Snell's house, where more cider was taken, the quarrel was renewed, in which Brashear either knocked or pushed Snell out of the door, who fell on some stones, which caused his immediate death. It was, as I thought, so evidently manslaughter that I did not exert myself as I otherwise should.

"I was astonished, and somewhat mortified, to hear that the magistrates disagreed. I became much interested in the prisoner, and hoped he would be admitted to bail.

"13th. The application to Judge Johnson has, as yet, been of no effect. He could only give an opinion, as one of the magistrates was absent. On my visiting the prisoner, he inquired for how much I would engage in his behalf. I answered, that if through my assistance he was cleared of the crime of murder, I would do it for $75, including the $10 which he has already promised me. He seemed inclined to engage me, and said he would send his father to see me when he again came up. If I am not feed, and can volunteer with a good grace, I shall certainly do so.

"This day I closed a bargain with Mr. Miller, the postmaster, on the conditions which I had before offered. In consideration of his procuring me to be made postmaster immediately, and the use of the small building called the shop, back of his house, I engage to give him $180 for four years, or so long as I shall hold the office, and to resign in his favor if he shall want the office again for his own use within six years. These terms I am convinced would be regarded as degrading, and we mutually agreed that they should be kept secret. I, however, feel conscious of no moral wrong, and see a prospect of some profit and many conveniences, counterbalanced, perhaps, by the inconveniences attending it. But if dissatisfied, I can resign when I please, and he will be at liberty to make conditions with any other person.

"14th. Removed my board to Arnold's, and my books into the post-office.

"17th. Learned to my sorrow that Mr. Henry was feed for the prisoner for whom I the other day appeared. It was done by the father, without consulting his son, and before he knew me.

"18th. Being determined to have something to say in the case, I offered my services to the prisoner without fee.

"22d. This day the prisoner was brought by habeas corpus before the circuit judge, in order, if possible, to procure bail. A question arose concerning the jurisdiction of the judge, but this was overruled. Before this happened, however, I was obliged to retire in consequence of a severe pain in my right knee.

"23d. Can hardly walk. The discussion on Brashear's case continued until this day, when he was recommitted.

"25th. Knee better, but not well. Began to write a speech for the trial of Brashear.

"28th. My knee nearly well. I am still writing on the speech, investigating miscellaneous points of law, and taking care of the post-office.

"31st. My health never was better. But I abuse the blessing I enjoy by too much indulgence of a most voracious appetite. I never ate so much in my life, either of food or fruit, and find it impossible to satisfy myself.

" *September 11th.* This morning received a letter from Mr. Sawyer, one of the associates for forming an emigration company, informing me that he was in Lexington, that a constitution was forming, that the thing would now go into effect, and requesting my presence there this day. After considerable trouble, I obtained a horse, and rode there. I found the business not perfected, and that I should be under the necessity of stopping three or four days.

" *12th.* I procured the constitution of the before-mentioned society, drawn up by Major Stackpole of Boston. There were many blanks in it, and some of the provisions are not satisfactory. Amendments were suggested, and it was given over to the further consideration of the moneyed men now in Lexington, who contemplate engaging in the business.

" *13th.* This evening we who have been forming a company for emigration, or rather for making our fortunes, had a conference. We are divided into two classes, called residents and non-residents. The non-residents are to purchase $ 190,000 worth of Georgia scrip from the owners of it in New England, and advance $ 61,000 for the purchase and improvement of land.

" There will be a board of directors chosen from the non-residents, in the choice or proceedings of whom the residents have no voice.

" With this scrip, and the necessary money, the directors are to purchase of the United States 100,000 acres of land, to be located, if Congress will permit, in the Indiana Territory. The scrip is to be purchased on a credit of ten years at six per cent interest, and the whole land is to be conveyed to three trustees, in trust, as security for the payment of interest and principal. Whenever three dollars per acre has been paid into the hands of the trustees, they, in conjunction with the directors, have power to give deeds in fee simple to purchasers. This money, instead of the land, will constitute a trust fund for the payment of the before-mentioned company's debts. It is, in the mean time, to be vested in bank or six per cent United States stock, and if, on the dissolution of the company, any surplus remain, it is to be divided like the other company property. The residents are entitled to equal shares of company stock, in consideration of which they settle on the company lands, procure settlers, and devote their whole attention to the business of the company. For their support they are each allowed $ 200 a year, or if they marry, $ 300, with the rent jointly of a house worth $ 6,000. They choose a chairman, and have a secretary, clerks, and a treasurer, the latter of whom is to be appointed by the board of directors. They are to enter into no private speculations, and are to take oath not to speculate on the company. By their consent and that of the board of directors all sales are to be made.

Residents and non-residents have the liberty to take up 200 acres of land for a farm, and one lot each in town. These are to be selected by the residents, and distributed by lot. The shares of the non-residents are transferable, but not of the non-residents, except by last will or testament, or by operation of law consequent on death.

" Any resident may be expelled for misconduct, with the consent of two thirds of the proprietors in value ; but is, at the dissolution of the partnership, to receive an amount of the profits in proportion to the time he was a member.

" The company is to continue ten years, unless sooner dissolved by the consent of two thirds in value of the proprietors. At the dissolution, after paying the company's debts, the overplus is to be equally divided among the shares. The company will consist of twenty ; ten of each sort.

" By act of Congress the Georgia scrip can be located only in the Mississippi Territory. The principal men in the company will petition for leave to locate in Indiana, and we are assured by some members that the petition will be granted. If not, there will be a location in the Mississippi Territory, where I have promised to go. Some of the company are very sanguine, and think we shall make fifty or sixty thousand dollars each, but I do not anticipate more than half that sum.

" To-morrow I shall return to Georgetown, and throw all my professional prospects to the wind. I consider it fortunate that I have made no arrangements to fix me here permanently. I expect to be employed in a few days on a journey to explore the Indiana Territory.

" *14th.* Returned to Georgetown determined to make arrangements to quit the profession of law, as I think prospects authorize it. Accordingly I sold the 'Laws of Kentucky' and Story's 'Pleadings' to Mr. S. Penn for $ 23, and desired Mr. Miller to free me from the arrangement I had made with him.

" It is, however, my intention, if I should be here the next court, to speak for Brashear, just to show the people that I can make a speech, and do not quit the profession for want of spouting talents. As I shall not be constantly employed in my new business until January or February next, I intend to employ the interim on the poem which I began at Mrs. Clay's. But not being able to find the few hundred lines which I wrote when there, I shall be under the necessity of writing them over again. I shall likewise remain at present in the post-office, and give time to Mr. Miller to make further arrangements. It is doubtful whether I resume practice, even if this business should fail. I was never pleased with it, and but partial success, with the means for obtaining speedily the good graces of the people fills me with disgust.

" Perhaps I shall, if I obtain the post-office, purchase the printing-

office and try my fortune as an editor. I should then have it in my power, free of expense, to obtain news earlier than any other editor in Kentucky.

" *20th.* I have labored continually for two days in reviewing and copying a speech for the trial of Brashear. I have now brought it into a form to suit me tolerably well.

" *21st.* Received a letter from Mr. Sawyer, at Lexington, informing me that they were ready for completing the instrument of our association.

" *22d.* Rode to Lexington. Did not find the instrument completed, but it is thought it will be ready to-morrow. Rode out to Mr. Clay's.

" *23d.* Returned to town. Read over the constitution and found most of my objections removed ; but am not, on the whole, satisfied with it. We residents are made too much the slaves of non-residents. However, some other alterations were made, which rendered it less exceptionable, but still the objectionable parts of the instrument, with the uncertainty of procuring the indulgence of locating in Indiana Territory, makes me doubtful of the propriety of engaging in it at all. On the whole, I returned to Georgetown, resolved to withdraw from the company within sixty days, the time granted to the residents to consider the subject, provided I can make an arrangement in Georgetown.

" The plan is to endeavor to induce Mr. Miller to surrender me the post-office, without my promise of resignation on request ; then to wait on Colonel Johnson, make my appointment to the post-office certain, and then purchase the printing-office. I should thus have an opportunity to open a correspondence with all the cities, and not be in danger of interruption by this request from Miller.

" After my arrival in Georgetown, I proposed the thing to Mr. Miller, who said he could not agree. I at length offered, if he would consent to my remaining postmaster, to permit him to find a deputy, take all the profits, and would even pay the postage of all letters he should send and receive. Nothing could apparently be more liberal ; yet he said he could not assent, but would think of it till to-morrow.

" *25th.* Miller and I have finally made an arrangement. I am to resign in his favor, if requested, after four years ; and within six, provided he shall become interested in the printing-office, if I shall then be the owner of it and request him. For four years I give him $ 180, for a building valued at $ 60 per year and the office. We have agreed to reveal the arrangement to Colonel R. M. Johnson, and ask him to recommend me.

" *26th.* I received a letter from W. G. Hunt, in Lexington, informing me that the constitution of the migration society would this evening be ready for signature, and requested me to come up. But I am tired of

obeying such summonses, and intend, even if I should not make an arrangement here, not to go until they are *actually ready.*

" *27th.* Called on Colonel Johnson, who promised me I should have his influence for the post-office if I would buy Henderson's half of the printing-office, but said he had better delay till he goes on to Washington. In the mean time, that I had better make a conditional bargain with Henderson, and undertake the paper immediately. I shall probably follow his advice, if I can make a bargain with Henderson.

" *28th.* Called on Henderson this morning. He thought he could not sell for less than $ 1,200, and I offered $ 800. I was, however, resolved to offer more, but as he seemed very indifferent to the business I left him with very little hope of being able to agree at all. However, I again called and made this proposal in writing, which I told him was an ultimatum. I offer $ 1,000 for his half of the office, payable in one, two, and three years ; one half in work of the office. He at first said he would not do it ;' but finally said he would think of it till noon, and then submit to me his ultimate proposal. But as he did not call on me, I again visited him. He said he had not had sufficient time to think of it, and was immediately going out to Colonel R. M. Johnson's. I wished to see Colonel James, and offered to ride out thus far with him. On the way he told me he was not anxious to sell at present, and unfolded his reasons. They were plans which he thinks would conduce to increase the profits of the office. He wished I had purchased Read's half, for he said he had long wished to engage with himself, in the establishment, some person of good education, and thought I would exactly meet his wishes. Believing his plan one which would conduce to mutual benefit, I proposed attempting to induce Mr. Read to relinquish his bargain, and offered the same for Read's half that I had offered him for his own. He seconded my proposal, and finding that Colonel James was not at home, I returned and visited Mr. Read. He was very willing to relinquish his bargain, and I now considered my fate as fixed. But some good or evil spirit which seems determined to thwart every plan of mine, because, I suppose, they are not for the best, led Read to examine his books and make some estimates as delusive as flattering, which induced him to change his mind. Henderson, Read, and myself had a long talk this evening, but he could not be persuaded to alter his resolution.

" On departure, Mr. Henderson told me that Read had hitherto never paid a cent of the expenses, but that unless he would relinquish, he should now bear his proportional part. He said Colonel R. M. Johnson could in a moment induce Read to relinquish, and said he would ride out and see him to-morrow. To this I assented.

" *29th.* Talked with Mr. Read to-day, and received from him proposals for relinquishing his bargain, on which I think we shall agree. Met him and Henderson in the evening and struck a bargain.

"*30th.* All the papers in our bargain before mentioned were executed. I give five notes to Mr. Henderson of $200 each, payable in one, two, three, four, and five years. The die is now cast, and I am fixed to Georgetown. God grant that I may not repent my bargain.

"*October 2d.* This day I came in possession of one half of the printing-office. It was a verbal agreement with Mr. Read that he should have the hands as boarders. This evening he complained to me that they would not come when his breakfast was ready, and seemed to attribute it to Mr. Henderson. I talked with Mr. H. and the hands, and found they had objections to boarding with Mr. Read at any rate. From what I could learn I believed their objections reasonable, and told them there should be no compulsion, and that we would satisfy Read as well as we could.

"This day commences the circuit court here. The grand jury found an indictment against Brashear a true bill; but as they had rejected the one laid before them by the Commonwealth, and drawn up one of their own, the attorney would not accept it. So they will have to begin again to-morrow.

"*3d.* Talked with Read, who did not want the boys to board with him if they were unwilling, but seemed to think he ought to receive some damages. I said if any damage resulted, I was willing to pay a proportional part, and so we separated.

"I composed a short address to the public, which was printed in the form of subscription papers.

"The court to-day proceeded to make up a jury, and spent the whole day. The number, twelve, was at length completed.

"*4th.* Spent the whole day in examining witnesses, and did not finish. I cannot but have some apprehensions for Brashear, there are so many black expressions attending the deed.

"*5th.* Completed the examination of evidence about noon. The case was then opened by Mr. Breckenridge. He spoke for about three hours, and was answered by myself. I spoke for about an hour and then sat down, more dissatisfied with my performance than I ever was before in my life. Yet I was soon after complimented for my excellent speech, and told that I made many cry. In the evening I was even told that it was said so great an orator had never spoken in Georgetown. But the fact was, I had not a perfect command of myself until I was more than half through, and absolutely forgot one third I intended to say. I was followed by Mr. Henry, who was interrupted by adjournment.

"*6th.* Mr. Henry finished, and was followed by Mr. Flournoy; these

two and myself were for the prisoner. Mr. Shannon then began, but was interrupted by adjournment at night.

"*7th.* Mr. Shannon concluded at dinner-time; the jury retired, and after dinner brought in a verdict of voluntary manslaughter. Ten years in the penitentiary.

"*8th.* Have received many flattering compliments concerning my speech. Flournoy said to some one that he was never in his life more disappointed and surprised. This evening, too, I was much mortified; for being at Mr. T. Herndon's, I was asked whether I had spoken for or against the prisoner. 'Zounds,' thought I, 'has not Fame told you?' But I was even obliged to tell them myself, for the partial jade had not put her head within those windows. But a little mortification is wholesome, for otherwise the human mind would run mad. Vanity, O vanity, the foe of improvement, the enemy of talent! In the evening after I had spoken I was walking the street and heard some one say, 'There was a great speech made in the court-house to-day.' 'That 's mine,' said vanity, and I stretched my ears to hear the next words, but, unfortunately, the person spoke so low I could not catch them.

"Well, one number of the 'Minerva Press' has come out in my name, and what say the public? Why the public says or cares very little about it. I have already repented of one article there inserted. I do not know whether I am censured for it, but it contains some observations concerning General Adair which I do not approve.

"Mr. Miller and I this day signed an agreement, and his resignation will this night be sent to the General Post-Office. I feel some of the terms as too degrading, but the bargain is for my interest. It will be kept secret. He resigns and rents me his shop. If I succeed him I agree to give $180 per year for four years, and after that resign if he shall wish to be reappointed within six. He agrees, if I shall own the printing-office, and request it, to become interested on my resignation, and conduct the correspondence. If I resign within four years, I leave to him the nomination of my successor; and if I approve, recommend him.

"*11th.* I have attended court but little this week, nor do I think the flattering reception I have met with will induce me to continue the practice of law. I observe with much satisfaction that I am now treated with much more deference than formerly. I have now in my head the plan of a religious publication, which I think will be attempted by Mr. Henderson and myself, if we can procure a sufficient number of subscribers.

"*17th.* I find myself now considerably occupied. I have formed an agreement with John Miller to come and live with me in the post-office. I give him his board, and instruct him in any branch he may be inclined

to study, for which I receive $80 per year,—$70 from George and $10 from himself, and his services in the post-office, when I shall be absent or necessarily engaged. I have been much pleased with him, and think we shall agree perfectly. He comes this evening, and stays for no limited time.

"A man applied to me to-day to bring a suit against another, and the temptation was so strong to make a little money, that I concluded, for the time being, to practice law. Perhaps I shall put out a sign, and continue practice at least till I know whether the printing-office will afford me employment.

"*18th.* This day issued proposals for a religious journal, to be published once in two months, and be called 'The Religious Intelligencer.' Its object is to subserve the interests of the Christian religion in general. Moved the post-office into the shop.

"*26th.* Affairs have gone on in a uniform train since the 18th. I, however, plainly perceive that the printing-office will cause me some embarrassment for the want of funds. However, after a year, I think, with proper management it will not only become a profitable business, but tolerably pleasant. Our foreman, Read, is an unpleasant fellow, ill-tempered, and sometimes drunk; we bear with him as well as we can, but do not think he will remain long with us.

"This day came on my appointment as postmaster. But I fear I cannot exercise its privileges until I get a commission. This is inconvenient to me, as I am anxious to enlarge my correspondence and circulate subscription papers for my paper and religious work.

"*28th.* Last evening a man was killed in an affray not far from town. It seems the parties were nearly all drunk, and who gave the fatal blow is a question which nobody can answer. Three or four have been taken and brought to town. Such are the miserable effects of drunkenness. Brashear has obtained a rule for a new trial, and is now out of prison on bail.

"*December 2d.* So it seems here is a hiatus of nearly a month. Close engagement in business has prevented my thinking of my journal.

"The men mentioned above had an examination of nearly a week's continuance, and were admitted to bail.

"About two weeks ago I became so dissatisfied with Mr. Read, our foreman, that, in conjunction with Mr. Henderson, I resolved to get rid of him. We accordingly had a conversation with him, in which we all kept our temper very well, and finished by concluding to separate. He said but one hard thing, which was, that he thought Mr. Lyle, one of the hands in the office, was put in as a spy on his conduct. But on my saying that what he said was false, and as base as it was false, he recanted and said he did not mean what he said. He had not followed

my directions, had violated my instructions in selecting matter for the paper, and had inserted pieces without ever bringing them to me. Ten dollars a week is something to save, for it does not come in hand every day.

"About the same time another trouble came upon me. I was invited out to Mr. Ward's, who, I found, wished to know everything I could tell him about Mr. Henderson's affairs. I discovered in the sequel that he owes Ward about $2,600, as security for which he has made over to him one half of the printing-office, and other chattels and accounts, by an instrument bearing date only two days after my purchase. I was at first startled, because I thought it was prior. He had likewise told Ward that he had transferred my notes to Colonel J. Johnson. As Ward will doubtless be obliged to take and sell the office, I wished to have some voice in the business as I am so intimately concerned, and mentioned to him Mr. Lyle, a hand in the office, as a proper person to purchase. I had before expressed a wish to Lyle to this effect, who I think would be glad of the opportunity. The next day I talked with Mr. Shellers, now our foreman, and found that Mr. Henderson owed him about $200, which he began to fear he should never get. He wished me to find out if my notes were transferred to Colonel Johnson, and if not, and it were possible, that I would get one of them for him. I promised, and the next day spoke to Mr. Henderson, and learned that but *one* of my notes had been transferred to Colonel Johnson, and he was willing that Shellers should have another. But learning that he was so much involved, and had not always told the truth, I began to be alarmed for myself. At first I resolved to come to a crisis, and have his half of the office sold at once; but on second thought, as his services will be essential in procuring subscribers to the religious work I have in contemplation, I concluded to keep myself in his debt as much as possible, and let the matter go on for a time; but I doubt not he must relinquish within a year, so great are his debts and so little his ability to pay them. Indeed, perhaps it will be the better for me the sooner it be closed. These embarrassments are almost intolerable.

"I have received my commission as postmaster, and on Monday, 27th ult., began to board at Thomas Theobald's. I give him $100 each for Miller and myself, and $18 per year for mine, and $15 for his washing. Thus my expenses to him will be $233, and $110 I pay to G. W. Miller, make $343,—somewhat more than the estimated profits of the post-office. Add to this $150 for other expenses, and it will cost me $493, say $500 per year to live.

"Some time in November I paid a visit to Mr. Alexander's, in Woodford. I take a lively interest in that family, for, from my own acquaintance, and the representations of some of my Yankee friends who have lived in the family, they are one of the most happy circles in the world.

"A few days ago I was much gratified with receiving a letter from Mr. Clay's two sons, enclosing me two dollars for a paper, one year. I wrote them an answer, and have since written to their father. This I considered myself bound to do, because I had not called on him when he was at home. I have also received a letter from my friend Flügel, likewise subscribing to the paper.

"A growing subscription seems to be making for my 'Religious Intelligencer,' and I am considerably occupied in the business which regards it. The plan which I have adopted has been to write to most of the postmasters in the State and other places, thus obtaining the names of the preachers, and then addressing them personally. Mr. Henderson is so much occupied with other business that he cannot attend to this.

"*10th.* I have gotten rid of half my troubles by dismissing Read, and I believe I should be rid of half the rest were I free from Mr. Henderson. He is very much in debt, and nothing but his usefulness to the office at the present time induces me to remain in partnership with him a moment. Indeed, if he does no more for the office this trip than he did the last, I think we shall break at once. I took away London, the negro, from his house, because he was not well-treated, and since then I have had complaints from all the other hands. Though the dismissal of Read has lessened the expenses of the office nearly one third, I think they may be lessened still more. My present plan is, that Mr. Lyle, a very careful and economical hand in the office, should buy Henderson's half, and then, with the aid of three or four good apprentices, we could do all the work without any journeymen at all. This would save about $500 more a year, and reduce the expenses to $600 or $700.

"*15th.* Read went away to Frankfort, and left his wife and family in a room adjoining the office, which we had rented of Mr. Davis, the present owner, for its use. I procured a room for her, and removed her at my own expense, and it was well I did, for that very night she was taken ill, and brought forth a boy. I wrote to Read a serious letter on his conduct towards his family."

CHAPTER VI.

"*1816, January 1st.* This year finds me involved in perplexity and vexation. My business at present is, I believe, the most uncomfortable in the world, and I am engaged in it with those who afford me little pleasure or prospect of gain. Mr. Henderson is gone, and some even express doubts whether he will return. His situation is indeed embarrassed, and, what is very singular, he never gave me the least hint of it. I have stopped all accounts which were opened in our names, and am determined on having a new arrangement the moment he returns.

"There was a ball here at Christmas, which I attended. On the evening of the ball I had an application to attend to a land claim in this county, on which a man by the name of Bullock wished to bring suit. The next morning I went out about eight miles with him, and spent the day in carrying the chain.

"In the evening I returned to Georgetown to superintend the publication of the paper. In the morning I again went out, spent the day in making out and serving ejectments, and at night was completely exhausted and sick.

"This claim covers upwards of eight hundred acres; one fourth part of which Bullock agrees to give me, should he recover, as a compensation for my services. If it be lost through my fault, I pay the cost; if through defect of title, he pays it. The prospect is good for recovering it.

"*10th.* After my agreement with Bullock, I began to revolve in my mind my future prospects, and eventually concluded that I had better release myself from the printing-office, except so far as relates to the editing of the paper, and accordingly laid a plan, by which the office was to be sold to Shellers and Lyle, while I should remain editor, and continue the practice of law.

"Accordingly, I proposed this plan, and at first it seemed quite likely to be effected. But on making a calculation from the past, Shellers was not satisfied, and suggested to me that I was probably sinking money every day. I sat down and made a balance of accounts, which likewise convinced me of the fact. The paper, the advertising, and the

job-work will not support the office. Just at this time, too, I received a letter from Colonel R. M. Johnson, in answer to one I had written, informing me that Colonel James had a mortgage upon the office even before I bought. This put me in great trepidation. I began to look around for security, and lay hold of everything which I could rightfully take into my possession. Mr. Henderson, however, returned four days ago. I went to see him, and brought him to my office that very evening. Here a conversation took place not very agreeable to either of us, which ended in an agreement that I should relinquish my purchase to him, and give him all the labor I have bestowed, on condition he should put accounts into my hands sufficient to secure me against my notes and every account which has arisen since I became interested.

"I had all the accounts for subscriptions to the paper made over on the spot, and an agreement to that effect lodged in the hands of T. S. Theobald. The estimated amount of these is more than $2,000.

"I declined having anything more to do with the paper, excepting as an editor, in which capacity I would continue to act until the return of Colonel J. Johnson. The hands, however, refused to work unless he would make them secure, which he did, by giving me liberty to collect accounts sufficient to pay them. But, after some deliberation, it was concluded to stop the paper at the next number.

"*16th.* The report of the intended stoppage of the paper raised a considerable ferment, and many advised me to proceed, but in vain. To-day, three days from its proper time, has been issued the last number of the 'Minerva Press.' During last week I carried out the subscription accounts, but find a considerable amount of them belongs to Chambers, and that four of my notes, instead of two, as I had been told, have been transferred to J. Johnson. I have not given up the office, nor shall I until I *know* myself entirely secure. I have now to go to work and collect accounts. Mr. Henderson allows me fifteen per cent on all moneys collected, and Chambers twenty on all out of the county belonging to him.

"I shall set out in a few days and make a business of it. I have made out the post-office returns for the last quarter, and find the commission much smaller than I expected. After paying Miller according to agreement, it will not leave me more than $60 per year.

"*18th.* Induced by the solicitations of the people here, I have this day, in conjunction with Shellers and Lyle, issued proposals for a new paper to be published here, which will be called the 'Georgetown Patriot.' Our determination is that we will not begin unless we have five hundred subscribers. Whether that number can be procured is at least doubtful. I am, myself, very indifferent about it, as I am certain it will be more for my final interest to continue the practice of law. I

have learnt by experience how vexatious is the business of an editor, or rather of an owner of a newspaper establishment.

"*21st.* I received a letter this morning from Colonel R. M. Johnson, who seemed, as I thought, to be a little displeased with a letter I wrote him some days ago, in answer to the one from him which informed me that Colonel James had a mortgage on the office. Suspecting that he had written more fully, and probably more freely, to Mr. Ward on the subject, I asked Mr. Ward. He told me that the Colonel supposed I must think he and his brother had acted very dishonorably with me in respect to the purchase of the office; that I seemed to think I was in bad hands, and that James was coming home soon, when he would probably release me, etc., etc. I felt very much hurt, as I had never harbored a thought that there had been anything dishonorable in them, although a suspicion, or rather a possibility of the thing sometimes flashed across my mind before I had an explanation from Henderson. I sat down and wrote to him, disclaiming in warm terms all ideas of the kind and making a statement of the facts in which I had been deceived by Henderson, and likewise requested Mr. Ward to write on the subject, who promised. I have no doubt but he will be satisfied, but care little whether he is or not.

"*22d.* On hearing that a young lady in town had said some fine things of me, I had a curiosity to see her. She is a sister of Mrs. Taylor, named Payne, in high repute. I called at her brother's, but did not fall in love, though I was pleased.

"*29th.* I intended to have gone on collecting business ere this, but could get nobody to stay in the post-office. I have written to Mr. Hough, now in Lexington, who I think will come. Should he not, Mr. Shellers will stay, and I shall set out on Wednesday or Thursday. It is a disagreeable job, and I wish it was done. Our subscription goes on tolerably well, but I still doubt of success.

"*February 1st.* Had a letter from Colonel James Johnson, in which he expresses much surprise at the sensitiveness which I displayed in my letters to his brother, and seems to be offended at one expression therein contained. It was that I would not hold property so subject to the control of any man, as by any possibility to influence the opinions which I must necessarily express. He seems to apply it to himself, but I intended no such application. It was intended to be a general idea, and I particularly excepted him. It gave me considerable pain; but I am resolved to maintain the opinion as well as the practice, though I may hazard the indignation of all the world. He says I likewise spoke roughly of Mr. Henderson. It is true that I did speak more roughly than facts would justify, but I was then under a mistake. I thought he had sold me property which was not his own. But the Colonel confirms Mr. Henderson's account that the mortgage has been redeemed, and, as he thinks, given up. Thus all this misunderstanding has arisen from Mr. Henderson's not communicating to me the real situation of the business. But sometimes I am careless whether the Johnsons are my friends or not; for if they were enemies, I should have an object for competition. At any rate, if they, in the present situation of affairs, become hostile to me, I shall be convinced that all they want of me is to make me a tool. But I flatter myself, if such be their plan, they will not find me so smooth to their hands as they could wish. But excepting only the offence which seems to be taken at that letter, I have no cause to suspect them.

"*3d.* The Colonel, it is said, will be at home in a day or two, and I intend to call on him immediately for an explanation. As I must fortify myself in some measure at the expense of Mr. Henderson, I have invited him to accompany me.

"The Colonel seems to be willing to take the office, and I think it best for me to give it up and quit the paper entirely.

"*4th.* Rode out to the Great Crossings with Mr. Henderson to see Colonel J. Johnson; but he had not come home. After my return, I sat down and wrote him a statement of the case, which I shall request Mr. Henderson to hand to him.

"*5th.* Mr. Hough, who will remain in my office during my absence, arrived to-day.

"*7th.* Set out on my journey. Dined at Berry's, and stopped for the night at Captain Eli Short's. Got eighty-five cents to-day.

"*8th.* Proceeded on to Nelson's. Went several miles in a circuit through the woods and hills; saw one deer, which was the first wild one I ever saw, and returned to Nelson's.

"*9th.* Went down upon the Crooked Creek road and settled with the subscribers there. This evening was excessively cold, and I was almost frozen before I reached Clarke's, on the road.

"*10th.* Though very cold, I started out before breakfast this morning, and visited two subscribers at some distance from the road. Before I reached the house of the first my whiskers and the lappels of my great coat were covered with frost. Here, for the first time, I got angry, and promised to warrant a man.

"Breakfasted at Arnold's, and then went on to Theobald's. Here was a collection of people paying the direct tax; and here I first became acquainted with Joseph Glenn, the deputy collector.

"*11th.* Having left a number of accounts with G. P. Theobald for collection, I went forward to Gain's. Here again there was a considerable collection on a trial, and among them several subscribers.

"There were several packets of papers left at Gain's, which Mr. Henderson had agreed should be left in other neighborhoods. Most of these

men should have received their papers in those packets. They declared to me they had never taken the paper from Gain's, and therefore would not pay. I proposed that they should pay for what papers they had received. To this they agreed, and supported each other in saying they had received but about twelve papers. For this number I settled with four of them, but discovered that they had imposed upon me. They had taken the papers from Gain's, and had received more than twelve papers. One of the men was high sheriff of Boone County, named Wigginton.

"*12th.* This day I went down into Mr. Wigginton's neighborhood to Ben Stevens's and Will Stevens's, satisfied myself that these men had imposed upon me, and returned to Gain's.

"*13th.* Drew out accounts against those with whom I had settled, and put those with all others which I had in this neighborhood into the hands of a constable, ordering him to warrant Mr. Wigginton without delay. Rode down to Boone court-house. Found there a Yankee by the name of Boson, a lawyer.

"Having learnt by experience how much confidence is to be placed in the people of this quarter, I put all my accounts into the hands of a constable. I shall pursue this plan for the future.

"*15th.* Having some business with Squire Grant, I steered for his house. He lives in a bend of Licking. You pass along two miles on a stupendous ridge, with the river at its foot both on your right and left. At length you pass off its end into a bottom of considerable size, and here lives Squire Grant. With improvements, the place might be made singularly romantic.

"I had a demand on this man for $30, from Daniel Bradford, of Georgetown. He had not the money, but said he would meet me the next day at Elijah Grant's, and pay the money. I pushed on to Elijah Grant's, where I again met with Glenn, collecting taxes.

"*17th.* Grant met me here to-day, but instead of making any arrangement, slipped away without my knowledge. I shall send a constable after him. This evening went on with Glenn to Grant's Lick.

"*18th.* This morning enclosed to a constable all my accounts in this neighborhood, and rode to Falmouth with Mr. Glenn. On the road saw two beautiful deer.

"Falmouth is a mean place, surrounded by poor land. The only favorable circumstance which attends it is the commerce of Licking. Poor land has, on account of the intercourse with Cincinnati through this channel, obtained a value superior to that of better land in other quarters.

"*19th.* Spent the day at Captain Smith's, it being impossible to pass the creeks, on account of the height of the waters.

"*21st.* Arrived in Georgetown. I have been uncommonly healthy during this expedition, notwithstanding the unpleasantness of the weather. Not many things worthy of remark have come under my observation, excepting the management of the newspaper. Ever since its commencement it seems to have been edited, printed, and carried in a way which would damn any paper. Mr. Henderson had procured a large number of subscribers on the ridge and on Licking. He sent a boy to carry a private mail, who was not only too young, but inconceivably careless. He received money and gave no credit. At the end of ten months the United States mail began to go over the ridge, and the private mail was discontinued. On Licking, most people had paid in advance. Many on the ridge had paid at the end of the year, and directed their papers to be discontinued. These circumstances made the whole business one tissue of vexation. Most of the accounts presented had been paid in advance, or the persons had directed discontinuances. It is not surprising that the paper lost its credit, and happy it was I quit when I did. Nearly a hundred of the papers should have been discontinued long ago. When I arrived here I found letters from various quarters making the same statements. If out of the $2,300 on the accounts I collect $1,000, I shall do more than I expect.

"The land through most of the counties where I have travelled is miserably poor compared with the land about Lexington; and so are the people. It would, however, make a fine grazing country, but unfortunately none of the inhabitants know how to make cheese. Even their butter is poor. Boone has some fine land, and so has Harrison. There are in this region a considerable number of deer and wolves, but no bears. I saw an old man of eighty out with his hounds, whose whole delight was the music of their voices. Attended a ball this evening, in honor of the Father of his Country. I have never been so merry since I have been in Kentucky.

"*23d.* Rode to Lexington to procure papers in the land suit in which I am engaged, but was unsuccessful. Called at Mr. Clay's. Rode to Woodford, and spent the night at Mr. Alexander's.

"*24th.* Went to Versailles, on a visit to Mr. Farnham. Found him well and in much better spirits than heretofore. I suggested to him that I would gladly have him come to Georgetown and become a partner with me, but he did not seem to approve the idea. Returned with Mr. Guilford to Mr. Alexander's. After considerable persuasion, Miss Marianne and Miss Victoria Campbell were persuaded to let me see some of their poetry. I had seen a piece of Miss Alexander's before, and was not surprised to find it excellent, but Miss Campbell's absolutely astonished me. I have seldom seen a poem of more genuine pathos. Mr. Guilford likewise showed me some of Miss Alexander's prose composition,

which would do honor to a professor. He likewise told me that Marianne had written a piece in answer to one I wrote and sent to him, in which the last line of every stanza was 'Fair Marianne,' making her last lines end 'Fair Amos.' The idea made me laugh, but it changed almost in a moment my feelings towards her, as it completely explained the nature of hers. They seem to be of that playful, unmeaning nature which characterized Eliza Lawrence, though not so perfectly developed. There was, too, a shadow of ridicule about it, which Love cannot bear. Not that I *loved* her, but that I had something of that feeling which is often matured into passion.

"*26th.* Rode out to see Major Herndon, who was present in the survey of Bullock's land. Could not obtain much satisfaction. Captain Branham was likewise present, but could remember nothing. On my return, I called on Colonel J. Johnson. I forgot to observe that on my return from my tour in the lower counties, I received a letter from Richard Miller, and a line from James, both stating that they were perfectly satisfied. James now wished to know what were my intentions. I told him that I wished to relinquish the office to him, and take in my notes. He consented to take it off my hands.

"*28th.* On calculating to-day how many subscribers we have, we found the number within our knowledge 270. There must be nearly 400, which is more than I expected.

"*March 19th.* Little has happened for some days worthy of remark. Feeling relieved from business, and being considerably confined to the office, my mind has been uncommonly restless. Sometimes I am studying law and investigating cases; sometimes thinking of poetry and forming plans for novels; sometimes trying experiments in mechanics, and endeavoring to discover the perpetual motion. I have, in my fancy, constructed many machines, but soon discovered the folly of them.

"*22d.* This day Mr. Regis Alexander and Mr. Guilford called on me. The latter has acceded to my proposition of entering into a partnership, and will be here for that purpose about the first of June. I hope our success may answer my warmest wishes. We will make one great effort, and if we fail, will fail like men.

"*April 1st.* This day is the first of our circuit court term. Mr. Guilford came over for the purpose of spending a week with me. I appeared in court and entered the action of ejectment which I had commenced in favor of Robert and Edward Bullock. The latter gentleman arrived here during the course of the day.

"*2d.* Bullock had considerable conversation with some of the tenants concerning a compromise, but they could come to no conclusion. In the evening I made proposals to Bullock, and offered to go down with him the next day and attempt a compromise.

"*3d.* We rode down to the land, and, after spending most of the day, a compromise was effected with nine of the tenants, on the grounds which I had proposed. They were that the land should be surveyed and valued according to law, and then the tenants should pay five sixths of the valuation of the land, or give it up and receive pay for their improvements. One fourth of the benefit hence resulting will accrue to me.

"*8th.* Mr. Guilford has left me again, and will return by the first of June, or sooner. We have talked much concerning building a distillery, but have come to no determination.

"*13th.* Cabell Breckenridge asked me, for his mother and sister, to ride out to their house. Being very desirous to visit there, I hunted up a horse and went with him.

"*14th.* Returned again to Georgetown, after one of the most agreeable visits I have ever made. I found Mrs. Grayson, a young widow, sister to C. Breckenridge, one of the most social and pleasant ladies I have ever met with. She is now beautiful, and must once have been a picture. I believe that Colonel Nichols, a widower, who called with me only to spend a few minutes, was even more entertained than myself; for by some means he did not get away until near 4 P. M. to-day.

"*20th.* This day the first number of the Georgetown 'Patriot' was published, of which I am editor. The arrangement is this, — Mr. Wood owns one half of the office and Colonel James Johnson the other. The latter gentleman becomes responsible for the whole expense of the business, and pays me $ 150 a year for editing the paper. It is not generally known what is the arrangement, as all the business is transacted under the name of Kendall, Shellers, and Lyle. I feel my situation somewhat delicate, but not half so much so as when I owned one half of the office; for if I now find that my course cannot be an independent one, I will quit.

"*23d.* Started off to the wedding of Samuel Theobald, about fifteen miles from this, in Fayette County. The evening was rather dull, as we had no amusement but cards.

"*24th.* Our amusement was the same as last evening. A little before night Dr. Henry and myself rode out to escort home some ladies, and after we had performed our task, concluded we would not return that night. So we started off to Mr. Robert Harrison's, but finally concluded we had rather go to Mrs. Breckenridge's. But we got lost in the woods, and did not arrive there until 8 P. M.

"*25th.* After breakfast, we set out on our return to Mr. Warfield's, the father of the bride. Having called on a very interesting lady on the way, a Miss Thomson, we arrived just as the company was ready to start for Mr. Theobald's father's, at Sander's Well. When we came to the Georgetown road we left the company and rode to Georgetown.

"*26th.* Rode down to the Well, where there was a party; but we had little pleasure, on account of the sickness of Mrs. Theobald's sister, Miss Warfield.

"*27th.* Returned to Georgetown quite restored to health by my dissipation.

"*28th.* I went to meeting this day, in town, not so much for the sake of hearing a sermon as for seeing a fine lady, with whom I had been in company yesterday. But lo! when I had come there, in came another young lady, a Miss A. Payne, who took full possession of my feelings. Now this is a confession not much to my honor; but nothing but truth shall appear in this journal. Well, I walked with Miss Payne to her brother's, in town, and spent the evening with her. I am extremely well pleased with this lady, and, in the blunt language of the clown, I would have her if she would have me. But I do not perceive any ground to hope that she would marry me, plain, poor, and a Yankee as I am.

"*29th.* A dance was proposed for this evening, and we succeeded in collecting a brilliant little party at Mr. George's. Miss Payne again attracted much of my attention, and I gave her a piece of poetry which was caused by the chat of a ball-room some time ago. I had, however, added one stanza, which contained a pun upon her name, —

'The victim sighed for Pain half mad,
    His blood ran through him boiling hot ;
'T was not for any pain he had,
    But for a Pain which he had not.'

But I could not tell whether she was pleased or not.

"*30th.* My newspaper is extremely popular so far, and we have received an accession of more than fifty subscribers since we started. The people seem to be extremely well pleased with my editorial address.

"*May 10th.* I am again considerably occupied in the duties of my various business. This day I was employed on a warrant-trying, and came off with success, though opposed by R. P. Henry. This is the third trial on which I have been engaged, and every time have been successful.

"*15th.* Went out this evening to Colonel J. Johnson's to consult him on our business. I proposed that in the approaching electioneering campaign I would insert the writings of neither side, but print them in handbills, if the parties wished it, and circulate them with the paper. The plan met his approbation, and he said he would suggest it to R. M. Johnson. My wish is to steer as clear as possible of censure on either side ; for I wish not to give offence for another's benefit.

"*18th.* Rode over to Mr. Alexander's on a visit to Guilford, accompanied by Mr. Clarke, a Yankee resident in Georgetown. I found them

all well, and Miss Marianne more interesting than ever. She has much improved her singing and playing upon the piano.

"*19th.* Visited a fine romantic place in the neighborhood of Alexandria, as this place is called, which Guilford has named Lovedale. In the midst of a beautiful amphitheatre of rocks rises a charming stream, which flows a few rods and again sinks beneath a wild precipice. It is a fit emblem of birth and death. At its rise everything is regular and beautiful ; at its end all is broken and gloomy. But had the fair Marianne been with me it would have been doubly beautiful, doubly enchanting. After some time spent in this pleasant retreat, we returned to the house. Were I to live there but a short time, I should be enthusiastically in love. Every time I see that charming girl she makes an impression which it takes days to wear away. What added much to the impression of this visit was the delight she expressed (but not to me) on reading some of my poetry. I had lent to Guilford a little select manuscript of it when he was last at Georgetown, which she had been reading. 'She kissed the pieces, and said I was a charming poet.' Half enraptured, I returned to Georgetown.

"*23d.* Bought of Colonel J. Johnson 12,000 copies of the Almanac which we are printing, for $ 200. It is my intention to make a business for a while of selling them, and I hope to make at least $ 100.

"*27th.* Mr. Guilford came over, and we adjusted our matters and commenced business in partnership.

"*29th.* Rode to Lexington and visited Mr. H. Clay. I found him a very agreeable man, and was familiarly acquainted with him in half an hour. It seems a great ferment is raised in Fayette as well as in Scott County with regard to the Compensation Bill, and Mr. Clay is likely to have a competitor.

"*30th.* Left Mr. Clay's and took dinner at Mrs. Breckenridge's. After spending three or four hours with the charming widow, returned to Georgetown.

"*June 4th.* There were long speeches in town to-day by the Congressional candidates. They spoke, in succession, upwards of seven hours. Very different opinions exist among the people ; some will support one, some the other, and some neither. I have the most difficult task as editor. There has been much grumbling by one and another ; but none are decisively angry. I shall endeavor to keep them in this state of half mad and half pleased.

"*5th.* We had clients to-day for the first time since our partnership. One man engaged us on a justice suit, and gave us two court actions in Franklin, and another gave us one suit in the circuit court of Scott. To-morrow I shall set out on a journey to Indiana, whence I shall not return under nearly a fortnight.

"*6th.* Set out on my journey, and rode as far as Snelson's tavern towards Vevay, thirty-eight miles. The road was very lonesome, there not being more than one house in the distance of twenty-two miles. The land is very poor in this direction, and can never support a dense population.

"*7th.* Passed on to New Fredericksburg, a town ten miles above Vevay on the Ohio, laid out lately by the Johnsons, — a sheer speculation. Went thence down the river to Ghent, a new town of the same kind of origin, opposite Vevay. My business on this route was to leave appointments for several postmasters, prepare for a mail, and leave subscription papers for the 'Patriot.' Passed over the river to Vevay, where I met my Saxon friend Flügel, who received me with great cordiality. He has a charming little wife, who is considerably out of health.

"*8th.* Visited several of the Swiss and their vineyards, and drank American wine. The flavor is not so agreeable as that of the imported, but it has more spirit. It makes excellent sangaree. They sell it for $ 1.50 per gallon, whereas in Switzerland they used to get about thirty-three cents. They are evidently growing rich, as may be seen in the improvement of their houses and plantations. We saw on one of the plantations, a pleasant old Frenchman, nearly fifty years old, who had been obliged to fly from France with his family, on the last abdication of Napoleon. He was formerly a professor of mathematics, in good circumstances ; but now, poor and an exile, with his spade and his rake he was making a garden on the banks of the Ohio. I was introduced to him, but not being able to speak French, or he English, we could have no conversation. As we approached, he came out to meet us, and as we departed he accompanied us a way. Notwithstanding his situation, he seemed to be happy, and I left him with feelings of pity, admiration, and esteem.

"*9th.* Crossed to the Kentucky side, and walked up the river three miles on a visit to Mr. Agniel, a Frenchman, who married the sister of my friend's wife. They could all speak English, and the time passed pleasantly. After dinner, the ladies visited another French family, likewise fugitives from the tyranny of Louis. It was that of M. Lakenal, lately a member of the National Institute, from which he has been removed by a decree of Louis. He has with him a wife and two young daughters, who returned with the ladies to Mr. Agniel's. They were all animation, but here again I wanted a language. It is surprising how these girls, in almost a wilderness, seem to be as lively, and accommodate themselves as well to their situation, as in the palaces of Paris. My friend confided to me his situation in business, which is not the most pleasant, though he has considerable property. There is no sale for it now, and he is much in debt. If his creditors were to come upon him he must inevitably break. On his asking my advice, I counselled him first to attempt to induce his creditors to take his property at a fair price, and if they would not, and he could not possibly raise the money, that he should secure it from being sacrificed under execution the best way he could. He had a beautiful lot on the second bank, which he said he had purchased for me, and wished me to come and live in Vevay, and take it of him at the same price he gave for it. I was so well pleased with its situation, and with the situation of the town, that I resolved to go there if I should leave Georgetown. I therefore bought the lot, with the privilege of relinquishing in six months.

"10th. Bade adieu to my friends, and left Vevay. Flügel, with a sister of his wife, whom he once wrote me was reserved for me, accompanied me out of town about three miles. She is a very innocent, good girl, but without education or beauty. Through a poor country and dreary road, I went on to Madison, twenty-two miles.

"11th. Left Madison and went to New London,—a new place laid out by one of that gang of villains who composed the Lexington Indiana Banking Company. He is now gone, and has left the people without titles to their lots, and they curse him soundly. In the neighborhood of this place, found a man whose evidence I wanted in the land case which I have to manage in Scott County, and agreed with him to come over. He was on the original survey. Went on thence to New Lexington, and thence to Charlestown, where I arrived about 9 P. M., having missed my way and found it again by mere accident.

"12th. Passed on through Jeffersonville to Louisville. The convention for forming a State government in Indiana is now in session, but it is doubtful what course they will take.

"15th. Went through Versailles to Alexandria. Mr. Farnham accompanied me to the latter place, unwilling, and yet willing. My admiration of the family there has been somewhat lessened by the duplicity and want of propriety which have sometimes been used towards both Farnham and Guilford, who are both enthusiastically in love with Marianne. In fact, I was tempted not to call at all, after hearing a tale by Farnham, and was consequently under much constraint while there. Indeed, his conversation, joined with a trifling indisposition, agitated me so much, that I was quite sick when I arrived, and was almost immediately obliged to go to bed.

"17th. Left Alexandria and returned to Georgetown. I have lost the pleasure I formerly received in visiting that charming family, and though I have always been received with cordiality and treated with politeness, I shall not often find myself there.

"July 23d. Multiplicity of business and some vexations have almost

made me forget that I kept a journal. The politics of the day are the most prominent matters of discussion, and excite considerable warmth. Having a newspaper under my control, I have had much difficulty, and once almost quarrelled with the Johnsons, to keep it clear of personal abuse. A piece was sent for publication which I refused to insert; but the matter passed off without any difficulty. Yet I am accused of subserviency to the Johnsons! I shall give Richard my vote, and feel perfectly inclined to be his friend, but not his tool. Though I disapprove of the Compensation Bill, I think it not a sufficient reason for rejecting him altogether. Little has been said in town until yesterday, when the people seemed almost universally inclined to talk, and some warmth arose. I came near having a quarrel with one man, and, had I been as warm as he, might have had a fight without any difficulty. I will not fight, but suspect I must prepare myself, as the man seemed very much inclined to insult me.

"There was but little business done at the last Circuit Court, and we had but a small share of that. About a week ago a fellow was committed here for horse stealing, and has employed us. I rode to Nelson County for him, to find a brother, but was unsuccessful.

"On my way I called and spent a night at Alexandria, the most agreeable that I ever spent there. I spent a night with Farnham on my return, who told me the whole story of his loves. He despises Guilford, who, by his account, has by his real or pretended sensibility often made himself ridiculous. But it is a fault which may easily be cured. They both love Marianne; but Farnham has the best chance for success. On the 4th of July Guilford delivered an oration here, and I a poem. They were received with great applause, especially the oration. They have both been published. The day passed away in great harmony, without any drunkenness or fighting. There was a ball in the evening, but I did not attend it on account of a headache.

"About two months ago my friend Flügel visited me, and persuaded me to lend him ninety dollars, which I could ill spare, and which I do not expect to get again without taking property. I was surprised that he should urge me so much when he knew my circumstances.

"30th. Politics have waxed very warm within a few days. There are several young men here who are very overbearing, and seem to be seeking occasion to quarrel with me. A few days ago I remarked an unusual degree of insolence, and was told by a friend that I should very likely get a fight upon my hands in consequence of some observation made by me about soldiers. It was a long time before I could recollect anything; but at length I remembered to have said once, in a conversation about the Compensation Bill, when sneeringly told that a representative might live as a soldier, that I presumed that no gentleman present

would be willing to live on the fare of a regular soldier. From this it had been circulated that I said, 'I hoped no gentleman present would condescend to associate with soldiers,' and gentlemen had threatened to insult me. I consequently thought proper to arm, and borrowed a dirk, with the resolution to insult no man, but if insulted to resent it, and if attacked, defend myself. I told my friends to contradict the story, and have heard nothing of it since. But to-day comes a new accusation, namely, that, after having said that I would publish no more concerning the Compensation Bill, I have inserted pieces in favor of it, thereby evincing that my object was to prevent communications in favor of the bill. This is entirely false. I did, however, say that I did not intend to publish any more, and requested my correspondents to turn their attention to other objects. But I never made an absolute promise in public or private that I would publish no communication; my object was to avoid receiving them from both sides. But R. P. Henry declined standing a poll, and in the piece which announced it took up the Compensation Bill. I could not refuse to insert that, and when I had inserted that, I could not deny a place to an answer. By this circumstance our paper has been again opened upon the subject. Some gentlemen have even gone so far as to threaten to discontinue; but I believe they will think better of it, and change their minds.

"We had a fight in town this morning, as a commencement of the election, between Dr. J. F. Henry and Samuel Theobalds. The public excitement is very great.

"August 30th. I have become very irregular in my journal, in consequence of having considerable business, but shall endeavor to give a sketch of passing events.

"The election passed away without any further trouble in town. Some gentlemen who seem resolved that I shall take a decided part in politics, and either defend or condemn the Johnsons in toto, still keep finding fault, and Drs. Ewing and Henry have discontinued their newspaper. Let them go, and every other man who will quarrel with an editor if he be honest.

"I commenced an attack on the 'Western Monitor' some time ago, and Mr. Hunt has since answered it, and we now have it regularly. But having great respect for each other, we find ourselves very much restricted.

"September 1st. I have for some time had a degree of partiality for Miss Anne Payne, and lately, when she was in this neighborhood, took considerable pains to get into her company. After her return home, Mr. Ford invited me to take a ride to her father's with him. I did so, and on the way learned with some surprise that he was very much attached to her, and was going with the express object of making a decla-

ration. I instantly resolved to stand aside and give him every opportunity, as he had committed so much to my honor. I therefore never hinted to him my own feelings, but cautiously endeavored to conceal them and promote his views. We stayed over night and most of the next day. In the evening no opportunity was offered; but in the forenoon of the next day Anne proposed a walk of a mile or more. But Anne Johnson, daughter of Colonel James, happening to be there, kept close by Anne Payne, both going and returning. They ran, jumped, and pulled Mr. Ford about (who is quite fleshy), evidently with the design of fatiguing him, and behaved so that I was disgusted, and thought they were making fun of him. But just as they got back, an opportunity was given him to say barely a word, and a word in answer, though entirely vague, has given him the strongest hopes. I, however, was so displeased with her conduct, that I left the place with very different sensations from those I had when I arrived there. Good by, Anne; I'll think no more of you.

"This day, on an invitation from Mr. Alfred Tarlton, I rode down to the Roman settlement in this county, and paid a visit to his cousins. I do not know the history of this settlement, but here are a number of Roman Catholic families settled together, who form a very respectable church. We attended meeting, but saw or heard very little but foolish mummery. It seems strange that people of this enlightened age can be pleased with such absurdity and nonsense. I paid all possible attention to the priest, but gained very little instruction or edification. We returned and dined with the ladies. I found I had entirely mistaken the disposition of Cecilia, the eldest of these ladies. I had seen her last winter at Mr. Jenkins's, in town, and almost fallen in love; but on being introduced to her at a ball, and attempting to converse, I was much disappointed."

From this time forward Mr. Kendall ceased to keep a regular journal, owing in part to indolence, and in part to the engrossment of his time by his various occupations. The little newspaper which he edited needed the support of all parties in the county to keep it in existence, and his policy was not to identify it with either of them. Congress had passed an act changing the compensation of the members from a per diem of eight dollars during the session to an annual salary of fifteen hundred dollars, with a retroactive provision, by means of which each member received a considerable sum beyond the lawful rate of compensation when the services were rendered. Colonel Richard M. Johnson had introduced the bill, and it had been voted for by the entire Kentucky delegation, with perhaps one exception. This act was seized hold of by political aspirants as a lever with which to operate against the sitting members, and its retroactive feature made it a powerful instrument. There was at once a general uprising of the popular mind against this measure, and Kentucky was in a ferment before the members reached home. Colonel R. M. Johnson called on Mr. Kendall soon after his return, and inquired what was his opinion and the opinion of the people. He was told that the opinion of the people and Mr. Kendall's opinion were against the retrospective features of the act, and that the only safety of the members who voted for it was in promising to sustain its repeal. Colonel Johnson took the stump and made a resolute effort to justify the measure; but he soon found it was all in vain. It was amusing to hear the Colonel, who was not an eloquent man, make a passionate speech in favor of the measure, and conclude by promising to vote for its repeal, because such was the will of the people. While Mr. Kendall maintained a position of neutrality in the paper he edited, and disapproved of the Compensation Bill, he openly declared his purpose to vote for Colonel Johnson, on the ground that a man of his patriotism and usefulness ought not to be thrust out of public life for a single error.

Every member of Congress from Kentucky who had voted for the Compensation Bill, except Colonel Johnson and Henry Clay, was defeated in this election, and these two were spared only upon their promises to vote for the repeal of the obnoxious measure. On the first day of the next session of Congress Colonel Johnson obtained leave to bring in a bill to repeal the act in question, and it passed with little or no discussion.

What a contrast between the excitement of 1816 and the quiet of 1856, after the passage of an act fixing the compensation of members of Congress at three thousand, instead of fifteen hundred dollars per annum, which also contained a retrospective provision precisely like that in the act of 1816. The former act produced a storm which revolutionized Congress; the latter, though identical in principle, and involving double the amount voted by the members to themselves, did not produce a ripple upon the ocean of public opinion. The secret of this popular inconsistency may probably be found in the fact that in 1816 the finances of the country were low, and no other existing question disturbed the public mind; while in 1856 the government had abundant means, and

the attention of the people was engrossed by the slavery question in connection with a Presidential election. And it is not to be disguised that the disposition of the manufacturing and other interests of the country, which profited by the mode in which the public revenue was raised, was to deplete an overflowing treasury by extravagant and reckless expenditures, thus introducing abuses and corruptions into the public service, and blunting the sensibilities of the people, who, scarcely knowing that they were taxed at all, became indifferent as to the manner in which the public moneys were expended.

During the war with Great Britain, from 1812 to 1815, all the banks in the South and West had suspended payment, and in aid of the government had issued a very large amount of their notes. After the close of the war they appeared to be in no haste to resume payment. The feature in Mr. Kendall's editorial career in Georgetown which attracted most attention was a series of articles in which he discussed the questions of currency, and called on the banks to resume specie payments. These articles won the approval not only of the public generally, but also of the officers of the Bank of Kentucky, who were gentlemen of the highest integrity and honor.

In September, 1816, Mr. Kendall had occasion to visit Frankfort, where he had some business with William Gerard, one of the editors of the State paper, called the "Argus of Western America." In their first interview, Mr. Gerard proposed to him to buy out his partner and undertake the editorial duties of the paper. He replied to this unexpected proposal by stating that he had no means of making the purchase. Mr. Gerard said that he was a director in the Bank of Kentucky, and would insure a loan or loans from the bank, which would enable him (Kendall) to meet the payments, which would not in all exceed two thousand dollars. Upon this proposal Mr. Kendall deliberated through a sleepless night, without coming to a conclusion.

It was in effect a proposal to abandon all his plans of life and adopt a purely literary and political career. Political strife had no charms for him; but just then party spirit had died away, and the time was called "the era of good feelings." The prospect therefore was, that he would be allowed to discuss principles and measures, and indulge his literary taste, without encountering the personality and asperity which had for many years characterized newspaper

discussions. On the other hand, he had never liked the practice of the law, and experience thus far had not commended it to his favor. His leading principle was, not to undertake a case where right was not on the side of his client; yet, through the representations of a lying thief, he once found himself engaged in successfully screening him from payment for the goods he had stolen. He had learned that in the higher courts justice is often sacrificed to precedent and forms of pleading, and that the lawyers' work is rather a struggle for forensic triumph than an effort to protect the innocent and enforce the right. In the land suit which he had undertaken, and pressed to judgment in the Circuit Court, the law itself seemed to him a violation of moral right. The land had been entered by a man in Virginia who had surveyed it; but he had not taken out a grant or improved it, and when he died bequeathed it to his sons. In the mean time it had been covered by a grant based upon a more recent entry, and the grantee, being probably aware of the older entry, had sold it out in small tracts at a very low price to actual settlers, giving them quit-claim deeds. On the eight hundred acres of land there were about eight settlers, who had built log-cabins, cut down portions of the forest, and brought considerable tracts into cultivation. Not more than half of them could read; but in concert with others in their neighborhood they had erected a school-house, and were trying to give their children an education. It was the labor of these men which had given the land its only value, and it seemed like robbery to take it from them. Yet the inexorable decree of the law did this. The hardships of the case, however, were somewhat mitigated by a compromise which Mr. Kendall advised.

These considerations inclined him to accept Mr. Gerard's proposition; but he did not then give a definitive answer. He consulted his partner and friends, and all of them, except Colonels James and Richard M. Johnson, advised him to accept the proposal. The Johnsons made a resolute effort to dissuade him from the purchase; but their known motive rendered their representations of little weight. They had quarrelled with Mr. Gerard, and were engaged in an attempt to break down his paper. They had thrown all their influence in favor of another newspaper in Frankfort, called "The Palladium," and had even obtained a promise from Mr. Kendall to write for it, before he was aware of their motives. Though he was the friend of the Johnsons, who had served their country

bravely in war, and were public-spirited in peace, he had maintained his own independence, and had not sympathized with their personal antipathies. He therefore listened respectfully to all they had to say, and then concluded to make the purchase.

On the 30th of September, 1816, he visited Frankfort and closed the bargain, agreeing to give $2,000 for half of the establishment, the amount being payable, one thousand on the first day of the succeeding November, and one thousand in one year thereafter.

Returning to Georgetown, he dissolved his partnership with Mr. Guilford, who determined to remove to Cincinnati. Mr. Miller, in whose favor he was bound to resign the post-office, if he resigned at all within a certain period, was dead, leaving a widow. Though he was under no obligation to do so, Mr. Kendall, having resigned in favor of another party for a consideration, paid the widow the amount he had agreed to pay her husband if he retained the office. The new postmaster, who had agreed to give two hundred dollars for the office, sold it not long afterwards to another person for five hundred. Though Mr. Kendall did not acquire the office for any purpose of speculation, intending to hold it permanently, he was never satisfied with himself for his participation in these transactions, and made up his mind that, if not corrupt, they constituted an abuse which the government ought not to tolerate. Yet these transfers of the post-office in Georgetown were effected through the agency of Colonel R. M. Johnson, then a member of Congress, who well knew their character.

The administration of the Post-Office Department at that time was extremely lax. Mr. Kendall found that no way-bills came to his office charging him with postage on any newspapers printed in Kentucky. Mentioning the fact to the former postmaster, he was told that bills would come embracing the whole quarter, at its close; but none came. Mr. Kendall then made out his account charging himself with the newspaper postage as accurately as he could, and wrote to the Postmaster-General stating the facts. No answer was received, and no remedy applied, and it is believed that very little of the newspaper postage collected in Kentucky at that time was ever accounted for.

After Mr. Kendall resigned, he forwarded an account showing the amount due from him to the Department, which was drawn for and paid. Long afterwards there came another draft upon him for the same amount, which was protested with an explanation, and thus the matter ended.

Mr. Kendall parted with his friend and partner, Nathan Guilford, with much regret. He was a man of very respectable talents, great kindness of heart, and marked simplicity of manners and language. Yet he was an inveterate deist, and appeared to entertain a perfect hatred of Christianity. On that subject there was no congeniality between the partners. Failing to make any impression upon Guilford by demanding what substitute he could furnish for human hope to rest upon, and warning him of the evil consequences to himself which would assuredly follow the public avowal of his opinions, Mr. Kendall begged and secured his silence on that topic. In after life, however, Mr. Guilford's prudence forsook him, and he paid the penalty of his folly. He took up the subject of common schools in Ohio, was elected to the legislature from Cincinnati, and procured the passage of an act embodying the original school system of that State. He was placed at the head of the Cincinnati schools, and a question arising as to the reading of the Bible therein, he gave free expression to his infidel opinions, which indiscretion not only deprived him of his office, but permanently impaired his influence and usefulness.

Mr. Guilford's marriage is directly traceable to his benevolence, which was one of his striking characteristics. He heard that there was a flatboat at the landing, on which was a family of emigrants sick with fever. He visited them, procured lodging for them in the city, and carefully attended upon them until their recovery. One of the sick was a beautiful young girl, who became his wife. And she was not unworthy of his love. When disappointments and misfortunes, operating upon a disposition naturally gloomy and a mind unsustained by any religious hope, had discouraged and reduced him almost to imbecility, she maintained her firmness and discharged her duties with admirable cheerfulness through all vicissitudes.

The following are extracts from a narrative written by Mr. Kendall soon after the occurrence of the events which it records : —

"About the middle of October I left Georgetown and came to Frankfort. Previous to this event, George Madison, who had been unanimously elected governor of this State, died, and the administration had devolved on Gabriel Slaughter, the lieutenant-governor. As I was on my way there, I amused myself by imagining what a peaceable and happy time I should have in Frankfort. There was little party spirit in the State ; all was quiet and harmonious. I had anonymously in the 'Argus' commenced an attack on the editor of the 'Western

Monitor,' which I intended to continue, as well for amusement as in support of the Republican party, which had suffered much in this State by the course which their leaders had taken with respect to the 'Compensation Bill.' Indulging in these reveries, I met Ben Taylor on the top of the hill above Frankfort, who told me the acting governor had appointed John Pope as his secretary. I was thunderstruck. I considered Pope the leader of the Federalists, and instantly foresaw a struggle between the parties which must end in the exaltation of the Federalists, or in the prostration of themselves and their leader. At that time I had not a thought of the course which affairs have since taken, but expected the contest would last for four years. I knew that much was expected from me by the Republicans, and both my interest and inclination gave me an instant resolution to take a decided stand against this act of the acting governor. As soon as I came into town, Mr. Gerard wished to know what course I thought we ought to pursue. I told him we had only one course to take, which must be anti-administration. After conversing with Mr. Bibb, we determined to publish whatever should be offered on both sides, and as soon as communications were offered in defence of the appointment, to express our own opinion. The lieutenant-governor was extremely anxious to prevent the papers in Frankfort from discussing the subject, and for that purpose held several private conversations with Mr. Gerard and the editor of the 'Palladium'; but it was in vain. They were inflexible. This act of the old man gave me a great contempt for him at the start. It was in itself mean and improper, and beneath the dignity of his office.

"On the 1st of November, 1816, I came out in a public address as co-editor of the 'Argus.' All parties were pleased with my address, and extolled me extravagantly. I received much attention from John J. Marshall and John Pope ; but I thought it interested and felt under no obligations. Because a quarrel was then existing between Mr. Gerard and the Johnsons, and because I had disapproved of the Compensation Bill, it was thought and asserted, that we would support Mr. Pope. I could not help smiling to see men who ought to know better, expect that we would yield up our political principles to a little personal dispute. Those men soon found their civilities useless, and entirely discontinued them.

"Before I came to Frankfort, as I have before mentioned, a controversy had arisen between Colonel James Johnson and Mr. Gerard, on account of some expressions of Gerard with respect to Richard M. Johnson, both in conversation and in the 'Argus.' Gerard was the personal friend of Ben Taylor (who had run against Colonel R. M. Johnson for Congress), and though he intended voting for Johnson at the commencement of the electioneering contest, yet on hearing Johnson abuse Tay-

lor, as he thought improperly, changed his mind and voted for neither. The controversy was carried on in the 'Palladium' and 'Argus,' and with some warmth. The original of the first piece was written by myself at the request of Johnson, who suggested to me all the ideas ; but when published it was in a shape which I entirely disowned. When I became an editor of the 'Argus,' I made the parties mutually agree that this controversy should cease. However, one piece appeared from Colonel Johnson which irritated Gerard and offended me. Gerard was eager for answering, but I dissuaded him from it, representing that it was giving our enemies an advantage at our expense, and that, as Republicans of the same principles, we ought by all means to put an end to the controversy. I could not, however, persuade him to forego the satisfaction of answering until I promised, if the attack were repeated, to take up the pen myself and endeavor to make them smart for it. Happily, however, nothing further was said on the subject. The 'Reporter,' at Lexington, which had all the feelings of Johnson, complimented me at the expense of Gerard, by expressing a hope that the 'Argus' would now retrieve itself from its doubtful character. I, however, answered that I did not receive the compliment with any pleasure, on account of the pitiful slander it contained against my brother editor. The writer of the compliment made an angry reply, and there it ended.

"The appointment of secretary was so generally disapproved by the people, that it was thought the Senate might be induced to reject it. On expressing some inclination to write on the subject, Mr. Gerard suggested to me that several numbers addressed to the Senators might probably have considerable effect. I accordingly commenced and wrote several numbers signed 'Cato,' which were quoted into many of the Kentucky papers. George Adams was at the same time writing articles over the signature of 'Montgomery,' addressed to the lieutenant-governor. I did not approve of the violence of his pieces, but would not object to their publication. They were answered by a writer under the name of 'Atticus,' and Adams replied in communications signed 'Snolus Bolus,' which I mostly wrote over, and in which I made some alterations. These pieces were vulgar, but contained some wit.

"If the nomination had been laid before the Senate when they first met, it is believed that body would have been divided more equally or have rejected it altogether. But it was delayed for several weeks, until Mr. Hunt could have time to electioneer and explain his conduct, so that every weak head (and there were many of them in the Senate) might be influenced to support him. It has since been ascertained that he wrote letters to gentlemen in the various counties, urging them to use their influence with the people to make his appointment popular, and with the Senators to procure a confirmation. Much pains was taken to

represent the appointment as popular, and many of the Senators were doubtless deceived even with respect to their own districts. The appointment was confirmed, twenty-two to eleven.

"Before I came to Frankfort, I had addressed to Hunt, the editor of the 'Western Monitor,' an anonymous letter in the 'Argus,' signed 'Derius.' He suspected me, as was apparent in his answer, and in my reply I gave him leave to publish my name. He did so, and we carried on a controversy in our own proper names, until it ended, as such controversies generally do, in personal invective. We had been very friendly ; but this broke our friendship, and though we have since met, it has been without cordiality. Yet many suspicious persons believed, or affected to believe, that we perfectly understood each other, and were quarrelling just for amusement! Unluckily, we were both Yankees, who are in this country a suspected people, and have to suffer for the follies of much worse men. In the contest with Hunt, I was accused of violence ; but I was more guilty of vanity. The Federalists thought that Hunt could write me down ; but, I believe, it was generally agreed that I had the best of the fight.

"The next editor with whom I came in contact was Doctor Anthony Hunn of Harrodsburg. He is a man of some talent, little education, and a great deal of vanity. He assailed me by a letter directed to me personally in his paper. I made some inquiries concerning him, and finding that he was more of a villain than a writer, I turned an anecdote concerning him into poetry, to the tune of 'Yankee Doodle,' which raised a great laugh upon him, and silenced him for a time.

"My next controversy was with a paper which was established last winter in Frankfort. As soon as it was found that neither the 'Argus' nor 'Palladium' was friendly to Mr. Pope, a third paper was established here under the name of the 'Commentator,' by Moses O. Bledsoe. This man had been a partner of Mr. Gerard for a short time, was afterwards married to a lady of some fortune, dissipated it all, and now, under the auspices and by the assistance of Mr. Pope and his friends, established this paper, in conducting which he took the message of the lieutenant-governor to the last legislature for his creed. We well knew that the great object of this establishment was our injury. Nevertheless, it was a considerable time before we took any notice of it. They procured Mann Butler, from Louisville, to write for it, and affected a character for conciliation and moderation. Soon after Butler came into the establishment he made an attack on the 'Argus,' and we retaliated by giving an account of the origin of the paper and the views of its friends, called it a hireling press, and Butler a hired writer. The consequence was an attack by Bledsoe on Mr. Gerard with a stick. No mischief was done, and as they gave no satisfactory answer, we repeated the charge, and kept up our fire. Butler's name did not appear in the paper; but as we knew he was a man unable to bear it, from extreme sensitiveness, all our observations were aimed at him by name. As we anticipated, he could not bear it; his friends were dissatisfied with him, and he with them, so that he concluded to quit the paper. He has since changed sides entirely; told me that he found there was more rancor in the no-party men than in us, and that he had reason to believe that what we had said of the 'Commentator' was true. He, however, declared with respect to himself, that he knew only Bledsoe in the bargain which he had made, and I believe he told the truth. He is a man of the best intentions, but easily deceived.

"At the commencement of the session of the general assembly last winter, I asked leave to take a seat in the House and report the speeches and proceedings. Leave was readily granted, and I continued to do it throughout the session. With the exception of two or three members, whose speeches, it was said, were much better as reported by me than as spoken by themselves, all the members of the House were not only satisfied, but pleased. It was not only gratifying to the members themselves, because it flattered them, but was very acceptable to the people. It gave an importance to our paper which brought it many subscribers, and made the representatives in some measure dependent on me. We were elected public printers without opposition, and with the exception of the attack by Bledsoe on Gerard, the winter passed away in tolerable quiet.

"Soon after I came to Frankfort a question arose whether or not the Constitution of the State required or authorized an election of governor to supply the place of George Madison. If I remember right it was mentioned to me first by Colonel Charles S. Todd, the secretary of Madison, who had been displaced by Slaughter to make room for Pope. He gave no opinion, but asked mine. The question then presented was, whether at the next annual election in August, another governor should be chosen to remain in office for the balance of the term for which Madison had been elected. I turned to the Constitution, and gave my opinion decidedly in the negative. I, however, drew up a list of reasons, both for and against a new election, and published them in the 'Argus,' without giving to the public any opinion. Little more was said on the subject until about the middle of the session of the general assembly, when Matthew Lyon, a man without political principle or honesty, addressed a few essays to the people on the subject. He is said to have been induced to this measure by some of his acquaintances in Lexington who told him he had been suspected of being a Federalist, and must redeem his character. These essays excited conversation, and some time after their publication, Mr. Mills introduced a resolution into the House of Representatives, providing for the raising of a com-

mittee for the purpose of inquiring into the constitutionality of a new election. This resolution was lost by a majority of only six. The friends of a new election were surprised at so great a vote in favor of it, and resolved to try their strength in a more formal manner. The people of Lexington were generally in favor of a new election; but their most efficient representative, Joseph C. Breckenridge, was opposed to it. Some of them, however, made him a visit, and he consented to bring the measure forward again. I had frequently heard him express an opposite opinion, and was astonished at his course, as I saw no reason for a change of sentiment. How he overcame his scruples I know not; but he asked leave to bring in a bill to provide for a new election of governor, and made a considerable display of learning, if not of eloquence, in its defence. The debate continued for the best part of three days. Breckenridge and Crittenden (John J.) were the principal advocates of the measure. Mills, to the astonishment of everybody, was in opposition, and said his only motive for introducing the subject before was to get an able report against it, which should go to the people and put down essays from abroad. The motive was an unworthy one, and the apparent duplicity of Mr. Mills's conduct on this occasion has effectually ruined his political influence. Thus by one imprudent step is the popularity founded on years of faithful services swept away in a moment. It now appeared that an immense majority were against a new election; the vote stood twenty-six to sixty-one, and the Senate immediately concurred without debate, three to twenty-one. My opinion coincided with that of the majority, but my feelings were all with the minority, among whom were my best personal friends. I reported the debate, and soon after the close of the session commenced its publication, with the intention of taking no part in the controversy. Gerard was in favor of the measure, and wished to come out on that side of it; but was restrained by me. At length, the decision of the same question by the legislature of New York, in a case precisely similar was received, which led me to an investigation. They provided for a new election both of governor and lieutenant-governor for a new term of four years. On examining the two Constitutions, I was surprised at the coincidence between them with respect to the executive department. About this time Mr. Bibb gave his opinion with his reasons, and directed my attention to the Constitution and a law of the United States by which a new election had been authorized on no better authority than was given in our Constitution. I now determined to write out the arguments, pro and con, and compare them together. I began with the pros, and when I came to the cons I could not think of any which would balance the weight of the pros. The latter, therefore, preponderated, and I formed an opinion in favor of an election of

governor and lieutenant-governor for a new term of four years. What influence dislike for Pope and Slaughter may have had on my mind I cannot tell; but I am sure that if it had any it was unconsciously. The question now was, What shall be done? A large majority of the State were doubtless of a different opinion. They might attribute our course to a dislike for men. Should we come out and strenuously advocate a new election, we would attack the decision of the legislature, and run the risk of losing not only the public work, but the support of the people. We did not, however, long hesitate; but determined to risk everything. I took up my pen and wrote a long argument before we commenced the publication. I took measures, by writing to several individuals, to have my articles republished throughout the State; for to us the contest was neck or nothing. On the 11th of April we began the publication, and continued it in five successive numbers. It drew to our paper several subscribers, but seemed at first to make but little noise. It was not long, however, before I heard that the friends of a new election throughout the country were taking that ground. The 'Commentator' here, which had abused and insulted us for our hypocrisy in not coming out on this question, found itself utterly unable to support the contest. The 'Western Monitor' said but little. My articles were republished in several papers, and generally read. Seeing no answer, doubting the event, and having nothing more to say, I was about to drop the publication, when a writer in the 'Commentator,' under the name of 'Plain Truth,' undertook to answer my articles. I copied his articles into the 'Argus,' and immediately after each article subjoined a reply under the name of 'Plainer Truth.' This was happily managed, and produced considerable effect. I began now to hear of some agitation in various counties, and of candidates coming out upon this question. Mr. Bibb came out publicly and harangued the people of Franklin; Jesse Bledsoe addressed a letter to the public, and became a candidate; the papers at Lexington assumed the same ground that I had taken, and William T. Barry came out in that county as a candidate for the Senate. The adherents of the lieutenant-governor, finding the proposed measure rapidly gaining ground throughout the State, redoubled their exertions, and published a pamphlet called 'The Constitutionalist,' signed 'A Kentuckian,' and written by George Robinson, Esq., afterwards a representative in Congress. My original plan for managing the controversy was, that after we had published two numbers, Mr. Bibb should come out in the 'Argus,' signing his own proper name, which was always his custom, and that after the conclusion the whole should be printed in a pamphlet. My object was to attract attention, by the weight of his name, before the publication of my third article, which was much the most important, and to follow up the effect of

newspaper writing with a pamphlet circulated liberally throughout all the counties in the State. But Mr. Bibb, though he had promised, was too indolent to write, and there was nobody to pay the expense of the pamphlets. But as soon as 'The Constitutionalist' appeared, the Democrats were eager to have a pamphlet in reply, and gave assurances of a liberal contribution. I therefore took up the pen. Many new ideas having been suggested in the discussion, I abandoned the track of my first argument and struck out a new course. In three days I produced a pamphlet of thirty-nine pages, which, at the suggestion of Colonel C. S. Todd, I called 'Free Suffrage.' The rough draft, with a little correction, without writing over, except about two pages at the end of the 'conclusion,' was sent to the press, and in a few days we struck off five thousand copies. This was a timely measure. The influence of 'The Constitutionalist' was considerable, and the current of public opinion in some counties evidently changing. But 'Free Suffrage,' which I took good care myself to distribute in every direction, soon changed the current and made it set more strongly than ever in favor of a new election. The contest was still maintained in the papers, and 'Plainer Truth' being too much for 'Plain Truth,' another writer came out in the 'Commentator' under the name of 'Truth.' This was Humphrey Marshall, famous in the politics of Kentucky, and a masterly hand at misrepresentation and abuse. His article contained only these two qualities, and was aimed at me too plainly to be misunderstood. He called me everything, and among the rest a knave or a fool. I then answered him under the name of 'A Fool,' pointed out who he was, etc., etc. He then gave a ludicrous description of me, which was laughable for its absurdity, to which I never replied.

"Everything was going on in a favorable train, but as if Heaven had really made mad those whom it intended to destroy, Mr. Pope undertook the writing of letters to various individuals to 'save the Constitution,' as he called it, or, in other words, to save himself. Among the rest he wrote to Charles H. Allen, a candidate in Henry County, wishing him to decline if Edward George of that county would offer, pronouncing the new election scheme 'wicked,' inviting him to patronize the 'Commentator,' which he called 'a very good paper,' telling him he 'would have no reason to regret it,' and concluding with the statement that he might 'be assured of his good will.' But the secretary mistook his man. Mr. Allen, though at first opposed to a new election, had changed his mind. Being questioned with respect to this letter, he showed it, and sent it to me for publication. I accompanied it with severe remarks, calculated to rouse the people, and show them the consequences of executive interference in their elections. The secretary was in a rage, and immediately replied by a hand-bill. In this he promised to address the people again before the election, and after that event to give them some account of his political conduct. This was a hasty and passionate piece of composition, in which he exposed himself to ridicule, which was so liberally bestowed in the next 'Argus' that he has been silent ever since. This man has effected much by private letters; but now he was caught in his own snare. His hand-bill was received with general indignation. His enemies pronounced it corrupt, and his friends imprudent. Scarcely anybody justified him except the newspapers which were in his interest.

"Notwithstanding all this, I had some fears with respect to the event. Accounts from the Green River section were contradictory; but the general impression was that a majority was opposed to the new election. In the middle section, a majority was on that side beyond a doubt. On the north side of the Kentucky, we were sure of a considerable majority. For myself, I was afraid that the majority in the House of Representatives would be too small to be overwhelming; that the Senate would oppose, and the question be lost. In that event, I should have regretted that I had ever taken it up. In Franklin County our prospect was rather doubtful. Mr. Bibb and C. S. Todd were our candidates. They were opposed by John J. Marshall and Richard Taylor. Marshall's friends were sanguine for him, but had no hopes of Taylor's election. Thinking their favorite strong enough to out-poll anybody, and preferring Colonel Todd to Mr. Bibb, because he has less talents and influence, they electioneered for Marshall and Todd. They did not see their error till it was too late to retreat. After a warm struggle during the three days of election, we beat them by a considerable majority, and triumphantly elected Bibb and Todd. On the evening of the close of the election, a multitude of our friends collected at Mrs. Price's, where they raised Bibb, Todd, and a number of others, among whom was myself, on their shoulders, and carried us around the room.

"We soon heard that the new election candidates had succeeded in every county except one on the north side of the Kentucky, in several of the middle counties, and almost universally in the Green River country, insuring to our party an overwhelming majority in the next House of Representatives. In April Mr. Gerard, either from fear of the event of the controversy in which we were engaged, or because he really wished to quit printing, proposed to sell out his part of the 'Argus' office and retire to the country."

It is natural that men born in the same country, though perfect strangers to each other, meeting in a distant land, should be predisposed to become friends. It was thus that Mr. Kendall had become the friend of John H. Farnham, while the one lived in the

family of Mr. Clay, and the other in the family of Mr. Alexander. About the time that Mr. Kendall settled in Georgetown, Mr Farnham began the practice of the law in Versailles. After the former removed to Frankfort Farnham visited him, and stated that, seeing no prospect of getting a living by his profession, he was desirous of getting a school for the present. Mr. Kendall then boarded with his partner, Mr. Gerard, in whose house he occupied a room. He entered warmly into Mr. Farnham's views, and offered, if he would come to Frankfort, to share his room and bed with him, and to get his partner to board him, and take in payment the instruction of his children. Under this arrangement Farnham came to Frankfort, and established a respectable school.

Farnham was a Federalist in politics, and sympathized with Mr. Pope and the lieutenant-governor. These circumstances would have been disregarded had he confined himself to the business of his school, or uttered his opinions with deference to those of others. But his manner was loud and confident; he indulged freely in sarcasm, and had a broad, meaning laugh, which was very irritating. Worse than all, he would spend long evenings with Mr. Pope, and without seeming to feel that there was any breach of honor in it, would detail to the editors of the "Argus" his private political conversations. Believing that a man who would fetch would carry also, especially as his avowed sympathies were with their adversaries, Mr. Gerard and Mr. Kendall became very reserved in their conversation with him. Finally, Mr. Gerard became so disgusted with his rude and ungentlemanly manners that he requested him to find board elsewhere. Though Mr. Kendall had found him a most disagreeable room-mate, who seemed to have no care for anybody's comfort but his own, he never had any altercation with him, and apparently they parted friends. Not long afterwards, a rumor was in circulation that Mr. Farnham was to become the editor of the "Commentator." This was more than confirmed by letters from the Green River country, where he was making a political tour, detailing his conversations, the leading feature of which was, that on his return to Frankfort he would become editor of the "Commentator," and "*knew enough about Mr. Kendall to write him down.*" Thus forewarned, Mr. Kendall, knowing that a vindictive controversy with his old friend was impending, determined to bring it to an issue as soon as possible.

In his first article Mr. Farnham assailed the "Argus," charging

it with malignity and falsehood in its course toward the "Commentator." The "Argus" retorted by giving the history of the "Commentator," alleged that it was established to promote objects of personal ambition; that Mr. Farnham's politics were of the Federal stamp, and that he was an hireling editor who had sold his talents to the ambitious men who had established that paper. In his reply, he said all this "came with an ill grace from one who was hired to write for the 'Minerva Press' and Georgetown 'Patriot,' and had now sold his pen to a printer in this town (Frankfort) for a fixed salary." Farnham very well knew that Mr. Kendall was a co-proprietor of the "Minerva Press" and the "Argus," and in the case of the latter Farnham was one of those who had advised the purchase. The "Argus" and "Commentator" were both weekly papers, published on the same day; but the issue of the latter containing these allegations was circulated before the former was ready for the press. To bring the matter to an issue at once, Mr. Kendall inserted a paragraph in the "Argus" declaring the first and last points made in Mr. Farnham's article "base and wilful falsehoods." This blunt and decisive contradiction, circulated within an hour or two after the publication of his own paper, enraged Mr. Farnham, who publicly announced his purpose to demand personal satisfaction. Mr. Kendall was soon advised of the threat, and being far Mr. Farnham's inferior in size and strength, he procured a dirk and placed it in his bosom. His office opened upon the street, and he was sitting at a table directing newspapers, when Mr. Farnham entered. He rose as Farnham approached, when the latter invited him to go into the street, saying that he desired some conversation with him. There were two journeymen at work in the office, and Mr. Kendall replied that he preferred that there should be witnesses to their conversation, bidding him to proceed with what he had to say. Farnham then said he wished Kendall to go out of his own premises, and invited him to go into a bookstore a few rods distant. To this proposition Kendall assented, and they left together for the bookstore. On their way Mr. Kendall observed Bledsoe and others of Farnham's partisans near at hand, their presence indicating a conspiracy to beat him, and repented that he had left his own office; but he deemed it inexpedient to retreat. In the bookstore Mr. Farnham began to interrogate Mr. Kendall, who answered somewhat at length, to gain time for the arrival of his friends, who had now begun to

flock in. At length Farnham came to a pause, evidently showing that he had the worst of the conversation, and began to falter in his purpose. Suddenly, however, he exclaimed that he had been charged with falsehood, and would not stand it, at the same time striking at Mr. Kendall with his fist. There was an instant rush upon them, which nearly threw them down. As he rose, Mr. Kendall drew the dirk from his bosom, but had no chance to use it. Farnham, when the rush was made, had sprung upon the counter, with the view of escaping into the counting-room; but Mr. Gerard, seizing his coat-tail, drew him violently back upon the floor and sprung upon him. Bledsoe, attempting to interfere, was taken in hand by the keeper of the bookstore, so that two fights were going on while Mr. Kendall, the cause of all the turmoil, was looking on with a dirk in his right hand. The *mêlée* lasted but a moment. Gerard had taken a large dirk from Farnham's bosom, and he raised it as if intending to thrust it through his body, when Kendall rushed forward and wrenched the weapon away, cutting his own fingers in the operation. He then had a dirk in each hand, but made no use of them.

The combatants having separated, it appeared that nobody was seriously injured except Mr. Farnham. One of his shoulders was dislocated by his fall from the counter, and his eyes were badly gouged by Mr. Gerard. The only hurt received by Mr. Kendall was a slight scratch in the face.

In his next paper Mr. Farnham repeated his false statements, and pretended to have evidence of their truth in Mr. Kendall's private letters. Mr. Kendall asked leave to take copies of those letters, which was refused. He then announced the refusal, declared there could be no such evidence in the letters, as no such facts ever existed, and challenged Farnham to publish them. The latter published a few extracts torn from their context, and put upon them false constructions, which were dissipated by a few words of explanation. He was denounced for using private letters, written in the freedom and confidence of youthful friendship, and at the same time defied to publish them entire, as the best refutation of his own charges.

At length he announced in the "Commentator" that any person could see the letters by calling at his room. Though Mr. Kendall knew what he had not said in the letters touching the matters under discussion, he did not remember what he had said about other matters. At his request a friend of his called and read the whole series, and reported that they contained nothing which could do the writer any harm, while they did contain that which would subject Farnham to universal contempt. He had made Mr. Kendall a confidant in his love affair with Miss Alexander, and that was one of the subjects treated of in this correspondence in the lightest and freest manner.

In the mean time Farnham continued to abuse Mr. Kendall in the " Commentator," in language which the latter did not care to employ in his own columns ; but finding that the continued attacks were producing some effect upon a certain class of readers, he resorted to the expedient of retorting in letters addressed to his assailant by name, printed in handbills, and enclosed with their papers to all the subscribers of the " Argus." These letters were marvellous specimens of ridicule and blackguardism ; but they had their effect. The upshot was, that Mr. Farnham incurred the contempt of his own political friends as well as enemies ; was expelled from the Masonic lodge of which he was a member, compelled to abandon his editorial position, and, in effect, was driven from the State of Kentucky.

It is not often that men can be found so utterly destitute of gratitude, delicacy, and honor as was John H. Farnham. After the battle was over, and he had fled to Indiana, Mr. Kendall being at Cincinnati, was offered by his friend Guilford a letter from Farnham to him, in which the latter had asked him for any facts within his knowledge which he could use to Kendall's detriment. Mr. Kendall declined to accept the letter, or even to read it. In after years he had become a Mason, and twice Masons came to him, probably at Farnham's instance, and proposed a reconciliation. His answer was, in substance, that when a man had wronged him through misinformation, mistake, or in a passion, he could forgive him and become his friend ; but the deliberate attack of this man upon his intimate friend, and the means resorted to by him pending the controversy, proved him to be rotten at the heart. He had no feeling which would induce him to pursue the fugitive beyond the Ohio for the purpose of doing him an injury, but no friendly relation could ever exist between them.

In July, 1817, a concerted effort was made to injure the " Argus," on account of the course it was pursuing in relation to Mr. Pope and a new election, by inducing its subscribers to dis-

continue their papers. A batch of twenty in Shelby County discontinued at the same time. Mr. Kendall wrote to some of his friends in Lexington informing them what was going on and invoking their active support. His letter appeared to be misunderstood ; for the gentleman to whom it was addressed called a few days afterwards and offered him five hundred dollars in cash, which offer he at once declined, stating that the only assistance he could accept was through a *bond fide* increase of his subscription-list. He knew not how the money was to be raised, or who was to contribute it ; but his object in rejecting it was the maintenance of his entire independence of all pecuniary obligations in his editorial career. As soon as the concerted movement against his paper became generally known, he received four or five new subscribers for every one lost.

In reviewing the contest in 1817, after the election, the " Argus " spoke of the " Commentator " as " a corrupt Federal press, established for our destruction," etc. Soon after that number of the " Argus " which contained these words was issued Mr. Kendall was passing from his lodgings to his office, which were but a few yards apart, bareheaded, with an inkstand in his hand, when he met Bledsoe, who, without saying a word, knocked or pushed him down, and when he attempted to rise repeated the operation several times before he was arrested. Mr. Kendall was unarmed, and his assailant possessed twice his physical strength. It was remarkable that, with the exception of a slight soreness in the chest from a blow, the former was not hurt in the least.

A few days afterward, being on a visit to Scott County, he mentioned to Colonel James Johnson Bledsoe's attack and its result. The Colonel remarked that Bledsoe was not satisfied, and would certainly repeat the attack. On learning that Mr. Kendall did not carry arms, he induced him to accept a small pocket pistol, then out of order and having no flint in it, with the view of having it repaired and carrying it in his pocket. On Mr. Kendall's return, about three miles from Frankfort, in a lonely part of the road, he saw Bledsoe with a friend, both mounted, coming to meet him. As they approached he saw Bledsoe change positions with his friend, for the evident purpose of coming within striking distance ; but affected to take no notice of the movement. The horses were so near each other that their necks lapped, when both parties raised their whips, Bledsoe exclaiming " Don't you deserve a damned

whipping, you infernal rascal," and both struck. Startled by the noise of the whips, the horses shot by each other, and Mr. Kendall, looking back, saw that Bledsoe was wheeling his horse for the evident purpose of renewing the attack, when thrusting one hand in his pocket, by a sudden jerk with the other he wheeled his own horse, exclaiming, " I will give you a damned shooting, you infernal rascal." Bledsoe sheered off, and rode on.

The thought that a man of twice his strength, accompanied by another bully, should thus attempt to intercept and beat him on the highway, so exasperated Mr. Kendall, that for half a mile he was resolved that as soon as he got to town he would put his pistol in order and shoot Bledsoe on his return. But it then occurred to him that it would be a more satisfactory revenge to tell the story immediately on his arrival, showing his weapon, and thus preparing everybody to laugh at Bledsoe for running away from a disabled and empty pistol. The cowardly attack and the inglorious flight went far to destroy whatever respect the public had for Moses O. Bledsoe, and finally he also abandoned the " Commentator " and left the State.

The following is Mr. Kendall's opinion of himself, as deduced from these personal rencounters, and written down soon afterwards : —

" So far as these affairs have enabled me to know myself, my opinion is that I have not so much of the daring in me as some men, but that I have nothing of cowardice. I have not felt intimidated at the time of the attacks nor lost my presence of mind, and the most I fear from a repetition of them is the necessity of killing him. I would rather disarm and take a whipping, if that were safe or would be esteemed honorable."

The rules of conduct Mr. Kendall had prescribed to himself as an editor were, that he would never knowingly assert an untruth about men, measures, or things ; that if betrayed into one by misinformation or mistake, he would, as soon as correctly informed, retract it, whether requested by an injured party to do so or not ; that no threats or violence should induce him to retract any statement which he believed to be true ; that if insulted, he would return the insult in kind ; that if assaulted, he would defend himself by any means at hand, if necessary by taking the life of his assailant, but would sooner take a whipping than run when attacked. As to duelling, he would not say that nothing could induce him to

fight a duel, but he would state his conviction that anything which could justify him to himself in attempting to take the life of a man in a duel, would justify him in deliberately shooting down his adversary in the street. Guided by these rules, he was never challenged or insulted, except in newspaper paragraphs, for which he was able to retaliate in kind.

Mr. Kendall's first political campaign had ended in an overwhelming victory.

The House of Representatives, at the preceding session, had by a vote of sixty-one to twenty-six decided against a new election for a fractional term, and had thus, in a degree, prejudiced the public mind against the measure in any shape. He changed the issue to an election of a governor and lieutenant-governor for a full term, thus displacing the acting-governor ; and it was interesting to see with what facility the original supporters of a new election abandoned their own project and adopted his. In achieving this result, however, he had been essentially aided by the known opinions of George M. Bibb, then a lawyer of high standing, though the labor of the controversy was originally all his own. As it progressed, however, W. T. Barry, Jesse Bledsoe, and many other prominent men fell into the ranks and swelled the victorious host.

It was at first thought that so decisive a demonstration of public opinion would settle the question ; but doubts soon arose whether the Senate, but one fourth of whose members were elected annually, would yield to the popular will. In the hope of operating on that body, Mr. Kendall wrote and published a series of articles, entitled, " The Federalism of Kentucky," the object of which was to satisfy the members that it was their duty to obey or resign.

During the summer and fall of 1817 Mr. Kendall travelled but little, his presence being required at headquarters. On one of his brief excursions he made a visit to the venerable Isaac Shelby, one of the heroes of King's Mountain, in the Revolutionary War, who had been Governor of Kentucky, and then lived on a plantation in Lincoln County. The old man was still vigorous in body and mind, and was possessed of a fund of interesting facts touching the early history of Kentucky. Not far from his house was the Knob Lick, which was of itself a great curiosity. The Lick was an extensive excavation in the side of a hill, dug by the tongues of buffalo. The earth of which the hill was composed was impregnated with alum and salt. Thousands of buffalo had for ages

come there to lick, until they had dug away one side of the hill.
Governor Shelby said that for some time after his settlement in
Lincoln County he procured most of his meat in this spot. His
practice was to hide behind a tree upon the brow of the excavation, rifle in hand, and from the hundreds, and sometimes thousands, of animals collected below, select a young fat buffalo and
shoot him down. Sometimes he would take this position for
amusement, and, when multitudes had collected, would suddenly
show himself and throw a club among them, when the whole herd
would take to flight through the forest with a sound like distant
thunder, which could be heard for miles. When not in a panic,
the buffalo travelled slowly, in broad, beaten paths and in a direct
line, departed from only when they met insurmountable obstacles.
Though at this time not a buffalo was to be found in Kentucky,
one of their roads was still to be seen passing over the very summit of an adjacent knob; for, like many human road-makers, they
had not learned that it is often less laborious to go round a hill than
over it.

At the session of the legislature commencing in December, 1817,
the House of Representatives passed, by a vote of fifty-six to thirty,
an act providing for an election of a governor and lieutenant-
governor at the next general election, to be held in August, 1818;
but, as had been expected, the Senate refused to concur. Some of
the most ardent advocates of a new election proposed to hold one
without the sanction of the legislature, on the ground that it was
only the exercise of a constitutional right ; but the more moderate
of the party, including Mr. Kendall, thought that course too
hazardous to be adopted, and recommended that a further attempt
be made at the next election to secure a majority of the Senate.
Their counsels prevailed, and it was resolved again to submit the
issue to the people.

Mr. Kendall reported the proceedings of the legislature, including sketches of the leading speeches, and the editors of the "Argus"
were elected public printers.

During the spring and summer of 1818 the new election controversy was still carried on, but with less bitterness than in the
preceding year. The Democratic, or New Election Party, again
carried the House of Representatives by a large majority, but still
failed to secure a majority in the Senate.

CHAPTER VII.

IN the mean time a new question had arisen, which began to
engross the attention of the people. In 1811 Congress had refused to renew the charter of the Bank of the United States then
existing, on the ground that such an institution was incompatible
with the Constitution. The financial difficulties of the government, during the war of 1812 with Great Britain, and the suspension of specie payments by most of the State banks, induced
many patriotic men, originally opposed to a Bank of the United
States, to think such an institution necessary to regulate the currency and internal exchanges, and give additional financial and political strength to the government.

There were in 1812–14 other causes of the weakness of the
government than the want of such an institution. The restrictive policy of Jefferson's and Madison's administrations, adopted
and persisted in to prevent the United States from becoming involved in the war growing out of the French Revolution, had
crippled the trade of the country and alienated the commercial
interest which then held most of its available wealth. Had a
National Bank then existed, it would have been under the control
of men whose feelings and interests were averse to the war, and
instead of strengthening the government it might have added
greatly to its embarrassments. Experience has shown how falla-
cious is the idea of regulating the currency by means of a National
Bank. Indeed, the scheme of sustaining a paper currency of uniform value throughout a country so commercial and extensive as
the United States, is an absurdity. If there be a paper currency
equivalent to gold and silver at the commercial centres, as at New
York, it will be worth more than gold and silver at distant points,
as at Chicago and St. Louis. The obvious reason is, that the difference of exchange between distant points and New York is almost always in favor of that city, and bank-notes equal in value
there to specie can be transmitted more cheaply than gold and sil-

ver. They in fact answer the purpose of bills of exchange, and
will as naturally flow towards those points whence the merchants
derive their supplies of goods, as water runs to the ocean. In an
extensive commercial community, therefore, a paper currency of
equal value everywhere is impracticable. Most absurd is the attempt to establish such a currency in a country full of local banks,
whose notes, though equal to gold and silver in their own immediate neighborhood, are below the par of specie at the commercial
centres, and cannot be used as bills of exchange. It is a general
law of currency, that when two kinds of bank-notes, or any other
medium, exist together in the same community, the least valuable
is the most current. If a man have notes of several banks, which
he esteems of different values, he will first part with those which he
thinks least valuable ; and as every man acts upon the same principle, it happens that the less valuable currency has the greater
circulation. This law accounts for the fact that so little gold and
silver circulates in company with ordinary bank-notes. But let
bank-notes be issued in the interior which are everywhere equal to
specie, and they will at once disappear from circulation, because,
being available as exchange, they are in that locality worth more
than the local bank-notes or specie itself, and are hoarded for sale
or remittance. The result would be the same if there were no
local bank-notes in existence.

But not only was the country led to expect a paper currency
everywhere of equal value from a Bank of the United States, but
this institution was expected also to equalize the domestic exchanges, a process almost as difficult, if not so absurd. It would
involve the necessity of an organization with offices in every considerable city and town in the United States, with authority in
each to draw bills on every other office, and transmit specie to
meet constantly accruing balances. Could all the trade between
the different sections of the country be carried on both ways by
bills of exchange, there would be no necessity for any considerable
transportation of specie under ordinary circumstances. There is a
visible flow of funds in large volumes from the West to the East
for the purchase of commodities for Western consumption; yet the
West is not drained. The funds return, not in so grand a volume,
but still with certainty, to keep up the ever-running stream towards the East. The process may be compared to the perpetual
flow of the Mississippi River, ever draining the great West, which

yet is never drained, because that which we see departing in mighty
floods returns in dews, snowflakes, and raindrops. So the volume
of funds, which perpetually flows from the West to the East, is
fed by funds carried from the East to the West by emigration and
by the trade in horses, hogs, cattle, hemp, grain, and other
products. No doubt an organization is practicable which shall approximate an equalization of the exchanges between different sections of the country, requiring, under ordinary circumstances, very
little transportation of specie ; but how are its expenses to be paid,
and who is to guarantee the fidelity of such an army of officers
and agents as it would require ?

In April, 1816, an act of Congress was passed establishing a
Bank of the United States. The arguments in favor of such an
institution were as follows:—

1. That it would greatly facilitate the fiscal operations of the
Treasury of the United States.

2. That it would regulate the currency by compelling the State
banks to resume and continue specie-payment.

3. That it would equalize exchanges.

4. That it would furnish, in its notes, a currency everywhere in
the United States of uniform value.

In every one of these objects, except the first, the United States
Bank of 1816 was a total failure.

As the failure was perhaps more signal in Kentucky than anywhere else, its operations in that State, intimately connected as they
are with this narrative, will illustrate its operations elsewhere with
sufficient precision.

It not only failed in Kentucky as it did elsewhere "to regulate
the currency by compelling the State banks to resume and continue specie-payments," but it compelled the State banks to suspend specie-payments after they had resumed.

After the close of the war of 1812 with Great Britain, the Bank
of Kentucky went to work, honestly and earnestly, in curtailing
its issues, and in the spring of 1817 resumed the payment of
specie.

About the same time a branch of the Bank of the United States
began operations in Lexington, and subsequently another was located at Louisville. They issued very few notes, and such as they
did issue, instead of entering into general circulation, were snatched
up and sent East to pay for goods, the branches receiving the notes

of the Bank of Kentucky for exchange; in all their transactions they soon accumulated heavy balances, which that bank, not being able to obtain the notes of the branches, found it impossible to pay otherwise than with its specie. The withdrawal of its notes from circulation, first to enable it to resume specie-payments, and then to sustain it in that ability under the adverse operation of the United States branch banks, began to operate disastrously on the prices of property and the means of debtors to pay their debts, and a cry for relief went up to the legislature. It was answered at the session of 1817–18, by the establishment of forty-three independent banks, scattered over the whole State. Their aggregate capital was fixed at $ 5,670,000, to be composed of specie or the notes of the Bank of Kentucky. During the year 1818 about half of these banks went into operation, and threw out their notes. For the moment this measure gave an impulse to speculation, though it greatly aggravated the trouble which ensued. Men reasoned that the establishment of banks would enhance the value of property in the towns where they were located, and they made extensive purchases of town property, borrowing notes from the banks to make the first payment, and relying on sales at advanced prices to meet the subsequent ones, and to yield them a profit. The operation ended in the ruin of most of those who had embarked in it. The United States branch banks received the notes of such of the new banks as were convenient to them and were supposed to be prudently managed, thus restricting their issues as well as those of the Bank of Kentucky; while the unchecked independent banks threw out their notes in profusion, filling the State with a depreciated currency. The failure of the Bank of the United States to "regulate the currency" was now conspicuous. It checked banks which needed no check, forced them to take in their notes, and furnished no substitute, thus leaving the field of circulation to the inferior banks at home and in other States.

The Bank of the United States at first made an attempt to furnish a currency everywhere of uniform value, which was one of the principal objects of its creation. It received everywhere in deposits and payments the notes of the principal bank and all its branches. The consequence was that the notes of the Western branches, being remitted Eastward as exchange, accumulated in the principal bank and Eastern branches, raising balances against the Western branches which at that time they had no means of

discharging otherwise than by the transportation of specie. About $ 20,000,000 of the capital of the bank consisted of United States five and six per cent stocks, and upwards of eight millions of stock notes fraudulently received by the bank in lieu of the payment of specie upon original subscriptions to the stock required by the charter. Its specie capital was, therefore, very small, though augmented by specie imported from abroad, to the amount of about $ 7,300,000 ; and having lost credit by fraudulent management, it became necessary to the preservation of its existence to call on the Western branches for payment of their balances.

In April, 1817, after the resumption of specie payments, the notes of the Bank of Kentucky in circulation, exclusive of its branches, amounted to $ 417,000. In November, 1818, its notes in circulation had been reduced to $ 195,000. At the latter date the Bank of Kentucky and branches were indebted to the United States branch banks $ 409,000. To maintain specie payments, the Bank of Kentucky in 1817 imported from the East and from New Orleans $ 240,000 in specie. As this bank was unable to meet the balances accruing against it in the United States branch banks, with unexpected rapidity, they had been suffered to accumulate on payment of interest ; but in November, 1819, the branches received peremptory instructions from Philadelphia to stop the interest account and collect the sums due without delay. It followed that the Bank of Kentucky suspended specie payments. But upon an agreement of the United States branch banks to receive payment in instalments of ten per cent every sixty days, one half in specie and the other in Eastern exchange, with interest on the amounts due, the Kentucky Bank resumed payment, having been in a state of suspension but a few days.

Soon afterwards, the directors of the Bank of the United States ordered their Western branches to receive in their business no currency but gold and silver and their own notes ; and about the same time ceased receiving their own notes from their private customers except at the offices whence they had been issued.

This course would have reduced the notes of the branches to a level with those of the specie-paying State banks in their vicinity, but for the fact that they were everywhere receivable for public dues, which gave them universal credit and rendered them still available as exchange. Of course, the notes of the branches still disappeared as fast as issued, and added nothing to the local cur-

rency of the country. Nor did the order not to receive the notes of the local specie-paying banks afford them any sensible relief. It merely compelled the customers of the branch banks to draw the specie from the State banks themselves for the purpose of paying balances and purchasing exchange, instead of using the local currency for these purposes, so that the drain of specie from the State banks continued as heavy as before. The Bank of Kentucky struggled manfully against this adverse current, but in vain. The immense diminution of the circulating medium had acted disastrously on the prices of property and on every department of trade, so that the banks found it impossible to collect the debts due them with sufficient expedition to meet their rapidly returning circulation, and general panic pervaded the public mind.

The United States branch banks in the West had been ordered to retrench their line of discounts twenty-five per cent ; but it was impossible to execute the order except to a very moderate extent. The Bank of the United States itself, owing to mismanagement and abuse, was on the brink of ruin, and was pressing its Western branches for remittances in specie, and while those branches were wagoning specie to the East, the Bank of Kentucky was wagoning it to the West to fortify its position. On one occasion it was said that wagons thus freighted passed each other on the Alleghany mountains.

At a meeting of the stockholders of the Bank of Kentucky, held on the 4th of May, 1820, a poll was opened in favor of and against the suspension of specie payments, and the question was decided in the affirmative by a large majority. On the same evening the directors voted unanimously to carry the resolution into effect, and the vaults of the bank were closed to the public, never again to be opened.

It was thus that the Bank of the United States checked the State bank and regulated the currency of Kentucky! It found there a sound local currency, issued by a bank managed with signal caution, ability, and skill. It was mainly instrumental in driving that currency out of circulation without furnishing a substitute, and compelling the bank which issued it to stop payment. Its branches continued to exist in Kentucky ; but with no more power to control the local banks and restore a sound currency than stranded whales have to control the motions of the little fishes which swim around them.

The Legislature of Kentucky, influenced, as most legislatures are upon such subjects, by men who wish to borrow money, had invited the Bank of the United States to locate branches in that State ; but like the poor frogs, at whose request Jupiter sent them a king in the shape of a serpent, the people soon began to repent the rash act of their servants. The first movement in any way hostile to the bank was an act of the legislature, passed at the session of 1817 – 18, imposing an annual tax of $ 8,000 each on the United States branch banks, estimated to be equal in proportion to the capital employed to that imposed on the Bank of Kentucky. This act imposed heavy penalties on the officers of the branches in case they refused to pay the tax. Their refusal was a matter of course, and the State commenced suit in its own courts for the recovery of the penalties.

In January, 1819, the Legislature of Kentucky passed an act imposing a tax of $ 60,000 each on the United States branch banks in that State, and requiring the sergeant of the Court of Appeals to collect it in a summary manner. The avowed object was to drive them out of the State. The banks, however, obtained from the judges of the United States Circuit Court an injunction to restrain the sergeant from executing the act of the legislature. In this condition was the controversy with the Bank of the United States in Kentucky when the Supreme Court of the United States, in the case of McCulloch *vs.* The State of Maryland, decided that the bank was constitutional, and that the States had no right to tax it.

In the mean time the suits commenced by the State for the recovery of the penalties imposed by the tax law of 1817 – 18 had been taken up to the Court of Appeals of Kentucky, where they were argued in the latter part of May, 1819. In December, 1819, the court, consisting of Judges John Boyle, William Owsley, and John Rowan, announced their decision, which was to the following effect : —

The judges were unanimous in the opinion that the Bank of the United States was unconstitutional, and on that account the State had a right to tax it and enforce the collection of the tax. Judges Owsley and Rowan were of the opinion that if the bank were constitutional the States would still have a right to tax it, from which opinion Judge Boyle dissented.

Judges Boyle and Owsley were of the opinion that the decision of the United States Supreme Court, in the case of McCulloch *vs.* The State of Maryland, affirming the constitutionality of the bank and denying the right of the States to tax it, was conclusive upon the State courts; from which opinion Judge Rowan dissented, maintaining that it was the duty of the court to sustain the State in the exercise of its admitted right, in order that the subject might be again carried up to the Supreme Court, thus giving that tribunal an opportunity to reconsider the whole subject.

Thus ended the efforts of Kentucky to enforce her taxing power upon the branches of the United States Bank located within her borders.

In the mean time, the State of Ohio had laid a tax of $100,000 on the branches of the Bank of the United States in that State, which, in September, 1819, was summarily collected. The bank commenced a suit or suits against the officers of the State in the United States Court, the result of which was that the United States Marshal, under the authority of the court, entered the treasury of the State, seized the money, and replaced it in the United States branch bank at Chillicothe, whence it had been taken.

Although the people of the West with almost entire unanimity believed the bank unconstitutional, and that the power of the States to tax its business, its stock, its income, and all its property was clearly within the reservations of the Constitution, yet they were not prepared to resist the United States tribunals by force, and concluded to await the peaceful remedies provided by our institutions.

The opposition of Mr. Kendall to the Bank of the United States began in 1818, when it was not yet two years old, and ceased only with its prostration under the giant blows of President Jackson, aided by its own corruptions. The complaints made by himself and many others about the management of the bank were met by an illiberal reply and defence of that management in the "Kentucky Reporter," published in Lexington, over the signature of "Sertorius." To his strictures Mr. Kendall began a rejoinder in the "Argus" of the 13th of November, 1818, over the signature of "Cato." These articles brought down upon him fierce denunciations from the newspapers which sustained the cause of the bank. He was called "a political incendiary," attempting "to produce civil commotion," guilty of "a base and open endeavor to

excite actual warfare between the State of Kentucky and the Government of the United States," etc., etc.

In his paper of the 12th of March Mr. Kendall indignantly repelled this charge.

In his next issue was announced the "momentous decision of the Supreme Court of the United States affirming the constitutionality of the Bank of the United States, and denying the right of the States to tax it."

In his paper of the 7th of May Mr. Kendall commenced a review of this decision in a series of eleven articles, showing what were then and ever have been his views in regard to the relative rights and powers of the several States and the United States, as well as the importance of preserving them as adjusted in the Constitution.

In No. 2 Mr. Kendall contests the argument of the Supreme Court deduced from the fact that a national bank had been established early in the history of the government, and that the principle had been recognized by many successive legislatures and acted upon in the judicial department in cases of peculiar delicacy "as a law of undoubted obligation." The force of this argument was denied, as well as its applicability to a popular government, where it is the province of popular opinion, operating through the right of suffrage, to reverse precedents set by their rulers, correct their abuses, and put a stop to their usurpations. It is sometimes a slow remedy, as in the case of the old Bank of the United States, in which it was many years before the popular voice could reach the subject through Congress, and when it did, justice to the stockholders of the bank who had, under the faith of the government, vested their funds in it, required that it should be permitted to live out its corporate term of existence. But by the refusal of Congress, on constitutional grounds, to re-charter the bank, the precedent set by its original incorporation was reversed, and its authoritative character destroyed.

He then shows that a proposed grant of power to Congress to establish corporations was directly negatived by the convention which framed the Constitution, and that in the discussions which preceded its adoption in the press and in the State conventions, the idea was never broached by its bitterest enemies or most ardent friends, that the new government would have power to establish banks or any other corporations. These facts were deemed con-

clusive evidence that neither the framers of the Constitution nor the people who adopted it ever imagined that Congress would possess any such power, and its assumption was ascribed to the disposition evinced by the leaders of the Federal party to enlarge the powers of the general government and restrict those of the States by implication.

No. 3 combats a position assumed by the Supreme Court, that the Constitution derived its authority from the people of the United States in mass, and shows that it was adopted by "each State or the people of each State, *acting for themselves only.*" It is shown that although an immense majority of the people inhabiting the United States had voted in favor of the Constitution, it could never have been binding on anybody until ratified "by the conventions of nine States," not by a majority of the aggregate people of nine States, and that if ratified by the unanimous vote of the whole people in all the States, except Rhode Island, it would not have acquired the least authority over the people of that State without their separate consent. The phrase, "We, the people of the United States," with which the Constitution commences, does not refer to the people of the United States *previously existing,* but to the people of *the United States then proposed to be formed;* and had only nine States ratified the Constitution, it would have included only the people of those nine States.

Its application was prospective, not retrospective: the people adopting it were not "people of the United States" until nine States had concurred, and had it not been ratified by that number of States, there would never have been a "people of the United States" within its true meaning. That the Constitution derives its authority from the States, and not from a majority of the people of the United States, is illustrated by the progressive manner in which it was adopted, by the mode of admission of new States, and by the process through which amendments are adopted, in all of which the people act by States, and not by a majority of the whole mass.

Nor is our government one of a popular majority of "the people of the United States" as created by the Constitution. While the House of Representatives approximates a representation of a majority of the people, the Senate is a representation of the States, in which the smallest has the same power as the largest, and no act of legislation can pass without the concurrence of a

majority of both. Nor is the President elected by a popular majority in which all the people of the United States have an equal voice; for, as the number of electors of President and Vice-President assigned to each State is equal to its representation in both Houses of Congress, it results that, everything else being equal, the voter in the smallest State has more than double the weight in electing the President and Vice-President of a voter in the largest State.

Neither in its origin nor in practice, therefore, is the government of the United States the government of a popular majority. In its origin the Constitution was a compact between States in their sovereign capacity, each agreeing with the rest to vest a portion of their powers in a common government. The very nature of the transaction required that the powers of this government should be accurately defined, for it was necessary that the United States should know what powers they possessed, and that the States should know what powers they had left.

No. 4 adverts to the inconsistency of the court in declaring that "the government is acknowledged by all to be one of enumerated powers," and admitting that "among the enumerated powers we do not find that of establishing a bank or establishing a corporation," and yet maintaining that such an act is constitutional.

It treats the provision in the Constitution authorizing Congress to pass all laws necessary and proper to carry into effect the enumerated powers, as unnecessary, if construed as an enlargement of their powers, being a grant of incidental powers.

The words, "all legislative powers herein *granted* shall be vested in a Congress of the United States," are quoted, and it is argued, that they necessarily imply a definite description of the powers granted, as such description is an essential part of every grant. The idea is illustrated by reference to grants of land described in deeds, and to powers in a letter of attorney. There must be a grantor and a grantee and a thing granted. The grantor must design to part with the thing granted, and the grantee must be willing to accept it. There can, therefore, be no such thing as implied powers in a constitution based exclusively on granted powers.

Attention is called to the argument of the court based on the omission of the word "expressly" before the word "delegated" in the tenth amendment to the Constitution, which declares that "the powers not delegated to the United States by this Constitu-

14

tion, nor prohibited by it to the States, are reserved to the States respectively, or to the people," and it is maintained that the avowed object of this amendment (which was more effectually to confine Congress to the granted powers), as well as the relation which the word "delegated" occupies in reference to the reserved powers of the States or the people, gives it precisely the same meaning as if it had been preceded by the word "expressly." How else can the reserved powers of the States or the people be ascertained? To know what is reserved we must know what is delegated, and how can we know what is delegated unless we can find it expressly granted in the Constitution?

The plan of the Constitution which divides the powers of government into two classes, the "granted " and the "reserved," is wholly incompatible with the idea of implied powers among the granted, and if by the omission of the word "expressly" in the tenth amendment it was intended to leave the way open for Congress to assume implied powers, and thus encroach upon the reserved powers of the States or the people, it was an imposition and a fraud.

No. 5 quotes the objections to the Constitution by Patrick Henry in the Virginia Convention, based on the prohibitions contained in the ninth section, which, he maintained, might be construed to authorize the exercise by Congress of all powers not expressly prohibited, and although this construction was repelled by its friends, it is now revived by Chief Justice Marshall, himself one of those friends, in the argument which he deduces from that section. This number concluded as follows: —

"Let us guard against the doctrine of implied powers, — guard against this opinion of the Supreme Court. The establishment of a national bank is as nothing compared with the powers which may be exercised under the protecting wing of this decision. The mind is lost in the confused multitude of implications passing before it, — mere phantoms in the opinions of good, easy politicians, but which may hereafter assume a form and substance as terrible to the government of the States as they are now unexpected in the minds of the people.

"The principle is determined, the foundation is laid, and unless the people resist, nothing is wanting to complete the work but a bold, energetic, skilful, and persevering master."

No. 6 is devoted to the examination of the argument of the Court, that the word "necessary," in the grant of power to Congress

to pass all laws "necessary and proper" to carry into effect the enumerated powers, does not mean "absolutely necessary," but only convenient, useful, or conducive to the end.

The word, says the court, "admits of all degrees of comparison": "a thing may be necessary, very necessary, absolutely or indispensably necessary."

To illustrate their argument they say: —

"It is, we think, impossible to compare the sentence which prohibits the laying of imposts or duties on imports or exports, except what may be *absolutely* necessary for executing its inspection laws, with that which authorizes Congress to pass all laws necessary and proper for carrying into execution the powers of the general government, without feeling a conviction that the convention understood itself to change materially the meaning of the word *necessary* by prefixing the word *absolutely*."

The reviewer proceeds to show that the difference is one of form rather than substance. It is not "absolutely necessary" to the execution of their inspection laws that the States should lay any duties at all on imports or exports ; for they might pay the expenses out of their ordinary revenues. If, therefore, this be a case of the superlative degree of necessity, as represented by the court, the States have no power to lay any such duties at all; for they are not *indispensable* to the execution of the inspection laws. It follows that "absolutely necessary" does not mean indispensable, but only "convenient" in the same sense which the court attaches to the word "necessary" in its most mitigated sense. In this case, however, the phrase "absolutely necessary" has reference only to the amount of money to be raised to pay the expenses of inspection ; and whether the word "necessary" be used with or without the prefix "absolutely," the meaning is precisely the same, its only effect being to express it more emphatically.

The court furnished a list of what they called the exercise of implied powers, not indispensably necessary, exercised by Congress under the grant to pass all laws "necessary and proper," etc. The court says: —

"The power to establish post-offices and post-roads is executed by the single act of making the establishment. But from this has been inferred the power and duty of carrying the mail along the post-road from one post-office to another. And from the implied power has again been inferred the right to punish those who steal letters from the post-office

or rob the mail. It may be said, with some plausibility, that the right to carry the mail, and to punish those who rob it, is not indispensably necessary to the existence of a post-office or a post-road. This right is indeed essential to the beneficial exercise of the power, but not indispensably necessary to its existence."

This example given by the court is most replete with sophistry, and most unfortunate for their argument. They say, "The power to carry the mail along the post-roads from one post-office to another is a power implied from the express power to establish post-offices and post-roads." Wonderful ingenuity! Miraculous skill in dividing things which are indivisible, — in splitting things which are unsplitable! Never till this elaborate opinion met the eyes of a wondering world, did the humble citizens of this Republic for one moment imagine that a *quality* could exist without *substance*, — that a *post-road* could exist without a *post*. As well might we attempt to make a man tailor without a man, a veteran army without veterans, a winged animal without wings, a wheeled carriage without wheels, a steamboat without steam, a stone-wall without stones, or a wise judge without wisdom! True, the government may designate a road and call it a post-road. So they may pass an act to raise an army and call it an army. But, nevertheless, the one is not a post-road until the post travels upon it, nor is the other an army until the men are enlisted. The *road* and the *post* make up the *post-road*. There might be a *post-road* without a road as well as without a *post*. The two ideas are inseparable. A grant of power to send a post would include the power to send it along the *roads* of a country; so, on the other hand, the grant of a power to establish a *post-road* includes the power to send the *post* along it. The same argument will apply to post-offices. Without a post there can be no post-office.

No. 7 criticises the positions of the court in maintaining, *first*, that without the constitutional grant to Congress of the power to pass all laws "necessary and proper" to carry into effect the enumerated powers, the power of Congress in the selection of means to that end would have been unlimited ; *secondly*, that its terms purport to enlarge, not to diminish, the powers vested in the government ; and, *thirdly*, that if it do not enlarge it cannot be construed to restrain the powers of Congress, all of which, taken together, it is maintained, leads to the logical conclusion that this provision in the Constitution means nothing at all!

After further strictures on the positions of the court, the reviewer proceeds to state what are his own views touching the meaning of the word "necessary" in this connection, as follows: —

"From the preceding remarks it is evident that the word 'necessary,' as applied to Congress in the passage of laws, must restrict them to the passage of those only which shall *necessarily* and *exclusively* tend to the execution of some power vested in that body. They have under this word a choice of means ; but the means chosen must conduce to the execution of their delegated powers, *exclusively* and *entirely*. They cannot rightfully pass a law which only in part tends to the execution of their powers ; the part which might not have this tendency would be unconstitutional and void. They have no right to pass laws which shall only incidentally and not necessarily tend to their object. They cannot rightfully use as means anything which has no necessary connection with the end ; much less can they bring under the denomination of *means* those things which may exist in the same shape, and operate on the community entirely independent of the end, and after it has been accomplished.

"The word 'proper' means that the laws which Congress may rightfully pass, in carrying into effect their delegated powers, must be such as do not violate the rights of any State or individual.

"The phrase 'necessary and proper' means that the laws passed must *necessarily* and *exclusively* conduce to the execution of a delegated power, and at the same time *not violate the rights of any State or individual*. It was used *to restrict Congress in the choice of means*, and prevent the assumption of new powers under the pretence of using them as the means of executing those which were actually delegated. This clause illustrates in the most powerful manner the intention of the parties to the national compact ; it tells us that Congress is not only limited in its powers, but also in the means of carrying them into execution. Nothing was left to implication, — *the incidental powers* as well as the principal, the *means* as well as the *ends*, are expressly granted, carefully restricted, and accurately defined in the expressions of the Constitution."

The reviewer then shows that the court appeared to attach no significance to the word "proper," with which "necessary" stands connected, and proceeds to give his own view of its meaning in the following words: —

"However 'necessary' a law might be, yet if it violated any State or individual rights it would not be 'proper,' and Congress would have no right to pass it. This is the obvious meaning of the word as used in the Constitution. If it meant merely *appropriate*, it would be superfluous; for that idea is contained in the word 'necessary,' whether it means convenient or something more. That a convention used the word without any meaning at all, or without intending that it should have some effect in defining the character of the laws which Congress might pass, is a supposition not admissible. To add a word without any meaning at all, or to take away the meaning of another, would indeed be an 'extraordinary departure from the usual course of the human mind as exhibited in composition,' especially when the latter word is coupled with the former and made a part of the same definition. The laws which Congress pass must not only be 'necessary' but 'proper' also. However 'necessary' a law may be, yet, if it be not 'proper,' Congress has no right to pass it. They must seek other means to execute the delegated powers, and pass laws which are *both necessary and proper*, or if no such law can be framed, then the delegated power cannot be executed. The word 'proper,' then, instead of enlarging the power granted by the word 'necessary,' actually restricts it, and confines Congress to still narrower limits.

"For example, Congress has a right to lay taxes on land, and the States have the same right. Both might exercise that power, and it might become absolutely *necessary* for the collection of the national tax that Congress should pass a law abrogating the State tax; but such a law would not be 'proper,' because it would violate the rights of the State.

"It might be absolutely necessary for the 'common defence' that a fort should be built on some spot of ground within a State; but Congress cannot purchase land for that purpose without the consent of the State. However urgent the necessity, if the State should refuse its consent, Congress could pass no law authorizing the land to be purchased and the fort to be built, because the act would violate a right reserved to the State; it would not be 'proper.'"

No. 8 contains an application of the principles developed in the preceding numbers to the case of the Bank of the United States.

It is not denied that Congress has a choice of means in the exercise of their enumerated powers; but those means must be "necessary and proper." That is to say, they must tend necessarily and exclusively to the execution of the delegated power, and at the same time must not infringe upon any right "reserved to the States or the people."

The argument in support of the constitutionality of the Bank of the United States is, that it is a necessary auxiliary of the treasury in managing the finances of the government.

The reviewer proceeds to show that the bank had no agency in assessing or collecting the revenues of the United States, whether from direct taxes, excises, or imposts. The only duty as an auxiliary to the treasury is specified in its charter, by which it is bound, when required by the Secretary of the Treasury, "to give the necessary facilities for transferring the public funds from place to place within the United States and the Territories thereof, and for distributing the same in payment of the public creditors, without charging commission or claiming allowance on account of difference of exchange, and shall also do and perform the several and respective duties of Commissioners of Loans for the several States, or any one or more of them, whenever required by law." These are all the acts which the bank is bound to perform as an auxiliary to the Treasury, and even these are contingent. If they shall not be *required* by the Secretary of the Treasury, or by law, the bank stands as disconnected from the government as any State bank. That government must, in the exercise of its powers, act through agents, is admitted; but it cannot therefore clothe its agents with powers wholly outside of the legitimate ends proposed to be accomplished. It may employ State banks or individuals to transfer the public funds; but it does not follow that they can enlarge the power of the State banks employed by it, or confer powers of banking on individuals. The government might make with an individual the same arrangement for the transfer and distribution of its funds as it made with the Bank of the United States, without its being "necessary" or "proper" to clothe him with power to issue his notes, build banking-houses, discount paper, buy and sell real estate, etc., etc. But if they could not constitutionally confer these extensive powers on an individual, whence the authority to confer them on any number of individuals associated for the same purpose?

The reviewer enumerates the powers conferred on the bank by its charter, and maintains that not one of them is "necessary" to the transfer of the public funds or the discharge of the duties of Commissioner of Loans. They all look to other objects having none, or if any, the most remote bearing on the business of the government.

The position of the court is, that the bank is the "necessary and proper" means of the government for executing the powers delegated to it by the Constitution. If this be true, it presents the

anomaly of a government raising a revenue by *taxing its own means!* At the start, it exacted a bonus from the bank of *a million and a half of dollars*. What was this for? Was it for services rendered by the bank to the government, or for favors extended by the government to the bank? If the former, it presents the anomaly of a government taxing its agents for the privilege of serving it; if the latter, it is conclusive evidence that Congress, in conferring such enormous powers upon the bank, had something in view besides the service of the government.

Though the power of Congress to create a corporation for any purpose, except in the District of Columbia, is denied, the reviewer assumes, for the sake of argument, that Congress may give corporate powers to its own agents or employees. Yet he maintains that they cannot, by such an expedient, enlarge the powers of the government. The corporate powers must be such only as an individual would possess if employed for the same purpose.

To illustrate: If Congress should deem it "necessary and proper" to create a corporation as means of executing the power "to establish post-offices and post-roads," they could not confer on such corporations powers which they do not themselves possess. The aggregate powers of the postmaster-general, deputy postmasters, and contractors might be vested in the corporate body; but does it follow that because they *use* roads, Congress could clothe them with power to *make* roads? Or because they use leather, they may make money by buying and selling leather? Or because horses, wagons, and stages are used by them, they confer on them power to make and sell them for profit? Or because they use blanks, they may establish and publish a newspaper? Or because they collect and transfer post-office funds, they may exercise all the powers vested in the Bank of the United States? The idea is preposterous. If corporations are to be used as means of executing the granted powers of Congress, they must, like other means, be "necessary and proper," tending *exclusively* to the end sought to be accomplished.

In No. 9 the reviewer undertakes to show particular cases in which the act establishing the bank is unconstitutional.

First. Congress has conferred on the bank powers which it does not itself possess. By the Constitution, Congress cannot purchase land within the States, for any purpose, without their consent, and, even with their consent, only "for the erection of forts, magazines,

arsenals, dockyards, and other needful buildings." Now the seventh section of the bank charter authorizes that institution, without the consent of the States, to purchase and sell "lands, rents, tenements, hereditaments," and the seventh clause of the eleventh section declares that the "lands, tenements, and hereditaments" which it may lawfully hold shall be only such as may be necessary for the convenient transaction of its business, or such as may be acquired in payment of debts. The bank, therefore, whether considered as the agent of the government or not, is authorized to purchase lands, not only without the consent of the States, but for other purposes than those only for which the government may make such purchases.

Secondly. If the opinion of the court be correct, Congress has bartered away a portion of its constitutional powers. If one bank be a "necessary and proper" means of executing its delegated powers, circumstances might make it equally "necessary and proper" to establish one or more additional banks. But the twentieth section of the charter requires the bank to pay the government a million and a half of dollars as a bonus, and the twenty-first pledges the faith of the United States that "no other bank shall be established by any future law of the United States during the continuance of the corporation hereby created." These provisions imply that Congress had power to establish other banks, but sold that power to the corporation then created. If, therefore, banks are "necessary and proper" means of executing the powers delegated to Congress, that body has sold a portion of its constitutional power to the Bank of the United States.

Thirdly. If the opinion of the court be correct, the act of Congress establishing the bank withdraws from the States a legitimate object of State taxation. The elucidation of this point is, however, deferred to the next number.

No. 10. The argument in this number may be summed up as follows: —

The States, before the adoption of the Constitution, enjoyed an unlimited power of taxation over persons, property, business, income, and every conceivable object from which a revenue can be collected.

Banking is a business, the right to pursue which is not originally derived from the laws, but belongs to every man in the community who chooses to pursue it. Until the law stepped in, and, from motives of public policy, took away the right, any man or association of men might establish a bank, and use their credit in the circulation of their notes as a currency as widely as their fellow-citizens chose to receive them.

Bank charters are, in their nature, but the restoration and regulation of the exercise of the right which had been previously taken away.

Before the adoption of the Constitution, the entire control of the banking business, with an unlimited power to tax it, belonged to the States. Did they give up the power to regulate or tax it by the adoption of the Constitution? Or if (as is denied) the power to regulate it in its bearings on the powers expressly granted to Congress is incidentally delegated, can the United States constitutionally exempt it from State taxation?

In adopting the Constitution, the States reserved to themselves or the people every power not by that instrument delegated to the United States. It follows, that the right to tax the business of banking carried on within their borders is reserved to the States in the most unlimited manner. Nor can it be taken away or infringed by means of the incidental power vested in Congress to pass all laws which may be "necessary and proper" to carry into effect their delegated powers; for however "necessary" it might be considered, it would not be "proper," because it would infringe upon the reserved powers of the States. To maintain that the reserved powers of the States can be swallowed up as a means of executing the powers granted to Congress, is not a whit sounder reasoning than to say that the States, in the exercise of their reserved powers, can nullify a power expressly granted to Congress. The one is just as sacred as the other, and not more so.

It is admitted that the States cannot tax the agents or the operations of the general government in their public character. They cannot tax a postmaster or a custom-house officer as such; but they may tax his poll as a citizen, and his business if a banker. Nor can Congress relieve the one or the other from State taxation because the party may be employed by the United States to perform certain public duties which cannot be taxed. Apply this principle to the bank. Admit that in its capacity as agent of the government for the transfer of its funds, and performing the duties of commissioners of loans, it cannot be taxed by the States, does it follow that they cannot tax it *as a bank?* If they cannot tax the

bank's *public* business, does it follow that they cannot tax its *private* business?

The reviewer contests the conclusion of the Supreme Court deduced from the provision of the Constitution, which declares that the laws of Congress and the treaties passed or negotiated in pursuance of that instrument, shall be "the supreme laws of the land," maintaining that this supremacy attaches not to every act which Congress may think fit to pass, but only to such as may in their application be confined exclusively to the execution of their own delegated powers, and do not infringe upon the reserved rights of the States or the people. He also contests the application which the court makes of this general principle to the case before them, which is in effect, that, *when a law of any State imposing a tax so operates as to defeat the operation of any law of Congress, such State law is null and void.* He shows that this position is not correct as a general proposition, even where both laws are constitutional, because on some subjects the powers of the States and of the United States are *concurrent* and *coequal.* The article concludes as follows: —

"The truth is, that the States have rights as well as the nation. Both are supreme to the extent of their powers. The national government is supreme over all the powers granted to it in the Constitution, and the necessary and proper means of carrying them into execution, subject, however, to any modifications and limitations therein prescribed. The States are supreme over all the powers reserved by them when they adopted the Constitution, and over the means of carrying them into execution; subject, however, to any modifications which may be prescribed in that instrument. Each has distinct powers, over which the other has no control. Each is supreme over its peculiar powers, and an attempt to control it in their exercise is an usurpation. There are some cases of concurrent powers. With respect to these the powers are *equal.* Neither is supreme over the other. Neither can control the other. Both are supreme over the object on which their powers are exercised; both have the right to dispose of it according to their will; but neither has the right to wrest it from the hands of the other. They may take it from any other hands, but not from the hands of an equal. During war, the several States have a right to raise and support armies, and so has the nation. These are concurrent and coequal powers. The States cannot prohibit the nation from executing this power, nor the nation the States. Both of them are supreme over the materials of which armies are composed, but neither of them are supreme over the other; and

when the materials are appropriated to the use of the one, they are not subject to the powers of the other, but become a part of the government or sovereignty which uses them. By this process, and no other, are these materials withdrawn from the supremacy of either party. Over the remainder, the State or national sovereignty remains unimpaired; or, if there be no remainder, no army can be raised, and the power cannot be executed. Such is the idea always entertained by the warmest advocates and supporters of our national Constitution.

"Among the concurrent and coequal powers of the State and national government is that of taxation. To the concurrency and coequality of this power there is but one exception, — the States cannot tax imports, and the nation can. Exports can be taxed by neither. Every other object of taxation is common to both parties. The power to lay and collect taxes over every other object is supreme and uncontrollable in both governments. If both tax, and the collection of its tax by one party absorb the property, it is as if it had been destroyed by fire. If anything remain, the other party may collect their tax; if not, they must lose it. They have no more power to wrest the property from the hands of each other than from fire, storms, and earthquakes. It is an authority above their control, beyond their reach, independent and supreme.

"Hence it follows that the States are just as supreme in levying and collecting taxes from all objects which they have reserved the right of taxing, as the national government itself."

This conclusion, so plainly deducible from the nature and expressions of the Constitution, was long since ably defended by *Alexander Hamilton*, in the "Federalist." To show the opinion of that *rigidly Federal* statesman, we subjoin the following extracts from his writings: —

"I affirm," says he, "that (with the sole exception of duties on imports and exports) they (the States) would, under the plan of the convention, retain that authority in *the most absolute and unqualified sense*; and that an attempt on the part of the national government to abridge them in the exercise of it, *would be a violent assumption of power unwarranted by any article or clause of the Constitution.* Though a law levying a tax for the use of the United States would be supreme in its nature, and could not legally be opposed or controlled; yet a law abrogating or preventing the collection of a tax laid by the authority of a State (unless upon imports and exports), would not be the supreme law of the land, but an usurpation of a power not granted by the Constitution.

"The inference from the whole is, that the individual States would,

under the proposed Constitution, retain an *independent and uncontrollable* authority to raise revenue, to any extent of which they may stand in need, by *every kind of taxation*, except duties on imports and exports.

"The particular States under the proposed Constitution would have coequal authority with the Union in the article of revenue, except as to duties on imports.

"There is no power on either side to annul the acts of the other."

These quotations are sufficient to show that Hamilton's opinion on this subject was variant from that of the Supreme Court. If Hamilton was wrong, the people were deceived into the adoption of a Constitution which they did not understand.

From what has been said, we think it sufficiently evident that, with respect to taxation, the States possess a power as independent and as supreme over the objects which they have reserved the right of taxing as that possessed by the national government. *Banking* being one of these objects, it follows that they have, in the language of Hamilton, "*An absolute and unqualified, an independent and uncontrollable authority*" to tax banking by "*every kind of taxation*," and "*that an attempt on the part of the national government to abridge them in the exercise of it*," is a "*violent usurpation of power, unwarranted by any article or clause in the Constitution.*"

No. 11, and last, is chiefly confined to illustration of the arguments advanced in the preceding numbers. The following passages are quoted: —

"To conclude. Instead of turning bankers, let Congress confine themselves to the powers delegated in the Constitution, and the means which tend *exclusively* to their execution. Let them not attempt to protect, under the wing of national supremacy, *the business, the property, or the stock* of our citizens from State taxation.

"The States reserved the right *to tax that business* when they adopted the Constitution. They cannot rightfully be deprived of it without an amendment to that instrument. But as the attempt by Congress has been sanctioned by judicial authority, we now have no remedy but a peaceful acquiescence and a speedy amendment to the Constitution. TAKE FROM CONGRESS THE ASSUMED POWER OF ESTABLISHING A BANK. It will deprive the national government of *no power*, of *no means* which they rightfully possess; but will wrest from their grasp a *new power*, a *private business*, which they have assumed the right of protecting under the pretence of its being the 'necessary and proper' means for the execution of their powers. It will put the two sovereignties on their original footing, and confine them to their legitimate powers and proper means.

"Should the broad principles advanced by the court hereafter be made the foundation of other usurpations, the States will be awake to a vindication of their rights."

We are now done.

It is not on account of the particular question which then agitated the country that so much attention has been bestowed on Mr. Kendall's review of the decision of the Supreme Court. The object is to show, *first*, the views then entertained by him in relation to the nature of our government, and the only safe and just rule of constitutional construction; *secondly*, his devotion to the Union, which he would not even hazard by anything looking towards forcible resistance to what he considered a most dangerous usurpation of the general government, subversive of a clearly reserved and most important right of the States, upon a principle which placed all their reserved rights at the mercy of Congress; and, *thirdly*, that his opposition to the Bank of the United States, which many years afterwards became somewhat effective, originated in motives higher than party spirit, self-interest, or personal ambition. No immediate effect was known to be produced by these articles, and none was expected. They probably had some influence upon the minds of the judges of the Kentucky Court of Appeals, who subsequently, notwithstanding the argument of the United States Supreme Court, were unanimous in the opinion that the bank was unconstitutional, though a majority of them deemed the decision of that court binding upon them. In this part of the opinion Mr. Kendall did not agree. His opinion was, that when the two governments, State and national, come to an issue involving the delegated powers on the one side and the reserved powers on the other, the Constitution has provided no common arbiter, and the question assumes the character of a dispute between two sovereigns or independent nations, having no necessary political connection with each other; yet, that the States ought not, except in a most extreme case, to resort to force for the vindication of their reserved rights, because they have the means of redress through patience, perseverance, and the ballot-box. To this remedy he looked forward in this case, and, though long delayed, it came at last.

While the discussions touching the Bank of the United States

were in progress, the circulating medium of Kentucky was undergoing a rapid diminution, which occasioned general embarrassment and individual distress. The condition of affairs was accurately described in an article headed "Alarming Times," published in the "Argus" of the 16th of April, 1819. In this the writer, Mr. Kendall, said:—

"Never within the recollection of our oldest citizens has the aspect of the times, as it respects property and money, been so alarming. Already has property been sacrificed in considerable quantities in this and neighboring counties for less than half its value. We have but little money in circulation, and that little is daily diminishing by the universal calls of the banks.

"What shall be done? Cannot the banks relieve us? If they can, they will not. Is not this a state of things which requires the interposition of the supreme power?

"Fellow-citizens, let us bury our private animosities and commune together on the means most likely to alleviate present distresses, and avert the calamities which threaten to cover our once happy State with bankrupts and beggars."

On the 13th of May, 1819, an imposing public meeting was held in Frankfort, which adopted with great unanimity a series of resolutions setting forth the distressed condition of the country, requesting the banks to suspend specie payments, cease for the present calling on their debtors, and make moderate issues of their notes; and recommending an early call of the legislature for the purpose of legalizing and regulating these measures, and devising other means of relief. A committee of correspondence was appointed, and entered zealously upon the duty assigned them, and in a few days meetings in several other counties responded to the proceedings at Frankfort.

So strong was the tide of public opinion in favor of relief, and so fearful was Mr. Kendall that some wild project among the many suggested by interested parties would be adopted, that he felt it incumbent on him to advise moderation.

But a spirit of opposition to the measures proposed sprung up, which exhibited itself through counter meetings, and in his paper of the 11th of June Mr. Kendall spoke as follows:—

"We have prated long enough about the encouragement of domestic manufactures; it is time to act. What is more ridiculous than to see men, clothed from head to foot in the drapery of England, declaiming

most pathetically upon the necessity of encouraging the manufactures of America! Let the people say to them, *Change your tone or change your coat; too long have we been insulted by useless cant, — give us a little practice, — set us an example of what you preach.* American manufactures would soon become generally used were they made fashionable. Great and influential men should set the example, — the rest will soon follow. Let them not seek for domestic cloth worth twelve or fifteen dollars per yard, but use a kind which our manufacturers can easily make, and any citizen readily procure. But if our great men will not do this, the object can be effected by the people themselves. Associations might be formed, extended over the whole country, the great object of which should be the *wearing* of domestic manufactures. Were the people true to themselves, they might soon create a market for their produce in their own neighborhood, relieve the country from its burdens, and make a *British coat* as infamous as *British principles*."

During the months of June, July, and August the Tennessee banks, the Cincinnati banks, and several of the Kentucky independent banks, stopped payment. In his paper of the 10th of September Mr. Kendall gave expression to his views touching banks in general, and the independent banks of Kentucky in particular, which will be sufficiently understood from the following extracts:—

"With respect to banks we would say a few words. Though the very thought of these institutions is disgusting, yet it becomes our duty to endure the disgust for the purpose of extricating ourselves from their toils or rendering them harmless. Could an amendment be effected to the Constitution of the United States which should prohibit any bank charter from being hereafter granted or renewed, either by Congress or the State, and thus gradually destroy the whole paper system, we should say, *Amen*. But we have no hope of so effectual a remedy. The interest of banks is too deeply rooted, prejudice in their favor has taken too deadly a hold to be unhanded even by the tremendous convulsions into which they have thrown the whole community. All declare the system a public curse, but few can think of destroying it.

"How shall they be rendered less injurious? How shall they be diverted, from their usual course of favoritism and individual aggrandizement, to the public good?

"We have intimated that we did not think the step best calculated to restore the currency of the State would be the repeal of all the charters of the independent banks. There are several in the commercial places which might, under the present state of things, continue to exist

with advantage to the State. But their charters require amendment. They have not at present sufficient responsibility. The public have not a sufficient assurance that they can obtain value for their notes. We think the following plan, communicated by 'Scævola,' a good one: Let the banks give security in the county courts for the payment of their paper when presented. In case of non-payment, the holder of the notes could bring suit on the bond, and recover their amount from the securities. This plan would be more advantageous than the responsibility of stockholders, because it would afford a more obvious and less tedious remedy. A course of this kind, we are satisfied, would afford more relief, and probably be of more service to the community, than an indiscriminate repeal of all the independent bank charters. But should the legislature prefer the latter course, or should they even abolish the whole system of banking on private capital, and make it entirely a public concern on public capital, we shall not view their course with much repugnance."

After the State elections in August, 1819, there was a lull in Kentucky politics. There was an occasional county meeting recommending relief, and a general understanding that something would be done by the legislature to mitigate the public distresses; but no particular measure had been so prominently recommended as to have become a topic of general discussion. Mr. Kendall took this opportunity to press on the legislature and people of Kentucky the importance of a system of common schools, in a series of six numbers, entitled "Sketches on Education for the Consideration of the People of Kentucky, and particularly the Members of the next General Assembly." No. 1 was intended to show that a republic cannot be well governed unless all or a majority of the people are capable of governing. Will natural genius fit a man for a representative or governor? No. Genius may excite public admiration, but it cannot inspire public confidence. Genius must be enlightened before it can be trusted with the reins of government. Of this fact the people are well apprised; and however brilliant may be the mind of him who offers himself for their suffrages, it is useful and solid intelligence alone which can inspire their permanent confidence. Why have we so many lawyers in our general assembly and in Congress? Is it because they possess greater talents than farmers, mechanics, and merchants? No; but it is because the business of their profession requires them to study, and thus they become more intelligent. Intelligence, not talents, gives them a superiority over every other class of society. Knowledge, when confined to a few, creates an aristocracy as marked and as effectual as distinctions of rank. The difference is, that the superiority which knowledge gives is real, and the people willingly acknowledge it; but the superiority which rank gives is fictitious, and the people acknowledge it by compulsion. Yet for all practical purposes there are lords and commons in the one case as well as in the other.

Let us produce equality, not by rendering anybody ignorant, but by rendering everybody intelligent. We would not put down the few, but would exalt the many. We would have no commons, but all should be lords. The man who has as much intelligence as his neighbor cannot be influenced by the authority of his opinions; they are equal; they feel themselves equal, and this is democracy.

Let us not be understood as advocating the destruction of our university or seminaries. They are essential parts in a perfect system of education, but in real usefulness they bear no comparison with the primary schools, which convey the elements of knowledge to all classes of our citizens. It is much more important that all should be well-informed than that a few should obtain an elegant education. Both these ends are desirable, and both may be attained. Free schools would convey to all that degree of knowledge which would fit men for the ordinary business of life, and arouse the genius of all those who are endowed by Nature with a capacity to excel in learning or shine in superior situations.

While the attention of the legislature is turned to the preservation of our seminaries and university, let their principal effort be directed to the creation of a system of free schools which will confer upon the people infinitely greater benefit than all other literary institutions put together.

Next to providing for the bodily comforts of its citizens, there is nothing to which a government should so ardently aspire as enlightening their minds. It is not so much the conferring of a single benefit as it is the construction of a fountain from which flow innumerable blessings. Man will take more delight in the society of man, and the pains and burdens of the body will be half destroyed by the pleasures of the mind. We shall see better sons, better husbands, better fathers, and better men. Beauty,

too, will be doubly charming. Enlightened by intelligence, women will rise in importance, and instead of whining sensualists, with more of weakness than virtue in their love and in their temper, we shall see dignified wives, uniting with the character of mothers the usefulness of instructors. How great, how glorious the object! How extensive and how efficient the means! Nothing is wanting but to give the means a direction to this great end.

Nos. 4 and 5 show that Kentucky had the means of establishing a large and productive school fund, the proceeds of which might be apportioned among the several counties, and disbursed under the supervision of the county courts, which might be authorized to lay a tax on their respective counties in aid of their portion of the public fund, divide the counties into school districts, appoint agents in each district, etc., etc.

No. 6 is devoted to the Transylvania University at Lexington, which is strongly commended to the liberality of the legislature.

On the 6th of December, 1819, the legislature of Kentucky met at Frankfort. The acting governor in his message earnestly recommended the establishment of a school-fund and common schools, and devoted a large portion of the document to the Bank of the United States, denouncing it as unconstitutional and dangerous, and contesting the principles laid down by the Supreme Court; and concluded by proposing a correspondence with the other States, to the end of securing amendments to the Constitution. On the third day of that month the Court of Appeals had given their decision, so that in December, 1819, the executive, judicial, and legislative departments of Kentucky concurred with almost perfect unanimity in the opinion that the bank was unconstitutional, and its establishment a dangerous usurpation.

But the legislative mind was engrossed by a subject of more immediate interest. The cry for relief had now become overwhelming; but there was great diversity of views as to the mode in which relief should be given. The legislature began by passing, on the 15th of December, an act suspending for sixty days all sales under executions issued on judgments, decrees, and replevin bonds, on the defendant's giving bond to have the property which might have been levied upon forthcoming at the end of that term. This act was vetoed by the acting governor, on the ground that it was a violation of that provision of the Constitution of Kentucky which

declared that "right and justice shall be administered without sale, denial, or delay." Also, that it was inequitable and unjust in declaring that securities in existing replevin and forthcoming bonds should not be released by this interposition. It was, however, passed over his veto by the constitutional majority of all the members elected to each house of the General Assembly.

The independent banks, established two years before, had become unpopular, owing to the general impression, no doubt to some extent just, that by fostering speculation they had increased, instead of alleviating the pecuniary embarrassments of the country, and the legislature, by a single act, swept the whole pestiferous brood out of existence. Some of them were well-managed, and judicious men desired that such should be preserved, not doubting that a general sweep, making it necessary that all should take in their notes and collect their dues, would add greatly to existing troubles.

The legislature spent several weeks in attempting to devise some general measure for the relief of debtors, and finally adopted one to the following effect. They passed an act granting an absolute replevy of one year upon all executions issued, not only on original judgments and decrees, but also upon replevin bonds and forthcoming bonds already in existence, which delay should be extended to two years unless the creditors would agree to receive in payment the notes of the Bank of Kentucky. That bank had suspended specie payments on the 5th of January, 1820, and its notes soon fell to a discount of about fifteen per cent.

By another act, passed at this session of the legislature, deeds of trust were put on the same footing as mortgages, so that sale could be made under them without a decree in chancery, thus subjecting them to all the provisions of the replevin laws.

A resolute though unsuccessful effort was made to procure the passage of a property law so framed as practically to postpone indefinitely the sale of property under execution, and thus prevent the collection of debts.

At this session of the legislature Mr. Robert Wickliffe, from the committee to which much of the acting governor's message had been referred, reported bills providing for the annual payment of certain sums of money out of the dividends arising from stock held by the State in the Bank of Kentucky, to the Transylvania University and the county seminaries; also further to endow those in-

stitutions; and also to appropriate for a school-fund all fines and forfeitures which were due, or might become due, to the State. Although Mr. Kendall did not like these measures in the aggregate, because they seemed designed to devote the public means, readily available, to the higher seminaries, leaving common schools to depend on a meagre and precarious resource, which could be made available only in the distant future, yet he advocated the passage of the school-bill in some shape. His language was, "It is no insuperable objection that no public funds are appropriated to this purpose. That object can be accomplished separately, or at a future session. Let us have a beginning; the benefits which will accrue to the community will insure the improvement and perfection of the system."

Two acts having relation to education were passed, one of them entitled "An Act to endow the Medical Department of the Transylvania University," and the other "An Act to appropriate Fines and Forfeitures to the Purpose of promoting Education."

The leaders of the Relief Party in Kentucky were not satisfied with the measures adopted by the legislature at the session of 1819–20, and continued to agitate the subject of a Property Law, in the hope of procuring its passage at the next session. Though Mr. Kendall was in favor of some degree of relief through a modification of the remedial laws and a temporary augmentation of the currency, he believed the legislature had already violated the Constitution of the United States and of Kentucky by interfering with sales under deeds of trust, and he feared more mischief still to the community from the passage of the proposed Property Law. Under these impressions he felt it his duty to avert the evil if possible, and entered upon a discussion of the whole question, — the source of value, the nature of money, a standard of value, the effects of a paper currency, and the operation of property laws. Denying that "labor" is the source of value, and treating "demand" as an effect rather than the cause, he looks into the human mind for the origin of value. The following is an extract from his first article on the subject, published in the "Argus" of the 27th of April, 1820: —

"VALUE AND A STANDARD OF VALUE.

"What constitutes value is not generally understood, and has been the subject of much controversy among men of learning and talents. Some say it is the labor which is spent in the production of an article;

some that it is the demand for it; while the people in general think it is the sum of money for which it will sell. All these notions are erroneous. Things have *value*, not because they are produced by labor, nor because they are in general demand, nor because they will sell or exchange for a certain number of dollars, *but simply because men desire to possess them. Desirableness is value.* In exact proportion that a thing is desirable it is valuable. Things which everybody possesses nobody desires, and of course they have no value. Hence there is no value in air, none in light, very little in water, although these articles are as essential to our existence as food. Were meat and bread as common as air and light they would possess no more value; they would not create desire. When Adam left the garden of Eden land had no value. The richest spots, or those most pleasantly situated or best cultivated, first assumed value because of the larger amount of sustenance they produced, or on account of the greater pleasure they afforded they became the objects of desire. Why are mountains of granite without value? Because they are not objects of desire. Place one of them near a large city and it immediately becomes immensely valuable. A sandy plain has no value; but let a city be built upon it, let the lots become desirable, and it immediately becomes a thousand times more valuable than the most fertile fields.

"With regard to the produce of labor, value is generally antecedent to the labor of production. It springs from our desire to possess that which labor may produce. Were labor to fix value upon its products, everything on which much labor has been spent would be very valuable. This notoriously is not the fact. A Danish captain once, with great labor, loaded his ship in Greenland with a bright sand which he thought contained gold. On his arrival at Copenhagen it was found to be mere sand and thrown into the sea. If labor fixes value, this sand would have been as valuable as gold. But labor could not make a thing valuable which was not desirable. Labor may be wasted. It may be applied to the production of that which nobody desires, which has no value. A man might spend years in setting out and cultivating an orchard of buckeyes, but he could not make them valuable, because nobody desires either the fruit or the wood of that tree. Yet the same labor might raise up an orchard of apple-trees which would be immensely valuable. Things do not become valuable because men spend their labor upon them, but men spend their labor upon them because they are valuable. As the desire for an article diminishes, its value decreases. Should a man set up a manufactory of hoops for ladies' petticoats, what success would attend him? His labor would not render the hoops valuable; they would be worth nothing, because nobody desires them.

[The reader will remember this was written in 1820.]

"From a desire to possess a particular article arises a *demand* for it. If the desire be general, so will be the demand, and they will rise and fall together. But the desire to possess an article, and, consequently, its value, are anterior in their origin to the demand for it. Demand is not, therefore, the cause of value. It is true, that demand and value generally increase or diminish with equal step; not because the one produces the other, but because they are both produced by desire, although value is the first born. A thing becomes desirable or valuable before there is a demand for it. The demand follows. If the thing be difficult of attainment, the desire for its possession usually increases, and the demand increases. But when the desire to possess it ceases, it has value no longer, and is no longer in demand. Writers who have said that demand created value, have mistaken the effect for the cause. What standard can be invented for the desires of men? Can the necessities, the comforts, the pleasures, the fashions, the opinions, and the caprices of man be reduced to any standard? Are they not ever changing like the winds of heaven? Measure never varies. A yard is always equal to the length with which it is compared. An acre is always equal to the surface with which it is compared. A quart is always equal to the quantity with which it is compared. These lengths, surfaces, and quantities never vary or change. Therefore they may be reduced to a standard which shall be uniform and last forever. But does value never vary? Will that which is now worth a dollar always be worth just the same sum? A yard, an acre, and a quart are always the same. But is it so with value? Is a spot on the Alleghany Mountains as valuable as a spot in Philadelphia? A yard, an acre, and a quart are the same fifty years ago and now, in Philadelphia and on the top of the Alleghanies. To reduce anything to a standard it must be made uniform. How can value, which depends upon the ever-varying conditions, tastes, and fashions of men, be made uniform? Measure and weight do not vary with the varying mind of man. No whim of ours can make a yard less than a yard, or a pound less than a pound. Not so with value. Assume a dollar as our standard for a gallon of whiskey, and will whiskey always sell for a dollar a gallon? No, because its value may change, and then our standard will not apply, — it ceases to be a standard. The desire for whiskey *may* diminish, a gallon may become no more desirable than half a dollar; or if the use of it were entirely to cease, the desire for it would also cease, and it would have no value whatever. To make a standard of value you must first make every acre of ground, every bushel of wheat, and any given quantity of any other article, at all times, in all situations and under all circumstances, sell for precisely the same amount. There must be no such thing as profit or loss, or buying or selling.

"We have said enough to show the utter impossibility of a standard of value, and that to talk seriously of any such thing is simply ridiculous. We may as well talk of a standard of hunger, thirst, opinion, fashion, caprice, and all those wants of the body and operations of the mind which make things desirable."

His second article, which treats of trade, the origin of money, and a standard of value, is as follows: —

"MONEY.

"Trade is carried on merely by the exchange of one desirable article for another. One man has meat and another bread. To the man who has meat, a portion of bread is more desirable than a portion of his meat. To the man who has bread, a portion of meat is more desirable than a portion of his bread. To gratify the desire which is thus excited in both, the one exchanges with the other a portion of meat for a portion of bread. Both make a good bargain, because they both get that which is more desirable than that with which they parted. This is the most simple operation of trade. Each obtains what contributes immediately to his own comfort. But most of its operations are more complicated. Two men have an equal abundance of wheat, and one of them has an abundance both of meat and bread. He exchanges a portion of his bread for a portion of his neighbor's wheat, not because he wants it for his own use, but because he can exchange it with a third person for clothing. Here we have the first glimpse of the principle whence originated money. The wheat in this instance is equivalent to money to the individual who exchanged his bread for it, not because he wished it himself or because it was desirable to him on its own account, but merely because he could exchange it for another article which he could use, or which was desirable. Yet it is the desire of the third person which gave value to the wheat, and induced the second person to take it of the first; and the second person desired to possess it because he could exchange it with the third. Whatever is received by one man for the purpose of exchanging it for something else, partakes of the nature of money. The more generally an article is exchangeable the nearer it approaches to money, and if it be universally exchangeable, that is, if every person will receive it for anything he has to spare, it is *money* to all intents and purposes. Money, then, is anything which is universally exchangeable. Government cannot make an article *exchangeable*, but it can reduce such an article to a fixed weight and measure, and thereby much increase the convenience of the exchange. Gold and silver derive their value from the universal source of value, — the desire of mankind to possess them. They were first used in the formation of utensils and ornaments. From their beauty and durability the articles made of these metals, and conse-

quently the metals themselves, became highly and universally desirable, — more so than any other article of the same weight and bulk. Hence they contained more value in the same bulk, and were in more universal demand, than any other article, and hence they became universally exchangeable, and assumed the character of money.

"Government did not give them this exchangeable quality; but finding they already possessed it, government took and divided them into pieces of different weights and sizes, putting on them certain stamps to designate their true weights and their real fineness. This saved the trouble of weighing these metals whenever they were exchanged for anything else, and guarded the community against counterfeit gold and silver. But these metals evidently did not derive their value from these stamps; but these stamps merely designated the value which they had before, and rendered it visible to everybody at the first view. Each nation affixes stamps of its own, which are not, generally, regarded by any other nation. English, French, Dutch, and the coins of all other nations pass among us only by their weight and fineness. When these are well known, they are received for a certain sum in our own money, to which their value is equal; but when they are not well known, we resort to the weight and fineness as ascertained by actual weighing and examination to ascertain their value.

"Hence it is evident that gold and silver have become money, not because government has put particular stamps or marks upon them, but because they are universally exchangeable, and contain more value in the same bulk than any other article. These metals have been stamped to gratify the pride of princes, by presenting their likenesses to their subjects and teaching them a lesson of reverence for their king on every piece of money they receive; but chiefly to designate the value of the metal which every particular piece contains. Other articles might be used for the same purpose, but with less convenience. The Spartans had iron money. To contain much value their coins were made of enormous size and weight. This article was not universally exchangeable, and of course they could not carry on trade in their own money. It was the object of their lawgiver to prevent trade. But it well may be doubted whether this provision *alone* would have produced so great an effect. In Mexico, before its conquest by the Spaniards, gold and silver were too abundant to contain great value in a small bulk. They were valuable, but not more so than would have been iron could the people have obtained it. Gold and silver were not coined by the government into money; but there was a valuable nut which was used among the people to a considerable extent as money. Among them it was universally exchangeable. Copper is used in many countries, and to a considerable extent in the United States, as money.

"From these principles it results that gold and silver, whether coined or uncoined, contain nearly the same amount of value, and the only advantage which they possess over every other article is that they contain more value in the same bulk and are universally exchangeable. Gold and silver are not the representatives of property, but they are property itself as much as iron, brass, houses, or lands. A silver bowl is as much property as an axe, and the silver out of which the bowl could be made is as much property as the iron out of which an axe could be made.

"When we exchange the produce of our farms or of our manufactures for eagles and dollars, we merely exchange one value for another. A dollar is as much property and more useful than a barrel of corn or a ham of bacon which we can never eat, because we can at any time exchange the dollar for something else. Property is evidently not confined to that which we can eat, drink, or wear, but extends to everything we possess which has value.

"Money is but a name for a particular species of property,—land, of another,—wheat, of another, etc., etc. Because these articles have different names they do not cease to be *property.*

"We have already said that the advantage which money has over every other species of property is, that it contains more value in the same bulk and is universally exchangeable.

"Any of the other species of property can always be had for money, but money cannot always be had for any other particular species of property.

"Money is constantly represented as a standard of value. Nothing can be more erroneous. The value of gold and silver is less variable and less fluctuating than that of any other article; but it is by no means uniform. Before the discovery of America the quantity of gold and silver circulating in the world was much less than it is at present, and its value was proportionally greater. But on the conquest of Mexico and South America by the Spaniards the immense quantities of the precious metals derived from that source in some degree diminished the demand, and, until lately, a diminution in the demand, and a reduction in the value of those articles has been, ever since, gradually progressing. This variation, although small in one year or ten years, has been considerable in four hundred years. Hence it appears that the standard of value, as it has been called, is itself fluctuating. There is less value in a dollar now than there was one hundred years ago. The idea of a *standard* precludes variation. What should we think of a yard which was longer one day than it was the preceding? What of a gallon that would hold more one day than it would the next? These standards, as well as that of weight, can be made forever unchangeable. They are made up of divisions and quali-

ties of matter, not of operations of the mind. There is a difference between them and value similar to that between matter and mind. The former you can divide and mark by lines and bounds; but the latter is invisible, intangible, and not subject to human control. Until the operations of mind and the various causes which put them in action are reduced to fixed rules, value can never be measured or reduced to a standard."

From Mr. Kendall's third article, treating of a paper currency, we make the following extract:—

"Of paper currency, as it is generally understood, there are two kinds,—bank-notes and government paper. Bank-notes are the *written promises* of certain corporations. When men borrow bank-notes, they merely exchange their promise for the promise of the bank. When I borrow one hundred dollars, I give my written promise to pay that *value* of gold or silver, and receive from the bank the *written promise* of the corporation to pay to me, or anybody who may be the bearer, that *value* in gold or silver.

"The advantage which I gain is, that the credit of the bank being much better established and more generally known than mine, the community will more readily confide in the due performance of its promises. The advantage which the bank gains is, that it receives interest on the value which I have promised to pay while its own promises made on the same transaction are not performed, or, in other words, before the notes issued to me return upon the bank and draw out the gold and silver.

"The other kind of paper currency is *government paper.* This is but an extension of the same principle. In whatever shape it may be issued it is but the mere *promise* of the government. It has no value in itself, it derives none from the stamp put upon it by government, but is a promise to pay the holder a certain value on demand or at some future period. If government makes more promises than it can perform, they become useless, and its currency depreciates. Within the memory of many men living, there have been two striking instances of abortive attempts to make the promises of government a circulating medium. The first was the *continental money* of our Revolution, and the second the *assignats* of the French. Why did our continental money depreciate and become useless? Because the paper dollars had no intrinsic value, and it was evident the government had promised what it could not perform. Laws were made to sustain it, but in vain. Had all the governmental money been made of gold and silver, would it have depreciated and become useless? We all know it would not. And why? Because the gold and silver are intrinsically valuable, but paper is not. When the

government gives the people a silver dollar it gives them something really valuable, but when it gives them a paper dollar it gives them a *promise* to give real value. If these metals and the paper derived their value only from being declared money by the government, a paper dollar would at all times be as valuable as a silver dollar. They would always remain a *standard of value.* But reason teaches that a promise is not so valuable as the thing promised, whether it be made by an individual, a bank, or a government. Not all the power of all the governments on earth can make a bit of paper as large as a man's hand as valuable in itself as the silver contained in a dollar. They may declare that it shall be a dollar, it may pass by that name, but it will have no more *value* than a linen rag.

"From these facts and principles we infer that it is as impossible for government to furnish to a country a circulating medium which has no intrinsic value as it is to give the same value to a scrap of paper which there is in a silver dollar. Every attempt at it will end in public embarrassment and loss."

Mr. Kendall was diverted from his purpose to discuss the subject of property laws on general principles, by the turn which was given to the discussion by other writers. He had in a very brief article corrected some erroneous notions commonly entertained in relation to the execution laws of the other States, derived from speeches made in the legislature. The accuracy of his statements was called in question in a communication signed "A friend to Relief," which he published, with the reply, in the "Argus" of May 18th, 1820. To this article "A friend to Relief" replied in the "Commentator," giving a personal turn to the controversy. In the "Argus" of June 8th, 1820, Mr. Kendall responded.

This "Friend to Relief" was, and continued to be to the day of his death, Mr. Kendall's personal friend; but at that time he was hopelessly involved in debt, though the owner of much real property. He was finally entirely ruined; and nine years after this controversy Mr. Kendall, satisfied of his integrity, appointed him, unsolicited, to a clerkship in Washington, which he held to the day of his death.

CHAPTER VIII.

WHILE Mr. Kendall was thus wielding his vigorous pen in the support of measures he deemed so essential to the prosperity of his adopted State, he mingled freely in society, evidently seeking one whom he could love, and whose love in return would satisfy the natural longing of his heart. The same discrimination and sound sense characterized his conduct in this as in other affairs. Fond of female society, in which his genial temperament and amiable manners made him a favorite, ready to mingle in the dance and contribute to the pleasure of others, he yet looked for more solid accomplishments in the woman who should be his wife. These he happily found in the person of Miss Mary B. Woolfolk, who, with her parents, resided at a small village in Jefferson County.

In October, 1818, they were married at her father's house.

The following have been selected from many letters written about this time:—

FROM MISS MARY B. WOOLFOLK.

MR. KENDALL,—I have perused the contents of your paper, and hope you will forgive me for having the boldness to write to you. But I write because I know what I have to relate I could not deliver verbally.

Before I proceed any further, I must tell you that I have an unfortunate brother and sister,—but you have heard of them, no doubt,—not capable of taking care of themselves, and it is designed by my father and mother for me to take them under my care at their death, if they should survive their parents. I feel it my duty, and never could be happy to see them anywhere else but under my protection after the decease of my parents.

I wish not to keep you in suspense, therefore, if you think you can grant me the privilege of taking care of my unfortunate brother and sister, and also give them your protection, and if my parents approve of our attachment, I do not blush to say that in spending the remainder of my life with you my happiness would be as great as I could expect in this world.

My father will provide for these children more liberally than the rest of us. I shall only have to take care of them.

MARY B. WOOLFOLK.

TO MISS MARY B. WOOLFOLK.

FRANKFORT, Wednesday Night, July 8, 1818.

DEAR MARY, — As John Russell will set out for home to-morrow, I cannot deny myself the pleasure of addressing to you a few lines. Perhaps you will think it improper for me to write you at this time; but I cannot believe that it will be wholly unacceptable to you. Determined to enjoy the pleasure of the moment, I leave the question of propriety to be settled by those who would sacrifice to etiquette all the tenderest endearments of life.

My ride from your house to Major Russell's was lonely, but so completely had I left my thoughts behind, that when I arrived there I could scarcely believe my own eyes; for I supposed I had not travelled half the distance. The next day I visited Newcastle, and yesterday morning arrived in this place, having ridden fifteen miles before breakfast. I found all well here excepting Bourbon, whom I did not find at all; for he was gone to Woodford. He has, however, returned in bad health and worse spirits, and is now walking the room sighing and groaning. Is it not singular that so many of us double the miseries of life by sad reflections and gloomy anticipations, when by a little exertion the present moment might be made to flit before us on golden wings? As much as we complain of the delusions of fancy, and the sad disappointments of dull reality, I sincerely believe that imagination creates for some persons more images of pain than of pleasure. We talk of air-castles which delight and deceive, but we might with the same propriety talk of *fire-castles*, which delude and torment. But of all the castles which fancy builds, those which yield us misery are the most useless and ridiculous. A reasonable being could not have any great objection to being deceived, when that deception gives him pleasure; but there certainly can be no more striking example of human folly than the man who makes himself miserable by fancying misfortunes which he never felt. The true philosophy of human life — that which I have long endeavored to learn and will always teach — is *to make the best of everything*, laugh at misfortune, think of the pleasures of life, and forget its miseries. The person who can practise this in perfection may, with propriety, be called happy. But though perhaps as cheerful as most men, I find I cannot perfectly practise the philosophy which I teach, and caught myself sighing as I penned the preceding sentence. Do not, I pray you, apply all the foregoing lecture to my friend Bourbon; for though his present temper has led to these reflections, he is generally far from being an unhappy man.

I called on Lucinda yesterday evening, and found her quite disappointed at not receiving a letter from you. She said she was very angry, and would scold you severely in a letter which I suppose will accompany this. She would not be pacified by my telling her that it was my fault; that I had returned to your father's much sooner than you expected; and that you had not time to write. However, I expect her wrath came from no lower region than the tongue, and that her heart all the time beat as warmly and affectionately for you as ever. . . . .

My dear Mary, I shall wait with great impatience the answer of your parents. It is not so much that I have any serious apprehensions that their answer will be an unfavorable one, as that I may see you again and hasten an event which daily becomes more near to my heart, and more essential to my happiness. I will not say that I enjoy no pleasure when deprived of your society, for it would not be true; but I can say with truth that in no other situation am I so truly and exquisitely happy. All other society has lost more than half its charms, and the scenes of our walks now want your presence to make them lovely. I do not exaggerate, — these are the words of *truth*, if not of soberness. You cannot, then, think it unreasonable in me to wish to hasten the time when I can spend with you every moment of leisure. Blessed with your love, with smiles and approbation of your parents, and above all with a pure conscience, I shall be too happy! But I may expect too much; Death's cruel hand may dash the cup of bliss from my lips, or mingle with it a drop of bitterness. I will not think so, — it cannot be possible. If I know myself, the man does not live who can justly accuse me of a single vice, and I am sure the world can say nothing of you which can change my feelings. It is not possible, then, that we can be separated; but in a few days I shall see you, with permission to love you as much as I please. That this day may not be far distant is my most fervent prayer, and I feel a pleasure in believing that its approach is not a matter of indifference to you. I intended to write only a few lines when I began, and lo! I have filled a sheet. Give my best regards to your mother, brothers, and sisters.

Yours, with affection,

A. KENDALL.

MISS MARY B. WOOLFOLK,
    Jefferson County, Ky.
By MR. RUSSELL.

TO MISS MARY B. WOOLFOLK.

FRANKFORT, July 12, 1818.

MY DEAR MARY, — . . . . I thought of you every minute, and believed that I should have been half cured if I could have had so dear and affectionate a nurse. Still I had no cause to complain, for Bourbon, who is in excellent health himself, was as attentive to me as a brother. But there was something still wanting, some person whose

eyes would seem to catch and share my pain, whose tender solicitude would make me forget my sufferings in a feeling of love and gratitude to her who would soothe it. Were you ever sick far from home, where nothing but the hand of cold civility administered to your comfort? If so, you know my feelings since I have been in Kentucky, by sad experience. If not, I leave the picture to be completed by your imagination. With the election and with sickness my time has been so much occupied that you will believe I have had time for little else. Yet I have examined the town from end to end for a suitable house, but have not been so fortunate as to procure one. There are two or three which can be had; but they are inconvenient for me, and I fear would be not only inconvenient to you, but disagreeable. I fear nothing is left me but a choice of evils, so few are the houses in this place to be rented. Before this time I never felt the want of property; but you have made me absolutely avaricious. I feel so anxious not only to satisfy you, but to place you in a situation superior to your most ardent hopes, that I would at this moment do anything which was not mean, dishonorable, or wicked, to become rich. But as Heaven has doomed me to temporary and perhaps lasting poverty, I must try to make up, in affection and kindness, what is wanting in wealth and splendor. Your desires are not enlarged, and, possessing you, I shall wish for nothing but to see you placed beyond the reach of want. Let God but give us a competency of the good things of this life, — all the rest of happiness depends on ourselves. "From *our own selves* our joys must flow." I scarcely need assure you, that the few days which I spent at your house were the happiest of my life. I never before felt in its full luxuriance the pleasure of loving and being beloved. Never shall I forget the moment when, on speaking of leaving your sister, you burst into tears. Dear Mary, those were precious tears, and sealed with drops more indelible than blood the obligation under which I feel myself to treat you always with the utmost tenderness. No, indeed, you shall not regret leaving the dearest, warmest friend and relation you have on earth, if the loss can be compensated by one at least as warm, whose happiness is irretrievably interwoven with your own. Yet I confess that woman risks much, very much, when in obedience to the impulse of affection she leaves those whose affections are interwoven with hers by natural ties for the uncertainty of a stronger and durable love in the bosom of a stranger. Many have wept that act of their lives in tears of bitterness. Many would prefer the once dreaded state of "single blessedness" to the miseries of a husband cruel, capricious, and improvident. I will not say I may be such towards you; for I feel that it is not within the bounds of moral possibilities. But I may be unfortunate, — can you smile upon adversity and meet even want with calmness? If so, I shall never be unhappy.

July 13. My health is completely restored, and my strength fast returning. When I shall see you I cannot now determine, but it shall be as soon as my business will permit. For our marriage I would propose the week beginning the 13th of September. Should any other time be more agreeable to you, I will cheerfully coincide if it be not much later. I should prefer an earlier period to a later one, for I have no doubt that, before that time, I shall be able to make all necessary arrangements. The day of the week I leave entirely and exclusively to you. . . . .

Yours, with affection,

A. KENDALL.

N. B. Should you think proper to write me, it will be received with the warmest pleasure.

TO MISS MARY B. WOOLFOLK.

HARRODSBURG, September 9, 1818.

DEAR MARY, — I am now in the court-house in this place reporting the trial of Samuel W. Daviess for the murder of Henry P. Smith. But little progress has been made in it, and I fear that I shall be detained here until some time next week. . . . .

I count the days and am eager for the arrival of October. It is seldom that I ever wished the hours "more swift," but now I do not care how speedily they wing their flight. I have been building a thousand air-castles for future life, contriving the plans of houses, yards, groves, and all the parts of a terrestrial paradise, in which I may live with an *Eve* who I am sure will not tempt me to sin. For the tree of knowledge of good and evil we will have the tree of love not forbidden, but always free, always delightful, always refreshing. But I know "the ills which life is heir to," and how soon Providence or misfortune may kill the warmest heart and darken the brightest hope. Yet I am sure that whatever ills are reserved for us will be our misfortune and not our fault. I have not time for more. You may expect to see me as soon as Monday evening the 28th instant. Until then, farewell.

Yours, with affection,

AMOS KENDALL.

TO HIS WIFE.

SUNDAY EVE, FRANKFORT, March 7, 1819.

MY DEAR WIFE, — I never before was half so sensible of the truth of the old saying, that we never know the value of a good thing until deprived of it. Would you believe it? since my return home I have been one of the most uneasy, discontented men in creation. I attempt to read, but cannot confine my attention to my book; I sit down to write, but in a few minutes become restless and impatient, get up, take my hat and walk out to find somebody to talk with. Though, as Guilford says, you sometimes trouble me a little with your questions, I had rather suffer — all, were it ten times worse, than my own feelings in your absence. In addition to this, the negroes vex me. The coffee is not made in time, the dinner is cooked badly, the cow is not milked, the house is not kept clean, or something is continually going wrong and conspiring to trouble me. I have been more peevish these few days than since I was a pedagogue. Like old Darby, most heartily do I wish my Joan back again, and, if possible, shall be more ready than ever to excuse her, if she sometimes gets out of patience with the negroes. I never felt more inclined to write a very *loving love letter* in my life, but that would, I suppose, be a very *vulgar, absurd,* and *unfashionable* thing in a husband writing to his wife. Indeed, I believe it is considered by most husbands very vulgar or very unfashionable to *love* their wives, or at least to let anybody know it. Though I would avoid a childish expression of passion or affection, yet I should feel it a sin not to love so good a wife as Heaven in its abundant mercy has given me, and I should feel myself a hypocrite not to own it. Ought I not, Mary, to be the happiest of men? God has "kept me from temptation and delivered me from evil." If mortal man can accuse me of an immoral act, I do not know it. He has prospered me beyond hope in the affairs of this world, and, above all, he has given me for a bosom companion one whose breast is purer than my own. I do indeed thank the giver of all good for these mercies, and could I enjoy no better heaven than I now feel, I would consent to be immortal. Do you not join me in this feeling? Yes, I know you do. I know your purity, your goodness of heart, and your sympathy with all my feelings. Malice could not keep us asunder, and I am sure that friends cannot make us unhappy. . . . .

                Your affectionate husband,
                                AMOS KENDALL.

TO HIS WIFE.

                                FRANKFORT, September 9, 1820.

MY DEAR WIFE, — You will see by the date of this letter that I am in Frankfort much sooner than was anticipated. The two letters which accompany this will inform you of my progress before I left Cincinnati. On Sunday evening last I crossed over to Covington for the purpose of riding a few miles that day, but had to wait for a gentleman whom it was necessary I should see. On Monday morning I started before sunrise. Licking River divides Covington from Newport. The innkeeper told me this river was fordable, but did not give me any description of

the ford, nor did I know that any was necessary. I put into the river with my horse, and had arrived within two rods of the Newport shore when he sunk down, so that the water came over his back. He plunged forward, striking the bottom with his hind feet, and reached the shore, which was so abrupt that in attempting to ascend it he fell upon his side, throwing me and my saddle-bags into the mud and water. I scratched out, and helped my horse out, but he, like an ungrateful dog as he was, as soon as I let go the bridle to pull the saddle-bags out of the river, took to his heels and made off. I followed him, with my saddle-bags full of water on my arm, crying "Whoa! whoa!" most piteously. But it did no good. I then made across a point to head him ; but when I arrived where I expected to meet him he was nowhere to be seen. I inquired of some men working near, but they had not seen him. The morning was cold, and I shivered. I thought it best to seek for a tavern, a dram, and a comfortable fire, so I poured the water out of my saddle-bags and set out for a tavern. I looked into one, which was too dirty for me, wet and shivering as I was. On my way to another I heard of my horse, which had been caught by a negro, without a saddle on. Another negro was despatched after the saddle, which he found in about half an hour, entirely wet and bearing sundry marks of bad usage. I at length took refuge in a tolerable tavern, took a stiff dram, found every thread of clothes I had drenched with muddy water, borrowed a pair of pantaloons, and had my clothes washed, dried, and ironed. My papers I dried myself. In about three hours I was again mounted and under way. Nothing in particular happened that day and the next, except that my horse appeared a little lame, got his back a little hurt, and I felt a little of the rheumatism lurking in my legs.

Your letter I got after I had written, and just as I was starting. It almost made me cry ; but then I thought your apprehensions were wrong. There are troubles enough in reality ; let us make none by the imagination.

                Your ever affectionate husband,
                                AMOS KENDALL.

TO HIS WIFE.

                                FRANKFORT, May 11, 1822.

MY DEAR WIFE, — I received your *short* epistle this morning, and was glad to hear that you continue to mend. God grant that you may be speedily restored to perfect health. To go down for you next Saturday will doubtless subject me to considerable inconvenience. However, I will endeavor to do it. Have everything ready to start on Sunday, and let us come a part of the way on that day, and finish our journey on Monday morning. I shall not bring down any horse but the one I ride,

and the boys must hire one or two, if necessary, in the neighborhood. Let them have all ready on Saturday night.

You will have heard all about the weddings before this time. Mr. Johnston got home this morning, and Sally Branham, with Thomas Smith, arrived this evening, — all well.

Several of the members have already arrived, and by to-morrow evening the town will be swarming.

I get more and more impatient of your absence, insomuch that I have become quite poetic. Were it of any use, I would apostrophize the sun as follows : —

        Roll on, thou glorious orb of day,
            Bid time more swiftly move,
        Chase pain with healing beams away,
            And give me back my love.

        My prattlers, too, with rosy cheek,
            Smiling around my knee
        So sweet, and Anne so meek, —
            Give, give them back to me.

        Truly on earth there is a bliss,
            Painless, without alloy, —
        Hearts that are pure may find in this
            A holy, heavenly joy.

Sunday Morn, May 12th. A comfortable night's sleep has done me good, nor do I remember a single dream wherewith to amuse you. There is certainly a pleasure in the forgetfulness which sleep brings upon us, and I have often thought if death only brought the same sweet oblivion, it would not be so very terrible a thing to die. But probably the chief pleasure of sleep is the relief from fatigue and trouble which we feel while our senses are sinking into drowsiness, and the refreshment of which we are conscious when we awake. As to mere senseless oblivion, in which we neither think nor feel, surely there can be no pleasure in that. Hence death, considered merely in relation to our bodily sensations, cannot be a source of pain or of enjoyment. But there is another reason why mankind do not die with the same satisfaction as they go to sleep. There are very few who are sure that by a change of worlds they will be gainers. When we go to sleep we are sure, or at least think we are, that we shall again awake ; but when we die we plunge into that dark and fearful gulf of which we can know neither the nature nor the bottom. Doubt or terror seizes the mind as it is about to take the fearful plunge, and it clings to life because it knows not the consequence of losing it. Now is the moment when those who are sincerely religious soar above the rest of mankind, and feel a full reward for the sufferings and contempt which they have suf-

fered from the world. Beggars become greater than princes, and the happy peasant in his cottage is elevated above the splendid monarch, whose pomp and glory but render him the more completely miserable. A right good sermon, on my word. I kiss your lips. Love to you and all.

                                AMOS KENDALL.

Mr. Kendall's comprehensive mind, always active and energetic, seemed determined to leave no branch of human knowledge unexplored. From the investigation of every subject he would deduce practical truths, inculcating important lessons of virtue and morality.

The following articles from his pen appeared from time to time in the "Argus" : —

From the Argus of Western America, of July 5, 1821.

. . . . With regard to the future character and principles of this paper, the past is the best and truest criterion by which they can be judged. In some points we may have been mistaken ; but we have never advocated anything which we did not think *right,* nor censured anything which we did not believe *wrong.* Though it is our study to pay due respect to the opinions, character, and feelings of all men, it is our pride that we are controlled by none. Our friends *know* this, and our enemies *believe* it. With regard to general politics, it is necessary to say but little. The old lines of party distinction are obliterated. Unfortunately for State rights and the principles of '98, many of their warmest and ablest advocates have gone over to the enemy. The national government, particularly the judiciary, are making encroachments which are lightly censured or passed over in silence. The expenses of the nation, particularly in the civil department, have increased beyond example and without reason. The public funds have been wasted by being put into the hands of army contractors and paymasters without sufficient caution or security. Our foreign policy has too much regard to the objects and principles of the Holy Alliance to do justice to neighboring republics which have attained their independence and are struggling to preserve it. Manufactures are left prostrate, and agriculture suffers by fostering foreign commerce. Indeed, there is enough wrong in the national government to excite anew the spirit of '98, were not the people distracted with local disputes and borne down with individual distress.

Could we relieve the people from debt, enable them to live comfortably in single blessedness or enjoy the bliss of mutual affection in the bosom of a happy family, put their names to the subscription-list of the printer, and pay him with cheerfulness and punctuality, we would cry *relief, relief* with the zeal of Stentor, if not his lungs; our goose-quill should work by night and by day, guiding many an arrow through the flinty heart which could resist a work so benevolent; every quarter of the State should echo our voice, and ten thousand honest, happy mortals sing our praises. Alas! we know the futility of such efforts and the wickedness of exciting hopes which must be disappointed. We might as well cry silence to the thunder, and bid the tempest cease. Things will take their course in the moral as well as in the natural world. When men raise their feeble arms and build their weak barriers, the flood is stayed but to accumulate a greater force and whelm them the deeper in the furious waves. To parry, to palliate, is all that man can do. So it is with the legislature. They may delay, may give facilities, but they cannot RELIEVE. *The people must pay their own debts at last.* This truth should be impressed upon them, their eyes should be turned from banks and the legislature to themselves, — their own power and resources. Few need despair. Industry never died with hunger. Economy never went without its reward. The legislature can do little, — the people can do much. Let both do what they can, and our country will soon be easy and tranquil, if not prosperous and contented.

Some are lost beyond redemption. They can be relieved only by a general bankrupt law, the passage of which rests with the national Congress, not with our legislature. Once we were bitterly opposed to this measure, but we have changed our opinions. Every week we see so many good and useful men lost to society and to their families, a burden to their country and themselves on account of irretrievable embarrassments, that we cannot resist the impulses of humanity which advise that they should again be restored to life and hope. How can a man be placed in a more gloomy and dreadful situation as to the affairs of this world than when, through folly or misfortune, he has involved himself in debts which a life of labor and suffering would not be sufficient to pay. Wife, children, and friends, the three blessings which God in mercy sends to man for the purpose of cheering his gloomy pilgrimage, become a source of the most acute distress. How can he see her suffer in penury and want, who, with unbounded affection has trusted herself and her fortunes to his guidance, and is chiefly dependent on him for the rank which she holds in public estimation? How can he see those little innocents, whom he has brought into being, grow up without the means of comfort or instruction? How can he see those friends who have lent their names or their money for his benefit, struggling with the tide of misfortune in which their confidence in his honor has overwhelmed them? If he be a man who feels, his misery must be

most poignant. The most distressing feature in his case is, *its hopelessness.* Give him hope, restore him to his family, to himself, to his country, let him start the race of life once more; perhaps he may profit by sad experience, make his family happy, and cause society to rejoice for the returning prodigal.

This is the only effectual relief. Let the State support her banking institutions, thereby giving facilities to those who by a struggle can extricate themselves from their embarrassments, and call on Congress for a general bankrupt law, — no half-way measure peculiar to merchants and traders, but extending through society and comprehending every hopeless case of pecuniary distress. The burden of debt will soon be lightened or thrown from our shoulders; the business and legislation of the country will return to their wonted channels, and all will unite in supporting and executing the laws, maintaining honesty and fair dealing, suppressing fraud and fraudulent transfers of property, while public morality and private virtue will meet with due encouragement and reward.

These are our present opinions and the course of policy which we advocate.

From the Argus of Western America, August 30, 1821.

HABIT IS SECOND NATURE.

Penn says we promised some "personal remarks against" him. This is not so. Such remarks were prepared; but his own course rendered them unnecessary. They were omitted; a statement of which fact is the only ground on which we predicate our promise. Towards us he used the lowest Billingsgate, the language of drunkards in their cups; and, shameless as he is, in a more sober moment he became ashamed of himself and apologized to his readers. We could not sink the man lower than he sinks himself. Before we acknowledge him "worthy of our *serious* attention" he must show himself so by preserving his own dignity and regarding that of others. Till then, his javelin will but poison the hand that throws it; and we shall treat him as we would a snarling brute, — provoke him merely that we may laugh at the folly of his self-destroying spite.

From the Argus of Western America, September 6, 1821.

Our last hit has provoked *Shadrach* to the utmost. Forgetting his promise to avoid personalities, he raves worse than ever. We begin to relent, — indeed we do. Perhaps it would be useful to take *serious* notice of him. Such an example might scare naughty children from vicious habits. A short history of his life would be a pretty little book. Perhaps we will undertake to write it. If so, the following may constitute a part of the

TABLE OF CONTENTS.

Penn's birth and parentage. — Why he was called Shadrach. — His mother's dreams bode no good. — Becomes a smart lad. — An apprentice. — Taste for sports of various kinds. — Residence at R——. — Adventures with Mrs. ——. — Deserves a horse-whipping, but don't get it. — Becomes an editor, first at Georgetown, then at Lexington. — Disputes. — Their result. — His wonderful courage. — Gambles. — Singular adventures one rainy night in Georgetown. — Turns merchant. — Breaks up his father-in-law, and causes an amiable family to be turned out of doors. — Adventures at Pittsburgh, Erie, Buffalo, and Detroit. — Is charged with attempting to defraud the revenue. — Thrown into prison. — Returns to Kentucky. — Is in a fit situation to become *a dependant.* — Establishes a well-furnished printing-office in Louisville. — How the means were obtained. — Returns to *wallowing in the mire.* — Meets a *leaden* gentleman one night in a by-place, who knocks out sundry of his teeth, and convinces him that it is not always safe to meddle too far, even with a woman.* — Like *Shadrach, Meshech, and Abednego* of old, he is cast into a burning, fiery furnace, not of real fire, but of whiskey, brandy, etc., in which, not like them, *he is burnt up.* — His epitaph: —

> This stone, though new, no news can tell
> Of him who haunts this mansion drear,
> Where'er he was, the world knows well,
> 'T was always true that PENN LIES HERE.

From the Argus of Western America, September 13, 1821.

SCHOOLS.

. . . . What has Kentucky done to elevate the moral character of her population and promote true equality? With a laudable ambition to further the progress of knowledge among her citizens, she has given lands to her county seminaries and lands and money to her university. From the miserable organization of the former, her bounty has been almost useless, and the latter has just begun to be useful. But what would have been effected had these institutions produced all the benefits which the legislature could desire? The blessings of education would have been extended to a large portion of our population, but an immense majority would have remained in the same condition as at present. Most of the farmers and mechanics have not the means of supporting their children in the towns, for the purpose of studying at academies or universities, and consequently they are effectually shut out from all the advantages which their more wealthy neighbors may receive from the public bounty. Did these classes of our citizens realize the wrongs

* He was less fortunate than the editor to whom he alludes, who was driven from his horse-whipping purpose by an empty pistol. But Penn takes the purpose for the deed. This is as near the truth as could be expected from him.

they suffer in this respect, their voice would soon be heard in the legislative hall asserting their superior claim to the munificence of the public.

What is it to them that our university and seminaries are liberally endowed? It only widens the distance between them and the more opulent citizens. It adds the aristocracy of learning to that of wealth, and increases the influence of the few over the minds of the many. Can such an appropriation of public funds, in a country where *equality* is the basis on which the government is built, be either just or politic? But we do not complain that the legislature "*have done what they ought not to have done,*" but that they have "*left undone that which they ought to have done.*" Instead of detracting anything from the universities and seminaries, we would add to their funds and their usefulness; but at the same time we would take measures to raise the great mass of the people as nearly as possible to the favored sons of the rich, who enjoy the benefits of the public liberality in the higher seminaries. In short, *we would establish a system of free schools, coextensive with the State, which should be open to the poor as well as the rich, and dispense the blessings of at least a common education to every citizen.*

It is in vain to say the State is *unable* to accomplish so extensive a project. The experience of other States shows that such assertions are not founded on fact. Massachusetts has a system which is supported *wholly by taxation.* New Hampshire has a similar plan. Connecticut has a school fund of more than a million of dollars, derived from her Western lands. New York has a system supported almost entirely by public funds. Compared with her population, Kentucky has more extensive means for introducing and perfecting a general system of free schools than any other State in the Union. To show her ability to accomplish this benign purpose, let us compare her resources which are applicable to this object with those already applied by New York.

New York has a white population amounting to about 1,300,000 souls; the white population of Kentucky is about 430,000. The white population of New York is about three times as large as that of Kentucky, and the children to be educated are consequently about three times as numerous. The annual expenditure on this object in New York is now $146,000; by the aid of which 6,332 schools are kept in operation during a part of the year; in 5,489 of which there were taught, during the last year, 304,559 children. Our white population being but one third as numerous as that of New York, an appropriation equal to one third of the funds there devoted to that object ought to produce the same effect in the State of Kentucky. Upon this estimate, $49,000 would set in operation and support, at least for a portion of the year, 2,111 schools, in which, according to the same ratio, there should be taught 101,520 children. There are in Kentucky sixty-eight counties, and this number would give thirty-one to a county. It is believed that on an average twenty would be sufficient for all useful purposes in this State.

But Kentucky may do more than New York. In the commencement of this article it was shown that this State will derive a revenue of at least $100,000 yearly from the new bank. Instead of $49,000, let $70,000 of this sum be appropriated exclusively for the support of common schools. An average of twenty schools in a county would give 1,360 schools in the State; and $70,000 divided among this number of schools would average $51 to each. In the Northern States, where this system prevails, competent teachers may be hired at $15 per month, exclusive of their board. At this rate, $51 would support a school nearly three months in each year, a period found sufficient by the experience of those States to give every child, the poor as well as the rich, a competent knowledge of reading, writing, and arithmetic, and, to the more studious, English grammar and geography.

Is not this an object worthy the attention of wise legislators? Can the profits of the new bank be more justly or more usefully appropriated? If the friends of an institution which has already saved many of our citizens from impending ruin will now complete their work of benevolence by using its profits for the extension of light and knowledge to the poor and indigent, they will render their fame as perpetual as their motives are pure. And how can its enemies better compensate the community for the evils which they apprehend from this novel experiment than by appropriating its profits to the advancement of knowledge? Let us unite in this great and philanthropic object. Should the bank fail, it will do no harm; should it succeed, the mind cannot grasp the innumerable and lasting benefits which it will shower down upon this community of free men.

From the Argus of September 20, 1821.

Shadrach Penn, after a week's deliberation, has replied to our "Table of Contents" in a long article. We have perused it very attentively, and see only the following sentence which throws any light on the subject. In relation to his mother's dreams he says, "Suppose he (the editor of the 'Argus') had declared that during the night the monkey was watching the wood-pile, and our mother dreamed the aforesaid monkey took from the above-mentioned wood-pile a small twig of hickory, and basted her son (himself) unmercifully."

Now this is very probable, and we will put it in the book. Hast any more materials for the work, Shadrach?

From the Argus of Western America, October 4, 1821.

AN ENGLISH TRAVELLER. — SCHOOLS.

We have read with great pleasure a new publication, "Views of Society and Manners in America," etc., "by an English Woman." So many illiberal slanderers from the "fast-anchored isle" have visited this country *but to abuse it*, that it is consolatory to our feelings to find one who has visited it *but to praise it*. The American reader will recognize in this book the features of a society and manners with which he is familiar; but except a few errors in immaterial facts, the chief fault in it is, that *it eulogizes us too indiscriminately*. It is our intention in this notice not to give a general review of the work, but merely to quote a few passages in relation to general education. It was an American ship in which she crossed the Atlantic, and, of the crew, she says: —

"It is worthy of remark that every man of the crew, from the old veteran to the young sailor-boy, could read and write, and, I believe I might almost say, *every* man could converse with you upon the history of his country, its laws, its present condition, and its future prospects."

Again, speaking of Americans, she says: —

"But there is yet a more important consideration, — *they are their own teachers;* not only can none shut the book of knowledge, but, by an imperative law, it is laid open before them. Every child is as fairly entitled to a plain but efficient education as is every man to a voice in the choice of his rulers. In his minority he is, in a manner, the ward of the ruling generation; his education is not left to chance; schools are everywhere opened for him, at the public expense, where he may learn to study those rights which he is afterwards called upon to exercise. In this union of knowledge with liberty lies the strength of America."

Here is praise too indiscriminate. What the writer says is true of New York and the more northerly States; but we regret to say that Kentucky is not entitled to one word of it. "A plain but efficient education," "schools everywhere open at the public expense," have engaged no part of the attention of our rulers. The education of the young and poor children is "left to chance," and is often totally neglected. Why will not our legislators, when it is so completely within their power, merit the encomiums which are thus liberally bestowed on our country? The following extract is of the same character as the preceding: —

"The State of Connecticut has appropriated a fund of a million and a half of dollars to the support of public schools. In Vermont a certain portion of land has been laid off in every township, whose proceeds are devoted to the same purpose. In the other States every township taxes itself to such amount as is necessary to defray the expense of schools, which teach reading, writing,

and arithmetic to the whole population. In larger towns these schools teach geography and the rudiments of Latin. These establishments, supported at the public expense, are open to the whole youth, male and female, of the country."

None of this general eulogium on our country belongs to Kentucky. We have no lands, no taxes, no public funds, whose proceeds are applied to the support of schools "open to the whole youth of the country." Equally great is the error of this liberal traveller, in relation to our young but rich State, when she says: —

"The child of every citizen, male or female, white or black, is entitled by right to a plain education; and funds sufficient to defray the expense of his instruction are raised either from public lands appropriated to the purpose, or by taxes, sometimes imposed by the legislature and sometimes by the different townships."

So far from having provided for the education of black children, we have done nothing for the white. In the following extract the writer has herself discriminated between different portions of our country: —

"In the education of women, New England seems hitherto to have been peculiarly liberal. The ladies of the Eastern States are frequently possessed of the most solid acquirements, the modern and even the dead languages, and a wide scope of reading; the consequence is, that their manners have the character of being more composed than those of my gay young friends in this quarter (New York)."

We will not undertake to say whether the preferences thus given to the women of New England, in point of education, be correct or not; but if the State of Kentucky shall hereafter be outdone by any State in the Union, either in the education of males or females, her legislators will be deficient in the duties which they owe to a liberal, rich, and growing community.

From the Argus, dated October 11, 1821.

OHIO AND THE FEDERAL COURT.

Our expression of satisfaction, in a former paper, relative to the manner in which the United States Bank had recovered the money collected from her by the State of Ohio as a tax, must not be understood as approving the decision of the court, but merely the peaceable manner in which its decrees were executed.

We are not ready to admit that the United States can rightfully, for any cause or under any pretence, by the authority of the President, of Congress, or the Federal Court, seize the keys of the State treasuries, enter their vaults, and take therefrom money which has been collected as a State tax, rightfully or wrongfully. The outrage is as great as if

State officers were to seize the keys of the National treasury and take therefrom, under the authority of any State, money which had been collected of its citizens as a national tax. According to our understanding of the Constitution, the States are as independent and uncontrollable in their power of taxation, both as to its objects and amounts, as the nation itself, excepting only in relation to imports. The nation has put her hand into the treasury of Ohio, and taken thence money collected by that State as taxes. We admire the calm and prudent temper of the people which could suffer the outrage in peace. It redounds to their eternal honor. The States can vindicate their rights without violence. The national government is their creature; they made and can mould it to suit their will. If the President, Congress, or the judiciary transcend their powers, they can be hurled from office, or the Constitution can be amended. He, therefore, who would use violence in opposition to the national authorities, is guilty of a crime worse than the usurpation he would resist. Violence would destroy the system which usurpation only impairs.

How shall the States resist the consolidating tendency of our national government, which the decisions of the Federal courts are annually making more apparent? Shall they permit the centre to attract and consume those glorious orbs which it was destined to enlighten and cherish? Few doubt the integrity of the Federal judges. But they are men. Did they not lean towards the source whence they derive power and receive support, they would not be human. Experience has shown that, however honest, they are not the proper tribunal to decide, where national and State powers come in conflict. They are one party. How can one party in a suit be an impartial judge?

When the President or Congress violate State rights, the people can turn them out. But how can they correct the national judiciary? That department is beyond their controlling hand. Even its errors are sacred. Nothing but corruption can expose their ermine to the vulgar touch. The public voice may cause them to pause for a while, but it cannot disarm them. The only mode for effectually correcting an erring judiciary is by *amending the Constitution*. But the fabric raised by Washington, Franklin, and their associates should be touched with reverence, and amended with caution. Derangement in its well-adjusted parts might produce greater evils than those which we now dread. But there seems to be one thing wanting, — a tribunal with acknowledged power to determine in the last resort the line which separates national and State authority. Might not a tribunal be established, to constitute which each State should appoint and pay one judge, the sole province of which should be to decide on appeals from the Federal or State courts where the question involved the constitutional rights of either government in relation to the other?

From the Argus of February 14, 1822.

We congratulate the editors of the "National Intelligencer" on the abatement of those gloomy forebodings which had given such a "sooty" appearance to the columns of their journal. To them the relief must be doubly welcome, as, by the indisposition of the members of Congress to make a nomination for the next Presidency, their own fears are entirely dissipated, and the people are rescued from that dangerous expedient which *they had recommended*. We are now told that there will be no *caucus* at Washington. This is well. We send men to Washington, not to make Presidents, but to make laws.

By some of the Eastern papers, favorable to the usual succession, hopes are expressed that the discussion in relation to the Presidency may still be suppressed. Mr. Walsh, editor of the "National Gazette," suggests that the printers ought to do it by refusing to publish articles on this subject. Indeed! Shall the printers conspire to suppress the discussion of a subject so important to the people? We caution our brethren of the type against being deluded by these *lords of the press*. There is a *design* in their efforts. They wish a President elected without discussion. They do not wish to see a lively interest excited in the country, by which they have much to lose and nothing to gain. To us a discussion appears necessary, *even now*. The minds of the people should be led to consider a Secretary of State as having no greater pretensions to the office of President than any other citizen. The charm of succession should give way to the right of unbiased election. No man should be considered a candidate by virtue of the office which he holds, but all should stand upon the level of equality. Is it so now? Do we not look upon the Secretary of State as a candidate for the Presidency from the moment of his appointment? Does not this appointment give him an advantage over every other candidate? Does not the impression that the present Secretary is to be the next President gain strength at every term? Where will it end? If not impaired by discussion and competition, will it not result in the uniform choice of the Secretary of State to the Presidency, without opposition, by which means each President will appoint his successor.

Every person acquainted with history, or the mind of man, will see the danger to which the silence of the press must inevitably expose us. Originally, a man ought not to have been elected to the Presidency or rejected because he was Secretary of State. But at this time, when this principle of succession has taken so strong a hold, the friend of our institutions will rather oppose than support the man who fills that office. Of the present Secretary we can only say, that we have always viewed him as a mild Federalist, who ought sooner to be trusted than

some apostate Republicans. That he would not go with *Otis and Co.*, in efforts to destroy his country, is an argument in favor of his honesty, but not of his correct principles. His father, John Adams, was as true a patriot as the Revolution produced; but was he a good President? To his son we have no enmity; but among those spoken of at present he is not our choice, and the station he holds does not lessen our objections.

With these views, it seems to us important that there should be a discussion in relation to the next Presidency, *even now*. It is not too early for the people to consider whether they will permit the *custom* of elevating the Secretary of State to the Presidency to become a *law*; whether all the Presidents ought to be elected from the North or the South, from Virginia or Massachusetts, or whether this honor shall sometimes be conferred upon the Middle or the West, upon New York, Pennsylvania, Carolina, Georgia, Ohio, or even Kentucky. In fine, every topic connected with this election, except, perhaps, the personal merits or demerits of the supposed candidates, are proper subjects for present discussion. Whatever, therefore, may be the course adopted by Messrs. Gales and Seaton, or by Mr. Walsh, our paper, even though it expose us to the charge of singularity, will remain open to this discussion.

From the Argus of March 21, 1822.

COMMON SCHOOLS.

The following circular has been prepared by the commissioners appointed by the last legislature to collect information and digest a system of schools. It is to be addressed to individuals in the various counties, and is published by request of the commissioners, with an earnest solicitation on their part that all persons throughout the State who feel interested in this important subject, will join in communicating to them the desired information, without a more particular application.

CIRCULAR.

SIR, — You are already apprised of the proceedings of our legislature at their last session, on the subject of education. We are appointed commissioners to collect information and digest a system for carrying into effect the benevolent purposes and munificent appropriations of the representatives of the people in relation to this important class of our common interests. Believing you to be friendly to the object, and willing to contribute whatever may be in your power to its accomplishment, we take the liberty of addressing to you this circular, and of calling to your attention the questions that are subjoined. Any information that you may be able to give will be gratefully received and faithfully employed. Letters may be directed to the commis-

sioner living within your district. We ask as early communications upon this subject as your convenience will permit. With great regard, we are, sir, yours,

> W. T. BARRY, *Chairman.*
> D. R. MURRAY,
> JOHN POPE,
> D. WHITE,
> J. R. WITHERSPOON,
> W. R. ROPER.

March, 1822.

QUESTIONS.

1. Has any county seminary been established in your county?
2. If so, what endowments has it received, and what is the present situation of its funds and buildings?
3. Is any teacher employed therein under the control or superintendence of the trustees?
4. What number of students are taught thereat, and at what price for each branch of knowledge?
5. Are there any academies in your county, established by law or otherwise, and what are their endowments?
6. Have they buildings?
7. What teachers are employed therein; what number of pupils are taught, and at what price for each branch of knowledge?
8. What number of common schools are now or usually taught in your county?
9. What number of children are taught therein, and what is the price of tuition?
10. What is the probable number of children who are growing up in your county without being sent to school?
11. What is the probable number of those whose parents are unable to give them a common-school education?
12. What is the size of the school districts into which your county has been laid off by the county court?
13. If a school were placed near the centre of each district, would it be practicable for all the children to attend it?
14. If not, how many would be excluded?
15. Could your county be otherwise districted so as better to accommodate those who would be sent to school?
16. Calculating from the usual number of children taught in the seminary, academies, and common schools, and the known prices of tuition, what is the probable sum paid annually in your county for the education of children?

To facilitate the collection of information, the State has been divided by the commissioners into five districts, and all letters should be directed to the commissioner residing in the district where the letter is written.

Any information, whether in relation to the condition of this State or the systems which have been adopted in other States, may also be communicated to Wm. T. Barry, Esq., Chairman of the Board, at Lexington.

As this is a subject of the utmost consequence, and as the accomplishment of the benevolent views of the last legislature will create an era in the history of Kentucky, not to be equalled in true glory by the most splendid military achievement, we earnestly hope that every citizen will feel interested in collecting the desired information, and will contribute his mite to the mass of intelligence which is essential to the framing of a system which shall realize the expectations of the legislature and the hopes of the country. The more minute the information, the less liable will the commissioners be to adopt erroneous principles and make false calculations.

To show what may be effected in the collection of information, we shall endeavor to procure and publish all the particulars on which the commissioners desire to be informed, so far as respects the county of Franklin.

we shall give a greater variety to our articles, both original and selected, than they have heretofore possessed. Not only politics, but agriculture, manufactures, commerce, education, literature, anecdote, poetry, morality, and religion will claim a considerable share of our attention. The longer we live, the stronger becomes our conviction that society cannot exist in a civilized state unless it be deeply imbued with the principles of religion. The promotion of that which constitutes the basis of all our social enjoyments, even by means of a common newspaper, cannot be wrong or impolitic.

We have some enemies. Our errors have been magnified into crimes, and our mistakes into wilful falsehoods. This is to be expected whenever we chance to run athwart the course of ambitious men. In the heat of controversy, however, we have been carried further than was justified by prudence or propriety. Like other men we cannot divest ourselves of human passions, and therefore we dare not promise that we will not hereafter be led astray. But, whenever convinced that we have, through misinformation, passion, or prejudice wronged any man, we shall not hesitate to do him justice, whatever may be thought or said by men who think it more honorable to stick to an error than to acknowledge it. Some of those who have shown themselves our enemies, we esteem, in the main, as honest men, and capable of being serviceable to the public; and whenever a proper opportunity offers, we shall show that we are not actuated by such feelings as they are. Though we cannot hope, so long as we are obliged to mingle in political contests, to live in peace with all mankind, yet we shall always endeavor to give no reasonable cause of offence. With this view, we are determined to avoid, as far as practicable, all interference between individual candidates, farther than their interests may be affected by the discussion of general principles.

With heartfelt gratitude we acknowledge the favors already received from the people and legislature of Kentucky; and so long as we remain honest and faithful we have no fears of losing their confidence and support.

AMOS KENDALL,
A. G. MERIWETHER.

From the Argus of February 26, 1823.

SUNDAY REFLECTIONS.

THE BIBLE. — The institution of a Bible Society in Franklin County naturally calls our attention to this ancient and venerable book. There is no man, whatever may be his religious opinions, to whom the contents of this volume are not highly interesting. It purports to give a history of the origin of our race, of the destruction of mankind by an

---

CHAPTER IX.

From the Argus of January 30, 1823.

TO THE PUBLIC.

THE undersigned have become sole proprietors of the "Argus" printing establishment, and this paper will be henceforth published by *Kendall and Meriwether*.

In relation to the principles which will govern our future course, it is not necessary to say much, because our political opinions are well known. The only charge we have lately heard against the "Argus" is, that it is too *democratic*. If we err at all, we prefer erring on that side, because it is the safest. The people had better have too much power than too little, because it is very easy to delegate power to our rulers, but not so easy to resume it. In all contests for power, therefore, where there is reasonable ground to doubt, we always have been, now are, and doubt not always shall be, in favor of leaving the contested power with the people. Nor shall we be deterred by any temporary loss or inconvenience from discussing principles freely and boldly; because we are satisfied that in the end "Honesty is the best policy."

But we have been editors so long to little purpose if we have learned nothing from experience. We are convinced that mere personal vituperation not only does no good, but degrades the press and lessens its beneficial influence on the community. Human nature is so prone to return abuse for abuse, with interest too, that it requires great command of one's temper to restrain it. But we are determined to make the effort, and, if possible, to preserve perfect decorum of language, whatever may be the provocation or whoever may offer it. Let it not be understood, however, that we shall suffer ourselves to be abused in silence. To repel the blackguard, it is not necessary to descend to his level.

As our individual attention will be bestowed upon this establishment,

---

universal deluge, of the patriarchal and pastoral manners of the early ages; gives us the system of laws, civil and religious, delivered to the Jews through the medium of Moses; contains the history of that people from a single ancestor almost to the dispersion of the nation; and relates to us the origin and progress of the Christian religion in its earliest stages. Merely as a history, it is therefore of great importance, and should be read with the utmost attention by every one who wishes to become acquainted with the events of antiquity.

To the admirers of morality and singleness of character it is also invaluable. From beginning to end it inculcates the existence of one God, the Creator of all things, and represents him as delighting in the devotion of his creatures to his service, their kindness towards each other, and their honesty and sincerity in all their dealings. Humility and self-abasement are everywhere represented as among the first of virtues, and man is called upon to bring his passions and appetites into complete subjection by giving up those possessions and pleasures which are dearest to his heart. Under the ancient religion, he who could, with perfect resignation, see the firstlings of his flock and the most precious fruits of his labor offered up as sacrifices to his Maker must have acquired a considerable control over the passions of his bosom. In Christianity, too, men have to make these sacrifices, — not of their flocks or their fruits, but of their pleasures and follies. Nor are these sacrifices less painful to the human heart than the firstlings and first-fruits of the old dispensation. Perhaps it requires even a greater effort, a more perfect control over one's desires and passions, to deny ourselves the gratification of our propensities than to surrender the most precious articles of our property. Infidels as well as Christians accord to the New Testament that it exhibits a system of more perfect morality than was ever taught by any other book. He who uniformly practises the rules there prescribed for the regulation of our conduct towards each other, will not only escape the censures of mankind, but the reproaches of his own conscience. "Do unto others as ye would have them do unto you." Language cannot convey the sum of all morality in a more brief, simple, and forcible manner. For its pure morality, therefore, independent of religion, the Bible, and more particularly the New Testament, ought to be possessed and read by every man who seeks to be honest, or admires that virtue in others.

But the Bible has still higher claims to the attention and perusal of man. It is the source of the Christian religion, which changes the heart and renders men moral and good by purifying the source whence all their actions spring. Religion produces pure morality as naturally as a pure fountain emits a pure stream. The Old Testament gives us an account of man's fall from that state of innocence in which he was

---

created, with many allusions to the future redemption of his race. The New Testament gives us a history of that redemption, and promises to man, in a future world, the happiness which he has lost in this. Almost every man who reads much and thinks much is religious, in theory at least. Some, indeed, disbelieve all religion, because they cannot understand its mysteries. As well might they disbelieve the existence of the most familiar objects in nature. Creation is full of mysteries, — by day and night mysteries innumerable roll before us, — we are mysteries ourselves. Whence came man? Who formed his beautiful limbs, and breathed into him the breath of life? Who gave form and variety to his senses, organized his brain, and set in motion his palpitating heart? Wilt thou say, it was God? If so, tell us in what manner the Great Supreme formed the first of human beings, and for what end? Is he capricious, and did he make man for nothing? Thou who refusest to believe in mysteries, art thyself the greatest mystery which thine eyes behold or thy thoughts embrace. Why not disbelieve thine own existence, and disbelieve even thy own disbelief, and think that thou dost not think, but that thou art all a delusion! There are few who deny that there is a Supreme Being, and that he created man; for to deny this would be to ascribe to man self-creation, which is not only a mystery, but a contradiction. If, therefore, God created man, he must, in the act of his creation, have exercised both upon his body and mind a direct and supernatural power. The very act of man's creation — an act which is proved by his existence — was a greater miracle than is ascribed to our Saviour in the New Testament, or to any of the prophets in the Old. Yet this miracle, the most extraordinary which the Bible records, is almost universally admitted to be true, even by those who reject religion on account of its mysteries.

For what end was man created? Merely to grow to manhood, play a few pranks before high Heaven, decay and die? A God influenced by such motives as the creation of an inferior being, would indeed be a mystery deeper and darker than that which shrouds the foundation of our religion. But this was not the design of man's Creator; the world was peopled for some higher and nobler purpose. What was that purpose? It is man's felicity, both in this and a future world, — it was *religion* and the *reward* of religion.

But some will not believe that God ever spoke to man, or held communion with his mind. Is there more mystery in communicating a thought to the mind than in creating that mind? He who made the mind could surely inspire it with a thought, and if the latter is too great a mystery to be believed, surely the former is also. Hence, he who believes that God created the mind ought not to think inspiration unreasonable, or reject religion because it purports to be a communication from God to man. Why should not the rules for the government of a moral agent come from the being who created him? Nothing is more reasonable or would seem to be more natural. God is a mystery, the universe is a mystery, the creation of man is a mystery, inspiration is a mystery; but the last is the least mystery of them all. Its mysteriousness is not, therefore, an argument against religion, nor against its emanation from the Divine mind.

These remarks are hastily thrown together for the purpose of exciting new thoughts in some of our readers, and calling their attention to an Old Book which is too much neglected. If the religion of our country be true, it is a matter of the highest importance for every one of us; and if it be false, it is the most moral and useful fable ever palmed upon mankind. To believe it can do no harm, and to disbelieve it may lead us to unimagined mischiefs. Let him who admits the existence of a God and the creation of man reflect, that he already assents to as great mysteries as religion presents, and that he can no longer, on that ground, refuse his credence to the whole system. But let him also reflect, that its beauties do not *consist in its mysteries*, but in its *influence over the hearts and manners of men*. If, on account of its mysteries, there is no ground to disbelieve it, there surely may be found in the beneficial effects which it produces the most forcible reasons to believe it a real emanation from the Great First Cause for the direction and benefit of the creatures of his power.

From the Argus of February 6, 1823.

OMINOUS.

The late news from England informs us that a considerable squadron of ships of war is fitting out in one of the ports of that country for a *Secret Expedition*. In the present state of the world, and with the neutral professions of the British government, what can be the object of this armament? There have been intimations in the English papers that Great Britain would not interfere with the affairs of Spain, that she would use her influence, if not her arms, to prevent the interference of others, and that Spain was to give her some equivalent for her friendship. What if this equivalent should be the island of *Cuba*, and what if to take possession thereof should be the ultimate destination of this secret expedition? It has always been the policy of the British government to secure all the commanding points in the commercial world, for the purpose of securing to herself the dominion of the ocean and controlling the trade of all nations. Next to Gibraltar, there is no point of the globe whose attitude is so commanding over the commerce of other countries as the island of Cuba. Look at the valley of the Mis-

sissippi and the empire of Mexico, whose chief outlet to the ocean and avenue to the commercial world is almost in sight of the Havana. The growing importance of the countries, and their vast resources, will render the commerce of the Gulf of Mexico, at some future period, not less important than that of the Mediterranean. The possession of a point which will subject all this commerce to the control of the British navy, and, in the event of war, enable them to destroy it, cannot but be a matter of the deepest interest to the British government. It is much more important to our government, and they should spare no means to prevent the possession of that island by the British. They would doubtless render it impregnable, so far as that end can be effected by the art of man, and for centuries it would remain a thorn in our side, controlling the commerce of more than half the Union. It would be better for us that it were sunk in the depths of the ocean, or that it were possessed by the Algerines, or pirates; for them we could conquer or expel. We have no desire to see this island annexed to the United States; for that would give reasonable cause for jealousy to our Mexican neighbors. It seems to us the wiser and the safer course to promote its independence, with a government confined to the island itself. In that case it would never be sufficiently powerful to endanger our commerce, and would be forever delivered from the grasp of Great Britain. In fine, its possession by that power ought to be prevented at all hazards; for it would be almost as fatal to the Western country as the occupation by her of the mouth of the Mississippi.

If, therefore, there be any ground to fear this event, we have a right to expect that measures will be taken to prevent it.

From the Argus of February 10, 1823.

SUNDAY REFLECTIONS.

RELIGION. — A belief in the existence of a Supreme Being is the basis of all religion. This belief may spring from either of three sources, or from all of them combined.

It is not reasonable to suppose that the first of men had no personal knowledge of the Being who created him. If he neither saw, nor heard, nor felt the Divine hand that formed his limbs and clothed his features in beauty, yet, when the senses first received the impression of external objects, and the mind awoke to intelligence, the new created being must have been conscious of the presence of that great Power which had thus raised him from the dust. That God would, after forming an intelligent being, leave him without a knowledge of the object of his creation, is not consistent with the plainest deductions of human reason. In this respect, therefore, our own reason entirely corresponds with the accounts

given in the Bible. Our reason teaches, that God would hold communication with man for the purpose of apprising him by what means and for what end he was brought into existence, and the Bible informs us that such was the fact. The first of men, therefore, had a personal knowledge of Deity, and could not but believe in his existence.

The second source whence a belief in the existence of God may be derived is the universe. Whence came the world and all it contains, the sun, moon, planets, and stars? Did they form themselves, or spring into existence by chance? Our little earth affords innumerable wonders, which nothing but Deity could frame; but what is earth compared with the universe? Many of the planets which wheel around our globe exceed it many times in magnitude, and the sun is immensely larger than them all combined. But the sun itself is but an unit among millions, but as a grain of sand compared with the universe. Look to the heavens full of dazzling spots which seem so small they are but a glimmer of light. What are they? The knowledge of man has not enabled him to ascertain. The most improved telescope — which presents the moon almost at our doors, gives the apparent size of that luminary to all the planets, and exhibits the sun as an almost unbounded field of fire whose unextinguishable flame is only broken by a few dark spots — is not sufficient to give magnitude to these twinklings of other worlds, so vast, so unmeasurable is their distance. All that these instruments can do is to aid the scattered glimmerings of other and countless luminaries, whose light the unassisted eye never caught and whose existence the mind of man never imagined, to concentrate and announce to him that there are wonders in creation which all his learning can never unfold, and which even his imagination could not grasp. What are these lamps of night which, to the eye of ignorance, are but spangles to ornament a seeming canopy of blue which surrounds this earth? Learned men suppose they are *suns*, illuminating other planets to us invisible. If this be so, how vast is creation! Suns innumerable, all have their planets wheeling around them, and all of those planets, perhaps even the suns themselves, are filled with innumerable existences. Who built and supports this stupendous system?

Who prevents world rushing upon world, and sun upon sun, filling the universe with confusion and fire? Who guides the comets in their fiery course, and prevents their driving from their orbits and whelming in ruin some of those innumerable globes between which they hold their harmless and unmolested way? He who can contemplate all this and not mentally, at least, shout *a God! a God!* must have shut his mind not only to the impressions of religion, but to the plainest deductions of reason.

The third source whence a belief in the existence of a Deity may be

derived, is the authority of others. Adam informed his posterity that there was a God who had made him, the world, and all it contains. The prophets and philosophers of old repeated to mankind the same information, all which is embodied in the Bible and handed down for the instruction of all future generations. If we have confidence in those who have spoken, if we believe them to be good men, we must believe that they have told the truth, and that there is a God who has held communication with them and made known his will to the children of his creation.

At this age of the world we do not witness instances of direct revelation from God to man. But to assert that they are not possible, and may not happen, is to strip Deity of his almighty power. The evidences we have of his existence are so conclusive, that a direct revelation is not necessary; for he who will not believe them, could not be convinced by a voice from Heaven. Indeed, there is not one man in ten thousand who does not believe in the existence of God, and thereby give his assent to the first principles of religion.

In the midst of his arduous labors Mr. Kendall was suddenly overtaken by domestic affliction in the death of his cherished and devoted wife.

Five years of nearly unalloyed happiness had been theirs. Death had cast no shadow over their peaceful household. Happy in the present, they cherished fond anticipations of future joys. The blow was sudden; scarcely did the stricken husband realize the sorrow in store for him before it fell with crushing force.

In the "Argus" of October 22, 1823, is the following: —

OBITUARY.

Died, at the residence of her husband, in Frankfort, on Monday night, the 13th instant, Mrs. MARY BULLARD KENDALL, wife of *Mr. Amos Kendall*, one of the editors of this paper.

In relation to her husband, three infant children, an affectionate mother, sister, brothers, relations, and friends, this dispensation of Providence is a cause of the most poignant grief; but in relation to herself, her confident hopes in a blissful immortality make it a cause of gratulation and joy. It is not easy for her surviving husband to portray her virtues, her feelings, and her hopes. He cannot even find language to express with adequate force the feelings of grief, admiration, and even joyful confidence which agitate his own bosom. Were he to say he has lost one of the best of wives, the praise would be faint. She did indeed arrive as near perfection as is generally granted to the lot of mortals.

Mrs. Kendall was the daughter of Mr. William Woolfolk, of Jefferson County, a plain, honest farmer, and was wholly raised in the country, far from the fashions and follies of towns. Though her opportunities were small, she had made considerable progress in most of the branches of a useful as well as polite education. When introduced into another and what is generally considered a more fashionable grade of society she readily accommodated herself to its manners without acquiring any of its vices. In relation to fashion, she was only desirous not to appear singular, — to excel in dress she had not the least ambition. She delighted in no company except where there was an unrestrained communication of kind thoughts and friendly feelings. Speaking disrespectfully of one's associates, neighbors, and acquaintances is a habit in which she never indulged, and when such was the tenor of conversation she sat in mute disgust. Her feelings on those occasions were known only to her husband, to whom alone she unbosomed her whole heart. Could the tale-bearers, the retailers of scandal, the creatures who remark with bitter envy on the superior dress, furniture, or equipage of their neighbors, know with what feelings this good woman was sometimes obliged to listen to their conversation, they would learn a useful lesson.

No wife ever entered more freely and fully into all the feelings, the plans, and opinions of her husband. If she had a foible in this respect, it was too strong an antipathy to those who had injured or spoken evil of him. Much sooner would she forgive and forget any wrong done to herself. In the management of her household she was industrious and economical. She regulated all her expenses by the ability of her husband, and was more than content to live humbly, that something might be accumulated for the education of her children and the comfort of old age.

In the management of her children she might be a pattern for many mothers. It was not her opinion that their manners, their minds, and their passions should be left to run wild until good sense or the effects of vice should teach them politeness and virtue; but she thought that restraint upon the passions and desires should be coeval with the dawn of reason, inculcated by precept, example, and even correction, until it should have grown into a principle and a habit. What her children might have been under the management of such a mother may be imagined from what they already are. In relation to their education, it was her determination not to send them to school while she could teach them anything at home; for she thought that as much is lost in our schools through want of discipline in the range given to the passions, and in the contraction of bad habits, bad thoughts, and bad language, as is gained by the increase of knowledge. It was also her intention that domestic labor and economy should form an essential part

of the education of her daughters, and that they should be taught all kinds of household labor, from knitting and sewing to spinning, if not weaving; for, said she, if they should be poor, the knowledge of these things will be necessary to their sustenance, and if they should be rich, so far from doing them harm it will enable them to know when their work is well done by others.

Both she and her husband looked forward with fond and eager hopes to the time when he would be able to retire from active life and political turmoil upon a small farm, where, in the enjoyment of a competency, they might rear their children, receive their friends with hearts light as the buoyant morning and brows unbent with care. Alas! how are as bright prospects as perhaps ever dawned upon mutual admiration and love forever overclouded!

On the 3d of October she complained of headache, although she appeared to be not materially indisposed. On that night she had considerable fever, but the next day and night her disease had not apparently increased, and no apprehensions were entertained that she was seized with the prevailing fever. On Saturday she became seriously indisposed, and on Sunday the disease had assumed a dangerous aspect.

Medicine afforded her but a temporary and delusive relief, and she continued sinking gradually until her dissolution, a little past nine o'clock on the night of Monday, the 13th instant. In the first part of her sickness she said it would end in death; but as the disease advanced she drew new hopes from what gave despair to her friends, and expressed a belief that she should live. For many months before her sickness she had become thoughtful on the subject of religion, and, soon after she was taken, sent for Mr. Holman, the Methodist preacher in this town, and invited him to read the Bible, sing, and pray with her. She told him she had not sent for him through any fear of the result of her sickness, but because, whether living or dying, she wished to possess the pearl of great price. She earnestly begged him and others to pray for her, and although she did not then profess to have been converted, no one could witness the earnestness which she exhibited without believing that the gates of heaven would be opened to her. When visited by her sister and one of her brothers, she told them among her consolations that she was near possessing "the brightest pearl that ever blazed." Subsequently she expressed a full confidence that she was prepared to die, and a perfect willingness to undertake the dreadful journey. During most of her sickness there appeared to be a kind of wildness in her mind and manner, giving rise at some times to the most good-humored remarks, and at others to expressions connected with death and immortality of astonishing force and sublimity. It seemed sometimes as if the spirit were bursting its cerement of clay, and giving expression,

by a mortal tongue, to its rapturous emotions as it ascended through the ethereal blue to the abode of eternal bliss. There, it is firmly believed, she has found an everlasting rest in the bosom of her God, where she will feel no more sorrow, no more pain, where the only thought that made death bitter — that of her children — is turned into joy by beholding how completely they are in the hands of that Being who does no wrong, and bereaves and afflicts his poor creatures for some good and benevolent end.

Her mortal remains were carried to Jefferson County, where they were buried beside her dear father, whom, in her sickness, she once said she should "see shortly." Before her interment, an excellent discourse by the Rev. Mr. Holman had spread comfort in the hearts of her relations and friends.

CHAPTER X.

The light in Mr. Kendall's household had gone out. A dark shadow clouded the bright visions of his youth and opening manhood. A widower with four small children, he deliberately forecasts the future. Self-reliant, resolute, and always hopeful, he determines to devote himself more assiduously than ever to his editorial duties.

National and State politics, education, morality, and religion constituted fields in which his mind delighted to range. His lucid and terse style, his cogent reasoning, and his exhaustive arguments, attracted attention, and soon won for their author a national reputation. Few journalists have so suddenly become famous. His appeals were to the intellect; he sought to convince men by force of argument. He always had a powerful ally in the consciousness that he was laboring in the cause of truth and right. Resting on high moral principle, incapable of suppressing the truth, fearless in the exposure of duplicity or falsehood, he was able to do valiant service in whatever cause he engaged in. Rarely descending to the use of blackguardism in his paper, he employed ridicule and satire as frequent weapons, but handled them with wise discrimination.

Engaged as he often was in acrimonious controversy, — for in those days Kentucky politics were of an aggressive and personal nature, — compelled to pass most of his time in his editorial sanctum, annoyed with pecuniary claims, physically weak, and anxious for the education of his children, he felt keenly the want of that sympathy and domestic happiness which for five years had been his.

Mr. Kendall's second marriage took place on the 5th of January, 1826, when he led to the altar Miss Jane Kyle, a lady twenty years his junior, whose parents then resided in Georgetown, Kentucky.

The sun again shone upon his household. However boisterous the outer world might be, at his hearthstone all was peace. No important change occurred in his domestic affairs till after the election of General Jackson in 1828.

As a correspondent, Mr. Kendall had few equals. Frank and honest in expression, mindful of the minutest details, choice in the use of words, he invested his epistolary style with grace and vigor hardly surpassed by the most eminent classical writers. It is doubtful if finer specimens of letter writing adorn the pages of English literature, even in its golden age, than the products of his ready pen.

Subjoined are a few letters written to his second wife :—

TO HIS WIFE.

CLEVELAND, OHIO, October 25, 1827.

MY DEAR WIFE, — I am here weather-bound. We have had rain more or less for five days successively. Last Sunday was the first of it. That day I rode twenty-nine miles ; on Monday came twenty-two ; on Tuesday, twelve ; yesterday I travelled forty. I have been wet several times, though not very much. Yet I have taken no cold, and am in excellent health.

The distance I had to travel is much greater than I supposed. According to my memorandum of distances, I have travelled three hundred and seventy-three miles, and it is upwards of six hundred from this place to my father's. The whole distance is not less than one thousand miles. Of course the time taken to travel it is much greater than I calculated. I have now been from home nearly two weeks, and it will take about three more to reach my father's. This will carry me to the middle of November. Then, if I stay with my parents two weeks, it will be the last week of November before I shall start back. Then, if I spend a week in Washington, it will be about Christmas before I can see you. The time I have been from you seems long already ; but what will it be before I get back ? I am sorry I took the children to their grandmother to stay until I come back, for I did not wish to trouble her so long with the care of them ; I wish they were with you.

Be sure to write to me and let me know all about yourself. Do not distress yourself about me at all, for travelling makes me more healthy than the still life I lead at home. Since the second day after I started, I have not been the least unwell, and I think I look much better. I

have been looking at the lake this morning. It has been so rough for five days that no steamboat or anything else runs upon it. The wind blew almost a hurricane last night. It has much fallen ; but the waves are nearly as high as ever. I went to the top of a hill, just at the water's edge, whence I could see, I suppose, thirty or forty miles up and down and directly in front, and there the lake seemed to meet the clouds. The whole was covered with foaming waves, tossing and roaring like a terrible storm in the woods. Below where I stood there was a beach of sand upon which the waves dashed up two or three rods. Some distance above, the shore appears to be perpendicular, and as the waves strike it they throw their foam ten or fifteen feet high. I then went down to the water's edge and amused myself with looking at the billows dashing up to my very feet. By to-morrow the lake will doubtless be calm, and then I shall start in a few hours for Buffalo.

Give my love to your mother and Elizabeth. You shall hear from me again as soon as I reach my father's, if not before. Probably I may write you again from Albany. I hope on this trip to do something which will be very beneficial to me hereafter. I cannot bear to be embarrassed in money matters, and if I can by any honest means extricate myself I shall not fail to do it.

Your affectionate husband,
AMOS KENDALL.

TO HIS WIFE.

TROY, N. Y., November 7, 1827.

DEAR JANE, — You will perceive by this letter that I am yet in the land of the living, though not at the end of my journey. I wrote to you from Cleveland, Ohio, and I wrote to Mr. Johnston from Rochester, in this State, so that you already know that I came safely down the lake. I know not what day my letter to you was dated ; but it was about ten o'clock on Sunday, the 27th October, that I went on board the schooner "Eclipse" for Buffalo, having been detained in Cleveland almost three days. The weather was still stormy, but the wind was fair, and we sailed, during the rest of that day, at the rate of ten miles an hour. The night was extremely dark, and the wind blew hard, with occasional rain, so that we were obliged to take in a part of our sail lest we should run upon some island coast in the darkness. In the morning there was an island right ahead, not far from the Canada shore. The wind blew harder than ever, and our vessel tossed up and down ten or fifteen feet upon every wave. I should have been alarmed, but I watched the captain and crew, and not perceiving that they were in the least moved I concluded there was no danger. They tacked ship and

stood out into the lake. It now began to rain so hard that I was obliged to quit the deck, where I had remained most of the time during daylight to avoid being sea-sick. I had not been long in the cabin when I began to get sick. As the day advanced the weather became more calm, and we landed at Buffalo about two o'clock on Monday, having sailed upwards of two hundred miles in little more than a day.

From Buffalo it was about twenty miles to the Falls of Niagara, and I intended to take the stage and visit them ; but my sea-sickness had made me feel so disagreeably, and the weather was still so bad, that I determined to go on board the canal-boat and make the best of my way to Albany. I left Buffalo about dark on Monday the 28th of October, and arrived at Albany, a distance of three hundred and sixty-three miles, on Monday night last the 5th of November. This is the most comfortable way of travelling in the world. There is in the boats a small cabin with windows, benches, and chairs, in which about twenty persons may sit very comfortably, warmed in cold weather by a small stove. They sleep at night in berths hung up by the sides of the cabin, which will contain twelve persons. If there are more passengers, they sleep on the floor. The berths are hard and not very comfortable. The boat moves so gently that you cannot tell, as you sit or lie in the cabin, that it moves at all, unless you look out. We travelled about fifty miles in twenty-four hours ; but the packet-boats, which carry nothing but passengers, travel seventy miles. I had pleasant company and a most agreeable passage, except that I had a terrible sick-headache one day, of which I was well the next.

On inquiry yesterday, I was told that my brother George had removed from Greenbush to Troy, which is six miles above Albany, and I came here in the stage. But on inquiry here I am told he has removed to Catskill, which is forty miles below Albany. If I were sure of finding him there I would go down ; but my information is somewhat uncertain. I am in this difficulty by not finding any letter from my father in Albany.

TO HIS WIFE.

DUNSTABLE, November 15, 1827.

MY DEAR JANE, — At last I have reached my father's house in health and safety. I have found my father and mother, brothers, and other relatives all well, but so altered by time that there are few of them whom I should now have known.

I wrote you, I believe, from Troy, N. Y. From that place I went to Albany, and after a day spent there went on board a steamboat for the city of New York. I arrived there, a distance of one hundred and fifty miles, in twelve hours. I found there an old classmate, and a gentle-

man to whom I had letters. I spent one day there, and then embarked in a steamboat for Providence, a distance of two hundred and ten miles, which we passed over in twenty-two hours. A stage received me there and carried me to Boston, forty-five miles. There I had to stay a day before I found a stage coming in this direction ; but the day before yesterday I again started, and was set down by the stage about two o'clock at Tyngsboro, four miles from my father's. This distance I walked, and got here before four o'clock.

I have had terrible weather for most of my journey. When I was in Troy and Albany the snow fell near a foot deep. The earth was covered until I came within fifty miles of New York, when it disappeared. I saw no more of it until I approached Providence, where the whole country was robed in white. As we approached Boston it again disappeared, and the day I spent in Boston there was a tremendous rain, which extended through the country, and left snow only in a few spots. The morning I left Boston the wind blew from the north almost a hurricane. The water dashed up on the wharves, and the sea was all in a foam. The wind was right ahead of the stage, and was so violent sometimes when we passed over hills exposed to the north that it almost stopped the stage. Many trees and some buildings were overturned. At length it began to snow, and when I reached Tyngsboro it was almost enough to blind one who faced it. For the first mile that I walked I could hardly get along, was often obliged to turn my back to the wind to get my breath, and thought I should have to turn into some house and give up my walk. But after I had gone a mile I came where the wind was less violent on account of the woods, and finally reached home without much fatigue. I saw my father and mother looking out at the window before I got near the house. My mother knew me as soon as she saw me ; but my father's sight is dim, and he did not recognize me until my mother had said, "It is Amos." There were a few tears of joy at the meeting, but they soon passed away. My father is much broken. In addition to the dimness of his eyes he is so decrepit that he can move about but little. He is a little deaf, and his memory seems impaired. My mother is scarcely altered since I saw her last. She looks young and healthy. She cooks, washes, and does all the housework for my father and herself, and for such an old woman is remarkably active. My father and she live in two rooms of their house, the rest being occupied by my brother Timothy. I do not think my father can live many years longer ; but my mother looks as if she might last many years. My father is seventy-three, and my mother seventy.

My dear wife, I hope never to be under the necessity of being so long separated again from you and my children. I should be quite happy

18

here, if I had you all with me; but now I feel very anxious to be back. In travelling here I have come nearly fourteen hundred miles, and occupied within two days of five weeks. My journey back will be much shorter and more rapid. I suppose the distance through Washington city to Frankfort is near one thousand miles; and I shall travel it in the swiftest steamboats and stages. When you get this, write to me at Washington. There will, I think, be time enough then for me to get it. I cannot hear from you too often.

I have had the worst cold since I left Albany that I have had these ten years. I caught it by staying on the deck of the steamboats to see the country as we passed. It has not made me sick, except that two or three nights I have had a little headache when I went to bed. It is now wearing away, and in a few days I hope to be clear of it. With this exception, and one spell of sick-headache in the canal-boat, I have enjoyed excellent health. God bless you.

Your affectionate husband,

AMOS KENDALL.

TO HIS WIFE.

WASHINGTON, December 15, 1827.

MY DEAR JANE, — I arrived here yesterday in perfect health, and this day took your letter out of the post-office. You request me to write to you when I start for home, but as I intend to travel as fast as a letter would go, I concluded I would send one on ahead.

A week ago last Monday morning I left my father's, and went to my brother Samuel's, who lives at Medford, five miles from Boston. I intended to take the stage for Albany on Tuesday morning, but had a fit of sick-headache on Monday night and was unable to start. On Wednesday night I went to Boston, and after going to bed and attempting to sleep, in which I did not succeed well, so great was the noise in the tavern, I was called up, and got into the stage before twelve o'clock. About a quarter past eleven the next night we arrived at Northampton, a distance of one hundred miles. The tavern-keeper told me I might sleep until one o'clock, and I paid him for my lodging and went to bed. But in half an hour, before I had got soundly to sleep, I was called up and again got into the stage. I had been stage-sick the evening before, and the loss of two nights' sleep had now worn me down very much. I was quite sick occasionally all day, but kept on, and arrived at Albany, or rather Greenbush, on the other side of the river, about nine o'clock on Friday night. There I met my brother John, who had come on two days before, and on Saturday morning we took the steamboat and went down to see my brother George, who lives forty miles below, at Catskill. I should hardly have known him, and he did not at first recognize me.

With him I spent the Sabbath, and on Monday again took the steamboat and went down to New York. Finding no conveyance to the South until Tuesday noon, I went to my sister's, who is living in the city. At noon I went on board a steamboat for Philadelphia, landed at Brunswick, and rode across to Trenton, twenty-five miles by land.

By daylight on Wednesday we started in a steamboat down the Delaware River, and arrived in Philadelphia about ten o'clock. My college room-mate lives in this city, and I stopped on purpose to see him. It was not until Thursday morning that I found him, and after spending a couple of hours most agreeably with him I took passage at noon in a steamboat for Baltimore. We landed at Newcastle, rode sixteen miles across the country to Frenchtown, took a steamboat again, and were in Baltimore about one o'clock at night. At five o'clock I took the stage, and landed here about ten yesterday. I have met here with a reception warm beyond my most sanguine expectations. Many men whom I never saw before appear to be my warmest friends, if it be possible that any could be warmer than many of those who know me. I have dined to-day with a Senator from New Hampshire, who was in college with me, and to-morrow I am invited to dine with the Speaker of the House of Representatives. I hope I shall be much benefited by my visit here.

When I shall set out for home I cannot tell, but it will be some day next week. I intend to travel as fast as stages and steamboats will carry me. When I arrived here I had hopes of getting away in two or three days; but I think now I shall find it for my interest to stay longer. In my business here I am likely to succeed as well as I could reasonably expect.

Sunday morning, December 16th. I was interrupted last night by the visit of several gentlemen, who remained with me till a late hour.

My friends here say that I look better than they have ever seen me, and I think myself my health is much improved. I am glad to hear that you are so well and cheerful.

I trust I shall have the means, on my return or very shortly after, to place my affairs in a more agreeable situation than they have been for some time past.

I am concerned about the children, — not because I have any fears that Madison and his lady will not take good care of them, but because I do not wish them to be troubled with them. But it will be too late when you get this to do anything about it, if nothing has been done, and I hope you will let the matter rest.

To be with my dear wife and little ones is now the strongest of my desires. Whatever may be our troubles abroad, if we are prudent and discreet towards each other we may always be happy at home, which is

the most valuable kind of happiness. It is better to have storms and misfortunes without doors and fair weather within than storms within and fair weather without. Nothing would delight me more than to be able to retire from the angry contentions of politics into the bosom of my own family, having little to do with the rest of the world. But I fear no such good fortune is in reserve for me. Give my love to your father and mother, to Sister Elizabeth, Alexander, and James. God bless and protect you.

Your affectionate husband,

AMOS KENDALL.

TO HIS WIFE.

WHEELING, December 26, 1828.

MY DEAR JANE, — You see I am safe on land, notwithstanding I have come more than four hundred miles in a steamboat.

Armistead will have informed you that we reached Covington, opposite Cincinnati, on the second night after I left you, about nine o'clock. Understanding that a steamboat was advertised to start for Pittsburg at nine o'clock the next morning, I got up and hurried over the river. The boat, however, did not start until past 3 P. M., and I had an abundance of time to write you, but Armistead was on the other side of the river. I went to see my friend Guilford, and we walked up to the canal. It had frozen over the preceding night, and no business was doing. Nearly three hundred houses have been put up in that city this year, and they now suppose it contains twenty thousand inhabitants.

At length we got under way. We had a mixed, but on the whole an agreeable company. There was an old lady who has lived about three years in Cincinnati, and is returning to Baltimore, who appears to be a Methodist, but I have not yet found out her name. There was another lady, about thirty-five, tolerably agreeable, who is going on to Baltimore with the old lady. Her name is Mrs. Jones. There were two young Virginians who have been travelling through the northern frontier counties and visiting some of the Indian tribes. There was a Dr. Dougherty, who lives at or near Steubenville, Ohio, but formerly resided in Kentucky. He was a very vain man, but very simple, always serious even about the merest trifles, and seemed not to be entirely in his right mind. I was told he had once attempted to drown himself. There was an old Frenchman, by the name of St. Leger La Harpe, with whom I became partially acquainted at Pittsburg in 1814, who appears to be a man of great learning and much good sense. We had also three or four other plain men in the cabin, and a dozen deck passengers. We read some, talked some, and played cards some for our amusement.

Night before last our old Frenchman was very sick, and we thought for a short time he would die. It was discovered that he had a box of opium in his pocket, of which he had been taking liberally, and our doctor declared he was attempting to take his own life. On inquiry, however, I found he was in the habit of taking it every day, and became satisfied that he needed nothing but sleep to relieve him. But our doctor declared he would soon be a corpse, and kept hauling up the old man's arms to feel his pulse, feeling of his feet, and disturbing him in every way, until some of the passengers insisted that he should let him alone and go to bed. The old man's box of opium was given to the captain. In the latter part of the night I heard somebody up, and drawing aside the curtains of my berth, there was the old Frenchman with a *jar* of opium before him on the table, cutting some of it up into small lumps for the purpose of swallowing. I begged him not to take any more of it; but he said he would take no more than he usually took. After taking a large quantity he again went to bed. In the morning he was tolerably well. He told me that trouble in his family had induced him to commence the use of it; that he cannot now live without it, and that he takes regularly eighty-four grains a day.

In the morning he alleged that he had lost his pocket-book, with about $70 in it. We had a search, but nothing was found.

Yesterday our doctor set out the table for cards again, but our old lady insisted that cards should not be played on Christmas. Finally, the young men made her a Christmas gift of their cards, and the old lady gave the doctor, who was the most forward, a very severe lecture. The balance of the day, until our arrival here, passed off in conversation upon religious and other subjects.

I am at a tavern kept by Mrs. Beck, a widow lady. The stage starts between twelve and one o'clock to-day, and reaches Washington in three days and a half. The river is full of ice this morning, and probably not another steamboat will come up. Kiss little Jane for me, and tell all the children their father thinks of them, and they must be good. You shall hear from me at Washington as soon as I get there.

Your affectionate husband,

AMOS KENDALL.

TO HIS WIFE.

WASHINGTON CITY, January 4, 1829.

MY DEAR JANE, — I wrote to you a few lines, two days ago, to inform you that I had arrived safely in this city. I have now had time to look around me a little, and form some opinion as to my future course.

You may prepare your mind for removing to this city in the spring. There is no doubt that such an office will be offered to me here as I cannot in justice to myself and family refuse to accept. I do not yet know precisely what it will be, or what will be the salary attached to it. The only doubt of my friend is, whether it will be a principal clerkship with a salary of $2,000, or an auditorship with $3,000. Of course I prefer the latter, and it is the opinion of my friends that I can get it, provided I will remain here until the arrangements of the new administration are completed. Although I dislike extremely to remain from you and my children so long, yet the prospect of securing $1,000 a year by it, for at least four years, ought not to be thrown away. I must therefore bear the privation of being separated from you until March, or at least until this thing can be made certain. I have procured employment here for the intervening time, which will, I hope, yield me at least $300, and I have a prospect of obtaining business on my way out, which will yield me something like $200 more. My compensation for bringing the vote is $269, which is $100 more than I expected, so that on the whole I hope I shall make $300 or $400 by this trip, besides paying my expenses.

Upon the advice of my friends, I have determined not to have any interest in a printing-office here. There are many good reasons why I ought neither to have any partnership with General Green, nor in and way come in competition with him. But it is probable that I can get him to give me $1,000 a year for writing for his paper. On the whole, I am quite confident of receiving an income here of at least $3,000 a year, and probably $4,000. This will at once place us in more comfortable circumstances. But, my dear wife, let us not think of being proud or extravagant. My first object will be to discharge my debts. That I hope to do by selling my Kentucky property. Our children are to be educated, and I am determined that shall be well done. This may all be accomplished, and yet we may enjoy all the comforts of life and all its pleasures that are worth enjoying. This city is the centre of extravagance. Many of the clerks and others, with an income sufficient to satisfy reasonable men, keep themselves poor by attempting to ape foreign ministers and the high officers of the government in their entertainments and parties. You may be sure I shall imitate none of this. I could show as handsome a wife as any of them, but it would give me no pleasure, and I am sure it would give you none, to make you a show at parties. So let us resolve to enjoy the comforts which this change of fortune is likely to bring us in private content and domestic happiness, without coveting or envying the parade with which we shall be surrounded.

Do not show this letter or speak of it out of the family, for all these

expectations may possibly yet be disappointed. Tell Mary Ann, Adela, and William that they must be good children, and learn their books well, until their father comes home, when he will bring them a present. Kiss little Jane for me. I hope to see her running about and beginning to talk when I get home.

Enclosed you have $20. Use it in any way you may think proper. Give my love to your father and mother, to Elizabeth, Alexander, and James. I must hear from you; write me immediately, and enclose your letter to Colonel R. M. Johnson.

Your affectionate husband,
AMOS KENDALL.

TO HIS WIFE.

WASHINGTON, January 15, 1829.

MY DEAR JANE, — Not one word have I heard from you and my little ones, directly or indirectly, since my arrival in this city. You know not how anxious I am to hear from you. I trust a letter from you is on the way, and I must content myself, until it comes, with writing you another.

I am becoming quite impatient to be with you. I do not believe I can content myself to remain here until the 4th of March; and indeed since the news of Mrs. Jackson's death, I have less inclination. That melancholy event will cast a gloom over everything, and prevent that display which otherwise would have taken place. It is supposed that the General is now on his way to this place, and will be here about the 1st of February. I now think that as soon as some of my friends can converse with him, and ascertain precisely what he intends shall be offered me here, I shall set out for Kentucky. Should he get here by the 1st of February, I shall be with you, unless I change my mind again, about the middle of that month.

On Tuesday night last I was at the wedding of a Miss Reynolds. There was quite a squeeze, but many more ladies than gentlemen, or else I looked at them more. I saw but one whom I thought pretty among them, and, thinks I to myself, my Jane would be prettier than she if she were only dressed as fine. So you may well suppose I did not fall in love with any of them. Indeed, I was introduced to but three, and they, I believe, were all married ladies. Except a few words, my conversation was with the gentlemen, several of whom I had before seen. Among my new acquaintances was Major-General Macomb, Commander-in-Chief of the Army. He is very sociable, and I was surprised to find him a Jackson man. He promised to call and see me, and I hope to find him a valuable acquaintance.

There is a great show here in the dress of the ladies, and great extravagance in entertainments. I do not like the ladies' dresses, however. They lace up too tight and expose their shoulders too much. Then their bonnets are too large, and apparently too heavy. They look as if they were not easy. In their countenances there is wanting that appearance of good health which so much adds to beauty.

I was invited to a party to-night at Dr. Cochrane's, in Georgetown, but I thought I had rather write to you than go. I am invited to another wedding on next Thursday night, at Mr. McLean's, the Postmaster-General. One of his daughters is to be married. If I am well I shall go.

Colonel Johnson is gone to dinner at Mr. Clay's. My old friend has not thought proper to send me an invitation. If he had, it would have been all the same.

This is about 7 P. M., and the dinner, I presume, is not yet over. You must know that the "big bugs" here pay no attention to the sun or the time of day in regulating their meals. They are above that. They invite you to dine with them at five o'clock, and the company gets together about six. They then sit down, and it is eight, nine, or ten before dinner is over. At the 8th of January dinner, which I was at, the company did not all leave the table until eleven o'clock, and then many of them could scarcely leave it at all. About one hundred and twenty persons drank two hundred bottles of wine, and the dinner cost us only five dollars apiece!

On the whole, if there is more extravagance, folly, and corruption anywhere in the world than in this city I do not wish to see that place. People of moderate income attempt to imitate foreign ministers, the President, and secretaries, and thus keep themselves poor, when by prudence and economy they might make ample provision for their families. There is great room for reform here in almost every respect, and I hope Jackson and his friends will introduce it.

Give my love to our little ones, — make them all good, so that when I get home none of them will know how to cry. I wish I could fold myself up in this letter, and be with you as soon as it will. But I must be patient, and so must you.

Your affectionate husband,
AMOS KENDALL.

TO HIS WIFE.

WASHINGTON CITY, January 23, 1829.

MY DEAR JANE, — I have not heard a word from you, except that Mr. Sanders, in a letter received yesterday, says my family is well. If

you have not written, write immediately when this reaches you, and enclose it to Colonel R. M. Johnson, Senator, etc. Our present news is, that General Jackson will leave home about the 20th of the present month, and as he will travel but slowly he will not be here until the 10th of February, or thereabouts. Should I leave for home as soon as I see and confer with him, still I cannot start until the 12th or 15th of February, so that your letter will have plenty of time to reach me.

Within a few days some of General Jackson's principal friends have started a project for running me and General Green together for the printing of Congress, with the understanding that we are to divide that and the patronage of the executive office between us. On account of the General's friendship for me last winter I refused to suffer anything of the kind to be done, unless with his entire approbation. I do not know whether any of them have conversed with him, and the result is doubtful. Green is a noble fellow in many respects, but he is perfectly wild in pecuniary matters, and imprudent in the management of his paper. I would not on any account have any partnership with him in money matters or in editing a newspaper. He would ruin me, as he certainly will himself, and we should never agree. But if the object now in view can be effected, I will take one half of the printing, and start a new paper myself. It is very uncertain, and I am very careless about it, for it would lead me a much more laborious life than an office with a salary, which I am sure to obtain if I will have it. Yet I should probably make more by one half of the printing than by any office, and for that reason I am willing to labor hard for a few years more, that you and my little ones may never be exposed to want.

Last night I was at a wedding-party at the Postmaster-General's. The concourse of people was very great. There were three hundred or four hundred, about one half of whom were ladies. It comprised nearly all the fashion of the city. But the crowd was such that there was very little enjoyment. The whole house, up stairs and down, at least eight rooms of tolerable size, was full to overflowing. At one time the whole stairway and the passages above were so blocked up that most of them could not get one way or the other. For my part, I did not venture up stairs, lest I should be caught between two or more of those very fine ladies and drifted — the Lord knows where. The ladies were splendidly dressed, to be sure; but I could give you but a poor account of their dresses, were I to try. There was no sitting down. The ladies walked, or were rather pushed about, hanging upon the arms of the gentlemen. I was not so unfortunate as to have one of them upon my arm, but I thought it would have given me some pleasure to have had you upon it, dressed with but half the elegance of many a beauty, so called, who was there. I do not know that you could match them in talking nonsense, and as for sense, it seldom ventures into such assemblies, and more seldom ventures *out* when it happens to be there. I snatched a cup of coffee and some cake from a waiter which, in the hands of a negro, was knocking to and fro in the crowd, and there was plenty of wine and spirits on the sideboard, if a body could only get to it. These squeezes generally last until eleven or twelve o'clock, but I came away a little after nine, and wrote a letter to my father after I got home. Are all the children good? Write me, that I may know whether I shall bring them anything. Give my love to all.

Affectionately, your husband,

AMOS KENDALL.

TO HIS WIFE.

WASHINGTON, February 10, 1829.

MY DEAR JANE, — Your letter of the 29th January was received yesterday. It gives me great pleasure to hear that you and my little ones are all well.

Last *night* I dined at the house of the Postmaster-General. I say *night*, because they have here adopted the ridiculous English custom of having dinner after dark. We were invited at *five* o'clock, went a little before *six*, and sat down about *seven*. The party consisted of Mr. Calhoun, Vice-President, General Scott, and Colonel Neale of the army, Mr. Ingram, Colonel Johnson, and four or five others, with half a dozen ladies. The table was highly ornamented and loaded with every kind of luxury. There was ham, beef cooked in various ways, mutton, turkey *with* bones and *without*, pork, chicken, partridges, canvas-back ducks, jellies, puddings, olives, grapes, raisins, custards, apples, and half a dozen things I know no name for; Madeira wine, sherry, champagne, and two kinds the names of which I do not recollect. Of course we could not dispose of all these good things, nor of a small portion of each of them, without spending an hour and a half at the table. Mr. McLean, who gave this entertainment, I suppose you know is a *Methodist*.

You seem to fear that if I go to such dinners and parties I shall have to give them. Not at all. These are given by very rich men or public officers who have $ 6,000 salary, and although many living on humbler incomes foolishly attempt to imitate all this style, it is not required or expected of them. I am told that these heads of departments do not even expect, when they invite those of less income, that their civilities will be returned. But it is otherwise among the humbler class, who throw away their living in this manner. If you go to their parties, having a family living here, you are expected to return them.

But I am a sort of *single man* now, and I can go where I please, — I mean to what *parties* I please, and nothing is expected of me in return.

I am glad you feel as I do in relation to this foolery of giving splendid parties. I should like once in a while to have a few friends to take tea and spend a social hour, without much expense or ceremony; but these great entertainments would suit my means as little as they would my taste.

I do not dislike your ambition to "*look fine.*" The more attention you pay to your person, the more I shall always love you. I do not believe any man of any taste can love a woman long who is not cleanly and neat in her person and dress. While I have the means, you shall be just as "fine" as your own taste desires.

With a "fine" face, "fine" clothes, and a "fine" mind well stored with "fine" things, you would be well fitted for any station into which fortune may throw you; and especially, to be always a *beloved* wife and a good mother.

If you can't persuade Eliza to be a little more moderate, I believe I had better not go home; for if I did, I should have to run away again, because I should be unable to pay her.

As the little girls claim only a doll, and William a horse, I shall have no difficulty on that score, even although James, Susan, and Peggy be added to the number.

Do ask Eliza whether she will not be satisfied with *a man?*

I still remain remarkably well, and my friends say I am gaining in flesh. God bless you, my dear wife.

Your affectionate husband,

AMOS KENDALL.

P. S. Tell your father that General Green has been elected printer to the House of Representatives to-day, by a majority of twelve votes over Gales and Seaton. There were for Green one hundred and seven, Gales and Seaton ninety-five, and six scattering, one of which was for your husband.

General Jackson is expected here to-morrow or the next day. I cannot tell whether I shall start from here before the 4th of March or not, until after his arrival. I will write to you as soon as I know myself.

TO HIS WIFE.

WASHINGTON, February 14, 1829.

MY DEAR WIFE, — I have had a private interview with General Jackson this morning, and he has assured me that I may rely on receiving a principal clerkship, with a salary of $ 2,000, or an auditorship with a

salary of $ 3,000. He would have no hesitancy in promising me the latter, did he not think it possible that some of those offices may be abolished, in which case I might be thrown out. He expressed his regard for me, and his disposition to serve me, in strong terms. I think I shall prefer the office with $ 3,000, and run the risk of its abolition.

I am advised to stay until I actually receive the appointment, which cannot be until the 4th of March or after. My friends advise me also to borrow a sum of money here sufficient to pay off most of my debts in Kentucky, that I may be able to sell my property there on better terms. It is probable I may do so.

I am inclined to think that I shall look out for a house in Georgetown. Rent is lower there, the people are said to be more agreeable, and the means of living somewhat cheaper. The distance from the public offices is only such as to afford me good exercise, and for most of the way there are now good side pavements.

I was at a small party in Georgetown night before last, at a Mr. Cochran's, who is an old man, and I believe an old resident. There was not so much parade as there is generally in the city, and the evening passed very pleasantly. Abraham Bradley was there, whom your father doubtless knows. The wife of one of Mr. Cochran's sons, about your age, I found to be the most agreeable lady I have met with since I have been here. If I had not had a wife and she a husband, I might have fallen in love with her. As it was, I thought only how much you would be pleased with her company.

Last night I was at *another* party in this city, where there was a plenty of *style*. It was given by a Mr. Dickens, who is, I believe, a $ 2,000 clerk in the Treasury Department, and I was told it was the second he had given within two weeks. But if I had known as much about him yesterday as I do to-day, I should not have gone. It is said he now wants some valuable office, and as a means of getting it, I suppose, he is wasting in extravagant parties all his salary in his present office. When I get to be a clerk I shall do no such foolish thing. Mind that, wife!

We have had about as cold weather here for three days as I ever felt for so long a time anywhere. It is not yet at all moderated. The river is frozen up for several miles below here. All my friends say I have much improved in appearance since I have been here, and I think I am some pounds heavier. I do not know what has improved me unless that I have worked a little *less* and lived a little *better* since I have been here than I did at home.

But I had rather work harder and live more roughly to be with you and my children than to live in this way. I hope our fortune will be so *good* for the balance of our lives that we shall not be again sepa-

rated. Tell the little girls and William that they must continue to be good, if I do not come home so soon as I expected. They must learn their books and mind their mother. When they come here to live, they shall go to the best schools I can find. Little Jane cannot understand what I say to her; but kiss her anyhow, and tell her it is her father. I have not written to your father. Always when I sit down to write home I think chiefly of you, so that my pen will write that way. You may read him as much of my letters as you choose. Let me see, how many are there to send love to? — little Jane, William, Adela, Mary Ann, your mother, your father, Elizabeth, Alexander, James, Susan, Peggy. Is there anybody else? If there is, give my love to them too. I kiss you, my dear wife.

Your affectionate husband,

AMOS KENDALL.

TO HIS WIFE.

WASHINGTON, February 25, 1829.

DEAR JANE, — I have been so closely engaged in writing circulars for members of Congress, for a week past, that I have had no time to write letters. I expect to get about $ 50 for my week's work.

The other day I had a long conversation with General Jackson. At the close of it, after saying many flattering things of my capacity, character, etc., he observed, "I told one of my friends that you were fit for the head of a department, and I shall put you as near the head as possible." I understood him to mean that I should have an auditor's office, which he has said to others he intended to give me. The salary of the office is $ 3,000. I think I can discharge its duties and make $ 1,000 more per year by my pen. Unless it shall be necessary that I should remain here a few days after the 4th of March, to take possession of the office and arrange matters, I think I shall start for home before that day. It is fortunate that I came and have remained here, for it will make a difference of $ 1,000 per year, I have little doubt. If I had not come, I should probably have been offered only a chief clerkship, with $ 2,000. I have no news to write you. The weather here has been exceedingly cold for two weeks. The Potomac is frozen up; the stock of wood in the city is exhausted, and it is selling from eight to twelve dollars a cord. The poor have suffered very much. On the 23d, Congress gave them fifty cords out of their stock, and I am told the same quantity was distributed from the Treasury Department. The weather has moderated, and the snow is thawing. If I start for home next week I shall probably not write again. Tell our babies I shall not forget the dolls and the horse. There is a fair here to-morrow, and I intend to buy something for all the children, and for James, Susan, and

Peggy. If there is a *man* for sale, I will buy one for Elizabeth, which I hope will pay all the debt she says I owe her. Alexander can get a *girl* for himself. Give my love to your father and mother. I believe I sent $ 20 in a letter, and forgot to mention it. I suppose you liked that better than to mention it and forget to send it.

God protect you.

Your affectionate husband,

AMOS KENDALL.

TO HIS WIFE.

WASHINGTON, March 10, 1829.

MY DEAR JANE, — I received your last letter on yesterday. I had before thought of trying to get some place for your father, but cannot do anything until I am myself appointed. I hope in a year or two, and perhaps sooner, to find some situation that will enable him to live near us, and comfortably. My regard for him would induce me to do it, but my love for you, and my desire in every possible way to promote your happiness, will make me much more anxious to accomplish it. After I get more acquainted here I shall know better what there is of which he is capable.

Since I commenced writing this letter I have seen Mr. Pickett, who intends starting to-morrow for Kentucky, and will visit Frankfort. He has kindly offered to carry such letters and other small matters as I may wish to send. You will therefore receive herewith a bundle containing the following articles as presents : namely, a reticule for Elizabeth ; a small feathered reticule for Susan ; two fashionable dolls for Mary Ann and Adela, of which Mary Ann is to have her choice ; a small doll for Peggy ; a horse, etc., for William ; a man-tumbler for James. The doll with the curled hair shows the fashionable mode for putting up the hair in this city at this time, and both of them have fashionable dresses on. If you want to be in the fashion, therefore, you must take pattern from the dolls.

In the ends of the boxes of the boys' presents you will see the end of a wire, which turns around, and the horse will caper and the man will tumble, to music.

Besides these, you will find a cape for yourself, a cap for your mother, a rattle for Jane, and some other trinkets for yourself and the little girls. I am sorry I cannot send Elizabeth a man just now. There are plenty for sale, but neither she nor I have money enough to buy. If she had $ 20,000 she could take her choice out of the whole assortment, and if she had $ 5,000 she might buy a decent fellow ; but as it is, I am afraid she will have to go without. It is a great misfortune, but I do not know that there is any help for it.

My year at Markley's house is up on the 1st of April. I do not wish to pay rent for nothing, and as I shall not probably be at home by that time, I wish you to have measures taken to clear the house and deliver it up to him. I think the best way will be to take out to your father's whatever you wish to preserve, and deliver up the balance to Ben Hickman to be sold. He has a judgment against me, I believe, in favor of somebody ; to satisfy that, it must be sold on three months' credit, and I shall have no trouble in collecting it ; and if there shall be more than enough to pay it, he can sell the whole and collect the money for me when due. The things which I do not wish sold are the shellwork boxes, the tea-caddies, the dressing-table, the bureau, and all those articles which my first wife left, including the pictures. In relation to all the rest of the articles you may do as you please, — and if there be anything among them which your father wants, let him have them. Let all my papers and newspapers be carefully preserved, but let all the books be sold, excepting the Bible. In fine, let everything be sold at once which will have to be sold at all, so that I may have no further trouble on that score. I will write to Ben Hickman on the subject.

I have not yet received my appointment, and do not expect it until the Senate adjourns, which will be in a day or two. In the course of a week I shall doubtless be in office. I shall make all possible haste to have its affairs arranged so that I may leave it, but shall not start until I hear from you. Do not, therefore, lose a day in writing to me. God bless you and my little ones.

Ever your affectionate husband,

AMOS KENDALL.

P. S. — Mr. Pickett had told me he should start at eleven o'clock to-morrow, but has just called and told me (ten o'clock at night) that he must start at seven in the morning. I intended to have got you something more elegant than the cape, but have no time now. So I send you that, with another kiss. There is a kiss on the piece of gold, — I have just put it there.

TO HIS WIFE.

WASHINGTON, March 22, 1829.

MY DEAR JANE, — I received my commission as fourth auditor last evening, and shall enter upon the discharge of the duties to-morrow. The salary is $ 3,000 a year. If now I had my affairs in Kentucky settled, and had my dear wife and little ones with me, I should be a happy man. I cannot say that I am very *unhappy* now, for my health continues excellent. I meet with nobody but friends, and am situated in a very agreeable family.

I do not recollect that I have given you any account of the family of

the Rev. O. B. Brown, where I board. Mr. Brown, though a Baptist preacher, is a cheerful, jolly man, who loves good eating and drinking and delights in a joke. He is scarcely ever serious except at prayers and in the pulpit. He is a clerk in the General Post-Office, and gets a salary of $1,400. Mrs. Brown is not an interesting woman either in her person or conversation ; but she is religious and very charitable to the poor, to whom she devotes much of her time and labor. They have an interesting, well-educated daughter of about eighteen years old, who is very sociable and entirely amiable in her disposition. A Mrs. Jackson, wife of Dr. Jackson, of the army, who is a son of Mrs. Brown by a former husband, has been residing with us, with her two children, for several weeks. She is quite handsome, and a very agreeable, sociable woman. Mr. Brown's three sons make up the family group. Having little to do, I have spent many hours with these ladies of late. Mary Brown has an album, in which she insisted that I should write some poetry. I wrote two or three pieces, the best of which is as follows : —

THE WILD-FLOWER.

On the white cliffs of Elkhorn, with cedars o'erspread,
    Where beauty and wildness in silence repose,
A gay little wild-flower raised up its head,
    By zephers caressed as in sweetness it rose.

Its beauties no culture could ever impart,
    No garden nor meadow can boast such a gem ;
All native it blossomed ; for never had art
    Transplanted its root or enameled its stem.

I saw it and loved it ; and now on my breast
    It breathes out its fragrance, its beauty displays ;
My heart leaps to meet it, in ecstasy blest,
    The dream of my nights and the charm of my days.

And O, thought of rapture ! not like other flower
    Does it droop on the air, life and loveliness flinging ;
But its charms and its fragrance increase every hour,
    And sweet little buds all around it are springing.

Did you ever see this wild-flower ? I wish I had it here, and my little buds with it. It would be sweeter than all the city flowers. I am afraid I have praised you too much to these ladies. Perhaps you cannot come up to their expectations. But you must excuse me, for what I cannot enjoy in seeing you I must make up as well as I can by talking about you.

Until I hear from you in relation to your own wishes, I shall do nothing about going to Kentucky or procuring and furnishing a house here. I hope, before this time, you have got my letter by Mr. Pickett, with the dolls, etc., and have written to me in reply. I do not like the idea of

being separated from you and the children until the end of the summer, but I must abide by your decision.

About three inches of snow fell here last night, and we have this morning a keen northwester. There is not yet the slightest appearance of spring.

I have no news. Give my love to all. Can little Jane talk or walk yet ?

Your affectionate husband,

AMOS KENDALL.

TO HIS WIFE.

WASHINGTON, April 6, 1829.

MY DEAR JANE, — Your letter of the 23d of March was handed to me by Mr. Pickett last night, and I should have written an answer then, had he not sat with me until after eleven o'clock.

I shall offer Mr. Johnston a clerkship here, and he has agreed to accept it. In a few days I expect to write him to come on. I am very anxious that Mary Ann and Adela shall be going to school, and I have been thinking of getting him to take charge of them and bring them on here. They will be pleasantly situated in Mr. Brown's family, and may be going forward with their education. Besides it will be very inconvenient to have so many children together when you come on, — there will be five of them. William, Jane, and the one that *is to be*, will be as many as we can well attend to on the road. Again, if I have to remain here sometime yet before I can go out, which is very probable, it is but fair that you should divide the children with me. It would be a great comfort and pleasure to have the little girls with me until I go out, and then I would leave them in safe hands here. I think I shall send Mr. Johnston to talk with you about it, and you will do just as you think proper.

Tell Elizabeth I don't believe a word about her *man*. But if she has made a bargain for one, I advise her not to wait my return before she has the bill of sale signed, sealed, and delivered. These men are a sort of wild animal, and when you have once caught them you had better tie them until they get tamed. If she don't secure this fellow soon, I expect to hear nothing of him when I get out. "Strike while the iron is hot," "Make hay while the sun shines," "A bird in the hand is worth two in the bush," "There 's many a slip between the cup and the lip," "Delays are dangerous," "Procrastination is the thief of love," etc., etc., etc. No, no, do not wait for me. "Never put off till to-morrow what you can do to-day." Then it will be such *hot weather* shortly. Who can this man be ? How delightful it would be if she could buy up old Bob Johnston and come on here with us !

I have been in office two weeks. I have applied myself closely to understand my duties. The labor is very light, and, when I am master of the laws under which I act, will consist of little more than looking at accounts and signing my name. Some days I spend five or six hours in disposing of the business before me, and on others it hardly takes one. If I had my affairs in Kentucky settled up, and my family around me, it seems to me I should be the happiest man in the world. I am more lively than I was when constantly poring over political matters, and I know I am in much better health. I am quite popular, too, among the ladies, and have made you popular by the fine things I have said of you. You will find a number of friends here, who never saw you.

I shall send you money to pay your father for all his expense and trouble of having my family with him, and to buy everything you want.

My dear Jane, you know not how much I desire again to clasp you in my arms. In the midst of all my enjoyments here, I still sigh for your society which nothing can replace. Well, when we get together again, I hope we shall love each other better, and never be again so long parted.

Give my love to your father and mother, Elizabeth and Alexander, Susan and Peggy, and all our babies. I should be delighted to see little Jane walking about. Kiss her for me. Give my best respects to Mr. and Mrs. Fenwick, and to Mr. and Mrs. Johnson.

Your affectionate husband,

AMOS KENDALL.

TO HIS WIFE.

WASHINGTON, April 22, 1829.

MY DEAR WIFE, — I have been so busily employed for some days in ferreting out some of the villanous transactions of my predecessor and others formerly in office here, that I have had little time for anything else. Nor have I yet got through with it; but I have snatched a moment to let you know that I am alive and well.

Enclosed you will receive $50. You have not acknowledged the receipt of any money I have sent you, not even my *golden kisses.* I should like to know whether all got safe to your hands.

God knows when I shall get away from here. These investigations into the conduct of the men lately in office are so important that they must be made and completed as soon as possible, that the government may recover the money out of which it has been cheated. I have discovered frauds in Dr. Watkins, who went before me in this office, to the amount of more than $7,000, and how much more will come to light I know not. Write me every two days and tell me everything.

In haste, your affectionate husband,

AMOS KENDALL.

TO HIS WIFE.

WASHINGTON, May 1, 1829.

MY DEAR JANE, — I have this moment received yours of the 18th April, which is postmarked at Frankfort on the 22d. In relation to the little girls, I gave up the idea of their coming on without you in a day or two after I wrote to you, and never wrote to Mr. Johnston anything about it.

The President has sent out instructions to have my predecessor arrested for frauds committed upon the government in this office. In a short time he will probably be brought to the city for examination. This circumstance has made it impossible for me to leave here as yet, and will detain me I know not how long. Indeed, I am learning things, from day to day, which make it very doubtful in my mind whether I do not owe it to my country and government not to leave this office during the present summer at all. If it shall so turn out, I shall make arrangements to have you and the children brought on with some safe attendant, — probably Mr. Johnston, — as soon as you are able to travel with entire comfort. I feel beyond description the privation of being separated so long from you and the children, and nothing but a sense of imperative duty would induce me to submit to it.

I sent you a few days ago $50. Enclosed you have $50 more. I have enclosed to you money several times, to be used by you or given to your father. Use this as you think proper. In none of your letters have you acknowledged the receipt of any money from me, and as you speak of borrowing money to fit out the children, I fear that you have not received it. I think I sent you once $20, at another time $30, and recently $50, besides two golden kisses (quarter eagles) worth $2.50 each. I hope you have received them.

In study and writing I make my office quite laborious of late. I spend about two hours in the office before breakfast; upwards of six more before dinner, which is about four o'clock, and sometimes I go up after dinner. But most of the time after dinner I spend in walking. Last evening I spent with Mrs. Decatur, the lady of the late Commodore Decatur. I found her an interesting woman, but not beautiful. But it is but little of my time that I spend at anything else than work.

I expect I shall have sold the printing-office before this reaches you. I wish I could sell the mill also. Give my love to all the babies, — to father, mother, sister, brothers, Susan, Peggy, not forgetting James.

God preserve you.

Your affectionate husband,

AMOS KENDALL.

TO HIS WIFE.

WASHINGTON, June 1, 1829.

DEAR JANE, — I have been anxiously expecting to hear from you for a whole week, but in vain.

I was sick a whole day last week, but have got over it entirely. The weather has been for some days remarkably hot. Within two days we have had a great deal of thunder, and the air is now cooler.

The case of Mr. Watkins is not yet disposed of. Everybody admits him to be guilty, but there is a motion to quash the indictments, on the ground that there is no law to punish a fraud on the United States. The question will probably be decided to-day. If I can, I shall be out as soon as I hear you are in a fair way to be able to travel.

I turned out six clerks on Saturday. Several of them have families, and are poor. It was the most painful thing I ever did; but I could not well get along without it. Among them is a poor old man with a young wife and several children. I shall help to raise a contribution to get him back to Ohio, where he came from, and intend to give him $50 myself. I shall send you more money in a few days, or carry it myself. If I go, I shall hire a private carriage to go out with me and bring my whole brood of little ones. Bless their sweet faces. I long to see them. Give them my love as well as to all the rest.

With unchanging affection,

Your husband,

AMOS KENDALL.

TO HIS WIFE.

WASHINGTON, June 8, 1829.

MY DEAR JANE, — After waiting almost three weeks to hear from you, I received your kind letter dated June, but without the day. I was sure that you had been sick and could not write, and I was becoming quite angry with Elizabeth and your father for not writing me something about it.

So you cannot come without me. Well, you *'shall* not come without me. As soon as the case of Watkins is disposed of, I intend to go to Kentucky. The grand jury is adjourned over to the 21st, and if there should be a trial at this court it will take nearly to the 1st of July. I cannot, therefore, hope to start earlier than the first of next month. But be with you I *will,* if I am alive and well.

I am sorry your father has been so hard pressed for money. If I could have known it at the time, I would have sent you more than I have. In this letter I expect you will find $50 more. Probably I will bring the next myself. If your father could get the post-office to take his paper, where could he get the capital to carry on a mill if he were

to rent one? Such a thing ought not to be undertaken without $1,500 or $2,000, which he cannot raise. I am in hopes I shall find something for him to do here yet, but I do not perceive anything about the office of which he is capable. He would not do for a clerk, and he is too old to be appointed a messenger. I hope I shall find him some superintending about the public grounds or buildings which he can fill with usefulness to the public. In the mean time he had better not think of renting mills, but live where he is until something can be done for him.

If Alexander will take pains to improve himself in writing, arithmetic, and in general reading, he may probably get a place as clerk in some of the offices, and be able to support his father and mother in advanced life. Your father or him, or both, I shall be ready to assist to anything which they can do with honor to themselves and advantage to the public.

So you don't think you are any better off, now "Jackson's elected!" Well, I confess you have not yet enjoyed much pleasure or advantage therefrom. But you have a *prospect.* $3,000 a year sure income is a little more comfortable to look upon than the subscriptions to the "Argus." We will live comfortably and genteelly, but economically, especially until my debts are paid off.

I cannot get boarding for my army for much less than $1,200, and I have determined to keep house. I can rent a good house in Georgetown for $175, and I must furnish it as well as I can. If I have not money to do it at once, I can hire furniture. So you may set your thoughts on keeping house in Georgetown. We shall be somewhat out of the way of the great parties in this city, and can live there more comfortably and cheaper. The society there is more plain and more agreeable. The house that I contemplate taking is in a charming neighborhood, on First Street, near Cox's Row. Perhaps your father will know something of the neighborhood. My lady friends in this city are bitterly opposed to my going to Georgetown to live, but those in Georgetown are quite delighted with it, or seem to be. You will see that my acquaintance with the ladies is quite extensive.

I am glad my sweet little ones are learning so well. Mary Ann ought to write me a letter, if it be not a very long one. Adela, I hope, will soon be able to write me also. How does the "old gentleman" come on? Little Jane, too, — I long to see her, and hear her say "Chick, chick," etc. Tell Mary Ann I remember something more about her than her "nose." To Elizabeth I am under great obligations for her attention to my children.

Give my love to your father and mother and the whole catalogue of the family. God preserve and bless you all.

Your affectionate husband,

AMOS KENDALL.

TO HIS WIFE.

WHITE SULPHUR SPRINGS, VA., August 7, 1829.

MY DEAR JANE, — I reached this place on my way to Kentucky last evening. I have determined to remain here for the purpose of drinking the sulphur water until Tuesday next, which will be the 11th, and then make my way to you as fast as I can.

The water of this spring is very strong of sulphur, and it operates freely. There are about one hundred and forty persons here, but except a gentleman with whom I rode two days in the stage, not one whose face I ever saw before, so far as I know.

Night before last I stayed at the Warm Springs. Nearly water enough to carry a mill boils up out of the ground, which is just about warm enough to bathe in. They have a fine bath prepared by clearing out the principal spring and building a wall around it. It is as big as a very large room, and about five feet deep. I went into it and remained in about ten minutes. It is delightful.

This whole country is nothing but mountains, with small spots of tillable ground between them. Yet by winding round in the valleys the road is not very mountainous. Indeed, it passes over the top of but one high ridge since we reached the mountains, and from that there is one of the most magnificent views I ever beheld. Back towards Washington the eye ranges over nothing but mountains, the most distant of which is the Blue Ridge, just visible in the horizon. To the most distant point visible it must be at least seventy miles. Scarcely a cleared spot, and I believe not a single house, is to be seen in all the vast prospect. Yet there are many farms and houses concealed in the deep valleys.

My health is pretty good, but I have not got entirely free from boils. It is to carry these off and purify my blood that I stop to drink this water. I hope five days will be sufficient for that. At any rate I can stay no longer. I have lost three days on the road already, two at Upperville and one at Winchester. When I start on Tuesday I shall go but ten miles that evening. It will take me three days then to reach the Ohio River. It may be a day or two before I can get passage down to Maysville. It will then take a day to go down and a day and a half to get from Maysville to Franklin Mills. It will therefore be about the 18th of the month that I shall see you, with Heaven's blessing. I did not expect to be so long on the road, but the distance is greater on this route than I supposed. It cannot be much short of six hundred and fifty miles.

As the mail does not go to the West until to-morrow evening, I shall not close my letter to-day.

CHAPTER XI.

EXTRACT from Mr. Kendall's review of the condition of the government during the first three years of General Jackson's term : —

"Delegated by the Republican Party in the several States to meet in convention and adopt such measures as, upon consultation, might be found necessary to concentrate their support upon a single candidate for the Vice-Presidency, we deem it our duty to review the condition of our government and country, and submit to our constituents the reasons which have induced our decision.

"All remember that in February, 1825, John Quincy Adams was elected President by the House of Representatives, through a coalition with Henry Clay, whom he immediately appointed Secretary of State. It was charged, that in this election Mr. Clay was induced to support Mr. Adams, in opposition to the will of the people, by a previous understanding that, in consideration of that support, Mr. Adams was to give him the first place in his cabinet, as a means of securing to him the succession. Upon this charge an issue was made up before the American people, who, after full discussion and consideration, pronounced a verdict of guilty, and consigned the delinquent to private life.

"General Jackson came into power by an overwhelming majority of popular and electoral votes. Of 1,150,508 popular votes given, he received a majority of 135,684. Of 261 electoral votes, he received a majority of 95. The people had a right to expect a cheerful acquiescence in their decision. They had a right to expect that no factious opposition, without just cause or legitimate object, would be got up against the man of their choice, and the administration of their creation. These just expectations were soon disappointed. The first act of General Jackson in the administration of the government had not been done, the acclamations of a delighted people, and the thunder of our country's cannon, which welcomed him to power, had not ceased to echo around the Capitol, when Mr. Clay, amidst a chosen band of hardy followers, proclaimed uncompromising war, and gave the signal to his distant clans. On his retreat to the West, and in his perambulations through the States of Kentucky, Ohio, and Indiana, he sounded the tocsin of alarm, and called his legions to the field.

August 8th. The water of this spring has a very favorable effect on me, and I think I shall derive much benefit from it. I have already formed several acquaintances, whose conversation enables me to pass an idle hour very agreeably. But a small portion whom I see are invalids. Most of them visit the springs rather for sport than health. There are some sick husbands with well wives, but more well husbands without their wives. The Virginians are very much in the habit of visiting the springs for weeks, themselves, and leaving their wives and daughters at home.

I do not know that I can write you anything more that would be interesting. In a very few days after this reaches you I hope to see you myself. Give my love to your father and mother and Elizabeth. I have forgotten her prize at last ! Shall I not have to pay it myself ? Give my love also to Alexander, Susan, and Peggy, and *especially* to my own little brood, Mary Ann, Adela, William, Jane, and *all the rest.*

With unabated affection,

Your husband,

AMOS KENDALL.

"In the mean time General Jackson entered upon the duties of the high station to which he had been elevated by a grateful people. A few individuals of doubtful integrity or dissolute habits were removed from office, and their places supplied with political friends. It was soon rumored that frauds and corruptions had been detected in the late incumbents, verifying the worst suspicions of those who had opposed the last administration.

"A new energy was inspired into all the public offices. The business which was in arrears for years was promptly brought up, and the receivers of public moneys, as well as disbursing officers of the departments, in all parts of the country and in distant seas, vied with each other in the promptitude with which their accounts were rendered. It is confidently believed that at no period in our government have public accounts been more faithfully rendered or more promptly settled than within the last three years.

"The new impulse immediately reached other portions of the public administration. Our foreign relations were found in a disordered state. A misunderstanding was pending with Brazil. This was speedily adjusted. Colombian cruisers had depredated upon our commerce, oppressive duties were levied in the ports of that Republic on the cargoes of American vessels, and circumstances had rendered our minister there powerless to do good. A successor was sent out ; indemnities were granted ; the duties were reduced ; and at length our vessels have been put on the same footing as those of Colombia in Colombian ports. With Mexico we had a suspended treaty. It has been ratified and confirmed with new and important stipulations. With Turkey we had no treaty, and the Black Sea was closed to our commerce. A treaty has been formed, which admits our vessels into Turkish ports on the terms granted to the most favored nation, and enables them to reach many Russian and Persian ports before closed to them. With Austria we had no diplomatic relations. A treaty has been formed extending to our commerce many advantages in her ports. Upon Denmark we had claims for spoliations of long standing. They have been recovered to the amount of more than $ 750,000. The last administration had lost a valuable trade with the British West Indies, and had sought to regain it zealously, but in vain. A new minister was sent out, and it was recovered. For twenty years our government had fruitlessly urged our claims on France. A new minister was sent out, and they are secured to the amount of $ 5,000,000, while the claim of that nation to exclusive privileges in our Louisiana ports is extinguished forever. France was obliged to send a fleet to enforce reparation for injuries done her commerce by the cruisers of Portugal. To us similar reparation, to the extent of about $ 112,000, has been accorded on demand.

The consequence of this improvement in our foreign relations is a commercial activity scarcely equalled in our history. The value of shipping, of wharves, of warehouses, of everything connected with commerce, has greatly increased. The shipyards are filled with new structures, and laborers find full employment and high wages. The farmer, the manufacturer, the mechanic, every class of society directly or indirectly participate in the advantages. At Boston alone, it is said, fifteen vessels were fitting out for the trade of the Black Sea ; the British West India trade has employed 36,914 tons of shipping ; the exports have been $ 1,441,700, and the imports $ 1,284,678 ; while our trade with other parts of the globe, relieved from a portion of the competition, is carried on with more spirit and better profit.

"The same energetic spirit entered the Treasury Department, and prepared it to realize all the benefits of our foreign relations in their improved condition. Among the custom-house officers and other receivers of public moneys, numerous peculators were discovered and hurled from office. The depredations of those who were removed within the first eighteen months of General Jackson's administration, in this department of the public service, were at least $ 280,000. The unrestrained power of the Treasurer over the public funds, by which they could be drawn upon his individual check, was taken away by a new regulation. Frauds in payment of fishing bounties were stopped, and two collectors, believed to have been engaged in them, removed from office ; in consequence of which there was a saving, in the first year of the administration in that branch of expenditure, of $ 51,271.41.

"A new and more efficient system of regulations for the revenue-cutter service has been introduced.

"From the improved condition of our foreign relations, and the energetic administration of the Treasury Department, the annual revenues of the nation have been increased about *four millions of dollars,* while the duties on coffee, tea, etc., have been taken off to the extent of about four millions. The receipts of 1832 will undoubtedly exceed those of 1828 by at least *six millions.*

"The War Department has long been completely organized, so far as it regards the army. That branch of its duties has been conducted according to the laws without material improvement. It is in its Indian affairs that the vigor of the administration has been most signally displayed. The idea of colonizing the Indians beyond the Mississippi was suggested by Mr. Jefferson soon after the acquisition of Louisiana. Mr. Monroe made it the topic of a special message to Congress, and from that time it became the settled policy of the government. Mr. Adams continued the same policy, adverted to it in his messages, and repelled the idea of Cherokee independence. Immediately after his accession to

power, General Jackson took hold of the subject with his characteristic energy. He changed the policy only so far as related to the mode of execution. It had before been confined to the removal of individuals ; he devised the plan of removing by tribes. Half a million of dollars were granted by Congress to aid in the undertaking. By a treaty with the Sacs, Foxes, and others, he acquired a tract of territory estimated at 16,860,800 acres for the use of the emigrating Indians. Treaties of emigration and change of lands have been made with the Delawares, Choctaws, Chickasaws, Senecas, Shawnees, Ottawas, Wyandots, and Creeks. The land acquired from these several tribes and bands is estimated at over 33,000,000 acres.

"The territories thus acquired are greater in extent than the States of New Hampshire, Massachusetts, Vermont, Rhode Island, Connecticut, New Jersey, and Delaware. They would make seven such States as Massachusetts, twenty-four equal to Delaware, and thirty-two larger than Rhode Island. General Jackson found more than half of Mississippi in the occupancy of savages ; he will leave it entirely free. A large part of Alabama he conquered in war, another part he has acquired by treaty, and the remnant will soon be emancipated. Entire bands are removing from Ohio. In Illinois and Michigan large tracts of country have been freed. If our venerable Chief be properly sustained in this energetic and humane policy, it is probable that in a few years, except in the cold and sterile region beyond Lake Superior, an Indian foot will not tread on this side of the Mississippi. We justly honor him for the preservation of Louisiana and the acquisition of Alabama amidst the terrors of bloody war. Shall we refuse him the meed of admiration and support for his peaceful achievements, for expelling an enemy from the bosom of the Republic, not by conquest and extermination, but by gentle persuasion, and advancing the interest of the savages as well as our own ?

"The Navy Department has felt beneficially the hand of reform. An end has been put to many abuses, frauds, and corruptions, which consumed its means and cankered the morals and honor of our navy. By these means a saving of more than half a million a year, or more than a million and a half in three years of General Jackson's administration, compared with the last three years of Mr. Adams's, has been effected without impairing the efficiency of the establishment. On the contrary, the number of officers, excepting midshipmen, has been increased, the force in commission has been as great, the public works in connection with our naval strength have been pushed with equal, if not greater effect. Energetic measures have been pursued in the examination and protection of live-oak timber ; the stores on hand have been largely increased, means have been adopted for their preservation, and greater care has been

taken to preserve from decay our vessels in port. The cruising grounds of our squadrons abroad have been extended to the coast of Africa, the Islands of the South Sea, and the Indian Ocean. Wherever an outrage is committed on our commerce, our national flag is soon seen. At the Falkland Islands our fishermen were seized and plundered ; our government promptly despatched a public ship to their rescue, and the aggressors have been punished.

"The Malays of Sumatra seized one of our trading vessels and murdered a part of her crew ; a frigate has gone to obtain reparation or avenge the outrage. Wherever our commerce seems to be in danger, some of our cruisers soon appear. The recent insurrections at Vera Cruz and Tampico had scarcely occurred before an American armed ship made her appearance to protect American citizens and their property.

"The present administration found the affairs of that department in a most deplorable condition. Negligence and credulity, to say the least, had possessed the head of the department, while corruption and fraud revelled in the principal accounting office. A fourth auditor was committing frequent frauds, directly applying the public money to his own use, and making unauthorized and extravagant allowances, that he might share the proceeds with those whom he favored. In one case upwards of $ 11,000 were allowed, when the original claim was less than $ 3,500, and had been repeatedly declared to be wholly unfounded, $ 1,000 of which were lent to the auditor and never repaid. In another case more than $ 30,000 were fraudulently allowed, and although the claimant was, after that allowance, $ 9,000 in debt, and had been two years out of office, $ 30,000 more were advanced to him out of the Treasury. Just before he was removed from office, the fourth auditor passed to his credit about $ 80,000 more ; but this settlement was arrested ; and in that single account the difference between the present and late auditor's settlement is about *one hundred and twenty thousand dollars.*

"On a review of the acts of our government since General Jackson came into power, it is difficult to perceive how it could have been better administered. In the management of our foreign relations, a success wholly unexpected and brilliant beyond example, has attended his efforts. His action at home, through the Treasury Department, is producing results in the extinguishment of our public debt which excite the admiration of the world and cheer on the friends of liberty in the Eastern hemisphere. Through the War Department he not only protects our frontiers, but removes from the bosoms of our States whole tribes and nations of ignorant savages and replaces them with a civilized population. Through the Navy Department, he protects our commerce in every sea. Through our Post-Office Department, he sends out light and

intelligence to all our people, like the swift rays of the glorious sun. It is difficult to imagine what more he could do than he has done, or how he could better do it.

"The opposition which was commenced against General Jackson before he had done a single official act has been continued with increasing bitterness, notwithstanding the signal success of his administration. He is charged with having turned out of office all who were opposed to him, when a majority of the office-holders at Washington are known to be in favor of his rivals. In that city the removals have been but one seventh of those in office, and most of them for bad conduct and character. In the Post-Office Department, towards which have been directed the heaviest complaints, the removals have been only about one sixteenth. In the whole government they have been only one eleventh.

"It is sometimes made a ground of attack that the President dissolved his first cabinet. Yet it is conceded by all that its materials were too discordant to do good, and that the existing cabinet is far its superior in talents and qualifications, as well as in harmony of feeling and concert of action.

"For want of better objections, it is often asserted that the President is in his dotage, — that he has lost the original vigor of his character and become the mere instrument of those around him. Many of us, within a few days past, have visited him, have witnessed his firm step, grasped the strong hand, looked into the undimmed eye, and heard the nervous language of him who, seventeen years ago, by the energies of his mighty mind and the valor of his fearless heart, repelled the storm of invasion and saved New Orleans. His bodily vigor is greater than it was then, and his mind retains its powers in their original vigor. He is destined yet to live, and with his firm grasp manage the helm of state until the storms at present raging shall be overblown.

"The means taken to annoy the President and break down his administration are most extraordinary. At the first session of Congress, after his inauguration, the Senate rejected on frivolous grounds many of his best nominations. It was with difficulty that the Indian Bill was got through. The President's recommendations were generally neglected. Nothing would Congress do to facilitate business in the public offices. The spirit of reform, wherever it appeared, was rebuked by them, and they legalized many of the frauds and corruptions which the vigilance of the executive had detected.

"At the next session, things were in the same condition. The Senate would permit the President to send only a *chargé d'affaires* to Turkey, when he desired to send a Minister, although they knew the apparent contempt of the Grand Seignior put in jeopardy our excellent treaty which had yet to be ratified. There was the same indifference as at the former session to the recommendations of the President and heads of departments. At the present session even a worse spirit seems to pervade a large portion of both Houses. They object to his arrangement with Great Britain, to his treaty with France, to his Indian treaties; they refuse or delay the necessary appropriations, recall his Minister to England, deny him the means of maintaining the mission in France, attempt to cripple the Post-Office Department, get up charges of fraud against his friends, never committed or thought of, and by some farfetched reasoning, endeavor to implicate him; go into endless and needless investigations, assert that the President encourages bullies to attack them, send spies to talk with him and misrepresent what he says, offer resolutions proposing to inquire into his private conversations, and by intemperate language and direct insult, excite as much personal feeling as possible, fill the land with feuds, charge to the administration the affrays which naturally spring out of their own violence, with the apparent design of giving employment in private altercation to those talents which ought to be devoted to the exposure of their designs and a vindication of the administration. The interests of the country are neglected or converted into electioneering engines; arrangements are made to throw into controversy as many exciting subjects as possible with the desperate hope of injury to the President from the part he may take; and almost half of Congress, instead of devoting themselves to such measures as may redound to the prosperity and honor of the country, appear to be altogether employed in schemes to put out one President and put in another; to prevent an election either of President or Vice-President by the people, that they may promote their personal views by corrupt elections in Congress. Thus do many members spend their time who were elected by the people and sent to Washington solely because they were expected cordially to sustain the President and his measures.

"His re-election by an expression of the public will, which shall frown into silence factious opposition, is deemed by us essential to the interests of our country, if not to the existence of the union. In the triumph of either of the three branches of the opposition, we perceive nothing but disaster to our institutions. The followers of Mr. Clay, by their injustice and insults to the South, if with their leader brought into power, would at once endanger the Union and probably dissolve it. The triumph of nullification would be disunion itself. In the spirit and principles of antimasonry our country cannot expect prosperity or repose. United as the three now are in opposition to the President, they would, if successful, produce an administration of the government without principle, without concord, without the power to do good, if not without the disposition. To sustain General Jackson, therefore, to give

him an evidence of increased public confidence and affection, to strengthen his administration and enable him to adjust the conflicting interests of our country to its altered condition, is, in our opinion, the duty of every patriot.

"A party, like a nation, to be *strong*, must be *just*. It must sustain its *true men*. When the attack is most fierce upon them, the more firmly must we rally to their support. When each man confides in those to his right and left, and when he knows that if the enemy's columns be concentrated upon him, thousands will instantly rush to his rescue, he marches on regardless of consequences to himself, and thinks only of achieving a common victory. A party thus united and resolute, always just to its friends and true to the country, is more irresistible than any army of veterans.

"At this moment, in our opinion, justice and true policy both require that the friends of Andrew Jackson shall sustain Mr. Van Buren for the Vice-Presidency. Victory is as certain as that the people are just. But if it were doubtful our decision would be the same. We had rather fall in an effort to *do justice*, than rise *by a cowardly abandonment of those who are exposed to danger only because they are our leaders*."

History of Amos Kendall's connection with the government of the United States, written by himself: —

"Soon after the presidential election in 1828, a young man named Overton, living in Lexington, Ky., called upon me and stated that he had just returned from a visit to General Jackson, at the Hermitage, and was authorized by him to inform me that it was his purpose to offer me an appointment at Washington. Not doubting that it would be an honorable one, I at once made up my mind to accept it; but I communicated the fact only to my wife and my partner in the 'Argus' office, and to them confidentially. There were two preliminary objects which I wished to accomplish, for the purpose mainly of neutralizing the aspersions cast upon my motives and character by Mr. Clay and his adherents pending the preceding contest. One of these objects was, to be made the bearer to Washington of the electoral vote of Kentucky for General Jackson, sealing my triumph over all my maligners and Mr. Clay in particular. The other was, to get reinstated by the legislature of Kentucky in the office of public printer, which I had lost in the previous local contests.

"The electors readily conceded to me the appointment of messenger, and in December, 1828, I repaired to Washington bearing the vote of Kentucky. My purpose was to deliver the package, and return with the view of securing the position of public printer; but my friends insisted that my presence was not necessary to the attainment of that

object, and persuaded me to remain in Washington until the inauguration of the new administration.

"Prior to the election of a printer by Congress, Major John H. Eaton, then in the Senate, proposed to me to become a candidate for the printing of that body, assuring me that Duff Green, editor of the 'Telegraph,' was unreliable and unpopular, and that I could certainly be elected. I declined the honor, unless Mr. Green, on being consulted, should consent to the arrangement. Although the printing of the Executive Departments, and the House of Representatives, which he was sure to receive, seemed enough to satisfy the desires of any reasonable man, yet as Green had fought the battle bravely in the very lion's den, I thought his desires ought to be gratified though somewhat too grasping. I declined even to confer with him on the subject, lest he should imagine that the idea of dividing the printing had originated with me; but I avowed my readiness, if, on being consulted expressly without authority from me, he should freely assent to such an arrangement. Major Eaton afterwards informed me that Mr. Green had been consulted, and refused to give up his claim to the printing of the Senate. Again the Major assured me that if I would consent to run I would be elected, Green's wishes and opposition notwithstanding. I, however, peremptorily declined.

"At that time I knew nothing of the management which was in progress touching prospective cabinet arrangements, and their bearings on aspirants to the Presidency, having in view myself nothing beyond the success of General Jackson's administration, and the permanent ascendency of Democratic principles. I was not consulted, and did not seek to know the reasons which controlled the selection of the new Cabinet Ministers. In only one instance was I in any way made acquainted with those reasons. John McLean, who was Postmaster-General under Mr. Adams, was a political friend of General Jackson, who gave him the option of remaining at the head of the Post-Office Department, or accepting a seat on the bench of the Supreme Court then vacant. He decided to remain in the Department, but was soon induced to change his mind by the management of Duff Green. Green was extremely proscriptive, and many postmasters were very obnoxious to him, some of them deservedly so. He presented certain cases to Mr. McLean, and asked whether he would remove them, and was answered in the negative. He presented the same cases to General Jackson, inquiring whether they ought not to be removed, and was answered in the affirmative. Mr. McLean was an aspirant to the Presidency, and very popular with the postmasters; and when he found that he should probably not be able to protect them from removal without losing the favor of the President and his friends, he changed his mind and signified that upon reflection

he preferred the judgeship. He considered the position, however, merely as a temporary withdrawal from the political theatre; for when, in conversation, I mentioned it as a very comfortable provision for one disposed to retire from political life, he promptly replied that he had no such intention, but should always hold himself at the disposition of his friends

"General Jackson reached the City of Washington in February, 1829. I saw him but once before his inauguration, and then it was in the company of several editors of newspapers. I said nothing to him in relation to an appointment. He did, indeed, ask how I should like to live in Washington, to which I replied that I thought I should like it very well.

"In the mean time, the Jackson members of the Kentucky delegation in Congress, of their own accord, sent me a recommendation to the President for an auditorship or chief clerkship expressed in too strong terms for me to present in person. I erased the chief clerkship and returned it to them, with my reasons for declining to present it.

"There was living in Washington at that time a singular woman, named Anne Royal, the widow of a Captain Royal, of the United States Army. She was homely in person, careless in dress, poor in purse, and vulgar in manners. But she had a tolerable education, much shrewdness, and respectable talents. She procured her subsistence by publishing books, in which she praised extravagantly those who bought her books or gave her money, and abused without measure those who refused, or had in any way incurred her displeasure. Some through love of flattery, and more through fear of abuse, contributed to her support.

"I was one day sitting with a friend in the gallery of the House of Representatives, when Mrs. Royal entered and seemed to be approaching us. My friend inquired whether I would like to be introduced to her, and I answered in the negative. She seated herself on the opposite side of my friend, and, after a pause, said to him, 'Why don't you introduce me to that gentleman?' He gave me an inquiring look, and I nodded assent. After another pause, she said to me, 'You are a Presbyterian preacher.'

"I replied, 'No, I have not that honor.'

"'Well,' said she, 'You are a Baptist or Methodist, — a preacher of some sort.'

"I answered, 'No, I am not even a professor of religion.'

"My friend now interposed and said, 'Mr. Kendall is the editor of the Kentucky "Argus."'

"She replied, 'I love the editors.'

"Observing a new book in her lap, I inquired, 'Mrs. Royal, is that your last publication?'

" ' Yes.'

" ' What is your price ?

" ' I make members of Congress pay me a dollar, but I sell it to other gentlemen for seventy-five cents.'

" I handed her the money and took the book.

" She soon after gave me a kind look and said, ' I begin to think you a clever fellow.'

" Thus cheaply I purchased my way into the good graces of Anne Royal.

" She subsequently commenced the publication of a weekly newspaper, called 'The Huntress,' at two dollars per annum, devoted chiefly to flattery and abuse. Of the former I for a time enjoyed my full share ; but alas ! for the mutability of human affairs, I fell from my high estate in the affections of this amiable lady, and became her antipathy in a very high degree. It was in this wise : I had become an auditor of the Treasury Department, with an annual salary of three thousand dollars. One day her ' Secretary,' so called, being a thin, spare, good-natured old maid, named Sally, who lived with her in the triple capacity of companion, servant, and messenger, called at my office to inform me that Mrs. Royal was sick and suffering for the necessaries of life ; that although she had a little food on hand she had no means of cooking it, being entirely out of wood. I gave her a note to the wood-seller with whom I dealt, requesting him to send Mrs. Royal a load of wood. A few days afterwards she came into my office in an unusually brusque and excited manner, when the following dialogue in substance ensued : —

" ' Well, Mr. Kendall, you sent me a load of wood, did you ?'

" ' I gave Sally an order for a load.'

" ' It was very mean in you, Mr. Kendall.'

" ' *Mean*, Mrs. Royal ?'

" ' Yes, mean, — you ought to have sent me a cord.'

" ' Well, I thought I was doing a *charitable* act ; perhaps I was mistaken ; perhaps I should have sent you a cord or half a dozen, but I only thought of enabling Sally to cook your food and relieve you from present suffering. You should judge the act, not by the quantity given, but by the motive of the giver.'

" Yet she was not to be appeased by anything I could say, and continued for some time to ring the changes upon the meanness of sending her a load of wood instead of a cord. I knew that she might be appeased by a moderate gratuity, but the spirit in which she had received this small favor awakened me to the evil of encouraging this kind of beggars and petty swindlers by any sort of countenance. Thus far I had in relation to Mrs. Royal been influenced more by thoughtless

amusement than any other motive ; but now I discontinued taking her paper and took no notice of her abuse, which, indeed, I never heard of except through the thankless kindness of officious friends.

" It was during my residence with Colonel R. M. Johnson that he made his celebrated report against putting a stop to the transportation of the mails on the Sabbath. Its authorship was erroneously attributed to me. After it was drawn up it was submitted to me, and my entire agency consisted in altering one or two words. Its composition in the main was doubtless attributable to the Rev. Obadiah Brown, the Baptist minister, in whose house the Colonel boarded. It was written with great simplicity and power, and had great effect on the popular mind, virtually settling the question for many years thereafter.

" My pecuniary means were at that time very limited, and I obtained temporary employment from the Postmaster-General in making out a list of post-offices by counties, for which I received an adequate compensation.

" It was quite surprising to me to meet so many men who claimed the merit of producing General Jackson's election to the Presidency, and had come to Washington to receive the appropriate reward. Among them was a small, spare man from Pennsylvania, who, at a Fair one evening, attached himself to me and entertained me with a long story of his achievements and his complaints. The former consisted chiefly in his having been, he said, the first man in Pennsylvania who had proposed General Jackson for the Presidency, and thus ' put the ball in motion.' The latter consisted in the fact that the importance of his services did not seem to be appreciated, and he feared that in the distribution of the offices he should be entirely overlooked. His reasoning was of this sort : —

" ' General Jackson could not have been elected if he had not been proposed. I first proposed General Jackson. Therefore I caused his election.'

" Thus, perhaps for an hour, walking to and fro, he entertained me, while I did not even know his name. Being anxious to know who it was to whom the country was so deeply indebted, I pointed him out after he left me to every person in the room whom I knew, and not one of them could tell me who he was. Meeting him in the same place on a subsequent evening, I continued my inquiries, and at length fell upon a man who was able to gratify my curiosity by telling me his name.

" A fine contrast was presented by a friend of mine from Kentucky, who had contributed by his pen and other means to the grand result. He had come to Washington for the purpose of securing an appointment in Kentucky. As we were walking along Pennsylvania Avenue,

he said to me, ' Mr. Kendall, I am ashamed of myself, for I feel as if every man I meet knew what I came for.' I replied, ' Don't distress yourself, for every man you meet is on the same business.' An exaggeration, but conveying a sad truth.

" The new administration was auspiciously inaugurated on the 4th of March, 1829. It was not creditable to the manliness of Mr. Adams and his cabinet, that none of them remained at their posts to receive their successors. They all fled as if an enemy was in hot pursuit. A beautiful contrast was exhibited by Mr. Van Buren and his friends twelve years afterwards. Mr. Van Buren, on General Harrison's arrival in the city, invited him to the White House, made him acquainted with its inmates, and entertained him as his guest until the inauguration. The members of his cabinet remained in their several offices until their successors made their appearance, received them courteously, and introduced them to their subordinates. Thus should it always be in a government like ours, in which changes are effected by the constitutional routine of regular suffrage, rather than the vicissitudes of civil war and its attendant bitterness.

" Nearly two weeks passed away after the inauguration, and I heard nothing of the expected appointment. Was there some mistake about the alleged promise of the President, or had he changed his mind ? At length a rumor reached me that the second and fourth auditorships were to be given to Major William B. Lewis and myself, but that the allotment had not been made. I called on Major Lewis and inquired which office he preferred. He replied, ' That in which there is the least work,' which he understood was the Second Auditor's. I said I preferred that in which there was the most work. The two offices were assigned to us accordingly. Nor was there in my expressed preference any affectation. Calling on the President to thank him for the appointment, I said to him in the course of the conversation, ' I suppose you will hold me responsible for the faithful performance of the duties of the office ?' He replied, ' Certainly.' Then said I, ' I ought to have the selection of my own clerks.' ' You shall have it,' was his prompt reply. Thanking him for the concession, I assured him of my purpose to manage the office on the same legal and moral principles that I managed my private affairs, and if ever satisfied that such a rule was impracticable in administering a public office, I would resign and go into private life. And while I remained in the Fourth Auditor's office I had the selection of my own clerks as effectually as if I had been the head of a department.

" By the Constitution and laws of the United States, all clerks in the Comptroller's, Auditors', and other subordinate offices are to be appointed by the heads of the departments to which they belong, producing this

incongruity that the heads of bureaus, deriving their own appointments from the President and Senate, removable only by the President, and held responsible for the faithful performance of the duties of their offices, are dependent on others, who have no rightful control over them, for their clerical force. And it has become one of the glaring abuses in our government, that clerks are often thrust in and thrust out of the bureau offices without consulting their responsible heads, and without due regard to the merits and qualifications of those put out or in.

" At length, on the 21st of March, 1829, I found myself installed in the Fourth Auditor's office, in which were then sixteen clerks, only one of whom was what was then called 'a Jackson man.'

" My predecessor, who had been one of the principal writers in favor of the late administration, did not wait to receive me.

" The first thing that struck me as being amiss in the office was the great number of letters for private citizens which came under cover to the Fourth Auditor, as means of avoiding the payment of postage. With the exception of a few special cases, in which I paid the postage myself, all such letters were returned to the post-office. That such an abuse existed, I well knew, but I knew little of its extent. On examining the law, I found there was a penalty of ten dollars attached to each illegal frank, and made up my mind under no circumstances to commit the offence. This resolution was sacredly adhered to during the eleven years I was connected with the government and possessed the franking privilege. Though one of my predecessors in the Post-Office Department had decided that a man having the privilege might frank his wife's letters, I found nothing in the law to warrant it, and rejected the precedent. Sometimes my associates in the government would allude with a sort of sarcastic pleasantry to my scrupulousness on that subject, and my uniform reply was in substance that I did not set myself up as a censor or judge of other men's conduct or consciences in the exercise of their special privileges ; but for myself I deemed it the safest rule to keep within the limits of the law. But I had few imitators in the Executive or in Congress.

" Within the first week of my official life, one of my clerks applied to me for a requisition on the Navy Department for money, stating that he was a disbursing agent for that department, for the purpose of paying small claims, and especially those originating at the Washington Navy Yard. It struck me as singular and incongruous that the Navy Department should have a disbursing agent in the office where its accounts were settled, and I asked the clerk under what law he acted. He replied he did not know, but that he had acted in that capacity for many years. I then stated that I must know his authority before I could take any further action.

"The result was, that there was not only no authority for the arrangement, but in some respects it was in direct violation of law. There was on the statute-book, unrepealed, an act of Congress requiring the Captain in command of the Navy Yard at Washington to perform the duties of Navy Agent at that station. So far as disbursements were concerned, that act had been long disregarded, and the duty transferred to a clerk in the Fourth Auditor's office. In addition to that duty, he paid small claims against the Navy Department upon the certificate of the Auditor, a practice introduced to avoid the labor and delay of running each of those claims separately through all the ridiculous forms of the Treasury and Navy Departments. A commission was allowed him on his disbursements, sometimes exceeding a thousand dollars a year. At the same time he was receiving one of the best salaries in the Fourth Auditor's office. His account was settled in the same office virtually by himself. Yet there was an act of Congress prohibiting clerks from receiving compensation for any extra service whatsoever.

"Having ascertained these facts, I informed the clerk that his operations must cease, and he must close up his accounts. His commissions were disallowed on the double ground that the whole arrangement was in violation of law, and that the allowance of compensation was prohibited by an act of Congress. The state of the case was reported to the Secretary of the Navy, who required the Captain of the Navy Yard to perform the duties of Navy Agent, until Congress should provide a regular agent.

"There was at that time a Navy Pension Fund of several hundred thousand dollars, the management of which was intrusted to the same clerk. His duties were to keep the accounts, invest the money, and reinvest it when refunded, and he was allowed a commission for this service also. Soon after my accession to office, the Hon. Michael Hoffman, who had been Chairman of the Naval Committee in the next preceding House of Representatives, called on me and invited my particular attention to that fund, stating that he had attempted in vain to ascertain what was its true condition during the two preceding sessions, the reports made in pursuance of his calls being unintelligible. Turning my attention to the subject, I called on the clerk for a report made out according to a form described by myself. After considerable delay, he made an unintelligible statement, which I returned, directing him to comply with the form I had prescribed. Without refusing to do so, he showed so much reluctance and made so little progress that I was sure there were circumstances connected with it which he did not wish to disclose. On the 1st of June he was removed from office, and his successor was instructed among his first duties to report the condition of the Navy Pension account. He found no difficulty in making out a

plain, intelligible statement. There had been no apparent embezzlement of the fund; but large amounts, after being refunded, had remained apparently to the credit of the agent in bank, some of them for more than a year, before they were reinvested, by which means the fund had lost many thousand dollars of interest. Whether the agent profited by the use of the money in any way, or whether it was a piece of gross neglect, was never ascertained.

"When I entered the Fourth Auditor's Office, I was totally ignorant of the process by which the Navy accounts were settled. To obviate this difficulty, I required successively a clerk in each branch of duty to meet me at the office before office hours, and go through the process of settling an account. I thus soon acquired a general knowledge of all the duties of the office."

The following fragment, from a journal kept by Mr. Kendall at this time, illustrates the assiduity with which he discharged his official duties: —

"JOURNAL.

"FOURTH AUDITOR'S OFFICE, March 23, 1829.

"Having qualified, taken possession of my office, and been introduced to my clerks, I took up the correspondence lying on the table. I found in enclosures directed to Tobias Watkins, Fourth Auditor, the following letters to other persons, viz: One to Gwynn Harris, from Philadelphia; one to Jos. H. Handy, from Portsmouth, N. H.; one to W. P. Zantzinger, from New York; one to E. McDaniel, from New York; one to J. Weed, from Boston; one to R. B. Maury, from New York; one to Eliza C. Porter of Alexandria, from Watertown, Mass.; one to J. I. Boyle, from New York; and four pamphlets to Dr. Cox, Dr. Huntt, Chas. Hay, and Tobias Watkins. All these I returned to the post-office, with a note to the postmaster, stating that I sent them to be disposed of according to law.

"My office appeared more like an editor's than an auditor's. Sixteen newspapers had arrived, and were on the table, since my predecessor had left the office on the 21st. I resolved to take no papers at the public charge which should not be useful to me in the performance of my official duties, and took a list of them for the purpose of ordering their discontinuance.

"A number of claims came in of midshipmen who have been attending at New York for examination. charging fifteen cents per mile for travelling from their place of residence, and $1.50 per day for remaining in New York, for which some of them charged ninety-two days. I inquired what law there was for allowing these accounts, and was told there was none. I inquired what regulation there was, printed or

written, and was told there was none. Mr. Gilliss, my chief clerk, informed me that it had been the custom to allow them for several past years. I laid them aside and consulted the Secretary of the Navy. He was not prepared to give an opinion, but instructed me to stop everything that I had any doubt about.

"After dinner, I called at the office with the chief clerk, and remained until night examining into the regulations of the office and the laws relative to the Navy. I instructed my messenger to have me a fire by half-past six in the morning.

"March 24th. I was at the office a little before half-past six, but the messenger had not arrived. I walked, and on returning found him making a fire. I prepared a circular and sent it to the editors of sixteen papers, — 'Baltimore Gazette and Daily Advertiser,' 'Constitutional Whig,' 'Political Arena,' 'Albion,' 'Free-Trade Advocate,' 'New York Morning Herald,' 'Atlas,' 'American and Commercial Daily Advertiser,' 'Richmond Enquirer,' 'Baltimore Patriot and Mercantile Advertiser,' 'Democratic Press,' 'Commercial Chronicle and Daily Marylander,' 'Evening Bulletin,' 'Phenix Gazette,' 'National Journal,' and 'National Intelligencer.' I added a note to the letter to the 'Richmond Enquirer,' requesting to be considered a subscriber.

"The following enclosures were received to-day. A letter to Jos. H. Handy, supposed from Charlestown, Mass.; one to Joseph L. Hughn, from Portsmouth, Va.; one to George Bealle, Esq., supposed from Carlisle, Pa.; and one to Gwynn Harris, from New York, all which were returned to the post-office.

"Mr. Hughn, who is Paymaster of the Marine Corps, came to remonstrate with me in relation to returning his letters, alleging that they were on public business, and were sent to the Fourth Auditor in pursuance of express directions to avoid a post-office account. I told him, that the law made it my imperative duty to return to the post-office all letters received under cover to me, and that as they were sealed I could not know that they were upon the business of the department. I told him I should abide strictly by the law, and if that were found to produce inconveniences, resort must be had to Congress to change it. He acquiesced by saying it would only delay public business one day. I replied that the law and not the auditor was responsible for that.

"George McDaniel, one of my clerks, called with a requisition signed by me yesterday, payable to —— Hutton, clerk, requesting me to expunge the name of the clerk and insert that of a messenger. On my inquiring why this change was requested, he informed me that there was a rule in the public offices, that no clerk should act as agent to settle accounts and draw money for any citizen; that the rule had not been enforced for some time past; that it had been revived at the

Treasury; that Hutton was drawing this money as agent for certain citizens who had assigned their account to him; that it could not be paid to him at the Treasury; and for the purpose of getting it, he had further assigned it to the messenger. After some examination and inquiry, I told him that the object appeared to be to evade a very wholesome rule, and that I could neither aid in nor countenance any evasions in this office.

"On investigating the case of the midshipmen, I found that the first payment of such claims was in 1820, for attendance at an examination in 1819, and that, by the decision of the Secretary of the Navy, the allowance extended only to travelling expenses, and that an allowance of a per diem was expressly prohibited. No further regulation, either of law or office rule, appears; but in 1825 accounts were first passed for the fifteen cents per mile and the $1.50 per diem. I submitted the case to the Secretary of the Navy.

"March 25th. Returned to the post-office one letter to Josiah Colston, from Pensacola; one to John McDaniel, from St. Michaels, Md.; one to John McBee, from St. Michaels, Md.; and one to G. Gilliss, from Baltimore.

"A claim was presented to-day for fuel by the Paymaster of the Marine Corps, charging twenty-four cords on his own account and twelve cords on account of his office, at seven dollars per cord, for the year 1828. On inquiry, I learned that the wood allowed to officers was originally paid in kind, and they were required to produce receipts to enable the department to fix the price; that the officers at Norfolk had agreed to commute for $3.50 per cord; that subsequently a commutation of $6 per cord had been allowed; that recently it had been extended to $7 a cord throughout the Union, and that the officers at Norfolk now claim and are paid the same sum as all the rest. Seven dollars is the average price in New York, where wood is highest, and this commutation only increases unlawfully the pay of the officers at the expense of the people. The subject must be examined.

"March 26th. Was sick to-day. Opened my letters in bed. Returned to the office a letter to R. Getty, from Philadelphia, and one to E. Fitzgerald, post-mark illegible. Received an insolent letter from Isaac Monroe, editor of the Baltimore 'Patriot,' in consequence of the terms in which I discontinued his paper.

"March 27th. Returned to the post-office two letters to Gwynn Harris, from Boston and Norfolk. Discontinued the 'Independent Citizen' and the 'Village Record,' which, with the 'Frederick Examiner' and the 'Scioto Gazette,' heretofore discontinued, make up twenty newspapers which I have discontinued.

"Had a conversation with the Secretary of the Navy. Found him much vexed with his clerks, and determined to change some of them. He expresses a full determination to reform his department, and fully believes that great abuses exist in the disbursement of public money under the rules or *customs* heretofore introduced.

"A gentleman long conversant with the public offices promised me a list of cases in which decisions had been given and public money paid from motives of favoritism, if not corruption.

"*March 28th.* Returned to the post-office a letter to J. N. Hambleton, from Pensacola; one to G. W. Hollins, from New York; one to E. McDaniel, from Norfolk; and one to George McDaniel, from New Berlin, N. Y.

"*March 30th.* Returned to the post-office a letter from Gloucester, Va., to A. K. Long, of Baltimore; also one to J. J. Boyle and J. M. Watson.

"Lieutenant Ross, of the Marine Corps, called and laid in a claim for transportation from New York. He had been attached to the ship 'Natchez,' and had come to Washington upon a permit of the commander, but without orders. He stated that he had presented his claim to Dr. Watkins, who refused to allow it, on the ground that he had no orders, but said he had since ascertained that he had allowed an account of his own son, also an officer of the Marine Corps, who had come to Washington under similar circumstances. I requested him to put his claim in writing, which he did.

"*March 31st.* Returned to the post-office a letter to E. McDaniel, from Norfolk, and one to Thomas H. Gilliss, post-mark illegible.

"I requested my chief clerk to inform me what allowance had been made to young Watkins for transportation, and under what circumstances. He examined, and reported to me that no such account had passed the office.

"George McDaniel informed me that money had been placed in his hands to pay the salaries in the office, and requested to know whether he was to proceed as heretofore. I told him to do so until further orders.

"*April 1st.* Returned to the post-office a letter from Pensacola to J. M. Hambleton, St. Michaels, Md.

"*April 3d.* Returned to the post-office a letter to George Bealle, from New York. I heard a day or two ago that this man was abusing me at Brown's Hotel, as 'a pretty auditor, indeed,' on account of my stopping the newspapers and sending back the letters. On turning to my memorandum, I find that I have heretofore returned to the office one letter to him. He does not like to pay postage, I suppose.

"George McDaniel stated to me that he had been employed for several years by the head of the Navy Department as a special agent to

pay off small claims accruing against the department; that a sum of money was placed in his hands at the commencement of each quarter for that purpose; that he had received one per cent on the amount disbursed, as his compensation; and he desired to know whether he should continue to act in that capacity. On inquiry, I found that this was a scheme which had been invented to prevent the trouble of passing small accounts through all the departments, but it seemed to me wholly unauthorized by law. I conversed with the Secretary of the Navy on the subject, but he was not prepared to give any opinion.

"Soon after McDaniel left me, Lieutenant Ross of the Marines called, and I told him the account of Lieutenant Watkins had never passed the office. He said Watkins had told him he was paid. I then stated that I would go and examine his account myself. He observed that he believed a Mr. McDaniel had paid it. It then occurred to me that it had been paid without having passed through the office. I called in McDaniel, and learned that he had paid it under the direction of Dr. Watkins, who was Lieutenant Watkins's father. He brought me the papers, from which it appeared that Lieutenant Watkins had come from the Mediterranean upon the permission of Commander Crane, on account of ill health, and that he had been paid for his passage from Smyrna to Boston and for his travelling expenses from Boston to Washington. No sick-ticket was produced, and I do not believe there ever was any. His transaction had been covered from my inquiries heretofore by this sub-system of paying accounts through a special agent, to whom the amount of the whole has been allowed in lump.

"Went up to the office after dinner, and with Captain Bennett, one of my clerks, went through the whole process of settling a purser's account. In the conversation which arose upon it, he informed me that a letter had been written by Captain Morris, commanding at Charlestown, in the Auditor's office, adopted by the Auditor, recorded and sent, directing the purser there to pay the officers money and take their receipts for wood. I requested him to show it to me to-morrow.

"*April 4th.* Captain Bennett showed me the letter referred to yesterday. It instructed the officer commanding at Charlestown to direct the purser to pay money to the officers in lieu of wood, at the usual market price, to take receipts for wood and not for money, and to forward on a certificate of the usual market price of wood in Boston. Though written by Captain Morris at Washington, it was directed to Captain Morris at Charlestown. Certainly this was a scheme to introduce false vouchers for the passage of accounts, upon the suggestion and with the aid of an officer interested.

"Discharged my assistant messenger. I did not know I had one until the 1st inst., when he presented an account as *laborer* for three

months' services. He said Dr. Watkins had employed him for some time and paid him in that way. I conversed with his brother, my messenger, and told him that he was safe, unless I in future should see cause to remove him, but that I did not feel myself authorized to employ his brother, nor did I think it necessary.

"*April 5th.* Called this evening and had a conversation of some length with the President. He approved the course I had pursued, recommended the utmost strictness in the passage of accounts, and thanked me for a variety of suggestions.

"*April 6th.* Sent to the post-office five letters, enclosed by officers, etc., at Smyrna to Dr. Watkins, to be forwarded to their wives, etc. There was an open note to the Doctor from one of them, named Hunter, requesting him to frank the two letters enclosed to his wife.

"One of my clerks, John McDaniel, presented me with an account of George Bealle, purser at Carlisle, with a note of my predecessor wafered at the bottom, stating that the Secretary of the Navy had decided that the purser at Carlisle was to receive the same compensation or allowances as the purser at Philadelphia. I inquired of McDaniel whether these allowances were the same, and he said they were. I then passed the account. Soon after Mr. Gilliss, my chief clerk, presented me with the account of the purser at Philadelphia, which contained an item of $2,200, I think, for paying mechanics and laborers. Mr. Gilliss stated that such a charge had been made for many years, but had never been allowed by the Auditor or Secretary of the Navy until last year, and that he thought the allowance not authorized by law, because there was no appropriation to pay it. I was clear in the opinion that it ought not to be allowed. He then told me he understood I had passed an account of the purser at Carlisle with a similar item in it. I was confident there was no such item in it, but remarked that there was one for clerk hire. He observed that I would probably find that to be in effect the same thing. I then sent for John McDaniel, and requested him to bring the account I had passed. He did so, and it contained an item of $600 for clerk hire. I inquired whether the purser hired any clerk. He replied in the negative. I inquired whether this charge was meant to correspond with the charge from Philadelphia for paying laborers and mechanics. He replied in the affirmative. I inquired whether there were any laborers or mechanics at Carlisle to pay. He answered in the negative. I then observed with some sharpness that it was a most broad and dishonest construction of the decision of the Secretary to maintain that it went to pay the purser at Carlisle for no services the same which was paid to the purser at Philadelphia for actual services, and that he ought before to have put me in possession of these facts. I took my pen and excepted the $600 from the allow-

ance. In a few minutes the purser, George Bealle, came in, and rather rudely claimed the allowance as a matter of right under the decision of the Secretary. I had some difficulty in keeping my temper, but restrained myself, and drew from him admissions that he neither hired clerks nor paid mechanics and laborers. I asked him what justice there was, then, in making such a charge. He pleaded that he had incurred other expenses. I told him to present a true account, then, and if the law authorized its payment it should be paid. He said he should have had no difficulty if he had presented it six weeks ago. I told him it was not my business to inquire what my predecessor would have done, but what it was right for me to do. He left me in no very good-humor.

"'What is this but a direct attempt to cheat by a false account? I fear this system has been carried to a great length; but I shall check it.'

"CIRCULAR.

"Having completed the contemplated arrangements in the office, the Fourth Auditor takes this occasion to apprise his official corps of the principles by which he expects them to be governed.

"Every man who receives a salary from the Treasury ought to consider himself hired by his fellow-citizens to labor in their service. Office in this country is not property. It is rather a contract between the people and the officer, by which the former promise to give a salary, and the latter to earn it. The duration of the contract, with all clerks, depends on the will of those to whom the people have given the power to appoint and remove. Clerks in this office hold their offices at the will of the Auditor and the Secretary of the Treasury. Independent of that will they have no right to their places. When that will decides on their removal, their rights cease. The present Auditor hopes that with him the painful business of making removals is at an end. Yet he wishes it distinctly understood that the continuance in office of each one of his clerks depends solely on the industry and fidelity with which he discharges his public duties. Determined to devote every energy of his body and mind to the service of that country by which he is employed and paid, the Fourth Auditor is resolved that no favor or affection, no personal consideration on earth, shall induce him to retain one about him who habitually violates the rules of the office and is negligent of his duties. The salaries of the office are competent to purchase the services of men of first-rate attainments and industry, and with such the office must be filled.

"Generally, a close devotion of only six hours each day to the business of the office will be required. He who devotes himself intently to calculation of figures or writing, will have the balance of his time for relaxation, exercise, family concerns, and rest. But surely, for the salaries paid, a rigid application of six hours a day to public duties is not unreasonable. The Auditor does not intend to limit himself to that number of hours or any other; he will be at labor whenever the duties of the office require it. But as he does not intend to be absent from the office during office hours, except upon public business, so neither will he tolerate absence and neglect in his clerks. It will give the office a bad name if those who are paid to be at work are seen traversing the city or country during office hours in pursuit of business or pleasure. Besides, urgent business may come into the office during their absence requiring special attention. But they must be at their posts during the six hours, whether they have anything to do or not, and they must be ready and willing to labor, before or after office hours, whenever the public interest may require it. In cases of sickness or family distress, the Auditor will not be backward to grant them every needful indulgence.

"At present the business of the office is somewhat in arrears, and no man need eat the bread of idleness. The Auditor is anxious that all arrearages shall be brought up, so that every account which is presented may receive instant attention.

"When the clerks enter the office they must lay aside all thought of everything but their official duties. They must not spend the hours of business in reading newspapers, or books, or writing private letters, or in any private concerns. For all those things, the public allows them sufficient time, morning and evening. Nor must they bring into the office loungers or idlers, or employ their time in conversing with friends or strangers upon other topics than their own current business. By suffering no intrusion to interrupt them, they will soon be rid of all intruders.

"It is natural for those engaged in public service to think lightly of public property. Without compunction they apply to their own use that which belongs to the people, when they would scorn to be guilty of a like act in relation to their neighbor. Yet it is in principle the same crime. He who applies to his own use the books or stationery of the public, is just as guilty in the eye of morality as he who takes his neighbor's property without leave and applies it to his own use. A public officer would be as justifiable in taking money from the Treasury, and bestowing it upon his family and neighbor, as he is in giving them a quire of paper from the public stock. It is by little and little that the moral sense is blunted and destroyed. It may be said there is no harm in taking, for our own use or giving to a friend, a few quills or a little paper which belongs to the public, because nobody will feel it. The transition is perfectly natural to a few cents, and a few dollars, and a few hundreds, until the Treasury is assailed and plundered of its thousands. It is important to guard against the slightest violation of principle. If we never suffer ourselves to do wrong in small things, we shall not be in danger of doing wrong in great things. Let me enjoin it upon the clerks of this office, in the use of the stationery, or whatever else belongs to the public, *to be as rigidly just as they would be in the use of that which belongs to their neighbor.* They will then not only never be *guilty* of extensive frauds, but they will never be *tempted.*

"Not only the public interest, but the reputation of our government and country require the practice of rigid morality by those engaged in public business. Gambling, intemperance, and extravagance ought not to be tolerated in the agents of the people. An habitual gambler can scarcely be a man of integrity. He who takes from his fellow-citizen thousands of dollars, re-

ducing his wife and children to beggary upon a fortunate deal of cards, would not long hesitate to take thousands from the government, if he thought he could do it without detection or responsibility. Such a man ought not to be trusted in public office. The intemperate man, if not led into other vices by his indulgencies, is no better than a lunatic. A madman ought as soon to be trusted in office. Extravagant habits of any kind, leading to expenditures beyond our income, ought not to be tolerated in a public officer. One whose income is fixed and certain has no excuse for exceeding it in his expenditures. Vain show and foolish aping of men of wealth in public agents, ought not to be encouraged. Much less ought government, by continuing salaries to vain and improvident men, give them credit in society and enable them to swindle farmers, mechanics, and merchants out of their produce, labor, and goods.

"As the Fourth Auditor will not knowingly appoint a gambler, drunkard, or grossly immoral man to any place in his office, so he should consider it his duty to remove any clerk who might contract such habits. He is proud to believe that the character of his office now stands unimpeachable on those points, and it shall be his pride, as it is his duty, to keep it so.

"In everything except the business of the office it will give pleasure to the auditor to treat his clerks as equals. He recognizes no superiority in one good man over another, further than a due discharge of public duties requires. While, therefore, he exacts a strict performance of every official duty from every clerk under his control, he shall consider himself no more than their equal as a man and a citizen, ever ready, by all just means, to promote their comfort, comply with their wishes, and increase their happiness.

"1. Every clerk will be in his room, ready to commence business, at nine o'clock, A. M., and will apply himself with diligence to the public service until three o'clock, P. M.

"2. Every clerk will hold himself in readiness to discharge any duty which may be required of him in office hours or out, and in no case where by laboring a short time after office hours an account can be closed or a citizen released from attendance at this city, must he refrain from continuing his labors after three o'clock.

"3. Newspapers or books must not be read in the office unless connected directly with the business in hand, nor must conversation be held with visitors or loungers except upon business which they may have with the office.

"4. Gambling, drunkenness, and irregular and immoral habits will subject any clerk to instant removal.

"5. The acceptance of any present or gratuity by any clerk from any person who has business with the office, or suffering such acceptance by any member of his family, will subject any clerk to instant removal.

"6. The disclosure to any person out of the office of any investigation going on, or any facts ascertained in the office, affecting the reputation of any citizen, is strictly prohibited without leave of the Auditor.

"7. No person will be employed as a clerk in this office who is engaged in other business. Except the attention which the families of clerks require, it is expected that all their time, thoughts, and energies will be devoted to the public service.

"8. Strict economy will be required in the use of the public stationery or

other property. No clerk will take paper, quills, or anything else belonging to the government from the office for the use of himself, family, or friends.

"Although it is necessary in transacting the business of the office that there should be implicit obedience to all just requisitions, and entire subordination of the clerks to the head, yet it will give the Auditor pleasure on all occasions to treat his clerks and their families as equals and friends. Forgetting every difference of opinion, he hopes and expects that all will be actuated by one spirit in the service of that country which protects all in their rights of property and conscience. He doubts not that he will find in them a prompt and efficient co-operation in every investigation and measure tending to expose delinquents, reform abuses, enforce the laws, and introduce rigid and just principles into the settlement of public accounts. It is thus only that we shall gain the lasting regard of good men, and, by restoring the purity, contribute to the lasting duration of the best government which Heaven ever gave, or man ever enjoyed."

CHAPTER XII.

THE fidelity with which Mr. Kendall, for five years, conducted the business of the Fourth Auditor's office, educing order from confusion, exacting strict accountability, and correcting abuses hoary with age, elicited numerous commendations from friends, and even for a time silenced the clamor of his enemies who practically adopted the maxim that the Jackson administration could do nothing right.

The following letter is a sample of many found among Mr. Kendall's papers:—

SHELBY COUNTY, KY., September 4, 1829.

A. KENDALL, ESQ.,

SIR,—Your friends and fellow-citizens of Shelby County have seen with great satisfaction the bold, prompt, and decisive manner in which you have employed the opportunities of your place in the present administration to crush the corruption which had raised such a fearful head at Washington. During past years that city has been signalized by official indulgences, political intrigues, and the venal application of the public patronage. You have honestly redeemed the pledges which your uniform course as editor, in vindicating the popular rights and the principles of democracy, gave to the public. You have given the example of an officer abolishing the *aristocratic privileges* which former incumbents had introduced into your station, by declining to use the public purse at once to administer to your personal indulgence, and to corrupt the organs of public information by refusing the franking privilege through the medium of your office, which had been previously allowed to all who desired it, and by cutting off the corrupt influence of executive legislation, which, under the name of construction, gave to a single department of the public service many thousands of dollars more of the nation's money than was authorized by law. But the example you have set in the case of Dr. Watkins is of the highest use to your country. It is calculated to bring back the public functionaries to a strictness in the conduct of their offices which will secure future accountability, and it is to be hoped will check the growth of fraud and peculation in our government, which seems to have struck so deep a root. Your honest vigilance in detecting, and boldness in denouncing and bringing to justice fraudulent defaulters and peculators, have brought down on you the vengeance of the aristocracy. You are charged with monstrous crimes which we disdain to mention in connection with your name, and you are invited to sue in Lexington for these libels on your character. Sir, your reputation belongs to your country, a country which will never suffer it to become a prey to the artifices of the bad men whose dangerous policy and violated faith it has fallen to your lot to expose. We trust you will scorn to submit your honest standing to the tricks of the bar and a jury of your enemies. The men who are arrayed against you have already given an evidence of the success with which they can suborn witnesses and influence a judicial tribunal. They cannot, however, control public opinion, by which they stand condemned, and by which you will be forever protected against their malicious invective."

Mr. Atwater threatens, and receives the following reply : —

WASHINGTON, July 15, 1831.

SIR, — Your letter of the 11th instant is just received. Although I had not time to answer all your previous letters, I urged forward your business as much as I properly could. But for the last paragraph in your letter, I should have rejoiced at the information I have just received, that your account has been adjusted and a balance found due and forwarded to you. That paragraph is as follows : "Unless I hear immediately from you my book will contain several pages I had hoped to have withheld. Human nature can only bear a certain amount of suffering."

I fear the receipt of this money will have the effect to suppress these "several pages"; and had not your account been adjusted, I should certainly have advised its delay until the appearance of your "book."

To be plain, sir, I understand this paragraph as a *threat* that, unless your claims be allowed, you will publish something derogatory to the administration. I hope I do not understand you correctly ; but if I do, I beg leave to inform you that when you again advance *such* arguments in support of pecuniary claims against the government, you must find some other advocate to present them.

With due respect,
Your obedient servant,
CALEB ATWATER, Esq.   AMOS KENDALL.

Mr. Kendall's early fondness for the study of Natural Philosophy and Mechanics lasted throughout his life, and the subject of per-

petual motion seems to have almost constantly haunted his mind. He insisted that such motion was contrary to mechanical principles, impossible, if not absurd ; yet some new project would occasionally prove that he had not ceased to ponder on the question, impracticable as it seemed.

The device referred to in the letter below was manufactured to his order, but before it was finished he discovered its impracticableness. Many other projects in the same direction occasionally diverted his mind, always with similar results.

PERPETUAL MOTION.

WASHINGTON, September —, 1831.

DEAR SIR, — When I was in New England I mentioned to you that I might wish to procure certain machinery with a view of trying some experiments on the laws of motion. So much has been said in relation to *perpetual motion*, and so many have deceived themselves with the notion that they had discovered it, that every one who speculates and tries experiments with a view to that result, is laughed at as a visionary. I do not join in that laugh. Although, *upon mechanical principles,* perpetual motion is an absurdity, and therefore impossible, I do not reject the idea that it is possible on other principles. Indeed, I know that it is possible, for we all witness it every day. The motion of the earth, moon, and planets is a *perpetual motion.* Astronomy taught me that this motion is maintained by the centripetal and centrifugal tendencies of these bodies. That is to say, — in relation to the earth for instance, — it has a tendency from its gravity or weight to fall into the sun ; but, having a motion, and all motion being, if left uncontrolled, in straight lines, it also has a tendency to fly off from the sun ; and these tendencies are so nicely balanced as to keep it revolving round the sun in a circle.

We have both these principles on the face of the earth. Every substance has gravity or weight, and tends to fall towards the centre. Here it is the centripetal power. Every wheel in motion affords a centrifugal power. The motion of wheels may be, and often is, so rapid as to throw upwards heavy substances from their peripheries in spite of their weight, thus overcoming the gravitating or centripetal power. The water flying upward from the top of a grindstone in rapid motion is familiar to every boy.

Now, can this centrifugal power be produced to such an extent as to more than counterbalance the gravitating power that produces it ? It has seemed to me that it might be. I have not been so confident as

to induce me to take much trouble or incur much cost for the purpose of ascertaining, but I have for many years been anxious to make experiments with that view. You know that by high gearing a small weight descending very slowly may be made to give rapid motion to a heavy balance-wheel. May not a machine be so constructed that a heavy balance-wheel thus put in motion shall come in contact with the small weight, and raise it back to the point whence it has descended in producing the motion ?

I am somewhat sanguine that this result can be produced, and would like to try various experiments to ascertain ; but here I have no opportunity, because the necessary apparatus is not at hand and cannot be readily procured. If you will obtain the apparatus and try the experiments, I will pay the expense if you will take the time and trouble ; and if anything comes of it, you shall share alike with me. I am not very confident, but so important would be the discovery and so valuable withal to those who make it, that I am willing to pay something for the experiment.

Enclosed I send you the drawing of a machine by which these experiments may be tried, not very accurately executed, but perhaps sufficient to direct you.

Your obedient servant,
AMOS KENDALL.

About the same time, despite the engrossing cares of his office, he invented what he called a "Cylinder Steamboat," the principles of which are stated in the following letter. The results of this invention were not equal to his expectations : —

CYLINDER STEAMBOAT.

WASHINGTON, December 24, 1832.

DEAR SIR, — Continued indisposition and a press of official business have prevented an earlier answer to your letter of the 1st inst.

The plan of my boat is exceedingly simple. Its basis is two or more hollow cylinders of large dimensions, with paddles on the exterior surface, which are to be rolled over upon the water by steam or other power. The whole structure for supporting the machinery, passengers, and freight, rests upon the ends of the axes of these cylinders, the room for their accommodation being between and above them from near the surface of the water upwards. I have no paddle-wheels or hull, the cylinders supplying the place of both, and the only parts of the boat which will touch the water are the cylinders and the rudder. The progressive motion is obtained on the same principle as that of a steam carriage, the cylinders supplying the place of wheels.

I trust this description will enable you to understand it without the aid of drawings, which could not be furnished without expense.

Another patentee claims the *principle* of my invention, but he has in fact no solid foundation for his claim, and has become anxious to compromise with me. Making the inquiries necessary in that controversy, I came to a knowledge of your patent, which, in some points, bears some analogy to mine. It seemed to me that the union of the three would secure all that has ever been patented on the subject, and would constitute the safest basis of proceeding, and probably the most profitable for all of us. In my opinion, neither your patent nor the other I desire to procure are in themselves of any value, nor can I imagine that mine will be of any great value ; but I can have its value tested, provided I can show to those who have the funds and the disposition to embark in it that there is no danger from other quarters. Hence, although I do not think either of the patents alluded to can injure mine in *law*, yet they do injure it *in practice*, and therefore it is that I wish to concentrate them.

I will therefore give you a nominal consideration for your patent, with an agreement that you shall have a small proportion of the net profits arising from mine, or from the united patents, should any accrue from them, without trouble or risk to yourself. And if you desire it, I will further agree to reconvey yours back again to yourself, if the matter shall not be tested by me in a reasonable time.

I beg to hear from you as soon as will suit your convenience, and the more definitely the better, as I dislike long negotiations.

Very respectfully,
Your obedient servant,
AMOS KENDALL.
Mr. W. W. VAN LOAN, Catskill, N. Y.

TO HIS WIFE.

CATSKILL, May 7, 1833.

MY DEAR JANE, — I am safely at my brother's, after a rapid and unpleasant journey. You recollect that I left you at ten o'clock on Saturday night. We arrived at Baltimore about four o'clock. The steamboat started at six. The morning was cold, with a raw easterly wind, and there was no fire on board which I could get at. We passed the railroad from Frenchtown to the Delaware, a distance of sixteen miles and a half, in about fifty-six minutes, going at the rate of seventeen miles per hour. At the Delaware we again took a steamboat, and were in Philadelphia at twenty minutes past two. Here I saw a few friends and walked out to the water-works, about two miles. At 6 A. M., on Monday, we were again in a steamboat. From Bordentown to Amboy there is now a railroad, but the cars are drawn by horses, which travel about eight miles an hour. At Amboy we again took a steamboat, and were in New York about 3 p. m. There we stayed until seven o'clock this morning, and arrived here about 3 p. m. The distance from Washington to this place is over three hundred miles, and we have been travelling but little over thirty-one hours.

I took an additional cold on Sunday morning, and on Monday was very hoarse. But it has almost entirely left me. I have felt very well all the way, have eaten heartily, and slept soundly. I intend to ride every good day several miles, and have no doubt I shall find great benefit from it.

Give my love to the children and to cousin, to your father and mother, Alexander, and the rest of the family. Tell Mary Ann and Adela that they must each write me a letter next Saturday. Tell William I shall inquire how he has behaved when I get home. I intended to direct him to go to Mr. Wheat's school, but I forgot it.

Affectionately, your husband,

AMOS KENDALL.

TO HIS WIFE.

CATSKILL, N. Y., May 17, 1833.

MY DEAR JANE, — I have not had a line from you since I have been here, nor a word from the family since Mary Ann's letter of the 11th, although the mail now comes from Washington here in a little more than two days.

This is Friday. On Tuesday evening last my brother and myself went up to Troy in a steamboat, where we visited an uncle and aunt and cousins. Aunt Wilson is sister to my mother, and, though a smaller woman, resembles her very much. Though once comfortable in the world, Uncle Wilson, by a series of misfortunes and accidents, has been reduced to poverty. The day and night preceding our visit he had lost about five hundred dollars in moulded brick, by an uncommon flood in the Hudson River. Yet both the old gentleman and lady, especially the latter, appeared to be perfectly cheerful under their misfortune, and resigned to their lot.

On Wednesday I went down to Albany and spent the night with Mr. Croswell, editor of the Albany "Argus." With him I also breakfasted and dined yesterday, meeting at dinner a number of warmhearted friends. At 5 p. m., my brother and myself went on board a steamboat, and arrived here, a distance of about thirty-five miles, about dark.

We have not had a fair day here for a week. The quantity of rain which has fallen is prodigious, and the damage done by the rising of

the streams very great. We found all the wharves in Albany and Troy under water, the houses on the lowest grounds flooded up to the second stories, and boats passing through the streets. Immense masses of lumber were on the wharves, a large portion of which has been swept away. The low lands all along the river are covered, and you may see numerous houses apparently standing on the water, with rows of trees, orchards, and forests growing out of it. The most melancholy part of the story is, that seven or eight lives have been lost, about or near Albany and Troy, in attempting to save floating property.

My friends at Washington write me that they regret my absence at this time; but perhaps it was well for me that I have been away. I should have given some explanation of Randolph's accounts had I been there, which might have exasperated him the more against me; but now it has been done by others. Some other matters have occurred also, which make me quite satisfied that I am here at this moment. Yet I have a strong desire to be with my dear wife and little flock, and nothing but Providence shall prevent my speedy return.

They all tell me here that I am very much improved. I feel nearly as stout as usual, and had the weather been good, so that I could have ridden on horseback every day, I have no doubt I should have been in more than my usual health. The cough I had is gone, but two days ago I took a little cold again, which I have not yet got rid of. But I have not taken a particle of medicine since I left home. Give my love to your father and mother and all the rest, "too numerous to be mentioned in a short advertisement."

Your affectionate husband,

AMOS KENDALL.

TO HIS WIFE.

BALTIMORE, June 6, 1833.

DEAR JANE, — I suppose you think I have forgotten you, because I have not written twice a day since my return to this city. Will you take any excuse? I will tell you the truth at any rate. Well, then, the truth is, I have had more writing to do since I have been here than I could accomplish with comfort to myself, and have postponed everything I could. Yesterday and to-day I have written over eleven sheets, and am not done yet. Will you forgive me now? If not, I will make it up some way when I get home. With the exception of one evening, I have been very well. As to the suit, we are just where we were a week ago. The lawyers talk of having it transferred to Washington, and making no further attempt with it here. If they go on, God only knows when I shall get home.

Enclose me Mrs. Moore's letters. I shall see the Major here. Do it

by to-morrow night's mail, or as soon as you read this. You have my love. Give a little of it to the children and the rest.

Ever your affectionate,

AMOS KENDALL.

TO HIS WIFE.

BALTIMORE, August 3, 1833.

MY DEAR JANE, — I have just received Adela's letter of yesterday, in which she says, "Mother is not well pleased at all at your not writing to her," and the sauce-box adds, "I think that it is too bad myself." So to prevent a fair outbreak in my absence, I have snatched up my pen just to let you know that I place some value on your good-humor. Really, if it would add to your happiness, — and no lady out of humor can be happy, — I would write every day, "I am well. How do you do? Your affectionate," etc.

I have succeeded here in my business quite as well as I expected, and go on in high spirits.

How come on my potatoes, the calf, cow, chickens, pigs, etc.? I think I was promised a letter once a day from one of the little girls, and have but one in a week! I am not "well pleased" myself, and you may tell Adela "I think it is too bad." Kiss John for me, and give my love to all the rest, and to your father and mother and family. Write me at New York.

Affectionately,

AMOS KENDALL.

TO HIS WIFE.

PHILADELPHIA, August 6, 1833.

MY DEAR JANE, — It has just occurred to me that it is no small part of my duty to keep you in a good-humor, and as I am left by myself a few minutes, I will spend them with you, — that is as nearly as I can.

In the first place, I am very well; in the next, I am in good spirits; in the next, I wish you were with me, — at least until to-morrow. I occupy a large parlor and a bedroom, with two doors, two windows, and a double bed, and eat by myself, unless a friend happens to be present when meals are ready.

Who do you think has just left me? No other than Robert J. Ward, of Kentucky. He tells me that he had a violent attack of cholera, but now he looks quite well.

Almost my whole time is taken up in receiving and talking with friends and men of business. This evening I am to meet a committee of a bank, — to-morrow morning another, and so on.

So you must excuse me if my letters are short. But what shall I say of you and the young ladies? It is their holiday now, and certainly one of them can take care of John while you write, or can write while you take care of him.

I send you a bushel of love, — measure out a quart apiece to the children, and keep the rest yourself.

With enduring affection,

AMOS KENDALL.

TO HIS WIFE.

PHILADELPHIA, August 9, 1833.

MY DEAR JANE, — To-morrow I expect to leave this city for New York. I had promised to dine out yesterday, but did not want to go, and a little bit of sick-headache came along very opportunely to furnish me with an excuse. I confess I should have liked a good dinner better. Three hours' sleep and a cup of tea put me on my legs again, and I am tolerably well to-day. But I am engaged for dinner again, and don't know what the wine may do for me.

I have been more successful here than I expected, and shall go on my way rejoicing, although the bank people abuse me in their newspapers most wickedly.

Have you got my turnip crop in? How come on the potatoes, etc? I got Mary Ann's letter to New York, and Adela's to this place, yesterday. They don't tell me half the news. "We are well, — hope you are so," is about all they say. Now, make them write me every particular, — or do it yourself, which would be better.

The women I have seen here are very ugly, but I have two pictures of beautiful girls hanging in my parlor. Looking at them, I have been more than half persuaded to have yours taken when I get back, for I think it would now be as pretty as they are, and if you should get so old and wrinkled that I can't love your beauty, I will look at the picture for your outside. Love to all.

Affectionately,

AMOS KENDALL.

TO HIS WIFE.

NEW YORK, August 13, 1833.

MY DEAR JANE, — I have just received your kind letter, and give you a thousand thanks for it. I dearly cherish a letter from you, because it comes in the language of a heart which I verily believe all devoted to me. It is also a good heart, which means no ill to any one, and although, like all of human mould, it has its foibles, they are less than those which belong to thousands and tens of thousands. We have seen adversity, and you have not been depressed; we are now in prosperity, and you are not elated. The same virtues of self-denial and economy we now practise will, at no distant day, make us independent of the world ; and surely we shall not be so unwise as to spend the evening of our lives, after toiling through the day, otherwise than serenely and happily. The scenes you speak of in relation to some of our friends will never occur between us ; and yet they should be a lesson to us and all married people to bear and forbear with one another. Let us never speak an unkind word to each other, and if one should escape from either in a moment of unguarded excitement, let the other not return it.

Poor Mrs. Riley ! and I may say, poor Mr. Riley ! See what a little adversity does for some people. It puts them out of heart and out of temper. Why should we, poor short-sighted creatures, when the storm is raging without, quarrel and make ourselves miserable within ? A man on whom the world frowns ought to smile upon his little family flock and make them happy, by showing that *he* is not miserable. Generally, the husband who carries a smile home will find smiles to meet him, and that which he might make a hell he can make *a heaven upon earth.*

But I sincerely hope the picture is exaggerated. Discontented maids and nurses are not always the most faithful retailers of facts, and should be listened to with great allowances. I hope you will not take Mary, for I am sure Mrs. Riley will think hard of it, whatever she may say. But if you have taken her, I have nothing more to say, and hope she will please you.

To-morrow I shall start for Boston. I intend so to arrange matters as to spend Sunday with my good old father. Soon afterwards, I shall be on my way back, but as I shall have to spend probably two days here, one day in Philadelphia, and one, or part of one, in Baltimore, I cannot be at home before the 25th or 26th of the month. Although I succeed rather better than I expected, the business is much more laborious. I wrote yesterday with my own hand eleven letters, seven of one page and four of two. Besides this, I am overwhelmed with civilities, most of which I am obliged to decline. You will readily see, therefore, that I have not much time to write letters of affection or amusement.

I have met here Mr. Van Buren, Mr. Livingston, and Mr. McLane. Mrs. Livingston was very sociable, and inquired after you. She told a story very flattering to me, which, although it was not in its circumstances true, I was too polite to contradict.

Said she, " I saw a lady to-day who has a kind remembrance of you."

Said I, " I am very happy to be kindly remembered by a lady."

She then said she had met with Mrs. Bache, of Philadelphia, and her

little daughter, who had come on in the steamboat with me from Philadelphia, and Mrs. Bache told her that I had found her in the boat without attendant or protector, and had kindly attended to herself and baggage, and provided a conveyance for her to her lodgings.

This being told before a considerable company, I heard it with all due modesty, saying to myself, " Either Mrs. Livingston or Mrs. Bache fibs most confoundedly."

The truth was this : Mr. Whitney came on board to see me as I started, and seeing Mrs. Bache there without an attendant, asked me if I would take charge of her, to which I answered "most certainly," and he introduced me to her. So I chatted with her occasionally on the way, and at her request got a hack for her at New York, handed her into it, she went one way and I another, and that is the last I have seen of her.

But, as I said before, Mrs. Livingston or Mrs. Bache represented the matter much more favorably than it was, and as I could not tell the truth without charging one of them with fibbing, I concluded to let it pass.

This is the sum total of my adventures with the ladies since I left Washington.

Well, I have given you a long letter.

With unabated affection,

AMOS KENDALL.

The great industry and ability displayed by Mr. Kendall in his office proved him to be qualified for still higher and more responsible duties.

The condition of the Post-Office Department had become a source of deep anxiety to the President. With astonishment he learned that its revenues were insufficient to meet pecuniary engagements ; contractors were pressing their claims, the credit of the department was in jeopardy, and its affairs in inextricable confusion.

Annoyed and embarrassed, the President turned to Mr. Kendall and urged upon him the task of rectifying these abuses, and of trying to bring order out of the chaos which reigned in this important branch of the government. Though the appeal was a forcible one, Mr. Kendall at first hesitated, but when urged upon personal grounds, he yielded.

To aid in the success of the administration which he firmly believed to be the triumph of true republican principles, he shrank from no sacrifice, thought no undertaking too arduous. He regarded

the President as the embodiment of truth and honor. The more others abused and slandered him, the brighter did his virtues shine in the eyes of Mr. Kendall. His admiration of the "old hero," as he delighted to call him, increased with time, and, to the day of his death, he could not listen to a reproach upon his character without repelling the slander with a vehemence which astonished and silenced the traducer.

Gigantic as were the difficulties anticipated by Mr. Kendall in assuming the direction of the Post-Office Department, the reality exceeded his worst fears.

Though his official conduct was as pure, honest, and faithful to the interests of the public as the highest standard of integrity could demand, he did not escape calumny and persecution. His former experiences had prepared him for the worst his enemies could do.

Any change in the cabinet was a sweet morsel for the opposition press, which pretended to see in it presages of new calamities to the administration and the country ; but that the friends of the government were justified in anticipating from this change most favorable results, the event abundantly proved.

On Mr. Kendall's retirement from the Fourth Auditor's office, he received a communication handsomely engrossed, signed by each clerk, and expressive of gratitude for his uniform courtesy, and bearing cheerful testimony to the fidelity and promptness with which he had discharged his duties ; to his untiring industry which led him to exact less service from his subordinates than he was ready to render himself ; and to his great ability and unblemished private character.

This voluntary expression of good-will was highly gratifying to Mr. Kendall, who carefully preserved the testimonial among his valuable papers.

The following extracts are taken from prominent papers at this time : —

"POSTMASTER-GENERAL.

" The rumor is quite rife that Major Barry is going to Spain as Minister Plenipotentiary, and that Amos Kendall is to succeed him as Postmaster-General. Mr. Kendall's pre-eminent talents and vigorous business habits give an assurance that the public interest will be faithfully as well as ably served should he assume that post. But the very fact that he is honest and intelligent will be the bitterest part of the potion to

the opposition. Apprehensive that he will deprive them even of a pretext for assailing that Department, the opposition press will open upon him with that virulence and abuse which is so characteristic of the party. Mr. Kendall may rest assured that his capability and honesty are sufficiently known, to leave him without a friend in the ranks of the opposition, and to cause him to be viewed as the worst of appointments for their purposes."

"THE POST-OFFICE DEPARTMENT.

" The opposition papers have announced the probable resignation of the present Postmaster-General, and the appointment of Mr. Amos Kendall to succeed him, and thereupon have commenced an indiscriminate and unlimited abuse of Mr. Kendall. It is well known that the inconsiderable difficulties which a disposition to accommodate the public has caused to grow up in the General Post-Office Department, furnish the last key for the cuckoo song of corruption by the opposition against the administration, and they are now afraid that if Mr. Kendall is appointed, that the last *pretext* for opposition will be swept from them. They know that his indefatigable industry, his honesty, his business habits, his acknowledged talents, and his knowledge of mankind will leave nothing undone which human ingenuity can effect to place the Department on that high and elevated ground which will disarm malignity of its opposition and leave nothing for its friends to wish for. We know nothing about a change, nor do we for a moment doubt the ability of Major Barry to place the department upon an invulnerable ground ; but we have no hesitation in believing that if the reported change is made, it will meet the approbation of the Democracy of the Union."

"AMOS KENDALL, ESQ.

" Letters from Washington state in positive terms that Amos Kendall is to take charge of the Post-Office Department as successor to Major Barry, whose delicate and declining health requires a change of climate and a less laborious station.

" We most heartily concur in the sentiments expressed by the editor of the Baltimore ' Republican ' in the following article upon this subject. Mr. Kendall is certainly one of the ablest men of the day, and under his skilful direction and management, the affairs of the Post-Office Department would be well conducted and wisely administered. It is a matter of serious regret to us that circumstances should render a release from the cares and responsibilities of this arduous station desirable to Major Barry, whose virtues as a man, and whose merits as a public officer have rendered him the object of general esteem and re-

gard ; but whilst we lament the necessity which compels us to anticipate the retirement of an officer so faithful to his duties, and so universally esteemed by the people, it affords good grounds for congratulation
to know that the place will probably be supplied by one so well qualified
in every particular, to give general satisfaction, as the gentleman whose
name heads this article. The editor of the 'Republican' says : 'The
opposition press is groaning in advance at the bare idea of the appointment of Mr. Kendall to the Post-Office Department. If the anticipation
is so afflicting, what will be the effect of the event ? That such an
event may happen is not improbable, if there be any truth in the mournful predictions of our adversaries. It may be that Major Barry's ill
health, aggravated by the persecutions of vindictive enemies, may render it agreeable to devote his acknowledged talents to the service of the
country in a sphere less laborious and equally respectable. It may be
that he may consent, at his own good time and convenience, to go on a
mission to Spain. It is known that he enjoys the undiminished confidence and friendship of the President, and that he will not be removed
or transferred but by his own choice. If he should retire, what is there
in the duties of the Post-Office Department to which the habits and
talents of Amos Kendall are not suited and adequate ? Does it require
untiring industry ?— he is known to possess it ; does it require talents
to rectify any malarrangement or to reform abuses which may have
sprung from defective organization of the Department?— who has quicker penetration to discover or greater firmness to apply the correctives ?
What more does the opposition require ? They would fain paralyze his
exertions by denunciations beforehand, and then complain of want of
success to which they themselves had contributed. But their efforts
will be vain. His success in the post of Fourth Auditor in overcoming
the prejudices that had been excited against him, is but an augury of
like success in the Post-Office Department, should he be appointed to its
administration. Amongst officers of the navy there is now an universal
admission of his capacity, his promptness, and his inflexible impartiality.
We challenge the opposition to mark our predictions and to note the
result.'

"The Albany 'Argus,' in alluding to the rumor that Mr. Kendall is
to be appointed Postmaster-General, makes the following remarks :
'We have no knowledge of the alleged intended change in the Post-
Office Department ; but we say with entire truth, that if Major Barry
should at any time retire from it, we know of no man to whom its duties
and responsibilities may be committed with greater propriety, and with
higher regard to the public interests, than to Mr. Kendall. He possesses certainly, in an eminent degree, every requisite qualification for
the trust. Indeed, upon this subject, if we had not the strongest affir-

mative evidence, the relentless spirit in which he had been pursued by
the harpies of faction and by the creatures of the bank, would afford of
itself sufficient proof of the purity of his character and the force of his
talents.' We agree with the editor of the 'Argus,' that in case there is
a change, no person is better qualified than Mr. Kendall to assume the
responsible duties devolving on the head of the Post-Office Department."

The following narrative, written by himself, contains an account
of Mr. Kendall's connection with the Post-Office Department :—

"During the short session of Congress, in the winter of 1834 – 35,
President Jackson said to me that a change was necessary in the head
of the Post-Office Department, and asked me whether I would accept
that position. Nothing could have been more unexpected than such a
proposition. No intimation had been given by me that any official promotion would be acceptable, and I am quite sure no one had recommended this arrangement to the President. Thanking him for his
kindness to me, I stated that there were, as I thought, conclusive reasons why such an appointment should not be made. Politically, I had
not occupied any of those prominent positions which the practice of the
government had made prerequisites for cabinet appointments ; that the
Whig Party, having the ascendency in the Senate, would certainly reject my nomination ; that my appointment would be looked upon with
jealousy by his own political friends in Congress ; and finally that I was
poor, with a large family, and being satisfied that I could never provide for them in public life, I had made arrangements to resign the
office I then held and go into private business. The interview was
closed by his requesting me to think of the matter a few days and call
again.

"In a second interview, I stated that my reflections had confirmed
my first impressions, and that my appointment was one which ought
not to be made, either on his own account or mine, and recapitulated
the objections to it previously raised. I added that as to myself, if
nominated to the Senate at once, I should be at once rejected, and if appointed after the close of the session, the prospect before me would be
the relinquishment of the favorable chance I then had of going into private business, a year's hard work in the Department, and being at its close
turned adrift by the Senate without property or income. But after
urging all these considerations, I concluded by saying that I would make
the sacrifice and take the office if it would give him any personal relief.
His reply was, 'There are many men who would be glad to accept the
Department, and I suppose would put everything right there ; but *I
know you will.*' What could I say more ? Believing that I could rely

more, to sustain myself, on what I could do in the Department, than upon
any existing claims to the position, I requested that the change should
be made as soon after the close of the short session of Congress as convenient, and my nomination delayed to near the close of the next long
session, to which the President readily assented. It was also understood that the arrangement should not be disclosed until after the
adjournment of Congress. There was a general understanding, however, that a change was to take place, and there was no lack of candidates for the position. One of them who aspired to it, and wanted my
recommendation, opened the subject by proposing to me to become a
candidate myself and offering to recommend me. Well understanding
that he expected me to decline and would thereupon ask me to assist
him, I affected to believe him in earnest, and he consented to call on
the President and urge my appointment, which, I afterwards learned
from the President, *he never did.*

"Soon after the adjournment of Congress it was arranged between the
President and Major Barry that the latter should resign the Post-Office
Department on the first of the succeeding May, and accept the mission
to Russia. It soon became known that I was to be his successor. The
1st of May arrived, and he did not resign. Certain parties, who had
reasons for not liking the proposed change, had persuaded him that the
mission to Russia was but a banishment, and that it would be degradation to accept it by making way for the promotion of one having so
little pretension as myself. The President, however, found means to
obviate the difficulty, and on the 1st of June, 1835, the proposed arrangement took effect.

"After it was understood between the President and Major Barry
that the latter was to resign, he wrote to the former a letter charging
his two assistants, S. R. Hobbie and C. K. Gardner, with being the
authors of all his official troubles, and asking leave to dismiss them.
No very specific charge was made against Major Hobbie, but Colonel
Gardner, who kept the books containing the accounts of the contractors
for carrying the mails, was directly charged with gross delinquency.
The President sent the letter to me, asking my views on the subject.
The chief clerk of the Department, whom Congress and the public had
fixed upon as the main cause of the mismanagement of the Department,
had resigned to avoid dismissal by order of the President, and I could only
look upon this movement against Hobbie and Gardner as instigated for
the purpose of transferring the stigma from the guilty to the innocent.
As such I denounced it to the President, who refused his consent to the
removal. Subsequent discoveries confirmed my impression. It was
true that Gardner's books had not shown the true state of the contractors' accounts, but it was only because the means of making them

accurate had been withheld from him, and as for Major Hobbie, he had
opposed even in writing some of the illegal if not corrupt allowances
which had been made to contractors.

"The Post-Office Department was then heavily in debt, as well to
contractors for carrying the mails, as to banks for money borrowed, and
was without credit. Its management had, at the two preceding sessions of Congress, been the subject of investigation by committees, and
by the members opposed to the administration severely condemned,
while by those in its favor it was but feebly defended. The general impression was that it had been reckless, and many denounced it as corrupt. Perhaps none believed that the head of the Department had
been corrupt, and his best friends who knew his amiable disposition and
his want of business habits, could readily comprehend how he might
have been misled by corrupt men about him.

"I retained Major Hobbie and Colonel Gardner in their places, and
took with me from the Fourth Auditor's Office two of my best clerks,
Robert Johnson and Joseph Perry, placing Johnson in charge of the
accounts. Preston S. Loughborough, a man of superior talents, whom I
had known from boyhood, and already a clerk in the Department, I
made my chief clerk.

"One of my first objects was to make myself acquainted with the
officers and clerks of the Department, and their several duties. For
this purpose I visited their rooms, examined their books, and asked all
needful explanations. While I was on this round, one of the prominent
clerks who had been suspected of being a secret agent of certain mail
contractors, after many professions of a disposition to serve me, suggested that he had the control of funds, and should be happy to accommodate me with loans. He received for answer, 'I never make myself dependent on those whom it is my duty to control.' 'A very correct principle,' he hurriedly replied. His assent to the principle came too late,
the prior offer being deemed proof of corruption, and as soon as convenient his services were dispensed with.

"The impression soon became irresistible that a few powerful mail
contractors, through favors to the officers and more influential clerks,
had really controlled the Department, and for their own selfish ends had
been the cause of all its embarrassments. To put an end to this source
of corruption, I announced to my subordinates that the acceptance of
any present of value from any mail contractor, or a free ride in stage
lines, steamboats, or railroad cars carrying the mails, would be cause for
instant dismissal, and that the rule prescribed to them I adopted for my
own guidance.

"In pursuance of this regulation, when presents and free tickets were
sent me, I returned them with polite letters, stating that they gave me

no offence, because I knew such things had been customary, but as I had prohibited their acceptance by my subordinates, I deemed it expedient to decline them myself. Once only there was an attempt to cheat me into a free stage ride. I had occasion to visit the West. There was a stage line from Washington to Frederick City, where it connected with the line from Baltimore to the West. Arriving at Frederick, I went to the stage-office to pay my fare to Wheeling. The agent told me I was to pay at Cumberland. There the agent told me he was instructed to receive nothing from me. Arriving at Wheeling, I enclosed the ordinary fare to Richard Stockton, the leading contractor, living at Baltimore. To avoid a similar difficulty farther West, I went to the stage-office immediately on arrival and paid the fare. In the course of the evening, one of the contractors who lived there brought to me at my hotel the money paid, which I politely declined to receive.

"Extensive curtailments of mail service had been recently ordered by the President, for the purpose of bringing the expenses of the Department within its income, and one of my first objects was to ascertain whether enough had been done to insure that end. The result was affirmative. Under these circumstances, it appeared to me easy to restore the credit of the Department. For that purpose I announced that at the end of the current, and every subsequent quarter, the amount due to contractors for that quarter would be punctually paid, and that pre-existing debts would be paid as fast as the Department should acquire the means. To ascertain whether anything could be done to hasten that result, my attention was turned to the mode in which its revenues were collected and disbursed. There were then about thirteen thousand post-offices in the United States. Those in the cities and the larger offices near them, not more than about a thousand in all, deposited their net receipts in the banks to the credit of the Department, whence they were drawn by its checks chiefly to pay contractors for carrying the mails. The other twelve thousand retained their receipts until drawn upon, and this was not done until their quarterly accounts were settled and the balance due ascertained at the Department. The practical effect of the system was not only to render the revenues derived from these offices in any one quarter unavailable for the whole or a large portion of the next quarter, but to allow the income of the small offices to accumulate on hand for several quarters before the Department deemed the amount worth drawing for. Inasmuch as on a vast majority of the mail routes the quarterly receipts were insufficient to pay for carrying the mail on those routes, it seemed to me practicable and desirable that the postmasters should pay over to the mail contractors on their respective routes the net income of their

offices at the end of each quarter. I made the suggestion to assistants and others of my most intelligent and experienced subordinates in the Department, all of whom pronounced such an arrangement impracticable. It did not seem so to me, and after mature reflection I determined to adopt it. As it was to be introduced on my sole responsibility, I resolved to arrange all the details myself. The books of the Department enabled me to ascertain precisely what was the amount required to pay for the transportation of the mails on each route, and, by reference to previous receipts, to estimate with sufficient accuracy the revenue accruing on that route. My purpose was to examine every mail route in the United States, and designate the offices which should pay directly to the mail contractors; also such as should retain their receipts until drawn upon; and also such as should be required to deposit them in banks. These details were all arranged by me in twenty out of the twenty-four States then in the Union, and in the other four by an intelligent clerk, whose aid I found necessary to get the new system in operation in the fall of 1835. The three classes of offices were called respectively 'collection offices,' 'draft offices,' and 'deposit offices.'

"Prior to the close of each quarter, every mail contractor was furnished with a list of the collection offices on his route, and he was required to call upon each postmaster, in person or by his agent, within two weeks after the close of the quarter, and demand his net income for that quarter, as shown by his own account current. Having made the demand at every collection office on his route, the contractor was required, after giving duplicate receipts to each paying postmaster, to return the list sent him, called an acknowledgment, noting on it the amount received from each office, and if any postmaster had failed to pay, give the reason for his delinquency. The adjustment was upon the principle that the contractors should not receive more than seventy-five per cent of their quarter's pay from the collection offices, and to secure their fidelity in making the demand, they were informed that the balance would not be paid until they satisfied the Department that they had called on every office and had reported the result truly. A circular was sent to the postmasters at all the collection offices, requiring them to close up their quarterly accounts immediately after the end of each quarter, and to pay over to the contractor on demand the entire amount which was admitted by his account current to be due to the Department, taking duplicate receipts. One of these constituted a voucher in his accounts.

"The deposit offices were required to make deposits more or less frequently, according to the estimated amount of their current receipts, the purpose being to prevent the accumulation of sums in their hands.

Each deposit, it was required, should be reported when made, and the certificate of deposit forwarded to the Department.

"The draft offices were only those reserved on routes wherever the post-office revenue exceeded seventy-five per cent of the contractor's quarterly pay, which were so situated that they could not conveniently be made deposit offices. Their proceeds were always drawn upon to pay contractors in their vicinity, in preference to checking upon funds in bank.

"The new system went into operation in October, 1835. Nothing could have been more satisfactory. It rendered the entire income of the preceding quarter available for payment of the quarter's expenses. Although the order to postmasters was expressly limited to the payment of the income of the preceding quarter, some of them paid over all the accumulations of all preceding quarters then on hand, so that a few contractors were overpaid. But no loss was incurred, the overpayments being set off against their next quarterly dues.

"Finding, in October and November, that the means of the Department would far exceed the demands upon it for the preceding quarter's service, I commenced paying the old debts, and thenceforward paid them whenever presented. A large portion of the debt was due to banks which did not press for payment; but during the winter of 1835 – 36, and early in the spring of 1836, the amounts due to them were all paid off.

"After I had acquired a partial view of the condition of the Department, in the summer of 1835 I told the President he must be satisfied if it were freed from debt before his retirement from office, on the 4th of March, 1837. About the 1st of April, 1836, I had the satisfaction of reporting to him that the Department was free from debt. This result was attained not only by rendering the current receipts promptly available, but by collecting the old balances in the hands of postmasters, generally small, but considerable in the aggregate, largely aided by an increase of revenue, and somewhat by suspension of payments to a few contractors who appeared to be overpaid.

"In the outset, I superintended the operations of the system myself, and carried on a large portion of the correspondence. Years afterwards I met with a man who had been a postmaster in the interior of Pennsylvania, and had on the first call of the contractor been in default. He informed me that he was surprised at receiving a letter in my own handwriting asking why he had not paid, and on replying that he was not at home when the contractor called, received another letter from me informing him that such an excuse, though accepted for the occasion, would not be deemed sufficient thereafter, because it was easy for him, if called away, to leave with his family, or whoever might have charge

of his office, the amount payable to the contractor. This case is mentioned as an illustration.

"It was one of the merits of the system that it brought all the collection offices under the direct supervision of the Department every quarter, and rendered defaults, without its knowledge, impossible. A leading principle adopted by me in its administration was to make postmasters and contractors feel that its eye was constantly upon them, not only collectively, but individually, so that no abuse could be practised and no neglect indulged in without its immediate knowledge. To that end it was made the duty of a special clerk to watch over the pecuniary concerns of the post-offices, to promptly require explanations of all postmasters reported in default by contractors, to see that the deposit offices made regular deposits as required, and in every case of neglect to demand an explanation, and to watch the accumulation of funds in the draft offices, and see that they promptly paid when drawn upon. He was required to report all delinquencies, as soon as ascertained, to the Postmaster-General.

"Under this system, the revenues of the Department, then over four millions of dollars annually, were collected and disbursed without any expense to itself.

"There had been many complaints about the irregular transportation of the mails in various sections of the country, and it was deemed my duty to inquire into the cause, and, if practicable, apply the remedy. The main cause was found to be unwarranted lenity towards the contractors. In all the mail contracts the Department stipulated for the power to fine the contractors for failures to arrive within the prescribed time, and other defaults, and although fines had been frequently imposed, they had been almost uniformly afterwards remitted, and thus the power was rendered practically nugatory. It was also soon perceived that on the principal mail routes the postmasters whose duty it was to report failures and their causes, were generally inclined to find excuses for the contractors, and were not in this respect a safe reliance for the Department. To insure efficiency in the transportation of the mails, it seemed necessary to introduce some system which should make the contractors feel that they were always under the direct supervision of the Department. For that purpose a new bureau was established, called 'The Inspection Office,' in which books were kept showing the time fixed in the contracts for the departure and arrival of the mails at the termini of every mail route in the United States. The postmasters at all these points were required to report periodically and without comment the exact time of the departure and arrival of every mail by filling up and returning blanks furnished them for that purpose. The contractors were informed that, in cases of failure, the Department would wait a reasonable time for their excuses, and if none were given would proceed to impose an appropriate fine, and that unless it were shown that the postmaster's report was inaccurate, or that the Department had made a mistake, no fine would be remitted, even though a good excuse might afterwards be given. This was necessary to insure punctuality and produce despatch in the business of the Department. A competent number of clerks were employed in examining the reports of postmasters, and entering all failures upon books which were first examined by the head of the bureau, and by him presented to the Postmaster-General, with his opinion as to the justice or propriety of fining the contractor. Every fine was at once charged up against the contractor, who was notified by letter.

"When I entered the Department there were two Assistant Postmaster-Generals, between whom the United States was divided, each having charge of the post-offices, mail contracts, and their execution, in his division. This arrangement, by burdening the assistants' minds with duties entirely dissimilar in their nature, did not seem to me conducive to promptitude or uniformity in the administration of the Department. I therefore separated the duties as follows : —

"All that pertained to the establishment, supervision, and discontinuance of post-offices was assigned to the first assistant, whose office was called 'The Appointment Office.'

"All that pertained to mail routes and the performance of contracts for carrying the mails, was assigned to the second assistant, whose office was called 'The Contract Office.'

"All that pertained to the performance of mail service under contracts, was assigned to the third assistant, whose office was called 'The Inspection Office.'

"Financial affairs, mail depredations, and miscellaneous matters were under the supervision of the Postmaster-General himself, through his chief clerk.

"I had long been led to dislike, from moral considerations as well as public policy, the use of fiction in law proceedings and the business of the government, and had, as far as I had the power, made them to conform to the truth. In the commissions of postmasters was found one of those fictions, which was not only false in fact, but involved a legal doubt, which might some day be solved to the disadvantage of the Department. The process in the appointment of postmasters was as follows : The appointment was by letter ; but the appointee was not recognized as in office, and entitled to enter upon its duties, until he had executed and returned to the Department a bond for the faithful performance of its duties, with acceptable securities. Having done this, a commission was sent to him bearing the date of his letter of appointment. The

commission was false, in the fact that it represented him to be postmaster from the date of his appointment, when he was not postmaster until the acceptance of his bond. I therefore changed the form of the commission so as to recite the preliminary proceedings in a preamble, and give it the date of its actual issue.

"An analogous evil existed in the omission of dates and the absence of regular records. Decisions of the Postmaster-General, involving thousands of dollars, had been recorded only on slips of paper, having no dates, and in one instance the only clue to $ 25,000 of Department acceptances was a list of them without date on a half-sheet of cap paper, with the initials of the gentleman to whom they had been handed. The practice of omitting dates. and sometimes giving false dates, pervaded all branches of the Department, making it extremely difficult to investigate satisfactorily some of its most important transactions. To put an end to this practice, I directed my subordinates to annex the true date to all their official transactions. I adopted the same practice myself. In the appointment office a journal was kept, which showed the decisions of each day. So did the books of the contract office. In special cases, the decisions, with the dates, were entered on the papers and immediately communicated to the parties interested, orally if present, and by letter if absent.

"It seemed to me remarkable, inasmuch as the law required the Department to accept the lowest responsible bidder, that for many years the most important mail contracts had been, at every letting, secured by the same sets of men. Prior to the first letting under my administration, one of those men called on me at my residence and inquired of me whether I intended to secure the contracts to the old and faithful contractors, as my predecessors had done. I replied that I should be very glad to retain them in the service, but as the law required me to accept the lowest responsible bid, I did not see how I could do anything to secure the contracts to them if they were underbid. He said it had been done through private understandings, prior to the lettings, between the contractors and the Department. He was told there could be no private understandings with me, and that the contracts would be given to the lowest responsible bidders, as required by law. He lost his contracts.

"There were two modes by which contracts had been secured to old contractors. One was by bidding so low that no man could afford to carry the mails for that price, with the understanding that the service was to be 'improved,' as it was called, by additional trips or increased speed, or under some other pretence, so as to make the contract a profitable one. By this process a bid of a few thousands sometimes became a contract of many thousands. The other mode of retaining 'old and

faithful contractors' was by means of what were called 'straw bids.' The contractors would themselves put in a bid which, if accepted, would give them a very liberal compensation. But as they could really afford to render the service for much less, they would engage irresponsible persons to put in a series of lower bids, the lowest being for the very lowest price they were willing to carry the mail. If there was no bona fide bid below their own, then all the lower bidders turned out to be vagabonds, who could give no security, and the contract was awarded to the old contractors upon their own bid. But if there was a bona fide bid below their own, then all the 'straw-bidders' disappeared, except the one next below the competing bona fide bidder who was found to be able to give security ; but his contract was soon assigned to the old contractors.

"By one or the other of these processes, 'the old and faithful contractors' had been kept in service, and all real competition on their routes effectually prevented.

"The law was already sufficiently explicit in requiring the acceptance of the lowest bid, and also in regulating allowances for bona fide improved service, and in those respects there appeared to be little chance of improving existing safeguards against abuses. The only effective preventive appeared to consist in honesty and sound judgment in the administration of the Department. It was otherwise with the 'straw bids.' The Department could not effectually defend itself against that abuse without additional regulation. The most effective preventive of this abuse, it appeared to me, was to be looked for in attaching additional responsibilities to bidders. This was effected by requiring all bidders to file with their bids the guaranty of two responsible citizens, whose competency should be abundantly certified, that the bidder should enter into contract with good securities for the performance of the service. Thenceforward all 'straw-bidding' ceased.

"Up to this time the post-office had not been organized as an independent Department of the government, though the Postmaster-General had, for some years, been recognized as a member of the cabinet. Nominally the Postmaster-General was in law a responsible agent of the government, receiving and disbursing the postage revenues, and accounting therefor to the Treasury Department. The settlement of his accounts, however, had become a mere form, and in effect he was in that respect wholly irresponsible. Here was a large revenue expended without appropriation by Congress, and without even nominally going into the Treasury.

"The Post-Office Law of 1835, drawn under my supervision, and passed with very slight changes, put an end to these anomalies. It organized the Post-Office as a separate and independent Department

It provided an Auditor in the Treasury Department for the settlement of its accounts. It provided that its revenues should theoretically, if not actually, go into the Treasury, and be expended in pursuance of appropriations. It took from the Postmaster-General all control over accounts, except in cases arising out of unforeseen contingencies. It legalized all changes made by me in the Department which required the sanction of law. But there were some important differences between this organization and that of the other Departments, suggested by my experience and observation as Fourth Auditor of the Treasury.

"'Specific appropriations' constituted one of the boasted reforms introduced into the government by President Jefferson. In the Navy Department, for example, the Secretary was required to estimate how much money he would require each year for pay, for provisions, for repairs, etc., and these sums were appropriated separately. By general laws the Secretary and his disbursing officers were forbidden to expend the money appropriated for one purpose on any other object, whatever might be the emergency. But in case the appropriation under any one head became exhausted, the Secretary never hesitated to draw upon some other head to supply the deficiency. To such an extent had this been done, that the Fourth Auditor's books showed that millions of dollars had been thus expended in violation of law, though perhaps every dollar was honestly devoted to the public service. In the settlement of the disbursing officer's accounts, they were charged under the head of the appropriation from which the money had been drawn, and credited under the head under which it had been expended, so that nothing was necessarily due from them, although their accounts could not be closed. There was nothing in the reports of the public expenditures made to Congress showing these facts. Those reports are not true reports of the actual *expenditures*, but only of *money drawn from the Treasury*. In this respect they are true. But there are always thousands if not millions of money remaining in the hands of disbursing officers unexpended, which are thus reported as expended. Thus it is that the object of specific appropriations is defeated, and the practical operation of the system concealed from Congress.

"The truth is, the system, especially in relation to the Navy Department, is absurd and cannot be strictly enforced without great detriment to the public service. A public ship is dismasted in the China seas ; the purser has plenty of money under the head of 'Pay' or 'Provisions,' but little or none under the head of 'Repairs.' The law must be violated, or the repairs cannot be made until he has sent to the Navy Department at Washington and received money under the head of 'Repairs.' Though this is an extreme case, it illustrates the absurdity of the system, — a system which does not accomplish the object for which it was introduced, and often makes it the duty of the public officer to disregard the law. The object of the system is to secure responsibility in the public expenditures. It fails in that, because the *actual* expenditures are never reported, and instead of facilitating the public service, when it affects it at all, it is as an obstruction. In this view of the subject, I came to the conclusion that although specific appropriations in certain cases, such as salaries, the erection of public buildings, and all similar objects are proper, they are not useful or desirable in reference to the current expenditures of the Departments. Specific appropriations cannot be of any use without *specific accountability*. My object was to secure the latter in the Post-Office Department without incurring the inconvenience of the former.

"The Act of 1836, therefore, directed the Postmaster-General to estimate the amounts which would be required for the service of the Department under certain specific heads, such as mail transportation, compensation of postmasters, mail-bags, etc., etc., the aggregate to be appropriated under the general head 'For the service of the Post-Office Department,' but to be accounted for under the specific heads of the estimate. By this plan specific accountability was secured, the possible necessity of violating the law by transfers avoided, a prompt settlement of accounts made necessary, the actual expenditures truly reported, and Congress enabled to compare them with the estimates, — a process impossible under the system of the other Departments. The appropriations were thus made for two or three years, and the accountability was as perfect as human ingenuity could make it; but so deep was the prejudice in favor of specific appropriations under all circumstances, that it always met with opposition in the Committee of Ways and Means, and finally its chairman, Mr. Cambreleng of New York, insisted on making a separate appropriation for each head of estimated expenditure. No possible good and not much possible evil could flow from the change in the Post-Office Department; but it was hoped that the example of that Department would lead to the adoption of the principle of specific accountability in the other Departments. To this day (1867) they retain the old system, reporting to Congress as expended all sums drawn from the Treasury, though millions may remain unexpended in the hands of public agents, and although other millions may remain unaccounted for in consequence of the non-rendition or non-settlement of their accounts. But of all this, under their system, Congress remains profoundly ignorant.

"Another important difference between the Post-Office as organized in 1836 and the other Departments consisted in the machinery for settling its accounts and obtaining payment of sums found due. In them the machinery for settling accounts consisted of auditors and comptrollers.

Accounts were first examined in the Auditors' offices and theoretically re-examined and revised in the Comptrollers' offices. Practically an effective revision was impracticable for want of a sufficient number of clerks in the Comptrollers' offices. For instance, — the Fourth Auditor's office contained sixteen clerks when I held it, and the Second Comptroller's contained eight to revise their work, and of these eight, three were employed in keeping books, balancing an equal number so employed in the Auditor's office. Practically, here were five clerks to revise the work of thirteen. Of course the re-examination was extremely superficial, and in many cases was entirely pretermitted, as I had abundant evidences. Instead of being an effective check upon the Auditor's office, the Comptroller's was more a shield to cover its errors and lessen its sense of responsibility.

"In the organization of the Post-Office, therefore, the revision of the settlements is dispensed with, and the action of the Auditor's office rendered final unless the claimant or the Postmaster-General shall be dissatisfied, in which event an appeal may be taken to the First Comptroller of the Treasury. The Postmaster-General himself has no other rightful control over accounts except in cases of a contingent nature not defined by law, regulation, or contract, — the Auditor being wholly independent of him.

"When the Fourth Auditor has passed an account he sends it with the vouchers to the Second Comptroller. When he has passed upon it, if anything be due, it is reported to the Secretary of the Navy. The Secretary issues a requisition for the amount on the Secretary of the Treasury. This goes back through the Second Comptroller's and Fourth Auditor's offices, where it is charged to the claimant and to the proper appropriation. It then goes to the Secretary of the Treasury, who issues his warrant on the Treasury for the amount. This has to pass through the First Comptroller's and the Register's offices before it can reach the Treasurer. The claimant has to go to seven different offices, and to two of them twice, before he can get his money. If the chiefs of all the offices are at their posts, and there be no unusual obstruction, it is still a hard day's work to get an unquestioned Navy or Army claim through the Treasury. In the Post-Office, such a Post-Office claim may be passed in half an hour. The Auditor reports it to the Postmaster-General, who draws his warrant on the Treasurer, which goes back to the Auditor's office, where it is charged to the claimant and to the appropriation, and thence it goes directly to the Treasurer. Thus a tedious and unnecessary circumlocution is avoided, and both time and money saved to the government and the claimant."

CHAPTER XIII.

"WHEN I entered the Department its accounts with some of the principal contractors were in a most confused state, as well as those of some postmasters, particularly those of James Reeside, Stockton and Stokes, and Samuel L. Governeur, postmaster in the city of New York. Not only did these contractors appear to be overpaid, but they had received large sums in acceptances which had been negotiated in various banks. I doubted the legality of these acceptances, and had no doubt of their impropriety. But as I felt bound not to pay these contractors anything until their current quarterly compensation should have cancelled the overpayments in their accounts, the means of paying the discounted acceptances all at once would be cut off; they would, unless some indulgence were extended, be discredited, and would probably be unable to continue the service. Under these circumstances I consented to furnish them with new acceptances, to be used only for the purpose of taking up those already discounted, upon their pledge of honor to apply them solely to that object, and ultimately take them up. Not believing that I had lawful authority to bind the government or the Department to pay out of its funds when nothing was due, the acceptances were made on the express condition of payment only in the event that the amount should be due when they came to maturity. Stockton and Stokes honorably redeemed their pledges; but Reeside suffered the acceptances to be protested, and withdrew from the service of the Department, though already indebted to it, as appeared by its books, many thousand dollars. This balance he did not contest. Yet, some years afterwards, in the trial of a suit against him in a Philadelphia court to recover judgment for it, he obtained a certificate from the jury that the Department was indebted to him about three hundred thousand dollars! And this amount was afterwards allowed by Congress with interest.

"By what means the decision of the jury or of Congress was obtained I never knew. In neither case was I called upon to testify. All I know is that no such claims were ever presented to me, and that Mr. Reeside did not, at the time, question the correctness of the settlement.

"The account of Samuel L. Governeur, postmaster at New York, had

not been settled for several years. Circumstances had led to suspicions of his fidelity. But though I had serious thoughts of removing him, occurrences, after I became Postmaster-General, determined me to retain him. I so informed him, at the same time stating that it was absolutely necessary for him to close up his accounts. His evasions and delays excited new suspicions. There was an item on the debit side of his account which he declared belonged to the account of James Reeside, the mail contractor, but had been put to his debit to conceal the true condition of Reeside's account from the investigating committees of Congress. He presented no evidence of the truth of the assertion, but it seemed from the nature of the item that it had no appropriate place in a postmaster's account; yet it was incredible that it should have been placed there without some reason. While the item was under consideration, the accountant of the Department brought me a half-sheet of cap paper on which was a list of acceptances amounting to $25,000, having at the foot the initials J. A. H., and my chief clerk stated that he had heard vague rumors indicating that the Department had had pecuniary transactions with James A. Hamilton, Esq., of New York. Upon the basis of these indications, I wrote to Mr. Hamilton. He promptly replied, that at some time in the administration of my predecessor, he was in Washington, and learning that the Post-Office Department wanted a temporary loan, he tendered his services to aid in the operation, that acceptances to the amount of $25,000 were placed in his hands for the purpose of raising money by getting them discounted in the banks; that he was unable to get them discounted, but that he raised $25,000 on his own credit and handed it to Mr. Governeur; that it was afterwards repaid by Mr. Governeur; that he had undertaken to raise the money on condition that his name should not appear on the books of the Department; and that the acceptances were still in his possession. This explained the mystery. Mr. Governeur had not charged himself with the $25,000 received from Mr. Hamilton, but in lieu thereof, had charged himself with sums advanced by him to refund that loan, thus converting an apparent credit into a debit. So wrong did this appear to be, that I had promised him to strike out the item unless the Department should be able to show why it was so entered. Mr. Hamilton's letter afforded the explanation. The account was rectified by transferring this debit to the credit side of his account, and charging him with the $25,000 received from Mr. Hamilton. But what could be said of Mr. Governeur? He had in this matter palpably attempted to cheat the government out of $25,000, by insisting on having this charge struck out, and concealing the fact that he had received that sum, not otherwise accounted for, in whole or in part. He was dismissed, and was found to be a defaulter in a large sum.

" But the case which illustrates more strikingly than any other in that Department the power of corruption in a government, and the fate of an honest man who endeavors to put a stop to it, is that of Stockton and Stokes. They had long carried the mails in post-coaches between Philadelphia, Baltimore, and Washington, and between Baltimore and Wheeling. They were of that class of ' old and faithful contractors' who procured a continuance of their contracts by ' private understandings between them and the Department,' had before the lettings, and by means of very low bids, afterwards ' improved.' They transported in their coaches, free of charge, prominent members of Congress, members of the Executive, judges, influential citizens, and not only the Postmaster-General, but all of his subordinates in the Department who were supposed to have influence there. When General Jackson went on to Washington in the winter of 1828 – 29, to enter upon the office of President, they refused to receive the usual fare from him, and not to feel under obligations to them, he sent to Mrs. Stockton a present of greater value than the fare. His private secretary, Major Donaldson, refused to enter an extra coach, gratuitously offered to convey him and his party from Frederick City to Washington, until they had paid the ordinary fare. It was these men who attempted to cheat me into a free passage from Frederick City to Wheeling, through instruction to their agents. Few, however, declined the tendered freedom of their coaches, and thus it was that the executive, legislative, and judicial departments of the government were in a great measure filled with men whose money they had saved by this apparent liberality. If this was not corruption, there is a moral difference between giving a man money for his influence or saving his money by a valuable service, the object being the same.

" Soon after I took charge of the Department, I learned that a large sum had been recently carried to the credit of Stockton and Stokes, apparently in consideration of services for which, if there was any truth in the reports of the committees of Congress, they had previously been overpaid. This discovery was very alarming in two aspects. First, it apparently added that sum to the responsibilities of the Department, already overwhelmed with debt. Secondly, if the reports of the committee on this case were to any extent true, here was a considerable amount, unknown to them, added to the allowances they had condemned, and presenting the question as to what was my own duty in the premises. It was my desire, as far as consistent with duty, to avoid conflict with the decisions of my predecessor, and at the same time to do my duty, whatever might be the consequences. I consulted the President, who remitted the matter to my discretion. As I was uninformed of the basis on which this allowance rested, and only knew that it was in conflict with the opinions of the committee, and therefore *prima facie* wrong, I

ordered its suspension from the credit of the contractors until a more mature knowledge of the affairs of the Department should enable me better to understand it. My predecessor was still in Washington, and on hearing of this decision was much excited, and meeting my chief clerk declared in his own words that ' Mr. Kendall shall not make a Toby Watkins of me.' I sent for him, and assured him that while I should do my duty in the Department, I should do it in a spirit of the utmost kindness towards him ; that if he did not make himself the partisan of the contractors, but left them to rely on his official acts as shown in the Department, there would be no quarrel between him and me ; that my action in this case was not definitive ; that as soon as I was able I should investigate the whole matter, and restore the credit if I found I could do so consistently with my duty to the public. As to the allowance, the only defence he set up for it was, that without it the contractors would be ruined, so great were their losses in attempting to expedite the mails. He left me in a good humor, promising to refer all parties who might question him as to his official acts to the records and files of the Post-Office Department.

" As soon as I conveniently could, I entered upon the promised investigation. I found that this was not a recent allowance, though lately entered on the books ; that it had been made on a loose slip of paper some time before ; that the slip was retained in the Postmaster-General's drawer until the committees of Congress were supposed to have finished their investigations ; that it was never seen by them ; and that the money was paid over to the contractors soon after the allowance was ordered, producing in whole or in part the apparent overpayment in their accounts on the books of the Department. This obviated the impression that it had added its amount to the debts of the Department, but it did not show that it had any basis in law or in services rendered. In short, the investigation conclusively showed that the entire allowance was nothing more nor less than a gratuity to the contractors, which might or might not have been necessary to save them from ruin.

" While this question was still undecided, a circumstance occurred which certainly did not aid the cause of the contractors. Major Eaton, General Jackson's first Secretary of War, and his wife were warm friends of Richard Stockton, the leading member of the firm of Stockton and Stokes. While I was investigating this affair, Mrs. Eaton called on Mrs. Kendall and told her that if she would induce her husband to allow this claim, Mrs. Stockton would give her a carriage and pair of horses.

" The investigation ended in making the suspension permanent, on the ground that the credit was an error, having neither law nor equity to sustain it.

" *Prima facie* it was impossible for me to conceive that the condemnation of the Department for its allowances to these men was sheer hypocrisy, designed merely for political effect, much less that Congress would in any way give countenance to the addition of one hundred and twenty thousand dollars to the hundred and odd thousand already allowed them, as the committee alleged, contrary to law. But I was mistaken. Stockton and Stokes petitioned Congress for relief, and that body, *without calling on the Department for information or explanation*, passed an act vesting the power to settle the claim in the Solicitor of the Treasury, a friend of the contractors, from the State of Maryland. Those who had denounced the Department for its illegal allowances were now dumb, and I did not think it my duty to volunteer information, although I had afterwards cause to regret that I did not then take steps to have a call made.

" The Solicitor of the Treasury, without calling upon me for any evidence contained in the books and files of the Department, or information of any sort, sent me an award allowing not only the entire amount originally claimed by Stockton and Stokes, but about forty thousand dollars in addition thereto, based upon claims which had never been heard of in the Department ! To say that I was shocked by the decision, is but a faint description of my sensations. I thought it my duty, if I could by any lawful means, to prevent the consummation of such an outrage on the Department. I therefore addressed a letter to the Solicitor, assuring him that the Department contained abundant evidence that nothing of this large sum was due to the claimants in law or equity, and asking him to withdraw his award, and allow me to present those evidences before him. To this he assented, and I furnished him with what seemed to me conclusive proofs that not a particle of service had been rendered the Department for the hundred and sixty thousand dollars which he proposed to allow. Nevertheless, he returned the award without any material alteration, except in one small item which in his haste he had allowed twice over. As there was no question of his legal power to allow all of the claims which had formed the basis of the legislation of Congress, I proceeded to pay those claims in full ; but I refused to pay the amount added by the solicitor upon new claims which had never been presented to the Department or Congress, had never been a subject of dispute, and of course did not come under his jurisdiction.

" Stockton and Stokes applied to Congress for the passage of an explanatory act or resolution to enable them to realize the balance of the award. No effective action took place in the House of Representatives. In the Senate it was referred to the Post-Office Committee, of which Mr. Felix Grundy was chairman. He called on me, as I at first sup-

posed, to obtain information ; but it soon appeared that his real object was to prevent my giving information, and induce me silently to acquiesce in the passage of a resolution directing the payment of the residue of the award. I reminded him that Congress had passed the original act implying that there might be something wrong in recharging the contractors with the sums in controversy without giving me an opportunity to defend my official action, which implication was strengthened by the action of the Solicitor, and now it was proposed to take another step implying that I had failed to obey a law, without giving me an opportunity to defend myself ; that it was due to me and the public interest that the committee or the Senate should call upon me to state why I had not executed the award in full. Upon his evincing a disposition not to do so, I became excited, and told him the time had come when *I would be heard* ; that I would no longer submit in silence to the imputations upon myself, and virtual plundering of the Department over which I presided, and if his committee did not call upon me for an explanation, I would send one direct to the Senate. He left me, himself greatly excited, and went to the President, Mr. Van Buren. What passed between them I never knew ; but the President sent for me, and suggested that it was unusual for the head of a Department, without being called on, to address the Houses of Congress, and proposed that I should make report of the case to him, and he would send it to the Senate. This course was finally adopted ; but Mr. Grundy found means to defeat my object. The report was referred to the Post-Office Committee without being read or printed, and of course went into the hands of Mr. Grundy. Years afterwards, when the merits of the controversy had become generally known, one of the members of that committee informed me that my report was not read in the committee ; that Mr. Grundy represented that it contained nothing which ought to prevent their favorable action on the claim ; and this member stated that had the truth been known, the result would probably have been very different. Upon the report of the committee, the Senate passed a resolution declaring, in effect, that the balance of the award ought to be paid. Had it been a joint resolution passed by both Houses and approved by the President, it would have had the authority of law, and the money would have been paid. Being a resolution of the Senate only, it left me in the same legal position as before, with the moral weight of the Senate against me. An attempt was made by Mr. Buchanan, afterwards President, and others, to induce Mr. Van Buren to order the payment of the money. probably with the view of forcing me to resign. Such would have been the effect of their successful effort, though I made no attempt to defeat them.

" Why no effort was made then or afterwards to pass a joint resolution

23

I do not know. I could not but attribute it to the conviction of the managers that so much light had already broken in upon the subject that it could not be gotten through the House of Representatives. Be that as it may, all further efforts in that direction were abandoned, and the claimants turned to the judiciary. I received a summons from the Circuit Court of the District of Columbia to appear before that court and show cause why a mandamus should not issue to compel me to execute the solicitor's award. This involved the question how far the head of a Department is amenable to the courts for his official action or refusal to act. The subject was taken as a cabinet question, and the defence assigned to Benjamin F. Butler, Attorney-General, and Francis S. Key, United States District Attorney. Under their direction, a plea to the jurisdiction of the court was put in. This, after long argument, the court overruled. Then, by a legal fiction and falsehood borrowed from the English courts, it was assumed that by the plea to the jurisdiction I had admitted the wrong, and had no defence upon the merits (though in my response I had claimed exemption on the merits), judgment was given against me, and a peremptory mandamus directed to be issued. An appeal was taken to the Supreme Court, which confirmed the decision of the court below, and then the balance of the award was paid.

"Thus it was, that by the manœuvering of corrupt men in Congress, and the false assumption of the courts, I was placed in the attitude of one who admitted himself to be a violator of the law, without an opportunity to show that from first to last I had acted in conformity with law and in obedience to my sworn obligations to the public. Thus, in spite of all my efforts, these corrupt men had secured payment of the whole one hundred and sixty thousand dollars awarded them by the Solicitor, not one cent of which I aver now (1867), as I did then, was due to them in law or equity. But they were not satisfied. They now commenced a suit against me in my private capacity, laying their damages at twelve thousand dollars, for my delays in payment of the award. I was rather gratified with this movement, because, I said to myself, I shall now have an opportunity to show that from first to last I have but done my duty. But when I offered to defend myself on that ground, the judges said, No ; you acknowledged that you violated the law in your plea to your jurisdiction in the mandamus case, and we cannot allow you now to take back that admission by showing that you did not violate the law. You are an admitted law-breaker, and the only defence left you is to show that you were not governed by a malicious design to injure the plaintiffs. It availed me nothing to prove, as I did by the officers and clerks of the Department, that no services had been rendered for the hundred and sixty thousand dollars awarded them by the

Solicitor, and that in nothing outside of this case had I shown any hostility to the claimants.

"The trial took place soon after the close of the embittered political campaign which ended in the election of General Harrison to the Presidency, in which I had taken a very active part. The jury was composed of eleven Whigs and one Democrat. They chose to infer malice without a particle of evidence, and found a verdict against me for about twelve thousand dollars. My counsel moved for a new trial, on the ground that the verdict was contrary to evidence, there being no proof of malice in the case. A new trial was readily granted, a strong impression having evidently been made upon the judges by the evidence, to such an extent indeed that one of them was heard to say that Mr. Kendall was the most persecuted man living.

"On the second trial, all pretext of malice was driven out of the case by proofs of acts of kindness and indulgence on my part towards the claimants. Indeed, it was proved that all the malice was on the other side, one of them having declared that the suit was brought, not to get money, but ' to punish the damned rascal,' and whatever they recovered would be given to the church. He was an Episcopalian. I was now very sure of a verdict in my favor ; but alas for the uncertainty of the law ! After the former trial, Judge Baldwin had decided, in the United States Court in Philadelphia, that a public officer was responsible in damages for any injury done or loss sustained by a private citizen through a violation of the law, whether it was malicious or not, and the judges in the District of Columbia considered themselves bound by this precedent, and so instructed the jury ! This left me without any defence. I could not show in this private suit that I had violated no law, because as a public officer, and with the concurrence of the President and Cabinet, I had had the audacity to question the jurisdiction of the court in the mandamus case, and now I was to be held responsible for this imputed violation of the law, whether I was right or wrong, honest or dishonest. Of course the jury had no alternative but to find a verdict against me for such damages as the plaintiffs might prove. And in doing this they were allowed an extraordinary latitude, and by means of counsel fees, hotel expenses, etc., rolled up an amount of alleged damages exceeding eleven thousand dollars, for which the jury gave a verdict.

"So I was convicted of honesty and fined for it. Prior to the first trial, I had made arrangements to remove to New York, and commence there the publication of a newspaper ; but the unexpected verdict on that occasion determined me to remain in the District of Columbia. Having no income from any source, I resorted to the publication of a small newspaper, called ' Kendall's Expositor,' by a hired printer, as means of subsistence for myself and family. This was so well patronized

that I was encouraged to purchase on credit the place adjoining the city of Washington, on which I have since resided, with the view of making it my permanent home. When the second verdict was rendered, I had paid nothing of the $ 9,000 purchase-money, and had no other property except household stuff and some unproductive and unsaleable Western lands on which the State taxes were about $ 150 a year. When the second verdict was rendered, I had learned so much of the uncertainty of the law, and my future was so dark, that I did not feel at liberty to ask any friend to become my security in an appeal bond, but resolved to take the case up to the Supreme Court by writ of error, which required no security, though it left my property exposed to execution from men whose only avowed motive was vengeance. I, however, wrote them a letter declaring my purpose, and proposing, in case of a stay of execution, to put all the property I had in the world in trust, first, for the payment of my other just debts, and secondly for the satisfaction of any judgment they might obtain against me in pursuance of the final decision of the Supreme Court. As my property was beyond their reach by execution, I had some hopes that they would accede to this proposition ; but the only reply I received was an arrest by the marshal, and committal to the prison limits of the district, then embracing the whole county of Washington. As the law then was, a judgment debtor was allowed to live one year within the limits, at the end of which he was required to surrender his property to be sold for the satisfaction of the judgment, on the penalty of going to close jail. Doubtless my persecutors anticipated the satisfaction of compelling me to sacrifice all my property by a forced sale at Washington, or of shutting me up in jail with men who were guilty of other crimes than being honest ; but they were doomed to disappointment.

"My newspaper subscription had fallen off after the first year, so that it afforded me an income scarcely equal to the support of my family. I had some debts, but not to a large amount. To avoid contracting more, with so poor prospects of being able to pay, I retired into a small unfinished frame house which I had caused to be erected on the place I had purchased in the country. There we lived very happily, though somewhat straitened for the comforts to which we had been accustomed. I had declared my purpose to go to close jail rather than surrender my Western lands to be sacrificed for the satisfaction of this unjust and cruel judgment, and my wife, with that cheerful acquiescence in all the vicissitudes of fortune which distinguished her whole life, declared her purpose to live with me there. Our anticipated residence in ' the Blue House ' (blue being the color of the jail), so called in contrast with ' the White House ' (the residence of the President), became the subject of many a family pleasantry.

"Such was the state of things when Congress met. The case had now attracted the serious attention of the country. Without any instigation from me, many petitions were sent to Congress in my behalf, and some of the State legislatures forwarded to that body resolutions recommending measures for my relief. The House of Representatives passed, without opposition, a bill providing for the payment of the judgment out of the United States Treasury, and it was sent to the Senate. There it was referred to the Post-Office Committee, of which Silas Wright was then chairman. He sent for me, and stated that the case was one in which I ought at once to be relieved, but that it involved principles on which the committee thought it important to have the decision of the Supreme Court ; that while they were ready to recommend the passage of the bill if I desired it, they would much prefer, with my consent, to recommend such a change in the law as would obviate the necessity of giving up my property, and allow me to remain in my then present condition until the Supreme Court should decide upon my case. To this course I assented, and instead of recommending the passage of the bill from the House, the committee reported, and both Houses passed, without opposition, a bill altering the general law so as to allow me and all persons similarly situated the privilege of the prison limits until the final decision of the Supreme Court, and one year thereafter.

"Thus my persecutors were thwarted in their design of forcing me into either insolvency or close jail.

"At the next session of Congress an act was passed abolishing imprisonment for debt in the District of Columbia altogether ; but having understood that one of the Judges of the Circuit Court had expressed a doubt whether it embraced cases wherein the debt or obligation was incurred before its passage, I deemed it prudent not to afford another opportunity for further acts of vengeance, and for this purpose took care not to pass the former prison limits.

"At length the Supreme Court announced their decision, which was in my favor. It was read by Chief Justice Taney, and only Justice McLean dissented. Thus were the authors of this malicious suit not only defeated in their designs, but virtually punished. Instead of sending me to prison or robbing me of $ 12,000, or any smaller sum, to give to the church, they had to pay all the costs of this long and relentless persecution, and see me triumphant at last.

"Nor did my triumph stop here. I now petitioned Congress for payment of my counsel's fees and all other costs and expenses which had been brought upon me by the honest performance of my public duties in my official relations with these parties. Both Houses, without a dissenting voice, passed an act for my relief.

"It was impossible for me to make out a detailed account of my expenses occasioned by this suit; but I estimated them as accurately as I could, and sent my claims to the Treasury with a short explanation. They were passed without hesitation, and both the Auditor and Comptroller afterwards assured me that had I charged a few thousands more it would have been allowed with equal promptitude. For the apparently universal conviction that I had but done my duty in this affair, I was undoubtedly indebted in a great measure to honest men among my political opponents. Most prominent among them was Elisha Whittlesey, many years a prominent member from Ohio. He was a man of strong prejudices but honest intentions. He was on the committee which investigated the affairs of the Department under my predecessor, and made a separate report, in which he charged that Stockton and Stokes had been paid over $100,000 more than they were entitled to by law. While the bill for their relief was before the House of Representatives, he offered several provisos prohibiting the allowance of certain items, not one of which was embraced in the contested account. Upon the election of General Harrison to the Presidency, he was appointed Sixth Auditor of the Treasury, in whose office the accounts of the Post-Office Department were settled. There he was brought in contact with those who were familiar with my administration in all its details, and especially with Peter G. Washington, chief clerk, one of the most faithful and efficient of public servants, who had been chief clerk of that office ever since its organization. From what he there learned, Mr. Whittlesey did not hesitate to acknowledge that he had entirely misunderstood the motives of my official conduct, and gave me full credit for integrity of purpose without regard to political considerations. He volunteered an explanation to me in person of his motives in offering the nugatory provisos in the bill for the relief of Stockton and Stokes, stating that not knowing or suspecting the true state of the case, he supposed I had recharged the illegal allowances exposed in his report, and his object was to prevent their restoration by the Solicitor. I expressed my gratification at this explanation; for, supposing he knew that the allowances suspended by me were not those condemned in his report, but were all in addition thereto, I could only consider his provisos as intended to keep up a show of consistency while he was in fact willing that Stockton and Stokes should not only retain the hundred thousand condemned by him, but should add thereto an hundred and twenty thousand more. Mutual respect was the effect of these explanations. The last time I ever saw that honest man and faithful public servant, he held the office of First Comptroller, and was lamenting in deep despondency the corruptions of the times. As I shook hands with him I said, 'Your palm and mine have never been stained by a bribe.' And it was without doubt his representations and those

of others who had been equally deceived that overcame the political prejudices of the Whig Party, and secured for me acquittal and indemnity by the unanimous assent of Congress.

"But what a lesson it is against legislating in the dark! And does it not illustrate the outrage of that rule of the courts, — I do not say of *law*, — which adjudges a party to be guilty of the matter charged who pleads to their jurisdiction? What is it but a judicial contrivance to punish without authority? I had violated no law, as I was advised by lawyers quite as learned as the court; yet, because I allowed myself under the advice of the President, to be made the instrument of ascertaining the line which separates the judicial and executive powers of the government, I was not permitted to show that I was not guilty of the offence charged, not even when, divested of their public interest, the proceedings assumed the character of vindictive persecution. Virtually, the Judges said to me, 'You dared to question our jurisdiction in the public case, and now, whether guilty or innocent, we turn you over without trial to the tender mercies of the plaintiffs in the private case.'

"Though in its progress this affair was most annoying, its consequences, under the direction of Providence, were most consoling. It established my reputation as an honest man, and a pure, faithful, and inflexible public officer.

"It probably saved my life. I had an invitation from Commodore Stockton for myself and family to the excursion of the Princeton, which was made awfully memorable by the explosion of his big gun. Two members of my family went, and I was prevented only by confinement in the prison limits. Had I been there, I should, without doubt, have been near the gun when it exploded. The Solicitor of the Treasury, whose action had led to my confinement, was one of the slain.

"By defeating my purpose of connecting myself with the press in New York, and confining me in Washington, it led me into connection with Professor Morse and his telegraph, to which I am indebted for three fourths of all I possess, and a release in my old age from all the cares of business.

"The private suit against me was defended with great ability by J. Hatch Dent and General Walter Jones, both of whom were confident of my acquittal had I been allowed to show that the Solicitor had exceeded his authority in allowing the new claims which were never known to the Department.

"Their fees of $2,000 were allowed and paid under the act of Congress for my relief.

"One of the prosecuting counsel was Major Eaton, whose wife had offered the bribe of a carriage and horses for the allowance of the origi-

nal claim. When he rose to address the jury I rose to leave the courtroom, stating that I feared I should be guilty of some outrage if I remained to hear him. Mr. Dent told me to sit down and look him in the face, which I did throughout his speech. The offered bribe was not the only or the principal ground of my excitement. Years before, when he had been vindictively assailed in his private and family and public relations, I had been his steadfast friend, and had, at the request of one of his family connections, without thought of fee or reward, revised and mainly re-written a pamphlet prepared by him in vindication of his honor, thereby establishing, as I thought, a claim upon his gratitude, though prior to that date disclosures not fit for record had satisfied me that my confidence had been misplaced. For some years after this, I passed him without speaking; but finally he took pains to confront me on the street, and say that it was professionally and not in personal hostility that he had appeared against me. I replied that there were relations which forbade one gentleman to appear against another professionally, and that I had supposed such relations existed between us. In reply to the expression of his hopes that the affair might be overlooked and forgotten, I assured him that all bitterness of feeling had passed away, though it was impossible for me to think or feel that he had done right."

In July, 1843, Mr. Kendall thus referred to his celebration of the birthday of the nation: —

"FOURTH OF JULY.

"We celebrated it in the prison limits of Washington, rejoicing in the liberty it gave our neighbors to go where they please."

In June, 1844, Mr. Kendall exults in his emancipation as follows: —

"FREE!!

"Sickness prevented our getting out a paper last week, or witnessing the closing scenes of Congress. Upon recovery, however, we find ourself released from the prison limits by an Act of Congress which effectually abolishes imprisonment for debt in the District of Columbia.

"We rejoice in our own emancipation, and more in the progress of a great principle. To all the guards which the law can throw around the rights of creditors, without touching the liberty of the debtor or bringing instant destitution or want upon the family of the debtor, we have no objection; but this putting of his body into prison or the prison limits because he cannot pay or will not pay, is a relic of ancient slavery as detestable as selling him to pay his debts. Let every species of

property and vested interest, excepting only such as is essential to the immediate comfort of the debtor's family, be subjected to execution for debt; but let man, created in the form of his Maker, be permitted to walk forth in his native liberty, until the safety of others requires his restraint.

"With the friends of liberty we cannot now but look back with gratitude and thanks to the persevering efforts of Colonel R. M. Johnson when in Congress, to effect this great reform. Though not successful, he sowed the seeds of that harvest which we this day enjoy."

When Mr. Kendall left the Department, the gentlemen who had been associated with him in office spontaneously addressed him the following letter: —

POST-OFFICE DEPARTMENT, May 25, 1840.

To THE HON. AMOS KENDALL.

SIR, — Your retirement from the head of this Department is an event that we regard with peculiar sensibility. It closes an official career eminent for ability and success, and terminates relations and intercourse which we have long enjoyed and highly valued. Our feelings will not allow the occasion to pass without the expression of our regret for its occurrence, our sympathies for its cause, and our ardent wishes for your future welfare.

The whole Union has felt the benefit of your official labors; but we alone have been the daily witnesses of the zeal, vigilance, assiduity, and skill with which those labors have been conducted. We have seen how successfully each emergency has been met by ample resources of mind; how much has been achieved, and how much preserved by that impulsive energy and supervisory scrutiny so rarely united in the same individual. Your reorganization of the Department established order, supervision, coercion, and efficiency. Your scheme of speedy returns and prompt collections largely augmented its revenues, enabling you to discharge an onerous debt, add millions of miles to the annual transportation of the mails, and accelerate their movements through the principal channels of communication. Your express mails anticipated railroads, and gave, with the despatch and regularity of steam, the extraordinary expedition demanded by the great commercial communities, at a period of intense activity in business. And your foresight and firmness, by denying the numberless importunities for mail improvements and extensions, and by timely retrenchments, warded off from your Department the disastrous effects of that great convulsion in monetary and commercial affairs, that has so deeply disturbed all the pecuniary interests of the country. It is gratifying to know that whilst so many interests afloat, like those under your charge, yielded to the fury of the storm, the deep-freighted bark at whose helm you stood was held steadily to her course, and guided in safety over the troubled waters.

We have also beheld, in their full array and proportions, the obstacles and difficulties you had to encounter, even from the outset of your career, where you found them thick sown in a previous season of derangement, like the dragon's teeth of the fable, springing up in every shape of resistance and hostility, armed with the artillery of the press, and the terrors of litigation, yet unable to divert you from the establishment of those reforms, and the maintenance of those principles of economy in expenditure and fidelity to engagements that form the distinctive traits of your administration. Vain were the demoralizing efforts of the day to make your Department *particeps criminis* with defaulting institutions, in imposing on the public creditor a depreciated and illegal currency; ineffectual the attempts at extortion, made through crafty combinations, or in the bolder exactions of licensed monopolies; unavailing the influence of friends, of party, or of station, to procure an act unapproved by a faithful sense of right in reference to principle or policy; and impotent the hand of sickness, though prostrating the physical energies, to repress the successful efforts of the untiring spirit in its devotion to the public service.

We separate from you under a grateful sense of the uniform kindness you have extended to us, and with sentiments of friendship for the man, won by the purity and simplicity of character, so happily united with the energy of mind and conduct, that commands admiration for the public officer.

May relaxation from toil give speedy restoration to health, and your future lot in life be as honorable and happy as your past career has been distinguished and useful.

We are, sir, most respectfully,
Your obedient servants.

This communication was signed by every gentleman then in the Department except six, who addressed him a private letter of the same import.

The following is a copy of the notice issued to postmasters: —

NOTICE TO POSTMASTERS.

POST-OFFICE DEPARTMENT, October 11, 1839.

The officers of this Department, from the highest to the lowest, are but agents to execute the laws. As executive officers, we have no right to consider the expediency of any existing law, our only duty being *to obey.* In addition to the duty of the private citizen to obey the laws, a duty next in binding force to moral obligations, we have taken an oath

faithfully to discharge the duties of our respective stations *according to law,* and to *defend the Constitution of the United States.*

The only currency which, by the Constitution and laws, is a tender for postages or in payment to contractors and others in the service of the Department, is composed of the gold and silver coins of the United States, and such foreign coins as Congress may from time to time prescribe by law.

The law *permits* postmasters to receive bank-notes of a certain character, not less in amount than twenty dollars; but if they receive such notes, they are yet bound to pay in gold and silver if demanded.

The law *forbids* the reception or payment of any bank-notes whatever of a less denomination than twenty dollars.

It *forbids* the reception of the notes of any bank which does not pay them on demand in gold or silver coin.

It *forbids* the payment on public account of any bank-note which is not equivalent to specie at the place where paid out.

It *forbids* the reception of the notes of any bank which, since the 1st day of October, 1838, shall have issued, reissued, or paid out any bill or note of a less denomination than five dollars.

These are the commands of the law. It is the duty of every postmaster, truly, faithfully, and without evasion, to obey them.

I deem it my duty, therefore, under present circumstances, to enjoin upon you strict obedience to the Constitution and laws in this respect, and to inform you that you cannot avoid your obligations without a disregard of your duty and your oath.

If a postmaster, therefore, receive or pay out any bank-note of a less denomination than twenty dollars; if he receive or pay out the notes of any bank which does not pay them on demand in gold or silver coin; if he receive or pay out the notes of any bank which, since the 1st of October, 1838, has issued, reissued, or paid out any note of a less denomination than five dollars; if he pay out any bank-note, though greater than twenty dollars, which is not equivalent to specie at the place where paid, — such postmaster is guilty of a dereliction of duty and a violation of his oath.

Your position, your oath, and your duty make you the standard-bearers of the Constitution and the laws in the several neighborhoods where you reside, and an example of rigid, fearless, and unhesitating obedience is expected from you, which shall not only prove your own uncompromising fidelity, but afford bright examples which shall inculcate respect for the laws of your country in all who surround you. It is but a step from the violation of the law to the disregard of moral obligation, and the latter often treads closely on the heels of the former.

While at the head of the Post-Office, Mr. Kendall prepared the following bill to facilitate the transmission of money by that Department, similar to the Money-Order Bureau afterwards so successfully introduced, but failed to procure its passage by Congress: —

FORM OF BILL TO FACILITATE EXCHANGES BY THE POST-OFFICE DEPARTMENT.

Be it enacted, etc., That the Postmaster-General be authorized to cause to be received by postmasters at such convenient points as he may designate, any sum of money not exceeding twenty dollars, to be sent by mail, and shall be permitted to charge therefor a commission not exceeding one per cent for one hundred and fifty miles or under, of two per cent for three hundred miles and over one hundred and fifty, of three per cent for six hundred miles and over three hundred, and of five per cent for over six hundred miles: *Provided,* that so far as it can be done without deranging the business of the Department, the sums received for transportation may be retained where received, and paid out at the places to which they are requested to be sent: *Provided also,* that all additional expenses of this operation shall be paid out of the commissions on funds received for transportation. *Provided further,* that if the commissions shall be more than sufficient to pay reasonable expenses, the Postmaster-General is required to reduce and graduate them to that standard.

REPLY TO INVITATION.

GENTLEMEN, — I have just received your letter on behalf of "the Democratic Citizens of Pittsburg and Alleghany County," inviting me to unite with them in celebrating the "centenary birthday of the author of the Declaration of Independence," on the 13th instant.

I am not a freeman in this "land of the free." I have not, like the negro slave, a kind master to give me "a pass." For attempting, when in a high station, to check extravagance and baffle corruption, for rejecting the favors of the powerful and meting out to them the same justice which is awarded to the weak, I have been amerced in the sum of $12,000, and not being able to pay it, am now confined to the jail limits of the county of Washington. The court said there was no evidence of evil intention on my part; the jury said my motives were not only pure but praiseworthy; a Whig Committee of Congress have declared that my conduct merited applause rather than censure; not a voice was raised in either House against the passage of an act to prevent my masters confining me in close jail; yet here I am confined to the jail limits, my interests abroad grievously suffering for want of my

personal attention, my credit destroyed, and myself subjected to heavy expenses in defending the case before the Supreme Court.

The utmost that is alleged against me is, that in my zeal to serve the public, I violated the law. Yet, strange as it may seem in *a land of justice,* the question whether I did violate the law has never been decided or tried. The courts have a rule that any one who calls in question their jurisdiction as to a matter in controversy, shall be treated as admitting that he has no other defence. When in this case I was proceeded against by mandamus, and, under the advice of the President and Attorney-General, resisted the claim to jurisdiction in the Circuit Court as an attack on the rights of the Executive, I was treated as admitting that the law and the facts were against me, contrary to my own belief and express declaration. And when sued for $100,000 out of my own purse (if so much should ever get into it) for this alleged violation of the law, the assumed admission in the mandamus case was taken as precluding me from showing that I had not violated the law, and honesty of purpose being also ruled out, I was left without defence, condemned without a hearing, fined for being honest, and imprisoned because I could not pay it.

You perceive why I cannot join you in honoring the memory of *Liberty's Apostle.* Nevertheless, I congratulate you that his doctrines have made great progress, and are still progressing. And if, as one of his disciples, I may be instrumental, by suffering persecution, in extending the range of their practical application, I shall exult in imprisonment.

With thankfulness for your remembrance of me on *such* an occasion, I annex a sentiment, and remain

Your friend,
AMOS KENDALL.

Jefferson's creed of government: "To punish rogues and protect honest men."

FROM HON. WILLIAM SMITH.

CULPEPPER COURT-HOUSE, VIRGINIA, July 6, 1837.

DEAR SIR, — I have noticed with much interest the extraordinary ground taken by the Circuit Court for the District in issuing a mandamus against you in your official character, and I have scanned with profound satisfaction your conclusive and unanswerable reply. The ground taken by the court would not only destroy that beautiful trinity, into which all power to be controlled must divide, but if maintained would indeed "make the judiciary the despotic branch."

You refer in support of your argument to only one of Mr. Jefferson's letters, that to Mr. Hay; but the same opinions are expressed in two letters to Mr. Adams, to be found in the fourth volume of his correspondence, pages twenty-two and twenty-six. In the latter letter the position is stated with great distinctness and simplicity, and therefore with peculiar power, decidedly more impressive than in his somewhat labored letter to Mr. Hay. I almost regret that you should have taken your last position, to wit, that you could not make the credit, because the books were not in your possession. This will enable the court to escape from the difficulty, and yet have the weight of judicial authority in favor of their decision.

I noticed also your scathing reply to Wickliffe. Can he be silent? If so, he ought to be doomed to everlasting shame. Let your enemies assail you, and do you maintain the same power in your replies, and it requires no seer to predict the consequences, — defeat, overwhelming defeat for your foes, — triumph glorious and transcendent for yourself. That you may be able to roll back (and I doubt it not) that torrent with which your persecutors have sought to overwhelm you, is the earnest wish of,

In haste, most truly yours,

WILLIAM SMITH.

AMOS KENDALL, Esq., Postmaster-General.

EXTRACT OF A LETTER FROM MR. VAN BUREN.

KINDERHOOK, December 15, 1842.

MY DEAR SIR, — Accept my unfeigned thanks for the friendly suggestions contained in your letter. They shall not be unheeded. I am grieved to hear of the troubles you have to encounter, and particularly in the affair of Stockton and Stokes. Certainly there cannot be found in the history of our government so wicked or so naked an act of injustice and oppression as that you have experienced in this matter. From beginning to end it has been an affair of wrong, and I should feel melancholy in believing that it is to continue so. The court will, I hope, do you justice, and if they do not, I should be sorry to think that Congress will not. . . . .

Very sincerely, your friend,

M. VAN BUREN.

The following testimony to the marked ability and success of Mr. Kendall's administration of the Post-Office Department is from a leading journal : —

THE POSTMASTER-GENERAL'S REPORT.

The report of the Postmaster-General, which was published in the "Advocate" of Saturday last, is a very concise and important document. It exhibits the admirable condition of the Post-Office Department in a strong light, which will not be easily perverted or darkened by the misrepresentations of the opposition press. There is, perhaps, no individual

connected with the present administration, who has received more abuse from the opposition, than the one now at the head of the Post-Office Department.

Notwithstanding all the blackguardisms and falsehoods that have been reiterated again and again by a corrupt and profligate press, that gentleman has kept along on "the even tenor of his way" in the discharge of his official duties, and his last report of the condition of the Department is a noble justification of his course, and a severe rebuke upon his calumniators.

"In 1835," says the report, "the Department was laboring under an extraordinary debt of $600,000 ; in 1837, it has a surplus of $800,000." Making a difference in favor of the Department of *fourteen hundred thousand dollars.* And this has been accomplished in the short space of about two years ! During this time the number of routes and post-offices has also been much increased, and the speed in the transportation of the mail on the principal routes greatly augmented.

The number of post-offices in 1835 was 10,770 ; in 1837, 11,009.

The number of miles of mail routes under contract in 1835 was 112,774 ; in 1837, 142,877.

The firmness and promptitude manifested by the Postmaster-General at the time of the suspension of the banks, and the carrying on of the financial operations of the Department from that time to the present according to *law*, and in the *legal* currency of the country, entitle him to the highest praise ; and he has already received from an intelligent people the appellation of "Well done, good and faithful servant !" while he has silenced a bitter opposition.

On the 1st instant, the Department had bank funds to the
amount of $430,645.57
Specie in post-offices reported subject to draft . . 410.662.81
Making the amount of funds on hand . . . $841,308.38

The able manner in which the Post-Office Department has been conducted should open the eyes and ears of every candid mind of whatever party. Are there not those who are opposed to the present administration who are willing to let facts like those which have been stated have an influence upon their minds in favor of the administration, rather than to suffer themselves to be misled by the misrepresentations of designing and corrupt men ?

TO HIS WIFE.

HERMITAGE, TENN., October 20, 1838.

MY DEAR WIFE, — I left Nashville after breakfast yesterday, and reached this place about eleven o'clock. The good old chief was at his gate, about as far from his house as our gate, waiting for the mail-car-

rier who brings his letters and papers. Although it was a raw cold day, he had on no overcoat, and his face was colored by the keen air. He received me with the utmost kindness, and inquired particularly after you and the children, expressing many regrets that you had not come with me. In these he was joined by Mrs. Jackson, who, with her husband and children, appears to be in good health, though the children, excepting a boy sixteen months old, look puny and pale. Major Donelson called to see me, last evening, in excellent health, and he also inquired particularly after you.

The General's house is a palace ; but I am not prepared to describe it. In the passages below and above, is the identical scene from Telemachus which ornamented the lower passage of DeKraft's House, though much more developed. I have a chamber assigned to me larger than any in that house, and most tastefully furnished. I am told to make myself entirely at home, and already begin to feel so.

Poor Earle died without knowing that he was seriously ill. He had but little pain, and a day or two before he died none at all. It was but a day before his death that any one supposed him to be in danger. He had had a steady, slow fever for some days, with a little pain occasionally in his limbs, back, or head. His medicine operated well, and it was thought his disease was slight. The pains left him, and he said he was well, excepting debility ; but from that time he became lethargic, although he could be roused without difficulty, and constantly said he was better. At length his fingers began to get cold, then his hands, then his arms, and all efforts to restore circulation in them were fruitless. He was unconscious of this coldness, and when the General and Mrs. Jackson attempted to restore the vital heat, he said his hands were warm enough. At length the coldness spread over his breast, and gradually his heart ceased to beat, and he died evidently without the least pain, and without any consciousness that his end was approaching.

Mrs. Jackson tells me that he had as many portraits of the General bespoken as he could have executed for years ; but that he had determined to take mine upon this visit, and often spoke of his anxiety to restore the beautiful little Andrew.

Mrs. Jackson's tomb is in a corner of the garden, about as far from the house as the gate of our garden is from ours. It is on the plan of General Van Ness's, near the Orphan Asylum in Washington, but has an obelisk upon the centre of the floor. It is all built of stone.

This is Saturday. Next Monday I propose to go to work. So many people are anxious to see me, and invite me to their houses, that I shall find it difficult to command my time without giving offence. But offence or not, I do not intend to miss the principal object which has brought me here.

I hope to find time to-morrow to write to Alva, and he may expect to hear from me in two days after you get this.

The "Globe" has been received here to the 8th October ; but I have as yet nothing from home later than Adela's letter of 30th September. I have no doubt an army of letters will soon overtake me. I rest in hope that all is well with you.

My love to our own and to your father's family.

All your own,

AMOS KENDALL.

MRS. JANE KENDALL.

The following letter is inserted as a just tribute to Hon. Horatio King, who, in 1839, was appointed a clerk in the Post-Office Department, and who for many years discharged with ability and fidelity the duties of Postmaster-General : —

TO THE POSTMASTER-GENERAL OF THE UNITED STATES : —

If you want a clerk in your office a gentleman of talent, integrity, and exemplary morals, of unwearied and persevering industry, of regular and economical habits, a good penman and correct draughtsman, a man in whom you may place the most implicit confidence in all situations and under all circumstances, and a Democrat to the core, sound, radical, ardent, and persevering, the undersigned most respectfully present and earnestly recommend as such an individual, Horatio King, Esq., of Maine.

In whatever situation he may be placed, you may rely that his services will be most invaluable.

ALBERT SMITH,
VIRGIL D. PARRIS,
R. WILLIAMS,
H. J. ANDERSON,
THOMAS DAVIS,

WASHINGTON, January 30, 1839.

In August, 1839, Mr. Kendall was summoned to the sick-bed of his venerable father, in Dunstable, Mass. Though unable to converse, his father recognized him, and died, apparently without pain, on the 12th of that month, aged eighty-four years.

He was a man of vigorous intellect, well informed, of positive character, for many years a deacon in the Congregational Church, above reproach in all relations of life, and conscientious in all his dealings. His piety was of that sturdy kind which rendered and exacted strict honesty. Incapable of conscious wrong to others, he plainly and unhesitatingly rebuked any deviations from the severest requirements of his religion.

CHAPTER XIV.

THE ORIGIN OF THE "GLOBE" NEWSPAPER.

EVEN before the organization of General Jackson's administration, General Duff Green, the editor of the "United States Telegraph," had lost, if ever he enjoyed, the confidence of many of the General's supporters. A majority of them in the Senate, at the session of 1828 – 29, were supposed to be averse to electing him their printer. Mr. Amos Kendall, being then in Washington, was informed by Major Eaton that he could have the printing of that body if he would consent to take it. He replied that he would consent only on condition that General Green should be consulted, and should give his assent; but he declined to consult Green himself, and requested that what had passed as far as he was concerned should not be communicated to that gentleman.

On a subsequent occasion, Major Eaton reported that Green had been consulted, and refused his assent; but it was proposed to elect Mr. Kendall notwithstanding, when the latter peremptorily refused to let his name be used. This refusal arose, not from any repugnance to the appointment in itself, but from an indisposition to interfere in any way with Green's expectations, however extravagant; for it could not be denied that he had established himself at Washington, risking everything in a doubtful contest, and there would be a seeming unfairness in depriving him of the anticipated reward of his labors, though his views might be grasping and unreasonable. Such an act, it seemed to Mr. Kendall, would sow the seeds of discord at the very outset of General Jackson's administration, to which he did not then doubt General Green's fidelity.

At the first session of Congress after General Jackson's administration was inaugurated, a combination was formed in the Senate to reject the editors of newspapers whom the President had appointed to office, and among the rejected was Isaac Hill, of New Hampshire, who had been appointed Second Comptroller of the Treasury. General Green called on him after his rejection, and strenuously endeavored to convince him that he had been rejected by what he called the "Eaton and Van Buren influence." This let new light into Mr. Kendall's mind. He had never before heard of such an influence. He knew that Green was the particular friend of Mr. Calhoun, and it seemed that the editors were to be rejected and sent back to their posts in the several States, under the impression that they owed their rejection to an interest adverse to Calhoun. As to Mr. Kendall himself, Green remarked that if rejected by the Senate for the Fourth Auditorship of the Treasury, to which he had been appointed, he might return to Kentucky and resume his editorial profession. When told that Mr. Kendall did not intend in that event to return to Kentucky, a new idea seemed to strike him, and it was singular that, when the vote was taken on his nomination, the Senate was equally divided, and he was confirmed by the casting vote of Mr. Calhoun, then Vice-President.

These incidents, and more of like tendency, created an impression among the friends of General Jackson that General Green was more the friend of Mr. Calhoun than of the President, and was already embarrassing the administration by intrigues looking toward the succession. It was their desire that General Jackson should be elected for another term, that he might establish the policy in relation to the Bank of the United States, and other subjects which he had initiated, and they apprehended that in this important measure they would not have the support of the "United States Telegraph." It seemed to them important, therefore, that another paper should be established at Washington, devoted exclusively to the support of the administration and its leading measures, without regard to the succession. It was not their object or desire to supersede the "Telegraph" as an official paper, or to deprive General Green of the printing of Congress, should he remain faithful, but to furnish an auxiliary paper, published semi-weekly, and sustained by its subscriptions, advertising, and job work.

When the project was broached to General Jackson, he entirely disapproved of it. He still had faith in the fidelity of the "Telegraph," and he feared collision between the papers should another be established. It was not long, however, before he began to

realize the necessity of such a paper as was proposed, and finally gave the project his tacit approval.

The several public offices were visited for the purpose of ascertaining whether they would give such a paper a portion of their printing. The responses were generally favorable; but Mr. Van Buren, then Secretary of State, replied that he not only would not promise, but would not give the paper a dollar's worth of printing should it be established. The reason he gave was, that were such a paper established its origin would be attributed to him, and he was resolved to be able to say truly that he had nothing to do with it.

In a consultation on the subject, Major W. T. Barry, then Postmaster-General, named Francis P. Blair, who was then writing for Mr. Kendall's paper in Frankfort, Kentucky, as a suitable person for editor, and Mr. Kendall undertook to correspond with him on the subject. Mr. Blair hesitated, and was induced to accede only by Mr. Kendall's assurance that he would bear an equal share in the responsibilities, upon the condition that he should at any time have the privilege of resigning the office he then held and becoming an equal partner in the new establishment.

This assurance was given, not because Mr. Kendall had any inclination to avail himself of the privilege, but only to overcome the hesitation of Mr. Blair, who thereupon determined to assume the position, writing Mr. Kendall that he should hold him responsible for the result.

Neither Mr. Blair nor Mr. Kendall had any capital to invest in such an undertaking. One condition insisted upon by Mr. Blair was that no publicity should be given to the project until he could have an opportunity to compound with his creditors, and particularly the Bank of the United States, to which he was heavily indebted. Under these circumstances, it was essential to make the new paper self-sustaining from the start. Its terms of subscription required payment in advance, and a printer was hired to print it. All the arrangements were made by Mr. Kendall before Mr. Blair's arrival, and he had only to ratify and execute what had already been planned. Only the name of the paper and its motto remained to be fixed upon. Mr. Kendall and Mr. Blair concurred in the name and in the sentiment embraced in the motto, "The world is governed too much"; but the phrase in which it is so briefly expressed was the work of Mr. Kendall.

Mr. Blair communicated frankly to General Green the objects

of his location at Washington, so far as they had reference to the public printing and the official position of the "Telegraph," and he was advised studiously to avoid any expression to which General Green could justly take exception. But the latter evidently had no faith in Mr. Blair's professions, and looked upon the new paper as intended to supersede his establishment and promote the elevation of Mr. Van Buren to the Presidency in opposition to his own favorite, Mr. Calhoun.

The first number of the "Globe" appeared on the 7th of December, 1830. Little notice was taken of it by the "Telegraph" until February, 1831, when General Green was elected printer to both Houses of Congress. Upon that event the "Globe" congratulated the friends of the administration on the disappointment of its enemies, who had anticipated divisions from the establishment of a new Jackson press at Washington. But the prospect of harmony, if there really was one, was of short duration. No sooner had the printing of Congress been secured, than the "Telegraph" began to throw out innuendos against the "Globe," of which the latter, however, took no notice. In a few days after the election of printer, Mr. Calhoun committed the fatal error of bringing before the public, both in pamphlet and through the "Telegraph," his correspondence with General Jackson touching the events of the Seminole war. On the 19th of February, 1831, the "Globe" came out with an article exposing Mr. Calhoun and vindicating the President. The "Telegraph" had already ranged itself on Mr. Calhoun's side. A sharp controversy ensued, which in a short time led to the repudiation of the "Telegraph," and the adoption of the "Globe" as the organ of the administration.

The "Globe" was still a semi-weekly paper, printed by contract. The position to which it had now attained required that it should be placed on an independent footing and published daily; but Mr. Blair had not the means to purchase the necessary materials. To raise the funds, he called on the friends of the President in Washington and elsewhere, who subscribed and paid in advance for six hundred copies of the "Daily Globe," at ten dollars per annum, and by this aid the "Globe" was made a daily paper. Thus, first and last, the "Globe" was established without a dollar of capital furnished by its proprietor, and, as Mr. Blair used to say, like the great globe we inhabit, was created out of nothing.

Mr. Benton is entirely mistaken in attributing the origin of the

"Globe" to General Jackson. General Green is equally in error in attributing it to Mr. Van Buren or his friends. It originated with those friends of General Jackson who regarded measures more than men, and desired his re-election for another four years, not so much for his own sake as to effect reforms in the government which no other man was capable of bringing about; chief of these was its severance from the banking power organized and exercised under the charter of the Bank of the United States. The "Globe's" subsequent support of Mr. Van Buren was occasioned by later events, which seemed to indicate that his administration would, so far as measures were concerned, be in effect a continuation of that of General Jackson.

REMOVAL OF THE DEPOSITS.

It is a significant fact that during General Jackson's controversy with the Bank of the United States, the Bank always carried a majority of Congress on every question which did not involve a direct issue between the members and the President. The latter's opposition to the Bank was well known; yet the act to recharter it was passed by a vote of twenty-eight to twenty in the Senate, and one hundred and seven to eighty-five in the House of Representatives. Although at the session of Congress in 1832–33, it was well understood that the General believed the Bank to be thoroughly corrupt and an unsafe depository of the public moneys, yet for the obvious purpose of deterring him from any measures for their transfer during the recess of Congress, the friends of the Bank procured the passage of a resolution declaring, by a vote of one hundred and ten to forty-six, that in their opinion the public moneys were safe in the Bank of the United States.

The politicians who had been accustomed to look upon Congress as the exponent of public opinion, believed this resolution to be conclusive against any further agitation on the subject of removal. Not so General Jackson and those friends of his who looked upon the destruction of the Bank as essential to the preservation of a purely republican government. They regarded the passage of the resolution in the face of abundant evidence of the corruption and abuses of the Bank, as only another exhibition of its dangerous power. The policy of the Bank was to them perfectly evident. So far from having, after the vote upon its recharter, adopted a system of gradual curtailment preparatory to winding up its affairs in

1836, when its charter expired, it had proceeded to add about twenty-eight millions of dollars to its discounts, thereby largely increasing its army of debtors and dependents. The year 1836, when the charter expired, was also the year of the presidential election, and the policy of the Bank was to keep quiet and strengthen itself, with the purpose of throwing its whole power into the canvass, and by its curtailments in the midst of the contest, under the plea of necessity in winding up its affairs, producing a degree of public embarrassment and alarm which would decide the presidential and congressional elections, and make sure its recharter.

The more intelligent adversaries of the Bank said that there was yet to be a desperate struggle with that institution; that their only hope of success therein lay in making it a direct issue between the Bank and President Jackson, backed by his invincible popularity; that this could be effected only by organizing a new system of public deposits, and depriving the Bank of the public moneys before the next presidential canvass began; and it was argued, if the Bank quietly submits to the change it will die in peace; if it makes battle, it will be conquered under the leadership of the hero of New Orleans, — in either event the question would be disposed of before the next political campaign.

For these reasons the removal of the government deposits from the Bank of the United States to the State banks was persistently urged by the writers for the Globe, Francis P. Blair the editor, and Amos Kendall, then Fourth Auditor of the Treasury, both of whom had been opposed to the Bank from 1817 downwards.

Louis McLane was then Secretary of the Treasury. Soon after the adjournment of Congress, in 1833, he sent for Mr. Kendall, and giving him the credit of understanding the subject better than any other man, said he wished to gain a full knowledge of the grounds on which a change of depositories was pressed. A discussion ensued which lasted more than an hour. It ended with a declaration on the Secretary's part, that his impressions were still against the measure, but that if the President made up his mind that it ought to be executed he would do it. Encouraged by this declaration, and anxious that Mr. McLane should enter upon the work with his whole heart, Mr. Kendall sent him his opinion written out at length, and placed a copy of the paper in the hands of the President.

Not long afterwards Martin Van Buren, then Vice-President, visited Washington, and was a guest at the President's House. He also sent for Mr. Kendall and warmly remonstrated against the continued agitation of the subject after the emphatic resolution adopted by the House of Representatives. This led to a discussion, in which Mr. Kendall presented to him all his views, financial and political, as to the effects of further forbearance upon the next presidential election. Still Mr. Van Buren maintained his opposition, until Mr. Kendall, becoming excited, rose from his seat saying that so certain to his mind was the success of the Whig Party in the next presidential election, and the consequent recharter of the Bank, that unless the latter were now stripped of the power which the possession and management of the public money gave it, he should consider further opposition useless and would lay down his pen, leaving to others this question and all that pertains to the politics of the country, adding, "I can live under a corrupt despotism, as well as any other man, by keeping out of its way, which I shall certainly do." Thus the parties separated, both somewhat excited.

A few weeks afterwards Mr. Kendall met Mr. Van Buren, when the latter at once said in substance, "I had never thought seriously upon the deposit question until after my conversation with you; I am now satisfied that you were right and I was wrong," and thenceforward he was one of the most steadfast friends of the measure.

Efforts were made to operate on the mind of General Jackson by telling him that if he did cause the deposits to be removed from the Bank, Congress, having resolved that they were safe there, would require them to be restored. On one occasion he mentioned this argument to Mr. Kendall, when the latter replied in substance, "If it were certain that Congress would direct them to be restored, still they ought to be removed, and any order by Congress for their restoration disregarded; for it is the only means by which this embodiment of power which aims to govern Congress and the country can be destroyed." "But," said he, "Congress will not undertake to overrule you if the measure be well-timed and prudently managed. Let the removal take place so early as to give us several months to defend the measure in the 'Globe,' and we will bring up the people to sustain you with a power which Congress dare not resist."

The discussion was vigorously carried on in the "Globe." Mr.

McLane was transferred to the State Department and William J. Duane was appointed Secretary of the Treasury. He had always been opposed to the Bank on constitutional grounds, and General Jackson, without consulting him on the subject, counted on his ready co-operation in the great measure impending. A sagacious Philadelphian sometime afterwards asked Mr. Kendall by whose influence Mr. Duane was appointed, and upon being answered, "I do not know," rejoined, "I can tell you, — it was Mr. McLane's, who supposed he would thus control two departments." The results justified this surmise.

Mr. Kendall was not personally acquainted with Mr. Duane, and only knew him as a writer of more industry than talent in the canvass which led to General Jackson's election. At the request of an ardent anti-Bank friend, he called on the new Secretary soon after his arrival in Washington, without intending to mention the Bank. His companion, however, introduced the subject, and perceiving that the topic was not a welcome one, Mr. Kendall turned the conversation and soon took his leave. He was, however, inclined to attribute Mr. Duane's unwillingness to talk on the subject to the indelicacy of his friend in touching at a first introduction on a serious matter which might involve his official action.

Not long afterwards, General Jackson left Washington on a trip to the North. While on his journey, he wrote Mr. Kendall a letter requesting him to ascertain what were Mr. Duane's views touching the removal of the deposits. This was a delicate service for an auditor of the Treasury Department, and would have been required only by one who never sympathized with that numerous class who, "dressed in a little brief authority," regard suggestions from any one of inferior station, touching their official duties, an insult to their dignity. Mr. Kendall, however, proceeded to comply with the request of the President. Having some official business with the new Secretary, he made that the pretext for a call, and after despatching it, entered into a general conversation, which he led to the subject of the Bank. Mr. Duane at once turned it upon some other topic. Without seeming to notice the diversion, Mr. Kendall followed his lead, but by degrees again came round to the Bank; again Mr. Duane evaded the point. The prospect was not very encouraging, but Mr. Kendall determined to try once more, and again following Mr. Duane's lead, for the third time approached the delicate topic; but with no better success than before. He now gave up the chase and reported the facts to the President.

At length the President called upon his Cabinet for their written opinions on the subject. Mr. McLane, then Secretary of State, submitted a strong argument against the contemplated measure, maintaining that the law had vested the control of the public deposits exclusively in the Secretary of the Treasury, and that the President had no right to direct or overrule him in the performance of his duties. In short, his opinion embraced nearly all the arguments against the measure which were afterwards urged in Congress. And yet, while he was Secretary of the Treasury, he had repeatedly declared that he would himself remove the deposits if the President made up his mind that it ought to be done.

Mr. Duane's opinion concurred with Mr. McLane's, though he assured the President that if in the end he found that he could not comply with his chief's wishes, he would resign his office.

Governor Cass, Secretary of War, excused himself from giving an opinion, on the plea that he did not understand the subject.

Mr. Woodbury, Secretary of the Navy, favored the measure, but gave no definite opinion as to the proper time for its execution.

Mr. Barry, Postmaster-General, was in favor of the removal.

The most decisive opinion in favor was that of Mr. Taney, the Attorney-General.

Thus the matter stood when the President, in conversation with Mr. Kendall, said, "They"— meaning, as it was supposed, Messrs. McLane and Duane— "tell me the State banks, through fear of the United States Bank, which can crush them at will, cannot be induced to take the public deposits and do the business of the government."

"Send me to ask them, and I will settle that argument," was Mr. Kendall's reply.

"You shall go," said the President instantly.

Mr. Kendall had a short time before spent several days in Baltimore, where he had been called on by the presidents of some of the banks who had evinced something more than a mere willingness to serve the government as keepers of its funds. The possession of six to ten millions of public deposits to bank upon, was no small temptation to the State banks, and it was believed that many of them would rejoice to be relieved from the power of the United States Bank, which was often capriciously exercised.

In pursuance of this understanding, the President proposed to Mr. Duane to suspend all further discussion of the subject until it could be ascertained whether a competent number of the State banks would receive the public deposits and do the business of the government appertaining thereto; if so, on what terms; adding that he should send Mr. Kendall as agent of the Treasury to negotiate with them. To this course Mr. Duane assented, and prepared a draft of instructions, which he sent to the President, who transmitted it to Mr. Kendall. These instructions were calculated to defeat the object the President had in view, by asking the *opinion* of the banks upon the financial topics then under discussion, in relation to which the banking interest generally was well known to be hostile to the administration. Mr. Kendall waited on the President, and told him he could not go under those instructions; that if he did, he would return loaded with documents full of party bias, and virtually in opposition to the measure the President wished to adopt; that the President did not want the opinions of hostile bank managers; all he wanted was to know whether they would receive the public money on deposit, and on what terms they would pay out or transfer it. The President replied, " Take the paper and modify it to suit your own views."

Mr. Kendall, retaining as much of Mr. Duane's draft as he could consistently with the main object of his mission, prepared amendments, confining his inquiries strictly to the ascertainment of the requisite facts, and handed them to the President. They were copied by his private secretary, and sent to Mr. Duane as his own emendations. Of course they were adopted, and Mr. Kendall departed, virtually self-instructed. He had two objects to accomplish. First, to remove a difficulty in the President's mind by showing that the State banks were neither afraid nor unwilling to become bankers for the government. Secondly, to ascertain the terms on which they were willing to become the financial agents of the government. In pursuance of the first object exclusively, he prepared a circular to be addressed to each bank, inquiring whether they were desirous of performing the service now rendered by the United States Bank to the government, should it be deemed necessary or expedient to employ another agent.

In pursuance of the second object, he prepared another circular to be addressed to such banks as should return a favorable answer to his first inquiry. It stated the conditions on which it was pro-

posed that the banks should receive the public deposits and do the incidental business of the government, corresponding in the main with those on which the Bank of the United States performed the same services.

Thus prepared, Mr. Kendall started on his delicate and important mission. At Baltimore he sent his first circular simultaneously to every bank in the city, and promptly received an affirmative reply from them all but one or two. He then sent to them his second circular, and, without waiting for a reply, reported progress and pushed on to Philadelphia.

There, also, nearly all the banks gave a prompt affirmative reply to his first circular. As at Baltimore, he then sent out his second circular, again reported progress, and proceeded to New York, where he received like encouragement.

Before he reached Boston his first circular was printed in the " National Gazette," which was the organ of the United States Bank in Philadelphia, together with editorial comments thereon. The editor called attention to the fact that the circular was wholly non-committal; that it gave no assurance to the banks of a purpose to employ them, whatever might be their answers; that it would seem soon enough for the banks to say whether they would serve the government or not when the government had made up its own mind to require their services; and that no direct answer to the inquiry contained in the circular seemed to be called for by the circumstances of the case. It cannot be denied that this was a reasonable criticism when addressed to those who did not know that the circular meant more than met the eye. But it came too late. The real object was accomplished by the responses of the banks in Baltimore, Philadelphia, and New York, and the last difficulty in the mind of President Jackson was already overcome.

Of the Boston banks, about thirty in number, only two gave an affirmative answer to the first circular. The rest either did not answer at all or gave indirect and evasive replies. With one of the former Mr. Kendall negotiated a conditional arrangement for the custody of the public moneys, reported progress, and turned back to New York.

There Mr. Kendall had much difficulty in making satisfactory arrangements with some of the principal banks, owing chiefly to their limited knowledge of the domestic exchanges. In that city were three banks, each with a capital of two millions of dollars,—

the Bank of America, the Mechanics' Bank, and the Manhattan Company, — all of which it was desirable to secure. Every director of the Bank of America was a Whig, and opposed to General Jackson's administration, while a majority of the boards of the other two banks were Jackson men; yet the Bank of America was foremost in yielding its support to the proposed measure of the government. The president, George Newbold, was a gentleman of comprehensive views, who did not accept the dogma of his party that a national bank was a necessary financial agent of the government, and he fully appreciated the wrong done to New York in depriving her of her natural advantages by the legislation of Congress, which undertook to make Philadelphia the financial centre of the Union. He also was sagacious enough to see that the gratuitous transfer of the public moneys, which was a bugbear to other banks, could be made a source of profit instead of loss. Little difficulty, therefore, was experienced in making acceptable terms with his bank.

The President of the Mechanics' Bank called at Mr. Kendall's room and delivered to him a written reply to his second circular. He was in the act of retiring, when he was invited to be seated until the document could be examined, as its perusal might suggest some useful remarks. The reply was found to be a refusal to serve the government on the terms proposed, for reasons which had little or no foundation. After finishing the perusal, Mr. Kendall expressed his regret that a bank on which the administration had relied in this emergency as one controlled by its friends, should reject the benefits to be derived from the government agency, particularly as the Bank of America had already acceded to the terms proposed. He then took up the objections urged in the document, showed that in all essential points they were without foundation, and concluded by appealing to the president to take back the communication, call his board together, and reconsider the subject. That official did so, and twenty-four hours afterwards handed in another document acceding fully to the terms proposed.

The Manhattan Company, which had thus far held back, now came forward and accepted in full the proposed terms.

No difficulty was then experienced in making acceptable arrangements with banks in Philadelphia and Baltimore, and having accomplished his object in a most satisfactory manner, Mr. Kendall returned to Washington and made his final report.

Some incidents worthy of note attended this mission. At Philadelphia, two men were frequent visitors to Mr. Kendall's room, who seemed specially anxious to ascertain the real intentions of the administration. One of them had a public appointment, which was virtually a sinecure, and he did little beyond watching for opportunities for private speculation. This gentleman frequently called on Mr. Kendall in New York also. While walking down Broadway one day he said to Mr. Kendall, "A good deal of money could be made out of this business." The prompt reply was, "I did not go into this business to make money, but to put down that infernal institution." Neither from the same nor any quarter did there come to Mr. Kendall any other suggestions which savored of speculation or corruption, though he was uncharitable enough to believe that a fortune was within his grasp had he been base enough to betray his trust-and his country by disclosing to the bank managers the real purpose of his mission, and undertaking to defeat the object of the President. Certain it is, that for a few days he held in his hands the threads of destiny, so far as the Bank was concerned.

The other person who was so attentive to him in Philadelphia was James Gordon Bennett, afterwards editor and proprietor of the New York "Herald." He had been previously associated with Mordecai M. Noah and James Watson Webb in the management of the New York "Courier and Enquirer," and when his associates, after obtaining accommodations to the extent of $ 52,000, went over to the Bank, he professed to remain loyal to the administration, and became editor of the "Pennsylvanian," a leading Democratic newspaper in Philadelphia. By his professions of loyalty, he drew Mr. Kendall into a private correspondence with himself on the Bank question, and sought to obtain all the information he could in personal intercourse. But soon after Mr. Kendall's return to Washington, Bennett began to throw out in the "Pennsylvanian," mysterious hints that a great conspiracy was on foot, of which he held the proofs. After attempting to work up the public curiosity in successive issues of his paper, he came out with a charge that the conspiracy was against the Bank of the United States; that the chief conspirator was Amos Kendall; and finally he published Mr. Kendall's private letters to him as proofs of his allegations. No notice was taken of the charge or the proofs, for, although the letters showed a determined hostility to the Bank and a strong

desire for its destruction, they showed also that the motives of the writer were patriotic and disinterested. While Mr. Kendall regarded the publication of these letters, without his consent, as conclusive testimony to the purity of his motives, yet the act was in itself so mean and dishonorable, that he never spoke to or recognized Mr. Bennett afterwards. What advantage, if any, the publication secured to Bennett himself, was never made known to the public. It doubtless had something to do with his secession from the "Pennsylvanian," whose patrons were generally Democrats, and his return to New York, where he established the New York "Herald," and by his successful profligacy has done more to corrupt the American press and the public morals than all the other profligate editors in the United States.

One morning, while Mr. Kendall was at New York on his outward trip, he was surprised to meet at the breakfast table of his hotel Louis McLane, Secretary of State, and Martin Van Buren, Vice-President. They sought an interview with him after breakfast, and suggested that an order should be given for a change in the government depositaries, to take effect on the first of the next January. He could not but suspect that Mr. McLane, finding that his argument based on the fears of the State banks had been utterly overthrown, had devised this scheme in the hope that Congress on meeting would interpose to prevent the execution of the order, and had induced Mr. Van Buren to aid him in carrying it out. But the strongest assurances were given that the real object of the project was more effectually to unite the friends of the administration in support of the measure, and it was urged that the postponement to the day named would prevent it from being regarded as taken in defiance of Congress. President Jackson was then at the Rip Raps, and it was proposed that Mr. Kendall should join them in writing to him in favor of this new scheme. His judgment did not approve of it; but deeming it desirable to maintain union and harmony in the administration, and believing it possible to sustain the measure in Congress, if the Cabinet and the friends of the President at Washington would give it their cordial and united support, he so far yielded as to write to the President in favor of the project, on condition that he could feel assured of such support. What the other gentlemen wrote to the President, if anything, he never knew. Whatever it was, their action had no effect in postponing the measure.

Learning from Mr. Kendall's reports that the State banks were not only not afraid to receive the public deposits, but would render to the government the same services, on substantially the same terms, as the Bank of the United States had done, the President determined that the change should be made before Congress met, and that he would "take the responsibility." His determination was announced in a paper giving his reasons for it, which was read to his Cabinet on the 18th of September, 1833.

The following is a summary of the reasons given by the President, which, in his opinion, justified and required a change in the depositaries of the public funds: —

That the Bank by asking for a new charter, knowing that he was opposed to it, made the question an issue in his second election, and he considered that event the verdict of the people against an extension of the Bank's existence.

That there was no reasonable ground for believing that any substitute would be provided by Congress, and it became the duty of the Executive to consider what should be done with the public moneys under existing laws, when the present charter of the Bank should expire.

That by the charter of the Bank, the Secretary of the Treasury was the only agent by whom the public deposits could be taken from it; that his power over them is unqualified, and has been so claimed and exercised from its origin, without dispute.

That it is obviously necessary to adopt some new system before the actual expiration of the Bank charter, and regard being had to the public interest and convenience, it was not too soon to act upon that necessity.

That, therefore, there were sufficient reasons for the proposed measure without regard to the conduct of the Bank, and that one of its effects would be to enable Congress to legislate on the subject before the expiration of the Bank charter.

But in the conduct of the Bank there were abundant reasons why it should be deprived of the use of the public money.

In the extension of its loans in sixteen months, ending in May, 1832, more than twenty-eight millions of dollars, when it knew the government intended to apply its heavy deposits then on hand to the payment of the public debt, and its secret arrangements with the holders of that debt to prevent the presentation of their claims, thus thwarting the policy of the government that it might retain the use of the public money.

In the fact that the Bank supports and controls, if it does not own, sundry leading presses of the country by means of extravagant loans on unusual terms and nominal security.

In its attempts through those presses to injure the credit of the Treasury by representing that the Bank sustained it, when it had millions of the public money in its vaults.

In its claiming over $ 150,000 damages on a protested government bill, when no such damages had been incurred.

In the violation of its charter by transferring its discount business from the board of directors to committees, systematically excluding the government directors from those committees, and thus attempting to withhold all knowledge of its transactions from the government.

And, finally, in applying its funds to the publication and circulation of political speeches and other matter intended to operate on the elections, and vesting in the President of the Bank unlimited power and discretion to use those funds for such purposes without accountability, under pretence of defending the Bank and enlightening the people as to its merits.

This important paper then sets forth in a vivid light President Jackson's own conclusions and his readiness to incur any needful responsibility.

The document underwent the severest criticism; but the facts stated in it were undeniable. The President's declaration that he did not desire that "any member of the Cabinet should do any act which he believes unlawful or in his conscience condemns," was specially denounced as insincere, in view of his subsequent removal of Mr. Duane because he refused to perform such an act; but it must be recollected that Mr. Duane had previously pledged himself to resign if, in the end, he could not concur with the President on this subject. This language, therefore, so far as Mr. Duane was concerned, merely implied that, if as the President most ardently desired, he, Mr. Duane, could not conscientiously perform the act, it was expected that he would, like a man of honor, redeem his pledge. The President did not expect or desire the Secretary to violate his conscience; but he did expect him to keep his word. In this expectation he was disappointed.

When the time for action arrived, Mr. Duane refused to act or resign. He had made up his mind to defeat the object of the President or become a martyr and claim "a martyr's crown." Though not a man of large mental calibre, he could not but be aware that in dealing with such a man as General Jackson, especially after proving false to his voluntary pledge, nothing short of martyrdom was his certain doom. And it is strange that he had not sagacity enough to perceive, that neither power nor fame was to be acquired by interposing himself with his broken pledges to protect a corrupt institution against the honest old patriot whose only object was to rescue his country from its demoralizing influences.

The President had no motive to disgrace Mr. Duane, and desired to part with him on friendly terms, but the latter preferred martyrdom. He was accordingly dismissed, and the Treasury Department was offered to Roger B. Taney, then Attorney General. Hearing of this offer, and fearing that Mr. Taney would not accept it, Mr. Kendall called upon him for the purpose of urging him to do so. As soon as Mr. Taney understood the object, he interposed and said in substance, " I have, as one of the President's constitutional counsellors, advised him to cause the public deposits to be removed from the Bank of the United States, and he proposes to act in accordance with my advice ; I, therefore, feel bound in honor to aid and sustain him in any position which he may think proper to assign to me." " But," said he, raising his hands and eyes towards Heaven, " in doing so, I give up the most cherished object of my life. I am not a politician, and have never sought political office ; the summit of my ambition has been a seat on the bench of the United States Supreme Court, and that desire I surrender in accepting the Treasury Department now." In this case, behold the result of honorable self-sacrifice ! He accepted the Treasury Department, and was rejected by the Senate ; Chief Justice Marshall died, and General Jackson nominated Mr. Taney to fill his place, and he was confirmed by the Senate. Thus the act which he considered a surrender of his hopes of attaining to a seat on the bench of the Supreme Court, led directly to his elevation to its highest place.

During all these discussions, Mr. Kendall but once made a suggestion to the President which had reference to the character of his Cabinet. This exception was when the latter informed him in a private conversation that he had made up his mind. "Then," said Mr. Kendall, "it is all important that your Cabinet should cordially sustain the measure." "They have all promised to do so," replied the President. This was a damper to Mr. Kendall, not

because he had the least thought of obtaining a place in the Cabinet, but because he did not believe some of its members would or could give the measure their cordial support. He had fully expected at least one resignation ; for he could not see how a man who had virtually taken the ground that the President had in this matter committed a gross usurpation, could honestly promise to support him in it, or could honorably remain in the Cabinet. But so strong was the old hero in his consciousness of right, and his confidence in public support, that he seemed to care little for the opinions of those around him when he announced, " *I take the responsibility.*"

At last the machinery of the government was ready for action, and Mr. Kendall was summoned to a Cabinet meeting, called for the purpose of selecting the State banks to be employed, and arranging the details of the proposed operation. No objections were made to any of the banks with which he had made arrangements, except the Bank of America. To that some opposition was shown on political grounds ; but it was promptly withdrawn when he stated the particulars of his negotiation in New York. The general plan advisable for carrying out the plan of the President, with the least possible derangement of the business of the country, had been discussed between Mr. Kendall and the more intelligent and discreet managers of the local banks, and was communicated in writing to the President and Secretary of the Treasury.

This communication shows not only the plan adopted, but the determination of the Treasury Department to adhere to it, notwithstanding some pressure from the State banks, who desired to have at once the possession of all the public deposits then in the Bank of the United States. The public deposits in that Bank and its branches amounted to millions of dollars, and it was reasonably calculated that any curtailment of accommodations in that quarter could be replaced by the State banks, strengthened as they would be by accumulating public deposits. But as soon as the Bank of the United States had discovered that the government was in earnest, it had begun to curtail its accommodations, and had already brought the State banks in debt to an amount which some of them would find it inconvenient to pay on a sudden call. As a precaution against any sudden hostile movement on this ground, it was deemed prudent to place in the possession of some of the State banks, confidentially, a considerable amount of trans-

fer warrants, with instructions to use them only in case of a menacing demonstration on the part of the Bank of the United States.

Another precaution was deemed advisable. Some of the State banks, in their intercourse with Mr. Kendall, had set up claims to a preference, on the ground of having accommodated the Post-Office Department, which was then embarrassed in its finances and under charges of gross mismanagement. Lest it should be charged that the government moneys were placed in the State banks for the purpose of bringing them within reach of the Post-Office Department, it was thought prudent, not only not to employ those banks, with one exception, but to require a pledge that the Department should not ask accommodations from any of those employed. Such a pledge was given by the Postmaster-General himself, both to Mr. Kendall and the President. Thus was this measure consummated, so far as the action of the President and the Secretary of the Treasury was concerned. Never was an important step taken with purer or more patriotic motives than those which actuated these functionaries and Mr. Kendall and the editor of the " Globe"; and never were details more carefully arranged to prevent public injury from a great change of policy. And it cannot now be doubted that the whole affair would have passed off with scarcely any perceptible effect upon the financial and commercial affairs of the country, had it not been seized upon as a pretext for an attempt to overthrow the party in power, and ultimately to procure the recharter of the Bank.

The change went into effect on the 1st of October, 1833. The Bank of the United States made no public demonstration of hostility. It was too completely within the power of the Treasury Department, through the large public deposits it retained, all of which were payable on demand, to venture on any open act of opposition.

It was Mr. Taney's desire that Mr. Kendall should become president of the Bank of the Metropolis, the deposit bank in Washington, and act as superintendent of the new system through that bank as its nominal head ; but the latter did not share this desire. As the president of that bank had promised Mr. Taney to make any change which might be required to further the views of the government, he was requested, through Mr. Kendall, to employ Mr. Reuben M. Whitney in the capacity of correspondent and

general agent of the deposit banks, with his head-quarters at the Bank of the Metropolis ; the object being to promote harmony of action throughout the new system. The president of the bank not only refused to admit Mr. Whitney into his bank, but denied his promise to the Secretary, maintaining that he was himself competent to conduct all necessary correspondence with the other deposit banks. Of course the idea of making his bank the head of the system was abandoned. Mr. Whitney was employed by most of the other banks as their agent at Washington, and most faithfully did he discharge his duties. Had his counsels been heeded, it is believed the deposit banks would not have stopped payment in 1837, and thereby compelled the government to establish the independent treasury.

In a few days after the new system went into operation, it was announced that the Union Bank of Maryland, to whose president Mr. Taney had confidentially intrusted two transfer drafts on the Bank of the United States, for one hundred thousand dollars each, had presented and cashed one of those drafts. Before the Secretary had time to procure an explanation, the same disposition was made of the other. Not receiving any satisfactory response to his letter of inquiry, Mr. Taney requested Mr. Ellicott, the president of the bank, to come to Washington. Mr. Kendall was in Mr. Taney's private office in the evening when Mr. Ellicott arrived. Mr. Taney told him he had sent for him for the purpose of ascertaining why he had used the transfer drafts confidentially placed in his hands, when the contingency upon which alone he was authorized to use them had not occurred. Mr. Ellicott made a stammering, incoherent statement about transactions in connection with a bank in Tennessee, and upon his conclusion Mr. Kendall said, " If I understand you, Mr. Ellicott, you have used those government funds to sustain a stock speculation." To this statement of the case Ellicott virtually assented.

Mr. Taney was excessively annoyed by this instance of bad faith. It exposed him and the President to charges of insincerity in the announcement that no government funds would be transferred from the Bank of the United States to the State banks ; but what made the matter more vexatious was the fact that Mr. Ellicott was his friend and special adviser in financial matters. Under other circumstances the offender would have been at once exposed and denounced. But such a measure at that time would have put a powerful weapon into the hands of the enemy. The mischief caused by the transfers was already done, and could not be retrieved by the disclosure of Ellicott's motives. On the contrary, such exposure would have been pointed out as proof that the entire movement had originated in similar motives, as had indeed been charged. The immediate consequence, therefore, was the dismissal of Mr. Ellicott with a reprimand. In the panic scenes which followed, he importuned Mr. Taney for more public money, under threats of stopping payment, until informed that he would get no more, whether he stopped or not. The ultimate consequence was that he was driven from the presidency of the bank.

Soon another source of disquietude was developed. Notwithstanding the pledge of the Postmaster-General, it appeared by the returns of the banks that the Post-Office debt in the Manhattan Bank, New York, had been increased from $50,000 to $100,000, and that the Department had procured a large loan from the deposit bank in Boston. On inquiry, it was ascertained that an agent of the Post-Office Department had represented to those banks that it was the desire of the Secretary of the Treasury that they should accommodate that Department. "What shall we do?" said Mr. Taney to Mr. Kendall. "If worst comes to worst," was the latter's reply, "tell the truth, and let every tub stand on its own bottom."

To guard against further injury, the deposit banks were quietly informed that it was the desire of the Secretary of the Treasury that they should not, under any representations, loan money to the Post-Office Department, and no other step was taken. To have even asked an explanation from the Postmaster-General could have done no good, and might have produced a quarrel and invited attack. The Secretary of the Treasury was in the presence, not of a liberal adversary who was ready to give credit for honesty of purpose, but of a watchful enemy prompt to avail himself of every opportunity to attack without regard to justice or truth. Yet no very serious assault was made on account of these particular Post-Office loans, though one was expected and dreaded, because it would necessarily lead to an exposure of the Post-Office Department and an explosion in the Cabinet.

The grumblings of the coming storm were soon heard in the distance. The United States Bank had already made extensive

curtailments, and measurably discontinued its operations in domestic exchange, of which it practically had a monopoly. The newspapers devoted to the Bank made the most out of the transfer warrants dishonestly used, and attempted to fill the country with alarms by predicting trouble. But one of the most significant signs was an announcement of Henry Clay, then on an eastern tour, in a letter dated at Philadelphia, October 14, 1833, being a reply to a complimentary letter from some of his political friends. Alluding to the removal of the deposits, he said: "But the time has arrived which I long ago apprehended, when our greatest exertions are necessary to maintain the free institutions inherited from our ancestors. Yes, gentlemen, disguise is useless; the time is come when we must decide whether the Constitution, the laws, and the checks which they have respectively provided, shall prevail, or the will of one man have uncontrolled sway. In the settlement of that question I shall be found where I have ever been."

This was the tocsin to rally the Whig Party for a desperate contest. Mr. Clay continued his progress eastward as far as Boston, going through Providence, visiting the principal towns around Boston, and returning by way of Springfield, Troy, and Albany. His partisans and those of the Bank rallied around him with a reawakened zeal which naturally inspired him with a belief that the day of his triumph over the "military chieftain" was at hand, and that the goal of his ambition, the highest office in the government, was at last within his reach.

The tone of the nullification organs showed that Mr. Calhoun was also mustering his shattered forces to array them with the followers of Mr. Clay on the side of the Bank. Elements, lately discordant and even antagonistic, were now combining for a last desperate assault on the man whose incorruptible integrity, inflexible will, and invincible popularity had overthrown all their schemes of personal ambition, consolidation, and revolution. Backed by the money and power of the Bank, this was a most formidable combination. To resist it the President stood almost alone. With one exception, his Cabinet were less than a "unit."

The semi-nullifiers, represented by the "Richmond Enquirer," were giving "aid and comfort to the enemy" by their doubts and carpings. The ambitious politicians who still surrounded General Jackson trembled in their knees, and were ready to fly. Almost

the only fearless and determined supporters he had around him were Mr. Taney, the editor of the "Globe," and its few contributors. They were a Spartan band, actuated by Spartan courage.

Congress met on the 2d day of December, 1833. On the 3d the President's Message was delivered, and on the 4th the Secretary of the Treasury submitted his reasons for removing the deposits. The President in his message fully presented the Bank issue.

Contemporaneously with the publication of the President's Message and the Secretary's reasons appeared a manifesto from the Bank, purporting to be a report of a committee, in which the paper read to the Cabinet on the 18th of the preceding September was reviewed with great severity. This manifesto began with an attempt to show that the President's hostility to the Bank was wholly attributable to the refusal of the Bank to allow itself to be used for political purposes. It asserted that "soon after the accession to power of the present Executive the purpose was distinctly revealed, that other duties than those to the country were required, and that it was necessary for the Bank in administering its affairs to consult the political views of those who had now obtained the ascendancy in the Executive. It is understood that soon after that event a meeting was held in Washington of the principal chiefs, to consider the means of perpetuating their own authority, and the possession of the Bank was among the most prominent objects of the parties assembled." All this is pure fiction. No such meeting was ever held, and the whole story was manufactured out of the most meagre materials. Having argued that the possession of the public deposits was a matter of right under their charter, the committee say, "In this case they are deprived of it by the unlawful interference of the President, who 'assumes the responsibility,' which being interpreted means, usurps the power of the Secretary."

Thus the Bank of the United States arraigned the chosen chief magistrate of the people before Congress and the world! It was, however, condescending enough to say, "The committee willingly leave to the Congress of the United States the assertion of their own constitutional power, and the vindication of the principles of our government against the most violent assault they have ever yet encountered;" which, being interpreted, means that the Bank has convicted President Jackson of outrage and usurpation, and is "willing" that Congress shall be his executioner!

In other respects the document was explanatory and argumentative, calculated to gloss over the wrongs charged by the President, except the application of the funds of the Bank to the publication and circulation of political documents; this was boldly defended as a measure of self-defence. Nobody had proposed to take from the Bank its charter, and up to the removal of the deposits no act had been done depriving it of any right claimed by it. The question was not whether the Bank should be permitted to live out the term of existence allotted to it by law, but whether it should have a new lease of life,—virtually, whether its existence should be perpetual. This was a question of constitutionality and high public policy with which the Bank had no right to interfere. It was not defending its present existence, which nobody attacked; but it threw its gold into the scale of parties for the purpose of so controlling the elections as to procure a prolongation of that existence.

On the 10th of December Mr. Clay led off in the Senate in opposition to the removal of the deposits, by proposing calls for information, and also a call for a copy of the paper read by the President to his Cabinet on the 18th of September preceding; accompanying his demand by condemnatory remarks. On the same day, Mr. McDuffie broke ground on the same side in the House of Representatives. On the 11th, Mr. Clay's resolution calling for a copy of the paper of 18th of September was adopted, and the next day a message was received from the President declining to comply with its request. His reasons were as follows:—

"The Executive is a co-ordinate and independent branch of the government, equally with the Senate, and I have yet to learn under what constitutional authority that branch of the legislature has a right to require of me an account of any communication, either verbal or in writing, made to the heads of Departments acting as a Cabinet council. As well might I be required to detail to the Senate the free and private conversations I have held with those officers on any subjects relating to their duties and my own.

"Feeling my responsibility to the American people, I am willing upon all occasions to explain to them the grounds of my conduct, and I am willing upon all proper occasions to give to either branch of the legislature any information in my possession that can be useful in the execution of the appropriate duties confided to them.

"Knowing the constitutional rights of the Senate, I shall be the last man under any circumstances to interfere with them. Knowing those of the Executive, I shall at all times endeavor to maintain them agreeably to the provisions of the Constitution, and the solemn oath I have taken to support and defend it."

As the paper had been published throughout the country, and had been made the subject of general comment, it is difficult to conceive what motive could have influenced the Senate in calling for it, other than the hope of making party capital out of the President's reply. Mr. Clay attempted to defend the call on the ground of established usage; but this is believed to be the only instance during the history of the government in which either House of Congress has called for a copy of any communication which had passed between the President and his Cabinet or any member thereof, oral or written. The motive of the call was made sufficiently apparent a few days afterwards, when Mr. Mangum gravely treated the President's response as an indignity to the Senate and an infringement of their constitutional rights, and moved its reference to a special committee, which was ordered, as a matter of course.

On the 18th of December Mr. Clay offered resolutions calling for copies of certain letters of Mr. Crawford, former Secretary, from which Mr. Taney had taken extracts in his reasons for removing the deposits; and copies of the correspondence of the agent of the Treasury with the State banks, relative to the government deposits, the preceding summer, and of his report, if he made one. The next day these resolutions were adopted, after a speech of considerable length from Mr. Clay, who denounced the reasons given by the Secretary of the Treasury for the removal of the deposits. This denunciation was repeated a few days afterwards, when Mr. Taney's reply to these resolutions was received.

On the 26th December, Mr. Clay offered the following resolutions, viz.: —

"1. *Resolved,* That by dismissing the late Secretary of the Treasury because he would not, contrary to his own sense of duty, remove the money of the United States in deposit with the Bank of the United States, and its branches in conformity with the President's opinion, and by appointing his successor to effect such removal, which has been done, the President has assumed the exercise of a power over the Treasury of the United States not granted to him by the Constitution and laws, and dangerous to the liberties of the people.

"2. *Resolved,* That the reasons assigned by the Secretary of the

Treasury for the removal of the money of the United States deposited in the Bank of the United States and its branches, communicated to Congress on the 3d day of December, 1833, are unsatisfactory and insufficient."

Mr. Clay advocated these resolutions in a speech which occupies near twelve pages of small type in "Niles's Register." The temper and general character of the speech may be understood from the following extracts. He began thus: —

"We are in the midst of a revolution, hitherto bloodless, but rapidly tending towards a total change of the pure republican character of our government, and to the concentration of all power in the hands of one man.

"By the 3d of March, 1837, if the progress of innovation continue, there will be scarcely a vestige remaining of the government and its policy as it existed prior to the 3d of March, 1829. In a term of eight years, a little more than that which was required to establish our liberties, the government will have been transformed into an elective monarchy, — the worst of all forms of government.

"Sir, I trust that the hopes and confidence of the country will revive. There is much occasion for manly independence and patriotic vigor, but none for despair. Thank God, we are yet free; and if we put on the chains which are forging for us, it will be because we deserve to wear them. We should never despair of the Republic. If our ancestors had been capable of surrendering themselves to such ignoble sentiments, our independence and our liberties would never have been achieved."

Having denounced the President's vetoes on various subjects, as well as his policy generally, and undertaken to show that he was guilty of usurpation and a violation of the Constitution and laws in the measures taken by him to effect a removal of the public deposits from the Bank of the United States, Mr. Clay concluded that portion of his argument as follows: —

"In that extraordinary paper he (the President) has proclaimed that the measure *is his own;* that *he* has *taken* upon himself the responsibility of it. In plain English he has proclaimed an open, palpable, and daring usurpation.

"For more than fifteen years, Mr. President, I have been struggling to avoid this state of things; — I thought I perceived in some proceedings, during the conduct of the Seminole war, a spirit of defiance to the Constitution and all law; — with what sincerity and truth, with what earnestness and devotion to civil liberty, the Searcher of all human

hearts best knows; with what fortune, the bleeding Constitution of my country now fatally attests.

"I have nevertheless persevered; and under every discouragement, during the short time I expect to remain in the public councils, I will persevere. And if a bountiful Providence would allow an unworthy sinner to approach the Throne of Grace, I would beseech him as the greatest favor he could grant to me here below, that he would spare me until I live to behold the people rising in their majesty, with a peaceful and constitutional exercise of their power, to expel the Goths from Rome; to rescue the public Treasury from pillage; to preserve the Constitution of the United States; to uphold the Union against the danger of the concentration and consolidation of *all* power in the hands of the Executive; and to sustain the liberties of the people against the imminent perils to which they now stand exposed."

Mr. Clay then entered into an examination of the reasons given by the Secretary of the Treasury for the removal of the deposits, condemning them throughout, pronouncing some of them false, and, in all cases wherein they were admitted to be true, justifying the conduct of the Bank, or treating them as frivolous pretexts. This portion of his speech he closed as follows: —

"The eyes and the hopes of the American people are anxiously turned to Congress. They feel that they have been deceived and insulted; their confidence abused; their interests betrayed, and their liberties in danger. They see a rapid concentration of all power in one man's hands. They see that by the exercise of the positive authority of the Executive, and his negative power exerted over Congress, the will of one man alone prevails and governs the Republic. The question is no longer what laws Congress will pass, but what will the Executive not veto. The President and not Congress is addressed for legislative action. We have seen a corporation charged with the execution of a great national work dismiss an experienced, faithful, and zealous President, afterwards testify to his ability by a voluntary resolution, and reward his extraordinary services by a large gratuity, and appoint in his place an executive favorite, totally inexperienced and incompetent, to propitiate the President. We behold the usual incidents of approaching tyranny. The land is filled with spies and informers; and detraction and denunciation are the orders of the day. People, especially official incumbents in this place, no longer dare speak in the fearless tones of manly freemen, but in the cautious whispers of trembling slaves. The premonitory symptoms of despotism are upon us; and if Congress do not apply an instantaneous and effective remedy, the fatal collapse will

soon come on and we shall die, — ignobly die, base, mean and abject slaves, — the scorn and contempt of mankind, unpitied, unwept, unmourned."

During the delivery of this speech, Mr. Clay was frequently interrupted by applause in the galleries, and upon its conclusion he was greeted with repeated cheers and clapping of hands.

These severe denunciations from a political leader of great eminence and popularity, were well calculated to alarm a large portion of the community. Those who had faith in Mr. Clay must have believed that President Jackson had laid violent hands on the money in the Treasury, and was meditating the subversion of the Constitution and the destruction of his country's liberties. These demonstrations from the leader of the Whig party were echoed by the leading Nullifiers, Mr. Calhoun in the Senate and Mr. McDuffie in the House of Representatives, and were repeated with aggravation by the Whig and nullification presses throughout the Union.

The policy of the consolidated Bank party was to rush headlong into the discussion of the subject in both Houses of Congress, and attempt to carry resolutions of condemnation by a storm of denunciation. Their majority in the Senate enabled them to do as they pleased in that body; but obstacles were encountered in the House of Representatives. Before the policy of the Bank party was understood, the papers relating to the subject in the House were referred to the Committee of the Whole; but after a severe struggle the vote was reconsidered and they were sent to the Committee of Ways and Means, a majority of which was understood to be in favor of the administration.

After this demonstration in that body, it became evident that the action of the Executive would be sustained unless means could be found to overawe the members. With that view a plan was adopted to create a panic in the country, to exaggerate the embarrassment already to some extent produced by the curtailments of the Bank, to attribute it all to the removal of the deposits, and stimulate the people to hold public meetings, and send memorials to Congress and the President demanding their restoration to the Bank of the United States as the only measure which would give relief.

A retrospect at this point of the course of the Whig and Bank press will more clearly explain the aims and the motives of their leading politicians.

Early in September, 1833, there were general complaints that money had become scarce and business was somewhat hampered. Mr. Niles, in his "Register" of the 7th of that month, announced that "a good many of the Eastern cotton factories have shut down their gates, ... whereby many persons are thrown out of employment and business generally is embarrassed." In the same paper he stated that "money is scarce," and he attributes it to the policy of the United States Bank in discontinuing its exchange operations in the West, and collecting into its vaults eleven millions out of the twenty-one millions of specie then estimated to be the specie circulation in the country, besides having five millions in Europe, while its balances against the State banks were heavier than usual; but he apologizes for this course on the part of the Bank on the ground that it might be suddenly called upon to pay over at once the entire public deposits. At that time no order for the removal of the deposits had been issued, and Mr. Niles knew nothing of the manner of the contemplated removal.

The "Globe" of the 20th of September announced that the public deposits would, "after the 1st of October, be made in the State banks, but that it is contemplated not to remove at once the whole of the public money now on deposit in the Bank of the United States, but to suffer it to remain there until it shall be gradually withdrawn by the usual operations of the government." And it was added, "This plan is adopted in order to prevent any necessity on the part of the Bank of the United States for pressing upon the commercial community; and to enable it to afford, if it think proper, the usual facilities to the merchants. It is believed, that by this means, the change need not produce any inconvenience to the commercial community, and that circumstances will not require a sudden and heavy call on the Bank of the United States so as to cause embarrassment to the institution or the public."

The Bank thenceforward knew that if its own policy should be pacific it had nothing to fear from any unusual call from the government; yet with specie enough in its vaults to pay the entire public deposit at once, it maintained its stringency under the pretext that it must be prepared for vindictive attacks from the Treasury Department. That Department might indeed have forced the Bank or some of its branches to stop payment momentarily by a sudden call for all its deposits in specie; but to pursue such a course would have been inexcusable and suicidal. To effect the

change with as little disturbance in monetary affairs as possible, was as much the interest as it was the duty of the administration. It was the Bank and its political adherents only who had anything to hope from pecuniary embarrassment and unwarranted panic among the people. Of course the politicians whose triumph was identified with that of the Bank, its army of debtors who dreaded the approach of pay day, and the dependent as well as the deluded presses united in a virtual conspiracy, first, to predict an increase of the moderate embarrassment already produced by the action of the Bank, then to augment and exaggerate it by all the means in their power, to attribute it altogether to the removal of the deposits, and finally to excite Congress and the country to a phrensy of panic in the hope of thus breaking down the President and his supporters, and by a change of administration procuring a recharter of the Bank. To all other motives was added personal hatred of the President, by the leaders of nullification and of the so-called "American system," who availed themselves of this last opportunity to gratify their revenge.

No adequate idea of the scenes that followed the removal of the deposits can be conveyed by any description. Perhaps the most satisfactory account of them will be a chronological narrative presenting the contemporaneous proceedings of Congress, the Bank, the press, and public meetings. "Niles's Register," though an imperfect and partisan record, serves us as principal authority for facts and documents.

It has been seen that as early as the 7th of September, about two weeks before the intention to remove the deposits was announced, Mr. Niles recorded the fact that there was pecuniary embarrassment in the country, which he attributed to the precautionary measures of the Bank of the United States. In his paper of the 12th of October he anticipates that the removal would "soon engross the attention of Congress and probably produce one of the most earnest debates which has ever ensued," and he adds, "The effect anticipated is gathering fresh force in a most severe pressure for money, which, if not soon relieved, must produce a paralysis in business. New enterprises are entered upon with extreme caution, and many mercantile and manufacturing operations are suddenly checked."

It was on the 18th of that month that Mr. Clay sounded the tocsin in Philadelphia.

On the 2d of November, Mr. Niles announced that the Bank had given instructions to wind up the affairs of its branch at Fayetteville, N. C., requiring its debtors to pay in instalments of one fourth every ninety days, and added, "Much pecuniary distress is apprehended on account of this proceeding, though as moderate on the part of the Bank as could be expected under the condition in which it is *violently* placed." And, ostensibly to create alarm in other quarters, he concluded by saying, "Similar orders have no doubt been issued, or will issue to other offices."

The same number contained an editorial announcing that "The money market is at this time in a very depressed state," which is attributed to the action of the government towards the Bank of the United States.

The number of November 23d contained a long editorial laudatory of the Bank of the United States, and depreciatory of the State banks, in which it is asserted that "there is an excessive pressure for money, and it will become heavier and heavier," etc.

On the 26th of December Mr. Clay delivered his great philippic, which has been already noticed. The spirit of that performance had already infused itself into the universal Whig, Bank, and Nullification presses, which now opened their batteries with a fury which indicated a determination that Mr. Clay's revolution should not continue "bloodless," unless the old hero would surrender at discretion.

Richmond, Va., seems to have been selected as the most promising field in which to open the campaign by public meetings. The jealousy of Executive power which had been engendered in Virginia during the administration of the elder Adams, had descended from father to son, and become a sentiment with the Democratic party of that State. It was only necessary to utter the words "Executive usurpation" to excite their lively apprehensions. Their organ, the "Richmond Enquirer," so far from approving, had faintly condemned the removal of the deposits, and carried with it nearly all of the leading Democrats of that State. It was, therefore, reasonable for the Whig leaders to hope for decided advantages from a resolute attack on that centre of the Democratic line which already seemed to waver. Accordingly, on the very day that Mr. Clay made his revolutionary speech in the Senate, a public meeting was held in Richmond which adopted a series of resolutions surcharged with the venom which the leader of the

Whig party was simultaneously pouring forth at Washington. They denounced the removal of the deposits from the Bank of the United States as "a palpable breach of the public faith, solemnly plighted to the institution by its charter," — "as an exercise of executive power in defiance of the legislative will, and of the contract made with the institution, plainly expressed in the act of incorporation," — and they denounced the President for the dismissal of Mr. Duane, and the appointment of Mr. Taney, under the circumstances; charging him with having "perverted and abused his constitutional power of appointment and dismission of officers, and assuming to himself an illegal, unconstitutional, and most dangerous prerogative"; as "an assumption by the President of full and absolute power over the public purse," having "a direct tendency to concentrate all the powers of government in his hands, and to convert our free, happy republican institutions into a simple monarchy." They resolved that "the pressure and distress which even thus early embarrass and endanger all the commercial interests and business of this great country, already so sensibly and so generally felt, must soon, in the apprehension of this meeting, be aggravated to an incalculable degree of mischief, and pervade every interest in the community"; that "no effective corrective of the evil can be devised, save only a removal of the cause that has produced it," — meaning the re-employment of the Bank of the United States as the only deposit bank; and that "no corrective which Congress can devise can be effectual unless it be speedily applied." They also resolved "that our fellow-citizens generally be requested to meet in their respective towns and counties, and to express their opinions upon the important subject of this meeting."

These resolutions were directed to be sent to all the Virginia members of Congress in both Houses, "in the hope that Congress will promptly devise means to correct the evils already experienced from the unhappy, illegal, and arbitrary measures of the Executive, and to prevent the yet greater evils that are to be but too certainly apprehended," etc., etc.

While Mr. Clay was holding forth at Washington, and his Whig partisans were speech-making and resolving at Richmond, the banks at Philadelphia were holding a meeting by their Presidents, and concocting a memorial to Congress requesting that the Bank of the United States might be reinstated in its former position as the fiscal agent of the government. This memorial was highly laudatory of the Bank of the United States, attributing to it in a very high degree the prosperity of the country, while it maintained that existing embarrassments and apprehensions were due solely to the action of the Executive in depriving it of the public deposits. It called that act "the disorganization of the whole moneyed system, and the whole revenue system of the country." Of course, the remedy which it proposed was a restoration of the deposits.

This memorial was presented to the House of Representatives on the 30th, and to the Senate on the 31st of December, the day on which Mr. Clay concluded the speech commenced by him on the 26th.

"Niles's Register" of the 28th of December spoke of "the present state and future prospects of the currency" as "solemn enough, dark and gloomy, and covered with an impenetrable veil that *must* soon be lifted, no matter what may be concealed; for the present state of things cannot last long. *We have* arrived at a 'momentous crisis'; we wish it was only one of the assortment of ten thousand which Mr. Ritchie used to *manufacture* on demand, or as convenience served; but we fear that it is a *real* one, when men must 'screw up' their courage to *bear* or *forbear*, as the case may be." The article then proceeded to record sundry mischievous rumors, and to state circumstances with a gloss calculated to aid in producing alarm and panic throughout the country.

On the 4th of January, 1834, it was announced that "The New York Board of Trade have petitioned Congress that the deposits may be restored to the Bank of the United States, and there was a mighty meeting of the people of Philadelphia, of all parties, on Tuesday last, at which resolutions concerning the pressure for money were passed."

The proceedings of the Philadelphia meeting were presented to the Senate on the 6th of January, and those of the New York Board of Trade on the 7th.

The meeting at Richmond, Va., was followed by meetings at Norfolk, Petersburg, Fredericksburg, Lynchburg, Leesburg, Staunton, Wheeling, Manchester, Falmouth, King and Queen County, and many other places; all telling the same tale about public embarrassments, denouncing the removal of the deposits, attributing the alleged distresses of the country to that act, anticipating still greater evils, and resolving that the remedy was to be looked for only in the restoration of the public money to the Bank of the United States.

Availing themselves of the advantage derived from the defection upon this issue of the "Richmond Enquirer," and the peculiar class of politicians whose organ it was, the Whigs and Nullifiers made a resolute effort to array the Legislature of Virginia against the administration. They were so far successful as to procure the passage of resolutions condemning the removal of the deposits, on the President's responsibility, as "a dangerous and alarming assumption of power," and instructing their Senators and requesting their Representatives in Congress to use all legitimate means for their restoration; but the practical effect of those resolutions was neutralized by another, declaring that the Bank of the United States was unconstitutional, and that it ought not to be rechartered.

On the 11th of January a large meeting was held in Fanueil Hall, Boston, which echoed the proceedings of meetings in Philadelphia and elsewhere, asserting the existence of a pressure for money, and great public embarrassment, which could be relieved only by a restoration of the relations which had existed between the government and the Bank of the United States.

In New York, the grievances of the Bank party found expression in a memorial to Congress, which was signed by about six thousand citizens, and then presented to and adopted by a large public meeting held on the 22d of January. This memorial attributed the financial difficulties of the country to the removal of the deposits, and prayed for their restoration.

A new means of agitation was devised in connection with this memorial. It was the appointment of a numerous delegation, purporting to represent all the mercantile, manufacturing, and mechanical interests of New York, "to proceed to Washington to present and enforce the objects of the memorial." This delegation visited Washington, exerted their influence with the members of Congress, made their representations to the President, Vice-President, and Secretary of the Treasury, and, returning to New York, reported to a public meeting called at the Merchants' Exchange for the purpose. Of the President they said, that he made "the most unqualified declarations that in no event would he ever consent to restore the deposits or to recharter the Bank of the United States; that he was determined to make the experiment of carrying on the fiscal concerns of the nation through the State banks, until the expiration of the United States Bank charter;

and if the experiment failed, some scheme might be devised of collecting and depositing the revenue without the intervention of any moneyed institution." They then stated that these views were confirmed by the Vice-President and the Secretary of the Treasury, Mr. Van Buren and Mr. Taney, and concluded as follows: "Your delegation regret to say that it is their sincere conviction that nothing is intended to be done by the government for the present; that no plan is under consideration for the future in respect to a national bank; that the administration is determined not to recharter the present United States Bank under any possible modifications, nor to propose any new bank; and, instead thereof, to rely upon State institutions until hard money can be made to supersede the actual paper currency of the country."

Except so far as relates to "hard money" these representations were undoubtedly correct. Information to the same effect had been previously received from the delegation, which gave rise to an excited meeting in the Park, the number present being estimated at 15,000 to 20,000. This meeting adopted the following resolutions:—

"*Resolved*, That in the opinion of this meeting, a national bank is indispensable to the prosperity of the trading community.

"*Resolved*, That we believe the only remedy for the existing distress is to recharter the Bank of the United States, with such modifications and restrictions as Congress in their wisdom may deem expedient."

At a meeting in the Exchange, a very large "Union Committee," so called, was raised, "with power to appoint delegates to proceed to Washington, Albany, and other cities, if thought advisable, to further the objects of their appointment; and, generally, to adopt such measures as may be deemed expedient "*in this crisis* of the public good."

Contemporaneously with these proceedings in the large cities, meetings were organized wherever the influence of the allied Whig and Nullification parties, constituting the Bank party, extended; and resolutions and memorials came pouring into both Houses of Congress,—nearly all of them of the same general tenor, asserting the existence of great public distress, attributing it to the removal of the deposits, and praying for their restoration to the Bank of the United States. Some of them went further, and petitioned for the recharter of the Bank; but the more adroit leaders confined

themselves to the deposit question, knowing they were stronger upon that than upon the question of recharter, and that the recharter must follow a restoration of the deposits. Nearly every morning for several weeks in the Senate, as these resolutions and memorials were presented, and on every practicable occasion in the House of Representatives, one or more of the Bank advocates would take occasion to expatiate upon the distresses of the people, echoing the allegations touching the cause and the remedy, and predicting still further calamities; and these lucubrations were daily reported and sent forth to the country to produce and aggravate the evils they predicted. To illustrate more clearly this course of proceeding we may recur to the proceedings of Congress.

On the 18th of December was presented the memorial of the Bank of the United States, complaining of a violation of its charter by the removal of the deposits, and asking redress.

On the 31st of December, a memorial from the Banks in Philadelphia, asking for a restoration of the public deposits to the Bank of the United States.

On the 6th of January, memorials of the Farmer's Bank of Lancaster, Pa., of the Board of Trade of the city of New York, and of the Board of Trade of Philadelphia. Mr. Selden of New York and Mr. Binney of Philadelphia made short speeches, intended to enforce the representations of their respective boards of trade.

On the 21st of January, the memorial of the Bank of Chambersburg; on the 22d, the proceedings of a numerous meeting in Cincinnati, and a memorial of many citizens of North Carolina.

On the 24th, Mr. Webster presented the proceedings of a meeting in New Bedford, and accompanied the presentation by a speech in which he depicted, in vivid colors, the alleged embarrassments throughout the country, declared that they were increasing, and called on the friends of the administration to say whether they had any plan of relief to propose?

On the 27th, Mr. Frelinghuysen presented the proceedings of a meeting at Newark, New Jersey, and dilated upon them in a speech of considerable length.

On the 29th, Mr. Frelinghuysen presented an additional memorial from Newark; and Mr. Wilkins presented one from Pittsburg, —to the allegations of which, in regard to the extent of public distress, he did not assent. This called up Mr. Webster, who defended the representations of the memorialists.

On the 30th, Mr. Wright presented to the Senate the resolutions of the Legislature of New York, approving of the removal of the deposits, and explained his own views on the subject. The following extracts will show what those views were, and may be taken as a truthful statement of the intentions of the President and his supporters at that period of the contest: —

"As to the fact of an existing pressure upon the money market, I believe that the recent extensive and sudden curtailment by the Bank of the United States in the facilities for credit which had before been lavished upon the community, has caused very considerable embarrassment to those in our commercial cities who had extended widely their moneyed operations, and who had made themselves dependent on these facilities; but at the same time, I believe that these inconveniences have been in an unimportant degree, either directly or consequentially, extended to other classes of citizens. I therefore believe, further, that the extent of the pressure has been greatly exaggerated, and that the motives for that exaggeration are to be found, primarily, in the belief that the present administration may be brought into disfavor with the people, and may be overthrown through the agency of the panic which is attempted to be gotten up; and, secondarily, in the hope that the same panic, if successfully produced, may subserve the interest of the institution by which it has been and is to be raised."

After declaring his unalterable purpose never to vote for the rechartering of a Bank of the United States, because he believed such an institution not only dangerous, but unconstitutional, and depicting the firmness and perseverance with which our fathers had resisted the moneyed power of Great Britain, Mr. Wright asked: —

"And have we, their immediate descendants, so soon lost their noble spirit? Are we to fold our arms and obey the dictates of a moneyed power, not removed from our soil and wielded by stranger hands, but taking root among us; a power spoken into existence by our breath, and dependent on that breath for life and being? Are our fears, our avarice, our selfish and base passions to be appealed to, and to compel us to recreate this power, when we are told that the circulation of the country is in its hands? — that the institutions of all the independent States of the confederacy are subject to its control, and exist only by its clemency? — when we see it setting itself up against the government, and vaunting its power; throwing from its door our representatives placed at its board, and pronouncing them unskilful, ungenteel, or incorrigible? Nay, Mr. President, when it lays on our tables, in this chamber, its

annunciation to the public, classing the President of the United States with counterfeiters and felons, and declaring, that, as kindred subjects, both should receive like treatment at its hands; I say, sir, are we to be driven by our fears to recharter such an institution, with such evidence of its power lying before us, authenticated by the Bank itself? Are we to do this after the question has been referred to the people of the country, fully argued before them, and their decision pronounced against the Bank and in favor of the President by a majority such as has never before in this government marked the result of a contest at the ballot-boxes?

"Gentlemen talk of revolutions in progress: when this action shall take place in the American Congress, then indeed will a revolution have been accomplished, and your legislature be the *sic volo, sic jubeo* of a bank. But, Mr. President, I do not distress myself with any such forebodings. I know the crisis will be trying, and I know too that the spirit and patriotism of the people will be equal to the trial.

"The country, Mr. President, has approved the course of the Executive in his attempts to relieve us from the corrupt and corrupting power and influence of a national bank, and it will sustain him in the attempt now making to substitute the State institutions for such a fiscal agent. I have full confidence in the ultimate and complete success of the trial; but should it not prove satisfactory to the country, it will then be time enough to resort to the conceded powers of Congress, or to ask from the people what, until every other experiment be fairly and fully tried, they will never grant, — the power to establish a national bank."

This speech of Mr. Wright was justly thought to indicate the inflexible determination of the President and his supporters not to restore the public deposits to the Bank of the United States, and to oppose, at every hazard, the recharter of that institution as well as the establishment of any other of like character. And coming from one of the purest and ablest men who ever adorned the halls of Congress, it could not fail to have a powerful influence on the popular mind.

Mr. Webster replied to Mr. Wright, basing his remarks on the assumption that the latter spoke the language of the administration, and predicting increased embarrassment and distress in all sections from the persistence of the government in its hostility to the Bank.

The zeal and exertions of the Bank orators, presses, and adherents now seemed to be redoubled throughout the country.

On the 3d of February, Mr. Shepley, who himself sustained the

administration, presented the proceedings of a meeting in Portland, Maine, repeating the cry of public distress, and praying for the restoration of the deposits. On the same day, Mr. McKean presented similar proceedings of a meeting at Pittsburg.

On the 4th of February Mr. Wright presented the memorial signed and adopted in New York on and about the 22d of January, which had been conveyed to Washington by an imposing delegation. He bore testimony to the respectability of the members of the delegation, and "considered that an expression of opinion coming from such a body was entitled to great weight."

Mr. Webster took this occasion further to intensify the panic which was spreading through the country, in a speech from which the following is an extract: —

"In the course of twenty years in Congress he had seen no such memorial. He had his doubts if in the whole history of our government any memorial had ever been presented in which such pains had been taken to give a respectful and emphatic expression of the deep, wide-spread, and earnest conviction of public suffering, as were exhibited in this memorial."

On the same day, on motion of Mr. Webster, the report of the Secretary of the Treasury giving his reasons for the removal of the deposits, and Mr. Clay's resolution declaring them unsatisfactory and insufficient, were referred to the Committee on Finance, of which Mr. Webster was chairman; and on the next day he made a voluminous report, which had been prepared with great labor and ingenuity. Its main features, however, were in accordance with the memorial of the Bank, presented near the beginning of the session, and it closed with recommending the adoption of Mr. Clay's resolutions. An extra number of this report was ordered to be printed.

On the 7th of February was presented an additional memorial, alleged to be "signed by a large and respectable number of the mechanics, manufacturers, laborers, and others of the second ward of the city of New York, without distinction of party, exhibiting the great state of embarrassment and distress under which they are suffering, ascribing it to the removal of the deposits from the Bank of the United States, and the only remedy for which, they consider, is the speedy restoration of the deposits, and the recharter of the Bank," etc.

Mr. Clay said, "the paper just read spoke a voice he was very

glad to hear, — it spoke the voice of freemen; of the laboring portion of the freemen of the country; and one that ought to be heard at Washington, and when heard will produce a proper effect."

This whole day was consumed in an excited discussion of various propositions bearing on the deposit question.

On the 10th, Mr. Southard presented a memorial of sundry citizens of Morris and Burlington Counties, New Jersey, of the same general tenor with those in favor of the Bank from other quarters, and followed the presentation by a speech of like import.

On the 11th, Mr. McKean presented a memorial of similar purport, brought by a delegation from Philadelphia.

Mr. Clay proposed that it should be printed with the names; and Mr. Webster, after making some remarks on the reality of the public distress, urged upon the Senate the necessity of action, and called upon those who had become sponsors for the administration to take the matter into their serious consideration, believing that they had power to save the country.

Mr. Mangum presented a similar memorial from Burke County, North Carolina.

On the 12th, Mr. Chambers presented a memorial, brought by a delegation from Baltimore, of the same general tenor as those from New York and Philadelphia.

On the 14th, were presented like memorials, as follows: One said to be signed by two or three thousand mechanics and artisans of the City of New York; one from a "great meeting" in Spring Garden, in the County of Philadelphia; one of a very numerous meeting in the Northern Liberties, Philadelphia; one of more than one hundred citizens of Tamaqua, Pennsylvania; one of over eleven hundred citizens of Southwark and Moyamensing; and several hundred additional signatures to the Philadelphia memorial, presented some days ago, containing over ten thousand names.

The memorial presented by Mr. Mangum being taken up, a long discussion ensued, in which Mr. Forsythe, Mr. Clay, and Mr. Webster bore a conspicuous part. The last-named gentleman concluded his remarks as follows: —

"The present is a moment of spasm and agony. The whole social and political system is violently convulsed. This, if no relief come, must be succeeded by a lethargy which will strike dead the commerce, manufactures, and labors of the community. This, sir, I think, is the real prospect before us."

Memorials and resolutions of the character heretofore described now came pouring in, in increased volume.

Mr. Clay, presenting a memorial, concluded a speech as follows: —

"If I have deviated from the beaten track of debate in the Senate, my apology must be found in the anxious solicitude I feel for the condition of the country. And, sir, if I shall have been successful in touching your heart and exciting in you a glow of patriotism, I shall be most happy. You *can* prevail on the President to abandon his ruinous course, and if you will exert the influence which you possess, you will command the thanks and the plaudits of a grateful people."

This speech contained a good specimen of the staple out of which the speeches of the Bank advocates in both Houses of Congress were at that time manufactured. Heated harangues, in which all possible changes were rung on "embarrassment," "distress," "executive usurpation," "revolution," and "fearful forebodings for the future," were daily sent out from the Capitol to alarm the people, and they found an echo in memorials and petitions signed by hundreds and thousands, nearly all pitched upon the same key. These again produced a new set of speeches, which went forth designed to increase the panic, produce new batches of excited memorials, overawe the House of Representatives, compel the President to recede from his position, and secure the recharter of the Bank.

On the 10th of March certain resolutions of the Legislature of Massachusetts were presented, drawn up in accordance with the current model, which were made the basis of an excited discussion, occupying most of the day's session.

On the 25th, a memorial was presented from Wilkesboro', and another from Halifax, N. C.; also, certain resolutions of a large public meeting of silversmiths, watch-makers, and jewellers of Philadelphia.

On the 26th, the proceedings of a meeting of 5,000 young men of Philadelphia, and another of 4,627 young men of the same city.

On the 27th, the memorial of 400 citizens of Augusta, Ga.; also a memorial of over 1,200 of the citizens of Lexington and Fayette

County, Ky.; also the proceedings and resolutions of a meeting of the citizens of Beaver town and county, Pennsylvania; and, on the 28th, the memorial of about 2,800 citizens of Albany, N. Y.

While these memorials were being presented, a debate had been in progress on Mr. Clay's resolutions, in which a large number of Senators participated; the principal champions on one side being Henry Clay and Daniel Webster, and on the other John Forsythe and Thomas H. Benton.

The example set by New York for the purpose of influencing the action of Congress, and if possible the President, by delegations sent to Washington bearing memorials numerously signed, had been imitated in other cities. Mingling with the members of both Houses of Congress, exaggerating the public distress, and predicting ruin to the country and political perdition to themselves, they zealously strove to induce the Democratic members to vote for the restoration of the deposits to the Bank of the United States. It was also a part of their programme to call on the President and verbally communicate to him the grievances of their constituents, and urge a restoration of the deposits and the recharter of the Bank. He received them courteously, and at first discussed with them the subjects of their complaint; uniformly declaring his fixed purpose never to consent to the restoration of the deposits or to the recharter of the Bank, or the incorporation of any similar Bank of the United States. These delegations undertook to report to public meetings, on their return, the results of their proceedings at Washington; and although all of them in the main truly represented the President's inflexible purpose as declared by himself, most of them did it with a coloring which indicated that their only object in seeking these interviews was to elicit something out of which they could make political capital. Under this conviction, the President resolved in future to receive such delegations courteously, hear them patiently, and dismiss them without discussion.

But once afterwards did he deviate from this determination. A delegation from Philadelphia was ushered into his room. He received them in that urbane manner for which he was distinguished, and bade them be seated. One after another they began to tell their doleful tales of public distress, and to utter their forebodings of awful disasters unless the public deposits were restored to the Bank of the United States; when one of them ventured to hint to

the President that if he persisted in his policy the people might seek redress by force. This roused the old lion.

"If that be your game," he exclaimed, "come on with your armed Bank mercenaries, and, by the Eternal! I will hang you around the Capitol on gallows higher than Haman's."

They felt that it was not "in vain" that he used the name of the Eternal, and were glad to escape from his presence. Years afterwards, one of that delegation passing along Chestnut Street, Philadelphia, saw the flag of the United States hoisted over the United States Bank building, which had been purchased for a custom-house; he stopped and exclaimed, "That is the greatest triumph ever achieved by mortal man!"

During this period the Whig and Nullification presses were actively at work attempting to fan the public excitement into an overwhelming panic, not only by circulating the daily outpourings of the Bank advocates in Congress, but by newspaper articles and the publication of memorials, preambles, and resolutions denouncing the President and the removal of the deposits; many of these latter being couched in most violent language, and some of them threatening the employment of force if the President could not peaceably be induced to abandon his policy.

The "Boston Courier" of the 20th January, says: —

"Saturday was the most tempestuous day on 'change we have yet had. The gloom was absolutely frightful. The intelligence of a large failure at Gloucester, involving the connections of the firm in this city to a large amount, was received on Friday evening, and followed, upon Saturday morning, by the failure of an old established house in Boston. Where is this to end but in general bankruptcy and ruin? . . . . Truly we see no reason to anticipate anything but a general closing up of all business at once."

The "Register" of the 8th of February contains many notices of panic meetings, discharge of laborers, reduction of prices, private bankruptcies, etc., etc., all tending to increase the public excitement.

Of similar character were the "Registers" of the 15th and 22d of February, the 1st, 8th, 15th, 22d, and 29th March, and the 6th of April. All sorts of facts and rumors calculated to excite and alarm the public mind were duly registered; accompanied by heavy documents and speeches vindicating the management and purity of the Bank, asserting its necessity as a means of maintaining a

sound currency, charging the President with a dangerous usurpation of power, and imputing to those who counselled and sustained him the most corrupt and mercenary motives. Nor were Mr. Niles and the other editorial advocates of the Bank content with exaggerating facts and circulating the most aggravated falsehoods, but they exerted themselves to the utmost to persuade the people that not only their pecuniary but their political salvation depended on a restoration of the public deposits to the Bank of the United States!

The "Register" of the 22d February contained an article from the "Lowell Journal," which says: —

"We learn with regret almost approaching to horror, that many of the Directors and Stockholders of the factories in this town are upon the point of deciding to stop the mills, etc."

The "Register" of the 1st March says: —

"We have fresh accounts of the proceedings of perhaps one hundred meetings, for the restoration of the deposits, in the current week. At some of those held in Virginia lately very strong language was used."

Again: —

"A great effort is making in Pennsylvania by petitioning the legislature, praying for its action, that the public deposits may be restored to the Bank of the United States."

The "Register" of the 8th March says: —

"That the distress which has *not*, as we fear, reached its extent on the sea-board, will reach the interior, must be expected. One thing is certain, *the present state of things cannot endure much longer*."

Even William J. Duane, always professedly opposed to the Bank of the United States, was induced to cast his feather into the Bank scale in a series of articles addressed to the people; apparently unconscious that by refusing to redeem his voluntary pledge to resign, if he could not conscientiously comply with the wishes of the great friend who had placed him in office, he had lost all influence over the popular mind, and was regarded with a sentiment stronger than dislike.

The organs of the Bank and of its political allies, during this period, continually gave out that the Bank was strong and invulnerable, having curtailed its discounts very little since the 1st of October, 1833, and having on hand about ten millions of dollars in specie. Care was generally taken not to state the amount of curtailments prior to the 1st of October, in anticipation of the course of the government, which had brought the State banks largely in debt, and induced the wise precaution of placing in their possession two and a half millions of dollars, in transfer drafts on the Bank of the United States, to be used only in case of a hostile demonstration on its part. Though the existence of the drafts would probably never have been publicly known but for the bad faith of the President of the Union Bank of Maryland, and although after he had used those placed in his hands, the real object of their issue was explained, and all parties knew they were precautionary, and intended for use only in case the Bank of the United States should attempt to break the State Banks, yet their issue was treated as a direct attack upon that institution. And when the question was, " Why does not the Bank, if strong as is pretended, relieve the public distresses of which there is so much complaint ? " the answer was, that it was compelled to husband its means as a resource against other possible assaults on the part of the government, whose obvious interest and object it really was to let it die in peace.

These drafts were made to figure not only as weapons of attack on the Bank, but also as violations of the Constitution, which declares that no money shall be drawn from the Treasury except in pursuance of appropriations made by law. As such drafts had been used from the organization of the government, for the purpose of transferring the public moneys from one depository to another, it was a new idea that this operation was drawing them from the Treasury, and untenable unless the Bank of the United States was the Treasury of the United States, — a position which some of the Bank advocates actually assumed !

Indeed, every subject which could, by any exercise of ingenuity, be used to feed excitement and disparage the President, was pressed into the service of the opposition. At the preceding session of Congress an act had been passed, under the lead of Mr. Clay, for the distribution of the proceeds of the public lands among the several States, etc.; which, having been sent to the President less than ten days before the adjournment, had been retained by him, and sent in at the commencement of this session with his veto. Thereupon Mr. Clay " commented in strong terms upon the conduct of the President in keeping back the land bill during the

whole recess, — a course which he considered as without precedent or justification, and calculated to rouse the country, if anything could provoke it, to denounce the present state of things." And this was made the text for numberless denunciations of the President for his repeated exercise of the veto power.

One of the duties imposed upon the Bank of the United States by its charter was to pay the public pensioners, and the State banks employed as depositories had agreed to render the same service without compensation. On the ground that the Executive had acted illegally in transferring this agency from the Bank of the United States to certain State banks, the former refused to hand over the pension books, papers, and funds, in its possession. General Jackson presented the case to Congress, in a special message, in which he said : —

" It (the Bank) places its refusal upon the extraordinary ground that the corporation has a right to sit in judgment upon the legality of the acts of the constituted authorities in a matter in which the stockholders are admitted to have no interest, and it impedes and defeats, as far as its power will permit, the execution of a measure of the administration, because the opinion of the corporation, upon the construction of an act of Congress, differs from that of the proper officers of the United States."

And he added : —

" The claim of this corporation thus to usurp the functions of the judicial power, and to prescribe to the Executive Department the manner in which it shall execute the trust confided to it by law, is without example in the history of our country. If the acts of the public servants, who are responsible to the people for the manner in which they execute their duty, may thus be checked and controlled by an irresponsible money corporation, then indeed the whole frame of our government is changed, and we have established a power in the Bank of the United States above what we derive from the public."

After the reading of the message in the Senate, Mr. Clay said : —

" It was his opinion that this agency had been confided to the Bank of the United States by law, and the Executive had no right to take it away from the institution, and that the doing so could only be regarded as a continuance of that career of assumption and usurpation which had been commenced during the last year against the Bank. He was glad the Bank had now resisted."

And this was added to the imputed crimes for which the President was denounced.

It would have been wonderful if all this agitation had produced no effect upon Congress or the country. There was no hope that the Senate, in which the Whig party, coalescing for the occasion with the Nullifiers, had a decided majority under their great leaders, Clay, Webster, and Calhoun, would sustain or even fail to denounce the measures of the Executive ; but it was confidently believed that a majority of the House of Representatives would not be found recreant, because, if they had no better reason, they would fear to encounter General Jackson's popularity among their constituents. Yet at one stage of the discussion, some of the truest members seemed on the point of yielding. One of the most devoted friends of the administration said to Mr. Kendall, " We cannot resist this tremendous pressure ; we shall be obliged to yield." " What ! " said Mr. Kendall, " are you prepared to give up the Republic ? This is a struggle to maintain a government of the people against the most heartless of all aristocracies, that of money. Yield now, and the Bank of the United States will henceforth be the governing power whatever may be the form of our institutions." The member remained true to the last. Indeed the President had a strong guarantee of the support of the leading Democrats, in the fact that the success of all their aspirations for future preferment depended on defeating the coalition which then rallied around the Bank.

The effect of the agitation upon the country was to impair credit, prevent the usual bank accommodations, compel many manufacturing establishments to curtail their business or suspend operations, paralyze trade, force a few banks to stop payment, and produce numerous bankruptcies. Strong efforts were made to prevent State banks from undertaking the business of the government, and to compel those already employed to surrender their contracts. The banks of South Carolina, at Charleston, refused to receive the public moneys on deposit ; the Branch Bank of Virginia, at Norfolk, which had undertaken the public business, was directed by the State and other stockholders to relinquish it ; and a majority of the stockholders of the Girard Bank, in Philadelphia, being waited upon individually, signed a paper requesting their board of directors to surrender their contract with the government.

On the 28th of March, 1834, Mr. Clay closed the debate in the

Senate on the removal of the deposits, when his resolutions were adopted in the following form : —

" Resolved, That the reasons assigned by the Secretary of the Treasury for the removal of the money of the United States deposited in the Bank of the United States and its branches, communicated to Congress on the 4th of December, 1833, are unsatisfactory and insufficient.

" Resolved, That the President, in the late executive proceedings in relation to the public revenue, has assumed upon himself authority and power not conferred by the Constitution and laws, but in derogation of both."

The first resolution was adopted by a vote of 28 to 18 ; the second by 26 to 20.

The resolution condemnatory of the President, it will be observed, specifies no particular act done by him in derogation of the Constitution and laws. Indeed, it was not easy to find such an act in all his proceedings. His only act was to remove one Secretary and appoint another. His constitutional power to do that could not be successfully called in question. Nor was the motive unconstitutional or illegal. It was to cause to be done an act which the Secretary of the Treasury could lawfully do ; an act which the President deemed necessary for the safety of the public moneys, and the preservation of a pure republican government. The first resolution does not, as it could not, denounce the act of the Secretary as unlawful ; and as there was nothing illegal in the means employed by the President, or in the end attained, it is obvious that there was nothing in the case which could be alleged as just ground for this imputation of crimes, or which, if susceptible of specification, would have formed just grounds for impeachment. This resolution, therefore, went upon the records of the Senate as a naked, causeless denunciation, the more inexcusable because it prejudged a case in which the President, had he been guilty of the crimes imputed, might have been and ought to have been put on his trial before the Senate as a court of impeachment.

This resolution called from the President a long and able protest, in which he denied the constitutional right of the Senate to sit in judgment upon his acts, otherwise than as a court of impeachment acting upon charges presented by the House of Representatives ; vindicated the right of the President to remove his subordinates for whose acts he is responsible ; claimed that his recent exercise of that power had become a duty, being necessary to the faithful execution of the laws; and charged that the tendency of the act of the Senate was to break down the independence of the Executive and disturb that apportionment of powers to the several departments so wisely adjusted in the Constitution. In its facts and arguments this paper was unanswerable; yet it was violently assailed in the Senate, and gave rise to a discussion which ran through several weeks, ending in the adoption, by the coalition majority, of resolutions to the effect that the protest "asserts powers as belonging to the President which are inconsistent with the just authority of the two Houses of Congress, and inconsistent with the Constitution of the United States"; that the President has no right to protest against the acts of the Senate and request them to put his protest upon their records; "that the protest was a breach of the privileges of the Senate, and that it be not entered on the journal."

Here again there was no specification of the powers inconsistent with the Constitution and the rights of Congress claimed by the President, and partisan orators were thus left to attach this condemnation to any of his acts or to any imaginary doings which it might suit their fancy or their malignity to invent.

On the 4th of April, 1834, the discussion was brought to a close in the House of Representatives by the adoption of the following resolutions, viz.:—

"1. *Resolved*, That the Bank of the United States ought not to be rechartered." Yeas 132, nays 82.

"2. *Resolved*, That the public deposits ought not to be restored to the Bank of the United States." Yeas 113, nays 103.

"3. *Resolved*, That the State banks ought to be continued as the places of deposit of the public money, and that it is expedient for Congress to make further provision by law, prescribing the mode of selection, the securities to be taken, and the manner and terms on which they are to be employed." Yeas 117, nays 105.

A fourth resolution was adopted by a vote of 171 to 42, providing for a committee to examine and report upon the alleged charges of abuse and corruption in the management of the Bank, with power to send for persons and papers, and to visit the Bank and its branches for the purpose of inspecting their books.

The adversaries of the Bank now felt that the battle had been fought and the victory won. Though these resolutions did not in terms approve of the removal of the deposits, they registered an

emphatic opposition to the recharter of the Bank, which was, in fact, the practical issue. The opposition complained that the resolutions did not take issue upon the sufficiency of the reasons given by the Secretary of the Treasury for the removal of the deposits. Practical results were the objects aimed at by those who prepared them. Some of those relied upon to sustain the administration by voting at the preceding session that the public deposits were safe in the Bank of the United States, stood measurably committed against their removal. In view of their position, it was deemed wise to take issue on the restoration rather than the removal. The Bank and its advocates had disti. tly admitted that the real issue involved was the recharter of the B_nk, and in this aspect of the case members opposed to that measure, though they thought the reasons for the removal insufficient, might still think there were sufficient reasons since accruing why they should not be restored. Yet the practical effect of approving their removal or disapproving their restoration was precisely the same. At the instance of Mr. Clay, the Senate subsequently adopted and sent to the House of Representatives two joint resolutions, one declaring the reasons of the Secretary insufficient, and the other providing that all public moneys received after the 1st of July, 1834, should be deposited in the Bank of the United States and its branches; but they were laid on the table in the House by a vote of 114 to 101.

Thus ended the direct action of the two Houses of Congress on the deposit question. For political effect, however, the agitation was kept up both in Congress and the country.

The Senate rejected the nomination of Mr. Taney, as Secretary of the Treasury, by a strict party vote.

The nominations of the four government directors of the Bank, John F. Sullivan, Henry D. Gilpin, Peter Wager, and Hugh McEldery, were rejected; and being again presented were again rejected. These gentlemen had committed the unpardonable offence of opposing irregularities and abuses in the administration of the Bank, and of reporting them to the President, from whom they derived their appointment.

The adversaries of the Bank confidently expected crushing developments in the investigation into the management of the Bank by the committee of the House of Representatives. It was known that after the investigation of 1832, large accommodations had

been granted upon nominal or insufficient security to political editors and members of Congress; some of whom, being enemies of the Bank, had suddenly become its friends; and, in one instance, a member of the committee was furnished the pages of the books which would show that a debt of a man then high in office had been charged to profit and loss. In short, it was believed that not only all that had been charged by the President and government Directors would be confirmed, but that other abuses and corrupt practices would be disclosed sufficient to settle forever the question of a national bank of a similar character. These expectations were not realized. The managers of the Bank refused to submit their books and papers to a thorough examination of the committee, imposing conditions which could not be complied with compatibly with the rights and dignity of the House of Representatives. Having visited Philadelphia, and exhausted in vain the means at their disposal to carry out the orders of the House, the committee returned to Washington and reported their proceedings, recommending among other things that the managers of the Bank be arrested and brought before the House for contempt. No action was had beyond an order for printing the Report, together with a minority Report made at the same time.

Although the deposit question, as well as the question of rechartering the Bank, was settled by the decisive action of the House of Representatives on the 4th of April, the public excitement seemed for a time rather to increase than diminish. This was attributable to two causes. The leading cause was, that the panic machinery was in full operation throughout the country when the vote in the House was taken, manufacturing cries of distress in meetings, memorials, and resolutions without number, etc., etc. These came pouring into Congress from day to day for several weeks, and their presentation was frequently attended by remarks designed to keep up the excitement. Men were hired to get signers to memorials, and in some instances copied names by the dozen from tombstones in the graveyards. In Baltimore some excited men held a meeting preparatory to organizing, with the avowed purpose of compelling the President to change his policy. Their object became known, and while the conspirators were holding a second meeting, a band of resolute men rushed in upon them, and they were glad to escape through the windows.

But the main object of the Whig leaders in keeping up the

excitement was now entirely political. Their Bank was doomed beyond hope; but they were not without hope that by means of the panic, and with the assistance of their Southern allies, they could carry the elections of 1834, and secure the ascendency of the Whig party. To give as much influence as possible to the panic documents sent to Congress, the Senate directed their Secretary to count and report the number of names attached to the memorials and petitions sent to that body in favor of and against the measures of the administration.

He reported the number of opponents of all classes to be 151,365, while those petitioning against restoring the deposits and rechartering the Bank were only 17,027.

It would have been remarkable indeed if these tremendous efforts had not produced some effect on the elections; but the gains of the Whig party in the various cities and States during the year did not at all alarm the President and his supporters. They knew that in the natural course of events, such violent and unscrupulous efforts must be followed by a reaction which would seal the fate of the Bank, and probably consign to private life its leading advocates.

Congress adjourned on the last day of June. A few days afterwards a correspondence took place between certain mercantile gentlemen of New York and the President of the Bank, in which it was virtually admitted that the restrictive measures of the Bank had been persisted in for no other purpose than to influence the action of Congress. The Bank at once put a stop to all curtailments theretofore ordered, and assented to the proposed policy of increasing its loans, giving as a reason "the adjournment of Congress without adopting any measures either of redress to the Bank or of relief to the community." Credit returned, business resumed its wonted channels, and the anticipated political reaction took place. But the country was strewn with wrecks of fortunes sacrificed to enable the Bank of the United States to control the government. Many a man has gone to the block and the halter for crimes less injurious to his country than that committed by the coalition leaders on this occasion. Their only apology must be looked for in the possible but strange conviction that the object sought to be attained was worth to the country all the distress, turmoil, and bankruptcy they were wantonly inflicting upon it.

So far as the political consequences of this contest were concerned, they may be summed up as follows:—

It made Mr. Van Buren President.

It made Mr. Taney Chief-Justice of the Supreme Court.

It made Col. R. M. Johnson Vice-President.

It made Mr. Forsythe Secretary of State.

It made Mr. Grundy Attorney-General.

It made Mr. Kendall Postmaster-General.

It extinguished the last hope of Mr. Clay to be President of the United States.

In conjunction with nullification, it separated Mr. Calhoun forever from the Democratic and every other patriotic party, and left him to rest his fame on the inculcation of doctrines which produced their bloody fruits in 1861.

Despairing of a recharter from Congress, the Bank purchased an act of incorporation from the Pennsylvania Legislature, and still carried on its operations under the name of the Bank of the United States. In common with the other State banks it stopped payment in 1837, and never resumed. Though declaring its entire individual ability, it discouraged a general return to specie payments to the last, and when the other banks could no longer be restrained it threw off the mask and exposed its insolvency. Its entire capital of thirty-five millions of dollars was dissipated and lost. Such a record as its books exhibited of loans to insolvent political men, evidently without expectation of repayment, of debts due by that class of men charged to profit and loss, of loans to editors and reckless speculators, and of expenditures for political electioneering and corrupt purposes, was never before exhibited in a Christian land. The ambitious author of all this ruin, who had aspired with the aid of his political allies to govern the government of the United States, and through his cotton speculations control the exchanges of the commercial world, and had been carried on men's shoulders as a sort of demi-god, had resigned the Presidency of the Bank and retired to private life, where he died miserably with the disease which consumed Herod of old.

So signal and awful was the destruction of the Bank and its ambitious President, so impressive was the lesson which it taught, that scarcely a voice has since been raised in favor of a national bank, and almost with one voice the country has borne testimony not only to the purity and firmness of the hero President, but to his wisdom and sagacity.

CHAPTER XV.

TO HENRY A. WISE.

WASHINGTON, February 20, 1837.

HON. HENRY A. WISE, *Chairman, etc., etc. :*—

SIR, — You will remember that while I was under examination before your committee, an anonymous letter was produced and made the basis of a question which the committee refused to let me answer, although expressly requested. Of that refusal I do not complain; but I complain that the anonymous letter was permitted to be put on your journals.

That letter, sir, is an atrocious libel on the President of the United States and on myself, and in all its essential parts is utterly false. I never made such a bargain as is therein described, nor has the President under such circumstances, or under any others, so far as I know or believe, confirmed the sales of any Indian lands purchased by a company in Boston.

This infamous libel has been placed upon your journal; it is presumed it will be reported to the House, and will thus be published. And where is my remedy? By the Constitution and laws of my country I am authorized to seek protection for my character, as well as my person, from the attacks of private citizens, in the courts of justice; but in this case members of Congress, around whom the Constitution spreads the shield of privilege, become the publishers, and the name of the libeller is withheld from me. Of this, I complain. By me the immunity of a member of Congress in the performance of his public duties will ever be held sacred. But I deny his right to extend the like immunity to every villain who has malice enough to stab, but not courage enough to meet the responsibility. I deny his right to receive and publish under his privilege any anonymous libel in any shape. It is, to say the least, an abuse of a constitutional immunity which was granted for purposes more noble and more just.

I ask, therefore, that the name of the libeller in this case may be ascertained and communicated to me. After placing the libel upon their journal, the committee, I respectfully conceive, cannot in justice do

less than place me in an attitude where I may avail myself of the protection and redress which the Constitution and laws promise in like cases to every citizen.

Very respectfully, your obedient servant,

AMOS KENDALL.

TO THOMAS RITCHIE.

WASHINGTON, Sept. 9th, 1837.

THOMAS RITCHIE, ESQ. :—

SIR, — In the "Richmond Enquirer" of yesterday, I find the following remarks, viz.: "The Postmaster-General may report, that 'this Department has been successfully conducted since May last upon the principle of dealing only in the legal currency of the United States'; but if Mr. Kendall means by this, that it has received and paid away only hard money, we take leave to differ from him. A committee of Congress has only to summon various postmasters before them to show the contrary."

I am sure it was not your intention to charge Mr. Kendall with reporting a falsehood to the President, and to invite a committee of Congress to convict him of it; yet such is the uncharitable construction which many have put upon this passage. Whatever may have been your meaning or motive, Mr. Kendall's report is too plain to be misunderstood, and the declaration of the President is literally true. It is not asserted, that no subordinate agent of the Department has, without the knowledge or direction of the Postmaster-General, received or paid nothing but "hard money." Doubtless there have been cases where contractors have voluntarily received paper from postmasters, and where postmasters have received it from the public; but it has been done without the sanction of the Department, and the fact does not militate against the declaration of the President. The *principle* upon which the Department has been managed is precisely as he declares. The deviations from that principle, if it exists, are too few in number to affect in any way the force of the example, or enable the opponents of the hard money system in the affairs of government, to base an argument upon them. All this I am sure you will readily concede, and give full weight to the argument which may be deduced from it.

I am one who has always given you credit for perfect honesty in your political opinions, and a strict adherence to the Constitution, according to its obvious meaning and intention. Yet, I cannot comprehend the chain of reasoning by which you are led to some of the conclusions which you are now pressing upon the community.

You admit that gold and silver are, by the Constitution, the only

legal tender in this country, and that every contract to pay money, public or private, is a contract to pay gold and silver. Upon these admitted principles, I do not comprehend the chain of reasoning by which you arrive at the conclusion that it is *honest* to force on the public creditors anything else. Yet you insist that the government ought to receive and pay to its creditors a depreciated paper, and you speak of them as *favored* because they are not compelled to receive less than their legal dues! Is this fair reasoning or a just conclusion? Instead of the public creditors being favored, do they not receive their just dues and no more; and are not the people *wronged* out of a portion of their just dues by being compelled to receive a depreciated currency? And when *a part* are wronged by the course of the banks, is it a just ground for honest complaint that *all* are not wronged in an equal degree? Honest complaint, it would seem, should seek to *repair the wrong* instead of giving it a wider range. It would aim at securing the inviolability of contracts guaranteed in the Constitution, rather than at reducing all to the same level of wrong in violation of its most sacred principles. Restore their rights, their *constitutional* rights, to an outraged people, and public and private creditors will stand on the same level. Do not deprive the public creditors of *their* rights, but restore to the people theirs. Compel your banks to fulfil their obligations to the country, and away with your relief laws. The *people*, the great mass, the honest planters, farmers, mechanics, and traders, who are not in debt, and have nothing to do with banks and speculation, would be relieved in a day, and you would find no ground to complain that public creditors are honestly paid according to their contracts, and thus have an advantage over private citizens.

There is another point on which, in all seriousness, I beg leave to ask you a few questions.

Do you believe "the hard money men," who formed our Constitution, ever contemplated the employment of banks, State or national, as keepers of the moneys in the Treasury?

If not, in what manner did they intend that the public moneys should be kept?

What did they mean when they declared that "no money shall be drawn from the Treasury, except in pursuance of appropriations made by law"?

Can this prohibition, without a violation of its plain letter and spirit, be construed to mean anything else than that the public money should go into the Treasury and there remain untouched and inviolate, until drawn out to pay the expenditures of the government in pursuance of appropriations?

Can it possibly mean that it may be handed over to banks or other corporations, or individuals, to be loaned out for gain or applied to their own use until wanted to meet appropriations? Or, if such be its meaning, of what possible use is the restriction?

Is the general government indeed such an imperfect body politic that it cannot safely keep its own money? Must it hand its purse over to strangers over whom it has little authority or control, suffer them to use its money for their own gain, and be subject in all its operations to be impeded and baffled by their mismanagement, indiscretion, or knavery? Is it not in the power of Congress to make the national Treasury as safe a place of custody as the legislatures of the States can make their banks? If, indeed, the general government has not under the Constitution powers and faculties adequate to the safe-keeping of its own money, the framers of that instrument sadly mistook the character of their own work, and have left a government, which they intended should be independent to the extent of its delegated powers, entirely dependent, not on the States as under the confederation, but on *the creatures of the States*, a set of soulless creatures actuated entirely by the love of gain, — to which honor, honesty, patriotism, all that is holy and sacred among men, will, as all experience teaches, be sometimes sacrificed.

It was not, sir, my intention to go into the general subject; but I have suffered myself to be carried thus far by the interest I feel in the prevalence of sound principles. A short time will satisfy you that your own separation from the Republican party, on the pending questions, does but strengthen the hands of our great enemy, a national bank; and that in fact there is no middle ground between depositing the public funds in "the Treasury," or in the vaults of our "legitimate sovereign," to whose restoration, through your secession and that of your friends, the friends of "the Bourbons" so confidently look.

Very respectfully, your obedient servant,
AMOS KENDALL.

"BABBLING POLITICIANS."

WASHINGTON, May 18, 1839.

SIR, — Your letter of the 13th inst., postmarked 15th, I received on the 16th.

You enclose a printed slip containing a letter purporting to be from me to "a friend in Kentucky," dated April 28th, 1833, and another purporting to be from me to "J. Monroe," dated March 24th, 1829; and you ask, "will you have the kindness to inform me if the letters herewith sent are correct copies *entire* of those written by you?"

Although I do not know the object of this inquiry, I have no objection to answer it.

The letter of 1829 is but a part of a letter addressed by me to Mr. Monroe, and whether that part be correctly printed I have not at hand the means of ascertaining.

Whether the letter of 1833 is a correct copy or not I cannot tell. About the time it bears date, I wrote a few private letters to friends in Kentucky, enclosing a prospectus for an extra "Globe." One of those friends had removed from the county where he had resided, and my letter to him, as I understood, was taken out of the post-office by some honest anti-Jackson man who had a curiosity to ascertain its contents, and by him sent to a newspaper editor for publication. The accomplices of this thief have put the letter through many editions since; but whether it has been "enlarged and improved" or not, I cannot tell, for I preserved no copy.

The object is to show an inconsistency between my professions and practice; but properly considered, the letters as printed show no such thing. The Auditor's Office *was* "filled with men of business." No man who came there to do business was annoyed by "babbling politicians." No "partisan feelings" entered there; but all men of all parties were treated alike in all their official intercourse with the office. The duties were discharged "in the spirit of reform which made General Jackson President." The same spirit I have endeavored to maintain in the Post-Office Department.

But, sir, could any man of sense understand me as meaning that I would not *think* of politics; that I would *have no opinion* upon political questions; that I would not *speak those opinions among my friends*; that I would not *write a word* about politics in my private letters? Did any one understand me as meaning that I would *fetter the pens, gag the mouths*, and *crush the thoughts* of my subordinates upon subjects in relation to which every freeman should have an opinion, and on proper occasions be at liberty to express it? I meant no such thing, as every reflecting man knows. I meant that "*partisan feelings*" should not influence the action of the office; that the clerks should not waste the time which belonged to the public, and annoy those who visited the office by "*babbling politics*"; and that the public business should be promptly and impartially performed, uninfluenced by party considerations.

If a *thief steals my private letters*, or an *eavesdropper catches my private conversations*, and gives them to the public, showing that I *have* political opinions and sometimes *express* them, is it any evidence that my office is filled with "babbling politicians"; that its acts are influenced by partisan feelings, "or that its duties are not discharged in the spirit of reform?"

That a portion of my enemies should pervert the stolen letter into

evidence of inconsistency, is not surprising; but that it should make an impression of that sort on honest and considerate men of any party, is "passing strange." I recognize the right of no man or set of men on earth to gag me in my private intercourse, and I would reject with scorn any office on earth if to be held on such terms. That which I would not submit to myself, I shall never attempt to impose on my official subordinates.

Yours, etc.,
AMOS KENDALL.

TO W. J. GRAVES.

WASHINGTON, January 31, 1840.

HON. W. J. GRAVES, H. R., Present : —

SIR, — I received this morning your letter of yesterday, alluding to certain remarks implicating my official conduct, made by you in the House on the preceding day. In that letter you say, "I propose to write out and publish my remarks; but before I do so, I have thought it but just to you to afford you an opportunity to answer whether all or any portion of my information be correct, so that if injustice has been done you, I may set the matter right in my written remarks."

You then inform me that you had reference to the case of E. W. Robinson, Esq., supposed to be a clerk in the Post-Office Department, who, it is said, is about to commence the publication of a newspaper at Frankfort, Ky., and you put to me several specific interrogatories touching that matter to which you request my reply with as little delay as my engagements will allow.

Now, sir, although I do not question the right of a member of Congress to become the retailer on the floor of the House of Representatives of the false and malignant gossip which taints the atmosphere of this city, I do deny his right to call on the party so slandered to aid him in escaping the responsibility of reducing those slanders to libels in a written speech. I very much regret that the idea of doing justice to me did not occur to you before you made your attack in the House. You admit it to be "just" that I shall have an opportunity to make the truth known before your speech be written, was it less just that such an opportunity should be afforded me before it was spoken? If before holding me up as delinquent in duty by remarks publicly uttered to be noted by reporters and scattered by letter writers over the whole Union, on no better authority than the second-hand information of a "highly respectable gentleman," you had done me the justice to inquire into their truth, I could have had no objection to putting you in possession of all the facts of the case within my knowledge. As it is, I deem it but justice to myself to decline affording you any assistance in

making up for the public a speech different from that you uttered on the floor of the House.

Very respectfully your obedient servant,
AMOS KENDALL.

TO HIS WIFE.

CINCINNATI, November 13, 1840.

MY DEAR WIFE, — I left Wheeling about noon on the 11th, and whether I go on to-morrow morning will depend on the state of my health.

Wheeling, where I remained over night, is one of the hottest Whig holes in the country; and in the night they saluted me by firing a cannon under the windows of the room where I slept; but offered me no other indignity.

In the steamboat about half the passengers were Democrats; but among the Whigs was Leslie Combs of Kentucky, and Baer, "the Buckeye Blacksmith," came on board at Portsmouth, Ohio. I had some jokes with Combs, and Baer once tried to get into conversation with me, but I did not encourage him. On the whole, the company was agreeable enough.

I have spent most of this evening at the house of my old friend, Nathan Guilford, who is one of the leading Whigs here; yet, a band of "Tip's" musicians collected before his house and sang several of their songs, winding up with divers groans, I suppose for my special amusement. The evening, however, passed off very agreeably, and I found the street clear when I returned to the boarding-house where I have taken lodgings.

I hope to get away to-morrow at 10 o'clock in the mail-boat, which will take me to Westport about 9 or 10 o'clock to-morrow night; but I shall not go unless I feel very well.

Give my love to the children; and if Fanny has been a good girl, tell her that her father sends her a kiss, and give it to her. The same to Mary Ann, and Mr. Gold, and to your father, mother, Alexander, and James.

Ever yours,
AMOS KENDALL.

In a political address, written in 1832, Mr. Kendall gives utterance to the following patriotic sentiments, foreshadowing the evils of secession : —

1. "*Our Federal Union must be preserved.*"

Men are beginning to think too lightly of the Union of these States. Some maintain that its value to the South is overbalanced by the evils of the present protecting system. Others insist if that system be abandoned it is of no value to the North. Both are wrong. If the evils of that system be as great on the one hand, or its benefits on the other, as the wildest enthusiasts on either side depict, there are yet advantages in *Union* which transcend them all. It preserves peace between twenty-four rival republics, covering a large space on this globe. It secures between them ready intercourse and free trade. It provides for the transmission and diffusion of intelligence with a safety and speed unequalled on earth. It maintains the pervading influence of certain great principles, useful alike to all ranks and conditions of men; such as the inviolability of contracts, an uniform tender in the payment of debts, and prospective legislation upon crimes and punishments. The dissolution of the Union would lead to frequent if not perpetual wars, — desolating our fruitful fields, exposing our peaceful cities to fire and sword, and deluging our country with fraternal blood. In addition to the devastations of war, taxes tenfold more heavy than the protecting system imposes would be required to support armies and navies, extended civil establishments and pensioners. Custom-houses would be multiplied on the borders of each State, as well as in the maritime ports; free trade at home would be lost without securing it abroad; all safe, expeditious, and cheap transmission of intelligence would be cut off; all fundamental principles violated in general anarchy; and our people reduced, like those of Europe, to labor only for the support of their rulers and those costly establishments which constant danger would make it necessary for each State to maintain.

Our people must not be reduced to this condition, "our Federal Union must be preserved." It is the *only* shield of the people. Its dissolution will soon be followed by the loss of all that is valuable in liberty. It will multiply beyond measure those who live upon the people's industry; and it will bring nothing in return but ages of taxation, misery, and blood. Our remedies for all abuses are *therefore within the Union*. To seek relief from existing evils in a dissolution of the Union is to rush through the flames of anarchy into the arms of slavery. With us, therefore, the Union is *sacred*. Its preservation is the *only* means of preserving our civil liberty. We look upon the enemies of the Union as the enemies of liberty.

2. "*The Constitution of the United States is a delegation of powers.*"

To this general principle all assent. Differences arise, however, in determining what is delegated. We are advocates of a strict construction. When doubts arise, the question with us is not whether a power be *necessary*, but whether it has been delegated. If it be *necessary* and not *delegated*, it cannot be exercised. To authorize its exercise, resort must be had to an amendment of the Constitution. Nor can a power

which conflicts with any provision of the Constitution, or violates any right of the States, be assumed and exercised as a means of executing clearly delegated powers. The general government cannot, in the use of means, enlarge its own powers, nor curtail those reserved to the States.

3. "*The State constitutions are limitations of power.*"

Were the people of the States to abolish their constitutions, as well as the Constitution of the United States, and elect legislatures untrammelled by instructions, the legislative bodies thus constituted would possess all political power, and be as omnipotent as the British Parliament. The State constitutions are, in their general character, *standing instructions* from the people to their representatives, forbidding the exercise of certain powers. In some instances they direct the performance of specific acts; but these provisions confer no power. They merely make it the duty of the legislatures to exercise certain powers which would have existed in just as full a manner if they had not been inserted; but would have remained undistinguished in the mass of legislative discretion.

4. "*The perfection of civil liberty is the power to do as we please, without infringing the rights of others.*"

Perfect men would need no government. Each one knowing his own rights and the rights of others, would content himself with quietly enjoying that which belonged to him, without molesting his neighbor. Neither life, liberty, nor property would be in danger from human violence, and therefore no laws would be necessary for their protection. In such a state, government would be unnecessary and unknown. Men would not choose legislators; for they would need no laws. They would not be taxed to support armies and navies, for there would be no enemy to encounter. They would not pay their money to build prisons and support the officers of the law, for none would commit violence upon their persons or depredations on their property. Each would be his own ruler, perfectly free and perfectly just.

It should be the object of government to place the honest and upright man, as nearly as possible, in this condition. It cannot make him *more free* than it finds him. Its only legitimate object is to *protect him in the enjoyment of his freedom*. He does not ask government to take the property of others and give it to him, or to subject their persons to his control. All he asks is that it shall protect him in the enjoyment of his property, and shield his character and person from the assaults of bad men. He is justly taxed and cheerfully pays a sum sufficient to support an adequate number of officers to perform these duties. He asks for no advantage over others; he only demands that others shall have no advantage over him. Men thus governed could enjoy " the

highest degree of liberty and equality of which mankind is susceptible in the social state."

The only use of government is *to keep off evil*. We do not want its assistance in seeking after good. Providence protects us, and leaves us to our own will. If Infinite Wisdom has deemed it inexpedient to infringe upon human liberty, even to promote human happiness, shall this prerogative be assumed by a fallible government? He is as much a slave who is forced to his own good, as he who is unwillingly plunged into evil. That government is as much a tyranny which forces the Laplander, contrary to his will, into the genial climes of the South, as that which drives the unhappy Pole to the frozen deserts of Siberia. Violation of human will is the violation of human liberty, and when it is not necessary to the protection of the rights of others it is *tyranny and oppression*, whether exercised *for good or for evil*.

Men do not complain of government for compelling the payment of just debts; for protecting their reputation, restraining the trespasser, punishing the thief, executing the murderer, and shielding them from the ravages of a foreign enemy. It is not for acts like these that discontents arise, rebellions are engendered, and revolutions break forth. These occur only when government departs from its legitimate objects, — "when the laws undertake to add to natural and just advantages artificial distinctions, to grant titles, gratuities, and exclusive privileges, to make the rich richer and the potent more powerful." A government perfectly just is not to be expected; because that very imperfection of our nature which makes it indispensable, necessarily mingles in its administration. But the more deeply impressed the people and public officers are with the legitimate objects of government, the nearer will it approach to perfection, less cause will be given for discontent, and less frequent will be rebellions and revolutions.

5. "*We consider ability, integrity, and fidelity to the fundamental principles of our republican institutions necessary qualifications for every office of honor or trust in our republic.*"

All concede the necessity of ability and integrity as qualifications for office; but in selections for executive and judicial offices, too little regard is generally paid to correct political principles. Perhaps it is unfortunate in a free government that office carries with it some degree of political influence. The respect of some, the interest of others, and his commanding position give to the opinions of a public officer more weight with the people than generally attends those of a private citizen. It is important, therefore, that public offices shall be held by men of correct political principles. The people do not hesitate to put men in office or out according to the principles which they profess and practise. It is the only process by which their own principles can be made to pre-

vail in the administration of their government. The same reason exists why other officers, not chosen by the people, should accord with them in their views of government and its administration. On this ground it may be maintained that it is the duty of those intrusted with the administration of the government, to fill all offices in their gift with those who have proved by profession and practice their devotion to the fundamental principles of our institutions. Would the Emperor of Austria or the Autocrat of Russia fill his cabinet, his bureaus, or his clerkships with known republicans in principle? They understand too well the effect of excluding their friends, and giving place and influence to the enemies of their despotic principles, to be guilty of such suicidal acts. Should republicans be less regardful of the principles which form the basis of their institutions and the means to give them practical effect? Should they place the offices of the republic in the hands of those who would destroy it? If monarchs are so true to *themselves*, should not republican magistrates be true *to the people*? Is it not *their duty* to fill the offices in their gift with men who have proved themselves *devoted to popular rights*?

Offices in our government are created for the good of the people, and not to provide places for the personal favorites of the chief magistrate or any other man or men. For the people are they established, and at the expense of the people are they maintained. They should be limited in number to the actual exigencies of the public service, and filled with men of talents, integrity, industry, and pure republican principles. No man has a *property* in the office he holds. It is a trust for the people, and whenever the people, or those whom they have selected to superintend that portion of their public service, think proper to place the trust in other hands, no *personal wrong* is done to him who is displaced. As a matter of expediency and humanity, individual inconvenience or distress should not be produced without cause; but in no case can the displaced officer complain that he is deprived of any *personal right*.

Dishonesty, indolence, imbecility, immorality, and anti-republican principles constitute, respectively, reasons which make it the *duty* of those having the power to change the incumbents of public offices. Not the convenience or interests of office-holders or their friends, but the *public good* should be the supreme law in all appointments and removals.

REMOVALS FROM OFFICE.

The following extract from a circular to postmasters designates the principles governing Mr. Kendall with reference to the removal of postmasters and clerks : —

"I have set out upon the principle of not suffering any party or other movement to procure the removal of good, faithful, and quiet men, whatever may be their political opinions, and I mean to persist in it. Brawlers of any party, who make politics instead of attention to their official duties their constant occupation, I mean to cut adrift from the public service, if I cannot otherwise conquer that propensity. All the support I ask for the administration from postmasters is a faithful, polite, and obliging performance of their duties, contenting themselves with the exercise of their own rights without attempting to proselyte others."

These are the principles upon which he steadfastly acted, and upon which, as he always maintained, every public officer of the government should act.

In more than one instance, when obliged to remove clerks for inefficiency, causing apparent hardship and distress, he made contributions for their relief from his slender private purse, having them conveyed indirectly to the parties, who never knew or suspected their benefactor.

RETIREMENT FROM THE POST-OFFICE DEPARTMENT.

Mr. Kendall was often admonished by attacks of indisposition that the arduous labor and constant demands of a faithful administration of the Post-Office Department involved a too severe strain upon his delicate though elastic physical organization.

In 1838 he intimated to the President his fears upon the subject, and in response received a letter dated August 6th of that year, in which Mr. Van Buren wrote: —

"I have read the account of the state of your health with great pain. Your retirement from a post for which you are so eminently qualified would be a positive and great detriment to the public service, and to be regretted on every account. Should your anticipations, however, be realized, we must make the best of it, and it would, I assure you, give me great pleasure to confer on you the mission to Spain if the retirement of the present incumbent puts it in my power to do so. This, we have strong reasons for believing, will be the case, as Mr. Gaston has declared his intention to return soon."

Finding, soon after this, his health somewhat improved, Mr. Kendall yielded to the wishes of others and continued to perform the duties of his office until May, 1840, when, greatly enfeebled by frequent attacks of sickness, he resigned his office and retired forever from public service. The following is his letter of resignation: —

POST-OFFICE DEPARTMENT, May 9, 1840.

M. VAN BUREN, *President of the United States:* —

SIR, — Impelled by a painful sense of responsibility for duties which feeble health renders it impossible for me to perform, I tender you my resignation of the office of Postmaster-General, to take effect as soon as my successor can be appointed.

For some months I have had this step in contemplation; but desiring to promote some beneficial changes in the Post-Office establishment, I lived in hope that the mild air of spring would bring with it a renovated health which would enable me to devote myself to these objects until the approach of another winter. In this flattering hope I have been disappointed.

Although I find no cause of regret in surrendering a high and honorable trust, and retiring to a private station, it is not without reluctance that I separate from the administration at a time when it is most violently and unjustly assailed; when, with vigorous health, I might do something more at the head of a great Department to exemplify the purity of its principles; and when the motives of the step I now take may be misunderstood by some and misrepresented by others. And this feeling is strengthened by severing my official relations with yourself and the gentlemen of your cabinet, from whom I have received so many evidences of confidence and kindness.

To correct any erroneous impressions, I shall omit no proper occasion to make known to my countrymen, that so far from being actuated by any dissatisfaction with you or your administration, I leave you with a respect and regard which have increased from the commencement of our official association, and with an abiding faith that the principles you maintain are the only ones which can preserve to the people of the United States the blessings of freedom and just government.

With enduring gratitude for the kindness I have uniformly received at your hands, I remain, personally and politically,

Your devoted friend,

AMOS KENDALL.

Perhaps no man ever laid down his honors with a prouder consciousness of having done his duty faithfully and fearlessly, unmoved by threats or calumny, undeterred from what he conceived to be the line of strict honesty by the favor of friends or the fear of enemies.

The "American Cyclopedia" does him but simple justice when it says: —

"He was also one of the earliest friends of common schools in Ken-

tucky, and succeeded in procuring the passing of an act to district the State, and to set apart one half of the profits of the Bank of the Commonwealth to constitute a school fund." While Postmaster-General, he "in one year succeeded in reorganizing the financial system of the Department, and in freeing it from the debt with which it had been embarrassed. In 1836 he procured from Congress a reorganization of the Department, on a plan suggested by himself, which has undergone no essential alteration since."

In reply to his letter of resignation Mr. Kendall received the following from President Van Buren: —

WASHINGTON, May 15, 1840.

MY DEAR SIR, — I received your letter tendering your resignation of the office of Postmaster-General, to take effect as soon as your successor can be appointed.

Though in some measure prepared for this event by previous intimations on your part, and from frequent observation of the effects produced by an unremitting assiduity in the performance of your high and responsible duties, yet this neither diminishes my sense of the loss which both the public and myself will sustain by your withdrawal, nor my regret at the occasion which renders it necessary.

To say that the manner in which you have performed those duties has met my entire approbation, is, I am sure, unnecessary, after an official intercourse in every respect so satisfactory. Still, I cannot in justice to my own feelings refrain from assuring you that the high opinion of your talents and integrity which I entertained when you became a member of my cabinet, has been steadily and uniformly augmented by a daily observance of the capacity, firmness, zeal, and disinterestedness with which you have uniformly administered the affairs of the Department over which you presided with so much honor to yourself and benefit to your country.

Be assured that I cordially reciprocate your expressions of personal regard, that I shall anxiously look for your early restoration to health, and will never cease to take a deep interest in your happiness and welfare.

I am, dear sir, very respectfully, your sincere friend,

MARTIN VAN BUREN.

To AMOS KENDALL, Esq.

Recruited and refreshed by a few months' rest, in February, 1841, Mr. Kendall began at Washington the publication of a small sheet, issued bi-weekly, called "Kendall's Expositor."

In his inaugural he thus sets forth the principles upon which he proposes to conduct his "little paper": —

WHAT IS DEMOCRACY.

The Democracy we advocate is justice between man and man, between state and state, and between nation and nation. It is morality. It is "giving to every man his due." It is "doing unto others as we would have them do unto us." It advocates the banishment of falsehood, fraud, and violence from the affairs of men. It is the moral code of all true philosophy; it is a fundamental doctrine of "Him who spake as never man spake"; it is the perfection of reason and the law of God.

Some teach that Democracy is incompatible with peace and justice. On the contrary, peace and justice are its natural fruits, and it is only in the degree that its principles are recognized in government that they are enjoyed by mankind. The first law of the universe is order; yet storms desolate the globe and earthquakes rend it. These appear to be violations of the universal law, and, in our limited view, they might so mingle earth and ocean as to destroy mankind, as they once did all but one family, and now do individuals, families, and cities. Why these evils exist, is known only to the Omniscient Mind; man cannot control them or mitigate their fury; all he can do is to ward them off by frail and temporary expedients.

By passion, error, and wickedness, storms are also generated in the moral and political world, which violate the law of order, break over the barriers of right and reason, and make man the victim of violence and rapacity. Why these wrongs are permitted, is known only to the Almighty Ruler; but man himself has power not alone to avoid or mitigate their effects, but in a measure to dry up their fountains.

In the physical world, he cannot ascend to the clouds and assuage the storm ere it reaches the earth; he can only build him a house, and resort to other expedients to shield himself from the rain, the wind, and the snow. In the moral world, he can do more; he can ascend to the sources of the evil; he can instruct the mind and improve the heart, not only his own but those of his fellow-men.

We should think a man mad who would refuse to build a house because he could not prevent the recurrence of storms; and is he less a madman who will refuse to take those equally essential and more effective steps to guard against storms in the moral and political world to which he finds himself exposed? When his buildings and fences are prostrated by a tornado, or swept away by an inundation, he proceeds to rebuild them in greater strength than before; and shall he have less

JOHN ANDREW-SON.

KENDALL GREEN, NEAR WASHINGTON.

courage and perseverance in his labors to secure himself and his children against those mischiefs which spring from his own passions and ignorance, or the passions, ignorance, and wickedness of his fellow-men? If he cannot exterminate the evil, is it wise not to take the steps within his power to mitigate its force and avert its calamities? Sad would be the condition of man if he were to make no exertion, bodily or mental, because he cannot do the work of Omnipotence. Despair is no part of the character of a Christian, a philosopher, or a democrat. He knows that perpetual resistance to evil is the duty and labor of his life. He knows that the physical condition of man can be ameliorated; for to that fact he has the concurrent testimony of history, observation, and experience. He knows that his moral condition may be improved; for he witnesses an advancement in virtue and knowledge, not only in individuals but in nations. He feels that he can aid in this progress both by precept and example. He can improve himself, he can contribute to the improvement of others, and he knows not to what degree of perfection his race is capable of advancing. In what he sees and knows, there is ground for glorious hope and unceasing exertion.

It is with a determination to emulate this spirit that we enter upon our duties as editor of this paper. Individually, perhaps, no man has more grounds for discouragement than the writer of this article. Though endeavoring to live a life of unsullied morality, and to do his duty in public stations without favor or fear, he has been hunted and pursued by a thousand presses, and ten thousand tongues, as if he was a robber and an outlaw. Without knowing why, thousands of honest men have been made to believe, by countless libels and slanders which it was as impossible to meet and refute as it is to catch in a bucket all the raindrops of a storm, that he is one of the worst of the human race. His life has been threatened, and his assassination publicly spoken of as a desirable thing. Men who profess religion, in this city, have used in relation to him expressions ill becoming the gospel creed, such as that "he ought to have his throat cut, and his house burned over his head." Recently, in Cincinnati, some of his friends were told that if they dared to give him a public dinner he should never leave that city alive. Threats, accompanied by shocking imprecations, are still occasionally uttered against his person. For acts when in office, as conscientious as ever flowed from the heart of man, he is pursued with a private suit, claiming $100,000 in damages, and a jury have been induced (honestly, he trusts, yet with a want of charity with which he hopes they may never be judged here or hereafter) to punish him with a penalty of $12,000, to be taken out of his private fortune, if so much he has.

All this comes upon him for resisting wrong, and attempting to do

right in office and out. If he had indulged in the profligate habits which prevail too extensively in this city; if he had wasted his substance and destroyed his health in intemperate eating and drinking, instead of devoting body and mind to the public service; if he had accepted the favors of powerful mail contractors, and paid them by extra allowances instead of resisting their exorbitant demands, and treating alike the humble and the high, he would not now, with broken constitution and in private life, be subjected to these persecutions.

But what of that? Shall we give up that consciousness of right which dwells within us, and become the advocate of bad principles and the associate of bad men to avoid the mischiefs which they bring upon us? What should we think of the man who, because an invading foe had plundered and burned his house, should join them in plundering and burning the houses of his neighbors? He is not less a traitor to his country than the man who abandons sound principles and good morals to escape the responsibility of being honest. Such a traitor we shall never be, though beggary and assassination be our lot.

No; we shall endeavor more strenuously than ever to prove, by precept and example, that moral rectitude is the basis of society and the surest guarantee of happiness.

That honesty in politics and in office is, if possible, more the duty of every good citizen than honesty in his private dealings.

That to cheat men out of their suffrages by wilful falsehoods, or out of their choice of rulers by illegal votes, is a worse treason than that for which men in some countries are hanged, drawn, and quartered.

That no law or institution is safe for individuals, communities, or nations which is not based on equal justice.

That, while violent changes are to be avoided, it is the interest of the people, and their right, gradually to bring back their laws and institutions to the standard of moral principle, wherever they have departed from it.

That to protect man in the possession of personal liberty, and the exercise of equal political power, is the first duty of government, and to protect him in the unmolested enjoyment of the honest fruits of his own labor and skill is its second.

That no man, state, or nation, has a right to interfere with or control the conduct of another, except in defence of his own rights and powers, or in fulfilment of his obligations as a member of society.

That in the assumption of men, states, and nations, to judge for others, instead of confining themselves to self-protection and the performance of their civil and social duties, leaving others "to their own master, to stand or fall," is found the source of much of that bloodshed, degradation, and slavery, which overspread the earth.

Aspiring to no office, neither having nor intending to have business connections with the government, and relying for our only income and support on the subscriptions of the people for our little paper, we feel as free as we are determined to expose the abuses of government in all its branches, while it is our firm purpose to avoid abuse altogether, and to deal in denunciation only when imperious duty shall require it at our hands.

In the fall of 1841, finding that in consequence of the proceeding against him by Stockton and Stokes he would be obliged to remain in the District for some considerable time, he negotiated for the purchase of a tract of about one hundred acres of land adjoining the city limits on the northeast, for a permanent homestead. He immediately began to build a frame dwelling, twenty-six feet square, intending it for a temporary habitation until he could erect a better.

In February, 1842, he moved into the house, then unfinished and scarcely comfortable.

The income from the "Expositor" having materially diminished, the idea of building a new house was abandoned for the time, and Mr. Kendall found serious difficulty in meeting his payments on the place. At one time he utterly despaired of fulfilling these pressing obligations, and sought relief by proposing to surrender the whole property to the party of whom he purchased, and become his tenant, expressing a willingness to sacrifice one half of his improvements. The proposition was declined in hopes of a better! Though he paid all he could, offered to restore the title of the property to the original owner and become his tenant, or to let him dispose of it if he could, the return for all this was the service of an injunction upon him, restraining him from cutting the wood.

There was every prospect of losing the farm, payments, improvements, and all; but the timely loan of $2,000 saved the place, and gave grateful relief to Mr. Kendall and family.

Having thus driven the wolf from the door, Mr. Kendall addressed himself assiduously to farming and editing. Kendall Green (the name by which he called his place) and "Kendall's Expositor" kept him fully occupied.

The possession of a piece of land he could call his own, and manage according to the dictates of his fancy, had long been with him a cherished dream. It was realized at last, though the real

Arcadia differed somewhat from the ideal. The difference was caused by the ghostly creditor whose unwelcome shadow too frequently darkened this coveted retirement.

Mr. Kendall was blessed with a wife who accommodated herself to her husband's circumstances, maintained a cheerful disposition, and practised the true philosophy of making the best of everything. Often has she remarked to the writer that she never enjoyed more real happiness than when living in the small, unfinished frame-house at Kendall Green. Their circle of friends was small, but the quality very choice.

In this situation the editor of the "Expositor" supplied his readers, at regular periods, with strong meat, calculated to develop the strength and muscle of the democracy.

His articles were noted for their simplicity, perspicuity, and vigor. Discarding learned phrases, he selected for the most part the pure Saxon. The little paper wielded an influence vainly sought by its contemporaries of larger pretensions, and won for its editor a reputation as a political writer attained by few if any in modern times. We subjoin a few extracts: —

A SHORT SERMON.

Text. — "Six days shalt thou labor, and do all thy work." — Exodus xx. 9.

My Fellow-Men: — This is the command of God! It is a part of the fourth commandment in the moral code given by God through Moses. In the Bible the whole commandment reads thus: —

"Verse 8. Remember the Sabbath day, to keep it holy.

"9. Six days shalt thou labor, and do all thy work;

"10. But the seventh day is the Sabbath of the Lord thy God; in it thou shalt not do any work, thou, nor thy son, nor thy daughter, thy man-servant, nor thy maid-servant, nor thy cattle, nor thy stranger that is within thy gates;

"11. For in six days the Lord made heaven and earth, the sea, and all that in them is, and rested the seventh day; wherefore the Lord blessed the Sabbath day, and hallowed it."

By the preaching you generally hear, you may have been led to suppose that this commandment makes but a single requisition upon you, and that is, to "remember the Sabbath day, to keep it holy." But a little attention to the language of the commandment must satisfy you that in effect it is a double commandment. It commands you to work six days, just as imperatively as to rest on the seventh. Look at it: "Remember the Sabbath day, to keep it holy." "Six days shalt thou labor, and do all thy work."

How can a command be given in more plain and imperative language?

"Six days shalt thou labor," not six days mayest thou labor; not six days mayest thou spend in idleness and waste thy time in unproductive folly. Six days shalt thou labor for the good of thyself, thy family, thy country, and thy race; I exact from thee only one day out of seven; but I command thee to labor the other six for the subsistence, the comfort, and the happiness of mankind.

That this is the meaning of the text is clear, not only from its language, but from its history. God himself worked six days before he rested one. "For in six days the Lord made heaven and earth, the sea, and all that in them is, and rested the seventh day." The commandment is founded on this example set by the Creator himself. The first part of that example is six days' labor; the rest on the seventh was but a consequence. He commands man, therefore, to do precisely what he did himself, — work six days and rest on the seventh.

Long before this commandment was given, man was doomed to labor as a part of the penalty for his first transgression. "In the sweat of thy face shalt thou eat bread," said God to Adam, Genesis iii. 19, "till thou return unto the ground." And St. Paul said, long afterwards, 2 Thessalonians iii. 10, "This we commanded you, that if any would not work, neither should he eat."

Thus we find that man was doomed to work; that he was commanded to work; and that he ought to have nothing to eat if he will not work. "In the sweat of thy face shalt thou eat bread," said God to Adam. "Six days shalt thou labor, and do all thy work," said God to Moses. "He that will not work, neither should he eat," said Paul to the Thessalonians.

Our country is not wanting in preachers of rest; but where are our preachers of work? How many sermons have we upon man's duty to rest on the seventh day, but how few upon his duty to work the other six! Yet, it may well be doubted, whether more moral evils do not flow from breaches of the working part of this commandment than of the resting part. Nay, do not gospel preachers themselves promote disobedience when they lead off men and women, during the six days, from their ordinary occupations, before they have done all their work? "Six days shalt thou labor, and do all thy work." There can be no escape from this command until all the work be done; and he who advises man or woman to leave his work undone, even for purposes most praiseworthy under other circumstances, counsels him to disobey a direct command of the Almighty.

But the evils arising from a breach of the commandment under such circumstances are but an atom compared with those which spring from the efforts of men to live without work.

Man is doomed and commanded to work. The world is filled with

misery, violence, and crime by perpetual efforts to escape his doom, in defiance of the command! Would every man be content to labor six days in seven, how much better would be his health, how much more happy his family, how much more prosperous his country! For attempting to escape his doom, and for bidding defiance to the command of the Almighty, he is cursed in his health, cursed in his family, and cursed in the troubles of his country. Did the evils fall upon the individual transgressor only, they would not be so much to be deplored; but it is necessary for those who live without work to get their subsistence out of the labor of others. Humble and honest men, who, cheerfully submitting to the doom of their race, and obeying the command, are content to work in their various avocations upon the land and the sea six days in the week, are grievously taxed to feed the rebels against God's authority who refuse to work. Grievous impositions are practised upon the true and obedient children of the Almighty, in as many ways as the first great Rebel can invent. One puts a crown on his head and tells them he is authorized by God to dispose of their property, labor, and lives according to his own will. He takes their substance to feed and clothe himself and family, his officers and armies; he compels them to sacrifice their lives in the conquest or plunder of other countries, for the gratification of his vengeance, ambition, or avarice. Others deck their heads with tiaras, coronets, and stars, and make the people work to keep them bright, and feed and enrich the haughty wearers. As the mass of mankind advance in knowledge, it becomes necessary to disguise under ingenious contrivances the process by which the products of their labor are taken from them for the support and emolument of those who refuse to work. The blasphemy of claiming a right to govern "by the grace of God" is no longer heard; but still the world has monarchs who "can do no wrong." One of these goes to war; the public "honor" and "safety" require that he shall have money to carry it on. Perhaps, not being able or willing to raise enough by taxation, he borrows a thousand millions of dollars, and then the "public faith" requires that the interest and principal shall be paid. If he borrow so much that payment of the principal becomes hopeless, yet "public faith," taking the place of the "divine right of kings," from generation to generation starves the families of those who obey Heaven's command to work six days in the seven, for the support of those who will not work at all ! !

We will not follow this chain of reasoning, lest we should seem to tread on what may be considered "holy ground." But we beg our readers to consider how much better would have been the condition of our own country if all our people had been content to obey the command, "Six days shalt thou labor, and do all thy work," instead of resorting to

so many expedients to live without work. How many have lost all they had, and made themselves and families miserable through life, by speculations entered into for the purpose of enabling them to live in idleness? What but this has caused the public distress of which we hear so much? What else has almost banished punctuality and moral honesty from the transactions of individuals and corporations? What else has created such bitter strife between man and man, and generated the agitation, profligacy, and crime which now stalk abroad in the land?

Does any one suppose that human legislation can cure the evils produced by a violation of God's commands? Vain expectation! If successful in putting bread into the mouths of those who will not work, human law-makers can effect it only by taking it out of the mouths of those who do. It would be relieving those who set at naught the laws of nature and of God, at the expense of the humble and honest men who yield them a practical obedience. There is a better and more just mode of relief. It is future obedience to God's commands. Let every man hereafter, instead of applying to the legislature of his State or to Congress for relief, labor six days in the week, and do all his work. Misery will vanish like the mists of the morning, and complaint will no more be heard in the land.

Let the legislatures and Congress, when asked to put bread in the mouth of idleness, say to the petitioners as St. Paul did to the Thessalonians, first epistle, iii. 11, 12 : "And that ye study to be quiet, and to do your own business, and to work with your own hands, as we commanded you; that ye may walk honestly towards them that are without, and that ye may have lack of nothing." And again, in his second epistle, iii. 10, 11 : "For even when we were with you, this we commanded you, that if any would not work, neither should he eat. For we hear that there are some which walk among you disorderly, working not at all, but are busybodies." And let the preachers of the gospel be advised to give more attention in their preaching to the doctrine of work. They may be assured that one of the best ways to persuade men to rest on the seventh day, is to induce them to work on the other six. Let them impress upon their hearers their obligation to keep the commandment as a whole. It is a double cord, and they cannot divide it without weakening its binding power and salutary effects.

DEATH OF PRESIDENT HARRISON.

This melancholy event occurred on Sunday morning, the 4th day of April, 1841.

Just one month from his inauguration, has General Harrison been summoned to the presence of the Almighty Ruler. He is no longer

responsible to the sons of men for his acts, and let the grave cover his foibles and his errors.

Upon his family this bereavement comes with peculiar force. What high anticipations are in a moment blasted! They have not enjoyed the elevation of their place long enough to find out how vain, and hollow, and delusive are the promises of happiness with which high station dazzles poor mortals. The rainbow of hope is made to vanish before they know how unsubstantial are its brilliant colors, and this it is, added to the pang which attends the severance of domestic ties, which makes them objects deserving universal commiseration.

Upon our country the effect of this dispensation cannot be at once perceived. Would to God the surviving leaders of the Whig party would mark the last words of their dying chief and let them sink deep into their hearts! As if half chiding an erring friend, perhaps with the dim and delirious recollection of some real scene which had passed in his cabinet, he said, "Sir, I wish you to understand the true principles of the government. I wish them carried out. I ask nothing more."

If his successor, throwing aside every other consideration, will obey this dying injunction, and carry out "the true principles of the government," our country, though she may mourn the loss of an honored son, may realize in the change more than she had a right to expect from his hands.

A FABLE.

Uncle Sam and his Dogs.

Uncle Sam had two dogs, Cesar and Pompey. Having but a single bone one day after dinner, he gave it to Pompey, and lay down to take a nap. He was scarcely asleep before Cesar began to quarrel with Pompey, who was quietly gnawing his bone in the corner. Cesar growled at Pompey, and Pompey growled back at Cesar. Cesar showed his teeth and bristled up his hair, and so did Pompey. Cesar put his paws on Pompey, and Pompey knocked them off with his paws. Cesar tried to bite Pompey, and Pompey tried to bite Cesar. In short, they got into a fierce fight for the bone, Cesar to get it and Pompey to keep it.

In the midst of the fight, one of Uncle Sam's sons came in. "Pompey," says he, "what are you quarrelling about?"

"Cesar wants my bone, and I am trying to keep it," said Pompey.

"You vile dog," says Daniel, "how dare you to fight for your bone? Father gave it to you to gnaw, and not to fight about! Here, Cesar, take the bone," and so saying he kicked Pompey out of doors.

By this time the noise had awakened the old gentleman, who came out to see what was the matter.

"Dan," says he, "what is this fuss about?"

"The rascal, Pompey," says Dan, "has been fighting for his bone, and knowing you did not give it him to fight about I gave it to Cesar, and kicked him out of doors."

"How came he to fight for his bone?"

"Cesar attempted to take it away from him."

"So Cesar began the fight?"

"Yes, sir."

"Ah, my son," said the old gentleman with a sigh, "you have done very wrong. Pompey would not have fought for his bone if Cesar had not tried to take it away from him; so that Cesar is the worse dog of the two. Indeed, Pompey was only defending the bone I gave him, and yet you punish him and reward his assailant. If you want to prevent quarrelling among the dogs about the bones I give them, you must first kick out of doors those who fight to get them; if those to whom I have given them then make a disturbance, kick them out too; but I seldom knew a dog quarrelsome so long as he was permitted to gnaw his bone in peace.

"Take a lesson from this, my son, and if you ever get to be President, and wish to prevent contention about the offices, first kick out of doors the office-seekers, and then kick after them every dog of an office-holder who will not gnaw his bone in peace."

ANOTHER SERMON.

TEXT. — "It is written, My house shall be called the house of prayer; but ye have made it a den of thieves." — Matthew xxi. 13.

This was the exclamation of Jesus, the Saviour, when he cast out of the temple at Jerusalem "them that sold and bought, and overthrew the tables of the money-changers." Trade and brokerage, with all their arts and falsehoods, had obtruded themselves into the temple of God, into the sanctuary where the Most High was wont to hold intercourse with the children of men, and the first effort of the great reformer was to drive them back to their appropriate haunts.

The great creation was God's first temple. His presence is in the sun, moon, and stars; in the earth, air, and sea. The mountains are his altars, and the ocean his laver. Incense ascends to him from all that is flowering and green; the day resounds with songs and praise; the night is mute with devotion and adoration. His voice is in the thunder; the lightnings are the twinklings of his eye. His power is exhibited in the raging wind, the rushing waters, the consuming fire, and the heaving earthquake; his goodness in the gentle breeze, the refreshing shower, the genial sun, and the earth glowing with beauty and teeming with comforts and delights.

In the midst of this temple man was placed, to adore the builder and enjoy perpetual bliss. God wanted no other house; and men needed no other place of worship. It was all that the Creator or created could want or desire. But what has man done? He has marred the building and converted it into "a den of thieves."

We shall attempt to point out briefly how this desecration has been effected, and then glance at the remedy.

1. The first step towards desecrating God's temple was the introduction of trade. There was no bargaining in Paradise until the Devil entered. The first bargain ever struck was between the woman and her tempter, in which she sold the happiness and immortality of herself, her husband, and her posterity for a promise as false and delusive as a modern bank-note. This bargain made men a bargaining race; and as the Devil cheated Eve, so have her sons and daughters been cheated unto this day. Scarcely a trade is attempted where a devil is not present whispering some kind of misrepresentation or concealment, to enable one party or both to circumvent their neighbor, and in nine tenths of the stores and shops which abound in cities and villages, the spirits of evil swarm like bees in a summer's day. Among clerks, he who can induce the daughters of Eve to make the most purchases by the arts which deceived their mother, gets the highest wages, being considered the best "salesman." And men who give a premium for the best imitation of the Devil's arts, and profit six days in the week by an incessant stream of falsehood, go to meeting on the seventh and affect to worship the God of truth that they may with more effect serve themselves and their real master during the coming six!

Yet trade in itself is not immoral. Exchanges of property among men, effected by frankness and truth, conduce to their comforts, their intelligence, and their virtue. The mischief lies in the falsehood and concealment which the desire to make many and good bargains tempts so many to commit.

2. The second step by which God's temple has been converted into "a den of thieves" is the invention of money. When money was first introduced among men, neither revelation nor history informs us. It was not of God's creation; the coining of money was no part of the first six days' work; nor did it constitute any portion of Adam's occupation in Paradise. We are told that, before the flood, the son of Cain was "the father of such as wrought in iron and brass"; but nothing is said of gold and silver or of money. How Noah paid the builders of the ark, or his descendants the workingmen upon the tower of Babel, has not been recorded. The first account we have of money in the Scriptures may be found in the twenty-third chapter of Genesis, where it is stated that Abraham bought the field of Machpelah for "four hundred

shekels of silver," verse 16: "And Abraham hearkened unto Ephron; and Abraham weighed to Ephron the silver, which he had named in the audience of the sons of Heth, four hundred shekels of silver, current money with the merchant."

In chapter xxxiii., verse 19, we are told that Jacob "bought a parcel of a field where he had spread his tent, at the hand of the children of Hamor, Shechem's father, for an hundred pieces of money."

Abraham weighed out the silver, and Jacob counted out the money, showing that in Jacob's time, if not in Abraham's, money passed by the count just as it does to this day.

The invention of money introduced no new principle into trade, but merely facilitated its operations. Gold and silver were always valuable in all trading nations, whether coined into money or not, and from the earliest ages could be readily exchanged for other property. Coining them is nothing more than dividing them into parcels of a definite and uniform weight, after being reduced to the same standard of fineness, so that, in being exchanged for other articles, they require neither weighing nor examination. They did not derive their value from being coined; but they were coined because they were intrinsically valuable, and of more uniform and more general value among mankind than any other article. Because they were valuable, and because their quality and weight when coined into money were defined by public authority, they became at an early age the most desirable property among mankind. The universal scramble was for that kind of property called money; the temple of God was desecrated, not only by buyers and sellers, but by money-changers; and to such excesses did the accursed lust for gold carry men, that an inspired Apostle said, "the love of money is the root of all evil."

Yet money in itself is no greater evil than any other article of merchandise. Honestly obtained, and prudently applied, it is a valuable auxiliary to human comfort and happiness, a powerful instrument in spreading the blessings of civilization and the light of truth. It is by the "love" of it, by the bad uses to which it has been applied, the gratification of man's vicious appetites and passions, the buying of men and women over to vice by its tempting lure, the hiring of assassins and armies to scatter death and desolation through families and nations, that money has been a tremendous engine in desecrating the original temple of God.

3. But the most effective cause of the downward career of human virtue now operating in the world, and especially in our own country, is the introduction of paper-money, and more particularly the notes of banks, companies, or individuals, to be used as a substitute for money. There were no banks or paper-money in Paradise. Men could be happy there

without them. For thousands and thousands of years, there were no bank-notes among mankind; all their business was managed very well without them. Although one might think from the importance now attached to banks and paper-money, that man cannot be happy without them, there is no trace of any such contrivance in the Old Testament or the New, among the prophets or the saints, or even among the moralists, philosophers, or lawgivers of Greece or Rome, of Egypt or Persia, of India or China. Neither Moses nor Jesus, Brahma nor Mahomet, Confucius nor Socrates ever taught or appear to have conceived such a method to make a people happy or a country prosperous.

It would seem that the arch-enemy of man became dissatisfied with the money of Abraham and Jacob, of the Greeks and Romans, of the Jews and Gentiles. It had too much of truth in it! The man who exchanged his lands, his produce, or his goods for it, received value for value. No failing individual, breaking bank, or tumbling government could in a moment reduce him and his family to poverty and want. His country might flame with revolution, invading armies might burn his house and desolate his fields, here is a kind of property which, buried in the earth until the storm has passed, may be dug from its hiding-place, unimpaired in its value, which will at once procure him the means of subsistence, or enable him to reach another land. This comfort and security to the humble man, limited and inadequate as it was, still left him with something of good. To deprive him of this resource, and provide means for inflicting new wrongs and tortures, the spirit of evil appears to have devoted the utmost exertion of his inventive powers, and the result was — paper money.

How this new invention operates to convert the temple of God into a den of thieves, we shall show hereafter.

In September, 1841, "encouraged by improved health, and stimulated by a desire to participate more largely in the discussion of the great questions which engrossed the attention of the country," Mr. Kendall issued his prospectus for the weekly publication of the "Union Democrat," "devoted to the preservation of the Union and the support of democracy."

TARIFF TAXATION.

Dialogue between two Farmers.

FARMER SMITH. Neighbor Jones, you are always talking about the tax that Congress has imposed on us by the bill increasing the duties on goods brought from foreign parts. I am sure I pay no tax to the government at Washington.

FARMER JONES. You don't! Don't you use salt in your family, and give it to your cattle?

FAR. S. Certainly; but I don't pay any tax on that.

FAR. J. You do indeed; the government takes from you one bushel out of every six, or makes you pay for five bushels as much money as would buy six if there was no tariff, and a little more.

FAR. S. I don't understand that; please to explain.

FAR. J. The tariff imposes a tax of twenty per cent on all the salt brought into the country, which the government makes the merchant pay to its collectors in the cities. On every five bushels he lands from the ships, the government makes him pay as much as one bushel is worth. That increases the cost to him one fifth. When he goes to sell it to the farmers, he adds what he pays the government to the price, and so makes the farmers pay it back to him. Do you understand it?

FAR. S. I think I do. If the merchant pays a dollar for two bushels, the government makes him pay twenty cents to the collector, and when he comes to sell it to us he makes us pay him a dollar and twenty cents for the two bushels.

FAR. J. Exactly; that is the principle; but the practical effect is worse than that. The merchant, you know, must have his profit on all the money he pays out for the salt, whether to the maker, the importer, or to the government. He adds the same rate of profit to the twenty cents paid for duty as he does to the one dollar paid for the salt. If his profit be twenty per cent, it amounts to four cents on the duty, so that for every twenty cents the merchant pays the government, the farmer pays twenty-four cents to the merchant.

FAR. S. Yes, yes; I see it now. But much of the salt we buy is made in this country, and they don't tax us on that.

FAR. J. It is all the same thing. The same tax which compels the importing merchant to raise the price of the salt, that comes from abroad, twenty-four cents on every dollar's worth, enables the maker of salt at home to increase the price of his salt twenty-four cents on the dollar's worth also.

FAR. S. I see that; but it don't go to the government.

FAR. J. Whom does it go to?

FAR. S. To the salt-maker, I suppose.

FAR. J. Exactly so; and in that way the tariff makes the farmer pay to the salt-maker twenty-four per cent more on every dollar's worth of salt bought of him than he would have to pay if there was no tariff at all.

FAR. S. Mr. Clay says this is to protect home industry.

FAR. J. Does that law protect your industry or mine, or that of any other farmer, mechanic, or day laborer, which compels us to give twenty-

four per cent. more for our salt than we would have to give if there was no tariff at all?

FAR. S. Well, well, I never thought of this thing before; I will go home and think about it, and then talk with you again.

TARIFF TAXATION.

Second Dialogue between two Farmers.

FARMER JONES. Well, I have been thinking about the tax on salt, and have had a talk with Tom Twist, our Whig candidate for the legislature.

FARMER SMITH. What says Mr. Twist?

FAR. J. He says, if the tariff did n't make us pay more than we should otherwise have to pay for our salt, the salt-makers could n't buy so much of our corn and meat, so that the tariff tax on salt improves our market.

FAR. S. Do you believe him?

FAR. J. Why it seems reasonable.

FAR. S. If a fellow should steal five dollars out of your pocket, and then buy your corn with it, would it do you any good?

FAR. J. Do me good to buy my corn with my own money! Nonsense.

FAR. S. Yet it would improve your market more than the tariff. The thief improves your market one hundred per cent upon the amount he takes from you, whereas the salt-maker, with the aid of the tariff, only improves it twenty-four per cent.

FAR. J. I'll tell Tom Twist about it.

FAR. S. No, no; think for yourself. It is because we farmers pin our faith too much on other men's sleeves that we are so much cheated and taxed.

FAR. J. Well, well, I did n't exactly understand you.

FAR. S. Tom Twist says, the money the tariff takes from us improves our market by enabling the salt-makers to buy more of our corn. Well, for the sake of argument, admit that Tom is right. The tariff now takes twenty-four per cent, which, we will say, improves our market for corn twenty-four per cent.

FAR. J. Yes.

FAR. S. Well, if it took fifty per cent, it would, on the same principle, improve our market fifty per cent, would it not?

FAR. J. Yes; it seems so.

FAR. S. And if it took eighty per cent, it would improve our market eighty per cent?

FAR. J. Yes.

FAR. S. And if it took one hundred per cent, it would make our market just as good again, would it?

FAR. J. Why, that would be the same thing as stealing my own money to buy my corn with!

FAR. S. Pretty much. You see now what Tom Twist's argument amounts to. If a small tariff improves our market a little, a large one will improve it much more, so that the higher the tax the better for the farmers taxed. What excellent markets we shall have when taxed to the amount of all we can earn and a little more!

FAR. J. It is strange what different conclusions men will come to. You and Mr. Twist, how different you make things look.

FAR. S. Look here, brother farmer, would n't you like to get a better price for your corn, in order that you may buy more salt than you do now, to give to your cattle?

FAR. J. Certainly, if I could get it honestly.

FAR. S. Well, if making us farmers pay twenty-four per cent more for salt improves our market for corn, by the same rule, making the salt-maker pay twenty-four per cent more for corn would improve his market for salt, would it not?

FAR. J. I suppose it would; "it is a poor rule that won't work both ways."

FAR. S. Well, the next time you see Tom Twist, do you ask him if it would not be a good thing to improve the market for salt; he will say yes; then tell him you have a plan founded on established principles, by which that object can be effected, and that is, that when he gets into the legislature he shall get a law passed making the salt-maker pay twenty-four per cent more for our corn, and then we can buy more of his salt.

FAR. J. Excellent! I'll put him up to it. Why should n't the law make the salt-maker pay more for our corn, if it makes us pay more for his salt? And why should n't taxing him improve his market, if taxing us improves our market?

FAR. S. Just so; let me know what turn Tom Twist will take to get out of that difficulty, will you?

FAR. J. That I will.

PARTY NAMES.

It is but fair to let every party select its own name. In the original division of parties in this country, one took the name of "Federalists," which then meant "Friends of the Union"; and the other, though not less friends of the Union, were content to take that of "Republicans." It was not long before the Federal party began to call themselves "Federal Republicans," and then the old Republican party began to take the name of "Democratic Republicans."

The conduct of the Federal party during the last war rendered the originally honorable appellation of Federalist so odious to the people, that those who had gloried in it sought to cast it off, and began to call themselves "National Republicans." This name, however, did not render them more acceptable to the people; their former principles and conduct were remembered; and they remained aliens to the confidence and honors of the country.

In the mean time a large portion of the old Republican leaders had become Federalists in principle, and the old lines ceased to be drawn, in Congress and out, although vast numbers of individuals still maintained their original faith in all its purity. This was the state of things when John Quincy Adams was elected President of the United States.

In the contest which ensued, original principles had less to do than the peculiar character of the election. The great mass of the old Federalists, with many Republicans, adhered to Mr. Adams; but there were not a few of the Federal party who supported General Jackson. There was at that time a general confusion of old parties, although the ultra Federalism indicated in some of Mr. Adams' measures and declarations began to excite alarm.

General Jackson's administration had not progressed far before that general shaking commenced which was destined, after a long agony, to separate parties on original principles, much better defined and understood than they were even in the days of Jefferson. The leading question tending to this result, related to a renewal of the United States Bank charter; and connected with this were internal improvements and the tariff. The Bank, possessing "the sinews of war," and a disposition to use them, was the only formidable adversary reviving Republicanism had to encounter. Its corruptions in attempting to arrest the grand reformation, are now recorded as a part of its history, and may everywhere be traced among its ruins.

In the mean time the Republicans began to call themselves Democrats. In former times there had been objections to this term, on the ground that our government is not technically a democracy; but that feeling had passed away. Every thing in our forms of government had been becoming more democratic from the adoption of our Federal Constitution. Scarcely a State constitution had been formed which did not bring the officers of government nearer to the people; and the general government, though not altered in form, had, particularly in the election of the President, and in the practice of the Senate, become more popular than was anticipated by those who framed it. That distrust of the people which prevailed to a great extent after the close of the revolutionary war had measurably ceased, and the principles and name of Democracy had become universally popular.

It became necessary that the party arraying itself against this new movement to introduce pure principles and practices into the General Government, should have a distinctive appellation. "Federal" would not do, and for some time they seemed at a loss. At length one of the Bank-bought organs in New York suggested the name of "Whig." This also was a popular name long borne by the friends of liberty in England, and, in contrast with Tory, favorably remembered in connection with our revolutionary history. The suggestion was well received by the enemies of Democracy, and they soon called themselves Whigs throughout the Union.

Who does not remember the language of the lamented Forsyth in the Senate, when this name became current in that body? While he admitted that his political adversaries had a right to choose a name for their party, he regretted that they had selected the term Whig, "for," said he, "it is an old and honored name, and I am sure they will disgrace it." He spoke the language of most Democrats. They were willing their adversaries should select the name by which they should be called; they conceded to them the title of "Whigs," though not without regret, knowing that their principles would soon become as well understood under that name as any other.

But while we concede to our opponents a right to select their own party name, we protest against their robbing us of ours, or forcing a new one upon us. The Democratic Republican party of this country have never disgraced their name. As the Federalists sought to obtain confidence by calling themselves Federal Republicans, so the Whigs are attempting to gild their already tarnished name by calling themselves Democratic Whigs. Indeed in some places, we believe, they drop the name Whig altogether, and claim to be Democrats! And while doing this, their organs are engaged in attempting to fix the term "Loco Foco" on the Democratic party! Some of them, among whom is the "National Intelligencer," uniformly class the parties as "Whigs" and "Loco Focos." This is not fair, gentlemen. Change your own name, if you please, as often as you disgrace it; but do not interfere with ours. Do not claim the right to name both parties, to put a new name upon us as often as detection dictates the necessity of taking a new one for yourselves, to rob us of a name we have honored to be disgraced by a party which dishonors all names. Take any other name but "Democrat," — we will call you by any you will stick to for a twelvemonth; the term "Democrat" is ours; except that, and you may disgrace every word in the dictionary, but you shall not, without opposition, reduce "Democrat" to the level of "Federalist" or "Whig."

Some Democrats, we perceive, are accommodating enough to adopt the name "Loco-Foco" prescribed by their adversaries. To the term itself

there is no peculiar objection; and if there were, the principles of Democracy would soon render it honorable. We object to it because "Democrat" is the most appropriate name, and already honored. It is not right that we should consent to honor a new name as often as our adversaries dishonor an old one. It takes the people some little time to understand the meaning and application of new names; and it is enough to concede to our adversaries the right to rid themselves of names which the people do understand, without suffering them to subject us to the disadvantage of names which the people do not understand. Much less should we suffer them to appropriate to themselves our honored name in place of their dishonored name. No, no; let us resist this insolence and stick to the name "Democrat."

Our general custom is to call one party Democrats and the other Whigs; and this we shall continue until the latter agree on some new alias other than "Democrat," under which to fight their future battles. The name of Democrat and the principles it indicates we will never surrender.

TARIFF TAXATION.

Third Dialogue. Farmer Jones, Farmer Smith, and Lawyer Twist.

FARMER SMITH. Brother Jones, I have brought our candidate along to hear an argument between you and him about the tariff tax on salt and the price of corn.

FARMER JONES. Well, I will say what I think, but can scarcely hope to hold an argument with so good a lawyer.

LAWYER TWIST. Thank you, farmer, for your compliment. Neighbor Smith says you want me to pledge myself, if elected, to get a law passed if I can to make the salt-maker pay twenty-four per cent more than the usual price for all the corn he buys. Did I understand him right?

FAR. J. Yes.

TWIST. Why, you are not so unreasonable as to want such a law passed.

FAR. J. Why not? The farmer is taxed for the benefit of the salt-maker twenty-four per cent on all the salt he buys, and why should not the salt-maker be taxed for the benefit of the farmer twenty-four per cent on all the corn and other products of the earth he buys? But the chief object of the protective tariff, you know, is to "improve the home market." And we want you to tax the salt-maker twenty-four per cent on all the corn he buys, for the purpose of improving his market for salt.

TWIST. A curious way that to improve a man's market?

FAR. J. Why curious, Mr. Twist?

TWIST. Why, is any one simple enough not to see that if you make the salt-maker pay me twenty-four per cent more than he does now, it

will lessen his profits and perhaps ruin his business? Improve his market, indeed!

FAR. J. My dear sir, don't you perceive that if you make the salt-maker pay me twenty-four per cent more than he does now for my corn, I shall have more money to buy his salt with, whereby his market will be improved, and he will sell more salt?

TWIST. And what good would it do him, pray, to sell more salt, if he has to furnish you with money to buy it, by giving you a higher price for your corn?

FAR. J. My notion exactly. But I want you to tell me now, what advantage it is to the farmers to sell more corn to the salt-makers and manufacturers, if they have, through a tariff tax, to furnish the money to buy it with?

TWIST. The tariff tax don't go to the manufacturer, but to the government.

FAR. J. The object of a protective tariff tax is to raise the price of foreign goods, and enable our manufacturers to sell theirs at higher prices. The tariff tax on foreign goods goes to the government; but this increased price or tariff tax on goods made at home, goes to the manufacturer, salt-maker, etc., and we farmers pay it. We give twenty-four per cent more for goods made in the country than we would have to give if there was no tax on the foreign goods. In this way the farmers are made to furnish the manufacturers, salt-makers, etc., with money to buy their own corn. This is the way the tariff improves the farmer's market. It taxes him twenty-four per cent on all the goods he buys, and does not confer on him a benefit of ten per cent in return, either in the greater quantity of produce sold or in its advanced price.

TWIST. It is very important, you know, that our country should be independent of foreigners, and that we should foster our own industry rather than that of other countries.

FAR. J. "Foster our own industry." That's exactly my notion again; but let me ask you one question on that point: Do foreigners pay any part of our tariff tax?

TWIST. No; it is all paid by our own citizens.

FAR. J. Very well. Then we tax our own citizens for the benefit of our own citizens, and what advantage is it to them to be taxed for their own benefit?

TWIST. Why, it is not altogether so. All are not taxed alike, nor do all profit alike by the tax. The tariff taxes all who buy foreign goods or products, or domestic goods of the same kinds, and by a moderate tax on all, enables our salt-makers and manufacturers to sustain their business and get rich.

FAR. J. Exactly so; to get rich by imposing on me, on Farmer Smith, and on every other farmer, mechanic, laborer, and professional man in the nation, a tax of twenty-four per cent on all we buy. This, you see, is taxing the many to enrich the few. A thousand are taxed to make one rich.

TWIST. Well, are not important advantages gained by it? Do we not make our country independent, and enrich our own people, instead of giving our money to foreign manufacturers?

FAR. J. I'll tell you what I think about that; but must first ask a question or two. Our country produces no silver, you know, and but little gold. Now, how does gold and silver money get into this country?

TWIST. Why, our merchants bring it in for our products or manufactures, sold for it in other countries.

FAR. J. How do British goods, French and Spanish goods and wines, and the manufactures and produce of all foreign lands get into this country?

TWIST. By the merchants, in the same way.

FAR. J. Then we sell something abroad for everything we buy from abroad?

TWIST. As a general principle we do; for we have no other way to pay for foreign articles.

FAR. J. You say, that when we buy foreign products and manufactures we encourage foreign labor, do you?

TWIST. Certainly.

FAR. J. Well, on the same principle, when foreigners buy our products and manufactures, they encourage our labor, do they not?

TWIST. Undoubtedly.

FAR. J. And is it not by our buying their products and manufactures that they get the means to buy ours?

TWIST. I suppose it is.

FAR. J. Then if we encourage their industry they encourage ours. The more they sell to us, the more they can buy from us; the benefit is reciprocal, and if governments would but allow free-trade we could exchange a great deal more than we do now. I hold that a perfectly free trade is the best protection for our labor. If the financial condition of the government would permit, I would abolish the tariff altogether.

TWIST. How no restriction at all upon the importation of foreign articles is to protect American labor, I think it will be difficult for you to show.

FAR. J. Not at all. We pay a tax, say of twenty-five per cent, including merchant's profit on the duty and charges, on all articles imported from foreign countries. I want to buy clothing for my children, and the merchant has cloth which, were it not for the tariff tax, he would sell at one dollar a yard; but that tax raises the price to a dollar and a quarter. I take five bushels of wheat to market for the purpose of getting money to buy the cloth with, and sell it at a dollar a bushel, making five dollars. With this five dollars I could buy five yards of cloth but for the tariff tax; as it is, I can get but four for it. Now, which system protects my labor best, that which gives me five yards of cloth for five bushels of wheat, or that which gives me only four yards for five bushels?

TWIST. I never carried my thoughts so far.

FAR. J. I beg you to run your thoughts over the system, and consider its bearings on every branch of American labor. To my mind the following principle is clear, viz.: —

The labor of a country is best protected when it is most free to exchange its products with the labor of all other countries. Every tariff tax imposed on exports or imports lessens the profits of labor, often in both countries, by lessening the amount which can be obtained in exchange for their products.

CRAWFORD'S STATUE OF WASHINGTON.

"De gustibus non est disputandum" (there is no disputing about tastes), says an old Roman maxim. If our statue of Washington were merely a matter of taste, we should have nothing to say about it; but looking upon it in a very different light, we feel called upon to enlarge somewhat upon the views heretofore expressed.

We protest against the ground assumed by many of our contemporaries, that in the statue of Washington, or any other work of the sort, the artist is at liberty to sport his fancy or indulge his genius at the expense of historical truth. Nor do we believe that such a license ever entered into the principles or practice of ancient sculptors. The exact imitation of nature was by them considered the perfection of the arts. Who that has read the history of the arts in Greece, does not remember the admiration expressed at the skill of the painter who represented grapes so true to nature on his canvas that the birds pecked at them, mistaking them for real grapes? If a Greek sculptor had been set to produce a statue of Themistocles, would he have considered himself at liberty to present to his countrymen the body and costume of an Indian Brahmin, surmounted with the head of the Athenian hero? If a Roman sculptor had been employed to make a statue of Cicero, would he have considered himself at liberty to place the head of the Roman orator upon the body of an Egyptian god?

The error of our contemporaries seems to us to have arisen from the fact, that many of the subjects of sculpture in ancient times were themselves wholly imaginary. Such was their Jupiter, their Hercules, their Venus; the whole race of gods and goddesses, their palaces and the regions they inhabited. Here the sculptor or the painter might give full scope to his imagination, and he who could infuse into his work the most of majesty, of strength, of beauty, or whatever other attribute the imaginations or superstitions of men ascribed to the particular object as its predominating characteristic, was justly considered the most eminent artist. Even here, however, the excellence consisted in the nearest approximation to ideal truth. The license which ancient artists justly exercised in delineating imaginary or invisible beings, our modern critics are inclined to permit in works purely historical. Do not antiquaries consider a statue of any distinguished man, now found among ancient ruins, as one of their greatest treasures, simply because it is presumed to resemble the original? Do they not attach a high value to every newly discovered delineation upon canvas or stone of ancient costume, utensils, instruments, or manners? Why is this, if it be conceded that ancient artists were at liberty to indulge their fancy at the expense of reality and truth?

If our statue of Washington had been found in the ruins of Herculaneum, it would have been considered the representative of some Roman hero, statesman, or god, so completely do the dress, the sword, the sandals, and all that appertains to the main work, belong to the Roman age. True, we have an ornament to the chair, mixed up with antiquity, the representation of an American Indian; but this would be taken rather as an evidence that the Romans were not ignorant of America than that the work belonged to modern times. Indeed, every beholder ignorant of the history of this work, and of the peculiarities of Washington's face, would take this statue to be, either a relic of antiquity or a modern imitation of ancient works of art. He would undoubtedly wonder by what rule of art or taste the American Indian was introduced into the company of the old Roman; but he could have no conception that the subject of the work was exclusively American. And we ask the admirers of this work, or rather of its plan, whether, except the face of Washington and the Indian upon the back of the chair, there is the least circumstance about it to identify it as belonging to this age or this continent?

They see our beloved Washington, most admired when delineated precisely as he was, converted into a Roman and thrown back almost two thousand years before he lived. They see him, not as he was, a man and an American, surrounded by the incidents of his country and his age, but in the dimensions of a giant, denationalized, banished, sent

back to antiquity as if his own character and feats were not "beyond all Greek, all Roman fame." Nor are the fictions with which he is surrounded the productions of modern genius or imagination, but mere copies from the works of the ancients!

Were there no passages in Washington's life worthy of the artist's genius? What of a devout cast can be conceived more imposing than Washington on his knees in the woods, pouring forth the whole of his mighty soul in earnest supplications to Heaven for the rescue and salvation of his country? What of a moral sublime could exceed the scene at the battle of Monmouth, when, on the approach of General Lee who marred the anticipated triumph of the day by an untimely retreat, Washington raised his voice in anger, and as his aid General Scott said, it seemed as if the leaves of the old oak under which they stood trembled with awe? Is there no room for genius in depicting the mingled joy, triumph, and gratitude to Heaven which must have illuminated the noble features of Washington when he saw the independence of his country secured by the capture of Lord Cornwallis and his army? And were there no incidents in the battles of the Revolution more worthy to adorn our hero's chair than fanciful scenes borrowed from a heathen mythology?

Statuary, when it pretends to present realities, should be as true as history. It should so present sensible objects that a thousand years hence they will convey, as far as they go, the exact truth in reference to the age in which they existed. The incidents and ornaments which surround the men whom it delineates in stone may be selected and arranged according to the taste and genius of the artist; but even these should have strict reference to the current age. If artists choose to indulge in works of fancy, let them do so; let them make as many Jupiters and Herculeses and Venuses and Titans and Neptunes as they please, and dress them as they like; but let them not put upon the bodies of these profane gods the heads of modern statesmen or heroes. Greece and Rome had their statuary, which was Greek and Roman; why should not we have a statuary all American? True genius will display itself, not in servile imitations of ancient art, but in making the new objects and combinations of modern times appear like reality itself upon the canvass and in marble. We do not despair of seeing a work of art which will make even the buff-faced coat and the cocked hat of the Revolution admired in a statue, so true to the reality shall be the work of the artist. In forming new combinations of real objects and adding to real scenes the enchantments of art, is the true, the broad, the almost uncultivated field of modern genius. American artists! this is your true field of glory. Study the excellencies of ancient art in Italy or Greece, or wherever you find them; but do not forget that

their chief excellence, at last, consists in their conformity to truth, real or ideal, — real when they profess to represent visible objects, ideal when the main subject is imaginary. But do not bring together those objects which are incongruous in nature or far separated in history. Do not, in historical works which pertain to modern times, put the bust of a man upon the body of a horse, or the head of a general upon the body of a Hercules. Do not borrow robes from the Romans to cover the nakedness of Americans, or substitute the sword of Rome, which enslaved the world, for the glorious weapon raised by our revolutionary fathers, whose gleamings are lighting mankind on the path of liberty. If you have not genius enough to make modern realities interesting, confine yourselves to works of mere fancy or to imitations of Greek and Roman originals.

It may be, that for these remarks we shall be considered barbarian in taste ourselves. One thing is certain, we shall never affect an admiration we do not feel, for the purpose of being considered a man of taste. Our taste, whatever name it may merit, cannot endure a figure which presents the head of a man upon the body of a beast, or the head of a beast upon the body of a man, the dress of an American on the body of a Roman, or the dress of a Roman on the body of an American. Such combinations, we think, belong either to the first or the last stages of the art; to the first, before its true objects and principles are properly understood, or to the last, when taste is vitiated and genius extinguished in vice and corruption, and not to that glorious middle age when practical virtue and cultivated mind teach men to recognize as beautiful only that which is true.

Upon the statue of Washington we look with mingled emotions of reverence and disgust. Who can but feel reverence on looking at those venerated features? But when the eye falls upon the body and its incidents, deep in our bosom is the feeling of sorrow and disgust that a head so sacred should be made to surmount objects so profane. But for the head, we should say, Remove it, put it out of sight, out of memory. As it is, we say to Congress, Do what you please.

In justice to the artist, we feel it our duty to add the tribute of our admiration for the manner in which the work is executed. On this point, we believe there is no difference of opinion. It is the design, and not the execution, which meets with extensive condemnation. And if what we have said shall wound the feelings of the artist, with whom we are not acquainted, we shall sincerely regret it. Our object is not to wound the feelings of any one, but simply to protest against, and prevent if we can, the introduction of what we call a barbarian taste into our works of art.

CHAPTER XVI.

OUR OWN AFFAIRS.

To the Democracy and to Practical Printers.

THE "Union Democrat" has been published six months, and numbers less than 1,200 subscribers. Of nearly 11,000 who took the first volume of "Kendall's Expositor," less than 1,600 have subscribed for the second. The entire subscription to both will barely pay expenses, and our current receipts are not sufficient to pay our printer. Our pecuniary arrangements were based on the confident expectation of receiving and retaining to both papers 8,000 to 10,000 subscribers. Of course they are all deranged, and we find our finances very much in the condition of those of the government.

Our friends attribute it to the hardness of the times, and we get kind letters from retiring subscribers; but "good words butter no parsnips." Our family must be supported, and creditors must be paid. For the means, we have no resource immediately available but our personal exertions. Lands we have, which we do not mean to give away, like our Whig economists; but it takes time to sell them, and they cannot be sold at this time without great sacrifice. Yet, unless better supported in our present business, we shall be obliged to abandon it, to sell property at whatever sacrifice, pay debts, and at the age of fifty-three begin the world again. To this turn of fortune, if it must come, we shall most cheerfully submit, though produced by responsibilities not originally our own, and by law expenses and damages imposed upon us in consequence of having been honest in office.

Could we give our time to it, we doubt not the number of our subscribers might readily be doubled. But cur health, which has been greatly improved by manual labor, requires that at least half of each day shall be so devoted, and the other half is not too much for that reading and writing necessary to make a paper interesting and instructive.

In May, 1842, after an existence of nine months, the publication of the "Union Democrat" ceased for want of adequate patronage.

PRESENTS TO PUBLIC MEN.

There is a mode of operating upon public men, common in this country, so nearly akin to corruption as to make the difference practically unimportant. The good will and kind feelings of the officers of government — inclining them to lean, perhaps unconsciously, to the interests of individuals, and sometimes producing the mischievous effects of direct bribes — are secured by presents, personal favors, and pecuniary obligations.

On taking charge of the Fourth Auditor's Office, we learned that some of the pursers of the navy and navy agents were in the habit of making valuable presents to the clerks who examined their accounts, thereby creating advocates in the office. We forbade the clerks receiving any present of value from those whose accounts they had to settle, on pain of instant removal.

A similar practice prevailed to a greater and more mischievous extent in the Post-Office Department. We were scarcely warm in our seat there, before presents from contractors began to come in upon us. On one occasion a whole deer, just killed, came down from the mountains and made its appearance one morning in the passage of the Post-Office Department. By a letter on our table, we learned that it was a present from a mail contractor. Said we to ourself, "An application for an extra allowance is not far behind."

The contractor, in his letter, requested us to send a piece to his old friend, Parson B. Availing ourselves of this request, we sent for the Parson, and delivered him the whole animal, not caring to eat meat for which we expected to be called on to pay out of the funds of the Post-Office Department. Sure enough, in a few days, here came the contractor with a project for an improvement in his mail service, which would increase his pay, and in other respects greatly promote his private interests. We were as little inclined to swallow his project as his present.

We were not two weeks in the Department before a clerk spontaneously offered to lend us money! In our heart we pronounced him a corrupt man, and took the first convenient opportunity to get rid of him. We have since ascertained that he was an agent and a spy of certain powerful contractors in the Department.

The subject of the *tariff* is usually considered a dry one, suited only for the consideration of legislators and politicians.

The luminous pen of Mr. Kendall invests this theme with so much light, clearing it of mystery, and bringing it within the comprehension of minds capable of reasoning upon any subject, that

we have deemed his articles worthy of insertion in full. The most of them were written in the spring of 1843.

TARIFF TAXATION.

The Principles and Effects of Duties on Imported Produce and Merchandise, whether for Revenue, Protection, or Retaliation, clearly illustrated by fact and argument.

A tariff is a duty or tax levied upon produce or merchandise transported from one country to another.

In most commercial countries, both exports and imports are thus taxed; but the Constitution of the United States forbids a tax on exports.

A tariff is a tax upon the surplus products of human labor, falling directly upon the domestic consumer, and indirectly on the foreign producer. It increases the prices of all the articles on which it is levied. If it be $33\frac{1}{3}$ per cent on the value of the article taxed, the importer pays $33\frac{1}{3}$ per cent more for it than he otherwise would. He gives four dollars for that which would otherwise cost him but three. Of that four dollars, three go to the foreign merchant or producer, and one to his own government.

But the amount of the tax does not ultimately come out of the importer. With him it is a part of the price of the goods, and in selling them to the merchant he charges it as such and adds his profit upon the whole. With the wholesale merchant the original cost, the government tax, and the importer's profit constitute the cost, and upon the aggregate of all three he calculates his profit. With the retail dealer, the original cost, the government tax, the importer's profit, and the wholesale merchant's profit constitute the cost, and he puts his profit upon all four. Finally, to the farmers, mechanics, and others, who purchase for consumption, the cost is made up of the original price, the government tax, the importer's profit, the wholesale merchant's profit, and the retail dealer's profit, all of which they refund out of the fruits of their own labor or the proceeds of their income. Thus:—

The cost of three yards of cloth imported into New York is three dollars	$ 3.00
The government tax is $33\frac{1}{3}$ per cent, or one dollar	1.00
Cost to importer	4.00
Importer's profit, say 5 per cent	20
Cost to wholesale merchant	4.20
Wholesale merchant's profit, say 10 per cent	42
Cost to retail dealer	4.62
Retail dealer's profit, say 20 per cent	$92\frac{4}{10}$
Cost to the farmer and other consumer	$5.54\frac{4}{10}$

If the goods pass through more hands, the cost to the consumer is still further increased. To the frontier settler who receives his foreign goods from the petty dealers in his vicinity, they undoubtedly cost on an average three times their original price.

The amount of the government tax is of course increased in the same ratio. In the foregoing case the government tax paid by the importer is	$ 1.00
Importer's profit, 5 per cent	5
Government tax as paid by wholesale merchant	1.05
Wholesale merchant's profit, 10 per cent	$10\frac{1}{2}$
Government tax as paid by retail merchant	$1.15\frac{1}{2}$
Retail dealer's profit, 20 per cent	$23\frac{1}{10}$
Government tax as paid by the farmer and other consumer	$1.38\frac{6}{10}$

Thus the farmer and other consumers pay *one dollar thirty-eight cents* for *every dollar* raised for government by a tariff tax of $33\frac{1}{3}$ per cent. If the tax be less, the consumers pay less for the article itself; if it be more, they pay more; but whatever the amount of the original tax may be, they pay the same rate of increase upon it arising from merchant's profit. Over our whole country, that increase cannot fall short of $33\frac{1}{3}$ per cent on an average. It may be less in the Atlantic cities where the goods have passed through few hands; it is much more in the distant interior, where dealers' profits have been multiplied.

For every $ 100, therefore, raised by a tariff tax, the people pay $ $133\frac{1}{3}$; for every $ 1,000, $ $1,333\frac{1}{3}$; $ $1,333,333\frac{1}{3}$ for every $ 1,000,000. If the government raise $ 20,000,000 by a tariff tax, the people pay no less than $ $26,666,666\frac{2}{3}$, and that when the tariff is *purely for revenue.*

Cost of Collection, etc.

Cheapness of collection is sometimes alleged to be one of the advantages of a tariff tax. The preceding facts show a cost to the people exceeding that which attaches to the collection of any other description of tax known among communities or nations. Yet it does not include the salaries and fees of those employed in the collection which come out of the amount of the original tax. Those expenses are probably 8 to 10 per cent more, and bring the cost to the people of collecting a tariff tax up to about 45 per cent upon the amount which actually goes into the Treasury.

The commission for collecting the United States direct taxes was, we believe, *five per cent*, and there are probably few taxes laid by States or corporations upon which the commission for collecting exceeds that rate.

Nor are its comparative advantages greater in reference to the number of persons employed in the process. The collectors at custom-houses, with their corps of officers, clerks, porters, and draymen, and the officers and crews of revenue cutters, are but a small portion of the number engaged in collecting a tariff tax. This kind of tax converts every importer of merchandise, every wholesale merchant, and every retail dealer in city and country, down to the pedler who sells pins and needles, into a collector of taxes for the government. Each is paid for his services by that portion of his profits which is based on the original government tax and forms a part of the price of the articles he sells, and the whole comes out of the farmers and other consumers at last. Our tariff revenue for the current year is estimated at $ 18,000,000. To get this into the Treasury the people pay to revenue officers, importers, merchants, and dealers of all sorts, at least 45 per cent, or about $ 8,100,000, making the whole amount paid by them $ 26,100,000.

Who Pays the Tax, etc.

Every man in the nation who purchases for consumption or use a single article embraced in the tariff, pays a portion of the tax and of the cost of collection. It encroaches upon the salary of the clergyman, of the public officer, and of the whole salaried corps in church and state. It breaks in upon the income of the clerk, the lawyer, the marshal, the sheriff, the justice, the constable, and all those who live by fees. These classes are remunerated, however, when the burden on their income is made too heavy, by laws and arrangements increasing their income. The importer if he resides in this country, the merchant, and dealer are themselves taxed in proportion to the amount of taxed articles they consume by themselves or their families. But when they feel the burden too heavily, they remunerate themselves by increasing the rate of profits on their merchandise.

Weight on Producing Classes.

Upon the producing classes, the farmers, planters, mechanics and laborers, the burden falls, not only without a possibility of remuneration, but aggravated by the increased salaries, fees, and profits it compels other classes to demand and exact.

Here is a farmer whose surplus profit for the year consists of three hundred bushels of wheat, worth one dollar a bushel, or $300 in cash. This is the amount he has to buy clothing and other comforts for his family, and farming utensils for his next year's operations. Suppose there is a tariff tax of 33½ per cent on articles of clothing, on iron, and in fact on every thing he wishes to buy. The importer's, merchant's, and dealer's profits and collectors' pay make it amount, by the time the

goods reach him, to 45 per cent. Of every $ 145 he pays for the goods, $ 45 is government tax and costs of collection. Of $ 290 spent by him, $ 90 is tariff tax. And, on his whole $ 300, he is taxed not less than $ 94.50. Thus almost one third of his entire income is swept away by the government tax.

Precisely the same is its operation on the mechanic and laborer. In every $ 14.50 they spend for tariff-taxed articles, $ 4.50, or almost one third, goes to pay the government tax and the costs of collection. Their income is but their labor converted into money, so that the government thus converts their labor to its own use to the extent of near one third of what is expended in earning the money thus laid out.

To the farmer it is the same thing as if, there being no tariff, a government collector were to stand at his gate and take out of his wagon forty-five bushels of wheat of every hundred and forty-five he sends to market ; or, in lieu of that, should stand at the door of the store and grocery, and as he came out with his purchases take from him four and a half of every ten yards of cloth, four and a half of every ten pounds of sugar, salt, nails, or iron of any description, and a like proportion of every other article purchased for the use of his family. It is as if a government collector took from the mechanic and laborer $ 4.50 out of every $ 14.50 earned by him, and intended for the purchase of foreign goods, or stood at the store doors and took from him four and a half out of every fourteen and a half yards or pounds they might purchase. The man standing *inside*, behind the counter, now, in effect, does the same thing.

Producing Classes without Remedy.

Nor have these classes any remedy in the legislation of the country, or an increased charge for their produce or their labor. No government can directly by law, in this country, raise the price of the farmer's produce, or the rate of the mechanic's or laborer's wages. So superabundant are the products of agriculture, that any effort to raise their prices above the natural level, directly or indirectly, is as vain as to attempt lifting the Alleghany Mountains from their base ; and it is scarcely less impossible to raise the wages of mechanics and laborers in general. If a momentary or local rise can be produced in their case by legislative acts, those acts produce an effect analogous to that of intoxicating liquors upon the human system, exciting and elevating but to leave them in greater depression. While, therefore, the legislatures may and do, by an increase of salaries and fees, shield the officers of government from the disastrous effects of an oppressive tariff tax, and the agents of corporations and other salaried individuals are shielded by similar means, the tax falls with unmitigated weight on the producing classes. Nay, its weight is made more ponderous and crushing by the increase

of taxes or charges in other shapes, necessary to reinstate the income of the merchants and all those who live by profits, salaries, and fees instead of labor.

The general practical result is, that a tariff tax is a tax upon the productive labor of the country. It takes from the farmer a portion of his surplus grain, cattle, or other marketable commodity : and in the same way extracts from the mechanic and laborer a portion of the products of his labor, whether it be in money or in other manufactured articles intended for market. In taking the proceeds of their labor, it deprives their families of a large portion of those necessaries or comforts they might otherwise enjoy.

A Blow at Trade.

A tariff, not of protection, enriches nobody. It lessens the trade of the country by diminishing the ability of the people to buy. We have seen that a tariff of 33⅓ per cent diminishes the means of the farmer to buy, to the extent of $ 45 in every $ 145. When there is no tariff he can purchase as many goods with $ 100 as he can with $ 145 under its operation. Abolish the tariff, and he can purchase the same goods for $ 100, and have $ 45 left to buy more goods with. So it is with mechanics, laborers, and every class of society. Of course, if the people can *buy* less, the merchants and dealers can *sell* less, and the importers can *import* less. The effect is a decrease in the trade of the country, corresponding with the diminution of purchases made by the people. Under a tariff of 33⅓ per cent, that diminution is not much short of one third. The merchant sells only 100 yards of cloth, bushels of salt, pounds of ironware, etc., where, if there were no tariff, he would sell 145. Probably the diminution of his sales is in fact much greater, for, in consequence of the increased prices, there are some who will abandon the use of the taxed articles altogether, or manufacture them at home.

Thus a tariff tax is a blow at the trade of the country, as well as at the comforts of the people ; and, of course, is a blow at the business of the merchant. His sales are cut off by the inability or unwillingness of some to purchase at the enhanced prices, and by the reduction of purchases by others ; while his profits on the sales made are broken in upon by the government tax on articles consumed in his own family. If he attempt to reimburse himself by increasing the charges on his goods, that operation of itself still further reduces the amount sold, and diminishes his general business. Gradually, the less wealthy of the commercial class feel themselves sinking, they know not why, and either become bankrupt or wind up and go into other business.

Merchants and dealers in general are not aware how intimately their interests are interwoven with those of the producing classes, and especially the farmers and planters. Any measure which increases the prices

cially the farmers and planters. Any measure which increases the prices of what those classes have to buy, diminishes the amount which the merchants can sell, and dries up their profits at their source. The merchant who supports a policy which increases the cost of the farmers' comforts or luxuries as well as his own, thinking to make it up to himself by increasing his rate of profits on goods sold, is like the fabled simpleton who "killed the goose that laid him golden eggs" that he might anticipate the treasure, instead of feeding, and nourishing, and making more productive his profitable bird. If our merchants understood their own interests, they would oppose all tariff taxation, and all unnecessary taxation of any sort upon farmers and planters, and all who live by labor. The more the government takes of their income, the less there will be for the merchant.

Effect on Foreign Producer.

The reflecting reader will have anticipated the effect which tariff taxation in one country has on the productive industry of other countries with which it has commercial intercourse. If the ability of our people to purchase foreign articles be reduced one third by a tariff tax, it follows that the foreign producers lose one third of their market in this country. The necessary consequence is, a reduction of their profits, followed by a reduction of their business in adapting itself to the reduced market. The extent of this reduction depends upon the proportion which their market in this country bears to their market in other countries. If we furnish their whole market, and by a tariff tax cut off one third of it, then their business must be reduced one third. If they find half their market here, then they lose one half of the whole. So of all other proportions. The consequence is, that laborers are thrown out of employment, establishments broken up, and inconvenience, often amounting to distress, is extensively felt. The capital and labor thrust out of one employment by foreign legislation, forces its way into others, disturbing them also, and it is some years before the great ocean of public labor settles down into regular channels and its wonted calm.

Reaction of Tariff Taxation.

But the mischief does not end here. There is a reaction back upon the country which imposes the tariff. All nations with whom we trade pay us in the products of their labor or the money for which those products have been sold in other nations. The ability of their people to buy of us is diminished by the inability of our people to buy of them. England buys our grain and meat, and pays us in manufactured goods. If we refuse to take her goods, which are the fruits of her people's labor, they are no longer able to buy our meat and grain, but must turn to other countries who are willing to make the exchange which we refuse. Every dollar added to the tariff tax may be properly considered as diminishing our foreign market *nearly a dollar and a half*, by taking from both our own people and foreigners the means to buy of each other.

Thus does tariff taxation act and react upon the nations of the earth. One cannot resort to it without disturbing the trade and industry of others who are connected with it by commercial ties. The blow falls most heavily on its own, but is felt around the globe. All the civilized world has become, as it were, one community in reference to industry and trade, and one of its members cannot be seriously wounded in those interests without affecting the whole. Every tariff tax is a *blow at the industry of mankind*, at their commerce, at their *shipping*, at their *wealth*, at *liberty*, and at *civilization*. What but that intercourse which attends the mutual exchange of the products of nations, is humanizing the savage, civilizing the barbarian, throwing the beams of intelligence into the remotest corners of the earth, and preparing mankind to live together in peace, as one family, realizing the blissful state which good men desire and the prophets have foretold?

Why preferred?

Why is a species of tax, expensive in collection above all others, burdensome to industry, disturbing to trade, anti-commercial, anti-philanthropic, and anti-liberal, so popular among the rulers of mankind? How is it that the people unite with their rulers in giving it a preference over others that would take from them less of their earnings, and leave the currents of trade undisturbed? *It taxes the people almost without their knowing it.* Rulers like it for that reason. When the people are required to pay money *directly*, they are apt to ask their rulers what they want it for, and whether a smaller quantity cannot be made to meet all necessary demands against the public. By approaching them stealthily, and taking money out of their pockets without their knowing it, the rulers avoid this annoying interference, and readily raise sums they would not dare to ask if each constituent knew, as he paid it, the amount exacted from him. The people like it, *because they do not understand it.* No man knows how much he pays, and multitudes never reflect that they are taxed at all. The tax is confounded with the price of the goods purchased, and in the merchant's bills is concealed under that disguise. If those bills could be made to *tell the whole truth*, public opinion would be very likely to change. For instance, if they read somewhat in this form, viz.: —

To one yard of woollen cloth	$1.00
To government tax thereon	45
	$1.45

Or if a government collector stood at the gate and took out of the farmer's wagon or cart, for public use, a third part of all the grain he sends to market, or every third horse, hog, or sheep, and whatever else he proposes to sell for the purpose of getting money to buy comforts for his family, or if the tax-gatherer stood by him in market and took from him 45 cents out of every $1.45 he received for them, his eyes would be opened to the effect of this tax. Or if the tax gatherer were to take his stand at every store and grocery and take from every farmer and other purchaser, as they come out, one fourth, one third, or one half of all the cotton and woollen goods, of all the nails and ironware of every description, of all the salt and sugar, and numerous other articles necessary to his business operations and the comfort of his family, he would be aroused to the truth on this abstruse subject. Yet there is now a tax-gatherer *inside* of every store and grocery, *standing behind the counter*, who performs this very office of taking for the use of government from every purchaser nearly one third of all the money paid by him for taxed articles; which, to the farmer, is the same thing as taking the same proportion of his grain or other produce sold to raise it. In the same manner, it takes for public account the same proportion of the mechanic's and laborer's toil, and of the income of every other class of society.

Our object, thus far, is to explain and illustrate the general effect of every species of tariff taxation, whatever may be the motive for levying the tax. There are circumstances which modify this general effect; but, being the result of general principles inherent in the structure of society, they cannot be in the main averted. We sometimes have snow-storms in summer and warm weather in winter; but they do not change the general character and effects of the seasons, flowing as they do from the fixed and unalterable laws of nature and of nature's God. Of some of the causes which modify the effects of tariff taxation we shall have occasion to speak hereafter.

A Protective Tariff.

Mankind, in all civilized countries, may be divided into two classes, *those who work* and *those who do not*. The *workers* constitute the great mass of the people; the *idlers* are but few. The latter employ themselves in devising schemes to appropriate to their own use the toil of the laboring millions, and in enjoying themselves upon the proceeds. Their modes of operation have been various. Bandits live by open plunder, and many ancient communities were little better. But an alliance with government has been the most ready and safe means by which the idlers have accomplished their object. War is one of their means. It enables them to plunder two countries at once, — their own

by taxation to feed, clothe, and pay their instruments, and furnish them with arms and munition, and the enemy's which they ravage and despoil. Nobody is enriched by this process but the chiefs; for it is but little of the plunder or prize-money that goes to the common soldier or sailor.

But war "kills the goose that lays the golden eggs." A few lions and tigers only can subsist upon the deserts it produces, leaving nothing for those more cowardly beasts, the jackals, the wolves, and the foxes. The idlers long since found that their true interest consisted in guarding mankind measurably from war's desolation, as the farmer does his sheep from beasts of prey, that he may profit more by their fleeces. From a few military chiefs, they became nobles, appropriating to themselves the lands of the country, with the labor of the cultivators, under the names of serfs or tenants. Nobilities have found allies in established churches, whose dignitaries, not content with the contributions, salaries, perquisites, and legacies they are able to extract from a willing people through their piety, superstition, and pride, surround the government also, and avail themselves of its laws to amass property and tax labor. A new order of spoilers has risen in modern times, in the holders of stocks representing the debt of nations, states, and corporations, the interest on which is exacted, directly and indirectly, from the sons of toil. With this order, "public faith" is much more sacred than "moral obligation"; and while they see private debts abrogated by thousands with perfect composure, they are shocked beyond expression at public "repudiation."

We have not room to follow these foxes through all the doublings and devices by which they approach and seize upon the fruits of other men's labor; but must come at once to the point in hand.

A Partnership.

Tariff taxation, in its deceptive and stealthy character, is well adapted to the genius and designs of the few who live without work. It is a ready means through which, by an alliance with government, they may extract from the people a goodly portion of their earnings. The government wants money, and so does the idler, or capitalist. The latter throws his weight and influence upon the former, and induces it to supply itself by means which fill his own pockets at the same time. Thus, a partnership is formed, the object of which is to *get as much money as possible out of the people in the easiest way*. It is like the partnership of church and state or king and nobility in other countries; and, so far as the labor of the people is concerned, quite as unjust and oppressive.

Government wants more money, and the question is, how shall it be raised? There are perhaps a thousand men out of five millions who employ their money (not their hands) in the manufacture of woollen

cloth. They say to the government, "*You may now help yourself and help us. Just lay a tariff tax of 40 per cent ad valorem on imported woollen cloths; and by thus raising the price of those imported you will raise the price of our goods, put money into your treasury and into our pockets at the same time.*" Congress yields to the suggestion.

How it operates.

Our present tariff on "all manufactures of wool or of which wool is a component part, not otherwise specified," including broadcloths, is 40 per cent ad valorem. That is to say, for every dollar the importer pays for the goods, he pays forty cents to the government. Let us see how this operates. In the first place, it raises the price of imported broadcloths in the following manner, viz.: —

Cost of cloth per yard, say	$1.00
Government tax or duty	$0.40
Importer's profit on duty, say five per cent	2
Wholesale merchant's profit on forty-two cents, the duty and importer's profit thereon, 10 per cent	4 4/10
Retail dealer's profit on 46 4/10 cents, (being the duty, and importer's and wholesale merchant's profits thereon,) say 20 per cent	9 2/10
Increase of cost to farmer or other consumer in consequence of duty	55 6/10
Whole cost to farmer or other consumer	$1.55 6/10

Hence it appears that the purchasers of foreign woollens pay, under our present tariff, more than 50 per cent over what those goods would cost them if trade were free. For every two dollars they pay for the goods, they pay a dollar and ten cents on account of government tax, only eighty cents of which go into the treasury; the other thirty being cost of collection or merchant's profit.

Of course, the effect of raising the price of imported woollens, is to raise in a like degree the price of those manufactured in the United States. That is the only object for which the manufacturers ask a protective tariff. Who gets the increase in this case? The manufacturer gets the same share as the government gets in the other case; that is, the manufacturer gets forty cents for every dollar's worth of his goods, and eighty cents for every two dollars' worth, more than he could if trade were free; and the consumers, by the same process, pay the same high commission for its collection. Perhaps the amount of importer's profit should also be added to the manufacturer's gain.

Thus the whole people are taxed upon all the woollen cloth they purchase, for the joint benefit of the government and manufacturers. This tax is enormous upon the people's purchases. Suppose those purchases, at the natural price, amount to $ 4,000,000, the duty of 40 per cent is $ 1,600,000, and the cost of collection, 33⅓ per cent, is over $ 500,000 more, making the enormous exaction of $ 2,100,000 from the people's labor.

How much of this sum goes to *each partner* (the government and capitalist) depends on the proportion which the goods imported bear to those manufactured at home. If a quarter part be manufactured at home, then the manufacturer gets $ 400,000 and the government $ 1,200,000. If half be manufactured at home, then each partner gets $ 800,000. If a quarter only be imported, then the government gets but $ 400,000, and the manufacturer $ 1,200,000. Just in proportion as the tariff becomes *efficient* in promoting the home manufacture, in the same ratio does the share of the government in the profits of this partnership operation diminish; and if it succeed so far in protection as to exclude the foreign article entirely, the whole tax, be it 40 per cent or 100, goes into the pockets of the manufacturer.

Sugar. — Illustration.

There are perhaps six hundred persons in the United States whose capital is employed in raising the sugar-cane and manufacturing sugar. The price of brown sugar in New Orleans, without any tariff, would not exceed three and a half cents per pound, and the price of imported sugar of the same quality in all the principal cities would be about the same. Our present tariff imposes a duty on the imported sugar of two and a half cents per pound, which at once raises its cost to six cents. Fortunately, we have data in the Treasury Reports and census to illustrate, with an approach to accuracy, the extent of this tax upon the people.

The amount of sugar imported into the United States in 1840, and not re-exported, was 101,108,633 pounds, and the amount produced by our own sugar planters was 155,110,909 pounds; making in all 256,219,542 pounds for the consumption of our people. The sugar-planters are one branch of the partnership with the government in taxing the people; and let us now see what is about their share of the proceeds under the present tariff. On every pound they make they get two and a half cents by this tax, that being the increase of price in consequence of the government tax on the imported article.

155,110,909 pounds produced at home, at 2½ cents tax, gives	$ 3,877,770.22
101,108,633 pounds imported, at 2½ cents tax, gives . .	2,527,715.82
	$ 6,405,486.04

Thus, of near six and a half millions of dollars exacted from the people, near *four millions* go to the sugar-planters, and about *two and a half millions* to the government. The planters' share divided among them gives over *six thousand dollars to each!*

But this is not the entire exaction from the people. The cost of collecting the planters' share of the tax in the shape of merchants' profit, is as much as the cost of collecting the government's share, or at least 33⅓ per cent, amounting to $ 1,292,490, and the cost of collecting the government's share at the same rate is $ 942,571, —

Making in all	$ 2,135,161
Add tax as above	6,405,486
Whole amount paid by the people	$ 8,540,647

Thus the people pay *eight and a half millions of dollars* to get *two and a half into the treasury*, the balance of *six millions* being a contribution for the support and emolument of the six hundred sugar-planters.

The price of sugar is nearly doubled by this tax.

The original cost per pound is about	3½	cents.
Add importer's and merchant's profits, 33⅓ per cent at least	1⅙	"
Making the cost to consumer	4⅔	"
Add the tariff tax to the original cost, and it makes the price	6	"
Add merchant's profit, etc.	2	"
Making the cost to consumer	8	"

Is there reason or good policy in such a tax? Is it *reasonable* that all our *millions* should be taxed to furnish an income to *six hundred?* Is it *politic* to pay eight and a half millions to get two and a half into the treasury?

Salt.

We have another apt illustration in the article of salt. In 1840 we imported 8,183,203 bushels, and manufactured 6,169,174. Our tariff tax is eight cents on the bushel of fifty-six pounds, the cost of which abroad does not average over eight cents. In public documents the price is stated somewhat higher; but the foreign bushel is eighty pounds, instead of our tariff bushel of fifty-six.

In this case the *partners* (consisting of the government and the salt-makers) divide between them $ 1,148,990, of which $ 654,656 goes to the government, and $ 494,333 to the salt-makers. But in addition to that sum, the people pay in merchants' profit or cost of collection at least 33⅓ per cent more, making the whole exaction from them $ 1,531,986, to get a little more than the third of the sum into the treasury.

Salt is an article of prime necessity, entering into the consumption of the poor equally with the rich, constituting an ingredient in the food of beast as well as man, and being the indispensable preservative of all meats as well for market as for consumption. What reason is there in making our farmers pay 133 per cent tax on this article, merely to enrich or sustain a few hundred manufacturers?

For Protection. — For Revenue.

We have data at hand to illustrate with equal clearness the difference in effect upon the people between a tariff for *protection* and a tariff for *revenue*.

By a duty of 2½ cents per pound on sugar the people are taxed about		$ 8,540,647
By a duty of 8 cents a bushel on salt they are taxed . .		1,531,983
Tax paid on the two articles		$ 10,072,630
Of this, however, there goes into the treasury from sugar, only	$ 2,527,715	
And from salt, only	654,656	
Making in all		3,182,371
Does not go into the treasury		$ 6,890,259
Deduct merchants' profit or cost of collection		1.722,564
Leaving amount paid for the support and emolument of sugar planters and salt-makers		$ 5,167,695

That is, for every dollar that goes into the treasury, the people pay over *a dollar and a half more* for the benefit of sugar-planters and salt-makers.

Cannot this double and triple taxation be avoided without resorting to a direct tax? Let us see.

The articles of coffee and tea are not produced in the United States. A tariff tax on them would operate as a revenue tax merely, having no effect to protect or increase the prices of any species of home product. The imports of tea in 1840 were 19,703,620 pounds, and of coffee 94,996,095 pounds. A duty of eight cents a pound on tea and two cents on coffee would produce the following results, viz.: —

19,703,620 pounds of tea at eight cents	$ 1,596,289
94,996,095 pounds of coffee at two cents	1,899,921
Total brought into the treasury	3,496,200
Add for cost of collection or importers' and merchants' profit, 33⅓ per cent	1,165,400
Whole amount paid by the people	$ 4,661,600

Hence, to get $ 3,182,371 into the treasury by the present duties on sugar and salt, the people actually pay $ 10,072,630; while duties on tea and coffee bringing into the treasury $ 3,496,200, would take from the pockets of the people only $ 4,661,600. *By shifting the duties from sugar and salt to tea and coffee, the people would save more than half they now pay.* This saving would be *more than sufficient to pay for all the sugar and salt they now use.* It would be much more than enough to *buy at a fair price all the salt and sugar made in the United States!*

A tariff, not of protection, takes from the people at least $ 4,000,000 for every $ 3,000,000 that goes into the treasury.

A tariff for protection takes a larger amount from the people in proportion to the extent of actual protection, and upon sugar and salt, our present tariff takes from them about $ 10,000,000 for every $ 3,000,000 that goes into the treasury. True, over $ 3,000,000 goes to the *protected* sugar-planters and salt-makers, but that only makes the matter worse.

What would our farmers think of it, if tax gatherers were sent by President Tyler to meet them in the road on their return from the store, and take away from them one pound out of two of all the sugar and salt purchased by them for their families and farms? What would they think of it, if he should hand half of it back to the sugar-planter to be sold over again, while the other half should be sold for the benefit of the government? However willing to give a fourth of his purchase for the use of government, would he think it quite right to give back another fourth to the sugar-planter? Is the farmer and planter of the North or South, the mechanic, the laborer, the merchant, or any other class bound by any moral obligation or constitutional compact, to give one fourth of their purchases of sugar back to the planters?

This, in effect, they now do, but by a different process. The first purchaser from the planter pays him, under the operation of the law of Congress, nearly twice as much for his sugar as it would otherwise be worth. By the time it reaches the farmer, the price is more than doubled. The same is the case with imported sugar, which constitutes one half, or thereabouts, of the farmers' purchases. The increase of price upon that half, or so much as constitutes the duty, goes into the treasury, and that upon the domestic half goes back to the sugar-planters. Without a tariff, sugar would cost the farmer five cents, and with it ten. Now, what is the difference to the farmer, whether, letting sugar come in free, you enable him to buy two pounds with ten cents, and then take one pound away from him, or raise the price to ten cents so that he can buy but one pound at first? In either event he has but one pound left for his ten cents. It is therefore a fair view of the present tariff tax on sugar, to represent it as taking from the farmer and every other purchaser *one half of all they buy*, a fourth for the use of the United States and a fourth to be returned to the sugar-planter to be sold a second time, after he has once sold and been paid for it at its full value. As the home product furnishes but half the quantity consumed, the handing back to the sugar-planter one fourth of all purchases for consumption is, in effect, handing back to him half of his crop.

The same principle applies to salt and salt-makers. Fully half of their products are virtually handed back to them after being purchased by the farmers, to be sold over again. They are enabled by the operation of the tariff to sell in the first instance at a double price, which amounts to the same thing, except that it is less trouble.

Arguments Answered.

Having illustrated the general nature and effect of a protective tariff, we proceed to answer the arguments of its advocates, after which we intend to dissect the most important parts of our present tariff, for the purpose of enabling each American citizen to ascertain how much he pays to support and enrich our young nobility.

It cheapens Manufactures.

So say a portion of the tariff advocates. Now, the avowed object of a protective tariff is to *increase prices*, so that the manufacturers may give good wages to their workingmen and yet make money themselves. The complaint is, that without a protective tariff to *increase* prices, the products of European "pauper labor" will undersell the products of American labor, thus throwing our laborers out of employment or reducing them to the level of foreign paupers. If the effect of a protective tariff is to *reduce* prices, it produces the very state of things *it is designed to prevent*, and those who wish to keep up prices *ought to petition for its repeal.* Who ever heard of the protectionists seeking to accomplish their object by *reducing* the tariff? When they petition Congress to protect American labor *by abolishing a tariff for protection*, we shall give them credit for sincerity in resorting to an argument so inconsistent and absurd.

There is now going the rounds of the Whig papers, a statement from Mr. Samuel Lawrence, a Lowell manufacturer, that cotton goods have fallen ten per cent in price since the passage of the late tariff law. Mr. Lawrence does not assert that this effect has been produced by that act; but others do.

Prices in general were sinking rapidly when that act passed. If cotton goods have fallen ten per cent, the farmer's produce and the laborer's wages have fallen *twenty, thirty,* or *forty* per cent. The Lowell manufacturers themselves have reduced the wages of their operatives twenty per cent. It is just as reasonable to ascribe to the tariff the universal reduction of wages and of prices as it is to ascribe to that cause the cheapening of cotton goods.

The truth undoubtedly is, that cotton goods have fallen *in spite of* the tariff, and would have fallen *much more* if it had not passed. The cause is the same which has cheapened almost everything else, viz., a *reduced demand.* The people do not use as many goods of any kind as they formerly did, because they cannot procure the means to purchase. Credit is nearly annihilated, and most men buy no more than they can pay for, cash in hand; and their means of raising cash are greatly reduced by the reduction in the prices of their produce, caused as well by a less consumption as by an increase in the value of the currency. The active circulating medium of the United States is not half as great as it was in 1837; and the necessary consequence is, that prices and wages have sunk, comparatively, in a degree somewhat corresponding. In many portions of the Union, about a fourth part of the currency has been withdrawn within the year 1842. But for existing debts this process would not be severely felt, because, all prices being reduced in an equal degree, the *same labor* though nominally at lower wages *would purchase the same amount of necessaries, comforts, and any kind of property.* But debts do not depreciate with the depreciation of property and labor under a currency improving in value, but are virtually increased. Under the operations of the last few years they have been doubled,—not by doubling the *number* of dollars due, but doubling the *value of each dollar.* That is to say, it takes *twice the labor* and *twice the produce*, or thereabouts, to command a dollar now that it did five years ago. The labor of the debtors, therefore, (and "they are legion,") is chiefly consumed in acquiring means to pay debts, leaving little surplus to purchase luxuries or even comforts. Thus the amount consumed by the people is diminished, the demand for goods is reduced, the amount manufactured accumulates, and the prices fall. To break the fall of prices *as to them*, the manufacturers procured the passage of the present tariff, not only leaving the rest of the community to feel the operation in its full weight, but taxing them in addition to relieve the favored few from their share in the general calamity. While their manufactures fall only ten per cent under the operation of causes which reduce almost everything else twenty or thirty, they endeavor to escape entirely by reducing the wages of their workmen twenty per cent, and thus put into their coffers as many dollars as they did when dollars were worth but half as much as they are now.

But most of those who maintain that a protective tariff cheapens manufacture, speak of it not as an immediate but as an ultimate result. They say, that temporary protection will enable our manufacturers to establish themselves, so that in a few years they will be able to dispense with protection and enter into competition with foreign manufacturers in the markets of other nations.

Do those who are influenced by this argument reflect what must be the condition of this country if this result should be brought about? The wages of English operatives in the manufactories are now barely sufficient to keep soul and body together. Yet they are in general as high as the manufacturers can afford to pay and make anything by their business. To undersell them in foreign markets or in our own without protection, our manufacturers must find means to manufacture cheaper than the British do. American *operatives* must work at wages still lower than the "pauper" wages of Europe. This cannot be, until the wages of every species of labor in this country are reduced nearly to the starving point; for laborers will not work in factories if they can get better paid elsewhere. The state of things which the tariffites promise us by way of inducement cannot exist, therefore, except as the consequence of poverty, privation, and suffering among our countrymen at least equal to that which now shocks us in details from the manufacturing districts of England. If a protective tariff dooms our country to this condition, who is there that will not look upon its promised *benefits* with repugnance and horror?

But, happily, centuries will pass away before the wages of labor *can* be so reduced in our new country. It is not at this time in the power of bad legislation to produce it, although the foundations of a system may be now laid from which such results may be seen through the vista of centuries to come. For centuries must labor, in all its departments, consent to be taxed by protective tariffs and other expedients before it will have sunk itself to the level of English operatives of the present day; for centuries must our farmers, mechanics, and every other class contribute their means to sustain an unnatural, hot-house competition before they will realize the *blessing* of *starving paupers* manufacturing *cheap goods* to compete with the same kind of goods manufactured in Europe by men equally abject. Is it not better to have *cheap goods* without the *paupers?* Is it not better to employ our own labor in raising food to feed the foreign paupers and take the goods manufactured by them in return, thus increasing their comforts and our own? Is not such a course more consonant with our interests, our true policy as a nation, with the benign principles of philanthropy and religion? Is it our *interest* to pay double prices for what we buy? Is it our *true policy* as a nation to heap vast wealth upon a *few*, and reduce *millions* to poverty? Is there *philanthropy* or *religion* in augmenting the want and wretchedness of foreign paupers by raising a class of paupers at home?

Although the general principle is sound, that a protective tariff increases the prices of manufactured articles to an extent greater than the duty, there are circumstances operating on particular articles which prevent this result; such as custom-house frauds, smuggling, and a rate of duty high enough to be prohibitory.

Custom-House Frauds.

In many countries custom-house officers are proverbially venal. For a bribe they admit goods with payment of none or but a small portion of the duties imposed by law, and the consequence is, that the importer sells at a lower price than if the duty had been rigidly exacted. In this country it is not alleged or imagined that the custom-houses are generally corrupt; but many facts have been developed tending to show that the custom-house at New York has not always been free from taint. When merchants pay fees or gratuities to custom-house officers or clerks under any pretence; when, baffled in attempted frauds at Boston and elsewhere, they order their ships to New York; and when the foreign trade accumulates and concentrates at that point with unnatural speed, as was the case a few years ago, there is ground for something stronger than suspicion. We firmly believe that one cause of the great concentration of our foreign trade at that point, when in its most flourishing condition, was attributable to enormous custom-house frauds, which kept down the prices of many highly taxed articles below what they would have been had the laws been faithfully executed, and yet gave to the importers enormous profits. For that belief we have reasons conclusive to our own mind.

Smuggling.

This is a kindred mode of keeping down prices and defeating the natural effects of a high tariff. With such a coast and such a frontier as surround our republic, it is impossible, when the temptation is strong, to prevent smuggling. Though a boy at the time of the embargo and non-intercourse, and living over two hundred miles from the Canada frontier, we well remember that some of the neighbors were notoriously engaged in carrying American produce into Canada and bringing British goods out, in violation of those laws. There were then not only custom-house officers but troops on the lines; but the country people with their sleighs and sleds laughed them all to scorn. They went and came in large parties, provided with axes, and if the old roads were guarded, they cut new ones in an incredibly short time, accomplished their object and dispersed before the government officers were apprised of their approach. Almost the universal feeling being against the government, it was not easy for its agents to obtain accurate information, and not always safe to act upon it when they had it. True, the Democratic party generally declared in favor of sustaining the laws; but it was with a feeling that the laws themselves were oppressive and unjust. Such at least was the impression of the country farmers from whom at that time all our information was derived.

During our high tariff, subsequent to the war, the same end was accomplished by different means. In addition to the ordinary process of smuggling, the Canada tailors sent their agents through New England offering to furnish ready-made clothing at perhaps one half what it would cost to buy the cloth from an American store and get it made up by an American tailor. They took the measure of such as agreed to purchase of them, and delivered the clothes at their houses. How many would be patriotic enough to refuse contracts so much to the advantage of their pockets, when all the risks fell upon the Canada tailors, every man must judge for himself; but it is an undoubted fact, that many a loud tariff advocate was clothed in a Canada-made coat, willing enough to relieve his own pocket from the tax he was willing to impose on his uninitiated neighbor.

These operations were carried on in heavy articles, the profit being so great in consequence of the increase of prices through our protective tariff as to justify the risk for even a third or fourth of that increase. But in light articles, such as silk and jewelry, smuggling particularly delights; and when the tariff is extravagantly high, it is as impossible to prevent our merchants from being supplied by illicit means as it is to make all men honest, or induce purchasers to believe it is not right to purchase at the lowest prices. So effectual is smuggling even in England, surrounded with "wooden bulwarks" and planted with bayonets as she is, in counteracting a high tariff, that the prime minister, Sir Robert Peel, lately declared in Parliament, that it was the natural check on this kind of legislation, and that in general 20 per cent was the highest rate of duties which could be imposed without bringing it into action. If such be the fact in England, (and coming from such a source, who can doubt it?) how can American Statesmen believe that a tariff of 30, 50, or 100 per cent can be maintained against this natural check in the United States, whose means of withstanding it are so incomparably less?

"Lead us not into temptation" is the best prayer ever taught to erring man. It is infinitely easier to keep men out of temptation than to deliver them from evils into which they may have been tempted. Legislators should remember this solemn truth when making laws for their fellow-men. If by law they increase exorbitantly the prices of goods, they tempt the importer to evade the law for the purpose of increasing his profits, and tempt the people to wink at or aid in it to save their money. There is a pervading sense running through the whole community that the law is unjust, and losing thus its moral force, it relies on terror only for its execution. To be respected and obeyed in a free country, laws should conform *strictly* and *palpably* to *moral principle*. An habitual departure from this standard by the government, confounds men's notions of moral right, depraves the citizen and

saps the foundations of human society. And it is a sad reflection, but still a truth engraved upon the tablet of history in every age, that governments generally make men worse instead of making them better. If men improve under them, it is on account of the *protection* they give to persons and property, not in following their *moral* examples. It ought not to be so, and would not be so, if our legislators took for their uniform guide the moral standard which all recognize as man's only true guide in dealing with his fellow-man. Far, far from this as the poles are asunder is a system of laws which takes from one portion of the people a part of their earnings for the purpose of enriching another. And the system becomes a *moral plague* when its exactions are carried so far as to make men feel *justified* or even *excusable* in committing or conniving at constant infractions of the laws. When legal restraints are set at nought, moral restraints lose their binding force; for as they *ought* to go together, the common mind does not readily separate the one from the other.

A Prohibitory Tariff.

When the duties are raised so high as to prevent the importation of an article, its price does not rise in proportion to the duty. On many articles our present tariff is prohibitory. Cheap cottons which do not cost six cents a yard, are required to be valued at twenty cents, and a duty of 30 per cent is imposed on this valuation. This, under the guise of a 30 per cent duty, is in fact a duty of more than 150 per cent, and entirely puts an end to importations. The price does not rise 150 per cent; for, independently of custom-house frauds and smuggling, the goods can be manufactured in the United States, not so cheaply perhaps as in England, but far below the actual duty imposed on their importation. The purchaser, therefore, instead of having three or four prices to pay, according to the general law of protective tariffs, only pays a *double* price, or a price much enhanced by the exclusion of foreign competition.

The same effect is produced by what are called *specific* duties, being duties levied upon the pound, the yard, the bushel, or other given quantity without regard to value. On iron wire, the duty is five cents a pound, which is about equal to its cost, or 100 per cent upon the value, effecting a prohibition. Wire will not rise in proportion to the duty, because it can be made in the country at a lower price, and yet with great profit.

When a duty is imposed on an article which is not imported at all, it produces no effect on the price. Our present tariff imposes a duty of three cents a pound on raw cotton; but it does not raise the price of cotton the fraction of a cent. And why? The home supply is more

than sufficient for the market, and none is imported. The same may be said of the duty of seventy cents per hundred weight upon flour, twenty-five cents a bushel on wheat, ten cents a bushel on oats, ten cents a bushel on corn, and nearly all the duties on agricultural products. They do not raise the prices a cent to the farmer, because the country yields more of those products than it can possibly consume. To put them into the tariff at all is a mockery or a fraud.

Specific duties and duties based on fictitious valuations, not originally prohibitory, may become so by a reduction in the value of the article, the effect being to increase the proportion which the duty bears to its original cost. If the cost of wire be five cents a pound and the duty five, it is a duty of 100 per cent upon the value; but if the cost be reduced to two and a half cents, it becomes, without any new action of Congress, a duty of 200 per cent. So if the actual cost of cotton cloth, arbitrarily valued by the tariff at twenty cents a yard, with a duty of 30 per cent superadded, be twelve cents, the duty will be 50 per cent upon the value; but if the cost fall to six cents, it becomes, without further legislation, a duty of 100 per cent. It is plain, that although a duty of 50 per cent, enormous as it is, may not operate as an absolute prohibition, a duty of 100 per cent would do so.

In all cases where the tariff is so framed as to be or become absolutely prohibitory, although prices are not kept up to the level of the cost and duty united, they are kept above their natural level just as long as the duties imposed continue to be protective. If home production be carried so far as to supply our own markets, as it now does with wheat, corn, and potatoes, cheaper than they can be brought from other countries, then and not till then the duty ceases to increase prices, ceases to be protective, and becomes a dead letter on the statute-book. That such a result never can be produced in this country until the wages of manufacturing labor sink to a level with the European standard, accompanied by the same state of poverty, suffering, and want, is as plain to the eye of reason as the most palpable demonstration of mathematical truth.

National Independence.

One of the most common and imposing arguments used by the tariff advocates is that it promotes our independence of foreign nations.

Political independence is a cherished object with every true patriot; but *commercial* independence is a very different thing. *Mutual dependence* runs through all society from individuals up to nations. "*It is not good that the man should be alone*," said the great Creator. To make him happy, it was necessary that he should have a "*help meet*," and she was created for that purpose. From that day to this the man has been

dependent on the woman, and the woman upon the man, while the children are dependent on both. This is the condition of man even in the savage state. As civilization advances, the bonds of dependence increase and strengthen. Family becomes dependent upon family, town upon town, state upon state, and nation upon nation. The farmer becomes dependent upon the mechanic, the mechanic upon the farmer, and both upon the merchant and the manufacturer. In fine, it is this state of dependence, by and through which all occupations exist, except hunting, fishing, and agriculture, and these are advanced by it. Make men *independent and you make them savages*.

Mutual interest is the basis of this dependence. The farmer does not build his own house, make his own hats, shoes, furniture, and farming utensils, because he can buy them with the produce of his farm cheaper than he can learn the various trades and make them himself. The same principle applies to all the occupations of society. Experience has taught mankind that their comfort and happiness are best promoted by a division of labor, assigning different portions to separate classes. It is this which has brought society to its present state, and is rapidly advancing the human family to its highest destiny. Yet it is, throughout, by a state of dependence that this great good has been effected, and every step in human progress makes that dependence wider and stronger.

Farmers are even dependent on each other. One's land is adapted to raising grain; another's is best suited for pasturage. By exchanging grain and meat, both are enabled to obtain twice as much of those necessaries of life as if each raised both cattle and grain. Would any man think them wise in refusing to exchange, and putting their families on short allowance, merely that they might be *independent* of each other? The various climates of the earth are adapted to different products, but all conducive to the sustenance, comfort, or pleasure of man. Shall the farmer in one climate refuse to enjoy these necessaries, comforts, or pleasures, merely because in exchanging his own productions for them, he creates a state of mutual dependence? This is not the order of nature or of nature's God. He has stretched his continents from north to south and thrown oceans between them, that man may exchange products with man in every latitude, and enjoy in the highest degree the blessings which Providence showers upon the earth. Through his beneficent arrangement, he has put it in the power of man in every region, from the ice-bound poles to the burning line, to procure and enjoy the products of every clime, and shall he repel the blessing lest it should make him *dependent*? Shall not the Northern man exchange the fruits of his labor for the sugar, the tea, the coffee, or the fruits of the South, because it will make him dependent on their producers? Shall he not use fabrics of cotton in his clothing or furniture, because the plant which produces it does not grow on his own mountains and hills? The notion is preposterous; *such* independence is ridiculous.

Those who employ this argument seem to forget that while *political* dependence is always one-sided, *commercial* dependence is always *mutual*. Being but an exchange of commodities, commerce always exacts an equivalent. Other countries buy of us as much as we buy of them; and if we cease to buy of them, they of necessity cease to buy of us. If the balance be against us with one nation, it is in our favor with another, so that the result is a general equation. Our condition in that respect is the condition of every other nation, so that on the whole all are alike dependent.

Is *this kind* of national dependence a thing to be deplored? We think not. On the contrary, it is a source of great individual profit and of innumerable enjoyments to the human family. It is also one of the strongest guarantees of peace among the nations. If nation could not war with nation without certain destruction to both, wars would cease. Just as near as the certain injuries of war approximate that result, in the same degree are the motives to avoid it increased, and to a like extent wars will be less frequent. What man, however malignant, will set his neighbor's house on fire when he knows that his own will be consumed in the same flame?

The United States are the last nation on earth which should fear a state of commercial dependence; for there is none which would suffer less from a suspension of commercial intercourse. We make, under all circumstances, our own bread and meat; and, with but slight inconvenience, we *can* make our own clothing. The destruction of commerce would make our labor less profitable and curtail our comforts; but, with the exception of a small portion of our population located on the seaboard, it would produce no actual distress. But let us suppose that the manufacturers of England obtained most of their bread and meat, as well as the cotton in which they operate, from the farmers and planters of the United States in exchange for their manufactured articles, and that these supplies should be suddenly cut off by war between the two countries, — what would be *their* situation? Having no lands like our farmers and planters, they could not ameliorate their condition by giving at once a different direction to their labor; but losing at the same time the market for their products which gave them wages and the supplies of cheap food which that market returned them, they would be cast out by tens of thousands to idleness and starvation. Dependent on us for her bread and meat, while we should be dependent on her only for articles of dress which in case of necessity we could make ourselves, it would be impossible that Great Britain could go to war with us with-

out endangering the existence of her government. There is no danger of our going to war with her so long as she does us anything like justice; and we may be sure of justice when it is her interest to be just. Our interest, therefore, lies in *increasing* the commercial dependence of the two countries, instead of diminishing it. Let our farmers and planters feed her laboring millions and take the products of their labor in return. Her almost entire exclusion from continental Europe is opening the eyes of her statesmen to the fact that if she would *have* markets she must *give* markets; and that to find vent for her manufactures in agricultural countries, she must receive in return the products of their agriculture. The misery and starvation of her people are forcing upon them the great practical truth that her artificial system of industry, built up by legislation in violation of the laws of trade, cannot be longer maintained by an exclusive policy; and that a return to the principles of free-trade is the only mode of saving her political system from bloody convulsions. The millions whom her protective system has led or forced into manufactories and workshops must be employed and fed at every hazard, and this can be done only by consenting to receive the surplus provisions of other countries in payment for the labor of their hands. Hence the advances which that country is making towards receiving the grain, the pork, and other agricultural productions of the United States. And shall not our farmers and planters be permitted to *accept* the market thus tendered to them? With surpluses of produce on hand, shall they not be permitted to feed the laboring paupers of England, and obtain their cheap goods in return? Shall they be debarred from a market by their own government, and at the same time compelled to pay double prices for what they buy? Is not this too heavy a tax to pay for the *commercial* independence of the Republic, which, after all, would be a curse rather than a blessing?

No, no; the interest of our farmers and planters, the leading interest of our country, with the prosperity of which that of every other interest which ought to be encouraged is inseparably connected, will be best promoted by the freest possible commercial intercourse with all the nations of the earth. Our national wealth, strength, peace, security, happiness, and political independence, will be advanced just in proportion as our agricultural products find their way into foreign markets. To obstruct the flow of trade inward or outward, under pretence of maintaining national independence, is as suicidal as for a farmer to refuse to buy of his neighbor or sell to him, under the idea of maintaining his individual independence. Yet how many plain and honest men are made to believe that to pay additional prices for what they buy is patriotic and praiseworthy, being necessary to maintain the independence of their beloved country?

The only country which for ages has maintained her commercial independence is China, and what is her condition? With fifty millions of men capable of bearing arms, we have just seen her whipped into submission by less than twenty thousand British and India troops? Shutting her people up within her own limits, admitting contact with foreigners only at a single port, she has for ages stood still in her solitude, while the rest of the world has been advancing. The British met at Canton, Ningpo, and Nankin the men of twenty-five ages past, and it should not create so much surprise that they slaughtered and dispersed the gathering myriads of China in 1843, as it does that Alexander with his 30,000 Greeks overthrew the myriads of Persia before the Christian era.

A protective tariff, by lessening or cutting off commerce with foreign nations, is a step in the road of Chinese policy. If it operated on all articles of import as it does upon some, it would make us another China, and secure all the blessings of commercial independence.

A Retaliatory Tariff.

We are often told that Congress ought to impose high duties on the products and manufactures of other countries, because they impose high duties on our products and manufactures.

That is to say, we ought to make *our* people pay an extravagant price for *foreign* products and manufactures, because other nations make *their* people pay an extravagant price for our products and manufactures.

Or, if the duties be made so high as to put an end to importations, it is saying to our own people, *you shall not buy and consume the products of another country, because its people cannot or will not buy and consume your products.*

The first and heaviest blow of retaliatory tariffs, in most if not all instances, falls upon the country which resorts to them. It is felt in the increased prices of what they buy, or in depriving their people altogether of a portion of their accustomed enjoyments. It is a certain tax upon their pockets or their comforts. Its effect upon the country at which it is aimed is secondary and uncertain. In any event, it can scarcely inflict a greater injury than first falls on the country which imposes it, because the one is the cause of the other. It affects the foreigner only by making our people too poor to buy of him. If a tariff does not increase prices, as some of its advocates sagely assert, a retaliatory tariff cannot affect in the least the one party or the other. But if it do increase prices, that increase falls on our own people, and the injury to the foreign producer can only be commensurate with the

inability of our people to buy, produced by that increase. If they find their entire market in this country, the injury to them may be serious; but if all the world be open to them, it will scarcely be felt.

But there is a *reaction* in this matter which ought not to be overlooked. How do we pay for the foreign products which we buy? In our own products, directly or indirectly. We send our products to other countries and take theirs in payment, or we sell for money in one country and with that money buy in another. Our trade with China produces a balance against us of eight or ten millions annually; but this is met by an equivalent balance in our favor with other countries. With Great Britain the balance is largely in our favor; we sell there more than we buy, and take the balance in specie or bills of exchange, and with them pay for teas in China. The result is the same as if all the rest of the world were one nation. As a general principle, the balance of trade is always practically equal; for if it be against us one year it is in our favor the next, by which the equilibrium is restored.

From these facts and principles it follows, that we cannot injure the market of foreigners among us without in an equal degree injuring our market among them. Just so far, therefore, as a retaliatory tariff injures the market of the foreigner, it injures our own market. By cutting off the trade of any nation with us, we cut off our own trade with that or other nations to the same extent. That which is called *retaliation* falls, *first*, on our own people, by increasing prices and lessening their comforts; *secondly*, on the nation aimed at, by injuring their market; and, *thirdly*, reacts on our own country and injures our market in an equal degree.

Can such legislation be wise? On the contrary, is it not, under ordinary circumstances, suicidal and ridiculous? I want pork, and my neighbor has it to sell; but I insist he shall take corn for it, which he does not want. He says to me, "Sell your corn to those who want it, and I will sell you my pork for the money, cheaper than you can get it anywhere else." I reply, "No, if you won't take my corn, I won't take your pork." To *retaliate* upon him, I exchange my corn with another neighbor for pork, *getting but half as much pork for it as I should have done if I had converted it into money and then bought the cheap pork of my first neighbor*. This is exactly the effect of retaliatory tariffs in general. And what difference would it make, so far as my interest is concerned, whether my first neighbor refused to take my corn because he did not want it or out of mere spite? If my neighbor will not do me a *favor*, shall I therefore do myself an *injury*?

Retaliatory tariffs are a *legislative war*, and can be justified on no other principle than a war of arms. It is a struggle of two nations to do each other harm. The nation which commences it is sure of injury itself, and finds its only just excuse in the prospect of compelling its neighbor to be more liberal and just. If there be none or but faint hope of such a result, it is a war of folly and madness. Every blow struck in it is a blow at the dearest interests of the human race, — at the value of labor, at the comforts of man, at the spread of intelligence, at liberty itself. Neither government can reach its adversary but through the bosoms of its own people, and every blow struck by either is echoed in the groans and lamentations of the citizens or subjects of both.

Why do we not retaliate upon China, which annually sells us teas to the extent of many millions of dollars, and takes almost nothing of our products or manufactures in return? It is the strongest case on the face of the globe; yet where is the statesman that *thinks* of attacking her by a retaliatory tariff? Where is the man who thinks it would be wise to make our people pay a double price for tea, because his Celestial majesty will not admit our corn, pork, and tobacco into his dominions? Why is this trade, the balance of which is so heavy against us, left unmolested? It is because on this matter reason is left to its natural conclusions without the bias of interest. The farmer, when he sips his tea, knows that his produce has paid for it. He does not see the whole train of operations through which he is enabled, with his wheat and his beef, to purchase the products of China; but he knows that such is the result. To him and to his country it makes no difference whether they go *directly* to China in exchange for the grateful beverage, or are exchanged for goods or money in England or elsewhere, and the proceeds, passing through a score of hands and as many nations, undergoing a new metamorphosis at every step, reach the tea-grower at last. If one half or the whole of the tea now consumed in the United States were excluded by a retaliatory tariff, does any one suppose it would have no effect upon our foreign markets? If so, it is a great error. Unless our other imports were increased, it would cut off our market abroad to an extent equal to the cost of the tea imported; for, to that extent, it would diminish the means of foreigners to purchase of us. While we see an enormous injury to ourselves *certainly* to spring from a retaliatory tariff on the great staple of China, we cannot perceive the extent of injury which would accrue to that Empire. No man, therefore, has the folly to propose such a measure.

It is only in reference to European nations with whom our trade presents a more favorable balance, that we hear the cry of retaliation. Is not *protection*, so called, at the bottom of it? Were there no rival interests in this country to be fostered at the expense of the working millions on both sides of the Atlantic, we apprehend that we should hear little of *retaliation*. Be the motive what it may, the result of every retaliatory duty is a tax upon every class of our own community, and a blow at our markets abroad.

What Tariffs are like.

In a dispassionate view of the subject, all sorts of tariffs, as well on exports as imports, are like *natural obstructions to trade*. They increase the cost of exchanging commodities between man and man, between nation and nation. That cost, left to the operations of free-trade, would consist of the expense of transportation and a reasonable commission or profit to those employed. A tariff seizes the product or manufacture in midway between the producer and consumer, and compels the carrier to pay to the government a tax sometimes exceeding its value. This, with a profit upon it, he embraces in the price he fixes on the article when he sells to the consumer. The effect is the same as if *the cost of transportation were increased to the same extent* by obstructions to harbors, rivers, or roads. Ought not causes which produce the same effect, to be considered of equal merit? Congress imposes a duty, for the purpose of increasing prices and lessening importations. Would it not be just as well to obstruct the navigation of our harbors, bays, and rivers, make breaches in our canals and break up our railroads, making foreign goods cost more to our people through a more expensive transportation, and thereby fostering manufactures in each section of the country? It would be precisely the same sort of *protection* to "American industry."

A foreign nation throws the folly to throw obstructions into her own harbors and rivers, and forthwith it is demanded by one class of sagacious statesmen that we shall retaliate *by throwing obstructions into ours!* This is a *retaliatory* tariff.

Why should we not consider *human* obstructions to trade with other nations precisely as we do natural obstructions? To some countries nature has denied good ports and navigable rivers, making trade with them difficult and expensive, — shall we, for that reason, refuse to trade with them as far as we can profit by it? To refuse to do so, would strike every man as ridiculous. And supremely ridiculous would it be to throw sand-bars into the mouths of our rivers because the rivers of other countries with which we wish to trade have sand-bars in them. Common sense teaches men to trade wherever they can make a profit. It teaches them to remove obstructions where they can, and submit to them where they cannot. If bad harbors and rapid streams will not allow *much* trade, they are content with *little*.

Why should not *legislative* obstructions to trade be treated in the same way? Is it not equally the dictate of common sense that we shall trade wherever we can make a profit, be it much or little? If foreign nations by legislative obstructions reduce our trade and their own, shall we reduce it still more by similar obstructions on our part? If Great Britain throw obstructions into the Thames, shall we throw

them into the Hudson? If she reject an advantageous trade with us in one article, shall we reject an advantageous trade with her in another article? Such is not the dictate of common sense.

A tariff is like a tax-gatherer standing in the highway to take from the farmer's wagon a fifth, a third, or half of the produce he sends to market, or a fifth, a third, or a half of the money or goods he gets in return. To make those goods cost him a fifth, a third, or a half more than they otherwise would, amounts to precisely the same thing; and such is the effect of a tariff. In case the tariff be protective, the agent of the manufacturer stands with the tax-gatherer, and they divide the proceeds between them.

A farmer sends out his corn to exchange with his neighbor for pork; but at each gate stands a tax-gatherer and takes a third of the corn and the pork for the use of the government and its partners, the manufacturers. Like this is the effect of a protective tariff.

The farmer has sold his produce and goes into a store to buy sugar and cloth for the use of his family. A tax-gatherer stands at the door, and as he comes out, takes from him every third pound of sugar and every third yard of cloth he has bought, and divides it between the government on the one hand and the sugar-planter and manufacturer on the other. Like this is the effect of a protective tariff.

The farmers of the land have their barns filled and granaries overflowing, when a prophet comes along and tells them that they will make money by *burning a third of their crops*. Would they believe him? Yet, what is the difference between burning a third of the crop, and adding fifty per cent to the prices of everything they buy with it? Without a tariff, two thirds of the crop would buy as much as the whole with a tariff.

Deceptions of the System.

OF A REVENUE TARIFF. — The whole system of tariff taxation is deceptive.

It is deceptive in this: It deceives the people as to the amount of taxes actually paid by them as well as the costs of collection. What farmer when he makes his purchases, is aware how much is paid by him in consequence of the tariff, over the natural price, on his axes, ploughs, hoes, scythes, sickles, chains, crowbars, harrow teeth, cart irons, horse-shoes, nails, spades, shovels, tongs, hinges, latches, knives, forks, ovens, pots, kettles, and every article of iron, steel, brass, pewter, tin, and copper that is used in building his barn, his house, and his out-buildings, in furnishing them, and in carrying on his business; on his coats, pantaloons, waistcoats, shirts, flannel, hats, shoes, socks, cravats and pocket handkerchiefs; on the dresses, shawls, bonnets, gloves, shoes,

hose, and other articles worn by his wife and daughters; on his sheets, blankets, counterpanes, comforts, beds, pillows, and pillow-cases; and on his sugar, salt, pepper, ginger, and the numerous condiments which make his food wholesome and palatable? If he would escape taxation on his drinks he must be a cold-water drinker; and even then he is taxed on the glass which brings the limpid beverage to his lips. But does he know *how much* tax he pays on his tumblers, his pitchers, his bottles, or on the windows which let the light of heaven into his dwelling while they exclude the cold of earth?

Does the carpenter know *how much* he pays on his planes and chisels, his augers and gimblets, his squares and compasses, his adzes and axes, or any or all the tools necessary to his trade? Does the blacksmith know the amount of tax he pays on his anvils and sledges, hammers and tongs, vices and files, any tool he uses or any species of iron or steel in which he works? Does the shoemaker know how much he pays on his awls and his hammers, his knives and his lasts, his wax and his thread, or on the leather he manufactures?

In fine, is there *any* man of *any* class or occupation who can tell *how much* tax he annually pays through his business or trade, his house and furniture, his food and raiment, his comforts and pleasures, under a system of tariff taxation. The most intelligent and reflecting are baffled in the attempt, and there are multitudes who seldom or never reflect that they are taxed at all. They pay the price charged by the merchant without knowing or recollecting that a fourth, a third, or a half of it is composed of a tax to the government and costs of collection.

Aside from all questions of protection, retaliation, and costs of collection, is that system of taxation a good one for a free people which *conceals from them what they actually pay?* Will any man who merits having a voice in his own government prefer having his *pocket picked*, as it were, for the support of the public institutions and authorities, to placing the amount *openly* and *directly* in the hands of the collector? Is there not, in this stealthy mode of collecting a revenue, an example of indirectness approaching to immorality, which a government desirous of promoting open dealing and sound principle ought not to set? Has not this system been the parent of all the real extravagance which has at any time prevailed in the administration of our government? When men do not know when or how their money leaves them, it cannot be expected that they will give much thought as to what becomes of it. But when asked for their money directly, they are very apt to ask in return *what it is wanted for*. When they see it go, — when they take it out of their pockets and put it into the collectors' hands, thus knowing to a cent how much they pay, — they will inquire for what this demand is made upon them, and insist that the exaction shall be confined to the necessities of the government.

Yet the indirect and stealthy manner in which a revenue tariff approaches the pockets of the people, is with modern statesmen the chief reason for preferring it to other systems of taxation. It enables them to take the people's money without being questioned about it, and that they consider a most excellent contrivance! Ought the tax-payers to think so?

OF A PROTECTIVE TARIFF. — Taking the money of the people without their knowing it, for the *bona fide* support of the *government*, may admit of some apology or excuse. But what can be said in defence of an *individual*, who, with his own hand or with the assistance of others, takes money out of his neighbor's pocket and applies it to *his own* use? What less than this does the manufacturer who gets Congress to pass an act raising the price of his goods, directly or indirectly, for the purpose of *increasing his profit?* Suppose the price of broadcloth to be a dollar a yard; Congress by law raises the price to a dollar and a half; the farmer buys two yards for three dollars which he could have bought for two if Congress had not interfered; thus one dollar of the farmer's money has been extracted from his pocket and put into that of the manufacturer. He is not conscious of it, however. The merchant tells him *broadcloths have risen;* and without knowing or understanding why, he pays his money and is content.

Is it believed that the system would last beyond a single Congress if the people universally understood precisely how it operates upon them? If each farmer, mechanic, laborer, lawyer, doctor, divine, and merchant distinctly perceived that this system takes from them large portions of their crops, earnings, salaries, fees, and profits, and hands them over to the manufacturers, iron-masters, sugar-planters, and salt-makers, not in *bona fide* remuneration for their goods and products, but merely to *enrich them* or *make their business profitable,* would they not all rise up against it with one voice? Would they not say to their rulers, "This is worse than the agrarianism which has been so strongly condemned? That takes the property of the rich and divides it among the poor; this takes the property of the poor and gives it to the rich. That divides the wealth of the country equally among the people; this puts the wealth of the country into the hands of a few. Both are violations of moral principle, differing only in policy and degrees of turpitude."

But the protective system does not content itself with clandestinely taking one man's money and giving it to another. It has various crafty devices to make its exactions effectual. One of them is the use of what are called *minimums,* which mean nothing short of *false valuations,* — *false by requirement of law!* The present tariff imposes a duty of 30

per cent *ad valorem* on certain cotton goods, and then provides that if they cost less than twenty cents a yard, they shall nevertheless be valued at twenty cents, and that the duty shall be 30 per cent on this false valuation. There are descriptions of cotton goods embraced in this provision which, we presume, do not cost in England four cents a yard, on which a *real ad valorem* duty of 30 per cent would be but little over one cent; yet, by means of this false valuation, it is raised to six cents, or one hundred and fifty per cent upon their cost. The consequence is, that all cheap foreign cottons are driven from our market, and the cunning manufacturers have it all to themselves without competition. It is as complete a prohibition as if Congress forbade their importation on pain of death. Following up the falsehood which the tariff law thus practises, many advocates of the system call it a *revenue tariff.* A tariff which from some articles *cuts off all revenue,* the people are told is a tariff to *raise a revenue!*

Specific duties is another mode, though less aggravated, of concealing the amount of the tariff tax. These are duties imposed upon the pound, the gallon, the bushel, the yard, or the article, or any given quantity of it, without regard to its value. The relative amount of this tax cannot be ascertained without first knowing the price of the article. If the tax be three cents a pound and the cost three, then it is a tax of 100 per cent; if the cost be six cents, then it is 50 per cent; if it be ten cents, then it is 30 per cent; but what it really amounts to *upon the value* is a sealed book to the people generally. When told that the tax is 30 per cent upon the cost of an article, they can form some estimate of its amount without an accurate knowledge of its cost; but when told that it is two, three, or more cents a pound, bushel, or yard, etc., they can form no idea as to what proportion of the price is made up of tax.

This point will be further illustrated when we come to dissect the present tariff.

Free-Trade.

What is *free-trade?* Many writers ridicule and sneer at the doctrine of free-trade; let us consider what it is.

I have corn and I want pork; my neighbor has pork and wants corn; we exchange. That is *free-trade.* That is the thing which the tariff advocates sneer at and ridicule. They tell me, "*Mr. K., your free-trade is a very bad thing for you; do you just pay the government a third of the price of the pork you get from your neighbor L., and let him pay a third of the price of the corn he gets of you, and it will be much better for both of you!*" That is the *tariff* policy. Which is best for farmers? The shoemaker makes shoes for his neighbors, and takes their grain, meat, and potatoes in payment. That is *free-trade.* Would it be better for

him and his customers to make him pay the government the value of one third of all he gets in exchange for his labor? That is the *tariff* policy. So it is with all other classes of society. *Free-trade* permits everybody to sell what they have *for the best price they can get,* and buy what they want *as cheap as they can.*

A farmer drives his wagon to market, gets the best price he can for his load, buys what he wants, and is on his return home. It is *free-trade* thus far; but at the boundary of his county or his town there is a little *toll-house,* the keeper of which makes him pay to the government a sum of money equal to one third of the value of all he has in his wagon. Is this better than *free-trade?* better than *carrying home the money he has left?* Would it be a good thing to have these toll-houses at the lines of all our towns, counties, and cities to take a third of all that *comes in,* or its value in money, from the farmers, planters, mechanics, and manufacturers who are always carrying the products of their industry to and fro for a market? Would it be better than *free-trade?*

Our Constitution establishes *free-trade* between the States. Would it be better for our farmers if toll-houses or custom-houses were erected on every road, river, or canal where it crosses a State line, to take from every passing cart, wagon, car, or boat, for the use of the government, one third of all the produce and goods transported in them, or their value in money? Would it have been *wiser* in Washington and his associates to have given us *such* a system instead of the *free-trade* they established? Few there are who will maintain that it would be a good thing for farmers to be taxed on the road to their neighbors, or at the town, county, city, or State lines, going or coming, with the products of their farms or the goods or other produce they have purchased by their sales.

What difference does it make whether the farmers or mechanics who exchange products, live on opposite sides of a *stone fence* or of the *Atlantic Ocean?* What difference does it make whether the articles coming in exchange for the farmers' products are taxed *at the gate* as they enter his yard, or at the *New York custom-house* where they enter his country? Is it not the same thing to him? Is it better for him that they should be taxed at *either* than that they should not be taxed at all? Is it better that the *tariff* should deliver them, taking from the farmer one third of their value at the same time, or that *free-trade* should deliver them without taking from him anything?

There is no mystery in *free-trade.* It is the simplest thing in the world. You may see it throughout the country, and nowhere more fully illustrated than in the village and city market-houses. Would the system there prevailing be bettered, if a tax-gatherer were standing by

and were to take from purchasers *five cents* for every *ten* or *fifteen* they spend for marketing? Or were to take from them every third or fourth pound of meal, bushel of meal, peck of potatoes, and every other article they purchase, which would amount to the same thing? And would it be better for the *countryman,* after he has sold out his marketing to the town-people, to have a tax-gatherer following him to the groceries and stores and taking from him *five cents* for every *ten or fifteen* he spends for family comforts? Is this interference between buyer and seller, taking from the former a third or half his money, better than *free-trade,* which would allow him to spend it all for his own benefit?

The principles of *free-trade* are the same between nations as between individuals. You may see them illustrated in every bargain between two women in the market-house. One sells as high as she can; the other buys as low as she can. In fact, trade between nations is at last nothing but trade between individuals. The parties are farther apart, and employ agents under the name of merchants to transact the business; but the principles which govern it are the same as if the parties lived in the same house. It matters not a fig whether the articles which pass from one to another are taxed in the hands of the agent or merchant, or in those of the final purchaser. Upon him falls the tax at last.

To talk of benefiting the farmer or any other class (excepting the *protected*) by *obstructing trade* through a tariff tax, is as absurd as to talk of doing him good by stationing a fellow on the road to knock a spoke out of his wagon-wheel every time he passes. What is the difference to him whether he pays a dollar for mending his wagon or as a tax on the goods he buys? Both are the reverse of free-trade; both are *tariff* policy.

If *free-trade* be a bad thing, what nonsense it is to clear out harbors, dig canals, make railroads, or good roads of any sort! Upon the anti-free-trade theory, sand-bars, rocks, and snags in the Western rivers, are very good things; they obstruct trade, render it *less free,* and *tax* it like the *best of tariffs!* Instead of petitioning Congress to *clear them out,* the anti-free-trade men of the West ought to petition them to *throw more in,* — to *fill* the Mississippi, Ohio and Missouri with snags and sawyers, rocks and sand-bars. By such means, foreign goods could be *kept out,* and the products of the country *kept in,* quite as effectually as by a tariff.

There is another plan to tax trade and "protect industry" equally effectual. It is to encourage *pirates* and *highwaymen.* Whether a third of the imports of the country are taken from their owners by pirates on the high seas or by the government and manufacturers through the custom-houses is quite immaterial so far as regards the interests of the people individually. Both would make goods cost more, would interfere with *free-trade*, would be equal to a *protective tariff*. And to "protect the industry" of each *section* of the country against interference from other sections, gangs of highwaymen on the roads to plunder wagons and rob merchants would be a most effectual expedient. All these things but increase the prices of imported goods, and what *but* that is the effect of a protective tariff?

Throw *revenue* out of the question, and what are the exactions of a protective tariff better than those of the bandit? Some Bluebeard or Captain Kidd stations himself off Boston harbor, in an armed vessel, and compels every ship that comes in to give up or pay him the value of one third of her cargo. How is this morally different from the Lowell manufacturer, through his agent in the custom-house, compelling every ship to pay for or surrender a third of her cargo for his benefit on her arrival at the wharf? Is not the effect the same? Is not the wrong just as great? But say you, "*one has law for it*, while the other *violates law*." Admitted; but *why should* one have law for it more than the other? Is it not just as right for Congress to *authorize plunder at sea* as to authorize it *on shore?* It is the *principle* and the *practical effect* to which we wish to call the attention of the country. Looking upon *protective tariffs* as the modern device to cheat the *workers* into the support of the *idlers*, and sustain unnatural and unjust distinctions in society, taking the place of the ancient plunderings, the vassalage, the tithes, and other contrivances of ancient times, now too well understood to be tolerated by the laboring millions, we desire to enable our countrymen to understand them in all their bearings.

Practical Exposition.

In a Report of the Committee of Ways and Means, made on the 23d February, 1843, in the House of Representatives, we find the following passage, viz. : —

"It also appears from a statement furnished by the Treasury Department that the average amount of duties on dutiable articles imported during the last quarter of 1842, is a little more than 35 per cent on their *ad valorem value ;* and, at that rate, an importation of $40,000,000 of dutiable articles during the year 1843 must produce a gross revenue of $14,000,000, which will yield a net revenue of nearly $13,000,000, the amount estimated by the Secretary."

Hence it appears that the tariff tax on all imported articles now subject to duty, averages over 35 per cent upon their value, and that of $14,000,000 estimated as their product, less than $13,000,000 will be net revenue, the custom-house expenses being over one million out of the fourteen.

From the practical results here exhibited let us see what is the amount which our people *actually pay* under the existing system.

Imports valued at $40,000,000 produce a gross revenue of .	$14,000,000
Add one-third, or 33⅓ per cent, for importers' and merchants' profits on the duties advanced by them	4,666,666⅔
Whole amount of tax paid by the people on their imports	$18,666,666⅔
Yet, after deducting custom-house expenses, there comes into the Treasury only	$13,000,000
Actual cost of collection	$5,666,666⅔

This is over 44 per cent, but one per cent less than our estimate under the head of "*Cost of Collection, etc.*" [See page 465.]

In this result the revenue feature only of our tariff is taken into consideration. If there were no "protection" in it, our people would pay *five and two-thirds millions* for the collection of *thirteen millions*. Is not this a monstrous *commission?*

But when we come to add the amount paid, under the *protective* features of the present tariff, upon articles grown or manufactured at home, the result is almost appalling. The precise amount of home manufactures purchased by our people, corresponding in character with those subject to duty imported from other countries, cannot be ascertained ; but we think it safe to say that they are at least equal to the imports, or, at their natural price, worth per annum $40,000,000. As the price of the imports is increased 35 per cent by the tariff, so the price of similar articles manufactured at home will be increased 35 per cent, which, upon $40,000,000, gives $14,000,000, equal to the entire gross revenue. *Not a dollar of this goes into the treasury*, but *every* dollar of it to the *sugar-planters, salt-makers, iron-masters, manufacturers, and a few minuter interests.*

But this also comes to the farmers, planters, mechanics, and other consumers, increased by merchants' profits equal to 33⅓ per cent, or $4,666,666⅔.

Here then we have the materials to form a satisfactory estimate showing how much the American people pay to get $13,000,000 of net revenue into their treasury, viz. : —

Custom-House expenses	$1,000,000
Cost of collecting the revenue tariff tax	4,666,666⅔
The protective tariff tax.	14,000,000
Cost of collecting the protective tariff tax	4,666,666⅔
	$24,333,333
Add net revenue	13,000,000
	$37,333,333

Thus it appears that out of THIRTY-SEVEN MILLIONS OF DOLLARS *paid by*

the people under the existing system only THIRTEEN MILLIONS *get into their treasury !* Of the balance FOURTEEN MILLIONS *is money transferred by legislative legerdemain from the pockets of the whole people to the pockets of a few sugar-planters, salt-makers, iron-masters, manufacturers, etc.*, FOUR MILLIONS AND TWO THIRDS is the cost of this operation, while FOUR MILLIONS AND TWO THIRDS is the cost of collecting the *revenue* tariff tax, and ONE MILLION the custom-house expenses.

Could *any* system of revenue be more expensive, more unjust, more iniquitous?

Let us see what would be the result of a direct tax on carriages, on watches, on silver-plate, and, if you please, on lands : —

Suppose the net revenue to be		$13,000,000
Commission to collectors 5 per cent . . .	$650,000	
Allow for losses 5 per cent more	650,000	
		1,300,000
Whole amount paid by the people		$14,300,000

Thus, to get thirteen millions of dollars into the treasury by any kind of direct tax, the people would be required to pay not over $14,300,000, whereas to produce that result under the *present system* they pay over $37,000,000 !

We do not *recommend* a direct tax ; we merely present what we believe to be *facts* for the consideration of the people.

A Home Market.

One of the delusive arguments of the tariff advocates is, that it produces a *home market*. The meaning of this is, that it increases the number of consumers of produce in comparison with the number of growers.

Does it necessarily follow that the increase of consumers is a good thing? If it be, why may not Congress pass an act to protect from destruction *crows and blackbirds, wolves and squirrels, rats and mice?* They are very considerable *consumers* without being producers. If *consumption* be a good thing, here is a way to obtain it without covering "the body politic" with "sores" in the shape of manufacturing cities.

But, say the tariff advocates, "the *manufacturing operatives give us something in return*." Yes, *at double prices*. I have ten bushels of wheat which I wish to exchange for articles of clothing ; what boots it to me whether the rats eat up half of it, or it be taken from me by a tax on cotton, linen, and woollen goods? Are not the rats just as good consumers as the manufacturers when they give me just as good a return?

But if the government ought to legislate with a view to increase the

proportion of consumers, there is a more effectual mode : *force the manufacturers to break in pieces all their machinery of modern invention and resort to the primitive modes of spinning and weaving.* They would then require five hands, probably ten, for every one now employed, and thus make a most important addition to the number of consumers. But, says the tariff advocate, "that would *greatly increase the price of goods*." Very well ; is not that the very end at which you aim by a protective tariff? "Aye ; but it would *increase the cost of manufacturing them*." Ah, that explains your real motive. You want to increase the *price of goods* without increasing the *cost of manufacturing them* and thereby *add to your profits*. While you *talk* of giving employment to laborers, increasing the number of consumers, making a home market for farmers, etc., etc., you are constantly introducing machines of iron, brass, and wood, *which neither eat nor drink*, to perform the work of men and women *who do*, and sending back your operatives to the occupations whence they came, or, as in England, turning them out to *steal or starve !* Yet you call on the farmers and others to pay an enormous tax to raise prices and make your *machine* labor profitable, to "*protect*" things of iron, brass, and wood from competition with the "pauper labor" of Europe !

What is the *fact ?* Has the building up of Lowell or Nashua increased the prices of the farmer's wheat or corn in Ohio, Indiana, or Illinois? Every man knows better. Has it increased the prices of the farmer's corn and rye raised in their *very neighborhood?* Every farmer fifty years old, who lives there, knows better. He knows that their prices, thirty or forty years ago, were higher than they are now. Southern and Western corn and flour have been brought, by means of these very manufacturing establishments, into competition with those of the New England farmer, at his own door, *reducing* prices there *without increasing them* in the regions whence the new supplies come. These are notorious *facts*, — the strongest of arguments. To *think* of increasing the prices of Western produce by building up manufactures and thus increasing the number of domestic consumers, is as idle as to think of affecting the volume of the Mississippi above or below by throwing the water over the levee at New Orleans with a bucket. The production of that teeming region is too vast to be affected by an operation so minute. The Mississippi must have *an ocean* to receive the waters of its innumerable fountains, and its valley must have *a world for a market*. To create a *home* market for its productions in New England or elsewhere by legislation, is just about as ludicrous an operation as digging a *home* reservoir to receive the waters of its mighty rivers.

As a man of the West we say to the general government, *clear out our rivers, protect us from piracy and war on the ocean, and give us the world for a market.* Do this, and in half a century we will show you results never surpassed in earthly beauty and productiveness since God planted the first garden among the four rivers of Eden.

Not a Sectional Question.

In the former discussions of the tariff, it was generally treated as exclusively injurious to the South and beneficial to the North. This was a mischievous error. That the system is more injurious to the North than the South will be obvious on a moment's reflection.

The amount of tax paid by the people of every section is in proportion to their consumption of the taxed articles. Of these, the laborers of the South, being chiefly negro slaves, consume very little compared with the laborers of the North, who are chiefly white freemen. The consumption of those who are called the higher classes in the North and South, is probably about equal. But taking the *whole population together*, there can be little doubt that the consumption of the North, compared with the whole number of souls, is at least three times as great as that of the South. Upon the small farmer who tills the ground he owns, it falls with manifold heavier weight in proportion to his means than it does upon the Southern planter with his hundred slaves. Indeed, its practical tendency is to throw the property of the North into the hands of a few, as that of the South now is, and make the mass of the white population work for them with as little practical benefit to themselves as the black slaves receive from their masters. There are some features in Southern slavery which are *humanity itself* compared with the factory system carried to its perfection as in England. The master is obliged to provide for and support his slaves in sickness and old age, and under all other circumstances, whether their labor be valuable or not. The factory laborers, after working for a mere subsistence when in health, are uniformly turned adrift to provide for themselves when sick and old, as well as when their labor is no longer profitable to their masters. The tendency of the protective system in this country is to make the whole population contribute to the wealth of the factory owners, — a portion of them by laboring *in* the factories, and another portion by tilling the soil and carrying on other business *out of* the factories, the profits of which are taken from them by protective tariffs and other taxes.

The difference between the North and the South is, that the recipients of these taxes, with some exceptions, live in the North. It is, therefore, to some extent, the transfer of wealth from one section to another. But is it any relief to the taxed farmer or mechanic of the North to see his income, in common with that of the Southern planter,

taken from him to build up an aristocracy of which he is practically to be made the slave?

The farmers and other classes in the Middle and Western States are affected by this system in the same manner as in the North. Upon the farmers of the West, however, it falls with additional weight. The farther imported goods are carried from the place of importation, the more hands they pass through, as a general rule, and the more is the tariff tax increased by the merchants' and dealers' profits thus accumulating.

With these arguments and facts, enabling every reader, we trust, to understand the subject of tariff taxation, and form some opinion of the amount he pays under the existing system, we must close this article. In "Kendall's Expositor" we shall give further illustrations of the effect of the tariff, from time to time, as we can obtain the information necessary to unravel its intricacies.

CHAPTER XVII.

The first number of the "Expositor" in 1843 appeared with a new heading, containing a picture of a pair of scales so nearly balanced as to require careful scrutiny to detect any deviation.

The following extract is from the leading article on

NEW THINGS.

Our new head presents itself to the reader. The scales are emblematic of Justice. We adopt them as indicating our intentions towards all our fellow-men. By making them a little one-sided, our artist may have meant to intimate that the human mind is incapable of being perfectly just under all circumstances. If our bias shall be no greater than he has given to our emblem, we shall come nearer to the eternal rule of right than falls to the lot of most men, however pure their intentions.

We omit the sword of Justice. To hold the balance is the utmost of our ambition ; execution we leave to others. We purpose weighing arguments with all practicable impartiality, and then submitting each case to the people, whose province it is to give judgment and order execution. Justice is Truth, and Democracy is Truth and Justice. To this cause we devote ourselves, believing it to be the cause of our country and our kind.

Our new volume opens with this number. The principles which will be recorded in it our readers already know. The arguments and facts by which we shall defend them remain to be developed. Our utmost talent and zeal are pledged to make our discussions instructive and interesting. What old Time may have to disclose for this year's record rests in the Almighty Mind. We have faith that whatever may happen to men or nations, the cause of human intelligence, human rights, and human virtues will be permitted to advance with accelerated speed.

The new year is already in progress. It is not too late, however, to wish our subscribers all sorts of happiness.

If Congress will be content to let currency and private business alone, modify the tariff so as to make it just, reduce the public expenditures, and take care to place the public credit beyond hazard or doubt, dismissing all thought of establishing banks, exchequers, or any other institu-

tion with the view of giving an unnatural expansion to the circulating medium, the people may hope for good times at no distant day. Industry and economy they have already learned, and the surplus products of their labor will soon bring them a wholesome currency in abundance, if Congress or the State legislatures do not corrupt it by their tampering. Their most earnest petition, prayer, and protestation to their rulers should be to let them alone in that respect, to preserve the public peace and the public faith, to protect them by general laws against violence and fraud, leaving them to their own means to accumulate wealth and raise themselves and families in the estimation of their fellow-men.

On the whole, the year 1843 opens upon us under favorable auspices. Rapidly advancing in the knowledge that government cannot make the people rich, but may make them poor, our countrymen are beginning in every section to demand that their governments shall content themselves with protecting their persons and property, leaving them to direct their labor and capital as they please, within the moral law ; getting rich or remaining poor as may result from their own management or fortune, under the dispensations of Him who controls the destinies of men and nations. Be it ours to inculcate reliance on themselves for relief and prosperity, and not on legislative acts which, in matters of general policy, can relieve one only at the expense of another, and can be generous only by being unjust. Confined to the prison bounds as we are, and to the prison walls as we may be, we shall rejoice in the advancement of our countrymen without, not only in their private fortunes, but in right modes of thinking; which will, in process of time, put an end to such wrongs as we suffer, and most others that flow from human government.

In February, 1843, Mr. Kendall announced his intention to publish the Life of General Jackson, as follows : —

LIFE OF GENERAL JACKSON.

Amos Kendall proposes to publish, in fifteen or more numbers, a Life of General Andrew Jackson, embracing the substance of all that has heretofore appeared in connection with the services of this distinguished man, together with many interesting incidents not noticed by his former biographers, and a complete history of his administration, concluding with an account of the manner in which, retired from the bustle of the world, he is quietly preparing to bid adieu to the scene of his glory.

This task has been undertaken with the approbation of General Jackson himself, who has kindly put into the author's hands his books and papers, public and private, and on obscure points favored him with his own recollections. With these materials, with the works already published, and with the contribution of facts and papers by many of the General's associates in civil and military life, aided by his own knowledge of events occurring within the last twenty years, the author hopes to produce a work worthy of the confidence and patronage of the American people.

The first number will embrace the General's early life, and a variety of revolutionary adventures and incidents not heretofore published. It will be illustrated by a first-rate likeness of the General, engraved on steel, and a print exhibiting him, when a stripling, saving from massacre a small party of men and boys, himself included, by attacking a band of about one hundred Tories who were rushing upon them in the night.

From his writings on political and general subjects we continue our extracts :—

MR. WISE.

This gentleman is now placed in a situation well calculated to excite reflection. In the violence and uncharitableness of party feelings, no man has in his charges done more injustice to others, and now the poisoned chalice is returned to his own lips.

We were told that while the Post-Office building was in flames in 1836, he wished that Amos Kendall was in their midst, and said that Amos had escaped him by a day, intimating that we had set the building on fire to destroy the evidences of some villany which he was about to elicit! At the moment these monstrous imputations were thrown out, the said Amos Kendall, having risen from a sick bed, was exerting every faculty of body and mind for the preservation of the books and papers he was charged with intent to destroy, and happily succeeded. But no exposure was made by Mr. Wise, and none attempted. What might have been charged under the Whig moral code of 1840, had the books and papers not been preserved, it is impossible to conceive. Perhaps we were as uncharitable as Mr. Wise; for we then thought that men like him and Stanly, who could so far forget their obligations to a fellow-man as to charge him with a flagrant crime without the least cause, were not too good to commit the same crime themselves, or by their instruments, and the exposed condition of the books and papers in a very combustible building was a source of great anxiety. One unsuccessful attempt was made to burn the building by setting fire to papers on the mantel-piece of the Postmaster-General's own room, thus bringing it home to us as near as possible; but the fire almost miraculously went out after burning to cinders a pile of loose letters and papers. Mr. Niles's apprehensions were so strong that he doubled the guard; and happy were we when we saw the whole safely transferred into the hands of the Whigs.

What villanies have they been able, with two years' possession, to bring to light? So far from finding anything corrupt in our administration of the Department, we believe the most violent are now ready to admit that our errors were on the other side, and that we were obstinately honest.

We know not whether Mr. Wise entertains this opinion; but we suspect he has not the least suspicion now that Amos Kendall burned the Post-Office building to conceal his villanies; and if he reflects upon the past as a good man ought, he will look upon recent events as but a providential infliction for his own injustice. If he view it in that light, they will do him no harm, but become the starting-point of a new and more honorable career.

In March, 1843, Mr. Kendall, amid the labors of editing the "Expositor," collecting material for and writing the Life of Jackson, and superintending the management of his farm, was so embarrassed with pecuniary affairs that, to extricate himself, he formed a partnership with his nephew, John E. Kendall, in a general agency for the prosecution of claims against the government, procuring patents, settlement of accounts, purchase and sale of real property, etc.

This business was to him always irksome and repugnant to his feelings. Necessity alone reconciled him to it.

THE END OF THE COMET.

The comet is gone without setting the world in flames. It seems even to have carried off a portion of the heat which warms the earth, and poor sinners are freezing to death instead of being burned up. The earthquakes appear to have exhausted themselves in shaking to pieces a few little islands instead of rending continents and breaking up the great globe itself. Within a few days, the weather has given decisive indications that "seed time" is returning, and doubtless "harvest" will follow. "The end is not yet," the calculations and predictions of the Millerites notwithstanding.

The idea that the great Architect is about to destroy this young world is an imputation upon his wisdom. It is not yet half peopled. It is just beginning to be useful. True, in the great deserts of Africa and Arabia, there is something like a bald head; but look at America and the isles of the ocean which seem to be creations of yesterday. Even Europe has scarcely arrived at manhood; and in most of Asia and Africa there are no signs of decay. The evident design of the earth's builder is not half accomplished. Civilization is to spread over

it; millions of intelligent human beings are to live where savages and wild beasts now roam; the principles of Christianity and the lights of science are to ameliorate the hearts and the conditions of men, and everything on earth be carried far towards perfection. When the globe becomes peopled to its utmost capacity; when improvement is no longer possible; when its fertile fields in every latitude begin to be covered with driving sands or perpetual snow; when mankind, from natural causes, disappear from its mountains and plains, — then may we expect the regenerating fire. Then will the material of our earth need working over to be made fit for some useful purpose in the economy of the universe.

Such is the revelation of nature, the dictate of reason, and the faith of that religion which believes there is nothing capricious in the character or acts of Him who rules all worlds. Nor is there anything inconsistent with it in the Book whence all sects of Christians deduce their creeds.

Let ancient women, womanish men, and timid children dismiss their fears. The world will roll on for the next six thousand years very much as it has done for the last six, with the difference that the human family will multiply faster and attain to a much higher rank in the scale of animate existences. The present preachings to the contrary are partly delusion, and partly fraud. In effect, they are another of those humbugs by which the artful and dishonest contrive to live in idleness upon the labor of their deluded followers. What trembling believer in the faith of Miller will not give food, raiment, and money to the herald that brings these startling tidings, and the more freely because all, all, is to be burned up within one short year! Millerism has the advantage of Mormonism in one particular: it fleeces the flock much quicker, and then turns it over to be roasted; but on the other hand, Mormonism pens and cherishes the flock, that it may be fleeced from year to year. Each plan is effectual in its way, and it is melancholy to behold rational beings who claim to be intelligent duped into supporting by their labor a set of idle knaves who become teachers of lies that they may live by the vocation.

GOVERNMENT.

The true functions of government are as yet but partially understood by the mass of mankind. It no longer rules by "right divine," and the principle is generally conceded that its proper object is the happiness of the people. But it has still too much of pageantry with it; people are in the habit of looking up to its functionaries as a superior class, of treating them with a deference not shown to merit in any other condition, and of conceding to them an extravagance of living and a liberality of compensation not approved or accorded in private life.

This is all wrong. The officers of the government are but agents of others to do business which they cannot do in person. They are entitled to the same respect as other agents, but no more. Their business is but a part of the business of society; more important than that of individuals, yet of the same general character. It is made up of transactions for men and with men, for the profit and advantage of men. The only difference is, that a greater number are interested in it, and more depends on its faithful performance.

The world will not be governed as it ought to be, until government shall be stripped of the majesty with which the arts and errors of ages have clothed it, and come to be considered as a part of the ordinary business of society; nor until those who administer it can travel abroad without other attentions than those bestowed on respectable gentlemen engaged in other concerns. Once, princes were made fools by being treated as gods and demi-gods; and the time has not passed away when presidents and secretaries may have their heads turned by parade and adulation.

The vanity inspired by such means would be of little consideration were it not for the consequences to which it leads. On one side, it makes the ruler feel as if he were superior to his fellow-men, and on the other it leads the people to concede to him a superiority. He ceases to feel or be regarded as the mere agent of the people, authorized only to transact certain things which they cannot do in person, and begins to exercise independent power, consulting only his own will. And the false majesty which is thrown around him dazzles the people into acquiescence, and thus the agent becomes the master. This is the most prolific source of misgovernment even in our own country.

We do not make these remarks in special reference to the present administration. They are the expression of convictions long settled, and never have we formed part of any pageantry to do honor to men in office. When President Monroe made his Western tour, in town meeting, at Frankfort, Ky., we opposed his reception under triumphal arches, with parades and speeches, and proposed that he should be welcomed only as we welcome other distinguished travellers. Being outnumbered, however, we became a mere spectator of the scenes which followed, declining, though strongly pressed, to be introduced to the President, although he was then accompanied by General Jackson, with whom we were most anxious to become acquainted. To do honor to him, we would have united in any public demonstration; for this repugnance does not extend to public benefactors not forming part of the government.

Much harm also arises from a misconstruction of the admitted maxim, that the proper object of government is to promote the happiness of the people. This idea, like many others, is not well expressed; the true meaning would be better conveyed by the following collocation of words, namely: "*The true object of government is to enable the people to promote their own happiness.*" It is to protect them from foreign and domestic violence, to render them secure in person, in property, in character, and in their respective pursuits; imposing no other restraints than are necessary to maintain the rights of others, and leaving them, under the benign influence of such laws only as are necessary to these ends, to work out their own happiness.

The proper functions of human government may be understood by considering those actually performed by the government of Heaven. That spreads the same sky over all. It presents the earth to the industry of man. It fans all with the same breezes, and "sendeth the rain on the evil and the good." Each man, under the protection of its general laws, is left to choose his home and occupation, to work or be idle, to accumulate wealth or live in poverty, without any special interposition to aid or prevent him.

Thus it should be with human government. To man himself Heaven seems to have left the regulation of all which man can manage. His laws should begin where Heaven's end, and be so formed as to carry out the same general principle. Their sole object should be to enable men to work out their own happiness unmolested by their fellow-men. It should be to protect men in their several pursuits, and render them secure in the enjoyment of their earnings. When it goes further, it becomes the source of those very evils it ought to prevent.

Most of the misgovernment on earth springs either from wilful wrong or a misconstruction of its legitimate functions. In the most liberal governments, even in our own, the agents of the people think it their duty to judge for the people as to the means which they shall adopt to advance their own prosperity. They undertake to think for the people in relation to their private affairs, to guide and direct them, as a father does his family, organizing their pursuits and directing their industry. It is vainly imagined that they can be made rich, prosperous, and happy by legislation. While a God of infinite wisdom deems it inexpedient to govern by special providence, his weak, erring, and presumptuous creatures deem themselves wise enough to govern by special laws. What Omniscience refrains from doing, they assume to do, and what is the result? Princes and paupers, masters and slaves, vice wallowing in wealth and virtue perishing in destitution, idleness taking the bread from the mouth of labor, the separation of society into classes and grades, grinding taxation and intolerable oppression, vice, envy, hatred, revenge, general demoralization, discontent, rebellion, and bloody revolution.

These are the results of attempting to promote the happiness of the people by interfering with the private pursuits of men.

The principles of our creed in relation to the duties of government are exceedingly simple. They are those of the moral code. To maintain a pure morality in the conduct of men is, in fact, the chief if not the only function of government. To prevent, by adequate punishments, violence, theft, calumny, and every act of man which injures a fellow-man, directly or indirectly, this is the proper province of human government. Mischief, and nothing but mischief, ensues from every attempt to direct or influence by law the honest pursuits of the people, to give advantages to a few not conceded to all, to establish or produce orders and classes, whether called kings, princes, nobles, and commons, or merely the rich and the poor. Distinctions of wealth are perhaps more mischievous than those of mere title, and, if they flow from the laws, just as wrongful to the mass of mankind. Wealth accumulated by fair competition, in honest pursuits, is the right of every man; but that which is derived from advantages which the law gives one man over another, is legalized plunder. The one is useful because it is the reward and stimulus of human industry; the other is injurious, because it encourages idleness and tricks on one side, and discontent and demoralization on the other. We shall pursue the subject.

GOVERNMENT (continued).

In our former remarks on government we endeavored to show that great and mischievous errors pervade the minds of men in relation to its dignity and its functions. We attempted to convince our readers, that it would be incomparably better for mankind if government were stripped of what is now called its majesty and dignity, and considered as it really is, a mere business matter, and its officers but ordinary agents to do for others what they cannot do for themselves. Inveterate habit makes the human race look upon government, even in this enlightened age, as something superhuman; and those in authority on the Eastern continent know how to avail themselves of that weakness to dazzle and deceive a thoughtless multitude. In France, particularly, as formerly in degenerate Rome, public shows and entertainments constitute a part of the government machinery.

The prophets and holy men of old looked forward to a time when there shall be little or no government among men. They characterize it as a period in the history of our race, when swords shall be beaten into ploughshares, and spears into pruning-hooks; when nation shall no longer rise up against nation nor learn war any more; when every man shall sit under his own vine and fig-tree, having none to molest or make him afraid.

It is universally admitted that nothing but the vicious propensities of men makes government necessary or desirable. If man never had the disposition to injure man, or nation to wrong nation, it is apparent that armies and navies, judges and sheriffs, jails, penitentiaries, and the gallows, would be of no utility. Whether mankind shall ever reach that happy state, we know not; but we do know that every improvement in the minds and morals of man is an advance towards it.

None but madmen or blind enthusiasts maintain that man can now exist in a state of society without government; but as it is the necessity of the case only which makes it his interest to be governed at all, it follows that the powers he should permit to be exercised over him should only be commensurate with the evils he designs to prevent. Whatever goes beyond that is a positive evil.

There is an axiom in relation to government which has misled many a mind. It is as old as the Romans, and was expressed by them in the words, "*non imperium in imperio*," meaning that there cannot be a government within a government. Adopting the same maxim, modern writers have maintained that sovereignty cannot be divided. The convenience of mankind has led them to expedients which have practically overthrown this ancient dogma and proved that there may be many governments within a government. No civilized society exists at this day under any other circumstances. In the United States we have: 1. The general government; 2. The State governments; 3. The county governments; 4. The city and town governments; 5. Parish governments; 6. Corporation governments, other than those of cities and towns.

Nor is it absurd to say, that sovereignty can be divided, whether we consider government or the people as the sovereign. In our country it is divided. One parcel of power is vested in the general government and another in the State governments, each exercising sovereign power over the same territory but over different objects. Within the States, there is a further subdivision, the State authorities, the county authorities, etc., etc., exercising jurisdiction over the same territory and people.

If it be said that all the local magistrates are dependent on the State, and not therefore sovereign or the representatives of sovereignty, it is answered, that this dependence, though a matter of fact, is not essential to their existence nor necessary to the exercise of the powers with which they are invested. Whence the impracticability of making the corporation of the city of New York, in the creation of its magistracy and the exercise of their powers as they now exist, wholly independent of the State, while the State should continue to exercise over it the same authority in other respects that it does now?

That state of things actually exists in regard to the State and national governments. Each has its powers independent of the other,

though exercised over the same territory and upon the same people. In the independent exercise of those powers, the one has no right to interfere with or control the other. If one commit an usurpation upon the other, there is constitutionally no common arbiter, and if one party do not yield, or there be no compromise, it becomes as much a question of peace and war as if the two governments occupied separate territories.

There may be more than two governments exercising independent authority over the same people and territory, provided their powers relate to objects entirely distinct. In one may be vested the power to make war and peace, and impose taxes adequate to sustain its operations; in another may be invested the power to regulate commerce; in a third, the power to make roads and canals; in a fourth, the organization and control of the internal police. In fine, there may be just as many governments over the same people and territory as there are separate functions to be performed by an agency of that sort.

If mankind would strip government of the factitious glare which gives it a mischievous influence over the public mind, let its powers first be reduced to the lowest degree that the present condition of society will admit, and the residue divided and parcelled out among as many jurisdictions as practicable consistent with the general interest. The power of peace and war is the most imposing, and most to be dreaded. It must of necessity be vested in one government; but that government need not be strengthened by an accumulation of other powers. They may be vested in other and independent authorities, thus lessening the influence of that most dangerous organization. Our general government was organized to a great extent on this principle; and if kept within its proper limits by a strict construction of the Constitution, would not be much to be feared. There is a perpetual struggle by one party in our country to enlarge its powers by a liberal construction of the Constitution, and the other does not always appreciate, as it ought, the importance of confining it to the strict letter of its power of attorney.

The State governments are susceptible of many salutary restraints not now imposed upon them. Their legislatures are considered omnipotent, except so far as they are specifically restricted by their own constitutions and that of the United States. Would it not be safer for the people to reverse the general principle, and, inserting in their constitutions a provision that they shall exercise no powers not specially granted, proceed to confer on them such powers, and no others, as the security of persons, property, and reputation may absolutely require.

One advantage of such a plan, and it would be no small one, would be to bring up each power for discussion and consideration by the people, and nothing could be granted without their express consent. We are quite sure that if this principle were adopted, many abuses by our State governments would be avoided, and the people would be much more secure from wrong and oppressive treatment.

The following is an account of the bursting of the gun on board the Princeton on the 28th of February, 1844.

AWFUL VISITATION.

Our readers will doubtless have heard of the explosion of the steamer Princeton's big gun, by which six human beings were in a moment hurried into eternity, and several others wounded.

It was on the 28th ultimo Captain Stockton had invited the ladies of the public officers, members of Congress, and many other citizens, to visit his noble ship and enjoy his hospitality. The day had passed in the highest enjoyment; all were gratified and delighted as well with the beauty of the ship as the good order of all and everything on board, and the cordiality of the Captain. The big gun had been twice fired, and notice was given that it would be fired no more. The ship was on her return from an excursion down the river, and had approached near her anchorage at Alexandria. The guests had devoured a sumptuous dinner, and while yet at the table, it was unfortunately proposed to have another gun. Without giving a general notice of the design, the Secretaries and Captain Stockton rose from their places and went upon deck for that purpose. The President rose to follow them, but was detained by a favorite song which was struck up by some of those still at the table. Mr. Upshur, Mr. Wilkins, Mr. Gilmer, Captain Kennon, Captain Stockton, Mr. Benton, Mr. Phelps, Mr. Maxcy, and many others, stood around the gun as it was being loaded. While the gunner was preparing the lock, Mr. Wilkins remarked, if he was Secretary of War he was afraid of that gun, and stepped back several yards from the position he had occupied. The next moment the gun exploded. The massive breech split into two parts, one of which killed Mr. Upshur, Mr. Gilmer, Captain Kennon, Mr. Maxcy, and Mr. Gardner, falling upon some of the bodies, and the other swept away a portion of the bulwarks of the ship and went into the river. One of the President's servants was also killed. Several small fragments of iron were thrown in different directions, one of which passed through the hat of Mr. Tyson, Second Assistant P. M. G., just over the top of his head. Captain Stockton, Mr. Benton, Mr. Phelps, and several others, were prostrated, but not seriously injured. Seventeen of the crew were wounded, some of them seriously.

The consternation and distress which ensued it is impossible to describe. The eagerness of the ladies to ascertain whether their fathers, brothers, and friends were among the victims, was almost frightful; and mournful was the condition of those in whose bosoms apprehension

became certainty. Their affliction and despair drew tears from the most firm.

The bodies remained on board during the night, and the next day were brought up to the city in coffins and deposited in the east room of the President's house.

Congress, the next morning, on receiving a message from the President in relation to the disaster, adjourned over to Monday, and all business in the public offices was suspended.

On Saturday the bodies, with the exception of Mr. Maxcy who was taken to his farm in Maryland for interment, were committed to the tomb in the Congress burying-ground, amidst an imposing military parade and a vast concourse of people.

Three of our own family were on board, and we should have been there had not the ship been out of the county of Washington, which constitutes our prison. While we, by being thus restrained of our liberty, were kept out of danger, the man whose action led to our restraint was among the slain. In this singular combination of events we find no gratification; but it tends to reconcile us to the ways of Providence, though men be his instruments.

CAPTAIN STOCKTON.

When this gallant officer became sensible of the destruction the bursting of his gun had produced, he exclaimed, in substance, " Would to God I had been the only victim." We can imagine the distress of a generous spirit which may reflect upon itself as the cause which has made so many widows and orphans. But we believe public opinion unanimously acquits Captain Stockton of all blame. The generous and the just sympathize with him most sincerely in his affliction. We trust and believe that he will rise manfully above it, and not be deterred by this calamity, great as it is, from still giving his country the benefit of his genius, only chastened and made cautious by so fearful a lesson.

THE SUB-TREASURY, — WHAT IS IT?

A treasury is a place where treasure is kept. The Constitution of the United States says, that " No money shall be drawn from the Treasury but in consequence of appropriations made by law; and a regular statement and account of the receipts and expenditures of all public money shall be published from time to time."

The obvious meaning of this provision is, that the " receipts," or money received shall go into the Treasury and remain there until drawn out by authority of law, when it becomes an " expenditure"; and the object of the published " regular statement " is, to enable the people to understand

how much has been received, how much has been expended, and how much remains in the Treasury.

The object was, that the public money should be kept for public uses legalized by Congress, and not applied to private or unauthorized ones.

When the government was organized under the Constitution, a Treasurer was appointed to receive the public money, carefully to keep it, and to pay it out only " in consequence of appropriations made by law." He gave bonds and entered upon the discharge of his duties. The collectors, who also gave bonds, were a sort of sub-treasurers. Neither they nor the Treasurer paid out public money except in pursuance of appropriation and Treasury warrants.

But there was a class of men who desired to obtain the public money for private uses. They did not like this system, which kept the money in the Treasury for the public only; and they set themselves at work to overthrow it. An ingenious plan was hit upon to abolish the Treasury, make the Treasurer a book-keeper only, and take the money which should be in the Treasury for the use of merchants, speculators, and other borrowers.

The plan was to hand over the public money to banks, not to be *kept*, but to be *lent*. It was called a deposit in bank; and the Treasurer's books showed heavy sums in the bank, when in fact there was not a dollar there, the whole having been loaned out, just as if it were bank capital. The nominal amounts in bank were called moneys in the Treasury. Thus the people were amused with the idea of a full Treasury, when, in fact, their money was all out in the hands of traders and speculators. Bank stockholders pocketed the interest, and the Constitution became in this respect a dead letter.

To perfect the scheme, a Bank of the United States was created, being the most convenient instrument through which the public money could be applied to private purposes.

For many years, the nation in fact had no Treasury at all. All its moneys went into banks, and were loaned out by them; and the balances reported to be in the Treasury were only the amounts which those corporations owed the United States.

In 1837 the balance thus reported to be in the Treasury was many millions; yet, the banks having suspended payment, the Treasurer could not command a dollar. It was all out of the Treasury, but not in consequence of appropriations made by law. When the appropriations came, the money was already gone.

This led those in the administration of the government to consider how it was that so many millions had gone out of the Treasury without appropriations or Treasury warrants. They soon perceived that not only the money was gone but the Treasury itself. We had a Treasurer but

no Treasury. Our Treasurer even, instead of keeping our treasure when we had any, had been metamorphosed into a mere book-keeper. Instead of being a keeper of treasure as the Constitution intended, he had become a keeper of books.

The remedy was obvious. It was to be found in a return to the Constitution and the establishment of a Treasury, in which the treasure of the country should be placed, not to be drawn out " but in consequence of appropriations made by law." It was, to make the Treasurer a keeper of treasure, as was originally intended, and as his official name implies, with such assistant keepers as the extent of our country and the business of the government rendered " necessary and proper."

Accordingly, to restore the Constitution, prevent the public money from being loaned out for private uses, and for the profit of bank stockholders, or " drawn from the Treasury except in consequence of appropriations made by law," Congress passed the Act of July 4th, 1840, entitled " An Act to provide for the collection, safekeeping, transfer and disbursement of the public revenue." The first section established a Treasury, that is to say, it provided a place where the public treasure should be kept, in the following words : —

" *Be it enacted, &c.* That there shall be prepared and provided, within the new Treasury building now erecting at the seat of government, suitable and convenient rooms for the use of the Treasurer of the United States, his assistants and clerks; and sufficient and secure fireproof vaults and safes, for the keeping of the public moneys in the possession and under the immediate control of the said Treasurer; which said rooms, vaults and safes, are hereby constituted and declared to be, the Treasury of the United States. And the Treasurer of the United States shall keep all the public moneys which shall come to his hand in the Treasury of the United States as hereby constituted, until the same are drawn therefrom according to law."

Inasmuch as most of the public moneys were received and disbursed at points distant from Washington, places of deposit were provided in the mints of Philadelphia and New Orleans, in the custom-houses at New York and Boston, and in rooms provided for the purpose at Charleston, S. C., and St. Louis, Mo., where the funds were to be received and kept under the charge of public officers bonded and sworn, for the purpose of being remitted to the Treasury at Washington, transferred to other depositories, or disbursed in payment of public dues, upon the order of the Treasurer and Treasury warrants issued according to law.

So far from allowing the keepers of the public money to use or lend it for their own profit or that of others, the seventeenth section of this Act provides as follows : " If any one of said officers, or of those connected with the Post-Office Department, shall convert to his own use in any way whatever, or shall use by way of investment in any kind of property or merchandise, or shall loan, with or without interest, any portion of the public moneys intrusted to him for safekeeping, disbursement, transfer, or for any other purpose, every such act shall be deemed and adjudged to be an embezzlement of so much of the said moneys as shall thus be taken, converted, invested, used, or loaned, which is hereby declared to be a felony; and any officer or agent of the United States, and all persons advising or participating in such act, being convicted thereof before any court of the United States of competent jurisdiction, shall be sentenced to imprisonment for a term of not less than six months or more than five years, and to a fine equal to the amount of the money embezzled."

Such was the measure of the Democratic party, which the Whigs nicknamed the "Sub-Treasury."

It was a plan to keep the public money for public uses, in compliance with the direct, positive, and unequivocal command of the Constitution.

It deprived no man of his rights, but prevented certain classes of men from using money which did not belong to them.

One of the first acts of Whiggism, when it came into power in 1841, was to abolish the Treasury.

They repealed the act passed by the Democrats to restore the Constitution and preserve the public money for the use of the public, virtually directing it to be placed in banks and loaned out by them for the profit of the stockholders and the use of the borrowers.

The difference between the two parties is here illustrated.

The Democrats obey the Constitution.

The Whigs disregard it.

The Democrats wish to preserve the public money exclusively for public purposes.

The Whigs wish to use it for their own purposes.

Little mischief has heretofore arisen from abolishing the Treasury in 1841, because the Whigs have spent the public money as fast as they could raise or borrow it. But we are told that the public deposits now begin to accumulate in the New York banks, and that speculation, vivified by the increased loans of the deposit banks, has again commenced its *ignis fatuus* career. We only want now a Bank of the United States to convert the Whig bankrupts, under the law of the extra session, into paper-money potentates and millionaire bankers.

OURSELF.

Our thanks are due to our friends in the Alabama legislature, and particularly to William L. Yancey, Esq., for their vindication of our

public and private character, and their sympathy for the condition in which fidelity to the public has placed us. In reading Mr. Yancey's speech, however, we find that he has been deceived by a new Whig lie, which we never before heard of. It is that on some occasion we had brought an action against somebody for a libel, and obtained but one dollar damages. We never brought an action for libel or slander in our life. Actions of that sort, when connected with political life, are like following a hornet which has stung you to his nest, for the purpose of making him individually responsible; you but provoke the stings of hundreds. We have always thought it most judicious, in such cases, to bide our time and destroy the nest. In 1828, we had some agency in destroying the nest; and, as it was rebuilt in 1840, we hope to be useful in destroying it again in 1844. In the mean time the insects may dab at us as they like, with stings blunted by former use; we shall aim directly at the nest.

But we shall be happy at all times to satisfy friends as to any passage in our life which to them may seem obscure. If a man lives who can justly charge us with ever doing a wilful wrong to our fellow-man, public or private, we have not understood our own motive in the act. Wrongs we have done, as every erring mortal must, who.has been called upon to do as much as we have; and wrongs we may again do without intending it. But to Mr. Clay we have done no wrong; he has not received full justice at our hands, and he never will. We intend, however, to approach the standard, and in what we say adhere most sacredly to the truth. Mark it, Democrats and Whigs; and when we depart from it reproach us.

NOT A SERMON;

But some Serious Reflections upon the Effects which the Moral Delinquencies of Man have upon the Creation around him.

A stranger might infer from the articles appearing in one portion of our newspaper press, that the people of the United States have not only abjured the Christian religion, but deny the existence of any Supreme Being who regards this world, or concerns himself with the affairs of nations or the conduct of men. Nothing in their estimation is so hypocritical as to profess a belief in God and providence; nothing so malignant as to point to events as governed by his general laws, or directed by his interposition; nothing so false as to impute the calamities of the country to the wickedness of its rulers.

We cannot conceive that any considerable portion of our countrymen concur in this opinion or are actuated by this feeling. They are not prepared to reject, not only the teachings of inspiration, but the evidences within and all around them, that there is a Being infinitely supe-

rior to ourselves, who has moulded and balanced the globes of the universe, opened the fountains of life, filled immensity with the wonders of his hand, and sustains the whole by his presence and his power.

Without conning over the lessons which nature teaches, let us turn to that book whence the Christian and civilized world draw their religion, and whose sublime precepts form the moral code, without some regard to which society cannot exist.

The very first principle presented by the Bible as the foundation of the Jewish and Christian religions is, that all the disorder and confusion, privation and pain, misery and death, which make this world a hospital, rocked with storms and resounding with groans, are attributable to man's transgressions. To Adam's violation of his Maker's command is ascribed not only all the corporeal suffering and mental agony which has fallen or may fall upon him and his race, until flames envelope the earth, but the pain and death of the entire brute creation, and even all the disorders of the physical world. Yes, the first principle of the Bible is, that one man's transgression of the moral law not only brought suffering and death upon the myriads of unoffending innocents which have sprung from his loins, but upon the beast of the field, the fowl of the air, the fish of the sea, the creeping thing however minute, the stalking monster however gigantic, on all the elements of creation, and on Nature herself.

It is now considered monstrous, by a portion of our press, to speak of the death of unoffending individuals as a Providential dispensation, connected in some inscrutable way with the moral conduct of others. To such we put the question in all seriousness, what have Adam's descendants of this day to do with his original transgression? Why should the gentle dove and innocent lamb suffer and die because Adam sinned? Why should man's moral conduct bring the eagle from his heights, or leviathan from his depths, a decaying carcass upon the plain or on the shore? Why should the depravation and derangement of man's moral faculties change the zephyr into a tornado, charge the clouds with thunder and let loose the lightning to shatter and kill, breathe malaria through the air and mix poison in the food of man and beast, cover the heavens with blackness and shake the earth in all its caverns, lift up the ocean and fling·down the mountains? Can ye answer this, ye arrogant men, who charge your neighbor with malignity, hypocrisy, and falsehood, because he tells you that your own moral delinquencies and the sins of a nation may have spread warning signs around you, and brought disappointment, suffering, and death upon those who were innocent of your crimes?

But let us look forward in the good book and trace this principle in the dealings of God with men.

Read in Genesis vi. 11, 12, 13, and 17; and also chapter vii. 20, 21, 22, and 23. What had the cattle, or the beasts, or the fowls of heaven, or the creeping things to do with the corruption and violence which induced the Ruler of the Universe to destroy everything "in whose nostrils was the breath of life"? What offence had the millions of drowning infants committed who were not yet old enough to breathe a prayer or lisp a curse? Yet, in consequence of man's corruptions and violence, "the fountains of the great deep were broken up," and the innocent and the guilty, "every living substance" on earth's broad surface, perished in the overwhelming flood. Christian, is it not so?

We have another signal illustration of the order of Providence in this world's affairs, connected with the history of ancient Egypt. In Exodus iv. 22 and 23, it is thus recorded: "And thou shalt say unto Pharaoh, Thus saith the Lord, Israel is my son, even my firstborn; and I say unto thee, let my son go, that he may serve me; and if thou refuse to let him go, behold, I will slay thy son, even thy firstborn." Here death to the son is threatened for the disobedience of the father.

Chapter v. 1 and 2. "And afterwards Moses and Aaron went in, and told Pharaoh, Thus saith the Lord God of Israel, Let my people go, that they may hold a feast unto me in the wilderness. And Pharaoh said, Who is the Lord, that I should obey his voice to let Israel go? I know not the Lord, neither will I let Israel go."

To satisfy Pharaoh who the Lord was, Moses was instructed to show him a sign, or a portent, or a miracle exhibiting supernatural power. Chapter vii. 8 and 9. "And the Lord spake unto Moses and unto Aaron saying, When Pharaoh shall speak unto you, saying, Shew a miracle for you; then thou shalt say unto Aaron, Take thy rod, and cast it before Pharaoh, and it shall become a serpent."

But Pharaoh was not induced by any signs or omens to take heed to himself and obey the command of his Maker; and as a further warning to him, the river was turned into blood. Verse 21. "And the fish that was in the river died; and the river stank, and the Egyptians could not drink of the water of the river; and there was blood throughout the land of Egypt." Here we are taught that the disobedience of the King of Egypt brought death upon the fish in the river and gave all his people blood to drink.

But the hardened monarch was not moved even by this sign; and others followed in rapid succession. Chapter viii. 3. "And the river shall bring forth frogs abundantly, which shall go up and come into thine house, and into thy bed-chamber, and upon thy bed, and into the house of thy servants, and upon thy people, and into thine ovens, and into thy kneading-troughs."

Upon the apparent submission of Pharaoh and the prayer of Moses, the frogs after being brought up from the river, were suddenly all destroyed. Verses 13 and 14. "And the Lord did according to the word of Moses ; and the frogs died out of the houses, out of the villages, and out of the fields. And they gathered them together upon heaps ; and the land stank." What myriads of the reptile creation are here destroyed not for any offence of their own.

Again the king became obdurate, and the rod of Aaron called into existence myriads of "lice upon man and upon beast." There next came " grievous swarms of flies into his servants' houses, and into all the land of Egypt ; the land was corrupted by reason of the swarms of flies."

Still did the obdurate monarch fail to take warning from these extraordinary occurrences, and it became necessary to bring upon him severer calamities. Chapter ix. 3 and 6. "Behold the hand of the Lord is upon thy cattle which is in the field, upon the horses, upon the asses, upon the camels, upon the oxen, and upon the sheep ; there shall be a very grievous murrain. . . . . And the Lord did that thing on the morrow, and all the cattle of Egypt died." Thus for the disobedience of Pharaoh alone, not only did the cattle of Egypt suffer death, but his people were deprived of a portion of their property.

The next sign was the sprinkling of ashes towards heaven by Moses, which became "small dust," and produced "boils, breaking forth with blains upon man and upon beast."

Read chapter ix. 14, 15, 18, 23, 24, and 25. Still these threatenings of divine wrath, and this display of almighty power, did not subdue the rebellious heart of this proud monarch.

Next came devouring locusts upon his land ; "before them were no locusts such as they, neither after them shall be such," which. "covered the face of the whole earth, so that the land was darkened ; and they did eat every herb of the land, and all the fruit of the trees which the hail had left, and there remained not any green thing in the trees, or in the herbs of the field, throughout all the land of Egypt."

Next "there was a thick darkness in all the land of Egypt three days ; they saw not one another, neither rose any one from his place for three days."

But something more heart-rending and awful than all these plagues was necessary to extort obedience from the tyrant of Egypt. Chapter xi. 4, 5, and 6. "And Moses said, thus saith the Lord, about midnight will I go out into the midst of Egypt. And all the firstborn in the land of Egypt shall die, from the firstborn of Pharaoh that sitteth upon his throne, even unto the firstborn of the maidservant that is behind the mill ; and all the firstborn of beasts. And there shall be a great cry throughout all the land of Egypt, such as there was none like it, nor shall be like it any more." Chapter xii. 29 and 30. "And it came

to pass, that at midnight the Lord smote all the firstborn in the land of Egypt, from the firstborn of Pharaoh that sat on his throne unto the firstborn of the captive that was in the dungeon, and the firstborn of cattle. And Pharaoh rose up in the night, he and all his servants, and all the Egyptians ; and there was a great cry in Egypt ; for there was not a house where there was not one dead." What had "the maid behind the mill," "the captive in the dungeon," the new-born infant, or the mother that bore it, to do with Pharaoh's transgression which brought on them this awful calamity ? Nothing whatever. It is all directly imputed to the disobedience and obduracy of the ruler of the nation. His moral delinquencies operating through the will or law of God, upon the material world around him, turned the river into blood, made it vomit forth frogs, changed dust into lice, bred swarms of flies and clouds of locusts. Pharaoh's heart was corrupt, and it corrupted nature around him. His depravity affected the elements, and produced thunderings and lightnings, fire and hail. It brought destruction and death upon herb and tree, reptile and fish, man and beast ; nor did the effects of one man's crimes cease until "there was not a house in which there was not one dead."

We have further illustrations of this great principle in the case of King David. How was he punished for his conduct towards Uriah and his wife ? 2 Samuel xii. 14. The Prophet Nathan tells him, "Howbeit, because by this deed thou hast given great occasion to the enemies of the Lord to blaspheme, the child also that is born unto thee, shall surely die." Here the innocent infant suffers and dies, to punish his criminal father.

1 Chronicles xxi. 11, 12, 13, and 14. We are told that David, in his pride, was tempted to number the children of Israel, which was offensive to Heaven. Thus, in three days, seventy thousand men were sent from time to eternity, for the crime of one man, while that man was permitted to live !

The Decalogue tells us that "the sins of the fathers" are visited "upon the children unto the third and fourth generation" ; and the book is full of instances in which families were punished for the sins of their head, and nations for those of their rulers.

In fine, it is an essential item in the creed of every Christian, not that the myriads of Adam's race alone die for his sin, but that it also produced the death of God himself in human form upon the cross, on which occasion, darkness covered the land, earth quaked, and the rocks were rent.

Does not the same relation exist between God and man now that did in the ages of Pharaoh and of David ? Do not man's transgressions now have the same effect that they did then on earth, air, and sea,

beast, fish, and fowl, the fate of families and the destiny of nations ? We have no prophets like Moses, or Nathan, or Gad, to point out the precise connection between cause and effect, between the moral conduct of man and the sign that warns him to reform, or the catastrophe that falls on him as a punishment. But the history of the past, reason, and experience should be a prophet to us. When we find extraordinary deviations from the regularity of nature's laws, always or frequently following extraordinary violations of the moral law, we ought to see a connection between them as clearly as if pointed out by the voice of inspiration.

PRIVATE CHARACTER. — POLITICS.

There are many men who maintain that in our political controversies the private character of candidates for office ought not to be brought in question. Is this sound doctrine ?

Is it safe to trust a man in public life who pays no regard to his moral or legal obligations in private life ? Every man will answer in the negative. How are the people to know whether a candidate is regardful of those obligations in private life without a discussion of his private character. There is a sense in which we admit the soundness of the principle. It is where nothing but mere faith is concerned, nothing which can influence or affect the public conduct of the candidate in its bearing upon the rights and privileges of his fellow-men. Such are abstract opinions and articles of religious faith, which have no bearing upon legislation or the administration of the laws. To call in question points of that sort is to infringe on the liberty of thought, and hold out inducements to hypocrisy.

But where in private life men disavow and deny the existence of all moral obligations, or where in practice they openly set it at defiance, it is absurd to say their private character in that respect is not a proper subject for discussion when they seek high places in society.

In like manner, if in private life a candidate for office be a notorious law-breaker, whatever may be his professions, his character in that respect is a proper subject for inquiry and discussion ; for the more elevated his position the more extensive is likely to be his practice, and the more fatal his example.

Indeed, it is infinitely more important that public officers should be moral and law-abiding men than that private citizens should. The whole community have a vital interest in the matter, and in those respects they have a right to know and discuss the private character of those who aspire to office.

Undoubtedly this practice is often carried too far, and made to embrace matters with which others have nothing to do. For instance, it

is nobody's concern what may be a candidate's religious faith, or to what sect he may belong. That is a matter between man and his God. Sometimes, indeed, when faith degenerates into fanaticism, and attempts to propagate itself by the aid of the civil power, it becomes a proper subject for discussion in electioneering contests, not in reference to its intrinsic truth or falsehood, but to its interference with the liberty and just rights of other creeds.

In fine, morality has much to do with politics ; but religion, separated from morality, nothing. It is only when religion ceases to be morality, and its professors attempt to encroach on the just rights of others, that it becomes a proper topic for political discussion, and then only in its abuses.

But the first question which ought to be asked when a man becomes a candidate and seeks an office of trust or power should be, is he a moral man ? This is but to ask, Is he not a murderer ? Is he not a peace-breaker ? Does he in private life respect the Constitution and laws of his country ? Does he take from others their property and rights without an equivalent ? Is he a thief, a swindler, or a gambler ? Does he pay due respect to those domestic relations which constitute the foundation of society and of human happiness ? All questions which relate to man's moral conduct are appropriate ; for the elevation of bad men not only endangers society by their direct power over its laws and institutions, but by their example, which is often quite as destructive.

Such are our opinions ; and when we hear men maintaining that the private character of candidates is not a proper topic for discussion, we always suspect that selfishness lies at the bottom of it, and that they know their own would not stand the scrutiny.

In October, 1844, Mr. Kendall announces the close of his editorial labors, in the last number of the "Expositor."

TO SUBSCRIBERS.

Another number of the "Expositor" will complete the fourth volume. As that number will be delayed until we can give the details of the approaching presidential election, it is proper to announce now, that the publication of this paper will cease with the present volume. This determination on our part does not depend on the event of the election, but is produced chiefly by the consideration that it yields us but a meagre income, not half sufficient for the support of our family, and we have no right to expect a better patronage in years to come than we have received in years past. We have nobody to reproach for our disappointment in that respect, and in private life shall continue to support Democracy with as much cheerfulness as if it had made us rich, although we cannot give so much time to its hallowed cause.

Our purpose is to devote ourself constantly and faithfully to the agency business in this city, — to the procuring of contracts, settlement of accounts, procuring of pensions and patents, and advocating just claims before the Executive Departments and Congress, and attending to any business here of a public or private nature with which our friends and countrymen may think proper to entrust us.

If our friends abroad will do us the favor to recommend us to those who have business in Washington, they will lay us under obligations which we shall be happy to repay. So far in life, we have served our friends and the public much more faithfully than we have ourself; and as the approach of old age admonishes us that we shall not be able to serve anybody much longer, may we not hope that our friends and the public will not only excuse us for giving a different direction to our labors, but aid us to make those labors conducive to the comfort and happiness of ourself and family ?

CHAPTER XVIII.

CONNECTION WITH THE TELEGRAPH.

WHILE Mr. Kendall was employed in the prosecution of claims, he fell in with Professor Morse, who was endeavoring, with little prospect of success, to get an appropriation from Congress to extend a line of his telegraph from Baltimore to New York; it being already in operation between Washington and Baltimore. Finding the Professor much discouraged, he inquired whether he had no project to render his telegraph profitable as a private enterprise, if he should fail in obtaining further aid from the government. On being answered in the negative, he rejoined that if the appropriation failed he would be 'glad to talk further on the subject. It failed, and Professor Morse asked Mr. Kendall for a proposition to take charge of his telegraph business.

The result was, in March, 1845, a contract between the proprietors of three fourths of Morse's patents and Mr. Kendall, by which the latter was to receive a commission of ten per cent on the first hundred thousand dollars which might be realized from the sale of their interest, and a commission of fifty per cent on all sums which might be thus realized over one hundred thousand dollars.

This agreement vested Mr. Kendall with full power to manage and dispose of Morse's interest in his patent-right, according to his discretion.

The contracting parties with Mr. Kendall were Professor Morse, who owned nine sixteenths, Alfred Vail of New Jersey, who owned two sixteenths, and Professor L. D. Gale of Washington, the proprietor of one sixteenth of the patent, the remaining fourth having been previously conveyed by Professor Morse to Hon. F. O. J. Smith of Maine.

A field worthy of Mr. Kendall's distinguished talents, and congenial to his taste, now stretches out before him.

From the discovery of electricity by Thales six hundred years

before the Christian era, to the moment when the idea of using it as a vehicle of intelligence occurred to Professor Morse on board the packet-ship "Sully," Wm. W. Pell, captain, on his return from Europe in 1832, but little had been done towards its practical application to the service of man.

Though this agent dozed through all these ages, scarcely recognized and not at all understood by mankind, at last it suddenly asserted itself as the swiftest and one of the most valuable servants of man.

Its marvels are innumerable, its magic incomprehensible. Tamed and harnessed by Professor Morse, it traverses with equal speed and certainty the depths of ocean, the snows of the mountain, and the burning sands of the desert. It outstrips the wildest fancy, passes Time himself in the race, and makes a circuit round the globe with the velocity of thought. It never tires, never grows old, has few bad habits, is perfectly docile, makes no mistakes, and, in fine, offers itself to man as his most faithful and obedient slave.

Much as we already know of its power and properties, he would be presumptuous who should venture to limit its triumphs to what has already been accomplished.

For a mind like Mr. Kendall's, this subject had a peculiar fascination independent of the pecuniary advantages which he confidently believed would follow its judicious management.

It is unnecessary to go into the details of his administration of these important interests. They called him frequently from home, involved him as agent in numerous law-suits, called into requisition his best executive ability in the formation and administration of new telegraph companies, and terminated in 1860. He could contemplate as their direct results, Professor Morse established in a condition of pecuniary independence, the other owners of the patent profited in the same proportion, and an ample fortune secured to himself and family.

The acquaintance formed with Professor Morse soon ripened into warm friendship, which knew no abatement or interruption. For twenty-five years their relations were not only intimate but often involved questions of the utmost delicacy touching closely the interests of both; but no jealousy, no distrust, no feeling tending to impair their most implicit confidence of each in the other's integrity ever occurred.

TO HIS WIFE.

NEW YORK, May 30, 1845.

MY DEAR WIFE, — I do not know when I shall be with you again. The people with whom we have to deal here move so very slowly that there seems to be no end to our negotiation. We have no reason, other than this tardiness and an evident desire to make as much money out of the telegraph as they can, to doubt that we shall in the end accomplish all we desire.

Mr. Butterfield has been with us to-day, and with some of his friends proposes to build a line of telegraph from Buffalo to Springfield, Massachusetts, there to connect with the line from New York to Boston, which also he is disposed to undertake if we do not make other arrangements. If this arrangement is consummated I shall consider our fortunes as *almost* made; but as "there is many a slip between the cup and the lip," it will not do to consider ourselves rich as yet. Mr. B. leaves for Washington this evening, and I shall ask him to take charge of this letter.

I remain *very* well, — *remarkably* well; but I do not like living from home. I must next time, if I can afford it, bring a part of home with me, yourself or Jane.

I send oceans of love to yourself and our dear children, including Edward and not forgetting Henrietta.

Your devoted husband,
AMOS KENDALL.

TO HIS WIFE.

NEW YORK, June 6, 1845.

MY DEAR WIFE, — Heigh ho ! I do not know when I shall see you again. We have just finished a long conference with the Executive Committee of the Amboy (Old Boy ?) Railroad Company. They have just begun to find out something about the magnetic telegraph, simple souls !

I find I have a little more patience than I once had; else I should curse and quit these New Jersey corporations. But it is so much our interest to get along their roads that I repress my feelings ; and the more readily because I am quite sure they will come to us in the end. When that end will come, I know not. Probably I can tell you more about it to-morrow, when we are promised a further interview. In haste,

Your devoted
AMOS KENDALL.

MRS. JANE KENDALL.

TO HIS WIFE.

NEW YORK, August 16, 1845.

MY DEAR WIFE, — Jane's letter of the 14th, with your *sweet* postscript, came to hand last evening. Take care to preserve yourself as well as the peaches, or the latter will "lose all their sweetness to me."

My cold did not leave me so kindly as I hoped. Thursday and Friday I was kept in my room, not very sick, but good for nothing. My nursing was none of the best, and I wished myself at home.

Nothing detains me here now but waiting for the caps for our telegraph posts, which were shipped from Portland two weeks ago, and are expected every hour. If nothing new occurs, I shall be off as soon as they come, but shall be detained a day or more in Philadelphia.

I should grudge the time more had I not with me a supply of General Jackson's papers, which enable me to progress with my book. I have worked at them to-day until I am wearied ; so you must excuse my brevity.

Jane does not send your love because postage is charged by weight ! A good idea. But she forgets that the god of love himself is outweighed by a feather. Send it along. Herein please receive more than all the heathen gods ever knew, and deal it out in universefuls.

Most affectionately,
AMOS KENDALL.

DEATH OF HIS SON.

Two days after writing this last letter, Mr. Kendall was startled by the receipt of the following : —

BALTIMORE, August 18, 1845.

Mr. KENDALL, — It is my melancholy duty to inform you of the following, received by telegraph a moment ago, announcing the death of your son William.

"6 o'clock 30 minutes, P. M.

"Mr. William Kendall, son of Hon. Amos Kendall, was, a few minutes ago, met and shot dead by Rufus Elliot, brother-in-law of John C. Rives."

Very respectfully your obedient servant,
HENRY J. ROGERS.

He hastened to Washington and found the distressing intelligence only too true.

An altercation of words with a friend, begun in jest, had resulted in a fearful tragedy.

William, then twenty-two years of age, the only surviving son by his first wife, the loved companion of a large circle of friends, of generous impulses and irreproachable character, having left his father's house a little before, full of life and vigor, is shot down in the street and carried home a corpse.

In this overwhelming affliction Mr. Kendall had the heartfelt sympathy of friends throughout the country.

Though the fondest hopes were in a moment blasted, he meekly bowed his head and received the stroke with true Christian fortitude and resignation, deeply chastened but not repining.

In the month of November following, another calamity fell upon his family in the death of his wife's mother and brother, under most distressing circumstances.

The following extract from a letter addressed to his nephew conveys the sad intelligence : —

"MONTICELLO, Mo., November 23, 1845.

"Yesterday, Saturday, about twelve o'clock, the wind blowing furiously from the northwest, a thick cloud of smoke was seen to rise by your grandmother and uncle on the outskirts of their farm. They hastened to save the fence and stacks of grain, which they had hardly reached when the fire, coming in a perfect tornado, overtook and completely enveloped them. Their clothes took fire and burned entirely off, burning their bodies in a most shocking manner.

Your grandmother was found to be lifeless ; Alexander lived until a quarter past ten that night."

They were buried in one grave, on the following Monday.

On receipt of the tidings at Washington, Mr. Kendall addressed the afflicted husband and father the following letter : —

WASHINGTON, December 12, 1845.

MY VERY DEAR SIR, — This morning we received the first news of "the awful calamity which has befallen you, and to-morrow morning your beloved James leaves us for the purpose of accompanying you to this city. Your remaining daughter, with the cordial and affectionate concurrence of her husband, invites you to come and live with us, and we both promise to do all in our power to make you comfortable and happy. The hand of Providence has been laid heavily upon us this year, but we have many ties of affection and many sources of enjoyment still left ; and, though we do not see how, all that has happened is designed for some good.

Jane has been much distressed during the day, but has become calm this evening.

Jane and the children unite in sending love to you.

Most affectionately your son, etc.,
AMOS KENDALL.

Mr. ALEX. KYLE, Clark Co., Missouri.

The invitation was accepted. The old gentleman constituted one of Mr. Kendall's family till 1852, when, in the 82d year of his age, he calmly yielded up his spirit with a full assurance of a blessed immortality.

The following letters, written in the fullest and most unrestrained confidence, illustrate better than any description the writer could give, the genial disposition, kindness of heart, and habitual trains of thought which were characteristic of Mr. Kendall's life.

TO HIS WIFE.

NEW YORK, November 7, 1846, 3.30 P. M.

MY DEAR WIFE, — I have never come so near being homesick since I became a husband ; yet I cannot leave here before the evening of the 11th (Wednesday next), without the danger of being compelled to return in a few days.

In this state of the case I enclose you sixty dollars ($60) of the eighty which I owe you, instead of delivering the whole in person as I expected.

Expecting to hear the gong for dinner every minute, and having barely time to get this into the mail after dinner, I must conclude by enclosing more *love* for you and the family than I do *money*.

Yours devotedly,
AMOS KENDALL.

Mrs. JANE KENDALL.

TO HIS DAUGHTER.

NASHVILLE, Tenn., January 4, 1848.

MY DEAR JANE, — On the 1st inst. I wrote to your mother, giving some account of my journey here, and I hope my letter will have come to hand before this reaches you.

I have met with many old acquaintances here, among whom is Mr. McIntosh, whom your mother will remember as jailor at Frankfort at the time of Beauchamp's execution. He is now keeper of the penitentiary here. He invited me to attend church with him on Sunday, where I heard an instructive and amusing New Year's discourse, — instructive for its religious statistics, and amusing for the plainness with which the pastor lectured his flock. By his statistics it appears that the Baptist church, to which he belongs, has largely increased within the past year in the South and diminished very considerably in the North. He attributed this diminution to the fact, that a large portion of their preachers in the North employ themselves in preaching abolitionism instead of the gospel.

This city is literally *founded on a rock*. A bank composed of strata

---

of hard blue limestone rises up on the southerly bank of the Cumberland River to the height of about 80 or 90 feet at its highest point from low watermark, and running back in a broad ridge about half a mile, there rises into a conical hill about 150 feet higher. A deep and broad valley surrounds this eminence, extending, in a circuit of about two miles, from the river above to the river below. The top of the rock is crowned with a grove of cedars, in the midst of which a new State house, which bids fair to be a magnificent building, is in progress of erection. It is built of hard blue and variegated limestone, or marble, quarried in the neighborhood and prepared in the penitentiary. Its foundations are as high as the tops of the church steeples in the city below, and it overlooks the surrounding country on every side to a considerable distance.

The best part of the city is on the broad ridge between the river and the hill ; but humbler dwellings have been erected in the valley, whence their poor tenants were driven by the late flood. The powder magazine which some time since blew up with such terrific consequences, was in the valley west of the city, where a portion of the ruins are yet to be seen.

I am located in the City Hotel, in a room with a Whig member of the legislature, with whom I get along quite cozily. He is a Taylor man, and does not believe Clay can be elected.

The stairway by which I approach my room bears marks of the scenes which sometimes occur in this region. There are a dozen bullet-holes in the plastering from the bottom of the stairs to the third story. The tale goes, that a husband suspected a gallant of being too well acquainted with his wife, and attacked him in the street with knife and pistol. The gallant shot the husband dead in the encounter, and fled to this house, pursued by a furious mob. As he ran up stairs, some twenty-five pistol shots were fired at him, none of which took effect. From the third story he fell or was thrown down between the winding stairways to the lower floor, about thirty feet, without serious injury ; whence the mob dragged him into the street for the purpose of hanging him to a lamp-post. Some of the cooler citizens interfered, and he finally escaped.

January 5. At this point in my letter, the carriage of A. N. Brown, late Governor of Tennessee, arrived for the purpose of taking me out to his residence, about three miles distant, where I spent the night. He has a splendid residence, and an agreeable wife, who invited me to visit them with your mother, and make their house our home, etc.

I hope to finish my business here this day or to-morrow morning, so as to return to Louisville by the next boat. There have recently been two explosions of those floating volcanoes, of which you have doubtless heard. These make engineers, etc., careful for a time, and travellers are more safe now than if they had not occurred.

Give my love to your mother, grandfather, brother, sisters, and cousins.

"Home! home, sweet, sweet home!
There 's no place like home!"

Your affectionate father,

AMOS KENDALL.

TO HIS WIFE.

STEAMER ISAAC SHELBY, KENTUCKY RIVER, February 4, 1848.

MY DEAR WIFE, — I feel like a young spark who has just set out on a trip to visit his sweetheart. To those sensations is added the anticipated pleasure of again being cheered with the smiles and greetings of beloved children and dear friends. On the whole, I am happier than the young spark; for there is a charming variety in my anticipations, while he has but one source of delight.

I write you because I cannot travel as fast as the lightning or even as Uncle Sam's mail. Early to-morrow morning I expect to reach Cincinnati, where I have two or three hours' business. That I hope to despatch and embark for Pittsburg before noon. There also, I must stop a few hours. The roads over the mountains, I am told, are in a shocking condition and may delay me. In counting up the days and hours which separate us, I cannot hope to see you in less than six days, and it is very likely to be seven or eight.

I met many old friends in Frankfort, and have been treated very kindly by old political enemies. It is very remarkable that Mr. Clay's old political friends in Kentucky, almost to a man, are opposed to his being a candidate for the Presidency again, believing that he cannot be elected, and doubting whether they can carry Kentucky for him. They are exceedingly anxious that he shall decline and let them all unite on General Taylor. This state of things, with some local quarrels among themselves, tends to make them kind towards the old sinners of the Democratic party. The members of the legislature are well disposed towards *our* telegraph, and I think will pass the necessary acts without opposition. Our work is going on bravely; we will have the telegraph in operation at Frankfort in ten days, and in less than three weeks will have up more than three hundred and fifty miles of posts, and one hundred and fifty wired. The O'Reillyites tried to get the Tennessee law repealed, but failed. Finding themselves in a sinking condition, they are letting loose the flood-gates of their wrath upon me in the fiercest manner. I think their reign is drawing to a close; but I wish I could be in this region to follow them up.

Benjamin Johnson has lost a beautiful daughter, about sixteen, and the whole of his family has been sick, chiefly with scarlet fever. I called

twice to see Mrs. Devine, but she was with Benjamin Johnson's sick family. Doctor, I hear, has been sick for two months, but is slowly recovering. I did not get out to Mount Pleasant, but saw Mr. Stedman. The late flood washed away his dam.

I learned from their son-in-law, Cox, whom I met in Frankfort, that Mr. and Mrs. Fenwick are well. I dined at Judge Monroe's, took tea successively at Tanner's, Russell's, and J. L. Moore's, and called upon Mr. and Mrs. Theobald, now keeping the Weisiger House, with whom I boarded at Georgetown, Ky., when I first commenced business in 1815. And on board this boat I find an old Lexington acquaintance of 1814. What an *age* has passed since I saw those faces, and how rapidly the sight of them sends the mind back over its varied and thrilling scenes! To me life seems to have been long, very long. Most men say it seems short. Does it seem long to me because I have experienced more changes, acted in more scenes, or had more thoughts? I do not know.

This morning was beautiful, mild, and sunny. Night approaches, and it is dark, cold, and snowing. O how comfortless is this little stateroom in which I write; how desolate and lonely is that narrow berth in which I must sleep! The boat shakes so I can scarcely write.

Take of my love all the heart can hold, and deal it out to father, children, cousins, and friends. Fear not that you will exhaust the store. It is like the widow's handful of meal and cruise of oil.

This boat seems to have gotten into a spiteful mood, — it is all jerk, jerk, jerk, — as if it were saying, "Good, sir, — stop now; Good, sir, — stop now"; and so on.

Your devoted

AMOS KENDALL.

OHIO RIVER, February 5.

Last night was so dark and stormy that our captain thought it prudent to stop.

TO HIS WIFE.

RELAY HOUSE, August 12, 1848, 9 P. M.

MY DEAR WIFE, — I am in a most fitting condition to give good advice. Let me advise you then, when you think of starting for the West some afternoon, just to inquire before you start whether any Western train of cars connects at this place with the evening train from Washington. If you do not, you may chance to find when you get here, that the evening train for the West went up at four o'clock, and that you will have to stay here until eight o'clock the next morning, when you might just as well be at home until six! Remember this piece of advice, and teach it to our children. It is an excellent

way to avoid feeling foolish after you have stopped here and find that you can neither progress on your journey, nor get back to Washington, nor forward to Baltimore.

The evening, however, is not without interest. The wind comes feeling around the house as if desirous of taking up lodgings here, every now and then dashing down a shower of raindrops, then, as it were, stopping to listen for the purpose of ascertaining what we inside think of it. Then about a thousand tree-frogs, with all sorts of tones, aided by crickets and grasshoppers out of doors and an accordion within, are giving us a most harmonious concert. Decidedly, this is more pleasant than chasing a locomotive all night through the hills and valleys of Maryland and Virginia, leaping the creeks, and threading the sinuosities of the Potomac. There is comfort in this, is there not? Then again, if I had not come down this evening, I should not have written you this letter, and who knows but the cars may run off the track to-morrow morning, and somebody sitting exactly in my seat may get his neck broken?

Doubtless it is best as it is, but do not forget my advice.

Give my love and advice to father and the children, not forgetting "inquiring friends."

Don't dream about my being thrown off the track to-night, for I ain't there.

Most affectionately, your husband,

AMOS KENDALL.

TO HIS WIFE.

STEAMER NOMINEE, Ohio River, Sunday, 8 P. M., October 7, 1849.

MY DEAR WIFE, — We left Wheeling about 9 A. M., yesterday, with a rise of six feet of water and a prospect of a rapid trip to Kentucky. But as the water runs less than four miles an hour, and our boat about ten miles, we found ourselves to-day getting ahead of the rise, and under the necessity of waiting for the water just above the mouth of the Guyandotte Creek, about 200 miles below Wheeling and 100 above Maysville. Here we found three boats, and have since been joined by another; and still another, attempting to cross a bar below, grounded in sight of us, so that there are seven steamers in a similar predicament. We shall probably be joined by several more to-night, or soon to-morrow, so that we can array a formidable fleet. I have hopes that we shall have water enough to progress to-morrow; but there is some uncertainty about it, and at the best, travelling all night from Maysville, I cannot expect to reach Frankfort before Wednesday morning.

I had as pleasant a journey as could be expected over the mountains, and reached Wheeling in thirty-six hours from Washington. The night

was cloudy and cold, and although I was abundantly warm, I took a slight cold, the effects of which have not entirely left me.

We were in the mail stage, and brought along news of the Maryland election to the little post-offices, which produced some funny scenes. The Upper or Cumberland district was represented by a Whig in the last Congress, but has now elected a Democrat. The Whig candidate's name was McKaig; the Democrat's Hamilton. The following dialogue took place at one of Mr. Collamer's post-offices in the Alleghany Mountains: —

POSTMASTER. Which party has carried the election, the Whigs or the Locos?

STAGE-DRIVER. The Democrats have carried every thing.

P. M. What, is n't McKaig elected?

DRIVER. No.

P. M. Nor Calhoun (for the legislature)?

DRIVER. No, he is beat worse than McKaig.

P. M. Well, *I don't care if the world comes to an end to-morrow.* What is the Loco majority?

DRIVER. I don't know exactly, — Hamilton has one or two hundred, and the Democratic State ticket still more.

P. M. I went to the election just to vote for McKaig and Calhoun, and if I had n't supposed they would have been elected I would n't have gone a step. They ain't both beat?

DRIVER. Indeed they are badly beat.

P. M. *You need n't leave no more mails here.* (A general laugh.) *Stop and make my coffin when you come back,* — *I can't live a day longer.*

I suppose this man was one of Mr. Collamer's new appointments.

In a few miles we arrived at another little post-office. As the postmaster came out for the mail, he asked, "Who is elected in this district?" The driver answered, "Hamilton." "*Glory enough for one day!*" exclaimed the "spared monument" of Whig mercy. Although it was near midnight, we saw several persons approaching the post-office, and as we left a hearty cheer came through the darkness, which was repeated until we were out of hearing.

This is not a first-rate boat; but I have a good state-room with a wide berth, and we have a very good table. A multitude of strange men and a few homely women constitute our company. There is not a face which I recognized; but one of the passengers says he has seen me at Washington. We have a Virginia judge on board, whom I took to be a crazy man. He walks *by* himself and talks *to* himself while the tobacco juice drips from his chin. Finally, however, I got into conversation with him, and found much good sense and intelligence under his slovenly exterior.

October 8. I was awakened this morning by the cheering sounds of preparation to start, a sure indication that the rise in the water had overtaken us. About sunrise we were under way, the rise in the night having been about seventeen inches. We are already running ahead of it again, having come about twenty-five miles, and expect to be obliged to wait again to-night. In hopes of reaching Portsmouth, Ohio, however, I shall close this letter with the view of mailing it there. The prospect is good for reaching Maysville to-morrow, in time for the stage which will take me to Frankfort on Wednesday morning.

The river is quite lively to-day. Two more boats came down last night, making nine in company or near each other, and as many as three or four have been in sight all the morning, passing and repassing each other, and we have met two or three going up.

A train of reflections occurred to me yesterday which I briefly noted down, and enclose the notes for your edification. Perhaps they were as useful as many sermons in church. Although everything was orderly in the boat yesterday, we had few signs of religion. The only ones I observed were a Quaker lady and the steward reading the Bible.

I trust that everything is progressing agreeably at home. What with the mechanics and our hired men, however, I cannot but have some concern for you. I know Joseph will do all he can to make things work smoothly, and I trust you will have no trouble with Mr. Richardson.

Give my love to father, Jane, Fanny, Marion, Adela, and the doctor, James and Anna, and remember me kindly to Mary, Catharine, and Joseph, by no means forgetting Aunt Chloe.

Your devoted husband,
AMOS KENDALL.

REASONS WHY MEN SHOULD NOT LIVE ALWAYS.

Men may be divided into three classes, namely: —
1. The bad in principle and profligate in habits.
2. The bad in principle and steady in habits.
3. The good.

The first class are their own enemies and the enemies of their race. Their habits in a few years disqualify them for physical enjoyments, and their destitution of principle cuts them off from mental enjoyment. Arrived at that state, earth becomes to them a place of constant torment; and if they were immortal, their torments would be eternal. It is better for mankind, and no worse for them, that they should be separated from the rest of their race and transferred to another world. It is but substituting one place of torment for another, while it prevents their interference with the happiness of others.

If the bad in principle but steady in habits were permitted to live always, increase of years would but increase their capacity for mischief. The Devil himself is represented to be a sober, steady being, never impairing his capacity for mischief by irregular habits. Analogous to him are sober and steady men without principle. And as they grow older, and gain knowledge by experience, reading, and observation, the more like him do they become; and if they were immortal, a large portion of earth's population would become little better than devils, keeping their fellow-beings in a state of constant annoyance and distress by their tricks and their crimes. And, in process of time, their own conduct becomes a source of torment to themselves without producing amendment. It is well that this class also should be separated from the rest before they know too much, and sent to associate with beings like themselves.

The good have no motive to desire immortality on earth. In addition to those physical sufferings to which all are subject, they are here associated with dissolute and unprincipled men, and necessarily suffer from their irregularities and crimes. Death is, therefore, a relief to them, rather to be sought than deprecated. It is a separation from the bad, a relief from physical suffering, and a transfer to a state of unalloyed happiness in congenial society, where the brawling profligate and the cloaked hypocrite never enter.

The economy of nature which limits the life of man is, therefore, wise. It does no harm to the bad, and is conducive to the happiness of the good. And if the bad go to a place of eternal torment, what reason have they to complain? If made immortal, just as they are, and suffered to live on the earth, their passions, habits, and crimes would make it a place of eternal torment to themselves, and in some degree to the better portion of their race. Is it unreasonable in a Superior Being to let them have just such an immortality as they choose?

TO HIS WIFE.

BROWNSVILLE, PA., December 4, 1849, 9 A. M.

MY DEAR WIFE, — We arrived here about nine o'clock last evening, after a series of ill luck, without any personal injury. At Frostburg, nine miles from Cumberland, a trace chain broke when we were ten or fifteen rods from the hotel, and the driver took out his team and left, not telling us what he intended to do. After sitting about an hour, some of the passengers went back to the hotel, and found him *put up for the night,* swearing that he would not, for all New York, drive such a team on such a night. It was dark and stormy, and the horses had shown a reluctance to proceed as well as the driver. In an hour more, however, we had found another driver, and went on through the night as comfortably as *seven men, one woman,* and *three*

children inside the coach would permit. In the morning, however, our forward axle-tree suddenly broke, and down went the right hand front corner of the carriage into the mud. Fortunately we were going at a slow gait, and the horses were instantly stopped. We crawled out upon the upper side of the wreck, and with a part of the passengers I walked on to the next village and got some breakfast. In about two hours our carriage made its appearance, supported in front by two wagon-wheels. It was yet a mile to Smithfield, where there were extra carriages. Just as we were entering that village a linch-pin of one of our wagon-wheels flew out, but it was fortunately observed by a passenger before we were again dumped down. Again we took to the mud and made our way to the tavern. In due time our relief carriage made its appearance, and there appeared on its side the letters and word "*L. W. Stockton,*" — a name of ill omen to me, said I to myself. But it turned out otherwise; for that same carriage landed us safely in this worthy city, which is neither upon a hill nor in a valley, but up and down a steep ascent. Within two hours we expect to embark for Pittsburg, and hope to be upon the Ohio the coming night.

About half the night, after leaving Cumberland, I was not at all well. The symptoms of illness then passed away, and I have been very well ever since.

The lady with three children lives in New Albany, and has been to Providence to visit her kindred. She is now returning without protector or attendant. She appears to be respectable and intelligent, and her children are evidently smart and as well raised as is common among good families in the West. But a woman who travels thus, except in cases of extreme necessity, is inexcusable. She is not only subject to perpetual annoyance, but herself and children are a continual annoyance to all around her.

You need not expect to hear from me again until I reach Cincinnati.

With abundance of love to yourself and the family, I remain, most truly,

Your devoted husband,
AMOS KENDALL.

P. S. — Send to the post-office to-morrow evening at 8.30 o'clock and you will get this letter.

In May, 1851, Mr. Kendall was summoned to Louisville, Ky., to the death-bed of Adela, the youngest of his two daughters by his first wife, who in 1839 had married Dr. F. B. Culver of Kentucky.

In this journey he was accompanied by his eldest and then only surviving daughter of his first wife, Mrs. Mary A. Gold, whose husband had died in Washington in 1847.

TO HIS WIFE.

LOUISVILLE, May 25, 1851.

MY DEAR WIFE, — Mary Ann will write you the particulars of Adela's illness and death. It is very consolatory to learn that she was conscious of her danger from the first, met the emergency with admirable firmness, and died at peace with all the world and with her Maker. Indeed, she conversed with such self-possession and calmness that persons visiting her would not believe that she was in any immediate danger.

Adela's chief concern seems to have been for her children, and it was specially in reference to them that she was so very anxious to see you, Mary Ann, and myself.

The day we started, Mary was somewhat sick in the cars, but felt pretty well after taking tea at Cumberland. But almost immediately after starting in the stages she became very sick, and before we reached Frostburg was so much worse that I was afraid to proceed. Besides, though I was better than when I left home, I began to feel fatigued and had misgivings about my own ability to stand a night ride over that terrible road. We accordingly stopped for the night, intending to take the morning line. In the morning, however, the stages were all full to overflowing, and we were obliged to remain until the next night. I took an empty stage coming from the West and returned to Cumberland, for the double purpose of ascertaining whether any message has passed from Louisville and securing seats in the stages. We had that night and the next day a rapid, rough, but on the whole a pleasant, ride to Wheeling, where we arrived about 8 P. M. on Wednesday. The Pittsburg packet of that day was already at the landing, and before 9 o'clock we were steaming down the Ohio at a rapid rate. On Friday morning about 5 o'clock, we found ourselves in Cincinnati, having made the run from Wheeling in thirty-two hours. We immediately transferred ourselves and baggage to the "Telegraph number Two," which started about 11 A. M., and landed us in Louisville at 10 P. M.; having made the run in eleven hours. Our real travelling time from Washington to Louisville was but three days and nine hours; and, including an entire day lost at Frostburg and six hours at Cincinnati, it was but four days and fifteen hours.

I shall be obliged to remain here certainly until the 30th inst., and probably until the 31st., but as soon thereafter as possible we shall hasten home by the Pennsylvania route. Having some preparations to make for the children, Mary Ann has not yet decided whether she will visit Frankfort or not.

Mr. W. C. Culver had a servant waiting at the landing, to invite us to his house, where Mary is now staying. I am at the doctor's. Mary Culver is one of the most kind-hearted little girls I ever knew. While

Adela was sick she could hardly be made to leave the house, and no sister could be more distressed. She is particularly devoted to Willie, and would be with him constantly if permitted. The poor little fellow is getting well very slowly; but I think will be benefitted by the journey. Eddy is as well as I ever saw him, and the doctor seems to be very well.

Give my love to father and the whole family.

Your devoted husband,

AMOS KENDALL.

The following characteristic letter was written to a defaulting telegraph operator:—

WASHINGTON, June 26, 1851.

——:——

DEAR SIR,—I received yesterday your letter of the 23d inst., and read it with great interest.

Early in life it would have been impossible for me to comprehend the degree of infatuation which it describes; but I have seen so much of poor human nature that no folly or crime now staggers my credulity. Although I never lost or won a hundred dollars by lotteries, games of chance, or bets of any kind, my little experience in early life taught me that my only safety consisted in abjuring such practices altogether; and although I never made vows which only expose men to double crime, I have, since the age of twenty-six years, declined playing for the value of a cent, or betting otherwise than in sport and for mere trifles. With the same steadiness I have, under all vicissitudes, refrained from all other habits and vices which corrupt the heart, exhaust the means, and shorten the lives of so many erring mortals. I do not mention these things boastingly, for I am sensible of most of those frailties which lead others astray, but my object is simply to show you, by my example, that the human will can be made by steady exertion to master our appetites and passions, and save us from the ruin which their unrestrained indulgence never fails to produce.

Your letter of itself is conclusive that you are not yet *entirely lost*. I believe you sincere in your repentance, and that you would now repair all the wrong you have done if you could. I trust it will not be like a sick-bed repentance, forgotten as soon as the God of mercy restores the blessing of health. Be that as it may, man cannot err in an humble imitation of his Maker, particularly as he cannot foresee the result of his mercies to his fellow-men.

You are undoubtedly exposed to a criminal prosecution as well as a civil action. It may be policy in the company to adopt the former course, by way of example, and I hear the president of the company has threatened it. He will be here in a few days, and I shall endeavor to

dissuade him from that course, and give you an opportunity to redeem yourself. I doubt, however, whether in justice to the company he can place you in another office. It is almost impossible that those doing business in the office can remain in ignorance of the facts, and the public, having neither the knowledge nor the charity which would induce it to look with forbearance on the past, might distrust the office on account of your presence in it. This loss of confidence is a part of the penalty you have to pay, and the company cannot be expected to assume it.

I have no doubt that all idea of proceeding against you in any shape will be abandoned if you can give acceptable security for the payment of arrears, even at a day somewhat distant. To this end your first efforts should be directed, and I shall urge on the president the policy of giving you full scope to make the attempt, and will promptly apprise you of the result. If this were satisfactorily arranged, you could *again* go boldly forth in search of employment.

The president, in a letter to me, mentioned an intimation of your purpose, in a certain event, to commit suicide! If any thing could destroy all faith in your good resolutions it would be the conviction that you deliberately entertained such a purpose *in any event*. If one event could produce such a catastrophe, another might, and how can we trust to the promises of one whose rash hand may at any moment put an end to his life and his promises by the same act? I doubt not the expression was used without any settled purpose in your heart, but the thought is often father to the deed, and always indicates in a less degree the same desperation. This world is on the whole a good world and a beautiful. It is full of pleasures to him who does not suffer a grain of disappointment or pain to outweigh a pound of hope and enjoyment. If it sometimes becomes a hell, it is the man himself who makes it such, and then to relieve himself he aggravates his folly by rushing into a worse one! He leaves one which his own will may convert into a comparative Paradise, and rushes into one over which he has no power! Dismiss all such thoughts, consider life as a thing over which you have no power, and make the best of it. Rise superior to your difficulties, which imagination magnifies into mountains. They are but mole-hills which a resolute will and steady effort may in one month demolish. Your talents, your business capacity, and prepossessing manners are by all conceded, and, notwithstanding the past, the future depends on your own will,—not a fitful changeable will, driven to and fro by every breeze of passion, appetite, or disappointment, but a firm, resolute, and persevering will, leading you steadily on in the paths of virtue, industry, and self-denial. In such a course it will be my pleasure to aid and cheer you on, as far as paramount duties will allow.

I remain your friend,

AMOS KENDALL.

TO HIS WIFE.

PHILADELPHIA, September 12, 1851, 8 P.M.

MY DEAR WIFE,—Can you keep cool? It is more than anybody can do in these parts. The thermometer is at 88° now, and has been at 98° to-day, so it is said. As I write, perspiration breaks out all over me, and even the hand with which I hold my pen glitters as with morning dew! There! the drops come trickling down my face as if sundry small fountains had broken out under my hair. O for home, among the cool shades of Kendall Green! The judges here think our trial will last five weeks! What do you think of that? And I have had the weakness to be persuaded to make a speech in the case! I hope we may finish it in two weeks; but I fear it will take not less than three.

I hope Mark has not worked his horses too hard these hot days. He should begin early, and about eleven o'clock stop until about four. Nor can men do much with safety in the sun for two or three hours after twelve o'clock noon.

Please let me know how the men come on, that I may give instructions if necessary.

I have not a word from the girls. Do you hear from them?

I am very well, though the heat and musquitoes have much disturbed my slumbers.

Give my love to Father Kyle, to Mary Ann and her four little gentlemen, to Marion and the servants. I hope you get along quietly and happily; and tell the boys that I shall inquire particularly when I get home which has been the best boy.

Your devoted husband,

AMOS KENDALL.

TO HIS WIFE.

WHEELING, November 15, 1851.

MY DEAR WIFE,—We reached Cumberland at 5 P.M. on the 13th, and in half an hour, with two others, I found myself wedged in upon the back seat of an old mail-coach, the front part of which was crammed full of mail-bags, on my way to Wheeling over the plank road. On the whole, it was the most uncomfortable night I ever spent in a coach. The coach seemed to have no more spring than a wagon; the seat was a bad one; it was very cold; and any relief by changing position out of the question. Yet we had some incidents to enliven us. One of the coach-doors came open, and one of my fellow-passengers put his head out to shut it and lost his cap. He did not think of calling upon the driver to stop until we had gone a considerable distance, and then he returned after a fruitless search, asking the driver to wait until he could find it, saying he could not lose it, for it cost him $15. The driver re-

fused and drove on, leaving him in the midst of an extensive forest on a dark and rainy night. We hoped for more room now; but it was not long before an outside passenger, to get out of the rain, wedged himself in alongside of us.

I had deposited my hat upon the mail-bags and put on my nightcap. In a few miles the other coach-door flew open and out went my hat. Happening to have my eye in that direction I saw it, and shouted lustily to the driver to hold on, which he did, muttering curses. I recovered my hat by a run of some two hundred yards, which was quite a relief to me.

The night was exceedingly cold, and in the mountains there were bunches of snow beside the road. In the morning we found ourselves in a better coach and milder climate, and had a pleasant ride to this city.

None but the smaller boats are running, and I have not yet determined whether I will wait for one leaving Pittsburg to-day or go on in the stages. Nothing but fear of a second night without sleep prevented my going on last night.

Lest they should make some mistake, I think the men had better not undertake the fence until I get back, though they may make preparations.

My love to all the family.

Your devoted husband,

AMOS KENDALL.

MRS. JANE KENDALL.

TO HIS WIFE.

LOUISVILLE, KY. May 14, 1852.

MY DEAR WIFE,—Having a short respite from business, I seize the opportunity and a broken sheet of paper (having no other at hand) to give some account of myself since I left Philadelphia.

The first day's journey brought us to the foot of the Alleghany Mountains near Hollidaysburg, where we slept, there being no night line over the inclined planes. No incident occurred worthy of note, except that at Lewiston a young lady with a very amiable and fun-loving face, was observed to enter the car and take a seat behind a young bachelor, whom I observed to become so interested that he could scarcely look ahead.

The next morning it so *happened* that she and I found ourselves in the same seat, and we soon became *very good friends*. A merry journey we had of it. The smitten doctor (for such he was) got into the car next ahead, and for some time he was upon the platform at every stop, looking in upon my companion. On one occasion the young lady, excited by a remark of mine, burst into a violent laugh just as he looked in upon her, and for an hour or so we saw no more of him. I did not fail to lecture her on her indiscretion in scaring Cupid by so broad a laugh, and she promised to be more cautious in future. After a while the doctor again made his appearance, and when we stopped for dinner he endeavored to play the agreeable. We had twenty-eight miles of stage riding after dinner, and the doctor got into the same stage with the young lady and myself, where we found another bachelor, and I contrived to keep them amused with themselves during several hours, over a very dusty road, at the end of which we were all clad in gray. Twelve miles of railroad took us into Pittsburg, where we arrived a little after dark. The first object of interest which presented itself was a large frame building all in flames from top to bottom and from end to end. About 9 P. M. we were located for the night.

Now, don't be jealous. This young lady had never crossed the mountains before, and was destined for a place called Kittaning, some distance up the Alleghany River, on a visit to an uncle's. A cousin who lives in the West attended her, but as he did not propose to return, she hinted she should be very glad to put herself under my protection back over the mountains. Nothing could have been more agreeable, of course; but as she proposed a visit of a month's duration, I remarked that my early return would deprive me of the pleasure. And what do you think she said ? It is perhaps not prudent to tell; but she said she would cut short her visit, for the purpose of returning with me, if I would let her know when I should return to Pittsburg that she might meet me there. *Of course, you know, I could not help* promising to give her that information by letter. What will come of it, there 's no knowing !

Whom should I meet on board the steamer but Mr. and Mrs. McKinley. They contributed to make the trip agreeable down the river; but it was barren of incident. The river bottoms and hills are now exceedingly beautiful, being dressed in fresh green of various hues, spangled with blossoms of white, red, and pink.

Our company have been three days in session, and have finished their business, except the election of officers, and for that purpose they will meet again at 9 A.M., to-morrow. The Western Smith had taken much pains and had published a pamphlet to make mischief; but though he had made some impression on the stockholders, I had no difficulty in baffling him at every point. Mr. Tanner will certainly be elected in his place, and then we shall have peace.

I shall have to remain here several days, perhaps a week, on important telegraph business, and shall remain a month, if need be, to put things on such a footing as to remove all necessity for my crossing the mountains again very shortly.

The company have reduced the treasurer's salary from $1,200 to $500, and Dr. Culver is not a candidate for re-election.

Friday Morning, May 5th.   You see I have procured some whole sheets of paper. The weather here is hot and showery, with thunder and lightning. It has put me a little out of sorts; but I do not think I shall have a sick spell.

I have received Mary's excellent letter of the 7th. Tell her not to be in a hurry to go North. Probably the weather is pretty well settled; but there may be another cold spell in a few days. If there should be, she may safely go as soon as it is over. Give my love to her, to father, Fanny, Marion; and remember me to the hands and the servants.

Your devoted husband,

AMOS KENDALL.

In behalf of a warm personal and political friend Mr. Kendall wrote the following: —

WASHINGTON, April 26, 1853.

TO THE PRESIDENT OF THE UNITED STATES : —

DEAR SIR, — Though I have the utmost repugnance to troubling you in any matter which relates to appointments, justice to an old friend and most deserving man makes it my duty to overcome it.

I allude to Mr. John M. McCalla. If there be any one who is entitled to the sympathy and support of a Democratic administration, he is the man. Of extensive acquirements, fine talents, unspotted character, and sincerely religious, he has for about thirty years, without regard to his own interest, fought the battles of Democracy, most of the time on a field where the fight was most ferocious and victory least to be expected.

When men deify a mortal, it is sacrilege to expose his vices. This was General McCalla's crime. He spoke the truth of the Whig idol, and will never be forgiven. Even some Democrats, with a consciousness that their own moral conduct will not bear the light, join in denouncing him who dares to expose vices which render men unsafe for public trusts, — that a common veil may conceal from the people the moral deformities of themselves and their adversaries.

With such men as General McCalla, any administration will be safe. If disparaging representations have been made to you, be assured they are slanders. To proscribe him is to proscribe fidelity and virtue ; to sustain him is to promote them ; and, as the admirer of both, I hope and trust this persecuted man may be provided for by this administration.

With confidence and respect, your obedient servant,

AMOS KENDALL.

TO HIS WIFE.

SPRINGFIELD, ILL., August 16, 1853.

MY DEAR WIFE, — I wrote you from Chicago on the 14th inst., and telegraphed you this morning on our arrival here.

We left Chicago at 8 A. M. yesterday, and travelled by railroad to La Salle on the Illinois River, and thence about sixty miles, almost all prairie, to Bloomington. For over forty miles there are but two houses near the road, and much of the distance not a tree was visible to the right or the left. All was one apparently interminable meadow of grass and weeds, in some places with an undulating surface, but generally quite flat, and ornamented with flowers, mostly of yellow and blue colors. Except an occasional team wending its way along the distant horizon, the whirring of a prairie hen scared from her covert in the grass, or a clumsy blue crane rising from the wet slues which intersect these immense pastures, there were for many miles no signs of animal life except the managers of the steam monster, and the living freight he seemed to be conveying from the regions of civilization to some unknown land beyond the horizon. It seemed, indeed, as if the cars had lost their way, and were plunging onward recklessly, without purpose or destination.

At length, about 2 P. M., we reached Bloomington, a scattered village on an oasis of woodland in a waste of grass. Hence to Springfield is about sixty-five miles, and this distance was to be travelled before eight o'clock this morning. There was no alternative, for no day line is run. There were but two post-coaches, and they were barely sufficient to accommodate the ladies and their attendants. Alvah and myself, with five others, were stowed in a covered wagon, whose springs were stiffened by age and compressed by a weight of baggage. We soon took the lead of the coaches, and *such a ride !* The jolting was unsurpassed. Alvah, who is no chicken in weight or dimensions, sat between me and another man on the front seat, and returning from one of his most exalted saltations he cracked the seat. It soon began to settle down in the centre, causing his companions to the right and left to slide down towards him into a most affectionate proximity. We, however, contrived to prop it up with a valise, so that it answered the purposes of a seat. We had but three teams in the sixty-five miles, and one team attached to a heavily laden stage-coach was driven thirty-five miles. The drivers were shockingly profane, and in some instances out of place, losing much time. There were many passengers desirous of reaching here in time to take an 8 A. M. train of cars to St. Louis, and they tried the effect of money upon the drivers. The upshot was, that our wagon got in about ten minutes before the cars started ; but the post-coaches fell a long way behind time, and all their passengers are detained here an entire day.

I was very glad you were not along. My bones are tied together by pretty strong sinews ; but your *flesh !* it would have been like the Arab's milk in his leathern bag, churned to butter by the trotting of his

camel ; or it would have been scattered along the road from Bloomington to Springfield !

But it was a gorgeous night. The moon was out in all her glory, clothing the broad prairies and clustering groves with mild and radiant beauty. Fleeting clouds tinged with silver light moved over the firmament, and summer lightning twinkled along the horizon. Alas, thought I, that such a *Paradise* should have such roads ! This is a beautiful country, — rich and beautiful almost beyond expression. Its beauty and richness, however, did not prevent our being made sore by our last night's jolting. A little cleaning up and a nap have made us almost "as good as new," except that Alvah is troubled with the "summer complaint," for which he is nursing himself to-day preparatory to visiting some of my lands to-morrow.

I cannot visit my Vermillion lands without taking a stage ride of about one hundred and fifty miles, to which my recent experience no way inclines me. The probability now is that after spending four or five days here I shall hasten home with all convenient despatch.

This is my birthday, — threescore and four years old. With what fearful rapidity is that never-stopping locomotive, Old Time, hurrying me on to that depot where I must rest until Gabriel's trumpet calls me up to take a longer journey. Do the loved ones at home think of me to-day ? And if so, is it with pleasure or with pain, or with something of both ? So it is with *me.* Has not life been happy with us ? There is pleasure in the thought. But there must be an end of it, — we must separate. There is pain in that thought. Yet hope whispers it will not be forever ; and *Faith,* what does she say ? She says it *shall* not be forever. Let us believe her, and cheerfully submit to the temporary separation imposed upon us by death, as we do to the distance which the necessities of life now cast between us.

Alvah sends his love to you and the family.

And believe me, age instead of cooling seems to increase the affection I entertain for you and my dear good children, one and all. Give my love also to all my little grandsons, including Willie Stickney. You know how to do it.

Your husband,

AMOS KENDALL.

MRS. JANE KENDALL.

TO HIS WIFE.

NEW YORK, September 3, 1854.

MY DEAR WIFE, — I appropriate a few minutes to give you a brief account of my adventures since I left home.

I arrived in Philadelphia a little after midnight, feeling stronger than when I left home. The next morning I breakfasted at six o'clock, and left at seven, in the earliest train, hoping to arrive at New York in time to take a twelve o'clock noon train up the Hudson River, and reach Utica early in the evening; but it was about half past twelve when I reached this city, and there was no other up-river train until about a quarter before 4 o'clock P. M. Here I found a message from Professor Morse, urging me to come on by the night line, apprehending that mischief might be done at the meeting called at 11 A. M., the next day, unless I were present. I took dinner at a restaurant about 1 P. M., and took the evening train, expecting to sup at Albany. The cars were late at that place, allowing no time for supper, and I proceeded on, hoping to find some refreshments on the way; but in this I was disappointed. The consequence was, that on arriving at Utica, at 3 A. M., I was thoroughly exhausted. A moderate meal produced no reaction, and the next morning I was scarcely able to sit up. The meeting was adjourned, though not on my account, from 11 A. M., to 3 P. M. My room adjoined that in which the meeting was held, with folding-doors between, and finding myself unable to sit up without danger of becoming wholly disabled, I opened the doors and lay down on my bed, where I could hear what passed. When it became necessary for me to say something in reply to Mr. Butterfield, I got up, scarcely able to stand, and went into the meeting. The chairman asked me to be seated as I spoke, and I had not proceeded five minutes before I felt decidedly better, and continued to improve as I spoke. The upshot of the meeting was, that we voted down Mr. Butterfield's project by a vote of 2,600 to something over 600.

By invitation, I removed from the hotel to a Mr. Walker's, who married a cousin of Professor Morse, where I spent a pleasant evening and quiet night, feeling quite as well on Friday morning as when I left home. Not inclined to take another railroad run of such length and rapidity, I took an afternoon train, which delivered me in Albany at 7 P. M., when I went immediately on board the steamboat Hendrick Hudson, ready to start. There, through the kindness of Mr. Palmer, Superintendent of the Telegraph Line, I found my passage already paid for, and a very comfortable state-room secured. I ate a moderate supper, rested well, and landed in New York at about 6 A. M. yesterday.

There were on the boat about three hundred and fifty passengers, among whom I did not recognize a single face as ever before seen by me, and I do not think there was one person who knew me.

I met here Mr. Swain and Mr. Hyde, and, after a session from about 11 A. M. to 11 P. M., closed my business with them very satisfactorily.

Until I ascertain to-morrow what more I can do here, I can form no opinion when I can get home.

I have written much more than I intended. Give my love to Mary

Ann and tell her I much regret the necessity of being absent during her visit. Give my love also to children and grandchildren, and take to your share as much as all the rest.

Your husband,

                 AMOS KENDALL.

MRS. JANE KENDALL.

The following reference to his health is extracted from a letter to Professor Morse, November 1st, 1854: —

"There is but a hope of receiving enough on your account to pay the drafts I have accepted, and make you a partner in the new company, from Louisville to New Orleans, before the first of February. Yet having done all we can, let us have faith that the Great Patron of the faithful and the true will not permit you or me to be reduced to the necessity of 'selling out at auction.' But for my Western lands I should have been on several occasions within the past year in very unpleasant predicaments myself. In every case, as the crisis approached, remittances came from my agents to meet it, sometimes wholly unexpected.

"But I think I have felt within the past year a sensible decay of my physical powers. Two serious attacks, altogether different from my ordinary sick spells, have admonished me that I hold life by a very precarious tenure. An ankle not yet recovered from a sprain given it last winter, has, in a great measure, cut me off from the exercise of walking. I can scarcely write an hour at a time without feeling exhausted in body, though, excepting memory, my mental powers seem to myself to remain unimpaired. However, I shall work on with cheerfulness and zeal, doing what I can to protect your interest and my own, trusting that a kind Providence will supply all my deficiencies and secure to you that triumph over all your enemies which your virtues and your merits so richly deserve.

"My family join me in kind regards to you and yours. We all hope to see you in Congress, 'Bashaw of three tails' as you are,* and I doubt not you will be as ready to join the Catholics and Episcopalians in defence of religious liberty as the Turk is in defence of his territorial right and sovereignty.

"Truly your friend,

            "AMOS KENDALL."

TO WILLIAM STICKNEY.

            LOUISVILLE, June 1, 1855.

MY DEAR STICKNEY, — I received yesterday your kind letter of the 25th ult., and mark what you say touching my not answering your letters. Be assured it arises from no indisposition to answer them; but

* Reference is here made to the testimonials Professor Morse had received from foreign governments in honor of his invention.

from the "engagements" of which you speak, and from the slowness and difficulty with which I now write, owing to a trembling hand and decaying physical vigor; that which was once a pleasure to me has become a labor, and hence I shrink from any correspondence which is not imposed upon me by some duty.

Fanny and myself had a very agreeable journey out; and both had excellent health until yesterday, when both were unwell, though not seriously, during the day. This morning both of us were in pretty good condition, so good that I saw her in the cars for Frankfort before 6 A. M. For a more particular account of her travels and adventures, I must refer you to Fanny herself.

I have had conferences with the lessees here, and have to-day submitted a proposition. I think we shall come to terms; but it is a little uncertain. They are hard business men, who recognize no principle in their transactions but strict legal rights, whether resting on moral right or not. I expect to close the negotiation this evening or to-morrow, and to join Fanny at Frankfort to-morrow evening or on Monday morning. Thence I propose travelling through Lexington to Cincinnati, by a railroad recently opened; thence by railroad to Wheeling; and thence by the B. and O. Railroad home; arriving about the end of next week.

This is likely to be a year of great abundance in the West. The fruit trees are loaded beyond precedent, and the growing crops never gave brighter promise. It has been somewhat dry; but within a few days past copious rains have put the wheat beyond the reach of drought.

The North Alabamians continue to cut down the telegraph almost every day. At first it was under the pretext that it produced the dry weather; but as they have had abundant rains, it seems now to be the mere spirit of mischief or ambition to carry a point. It is said they were encouraged by a preacher who proclaimed from the pulpit that God had sent the dry weather to punish the world because man had got to be "too smart" in reducing his lightning to human uses. Give my love to Jeannie and Willie, to your mother, sisters, and brother, not forgetting Willie Gold and Mrs. Eddy.

Affectionately, your father,

            AMOS KENDALL.

TO REV. G. W. SAMPSON, ON "PREDESTINATION."

            WASHINGTON, October 15, 1856.

REV. G. W. SAMPSON : —

MY DEAR SIR, — Will you excuse a few plain observations from a hearer who is generally instructed and edified by your preaching? However they may strike you, they are conceived in a spirit which, I trust, is truly Christian.

It is perhaps my own fault that your sermon of to-day, and I may say of last Sunday also, did me harm instead of good. My mind and heart revolt at every attempt to penetrate the counsels of God in cases palpably beyond the reach of human intellect. It always strikes me painfully, as a sort of sacrilege, — an attempt to penetrate God's secrets; to eat the forbidden fruit over again.

There are apparent contradictions in the Book of Revelation, as well as the Book of Nature, which it is worse than idle to attempt to reconcile. God is almighty. He could prevent evil in the world if he would. Why does he not prevent it? Can human reason give a satisfactory answer? Why should an almighty, all-wise, and all-good God make a world to be filled with sin, suffering, sorrow, and pain? Can reason tell us why? Why, instead of making everything immutably good, did he make man fallible, and permit him to fall when he could have prevented it, and thus make it necessary to sacrifice his Son for man's redemption? To our limited reason, all this seems capricious and cruel.

To say that a thing existed or took place from eternity, is to human reason the same as to say that it never came into existence at all. We cannot conceive an act done which is not done in time. We cannot think of decrees of foreordination or of foreknowledge without connecting them with time. Nor is the connection obviated when told that these things existed "from eternity"; for of eternity itself we have no conception as a thing to be separated from time. Our hearts beat in time, our minds think in time, and all our acts are done in time. We cannot penetrate the future or the past without measuring by time the flight of our imaginations. And of course our minds cannot conceive how God can have plans or designs which had no beginning.

You truly say, the foreknowledge of God finds a place in heathen philosophy and human reason as well as the Bible. I do not complain of implicit faith in that doctrine. What I complain of is, all attempts to reconcile the doctrine and its necessary premises, foreordination with human accountability. Human reason deduces from it the conclusion that most of mankind were created to be damned without a possibility of salvation, while a smaller portion are born to be saved without a possibility of going to perdition. Nor is it a satisfactory explanation to say that their will was free; for the doctrine presupposes that all the motives which were to influence their wills, and the act of the will itself, were inevitably fixed and foreknown long before man had an existence.

Nor have I ever heard an illustration from you, or any one else, which was sufficient to reconcile predestination with human accountability. Take the one used by you to-day. You presented the case of a city afflicted by a destroying pestilence, to whom a deliverer appears and offers to remove the whole population to a place of safety; but while a few only accepted the offer, the majority chose to remain and perish, and you asked whether their perdition is his fault or their own? To make the case parallel with that of the human family, we must suppose that the deliverer himself had foreordained the pestilence, and had also foreordained the refusal of the people to fly to a place of safety; so arranging events and motives, even before they were born, as to make it impossible for them to decide otherwise. Could human reason, in such a case, comprehend the justice of the deliverer, to say nothing of his mercy for the perishing multitude?

The decree of God is stronger than a tyrant's chain. Suppose a tyrant has cast into prison and bound in chains a multitude of his subjects. Predetermined that the doors shall not be opened nor their chains knocked off, he sets fire to the prison, and calls upon them to fly for their lives. Such, in the eye of *human reason*, is the gospel to that portion of mankind which was ordained to perdition before the world was created.

Shall we therefore reject it? Not at all. We are to take for granted the attributes of God as disclosed in Nature and Revelation, and take also for granted that there is something unrevealed which would reconcile God's supremacy with man's accountability. Our consciousness of freedom and responsibility is enough for us, without attempting to penetrate into God's secrets.

Now, my dear sir, would it not be better to give this turn to the whole subject instead of bewildering the minds of hearers with disquisitions upon points which must be assented to *on faith alone*, and affording to cavillers the poor excuse that their sins are inevitable, having been ordained by God himself. The whole Christian system, worship, prayer, every inculcated duty of man to man and man to God, is based on human liberty and accountability; and, it seems to me, it may well be left to God in his own good time, if he should ever deem it expedient, to explain how the consciousness he has implanted within us is consistent with his foreknowledge. That it is so, we are bound to believe; but *how* it is so, is known only to the eternal mind. There let the secret rest.

Your liberality will excuse the liberty I have taken. I did not feel quite so good when I left the church to-day as when I entered it, and I concluded to tell you why, not for your guidance, but for my relief and your consideration. Perhaps I am mistaken in supposing that preaching on these incomprehensible subjects is as unprofitable to others as it is to myself.

Most sincerely your friend,

AMOS KENDALL.

CHAPTER XIX.

FOUNDING THE COLUMBIA INSTITUTION FOR THE DEAF AND DUMB.

THE existence of this institution, organized in 1857, and which has already "become one of the brightest jewels in the coronet of the Republic," is due to the liberality of Mr. Kendall. With a heart full of sympathy for the unfortunate, he always carried a hand ready to relieve their wants and improve their condition, as far as his means would permit.

The gift of a house and two acres of ground adjoining the city, in October, 1856, valued at that time at about ten thousand dollars, was the nucleus of the hundred acres of ground and the noble group of buildings which Congress, in its appreciation of this great charity, has provided for the education of the deaf and dumb of our country. The origin and progress of the institution may be seen from the following address of Mr. Kendall at the first commencement of the National Deaf-Mute College, held in Washington, June 23, 1869:—

MR. PRESIDENT, LADIES, AND GENTLEMEN, —

This occasion brings to me a train of interesting memories. About fifteen years ago an adventurer brought to this city five partially educated deaf-mute children, whom he had picked up in the State of New York, and commenced exhibiting them to our citizens in their houses and places of business. He professed a desire to get up an institution for the education of unfortunates of that class in the District of Columbia, raised considerable sums of money, and gathered a school of about sixteen pupils. Apparently to give respectability and permanency to his school, he sought and obtained the consent of some of our leading citizens to become its trustees. It soon appeared, however, that he had no idea of accountability to them, and only wanted their names to aid him in collecting money to be used at his discretion. On being informed by the trustees that such an irresponsible system was inadmissible, he repudiated them altogether.

In the mean time, an impression had gone abroad that he maltreated

---

the children, and it led to an investigation in court, ending in the children being taken from him and restored to their parents, except the five from abroad, who were bound to him who now addresses you as their next friend.

The trustees then had a meeting to determine whether they would abandon the enterprise or go forward. Having in the mean time understood that there were from twenty to thirty of their fellow human beings in the District who, from deafness or blindness, were cut off from all means of education in the ordinary schools, they determined to go forward. They adopted a constitution, raised contributions, hired teachers, and opened a school in a house set apart for that purpose at Kendall Green.

At the session of Congress, in the winter of 1856 – 57, they procured an act of incorporation, containing a provision for the instruction of the indigent deaf and dumb and blind in the District at the expense of the United States. This act, by allowing the institution to receive pupils from all the States and Territories, and leaving all details as to the objects of study, the arrangement of classes, the length of time the pupils should be taught, to the discretion of the directors, enabled it to expand, should it ever become practicable and desirable, into a great national institution, in which all the higher branches of science, literature, and art should be taught.

The institution was organized under its charter in February, 1857. In May of that year the board of directors was so fortunate as to secure the services of E. M. Gallaudet, Esq., under whose energetic and prudent management, first as superintendent and then as president, the institution rapidly advanced to the front rank of similar institutions, not only in our own country, but throughout the world.

At his instance an act of Congress was passed in April, 1864, authorizing the institution to confer degrees and issue diplomas. The time seemed now to have arrived for carrying into effect a project vaguely entertained from the origin of the institution. The State institutions taught little else than those branches of knowledge taught in the common schools. The deaf and dumb in the various States, desirous of attaining or able to attain to a higher degree of culture, were not numerous enough to justify the maintenance of a college in each State for their instruction; but it was believed there were enough of that class in all the States to sustain one such institution. And where could that be so appropriately located as at the seat of the general government? Influenced by these considerations, and in the belief that there were enough deaf-mutes partially educated who panted for higher attainments, and would find means to pay for them, the directors, in the summer of 1864, organized a new department in their institution, denominated the

---

"National Deaf-Mute College." In the mean time they had been relieved by Congress of the charge of the blind, and authorized to take the deaf-mute children of soldiers and sailors.

Thus has our institution been matured; the progress of the college has been most encouraging, and buildings for the accommodation of all its departments are springing up on the confines of your city, an ornament to your surroundings, and a testimony to the benevolence of our people and our government.

In ancient times it required the exertion of Divine power to enable the dumb to speak and the blind to see. The restoration of sight and hearing was the subject of miracles in the time of Christ. It was a part of his holy mission to cause the deaf to hear. We do not claim that there is anything supernatural in the teaching of the dumb in this our day; but is it not the fruit of that love to our neighbor which Christ taught his disciples, and that use of those faculties of the mind which God gave to man from the beginning?

What more noble invention has Christian civilization brought to man than the means devised to teach the blind and the deaf to read and write? And what more godlike charity can there be than in furnishing the means to enable these unfortunate children of darkness and of silence to receive the lights of knowledge and religion, virtually to enable the blind to see and the deaf to hear? And where shall our benevolence stop? Shall we be content to merely fit them for the animal drudgeries of life, or shall we enable those who have aspiring minds to soar into the heights of science and art, to solve the problems of nature and admire the wisdom of God?

But the subject is not merely one of benevolence; it is also one of public policy. How many hands are made permanently useful to society, and how many minds are awakened to aid in the progress of our age, by the deaf and dumb institutions?

It is an accepted proposition that, the brain being unimpaired, the destruction of one of the senses renders the rest more acute. If the sight be lost, the hearing becomes more distinct; if the hearing be lost, the eye becomes more clear and piercing. Why then may it not be, that persons deprived of hearing are more fitted to excel in some branches of learning than those in the full possession of all their senses? Silence and seclusion are conducive to study and meditation. In the silence of the night the astronomer can best study the heavens. In the silence of the desert and cave the hermit can best meditate on the vanities of life and the attributes of God. And is it unreasonable to hope that men whose atmosphere through life is silence, may, if allowed the benefit of a superior education, become prominent in all those branches of learning to the acquisition of which silence is conducive?

Why may we not expect to find among them our most profound mathematicians and astronomers, our most clear thinkers and chaste writers, our most upright men and devoted Christians?

My dear young friends of the graduating class, although you have been well taught, not only in books, but in your duties to God and man, I desire to say a few words to you at parting.

There is an old book, seemingly considered almost obsolete in some of our colleges and seminaries of learning, and yet it contains the earliest record of the principles and precepts on which are based all order, all law, and all religion that deserves the name or is useful to man. That old book is the Bible. I beg you to read and study it, not merely as religionists, but as men seeking after truth. You will find in it, as you doubtless have found, much that you cannot understand, and some things that may stagger your faith; but you will find this great principle running through it from beginning to end, that obedience — obedience to the law and rightful authority — is the only guarantee of human happiness, national and individual, here and hereafter. The lesson is first taught in the story of Eve and the apple, — whether fact or allegory it matters not, the teaching is the same. It is repeated throughout the book, from Genesis to Revelation, in narratives, in parables, in promises, in threatenings, in songs, in prayers, in prophecies, in famines, in pestilences, in wars, desolations, and captivities. All, all are represented as flowing from disobedience to lawful authority. And is not this book (in some parts the first of all books) worthy of profound study, if it were only to see whence came that principle on which all order, law, and just governments are based, and to trace it through the ages down to our own day.

I know not what your religious opinions are. You go out into the world at an era when society is shaken as by an earthquake. So wonderful have been the inventions and discoveries of modern times that men's faith in everything old seems to be shaken. Strange and absurd theories, reversing the order of God and nature, are broached and find believers.

Remember, young men, that whatever else may change, the moral principles inculcated in the Old Book are unchangeable, and if its religion be called in question, tell the caviller to hold his peace until he is prepared to offer a better. Sweet is the Christian's hope, and none but a devil incarnate would seek to destroy it."

To the day of his death, Mr. Kendall did not cease to feel a deep interest in the success of this institution; which he often visited, and where he loved to take by the hand those children of silence whose eyes looked the gratitude they could not speak. These

occasions always filled his warm heart with tender emotion, manifested by the falling tear and the quivering lip. Had he done nothing else, his name would be cherished in grateful remembrance by hundreds of deaf-mutes, the darkness of whose minds has been dispelled by the lights of knowledge, and who have been elevated from ignorance and dependence to positions of influence and responsibility.

The only deaf-mute college in the world, its success has been fully established, reflecting honor not only upon its founder but upon the country which has so generously contributed to its support and development.

In 1864 Mr. Kendall relinquished the Presidency of the Institution to Edward M. Gallaudet, then Superintendent, to whose talents and energy it is largely indebted for its great prosperity and present distinguished position.

The original board of directors consisted of the following gentlemen, who contributed to the support of the Institution: Amos Kendall, *President;* William Stickney, *Secretary;* George W. Riggs, *Treasurer;* Wm. H. Edes, Judson Mitchell, J. C. McGuire, D. A. Hall, and Byron Sunderland, *Directors.* Of these Messrs. Stickney, Riggs, McGuire, and Sunderland alone survive.

Though Mr. Kendall had retired from the stormy sea of politics into a haven of domestic retirement, he was a careful observer of public events, and was among the first to hear the mutterings of that storm which was so soon to burst with all its fury upon the good ship of state.

In feeble health and heavily burdened with the cares of the telegraph, he yet considered the interests of his country paramount to all others, and was ever ready to resume his pen, if by so doing he could contribute in the least to avert or diminish the threatened evil.

The following extract of a letter, written at this time, forcibly sets forth his apprehensions of coming events: —

WASHINGTON, August 19, 1856.

GENTLEMEN, — I received yesterday your letter of the 16th inst., inviting me to address the "Grand Mass Ratification Meeting" to be held at Tammany Hall, on Thursday evening, the 21st inst.

Would that I were able to address that meeting in a voice which should reach, not only every man within the precincts of Tammany Hall,

but also every true American, native born and naturalized, from Canada to Mexico, from the Atlantic to the Pacific.

Say what we will about the impossibility of a dissolution of this glorious Union of States, such a catastrophe is possible, and events are fast hurrying us to the precipice. The union of some of the churches, whose ties ought, if possible, to be more sacred than our political bonds, is already dissolved; in others the breach is becoming year by year wider and wider, and all religious and benevolent institutions are threatened with disruption. Mutual defiances are passing between men at the North and men at the South, attended occasionally by scenes of violence between individuals, which need only an accession of numbers to each side to become a most embittered and bloody civil war! And Congress has just adjourned without making appropriations for the support of the army, when every man of them knows that nothing but its presence in Kansas prevents that territory from becoming the seat of an exterminating civil war, which would almost certainly extend through the centre of the Union to the Atlantic coast. Is the country ripe for this? Are Pennsylvania, Delaware, Maryland, and Virginia willing to become frontier States of two empires, whose people shall be embittered against each other with an intense hatred arising out of mutual injuries? Are Ohio, Indiana, Illinois, and Kentucky prepared to see the Ohio River, now the channel of peaceful commerce, converted into a river of blood, whose fertile shores and thriving cities shall be alternately ravaged by fire and sword? Are the people of all these confederate States, North and South, prepared to see their sons dragged from their fruitful fields and smiling hearths, to be slaughtered in intestine war, and all the fruits of their labor taken from them to support standing armies?

Let no man shut his eyes to the danger, or imagine that the consequences are exaggerated. The signs of the times are, as it were, written upon the heavens, and should this Union ever be dissolved in consequence of the question which now agitates it, it will be as possible to unite fire and water in harmonious action within the same furnace as to preserve peace between our dissevered communities. Thrust asunder by one grand explosion, the shattered fragments would dash against each other on a sea of anarchy, and finally sink and be lost beneath the calm of despotism.

In December of the same year he addressed the following earnest appeal to James Buchanan, then President elect: —

WASHINGTON, December 7, 1856.

DEAR SIR, — Permit me to congratulate you most sincerely on your election as President of the United States. Though fortunate enough

not to need or desire any personal favor at the hands of my government, I have never before felt so deep an interest in a presidential election, because never before, since the adoption of the Federal Constitution, has our government been in such imminent danger.

The interest I have felt in your election is now transferred to your administration, because I believe it to be in your power to give such a turn to political opinion and action as will avert all danger to our glorious Union for many future years.

In addressing one so much observation and experience on a subject which has necessarily commanded his most serious attention, I feel that I expose myself to the charge of presumption, but I console myself with the reflection that if, as is most likely, I shall not advance an idea which is new to you, this letter can do no harm, while it will in some measure allay my own anxiety for the future in the possibility that it may do some good.

We cannot shut our eyes to the fact that there has been in the South, ever since the days of nullification, a small disunion party. Their policy has been, both as to measures and men, so to shape their course as to produce a nation between the North and the South, in the hope and with the design that the disruption of the Union would be the result. This party has generally acted with the Democracy, while they have sought to break down that party by proscribing leading Democrats of the North. It was this course which originally gave strength to Freesoilism in the North; some Northern politicians having thrown themselves upon that measure through resentment and for revenge.

In the late contest this party supported you, not, as I verily believe, with any desire to secure your election. Certain it is, that they were the only party which jeopardized your election. Their defence of Brooks's attack upon Sumner, their justification of Missouri outrages in Kansas, their ultra pro-slavery doctrines, their annunciations in favor of a renewal of the African slave-trade, and constant threats of disunion, were all calculated, and I believe designed, to exasperate the Northern mind and produce the election of Colonel Fremont. And by taking the ground that if Fremont should be elected, the Union would at once be rightfully dissolved, they prepared the public mind for the catastrophe they hoped to witness.

The conduct of these men operated against your election in another way. For obvious reasons, no States are more devoted to the Union than Maryland, Kentucky, Tennessee, Missouri, and Louisiana. The conduct of your disunion supporters in the South enabled artful men in these States to represent you as a sectional candidate, whose fidelity to the Union was doubtful, and the vote for Fillmore sprung from the thorough-going Union sentiments of those States. In fine, it is my firm conviction, that but for the attack on Sumner, the outrages in Kansas, and the justification of those acts in the South, there would not have been a serious contest in the late election.

On the other hand, there is a small but growing disunion party in the North, and nothing can be more dangerous than the principles upon which the self-styled Republican party is organized, and nothing more unprincipled than the means adopted by them to gain power. Few of them are in favor of a dissolution of the Union ; but they are sapping its foundations and casting firebrands amidst its drapery. Let them succeed in arraying a consolidated North against a consolidated South, and maintain that array of parties through a succession of elections, and the end aimed at by Southern disunionists will be attained.

We have already premonitory indications of the game designed to be played by these extreme parties during your administration.

Governor Adams of South Carolina, and various disunion newspapers are out in favor of a renewal of the African slave-trade, thereby furnishing materials for Northern agitators, while the Kansas question is renewed in the House of Representatives, to prevent the disbandment of the Republican party.

Now, the safety of the Republic requires that these parties shall be deprived of the power to excite their respective sections of the Union against each other. But how is it to be done ? To my own mind the way seems clear. Let your administration, as the head of the Democratic party, assume and inflexibly maintain two positions, namely : —

First. The Federal Union shall be preserved, as organized by the Constitution, in its letter and spirit.

Second. Inflexible opposition to any further agitation of the subject of slavery in the Territories or elsewhere.

Let it be understood that no man who *talks* about a dissolution of the Union, or maintains political relations with disunionists South or agitators North, is to be considered a friend of the administration or a member of the Democratic party. In short, let the Union sentiment, in the spirit of the Constitution, be embodied as the leading element in the administration and in that party.

Many a patriotic man has been pained and disgusted by the continual harping about the dissolution of the Union by some of the Democratic papers, and even those in Washington. Let all this be made to cease ; let the public mind be led to have faith in procuring remedies of all existing evils *within* the Union and not out of it. Particularly let any newspaper which may be supposed to speak the sentiments of the administration, be an example of unwavering faith in the perpetuity of the Union, while it advocates the rights of the States with no less firmness and zeal.

The slavery question now rests where the Constitution left it. Whether it was wise to repeal the Missouri Compromise, it is unnecessary to decide. I always thought it a violation of the spirit of the Constitution, which presupposes that a State has been organized by the people composing it, before Congress has anything to do with it as a State, and that for Congress to interfere before admission, with a view of shaping its institutions, is as inadmissible as their interference to alter them after admission. The true principle has been restored by the Kansas-Nebraska act, and there is no difficulty in defending it in the North as well as in the South, if it be carried into effect in good faith, and the Northern mind be not excited by the taunts, violence, and extreme opinions divulged by Southern disunionists.

I have thus very hastily, but I hope intelligibly, sketched out the views I entertain in relation to the present and future political condition of the country. I have no apology for obtruding them upon you but the desire to see my country maintain its unity, and my government its purity, through my few remaining years, and die in the hope that my children's children may enjoy the same political blessings which have been my invaluable inheritance.

Hoping and believing that your administration may be an honor and glory to yourself, and a blessing to our expanding country and its increasing millions,

I remain, with the highest respect, your obedient servant,

AMOS KENDALL.

HON. JAMES BUCHANAN.

GENERAL JACKSON.

WASHINGTON, June 2, 1858.

HON. A. P. HAYNE, *United States Senate :* —

MY DEAR SIR, — You ask me for my opinion of General Jackson as an administrative officer of this government, which I cheerfully give.

No man ever excelled General Jackson in integrity and patriotism. To save his country by honest means was the height of his ambition. On every subject which required his official action, he sought for information in any and every quarter from which it could be obtained, and listened with attention to every opinion. Upon facts and opinions thus collected, or circumstances within his own knowledge, no mind was ever more prompt in arriving at correct and safe conclusions. He never stopped to calculate political consequences.

He took it for granted that in doing right his country would sustain him, and how gloriously have results justified that faith !

Yours very truly,

AMOS KENDALL.

In May, 1860, Mr. Kendall was invited by many friends in Washington to deliver a lecture before the Young Men's Christian Association in that place. Accordingly, on the 15th of May, he complied with the request, and gave the following lecture in the Smithsonian Institution, upon

CHRISTIANITY AND ITS LEGITIMATE INFLUENCE UPON HUMAN SOCIETY AND GOVERNMENT.

The theme selected for this occasion is Christianity and its legitimate influence upon human society and government.

It is not designed to attempt a development of the mysteries of Christianity, which lie beyond the scope of finite mind, and claim man's assent by Divine authority alone. Suffice it to say, that because man cannot understand is not a conclusive reason why he should not believe. If men's faith were limited to their comprehension, they would disbelieve all existence, material and spiritual, even their own. Who can comprehend how this globe and all the heavenly bodies came into existence ? Who can comprehend how matter can be created or annihilated, or how it can exist from eternity to eternity ? Who can comprehend how it is made to appear in the ten thousand forms of herb and flower, shrub and tree, fish and fowl, insect and reptile, beast and man, and how through death and resurrection in a new form of life it is made to pass in an unceasing round through various forms of mineral, vegetable, and animal existence ? Who knows by what principle the flower shoots up its slender stem and the tree its mighty trunk towards heaven, contrary to the laws of gravitation ? If you believe man to be altogether a material being, can you comprehend how matter can be made to think ? If you believe him to be partly material and partly spiritual, can you comprehend how the two natures are so combined as to enable the spirit to think and speak and act through the body ?

Mystery is not peculiar to the Christian religion ; and instead of solving mysteries, infidelity multiplies them. If the existence, nature, and attributes of matter and of spirit be mysterious, to deny the existence of the one or the other plunges us into deeper mysteries.

Some have denied the existence of matter, thus rejecting the evidence of their own senses. Does that relieve all nature from mystery ? A greater number have denied the existence of spirit, even of God himself. Does that relieve our minds from mystery ? If the first man was not created by Divine power, how did he come into existence ? Did one mass of matter organize itself into a man, and another into a woman, without a pre-existing, intelligent, plastic power to mould the form and inspire the brain ? Until we see human forms in the maturity of man-

hood rising out of the earth around us, with power to think and speak and act, or at least witness some advance in animal life from the reptile through the insect towards the monkey and the man, we cannot but suppose there is less mystery in the belief of a Creator God than in the theory of accidental or self creation. And when we look beyond man to the grand universe, composed of the sun, planets, moons, and stars, extending through inconceivable distances, but all constituting one vast machine in harmonious action, is it possible to conceive that it is the creation of chance ? Surely, there is less mystery in believing that it is the work of a mind more vast than itself, which gave it form and motion, and prescribed the laws by which it is governed.

A belief in the mystery of a God is the first article in the Christian creed, and who can reject it without involving himself in theories a thousand times more mysterious ?

In the dealings of God with man, according to the Christian system, there are also mysteries equally beyond the comprehension of the human intellect. Human reason asks in vain why God should create man in innocence and permit him to fall ; why he should suffer sin and pain and death to invade his creation ; why it was necessary for him to become incarnate and suffer a human death for man's redemption ; why he should hold man responsible at all for acts of transgression which he foresaw and foreordained as an essential part of the world's drama. Vain is every effort of human reason to reconcile man's responsibility with God's omniscience, omnipotence, wisdom, and goodness. Such attempts only bewilder the minds of teachers and hearers, and tend to shake men's faith in the justice of their Maker. Better tell them to have faith in their God, and not attempt by their glow-worm intellect to penetrate the recesses of earth and heaven, which only the sun of Omniscience can reach and illumine. Tell them to have faith that God's justice and wisdom are compatible with their free agency, and thus turn their thoughts upon their practical duties as accountable beings.

That we are free agents is proved by our consciousness. We know that we can talk or be silent, that we can stand or sit, lie down or walk ; that we can choose between good and evil, and that every sin and every crime is our voluntary act, for which something within admonishes us that we are responsible. On this point, human reason and Christianity are in perfect accord. If man cannot understand his mysteries, he can understand why he should be held responsible for his own voluntary acts. And on this basis Christianity rests, as an institution for the benefit of man during his residence on earth. In its mysteries it rests upon faith ; as a practical institution it rests upon works. It is in the latter aspect that we now propose particularly to consider it.

It cannot be denied that Christianity prescribes rules of conduct, which, if universally observed in their true spirit, would insure to the human family here on earth the highest degree of development and happiness of which man is capable.

They begin with the family relations. They teach us that "every man should have his own wife, and every woman her own husband." They command wives to submit themselves to their husbands, and husbands to love their wives. They declare, "So ought men to love their wives as their own body." Perfect fidelity to the conjugal relation is urgently inculcated; and so sacred did the author of the religion consider this relation, that he declared it could not be dissolved by human authority, except for infidelity. "What God hath joined together," said he, "let not man put asunder."

Reason, philosophy, and the experience of mankind concur with Christianity in the principle that the union and fidelity of one man and one woman in the married state is the domestic arrangement most conducive to the physical and mental vigor, the virtue and advancement of the human race. It is indeed the only safe foundation of civilized society.

The duties of children to parents, and of parents to children, are also prescribed. "Honor thy father and thy mother" is an injunction accompanied with the suggestion of long life as a reward. "Children, obey your parents in all things" is a repeated command, and this they are told "is well pleasing unto the Lord."

"Fathers, provoke not your children to anger lest they be discouraged; but bring them up in the nurture and admonition of the Lord." In other words, "Be kind to your children, and instruct them in all their duties toward their Maker and their fellow-men."

The duties of servants to masters, and masters to servants, are inculcated by precept, in language too plain to be misunderstood.

But Christianity does not stop here. It teaches man to consider his fellow-man his brother, no matter what may be their relative positions in human society. "Thou shalt love thy neighbor as thyself," is enjoined upon him as his highest duty, except the love and worship of his God. By the story of the Samaritan who fell among thieves, the author of Christianity himself teaches us that by the term neighbor, in this commandment, we are to understand every human being. The command is, therefore, to love every human being as we love ourselves. And lest there should be left room to make an exception, men are required even to "love their enemies." "I say unto you, Love your enemies, bless them that curse you, do good to them that hate you, and pray for them that despitefully use you and persecute you." And wherefore does Jesus thus command his followers? "That," says he, "ye may be the children of your Father which is in heaven," — in other words, that ye may be true Christians.

In this injunction to love our neighbors as ourselves, is condensed the essence of true Christianity in its human aspect. But, lest the duties comprehended under this general precept should not be fully understood, many of them are specified in detail. That violence ought not to be retaliated by violence, or wrong by wrong, we are admonished not to resist evil, and are told "whosoever shall smite thee on the right cheek, turn to him the other also," and "if any man sue thee at the law and take away thy coat, let him have thy cloak also." We are also instructed that we should have unbounded charity for the faults of others; that we should not judge others; that we should not be revengeful, but forgive injuries, and return good for evil; that we should be merciful as God is merciful; that we should be humble, preferring others to ourselves; that we should visit the sick, feed the hungry, and clothe the naked; that we should curb the tongue, not returning railing for railing, nor speak evil of any man; that we should improve our talents, be industrious in our business, provide for our families, deal justly with all men, avoid envy, hatred, and jealousy, not covet our neighbor's possessions, be content with our lot whatever it may be, avoid even the appearance of evil, — and in all things do others as upon a reversal of our relative positions we would have others do unto us.

How beautiful the picture of a society, all of whose members should be governed by these precepts!

There is another Christian duty emphatically enjoined by the Book, which ought to be the Christian's creed; it is obedience to government, and submission to its laws. This injunction has no reference to any particular form of government, nor to the character of its laws. It applies alike to despotisms, monarchies, and republics; to the decisions of a despot, the decrees of a monarch, and the laws of a republic, however oppressive and unjust. Paul, in his directions to Titus as to what he was to teach, says: "Put them in mind to be subject to principalities and powers, to obey magistrates." In his Epistle to the Romans, he enjoins upon them submission to the powers of the existing government, denouncing resistance as punishable with damnation in the world to come.

Christianity is not a civil or political institution. Its faithful ministers are not politicians. Jesus himself could not be tempted into the expression of a political opinion. All its early teachers, both by precept and example, inculcated obedience to the laws as an essential Christian duty; and when those laws required them to violate their duty to their God, instead of resorting to resistance and rebellion, they made a merit of meekly accepting the penalty, though it were death itself.

This injunction becomes more emphatic from the consideration that the governments of the world were then in pagan hands, and the author

and teachers of the new religion were members of a community which had but recently passed under the yoke of the Romans. It was, therefore, a foreign and pagan government to which the Jewish Christians were commanded to be obedient, and it is believed not one of them took part in the subsequent insurrection, ending in the destruction of Jerusalem, though the object was to recover the independence of their country. It was in accordance with their own doctrine that the author and early teachers of Christianity, in submission to unjust laws, unresistingly and uncomplainingly laid down their lives. How incomparably less effective would have been their precepts in all future time had they perished in rebellion, or had they overthrown by violence the government by which they were persecuted!

Nor does Christianity denounce any institution which it finds among men. It addresses, *individually*, husband and wife, parent and child, master and servant, citizen and stranger, ruler and subject, and teaches them their duties in the positions where Providence has placed them. Far from enjoining or even recommending a change in existing relations, it emphatically urges every one to be content with his lot, and cheerfully render all the services appertaining thereto which are required by human society. It teaches us that in the sight of God all men are equal, and that existing inequalities in the relations which men bear to each other on earth are but transient in their character, and that cheerful submission to them is an essential part of preparation for that eternal equality which we may all so soon enjoy.

True Christianity, therefore, is an institution, even in its human aspect, entirely distinct from all other institutions. It proposes to change *men* and *not* institutions; to make men happy under *all* institutions, — happy when earth and all it contains shall be remembered as a long past vision.

So long as Christianity was kept entirely separate from government; so long as its ministers and professors had nothing to do with making or executing the laws; so long as they preached and practised non-intervention in, and implicit submission to, the regulations of society, meekly bore persecution, and, when necessary, sealed their doctrines with their blood; so long, in short, as they considered themselves ministers of "a kingdom not of this world," whose only function was to fit men for the heavenly kingdom, leaving all earthly reforms to flow from that fitness, — the new religion was fast fulfilling its mission of peace and universal brotherhood among men. No worldly interest was then to be subserved by hypocrisy, and the palpable sincerity of Christians, attested by their sufferings and their resignation, was rapidly extending their faith throughout the known world. But when Christianity allied itself with government, all was changed. Then the commands of human law were substituted for the

precepts of the gospel as means of converting men to Christianity; then the peaceful missionary was substituted by the ferocious warrior; then the cross, theretofore the emblem of peace and universal brotherhood, became the fiery ensign of war, under which man went forth to slaughter his fellow-man. What atrocities were committed for a series of ages in the abused name of Christianity! Not only were the heathen required to become Christians under penalty of death, but Christian pursued Christian with confiscation, imprisonment, and torture for the purpose of enforcing uniformity of faith and practice.

The general mind of modern Christendom revolts at these atrocities, so repugnant to every precept of Bible Christianity. But has this enormous abuse been wholly eradicated? Is not Christianity still connected with government throughout most of the civilized world? Does it not, almost everywhere, lean upon the civil power for support? Is not hypocrisy encouraged by religious tests as qualifications for public office? Are not worldly ends sought to be accomplished by its denunciations and anathemas? Do its ministers everywhere content themselves with endeavoring to fit men for heaven? We boast of the advancement of our own land over all others in its separation of the civil from the religious elements of society; but are we free from the taint which has corrupted Christianity through all ages since the days of Constantine? Do its ministers with us keep themselves entirely aloof from politics and the civil power? Do we never see them in public offices, in State legislatures or in Congress? Do they without exceptions teach obedience to servants and submission to the laws? Do they, like the author and early teachers of Christianity, enjoin upon every one not to judge or envy others, to be content with his own lot, to render all service required of him with alacrity and cheerfulness, to endure wrong, and even submit to undeserved chastisement without resistance or complaint, and all this as an imperative Christian duty? In short, *do they content themselves with endeavoring to fit men for heaven?*

Does it follow that bad institutions and laws shall remain unchanged, or that the teachers of Christianity shall have no agency in effecting a reformation? Far from it. *Every faithful Christian teacher is an apostle of reform in all the relations of life.* But his only legitimate means are the example and precepts of the early teachers of his religion. He is restricted to the reformation of the *individual*, the husband and the wife, the parent and the child, the master and the servant, the ruler and the ruled, — to the *individual man* in all his relations with his fellow-man, thus fitting him for heaven. He thus fertilizes the soil and cherishes the root; a glorious foliage and abundant fruit are the necessary but noiseless result. Silent, effectual, but irresistible, when wielded by men imbued with their spirit, are the truly Christian weapons of reform. It is the wisdom, the glory, and the beauty of the Christian system that, by means perfectly unexceptionable even to antichristian minds, it aims to improve society through its elements, and government through its constituents. In fitting men for heaven, it fits them to become the instruments as well as the subjects of all needful reforms in society and government.

Let the Christian teacher strictly follow the path which is laid out before him. Let him strive to prepare the individuals around him for heaven, by the quiet and inoffensive means prescribed in the Book wherein he seeks instruction and learns wisdom, — the Book which he professes to receive as the word of God. If he cannot make men perfect, he may make them better. If he cannot by such means make human institutions perfect, he may aid in improving them. By faith and perseverance he may do something towards advancing mankind in the path towards that millennial perfection to which the Christian aspires. As the tiny insect labors from age to age in piling atom upon atom on the bright coral column, until his wonderful structure rises from the ocean's gloomy depths to the light and heat of a tropical sun, and forms an island radiant with foliage, fruit, and flower, so let the Christian teacher labor on from age to age and from generation to generation in the certainty that he is advancing the true interests of his fellow-man, and in the faith that he is instrumental in building up a glorious moral structure for the habitation of man, which the waves of time shall never sweep away.

Shall man do nothing because he cannot do everything? Shall he despise all knowledge because he cannot make himself omniscient? Shall he not teach men honesty, industry, fidelity, benevolence, and every virtue because he cannot make all men honest, industrious, faithful, benevolent, and virtuous? Progress is the motto of the age. Let this progress not be confined to discovery, invention, science, and art. Let it be seen also in morals, in the love of man for man, in more general conformity with Christian precepts. In them there is no room for reform, — they are unchangeable.

Here is something fixed amidst the convulsions of a changing world. They are the rock in the ocean on which the weary bird of passage may rest above the reach of the raging surge. Their principles are the basis of all useful reforms in society and government, whether men think so or not. Take these precepts as your guide, young men of the Christian Association, and you may safely shout *Excelsior!* and with alacrity and zeal join in the glorious race of human progress.

In 1860 he sets forth the then deplorable condition of the country, in a letter to Colonel Orr, of South Carolina, which not only

breathes the loftiest patriotism, but anticipates with almost prophetic vision the impending calamity.

MR. KENDALL'S LETTER TO COLONEL ORR.

WASHINGTON, September 10, 1860.

HONORABLE JAMES L. ORR : —

MY DEAR SIR, — Your letter of the 15th ult. reached Washington while I was absent in the North.

Though I did not contemplate, when I wrote you on the 9th ult., anything beyond a limited private correspondence, yet, having no opinion on the portentous condition of public affairs which I have a motive to conceal, or am ashamed to avow, I cheerfully comply with your suggestions.

You quote from my former letter the declaration that "my mind is equally clear that the South has long had a peaceful remedy within her reach, and has it still, though impaired by the recent conduct of some of her sons," and you ask of me a full explanation of my opinions on that point, as well as "the remedy to be resorted to by us (the South) should the government in November pass into the hands of a party whose declared purpose is to destroy our property, amounting in value at the present time to three billions one hundred and fifty millions of dollars." You ask, "Can it be prudent, safe, or manly in the South to submit to the domination of a party whose declared purpose is to destroy such an amount of property, and subvert our whole social and industrial policy?"

In a subsequent part of your letter you call my attention to certain grievances endured by the South, and conclude your commentary thereon as follows : —

"Is it wise, if we do not intend to submit to such consequences, to allow a Black Republican President to be inaugurated, and put him in possession of the army, the navy, the treasury, the armories and arsenals, the public property, in fact the whole machinery of the government, with its appendants and appurtenances? If the South should think upon this subject as I do, no Black Republican President should ever execute any law within her borders, unless at the point of the bayonet and over the dead bodies of her slain sons."

I shudder at such sentiments coming from one whose sincerity I cannot doubt. The time was when 150,000 men tendered their services to the President to aid him if necessary in executing the laws of the United States ; the time will be when 200,000 will volunteer for a like purpose, should resistance be made to his legitimate authority, no matter by what party he may be elected.

There seems to me to be in the course recommended to the South, in the event of Mr. Lincoln's election to the Presidency, a fatuity little

short of madness. Would you pull down the canopy of heaven because wrong and crime exist beneath it? Would you break up the earth on which we tread because earthquakes sometimes heave it and pestilence walks its surface? The Union, sir, is too precious to the people it protects, North and South, East and West, to be broken up, even should a Black Republican be elected President next November. Should the attempt be made, an united North and three fourths of a divided South would spring to the rescue. No, no, the remedy for the evils of which you justly complain are to be found within the Union, and not among its bloody ruins.

I admit that the grievances which you enumerate are hard to be borne ; but a few Southern men are not without responsibility for their existence. The general sentiment of the country, North and South, at the close of the Revolutionary war was antislavery. It has changed in the South, but remained unchanged in the North. There, however, it has been roused to unwonted activity by the preachings of fanatics and the denunciations of political demagogues, aided not a little by the art, the language, and the violence of Southern disunionists.

It is needless to give in detail all the causes which have brought the politics of the country to their present deplorable condition. Suffice it to say, that you have long had in the South a small party of able men whose aim has been to destroy the Union ; that, as a preliminary to their main design, they have sought to break up the Democratic party ; that their means for accomplishing this end were to act with it, and force upon it every possible issue obnoxious to the general sentiment of the North ; that they have dragged after them the true Union men of the South, partly through their fears of being considered laggard in their devotion to Southern interests, and partly through ambition for political distinction ; to make the Democratic party as odious as possible at the North, they became the advocates of slavery on principle, justified the African slave-trade, and denounced the laws prohibiting it. By these acts and frequent threats of dissolution, they enabled the enemies of Democracy in the North to denounce them as pro-slavery men, and to all this, they added occasional taunts that they were no more to be relied upon for the protection of Southern rights than their opponents. By these means the Democratic party was reduced, before the last presidential election, to a minority in most of the Northern States, and, in the residue, had the utmost difficulty in maintaining their ascendancy. In the mean time the Union men in the South had measurably ceased to consider the Democratic party as friendly to the Union ; and the Union sentiment, particularly in the border slave States, whose interest in its preservation is pre-eminent, sought expression through the American party. To such an extent had the Democratic party been weakened by

the insidious policy of their disunion allies, that they had the utmost difficulty in electing an old practical statesman over a young man who had nothing to recommend him beyond a few successful explorations of our wilderness territory.

There were those who foresaw that longer affiliation with Southern disunionists would inevitably destroy the ascendancy of the Democratic party, and a feeble and fruitless effort was made to induce the President to lay the foundation of his administration on the rock of the Union, and cut loose from those who were seeking to destroy it. For reasons, no doubt patriotic, but to me inexplicable, the reverse of that policy was pursued. The support of the Lecompton constitution, which the country generally believed to be a fraud, was made the test of Democracy ; one leading Democrat after another was proscribed because he would not submit to the test, and as if to deprive Northern Democrats of the last hope of successfully vindicating the rights of the South, an act was passed for the admission of Kansas into the Union at once, provided she would consent to become a slaveholding State, but postponing her admission indefinitely if she refused.

In your published letter, you justly condemn the seceders from the Charleston Convention, who, you think, ought to have remained and prevented the nomination of a candidate who is obnoxious to the South. Do you not perceive, sir, that the secession was a part of the programme for breaking up the Democratic party? And is it not palpable that after absolutely vacating their seats at Charleston, they went to Baltimore for the mere purpose of more effectually completing the work of destruction by drawing off another detachment? I, sir, entertain no doubt that the secession was the result most desired by the disunionists ; that the object of the new issue then gotten up was merely to form a pretext for secession, and that its adoption was the last thing they desired or designed.

Glance a moment at a few facts : Alabama, led by an open disunionist, went to Cincinnati in 1856, under instructions to secede unless the equal rights of all the States in the Territories should be conceded and incorporated into the platform of the Democratic party. The concession was made, and they had no opportunity to secede.

They came to Charleston under the same leader, again instructed to secede unless the convention would put into the platform a new plank, the effect of which, if adopted, would be further to disgust and alienate the Northern Democracy. In this instance the *sine qua non* was not complied with, and the disunionists floated off on the rejected plank into an unknown sea, unfortunately carrying with them a large number of good and true Union men.

And what is this principle, the non-recognition of which has rived asunder the Democratic party, and apparently threatens the dissolution of the Union? It is, that *it is the right and duty of Congress to legislate for the protection of slave property in the Territories.*

Now, I take it upon me to say that a more latitudinarian and dangerous claim of power in Congress never was advanced by Federalists of the Hamilton school. Look at it in a constitutional and practical light; if Congress have the right to legislate for the protection of slavery in the Territories, they have a right to legislate for the protection of all other property; and if they have a right to legislate for the protection of property, they have a right to legislate for the protection of persons. The assumption that they can legislate for the protection of slave property leads, logically and inevitably, to the conclusion that they have the power to legislate for the Territories in all cases whatsoever. If you can put your finger on the grant of this power in the Constitution, please put it also on its limitations, if any can be found.

Upon this principle, Congress may acquire an empire outside of the organized States, over which it may exercise unlimited power, governing it as the Roman Senate did their conquered provinces. And this under a Constitution which jealously restricts the exclusive power of legislation by Congress to a few spots of land purchased, with the consent of the States, for special objects, and grants no power of general legislation over a Territory whatsoever.

To verify these positions, we need only advert to the Constitution. Among the grants of power to Congress is the following : —

"To exercise exclusive legislation, in all cases whatsoever, over such district (not exceeding ten miles square) as may by cession of particular States, and the acceptance of Congress, become the seat of the government of the United States, and to exercise like authority over all places purchased by the consent of the legislature of the State in which the same shall be, for the erection of forts, magazines, arsenals, dockyards, and other needful buildings."

Mark the jealousy with which this power is restricted. For the protection of the government, even, it is limited to a territory not exceeding ten miles square, and it cannot be exercised over "the forts, magazines, arsenals, dockyards, and other needful buildings," situated within the States, unless the lands on which they shall be located shall be first purchased with "the consent of the legislatures" of those States. Is it conceivable that the wise men who restricted the exclusive power of legislation in Congress to a territory not exceeding ten miles square, did, by any indirection, grant that power broadly enough to cover the whole continent outside of the organized States, should it be annexed by purchase or conquest?

The following provision is the only one in the Constitution which has been chiefly, if not exclusively, relied upon to sustain the position that Congress has any power whatsoever to legislate over the Territories, namely : —

"The Congress shall have power to dispose of and make all needful rules and regulations respecting the territory or other property belonging to the United States."

The word "territory" used in this provision obviously means *land,* and nothing else. The United States, at the time when the Constitution was adopted, owned an immense amount of land north of the Ohio River, and these lands Congress was authorized to "dispose of." That the word "territory" means property, is conclusively shown by its connection with the words "and other property," — "territory and other property." The territory spoken of, therefore, is property in lands.

"Rules and regulations" are a grade of legislation somewhat below the dignity of laws; but admitting them in this case to have the same effect, on what are they to operate? Simply on the property of the United States, not on any other property, nor on persons, except so far as they may be connected with the public property. To this extent, and no further, is the power of Congress to legislate over a Territory granted to Congress, and whenever all the lands and other property are disposed of, the "rules and regulations" become obsolete, and the power of legislation granted in this clause is thenceforth in abeyance.

Moreover, this grant of power extends as well to property within a State as within a Territory. In a State the general power of legislation is in the State legislature; yet the power of Congress to make "rules and regulations" respecting public property, is the same in a State as in a Territory. The scope of the grant can, of course, be no greater in a Territory than in a State, and it necessarily follows that this clause of the Constitution confers on Congress no general power of legislation, either within States or Territories.

It is not a satisfactory reply to this argument to say that such a power has, to some extent, been exercised. Is it better to acquiesce in and extend the usurpation than to put a stop to it, as in the case of the United States Bank, by bringing the government back to the constitutional test? Which is safest to the South, the constitutional principle that Congress shall not legislate for the Territories at all, or the adoption of a principle unknown to the Constitution, which, in its general application, would not only defeat the object it is advanced to promote, but would enable the free State majority to surround the slaveholding States and encircle the Union with an empire outside of the organized States, over which that majority should exercise the power of unlimited and exclusive legislation? If such an idea be chimerical, the apprehension is not chimerical, that the Black Republicans, should they acquire the control of all branches of the government, will use the claim

now set up for Congressional legislation over one species of property in the Territories, as an apology for assuming the power of general legislation, involving the power to destroy as well as to protect.

It by no means follows that the people who may occupy a territory of the United States constitute an independent community, with all the attributes of sovereignty. Though the Constitution of the United States does not apply to them, they live under another constitution of powers, perhaps more limited. I mean the paramount law of necessity. They are in the condition of bands of hunters or miners located in the wilderness, who may adopt such rules and regulations as may be absolutely necessary for the protection of person and property, until Congress acknowledges their independence by admitting them into the Union on the same footing with the original States. At that moment, and not before, the powers of a limited sovereignty accrue to them, and may be exercised to protect or destroy local institutions which may have grown up while the legislative power was limited to the absolute necessities of the occasion. If it be said that the law of necessity may be transcended, and regulations adopted to destroy some kinds of property instead of protecting it, I answer that such regulations would be an assumption of power not justified by the law of necessity, analogous to usurpations of power in organized communities, remediless, perhaps, but for that reason none the less unjust.

If this be not the true theory in relation to our Territories, when does sovereignty therein begin? Is the first settler a sovereign? Does sovereignty accrue when there are ten, or one hundred, or one thousand, or ten thousand settlers? Where shall we draw the line and pronounce that on this side the settlers live under the law of necessity, and on that they become rightfully sovereign?

The Constitution of the United States was not made for Territories but for States, as its name implies. It has, by strict rules of construction, nothing to do with Territories outside of the States united, beyond the protection and disposition of the common property therein. It seems to contemplate that the Territories shall be left to themselves until they shall have a population adequate to the formation of a respectable community, when their independence should be acknowledged, and their admission into the Union granted, on the sole condition that they adopt a republican government.

But if there be a doubt as to the power of Congress to legislate for the Territories, is it not safer and more consistent with Democratic principles to deny the power than to assume it? Some of the original States, when admitted into the Union, had not the population of a third-rate city of the present day, and no harm would be likely to arise by leaving the Territories to themselves until they have double the population of Delaware or Rhode Island in 1789. But would it not be incomparably better to admit them into the Union as States, with a much less population, than to leave them to be a bone of contention among demagogues and disunionists, disturbing every essential interest of the country and jeopardizing the Union of the existing States?

Let us briefly consider the practical workings of the remedy for Southern wrongs which you suggest, in case a Black Republican is elected to the Presidency. You ask, "Is it wise, if we do not intend to submit to such consequences, to allow a Black Republican President to be inaugurated," etc., and you say, "if the South should think upon this subject as I do, no Black Republican should ever execute any law within her borders, unless at the point of the bayonet and over the dead bodies of her slain sons."

I know there are men in the South who would sacrifice their lives and endanger the communities in which they live, upon a point of honor, and that such men often fire up with unwonted fierceness if reminded of the probable consequences of their own rashness. But the time has come when consequences should be looked in the face, not for the purposes of defiance, but that we may consider whether the policy which would lead to them is required by Southern interests or honor.

How do you propose to prevent the inauguration of a Black Republican President should such an one be unfortunately elected? Will you come to this city with an armed force and attempt to prevent an inauguration by violence? In that event, force would be met by force, and there would be instant civil war, in which the country and the world would declare the South to be the aggressor.

He *would* be inaugurated here or elsewhere in spite of you. Well, suppose you then attempt to secede from the Union, and resist the execution of the laws? Every lawyer in the South knows that every citizen of every State is as much bound by the laws of the United States constitutionally enacted as by the laws of his own State, and that it is as impossible for the State to relieve its citizens from allegiance to the United States as it is for the latter to relieve them from allegiance to their own State. And it is the sworn duty of the President to take care that the laws of the United States shall be faithfully executed upon every citizen of every State, and, as long as we have a faithful President, they will be so executed, if the courts, the marshals, the army, and the navy remain faithful to their respective trusts.

I know that much has been said in the South about reserved rights of nullification, secession, and not coercing a sovereign State, etc., when in fact the conventions representing the people of the several States which adopted the Constitution made no such reservations, but bound their constituents, one and all, to allegiance to the Constitution of the United States, as firmly as similar conventions bound them to the State constitutions. And although the general government cannot, technically, coerce a State, it can rightfully coerce all the citizens of a State into obedience to its constitutional laws. The pretended reserved rights of nullification and secession, therefore, are in effect nothing more nor less than an outspoken rebellion when wrong and oppression become intolerable. But when the crisis comes, there are two parties who must necessarily decide, each for itself, whether circumstances justify the act, — the seceders and the government of the United States. And do you conceive that the mere election of a President entertaining obnoxious opinions, or even entertaining hostile designs against the institutions of the South, checked, as he must necessarily be, by the Senate and judiciary, if not by a House of Representatives, without one overt act, can justify any portion of the South even to their own consciences in an act of rebellion?

There is one notable feature in the attitude of the South. The cry of disunion comes, not from those who suffer most from Northern outrage, but from those who suffer least. It comes from South Carolina, and Georgia, and Alabama, and Mississippi, whose slave property is rendered comparatively secure by the intervention of other slaveholding States between them and the free States, and not from Delaware, and Maryland, and Virginia, and Kentucky, and Tennessee, and Missouri, which lose a hundred slaves, by abolition thieves, where the first-named States lose one. Why are not the States that suffer most, loudest in their cry for disunion? It is because their position enables them to see more distinctly than you do, at a distance, the fatal and instant effects of such a step.

As imperfect as the protection which the Constitution and laws give to their property undoubtedly is, it is better than none. They do not think it wise to place themselves in a position to have the John Browns of the North let loose upon them, with no other restraints than the laws of war between independent nations, construed by reckless fanatics. They prefer to fight the Abolitionists, if fight they must, within the Union, where their adversaries are somewhat restrained by constitutional and legal obligations. No, sir; Delaware, Maryland, and Virginia, do not intend to become the theatre of desolating wars between the North and the South; Kentucky, Tennessee, and Missouri do not intend that their peaceful channels of commerce shall become rivers of blood to gratify the ambition of South Carolina and Alabama, who, at a remote distance from the present danger, cry out disunion.

I have said that the South has all along had a peaceful remedy, and

has it still. The Union sentiment is overwhelming in all the Middle and Western States, constituting two thirds of the Republic. Pennsylvania, Ohio, Indiana, and Illinois are as little inclined to become frontier States as Maryland, Virginia, and Kentucky. Had the present Administration cut loose from the disunionists, instead of virtually ministering to their designs, and planted itself firmly on Union ground, the secessions at Charleston and Baltimore would never have occurred, the "Constitutional Union Party" would have been an impossibility, the Democracy would have recovered its ascendancy in the North, and an united party, embracing two thirds of the North and of the South, would now have been marching to certain victory next November.

What ought to have been the preventive must now be the remedy. Should Lincoln in November next secure a majority of the electors, patriotic men, North and South, without waiting for his inauguration, irrespective of party lines, must band together for the triple purpose of preventing any attempt to break up the Union, checking the Republican party while in the ascendant, and expelling them from power at the next election. Let the toast of General Jackson, "*The Federal Union, it must be preserved*," become the motto of the party; while strict construction of the Constitution and a jealous regard for the rights of the States shall be its distinguishing principle and unwavering practice. Let the constitutional principle be adopted, of no legislation by Congress over the Territories; or throw aside altogether the mischievous issues in relation to them, of no practical utility, gotten up by demagogues and disunionists, as means of accomplishing their own selfish ends. Let them inflexibly refuse to support, for any Federal or State offices, any man who talks of disunion on the one hand or "irrepressible conflict between freedom and slavery" on the other. Throw aside all party leaders except such as "keep step to the music of the Union," and are prepared to battle for State rights under its banner.

Be this your "platform"; let the South rally upon it as one man, and I would pledge all but my life that at least one half of the North will join you in driving from power the reckless assailants of your rights and institutions. But whether the South come up to the rescue or not, I foresee that, in the natural progress of events, the Central States, from the Atlantic to the far West, will band together on this ground, leaving the Abolitionists of New England and the disunionists of the South to the harmless pastime of belching fire and fury at each other at a safe distance, protected by the patriotism and good sense of nine tenths of their countrymen, against the evils they would bring on themselves.

Can you doubt the success of such a reunion? Not an advocate of disunion, under any probable circumstances, can be found among the candidates for the Presidency and Vice-Presidency.

The supporters of Bell to a man, the supporters of Douglas to a man, and more than three fourths of the supporters of Breckinridge, are staunch supporters of the Union, and staunch adversaries to Northern interference with Southern institutions. When convinced of the folly and madness of their warfare on each other, as they will be after the election, if not before, they band together in a common cause, and that cause the preservation of our glorious Union and its invaluable Constitution with their attendant blessings, will they not be irresistible?

How much more hopeful and cheering is a prospect like this than the contemplation of standing armies, grinding taxes, ruined agriculture, prostrate commerce, bloody battles, ravaged countries, and sacked cities. This Continent, like the Eastern world, is destined to have its "Northern hive." Shall its swarms be repressed by the strong hand of the States united, or are they, by a dissolution of the Union, to be let loose upon our South, like the Goths and Vandals upon Southern Europe? True, their blood might, in that event, fertilize your desolated fields, but your institutions, like those of the Roman Empire, would sink to rise no more.

These are the thoughts of an old man whose only political aspirations are, that when he dies he may leave his country united, happy, and free.

With sincere regard,

AMOS KENDALL.

The following letter was addressed to the editor of the "Constitution," the administration organ at that time in Washington, but he refusing to print it, it was published in the "Evening Star."

WASHINGTON, October 2, 1860.

TO THE EDITOR OF THE CONSTITUTION, — Your paper for a few days past has forcibly reminded me of the days of President Jackson, when *Amos Kendall* was the theme of a thousand scribblers. Circumstances, however, have somewhat changed. Then he was abused by the enemies of the old hero and his administration; now, by the organ of an administration which claims to be his friend. Who has changed? Is it Amos Kendall, who has not uttered a sentiment which is not an echo of those avowed and acted upon by that purest of patriots? Or, is it certain men who claim his mantle while they repudiate his most dearly cherished principles? When he heard disunion foreshadowed in dinner-table speeches, he rebuked it in his celebrated toast, "THE FEDERAL UNION, *it must be preserved*"; and when he saw the sentiment about to be reduced to practice, by his eloquent and patriotic appeal he called into existence one hundred and fifty thousand volunteers to preserve it. Because I alluded to that fact, and expressed the opinion that, should a similar emergency arise, two hundred thousand would respond to a

similar call, you denounce me as a bloody monster ready to slaughter "women and children!" Yet, no eulogy is too strong for you to bestow on General Jackson.

You are right in the caption with which you head your comments upon my letter to Colonel Orr: "*Threats will never bring peace*." For months past, the papers controlled by the enemies of the Union in the South have teemed with threats of disunion in the event of Mr. Lincoln's election, and my letter was in response to a startling threat of that description. There will not be peace until these threats cease, or until Southern Union men cut loose from the enemies of the Union and cordially unite with the friends of the Constitution in the North to put down Black Republicanism on the one hand and disunion on the other. I made no threat; you have misapplied the sentiment of your caption.

Your strictures upon myself need no reply. If I have not, during a life of seventy-one years, a large portion of which has been spent in public positions, established a private and political character which no name you can give me can mar, and no association in which you can place me can taint, it is useless for me to care for the future. It is a higher aim than self-defence or self-distinction which induces me to resume my pen.

Sir, it is a sad sight to see the organ of a Democratic administration attempting to establish the doctrine that it would in any event be a crime in the President to defend the Constitution and enforce the laws of the United States constitutionally enacted. Disguise it as you will, your doctrine amounts to this and nothing less. Already the peculiar organ of nullification in the South is recommending secession while Mr. Buchanan is still in office, upon the assumption that he may not enforce the laws and defend the Constitution, which by his official oath he is bound to do. Doubtless the assumption is unwarranted, though justified by the tone of his acknowledged organ.

But let it be remembered, that the question is not now what the South ought to do in case of an actual and irremediable outrage upon her rights and institutions. The threat is *to secede* if *Mr. Lincoln shall be elected*. Will his mere election absolve the people of the South from their allegiance to the Constitution and laws of the United States, or relieve the President from the duty of defending the one and executing the other? This is the real question under discussion. You talk about *coercing States*. States are not the subjects upon which the Constitution and laws of the United States operate. They cannot commit treason nor be hanged as traitors. But neither can they, by any act of theirs, absolve their citizens from their allegiance to the United States.

The Constitution contains the following provisions: —

"This Constitution, and the laws of the United States which shall be made in pursuance thereof, ... *shall be the supreme law of the land;* and the judges in every State shall be bound thereby, *anything in the constitution and laws of any State to the contrary notwithstanding.*"

The same Constitution declares, that "Treason against the United States shall consist only in levying war against them, or in adhering to their enemies, giving them aid and comfort."

It also declares, that the President "shall take care that the laws be faithfully executed," and prescribes to him the following oath : —

"*I do solemnly swear (or affirm), that I will faithfully execute the office of President of the United States, and will, to the best of my ability, preserve, protect, and defend the Constitution of the United States.*"

Now, suppose Lincoln were elected, and a-citizen of Charleston, acting with or without the sanction of the State authorities, having a cargo of sugar entering the port, should refuse to pay the legal duties, and with an armed party should resist the officers attempting to collect them, thus levying war against the United States, do you think the President would be faithful to his duty and true to his oath if he did not, if necessary, use the militia, the army and navy, in "*taking care that the laws be faithfully executed,*" and in *preserving, protecting, and defending the Constitution of the United States ?* Could he, without official perjury and becoming a traitor himself, fold his arms and say *this would be coercing a State,* and under such a plea suffer the Constitution and laws to be subverted ? If bloodshed ensued, who would be responsible, the President who would be, "*to the best of his ability,*" attempting to perform his sworn duty, or the traitors who were attempting to subvert the government ?

Your doctrine I suppose is, that the State authorities or a State convention may declare a State out of the Union, and thus absolve all its citizens from allegiance to the United States.

Now, each State, by a convention elected by the people, agreed with every other State, by the adoption of the Constitution, that all its provisions and the laws passed in pursuance thereof, should be "*the supreme law of the land.*" They all agreed to take a portion of the powers theretofore possessed by their respective State governments and vest them in a common government, (based on precisely the same authority as their State governments,) whose Constitution, and the laws passed in pursuance thereof, should be above the reach of all State authority. How then can any act of a State absolve its citizens from obedience to this "*supreme law of the land,*" declared by its highest authority, a convention selected by the people, to be binding, "*anything in the constitution and laws of any State to the contrary notwithstanding*" ? To me it is a wonder that any man can entertain an idea, to my mind, so absurd. The theory of our government obviously is, that the citizen owes allegiance to his State government *to the extent of its reserved powers,* and to the general government *to the extent of its granted powers,* and that no act of the general government can relieve him from allegiance to his State, and no act of his State can relieve him from his allegiance to the United States.

Let me not be misunderstood. I do not deny the right of rebellion in the people of any State when unconstitutional outrages shall be committed on their rights and institutions, and all hope for redress by peaceful means has vanished. But I deny that the language of aspiring demagogues, or the election of one of them to the Presidency, would constitute such an outrage, though a just cause for alarm. I also deny, that in such an event, the South would be without hope of redress. It is not to be found, however, in personal denunciations of eminent Democrats, in attempting to force on the Democratic Party new and useless issues, or in threats of disunion. Let all this cease now and forever. Be just to the Northern Democracy ; in devotion to the Union emulate Washington and Jackson, and you will rally an irresistible force, who, by the aid of the ballot-box only, will rescue your institutions from danger, and firmly maintain every constitutional right.

You say that Southern men are "demanding only their constitutional right." Do you think they have a "constitutional right" *to destroy the Constitution ?* Such indeed is the claim of a right to secede from the Union, if based on any other ground than a right of rebellion for gross and irremediable wrongs.

You say that the South Carolinians "will even suspect that he (meaning me) is governed by disappointment and the revenge consequent thereon," and that "under other circumstances he entertained another sort of sentiments."

I plead guilty to the charge of disappointment, though it has filled me with sorrow rather than revenge. My disappointment was in the apparent fact that the present administration had not the sagacity to perceive that their policy would inevitably destroy the Democratic party, and minister to the designs of those whose ultimate object is the destruction of the Union.

As evidence of *my* inconsistency you quote certain sayings of *Senator Douglas !* I might with propriety demur to this testimony ; but I adopt those quotations as in the main my sentiments then and now, unchanged and unchangeable. I believe that fidelity to the Constitution in the North and in the South is the only means by which the Union can be long preserved. I do not doubt that when the theory of Senator Seward, false in fact and treasonable in effect, that slave labor and free labor cannot exist in the same community, becomes the settled rule of action in the general government, the Union will come to an end. But

my faith is equally strong, that it is in the power of the friends of the Constitution in the South, by a cordial union with its friends in the North, to avert this catastrophe and all its consequent calamities.

In further response to the charges of disappointment and inconsistency, coming from the organ of the administration, I send you for publication with this letter a communication addressed by me to Mr. Buchanan before his inauguration.

I have no reproaches for the President because his views did not coincide with mine. Which were best adapted to preserve the Democratic party and the Constitution let the country decide.

In conclusion, I implore you and those who act with you to abandon your denunciations of men with whom you must ultimately act in preserving the Constitution and State institutions, if they are to be preserved at all. Do not further verify the old maxim, that "*Those whom God would destroy, he first makes mad.*" That the cordial co-operation of the supporters of Breckinridge, Douglas, and Bell might have prevented the triumph of Black Republicanism, and may hereafter render its triumph transient and innocuous, no observing man can doubt. Why then not labor to bring them together, instead of thrusting them further apart ? Is the new-fangled dogma on which the Charleston convention split, or any theoretical claim to a right of secession, of more importance than the preservation of the Union, the Constitution, the peace, the happiness, the prosperity, and the glory of our country, — hitherto unequalled by those of any other people on the face of the earth ? Or shall Black Republicanism in the North and secessionism in the South be allowed to cut asunder our bond of Union and divide us into hostile States, occasionally drenching our own joyous fields in the blood of their cultivators. Any man who thinks this Union can be peacefully broken up, or, if it could, that peace could always be maintained between its fragments, shuts his eyes to the events of our own age, and is deaf to the lessons of history.

AMOS KENDALL.

The letter to Colonel Orr had a wide circulation through the country.

From the many favorable notices of his letter, the two following are selected as fair samples of the whole number. The first is from the "State Sentinel" of Harrisburg, September 29, 1860.

"LETTER FROM AMOS KENDALL.

"No name is more familiar to the American people than that of Amos Kendall ; and no man is more universally respected for his intellect, integrity, and moral worth. At one time an active politician, the bosom friend and confidant of General Jackson, a cabinet officer of that patriotic old President, he made his mark by the intelligence and stern justice with which he discharged his duties, and by the tenacity with which he clung to the President through the troublous times of his administration. Next to Jackson himself he was the favorite of the party, and is perhaps the most notable individual now living who represents the principles of the old hero. Any advice from him, at any time, would command respect, and a letter from him now, on the subject of national politics, cannot fail to attract universal attention. We publish such a letter in to-day's 'Sentinel,' addressed to Honorable James L. Orr, of South Carolina. It covers the whole ground of contention, and shows conclusively who are right and who are wrong ; and portrays in strong and eloquent language the inevitable results of the mad doctrines of the Abolitionists on the one hand, and the sectionalists on the other, if carried to their logical conclusions. Mr. Kendall has long since retired from active political life, and looks upon the stirring events of the times with the eye of a philosopher, statesman, and patriot. Whoever reads his able letter may well imagine, as we do, that the spirit of the old hero was near him, and every word is an invocation from the other world to the people of this Republic to frown upon all the attempts now being made to weaken the Constitution and dissever the Union."

The following is from the "Daily Enquirer," of September 27, 1860, published in Memphis, including the fancy sketch by Miss Harriet Martineau.

"AMOS KENDALL'S LETTER.

"Honorable James L. Orr has called forth a letter from one of the most renowned Democrats of the old *régime* yet on the stage, and adverse enough to Mr. Orr's politics it is. Mr. Kendall's letter is done in admirable style. It is evidently the work of a master of first-class abilities, and of long and thorough practice. Politics of past times dwell pertinaciously in his mind, but their recollection serves to illustrate and point out his views of present questions. Barring some of his old party leanings and his defence of Douglas's distinguishing doctrine, his letter is one of the ablest Union papers of the season. He prefers with Crittenden to fight the Abolitionists in the Union, if fight he must. He says the Union sentiment is overwhelming in all the Middle and Western States, constituting two-thirds of the Republic. Pennsylvania, Ohio, Indiana, and Illinois are as little inclined, he says, to become frontier States, as Maryland, Virginia, and Kentucky. He sees one notable feature in the attitude of the South : —

"'There is one notable feature in the attitude of the South. The cry of disunion comes, not from those who suffer most from Northern outrage, but from those who suffer least. It comes from South Carolina, and Georgia, and Alabama, and Mississippi, whose slave property is rendered comparatively secure by the intervention of other slaveholding States between them and the free States, and not from Delaware, and Maryland, and Virginia, and Kentucky, and Tennessee, and Missouri, which lose a hundred slaves by abolition thieves where the first named States lose one. Why are not the States that suffer most loudest in their cry for disunion? It is because their position enables them to see more distinctly than you do, at a distance, the fatal and instant effects of such a step. As imperfect as the protection which the Constitution and laws give to their property undoubtedly is, it is better than none. They do not think it wise to place themselves in a position to have the John Browns of the North let loose upon them, with no other restraints than the laws of war between independent nations, as construed by reckless fanatics.'

"Mr. Kendall is now in his seventy-second year. In 1834, Miss Harriet Martineau being in Washington, thus writes of him as one of the most important personages of the day. She was well acquainted with Webster and Clay, and it is thought that her picture of Kendall is tinged with the unfriendly hues of a rival party ; but she thus speaks : —

"'I was fortunate enough once to catch a glimpse of the invincible Amos Kendall, one of the most remarkable men in America. He is supposed to be the moving spring of the administration ; the thinker, planner, and doer ; but it is all in the dark. Documents are issued, the excellence of which prevents their being attributed to the persons who take the responsibility of them ; a correspondence is kept up all over the country, for which no one seems answerable ; work is done of goblin extent and with goblin speed, which makes men look about them with superstitious wonder ; and the invisible Amos Kendall has the credit of it all. President Jackson's letters to his cabinet are said to be Kendall's ; the Report on Sunday mails is attributed to Kendall ; the letters sent from Washington to remote country newspapers, whence they are collected and published in the "Globe," as demonstrations of public opinion, are pronounced to be written by Kendall. Every mysterious paragraph in opposition newspapers relates to Kendall ; and it is some relief that his now having the office of postmaster-general affords opportunity for open attack upon this twilight personage, who is proved by the faults in the post-office administration, not to be able to do quite everything well. But he is undoubtedly a great genius. He unites with his "great talent for silence" a splendid audacity.

"'It is clear that he could not do the work he does (incredible enough in amount any way) if he went into society like other men. He did, however, one evening, — I think it was at the attorney-general's. The moment I went in, intimations reached me from all quarters, amid nods and winks, "Kendall is here" ; "That is he." I saw at once that his plea for seclusion (bad health) is no false one. The extreme sallowness of his complexion, and hair of such perfect whiteness as is rarely seen in a man of middle age, testified to his disease. His countenance does not help the superstitious to throw off their dread of him. He probably does not desire this superstition to melt away, for there is no calculating how much influence was given to Jackson's administration by the universal belief that there was a concealed eye and hand behind the machinery of government, by which everything could be foreseen, and the hardest deeds done. A member of Congress told me this night that he had watched through five sessions for a sight of Kendall, and had never obtained it till now. Kendall was leaning on a chair, with head bent down, and eye glancing up at a member of Congress, with whom he was in earnest conversation, and in a few minutes he was gone.'"

After the publication of the foregoing letter to Colonel Orr, Mr. Kendall was persuaded by many friends of the Union to continue his efforts for the maintenance of peace and the Union. Yielding to these solicitations, though almost despairing of success, he wrote a series of articles upon Secession, which were published in the "Evening Star" of Washington. The editor of that paper, in announcing the publication, said : —

"If there lives a man entitled to be heard attentively and respectfully upon such a subject by the Democratic party, that man is surely Amos Kendall, the right-hand man of Andrew Jackson, in times as trying to the party and the country as those now upon us. In those times, next to Jackson's, his mind was the controlling one in the government ; stamping the impress of its patriotism and will more indelibly upon the future of the United States than those of all the rest of Jackson's constitutional advisers. Long since entirely disconnected with politics, and now at a very advanced age, if any man can approach the discussion of such a subject in such times unbiassed by any other than the purest considerations, that man is Amos Kendall."

WASHINGTON, November 16, 1860.

To THE EDITOR OF THE EVENING STAR : —

The annexed article was prepared for the "Constitution," but its editor, avowing himself a Secessionist, closes his columns against the friends of the Union ! The writers for his paper denounce as no true Democrat all who deny this new doctrine of secession, thus setting up a new test of Democracy.

From boyhood I have considered myself a Democrat, reared in the school of Jefferson, in whose words or acts I challenge any one to find the trace of a thought giving color to this doctrine.

I have some claim to be heard by Southern people. Like hundreds of others in the border slave States, I have suffered by abolition thieves. When at the head of the Post-Office Department, I incurred violent denunciations by denying the right of the Abolitionists to distribute their incendiary papers and documents in the Southern States through the United States mails and postmasters, by justifying the postmaster at New York for refusing to mail them to Charleston, and the people of Charleston for seizing and burning them in the street. Moreover, I am an old man, whose political race is run ; who has no motive of ambition or gain to influence him, nor any inducement to take up his pen, but such as is common to all who have property to lose or families to leave behind them.   AMOS KENDALL.

PREFACE TO A SERIES OF ARTICLES ON SECESSION.

The troubles of our country arise entirely from a defective political education, both North and South. The tendency of the Northern mind is to consider the United States a consolidated republic for all purposes, while that of the Southern mind is that they are not consolidated for any purpose. The North is consequently inclined to claim for the general government powers which it does not possess, while the South is inclined to deny to it powers which it does possess.

When the Constitution says, "We, the people of the United States," it means all the people of all the States, as truly as if all had been assembled in one mass and had unanimously "ordained and established" that instrument. The only reason they acted through State conventions was, that each State was an independent sovereignty, which could not be divested of any of its powers without its own separate consent. The State conventions which adopted the Constitution in effect accomplished two objects, namely : —

First, they divested their respective States of certain powers which it was proposed to vest in another government. In this they acted separately from the people of the other States.

Secondly, they agreed with all the people of all the other States to vest those powers in the government of the United States, and that the Constitution and laws of that government should be "the supreme law of the land." In this they acted jointly with the people of all the other States.

The consolidation, to the extent of the granted powers, but no further, was just as effectual as if there had been no State governments in existence, and the whole people of the United States had acted in one convention.

In the same sense, each State remained a consolidated government to the extent of its reserved powers, but no further. To that extent they remained just as foreign to the general government and to each other as Great Britain is to France. One State, or the people of any one State, have no more to do with the laws of any other State regulating the rights of property, or the relations between man and wife, parent and child, master and apprentice, or master and servant, than they have with the laws of Great Britain and France, nor are they any more responsible for those laws than they are for the laws of the African kingdom of Dahomey. It is difficult fully to possess most Northern minds of these ideas, and hence their notion that Southern slavery is "our great national sin," which, if a sin at all, is only the sin of those States which tolerate it.

Equally unsound in principle, and much more fatal in its consequences, is the Southern idea that our Constitution is nothing more than a treaty between independent nations, to which the States and not the people are parties, and which any one State may repudiate at will, not only without the consent, but to the manifest injury and even total destruction of her sister States. The argument is, that the States did not and could not part with any portion of their sovereignty when their people adopted the Constitution. If this be true, they can no more part with any portion of their sovereignty hereafter than they could heretofore ; and they may, whenever the notion seizes them, secede from any new confederacy into which they may hereafter enter, as they claim a right to do from the present Union. The principle is not only unsound, but, if recognized, is fatal to the idea of any stable government, whether in the existing Union or any future confederacy of States. In an instant, as it were, the weakest member of such a confederacy may, as South Carolina has done now, throw everything into confusion, break up the business and depreciate the property of all the other members, seize their forts, arsenals, ships, and munitions of war, and for all this there will be neither remedy nor redress because the little State is "sovereign," and nobody has a right to "coerce" her !

"O reason, thou hast fled to brutish beasts, and men have lost their wits !"

SECESSION. — No. 1.

THE ORIGIN OF THE FEDERAL UNION. — TO BE PERPETUAL BY COMPACT BETWEEN THE STATES. — THE ARTICLES OF CONFEDERATION THE ACT OF STATE LEGISLATURES. — THE CONSTITUTION THE ACT OF THE PEOPLE. — SOVEREIGNTY MAY LIMIT ITSELF.

To THE PEOPLE OF THE SOUTH, — I propose to discuss the doctrine of secession in a few short numbers, and commence by showing the origin of the Federal Union, constituting the United States of America.

When, in 1776, the British Colonies, constituting the original members of our Federal Union, became independent States, each State was an independent nation, possessing all the powers of unlimited sovereignty. They were then acting in concert against British oppression; but it was not until more than two years afterwards that a formal compact of union was consummated. That compact was styled, "*Articles of Confederation* and PERPETUAL UNION *between the States*," naming them.

A part of the 13th article of this instrument reads as follows:—

"And the articles of this Confederation shall be inviolably observed by every State, and the *union shall be perpetual*."

The form of ratification of those articles was as follows:—

"And whereas it has pleased the great Governor of the world to incline the hearts of the Legislatures we respectfully represent in Congress, to approve of, and to authorize us to ratify, the said Articles of Confederation and Perpetual Union, Know ye, that we, the undersigned delegates, by virtue of the power and authority to us given for that purpose, do, by these presents, in the name and in behalf of our respective constituents, fully and entirely ratify and confirm each and every of the said Articles of Confederation and Perpetual Union, and all and singular the matters and things therein contained. And we do further solemnly plight and engage the faith of our respective constituents, that they shall abide by the determinations of the United States in Congress assembled, on all questions which by the said Confederation are submitted to them; and that the articles thereof shall be inviolably observed by the States we respectfully represent, and that the Union shall be perpetual."

To this instrument South Carolina became a party by the authorized signatures of her delegates, Henry Laurens, William Henry Drayton, John Mathews, Richard Hutson, and Thomas Heyward, Jr.

The advocates of secession base their argument, not on any right reserved or in any way alluded to in the Constitution, but on the inherent sovereignty possessed by an independent State; which, as they say, enables her to set at naught, whenever she chooses, any and all her compacts with other States. Without commenting upon the unsoundness and demoralizing tendency of this doctrine, we ask secessionists to say, whether South Carolina, after solemnly plighting her faith that she would abide by the articles of Confederation, and that "*the Union should be perpetual*," could, at will, rightfully secede and break up that Union? Surely, the wise men of that day did not understand that by means of the sovereignty of any discontented State she could rightfully leave the Union, her plighted faith notwithstanding, or they would not have trifled with each other and the world by such a stipulation. They evidently thought that a sovereign State had power to limit its own sovereignty by compacts with other States, which should be of *perpetual obligation*.

There is, however, a striking difference in the authority by which the Articles of Confederation and our present Constitution are sanctioned. The former rested on the authority of the State legislatures, acting through their delegates in Congress; the latter on the authority of the people of each State, acting through delegates in convention. The Constitution, therefore, rests on the highest authority known to republican government, the people themselves, not the people of the United States, *in mass*, but the people of each and every separate State, and in that sense emphatically "the people of the United States," as asserted in the preamble.

Now, if the *legislatures* of the States could bind them to a "perpetual Union," their sovereignty notwithstanding, (as they actually did, unless we suppose that the men of that day were totally ignorant of the legal effects of their own acts,) surely *the people* of the States, the original sovereigns, could do the same thing. That they have done the same thing, and have provided in the Constitution itself the means of perpetuating the Union, we shall endeavor to show in future numbers.

AMOS KENDALL.

WASHINGTON, November 16, 1860.

SECESSION.—No. 2.

TO STRENGTHEN THE UNION WAS THE LEADING OBJECT OF CONGRESS IN RECOMMENDING, THE CONVENTION IN FRAMING, AND THE PEOPLE IN ADOPTING, THE PRESENT CONSTITUTION.

TO THE PEOPLE OF THE SOUTH,—In our first number we have shown that the States composing the Federal Union, from 1778 to 1789, had solemnly plighted their faith to each other in the articles of Confederation that *the Union should be* "*perpetual*." These articles constituted the Constitution of the United States until 1789, when they were merged in our present Constitution.

We will now show that the object of the change was not to relieve the States from their *perpetual obligation*, or in any way to weaken the Federal Union, but to give it greater strength, and furnish it with means to perpetuate itself by relieving it from dependence on the States for the execution of its acts.

By the Articles of Confederation, Congress had power to determine the amount of revenue necessary to be raised for the service of the United States, and apportion it among the States; but whether the necessary taxes should be levied or duties imposed and collected depended on the State authorities. The consequence was, that not long after the close of the revolutionary war, through the refusal or neglect of some of the States to fulfil their Federal obligations in that respect, the United States found themselves without means to support the public credit or

---

perform the functions then intrusted to them. It therefore became necessary that the United States should have power to levy taxes and duties, and collect them, without the aid or interposition of the States. This required that the United States should have independent legislative, executive, and judicial powers, together with the means of executing their acts and decisions. To such a pass had the neglect or misconduct of some of the States brought the affairs of the United States, that there was imminent danger of a dissolution of the Union from the want of self-sustaining powers.

The history of the United States for some years after the close of the revolutionary war, is replete with difficulties growing out of weak and unstable governments, and with expedients, proposed by the statesmen of that day, to put an end to them. Finally the minds of all intelligent and patriotic men settled down in the conviction, that an effectual remedy was to be found only in a thorough revision of the Federal Constitution, and the delegation to the United States of sufficient powers to enable them to command respect at home and abroad, and especially to preserve the Federal Union. This conviction found expression in a resolution of Congress, adopted on the 24th of February, 1787, in the following words:—

"*Resolved*, That in the opinion of Congress, it is expedient, that on the second Monday of May next, a convention of delegates, who shall have been appointed by the several States, be held in Philadelphia, for the sole and express purpose of revising the Articles of Confederation, and reporting to Congress, and the several Legislatures, such alterations and provisions therein, as shall, when agreed to in Congress, and confirmed by the States, render the Federal Constitution adequate to the exigencies of government, and *the preservation of the Union*."

There was already, by compact, a "perpetual Union"; and this perpetual Union it was the avowed object of Congress to preserve, by a revision of the "Federal Constitution." South Carolina was present by her delegates, and doubtless voted for the resolution.

The several States concurred in this recommendation, and in appointing their delegates, recognized and designated the objects in view.

Virginia stated the object to be, "devising and discussing such alterations and further provisions as might be necessary to render the Federal Constitution adequate to the exigencies of the Union."

North Carolina stated the object to be "to discuss and decide upon the most effectual means to remove the defects of the Federal Union, and to procure the enlarged purposes which it was intended to effect."

South Carolina stated the object to be "devising and discussing all such alterations, clauses, articles, and provisions as might be thought necessary to render the Federal Constitution entirely adequate to the

---

actual situation and the future good government of the confederated States."

All the other States stated their object in similar language, all concurring in the project of giving additional power and strength to the "perpetual union" already in existence.

The object of the Convention which framed the Constitution, in this respect, is shown in the letter signed by "George Washington, President," transmitting that instrument, as framed by them, to the President of Congress. He says:—

"In all our deliberations on this subject we kept steadily in view that which appears to us the greatest interest of every true American, THE CONSOLIDATION OF OUR UNION, in which is involved our prosperity, felicity, safety, perhaps our national existence."

Thus we have, distinctly avowed, the leading object of Congress which recommended the calling of the Convention, and of the Convention itself after they had finished their work.

The Convention proposed that the Constitution framed by them should be submitted for ratification, not to the legislatures of the States, but to a convention in each State chosen by the people thereof, and Congress adopted their recommendation. Conventions were held, the proposed Constitution was ratified, and thus became the act of the people. Their objects in ratifying it are set forth in the preamble, and foremost among them is the increased stability of the Union.

"We, the people of the United States," say they, "*in order to form a more perfect union*," etc., "do ordain and establish this Constitution for the United States of America."

It was unnecessary to repeat in the Constitution that the Union should be perpetual, because on its face it purports to be of unlimited duration, and contains within itself the means of perpetuating its own existence. The ratifications of all the States were unconditional, and, in the language of Mr. Madison, bound them "*forever*."

The State of Vermont was not a member of the "perpetual Union," established by the articles of Confederation, but when she came in under the Constitution, she expressly recognized its perpetual obligation. By her convention she declared that on her admission into the Union by Congress, the Constitution of the United States should (in their own words) "*be binding on us and the people of Vermont* FOREVER." Yet, who at that day supposed it was more binding on the people of Vermont than it was on the people of South Carolina?

It thus appears that Congress, the State legislatures, the Philadelphia Convention, and the people of the States in exchanging the Articles of Confederation for our present Constitution, intended to give additional strength and security to the Union. Yet, if the doctrine of secession be sound, they did not understand their own work, and exchanged a "perpetual Union" for one which any discontented State may break up at pleasure !

In another article, I shall endeavor to show that the men of that day did not fail in their object, but in fact added strength and stability to the pre-existing Union.

WASHINGTON, November 19, 1860.   AMOS KENDALL.

SECESSION. — No. 3.

HOW THE FEDERAL UNION WAS MADE STRONGER BY ITS NEW CONSTITUTION. — IT ESTABLISHED A GOVERNMENT INDEPENDENT OF THE STATES IN THE EXERCISE OF ITS POWERS. — WE LIVE UNDER TWO GOVERNMENTS, EACH HAVING ITS OWN EXCLUSIVE POWERS.

TO THE PEOPLE OF THE SOUTH, — We have shown in our first number that, in 1778, the States which had previously declared their independence of the British Crown entered into a Federal Union, solemnly stipulating with each other that it should be "*perpetual.*"

We have shown in our second number that the Congress of 1787, which recommended the Convention of 1789, the State legislatures which appointed the delegates, the Convention itself, and the people of the States who ratified it, declared their leading object to be to strengthen and perpetuate the "perpetual Union" then in existence.

To assert that they failed in their object, and exchanged that Union for one which exists only at the will and pleasure of each individual State, is to impeach the wisdom of the whole generation of revolutionary statesmen, and render further argument unnecessary. But more effectually to refute the modern claim of secession in each State, we propose to show that the statesmen of 1787 – 89 did not fail in their object, and actually gave to their country a Constitution which contains within itself the means of perpetuating its own existence.

How did they go to work to effect that object? They changed the Confederation into an effective *government*, giving it the means of carrying on its operations *without the aid and in spite of the interference of the States.*

The Constitution, when it came from the hands of the Convention, was but a proposition to the States. It contained the frame of a government complete in its legislative, executive, and judicial departments. It proposed to the sovereign people of each State to divest themselves of certain powers, and vest them in the United States and in the government thus formed. It proposed to vest in Congress, power to pass all laws necessary and proper to carry the granted powers into effect. It proposed that these laws should be "*the supreme law of the land,*"

"*anything in the constitution or laws of any State to the contrary notwithstanding.*" It proposed that the members of Congress and of the State legislatures, and all executive and judicial officers, both of the States and the United States, should be sworn to support the Constitution. It prescribed a special oath to the President of the United States, to the effect that he would "*faithfully execute the office of President, and to the best of his ability preserve, protect, and defend the Constitution of the United States.*" It required him to "take care that the laws be faithfully executed " ; and, to enable him to perform that duty, and to " preserve, protect, and defend the Constitution," it proposed to put at his disposition the army, navy, and militia of the United States. It proposed that levying war against the United States by any of their citizens, or giving their enemies aid and comfort, should be treason, punishable as Congress might direct. Finally, it proposed modes of amending the Constitution, by the assent of the legislatures or conventions of three fourths of the States.

The sovereign people of South Carolina, through their convention, acceded to this proposition in all its parts. Upon the sole condition contained in the instrument itself, that nine States should do the same thing, they consented and agreed to part with a portion of their sovereign powers, or rather to put them into a common stock, and vest them in a common government, whose laws, passed in the exercise of those powers, should be beyond the reach of all State authority. Nine States did consent to do the same thing ; the condition precedent was fulfilled ; the Constitution became a compact between the ratifying States ; and since the organization of the new government in 1789, the people of the United States have been living under *two governments* deriving their powers from the *same source*, that source being the *sovereign people of the several States.* Each government, however, has a distinct class of powers, the United States possessing all that relate to foreign nations, and a few relating to interior affairs, in the due exercise of which all the States have a common interest, while the States retain all powers relating to domestic institutions, rights of person and property, — in fine, all powers of legislation and government not granted to the United States in the Constitution.

Each government, *acting within its own sphere*, is just as independent of the other as if they were wholly foreign and separated by oceans, and if one infringes on the *incontestable* rights of the other, the remedies are only such as exist between independent nations.

The Constitutions of the two governments, however, differ in this : The State constitutions are compacts between individuals for their own government, which can be altered or abolished by the citizens of the State, while the Constitution of the United States is a compact between

the sovereign people of each State with the sovereign people of every other State, acting through conventions, which cannot be changed without the consent of all the parties to it, though it may be altered in the manner prescribed in its own provisions.

The laws of the United States, like the laws of the States, reach and bind every citizen, high and low, and while the United States cannot absolve any one from his obligation to obey the State laws, so neither can the States absolve any one from his obligation to abide by the laws of the United States. Each government has its own judiciary, and enforces its own constitutional laws, without the aid and in spite of any attempted let or hindrance from the other. Such, at least, is the true theory of our institutions.

Does not the foregoing statement of incontestable facts show the unsoundness and absurdity of the doctrine of secession ?

In another paper special attention will be paid to the argument by which the secessionists attempt to maintain their modern doctrine.

WASHINGTON, November 21, 1860.   AMOS KENDALL.

SECESSION. — No. 4.

NOTICE OF SECESSION ARGUMENTS. — SOVEREIGNTY NOT INDIVISIBLE NOR INHERENT. — INDEPENDENT STATES CAN MERGE OR SURRENDER THEIR SOVERIGNTY IN WHOLE OR IN PART. — IN THIS COUNTRY IT HAS BEEN DIVIDED, A PORTION TRANSFERRED TO THE UNITED STATES, AND A PORTION LEFT IN THE STATES. — MR. MADISON'S VIEWS.

TO THE PEOPLE OF THE SOUTH, — Secessionists maintain that each of the United States retains all its original sovereignty ; that the United States possess no sovereign power ; that their government is a mere agency for the States ; that any of the States may at will dismiss this agent, and thus relieve its people from all obligation to submit to its Constitution and laws. One fundamental position assumed by the secessionists is, that "SOVEREIGNTY IS INCAPABLE OF DIVISION."

If this be true, how happens it that there is more than one sovereignty in the world ?

Old Adam, we suppose, was the first sovereign, and if "sovereignty is incapable of division," how happens it that there are so many sovereigns among his descendants ? If this position be sound, there is now but one sovereign on earth, and that is vested in *all mankind* as one consolidated mass. South Carolina has been in rebellion against this "one and indivisible " sovereignty since 1776 at least !

How came South Carolina to have any sovereignty at all ? She formed a part of the British Empire, whose sovereignty, according to this argument, or assumption rather, was and is "indivisible." She is, therefore, still a part of the British Empire, though in a state of rebel-

lion, and ought to return to her allegiance ! But if they mean that the sovereignty of any one nation cannot be divided, the position is equally absurd, as we shall hereafter show.

It is another fundamental position of secessionists, that "SOVEREIGNTY IS INHERENT." Inherent in what ? Secession answers, "In the States." But how did it *get into the States ?* Surely they were not sovereign while they formed parts of the British Empire. They then had no "inherent" sovereignty. Did the Declaration of Independence make them sovereign ? That was the act of Congress. If that gave them sovereignty, they derived it from their own creature, and Congress must have been sovereign before they could impart that quality to their constituents. That sovereignty was inherent in Congress, nobody pretends ; to say that it was inherent in the Colonies, while parts of the British Empire, is absurd ; and if it be "indivisible " and "inherent," pray where did they get it, and when did it begin to be "*inherent ?*" And what became of the "indivisible" sovereignty of the British Empire when it was divided into twelve or thirteen independent States ?

The truth is, sovereignty is not "*indivisible*" nor "*inherent.*" It has been divided and subdivided, acquired and lost, restricted and enlarged, times without number, and by various means, during the world's history.

But, without caring how or where the States got their sovereignty, we are ready to admit that they were sovereigns in 1776 ; but we maintain that they could and did modify their own sovereignty in the adoption of the Constitution. Can any one doubt that the people of each State, if they had been so minded, could have united with the people of all the other States and formed a consolidated government ; that all their sovereignties could have been merged into one sovereignty, and that the States could thus have been extinguished ? The history of the world is full of examples of two or more nations being merged into one, and of one divided into two or more ; of sovereignty lost by conquest or by voluntary surrender, and sovereignty acquired by rebellion or voluntary association. To say that a State cannot surrender or merge her own sovereignty, is to deny the existence of sovereignty itself ; for how can a State be sovereign which cannot dispose of herself ? And if a State can merge her *entire* sovereignty in that of other States, cannot she merge a *part* and retain a *part ?* To say that she cannot is also to deny her sovereignty ; for sovereignty, according to secession logic, possesses *all* political power, while, by the same logic, it cannot divide itself, and therefore does *not* possess all political power ! The argument is a *felo de se*, — it destroys itself.

When secessionists say that sovereign power cannot be invested in the *government* of the United States, they utter a truth which is equally applicable to the governments of the States. Both governments are *agents* in the same sense, and both of them are *governments* in the same sense. What is a State? The people composing it. What is the United States? The people composing them in the sense of the Constitution where it says, "We, the people of the United States." The grants of the Constitution are to the United States, meaning the people thereof and not to their government. The powers reserved in the Constitution are reserved to the States, meaning the people of the States, not their governments. When the Constitution says there is such a thing as "the people of the United States," there must be such a people in some sense, and in *that people* is vested and merged the sovereignty of the people of the States, so far and so far only as it covers the powers granted in the Constitution. In reference to all their reserved powers, the people of the States remain as sovereign and independent as they were in 1776.

If I had entertained a doubt of the correctness of my own views on this subject, it would have been obviated by the following lucid and unanswerable exposition I have recently met with in one of Mr. Madison's letters:—

"In order to understand the true character of the Constitution of the United States, the error, not uncommon, must be avoided of viewing it through the medium either of a consolidated government or of a confederated government, whilst it is neither the one nor the other, but a mixture of both. And, having in no model the similitudes and analogies applicable to other systems of government, it must, more than any other, be its own interpreter according to its text and the *facts of the case.*

"From these it will be seen that the characteristic peculiarities of the Constitution are: 1. The mode of its formation; 2. The division of the supreme powers of government between the States in their united capacity and the States in their individual capacities.

"1. It was formed, not by the governments of the component States, as the Federal Government for which it was substituted was formed. Nor was it formed by a majority of the people of the United States, as a single community in the manner of a consolidated government. It was formed by the States; that is, by the people in each of the States acting in their highest sovereign capacity, and formed consequently by the same authority which formed the State constitutions.

"Being thus derived from the same source as the constitutions of the States, it has, within each State, the same authority as the constitution of the State; and is as much a constitution, in the strict sense of the term, within its prescribed sphere, as the constitutions of the States are, within their respective spheres; but with this obvious and essential difference, that being a compact among the States in their highest sovereign capacity, and constituting the people thereof one people for certain purposes, it cannot be altered or annulled at the will of the States individually, as the constitution of a State may be at its individual will.

"2. And that it divides the supreme powers of government between the government of the United States and the government of the individual States, is stamped on the face of the instrument; the powers of war and of taxation, of commerce and of treaties, and other enumerated powers vested in the government of the United States being of as high and sovereign a character, as any of the powers reserved to the State governments.

"Nor is the government of the United States, created by the Constitution, less a government, in the strict sense of the term, within the sphere of its powers, than the governments created by the constitutions of the States are, within their several spheres. It is, like them, organized into legislative, executive, and judiciary departments. It operates, like them, directly on persons and things. And, like them, it has at command a physical force for executing the powers committed to it."

Here Mr. Madison describes the sources of error into which different classes of politicians fall in considering the nature of our government, one class considering it a consolidated government and the other a mere federation, "*whilst it is neither the one nor the other, but a mixture of both.*" It was the error of federalism to consider it consolidated; it is the error of secessionism to consider it a mere confederation; it is the creed of Jeffersonian and Madisonian republicanism that it is "neither the one nor the other, but a *mixture of both.*"

In another number I shall show the utter incompatibility of secession arguments with the language and substance of the Constitution.

                              AMOS KENDALL.

WASHINGTON, November 23, 1860.

SECESSION.—No. 5.

WHERE THERE IS ALLEGIANCE THERE IS SOVEREIGNTY, AND THERE CAN BE TREASON ONLY WHERE THERE ARE BOTH. — MISTAKE SOMEWHERE. — THERE IS TREASON AGAINST THE UNITED STATES. — SECESSIONISM CLAIMS THE POWER OF ABSOLUTION FROM ALLEGIANCE, CRIMES, AND OATHS.

TO THE PEOPLE OF THE SOUTH, — Secessionists deny that the United States are anything more than a partnership, and they represent the general government to be a mere agency, of which the Constitution is the power of attorney, and from these assumptions they deduce the conclusion that the United States can neither possess sovereignty nor command allegiance.

The Constitution itself, on its face, negatives this conclusion. It recognizes such a crime as treason against the United States. Now, treason is "*the breach of allegiance from a citizen or subject to a sovereign.*" Where there is no sovereignty there can be no allegiance, and where there is no allegiance there can be no treason. By recognizing such a crime as treason against the United States therefore, the Constitution asserts sovereignty in them, and claims allegiance.

The first Congress assembled under the Constitution passed "An act for the punishment of certain crimes against the United States," the first-named of which is *treason.* It enacts that "if any person or persons *owing allegiance to the United States of America* shall levy war against them, or shall adhere to their enemies, giving them aid and comfort within the United States or elsewhere," etc., etc., such person or persons "shall suffer death."

The same Congress passed another act touching the army of the United States, which required every officer and soldier to take an oath to "*bear true allegiance to the United States of America.*"

There must be a mistake somewhere. Either George Washington, and the Convention which framed the Constitution, the whole people who adopted it, and the first Congress convened under it, must have been mistaken, or our modern secessionists must be greatly in error. All the former, without exception, and it is believed every member of Congress and every United States judge for at least forty years after the Constitution was adopted, fully believed the United States to be a *limited sovereign,* to whom every citizen owed allegiance. Are they less likely to be right than the modern enemies of the Union? Who is it that "owes allegiance to the United States," and can commit the crime of treason against them? We answer, *every citizen of every State,* all of whom are also citizens of the United States, the two descriptions embracing precisely the same persons. Every citizen of every State, therefore, owes allegiance to the United States, not in his character as a citizen of a State, but in his character as a citizen of the United States.

Now, can any State absolve its citizens from their allegiance to the United States? In other words, can a State abolish the crime of treason against the United States, so far as its own citizens are concerned? Can it do this, though it has, by its highest sovereign authority, stipulated with all the other States that its citizens shall be deemed traitors, if caught levying war against the United States, and after stipulating that their Constitution and laws shall be "the supreme law of the land," "anything in its own constitution and laws to the contrary notwithstanding"? To say that a State can, directly or indirectly, absolve its citizens from allegiance to the United States, and from the guilt of treason should they be found in arms against the United States, is to say that the people of a State can at will absolve themselves from every human obligation, and bid defiance to constitutions, compacts, laws, and all government. The principle goes further, and assumes a power to absolve men from their self-imposed obligations to their Maker. The law-givers, judges, and governors of the States have taken a solemn oath to support the Constitution of the United States, and many of their citizens have sworn to bear them true allegiance. Secessionism maintains its power to ab-

solve the law-givers, judges, governors, and citizens of the State, though also citizens of the United States, from their obligations to their God incurred by these oaths. Secession does not stop there. It even undertakes to release the United States law-givers, judges, and officers, and the President himself, from the obligations of *their* oaths! Though the President swears that he will, to the best of his ability, "*preserve, protect, and defend the Constitution of the United States,*" secessionism undertakes to release him from his oath within any State by declaring it no longer a member of the Union. It denounces the mere suggestion that he has any right to attempt "to preserve, protect, and defend the Constitution," though he may have ample "ability" to do so, should the people of any State declare themselves absolved from their voluntary compact with the people of the other States.

This pretended "indivisible" and "inherent *sovereignty*" arrogates to itself a power not now claimed by priest, pope, or potentate; a power to release itself from its own most sacred obligations; a power to relieve citizens from allegiance to their government; a power to absolve law-givers, judges, governors, and presidents from the obligations of their oaths.

There are some miscellaneous matters not yet touched upon, illustrating the absurdity of this doctrine of secession, which will form the subjects of another number.

                              AMOS KENDALL.

WASHINGTON, November 30, 1860.

SECESSION.—No. 6.

SECESSION ARGUMENTS FURTHER CONSIDERED. — THE CONSTITUTION A SINGULAR POWER OF ATTORNEY. — WHAT IS TO BECOME OF LANDS CEDED BY THE STATES? — SECESSION AN EASY WAY TO PAY DEBTS, AND GET OUT OF WARS.

TO THE PEOPLE OF THE SOUTH, — "Allegiance" to an agency! "Treason" against an "agency"! An agency which has power to enact and enforce laws! An agency divided into three departments, — legislative, executive, and judicial!

Such is the political monster into which secession converts the United States and their government. The Constitution is a mere power of attorney, forsooth! A singular power of attorney which creates the very being it clothes with power! But if it be a mere power of attorney, why was it called a Constitution? And if the government was a mere agency for the States, why was it not called an agency? Why was not the preamble to the Constitution made to read, "We, the people of the United States," etc., etc., "do ordain and establish this *agency* for the United States of America"? Why was it not made to say that "all legislative powers herein granted shall be vested in a Congress of the United States *agency*"?

Why not have said, "The House of Representatives of the United States" agency? "The Senate of the United States" agency? "The President of the United States" agency?

Why not have sworn the President "to preserve, protect and defend" *the power of attorney* constituting the United States agency? Would this have been ridiculous? If so, it is because the fundamental arguments of secessionists are ridiculous.

Why were not the judges of the United States called judges of the United States agency, and their jurisdiction defined to extend to all cases arising under *the power of attorney*, the laws of the agency? etc., etc.

Why was it not provided that the United States *agency* shall have power "to lay and collect taxes, borrow money, regulate commerce, coin money?" etc., etc.

If the Constitution be a mere power of attorney it contains some very singular provisions. It is not usual for parties giving powers of attorney, revocable at will, to restrict their own powers. But in the power of attorney which we call the Constitution, the principals bind themselves *to their agent*, that they will not exercise some of their own powers. "No State," says the pretended power of attorney, "shall make anything but gold and silver coin a tender in payment of debts, pass any bill of attainder, *ex post facto* law, or law impairing the obligation of contracts, or grant any title of nobility." Now, is it not very singular, that the States, in giving a power of attorney to an agent, should thus tie up their own hands in matters not at all involved in the powers conferred upon their agent? Does it not make the Constitution look a little more like a compact between the States than a joint power of attorney to a common agent?

But the oddest feature in the Constitution considered as a power of attorney given by the States, is the provision which relates to amendments. It provides that amendments when proposed in a manner specified, and "ratified by the legislatures of three fourths of the several States, or by conventions in three fourths thereof, *shall be valid to all intents and purposes as part of the Constitution.*" Now, who ever thought of amending a power of attorney, either enlarging or restricting the powers of an agent, without the concurrence of *all the parties originally granting it?* We have now thirty-three States, twenty-five of which can make any change they please in the Constitution, and the other eight will be bound by them. Here, then, is the anomaly of a provision in a power of attorney binding on eight parties who have not given their assent to it! Is there a parallel to such "*a power of attorney*" in the world's history?

But let us look at this question in another aspect. Many of the States have ceded to the United States from time to time large tracts

of territory, including soil and jurisdiction, as well as small tracts for forts, arsenals, dockyards, and other needful buildings, and for the seat of government. Over the District of Columbia, and many more of these tracts, the jurisdiction of the general government is exclusive. Is not the United States their sovereign? If not, who is? And if the United States be their sovereign, they are something more than an agency.

In case of the secession of a State which has made one of these grants, does the property return to her? Virginia owned nearly all of Ohio, Indiana, and Illinois. Should she secede, would all these regions revert to her, on the ground that she could not part with her sovereignty or divide it? So, most of the territory embraced in Alabama and Mississippi was ceded to the United States by Georgia. Should she secede, does it all revert to her?

The truth is, that all the States making these grants supposed they were making them to a *government of perpetual duration*, and not to an agency which might be broken up by the smallest State in the Union. They had no conception that under the "more perfect Union" formed by the Constitution, any State could recover its ceded property or its ceded powers by seceding from the Union.

Look at the principle in other aspects. There is a national debt; could South Carolina evade the payment of her portion of it by seceding from the Union?

See what sort of a government a recognition of a right of secession would leave us: —

A State don't like an existing tariff, and she secedes.

A State don't like a direct tax which Congress finds it necessary to impose, and she gets rid of it by secession.

Congress lays an embargo, and Massachusetts opens her ports by secession.

Congress declares war, and South Carolina, thinking it more for her interest to sell cotton to the enemy than to furnish men and money for the war, makes peace for herself through secession?

Is this the "more perfect Union" which our fathers made "to establish justice, ensure domestic tranquillity, provide for the common defence, promote the general welfare, and secure the blessings of liberty to themselves and their posterity"? The blood of Revolutionary warriors cries from the ground, and the manes of Revolutionary statesmen shout from their tombs, "No, no! Secession is Treason."

A few remarks about the attitude of South Carolina, and the idea of "coercing a State," will form the topics of another number.

AMOS KENDALL.

Washington, December 7, 1860.

P. S. — That "secession is treason" is not an original thought. In

1808, Massachusetts threatened to leave the Union on account of the injury to her commerce caused by the restrictive measures of Jefferson's administration. In December of that year, the Virginia electors who had voted for Mr. Madison, dined together, in company with many other distinguished citizens. Among the regular toasts was the following: —

"*The Union of the States:* The majority must govern. *It is treason to secede.*"

Spencer Roane presided, and *Robert Taylor* was Vice-President. There were present Governor Cabell, Hugh Nelson, J. Peyton Randolph, John Preston, Thomas Ritchie, and many other prominent Virginians.

SECESSION. — No. 7.

Coercing States an Artful Fallacy. — Every Government is a Government of Coercion. — The United States Government coerces Individuals, not States. — The States cannot absolve the Mail Robber or Traitor from Guilt or screen him from Punishment. — An Act of Secession not Treason, but Nugatory. — Actual Armed Resistance to the Execution of the United States Laws is Treason, whose Penalty is Death.

To the People of the South, — The unprejudiced reader cannot, I think, fail to be satisfied that our Constitution is the work of the people of all the States, and is just as much in effect, though not in form, a compact between *all the people of all the States* as the constitution of a State is a compact between the people of that State. But whatever it may be in its origin, *in its operations it ignores the States altogether.* By its legislative, executive, and judicial powers, *it acts directly on every citizen of every State* as effectually as if no State government existed.

Those who have been for years endeavoring to smooth the way for a dissolution of the Union, have specially denounced the idea that the general government should think of maintaining its authority or existence by *coercing States.* Who threatens to "*coerce States*"? The States are not citizens or subjects of the United States.

The laws of the United States are not made for States, but for citizens of the United States, regardless of the other bodies politic of which those citizens may be members. A citizen of the United States does not cease to be a citizen even by becoming a member of a State legislature, a judge, a governor of a State, or even a member of a State convention. If the governor of a State were to be detected in robbing the mails, or counterfeiting the coin of the United States, he is punishable in the same manner as the humblest citizen; nor could any act of the State, through a convention or otherwise, screen him from punishment. The Constitution and the laws of the United States, constitutionally enacted, are "the supreme law of the land," and the

citizen owes obedience to them, from which he cannot be relieved by State authority. Can a State by legislation, resolution, judicial decision, or any other device, *pardon the mail robber?* If she attempt to do so, by the resolutions of a convention or otherwise, and the United States proceed to punish him notwithstanding, is *that coercing a State?*

Every government which deserves the name is a government of coercion. To give that character to the government of the United States was the leading object of Washington and his compatriots in framing our present Constitution. For this, it was clothed with the legislative, judicial, and executive powers, and with means to execute them. To make these means effective, it expressly places the Constitution and laws of the United States, constitutionally enacted, beyond the reach of State authority.

Treason has among all nations been considered a crime of the highest enormity. That crime is defined by the Constitution to be "levying war against the United States or giving aid and comfort to their enemies," and the laws of the United States prescribe death as the penalty. Now, can any State interpose to screen a traitor from punishment any more than a mail robber, when convicted under the "supreme law of the land"? And is the punishment of a traitor to be denounced as *the coercion of a State?*

The truth is, that whatever the convention of South Carolina may resolve, *she cannot release her citizens from their allegiance to the United States.* Any ordinance of her convention purporting to do so, will be absolutely null and void, and all her citizens will still be citizens of the United States. In itself it will not be treason, because it would not be "levying war against the United States," and the general government would not be bound to take any notice of it. But if any citizen of South Carolina, acting under the pretended authority of a convention or the legislature, shall be found "levying war against the United States," he will be guilty of treason, and incur the penalty of death.

What it may become the duty of the general government to do, should the political leaders of South Carolina delude her people into the crime of treason under the pretext that a State convention can release them from their allegiance to the United States, it is not my province to anticipate. My object is to dispel delusion as to the pretended right of secession, and enable every citizen to understand the awful responsibility he will incur, should he, under cover of an unconstitutional and void act of his State, be found resisting the execution of the laws of the United States.

The slang about not coercing States, as well as the doctrine of secession, are the invention of the enemies of the Union; devised for the purpose of making disunion easy, by impressing the popular mind with the belief that so far as regards the people of each State, the decrees of a State convention are "the supreme law of the land," — "the Constitution and laws of the United States," notwithstanding.

And thus, the whole theory of the government is reversed, and the States are thrown into a revolutionary state, where the will of each is a law to itself.

The right of rebellion against intolerable wrong and oppression, nobody in this country contests. Why does not South Carolina place herself on that ground? Is it because the wrongs of which she complains are, in her opinion, not sufficient to justify her in the opinion of her own people, or those of other States, in rushing headlong into revolution? And is she, therefore, compelled to conceal the true character of the movement under a new name and a pretext of inherent right?

In one or more numbers I propose to examine the wrongs of the South, and treat of the remedies.   AMOS KENDALL.

WASHINGTON, December 8, 1860.

P. S. — Since the foregoing was written I have read the admirable and unanswerable argument of the President against the pretended right of secession; but its force on the public mind is much impaired by the conclusion at which he arrives. It is very true that the Constitution confers no power on Congress to declare or carry on war against a State; for such a power would have been inconsistent with its leading principles. But it does confer power to coerce *every citizen of a State* detected in the violation of its provisions and the laws of the United States. The power is in no way affected if the transgressor be sustained by all the authorities of his State, who may become his accomplices; themselves punishable, not as State officers, but as citizens of the United States.

The truth is, the *right* of the United States to enforce their own laws on every citizen of every State, no matter what the State may enact or resolve, is as perfect as any granted right can be; but the times and modes of its exercise depend on circumstances, and to some extent on the discretion of the public authorities.

SECESSION. — No. 8.

FATAL ERROR OF THE NORTH. — THE STATES FOREIGN TO EACH OTHER IN RELATION TO DOMESTIC INSTITUTIONS. — UNCONSTITUTIONAL LEGISLATION NOT NULLIFICATION. — HOSTILE ACTS NORTH THE MOST EFFECTIVE ARGUMENTS OF SECESSIONISTS. — THE SUFFERERS ARE THE BORDER SLAVEHOLDING STATES, AND NOT SOUTH CAROLINA.

TO THE PEOPLE OF THE SOUTH, — If a portion of the people of the South have been deluded into the idea that they have an inherent right

to secede from the Union, a delusion equally fatal has been practised upon the public mind of the North. It is in the inculcation of the idea that they have any right to interfere with the existence of slavery in the South. They do not realize the fundamental principle of our institutions, that so far as regards the reserved rights of the States they are as foreign to each other as are Great Britain and France. Massachusetts has no more right to interfere with the relations of master and slave in South Carolina than South Carolina has to interfere in the relations of master and apprentice, man and wife, parent and child, in Massachusetts. A man in Massachusetts has the same right to the labor of his wife, his son, his daughter, and his apprentice, that a man in South Carolina has to the labor of his slave. It is not a natural right, but a right originating in the laws of an independent State, with which no foreign States or people have any right to interfere. If our States were not united for general purposes under one Constitution, the interference of one State or its people with the institutions of another would be impertinent and offensive, and might be carried so far as to afford just cause of war.

Under our present Constitution, not only does every State reserve an unlimited control over its domestic institutions, but it is one of the conditions of union that "no person held to service or labor in one State under the laws thereof, escaping into another, shall, in consequence of any law or regulation therein, be discharged from such service or labor, but shall be delivered up on claim of the party to whom such service or labor may be due."

This is the language of the Constitution, the supreme law of the land, which all State legislators and judges are not only bound, but are sworn to support.

The provision has two aspects. In one of its aspects it provides, in substance, that no apprentice or slave owing labor to his master under the laws of one State, shall, on escaping into another, be relieved from that legal obligation by legislation or judicial decision in the latter State. Every State judge, therefore, who decides that an apprentice or slave is free as soon as he escapes from one State into another, as from Kentucky into Ohio, or from Virginia into New York, not only violates the Constitution but also his oath to support it.

The other aspect of the provision is that which requires that the fugitive, apprentice, or slave, shall be delivered up to his master. It does not say by what agency he shall be delivered up; but if the several States were actuated by the spirit of harmony which ought to pervade the Union, they would lend their agency to carrying into effect this provision as well as every other part of the Constitution. The least that could be expected of them, if they wish to preserve

the Union, is not to obstruct the Federal authorities in their efforts to make effective this provision of the Constitution. But several of the States, instead of aiding to give effect to the Constitution in this respect, or even maintaining a passive attitude, have done their utmost, by legislation and otherwise, to render this provision nugatory. Their legislators have by their acts defied the laws of the United States, and violated the Constitution, together with their oaths to support it. These acts afford the most effective argument now wielded by the secessionists, because they constitute a just cause of complaint; and they furnish pretexts for charging the offending States with nullification.

While these acts are an outrage upon the Constitution, they are far from constituting "nullification" in the South Carolina sense of the term. In that sense, "nullification" is a sovereign act of the people of a State, not susceptible of revision by any earthly tribunal, rendering any designated act or acts of Congress inoperative and void within the limits of that State; whereas these offensive acts of the States do not profess to render void any act of Congress, (though designed to obstruct the operation of a particular act,) nor to be beyond revision by the Federal judiciary, which will undoubtedly pronounce them unconstitutional and void as often as an appeal shall be made to them. Whether, with this remedy always at hand, they constitute a just cause for rebellion and revolution may well be doubted.

The practical effect of those laws is not so much to prevent the recovery of fugitive slaves as it is to encourage negro stealing and demoralize Northern sentiment on that subject. There will always be thieves of other property as well as negroes, whose operations no State can prevent, but so far from attempting to restrain the negro thief, he is encouraged and sustained by legislative enactments, void though they be.

That a portion of the Northern States and people have grossly violated the rights of Southern slaveholders under the Constitution, does not admit of a doubt. But who are the sufferers, and what is the remedy?

The sufferers are almost exclusively the border slaveholding States, — Maryland, Virginia, Kentucky, and Missouri. They have lost slaves, in consequence of Northern agitation and legislation, by thousands; while South Carolina, secure by a double cordon of slaveholding States intervening between her and the haunts of the negro thieves, has lost few or none from that cause. Yet, without consulting them in a matter which concerns their interest a thousand times more than her own, she tells them their only remedy is in a dissolution of the Union; and, with a white population scarcely exceeding that of the city of Baltimore,

she plunges into the sea of revolution, expecting to compel these great States to follow her.

We will examine the remedy she proposes, and consider whether there is not a better.   AMOS KENDALL.

WASHINGTON, December 11, 1860.

SECESSION. — No. 9.

REMEDIES FOR EXISTING EVILS PROPOSED BY SOUTH CAROLINA. — THEIR ABSURDITY. — THE AVOWED NOT THE TRUE MOTIVE. — OPENING OF AFRICAN SLAVE-TRADE THE LEADING OBJECT. — ITS EFFECTS ON THE BORDER SLAVE STATES. — THEY ARE TO BE USED TO EFFECT "PEACEFUL SECESSION," AND THEN "COERCED" INTO TERMS, OR LEFT AS A BARRIER AGAINST ABOLITIONISM.

TO THE PEOPLE OF THE SOUTH, — Let us briefly consider the remedies which South Carolina proposes for the wrongs of which the South complains.

They complain that Northern men intend to exclude slaveholders from the Territories, which are the common property of all the States, and, as a remedy for this prospective grievance, South Carolina proposes to *give up the Territories altogether!*

They complain that some of the Northern States have violated the Constitution by passing acts to impede the execution of the Fugitive Slave Law, and as a remedy for this violation on their part, South Carolina proposes to *abolish the Constitution altogether!*

They complain that the Constitution and laws of the United States are not sufficient to prevent the abduction of slaves, or secure the rendition of fugitives, and South Carolina's remedy is, *to relieve Northern negro stealers from those restraints, and give up all claims to the rendition of fugitives.*

They complain of the "underground-railroad" by which slaves are transported to Canada, and, as a remedy, South Carolina proposes to *save the cost and trouble of transportation by virtually bringing Canada down to the Ohio River and the borders of the slaveholding States!*

They complain that there is a party in the Northern States which is seeking the overthrow of Southern institutions, and South Carolina's remedy is *to drive all other Northern men into that party!*

They complain of the sympathy expressed by a few madmen in the North for John Brown, and South Carolina's remedy is *to remove every barrier to the organization of powerful filibustering expeditions against slavery on the very borders of the slaveholding States!*

In every one of these cases the remedy she proposes would aggravate the injury beyond calculation, though in these particulars it would fall lightly upon her. Ensconced as she is upon the seacoast, surrounded by a double and triple circumvallation of slaveholding States, she does not lose one slave by Abolition thieves, where Maryland, Virginia, Kentucky, and Missouri lose hundreds. If her remedies were adopted, they would expose those States to a constant border-war and the loss of ten slaves where they now lose one ; while the statesmen of South Carolina might still sleep quietly in their beds, undisturbed by the increased perils and losses brought on other parties by their mad ambition.

It is inconceivable that the evils of which the South justly complains, inasmuch as they affect South Carolina very little if at all, constitute the *real* motive with her leading men for plunging into a revolution, the only effect of which, if peaceful and successful, would unquestionably be greatly to increase the losses and dangers of other States without the least benefit to their own State.

There must be some other motive not openly avowed, which stimulates them to take this desperate plunge. What that motive is, I think I understand.

Already the men who expect to lead in the Southern Confederacy have declared themselves in favor of reopening the African slave-trade. They have no hope of the accomplishment of that object so long as their respective States constitute a portion of the present Confederacy. But should a new confederacy composed of the cotton States be established, undoubtedly one of their first acts would be to legalize the African slave-trade. Its immediate effect would be to depreciate the value of slaves more than fifty per cent throughout all the slaveholding States ; for while the cost of a good hand from Virginia in the cotton States is not less than $ 1,000, able hands brought direct from Africa under an unrestricted slave-trade, can soon be purchased for $ 200. And if the Southern Confederacy should then conquer Mexico and annex Cuba, what a magnificent empire it will become !

But in the mean time, what is to become of the border slaveholding States ? They have no desire to open the African slave-trade, and no interest which can be subserved by it. On the contrary, such a measure would at one blow annihilate more than one half the value of their slave property, while the breaking up of the Union would expose the residue to increased perils.

I venture to predict that Virginia and the other border slave States will never be allowed to join the Cotton Confederacy, should it be established, unless it be with the clear understanding that they will assent to the reopening of the African slave-trade. They are now to be used for the purpose of effecting the *"peaceful secession"* of the cotton States, and to ward off from them the perils of disunion ; but when that object shall have been effected, they will be required to submit to the terms of the seceders, and in any event remain a barrier between them and

the abolitionism of the North, relieved from the restraints of our present Constitution and laws.

In another number we will consider the possibility of a practical remedy for the real evils endured by the South.

           AMOS KENDALL.

WASHINGTON, December 15, 1860.

SECESSION. — No. 10.

DISUNIONISTS SOUTH AND ABOLITIONISTS NORTH NOT TO BE CONSULTED. — THE UNION MEN NORTH AND SOUTH MUST SAVE THE UNION. — THE BORDER SLAVE-HOLDING STATES MUST BE APPEASED. — NO GENERAL HATRED OF THE NORTH AGAINST THE SOUTH. — GARRISON AND KEITT.

TO THE PEOPLE SOUTH AND NORTH, — In considering the remedies for the present difficulties of our country, it is essential to understand the elements with which we have to deal. There are two classes of men whom it is needless to consult.

The first of these is the South Carolina leaders and their confederates in other States, who have long desired the destruction of the Union, and avail themselves of existing circumstances as a pretext, so far as they are concerned, to accomplish their cherished object.

Nothing, as these men openly avow, will deter them from their predetermined course ; and, if they be consulted at all, their policy will be, as it has been in their connection with the administration and their control of its newspaper organ, to prevent all compromise and hasten the dissolution of the government. To consult such men, when seeking means to preserve the Union, is but to take enemies into your counsels.

The other class, whom it is not only unnecessary but dangerous to consult, are the extreme men of the North, who would at once rush to civil war for the preservation of the Union, without listening to the just complaints of the Union men of the South. They do not seem to reflect that secession arguments on the one hand, and Union arguments on the other, are, in the border slaveholding States, addressed to men who a ̇. smarting under a sense of wrong and outrage from Northern interference with their domestic institutions. It is but natural that men so situated should listen with complacency to those who promise them relief and satisfaction by means however desperate.

Keeping clear of the disunionists *per se* on the one hand, and those who would at once rush into civil war on the other, let the lovers of the Union, North and South, particularly those of the border slaveholding and the Middle free States, on whom the calamities of disunion must most heavily fall, confer together and devise, if possible, a peaceful remedy for existing wrongs. This is not a very difficult task if approached in the spirit which gave birth to the Constitution.

To secure the cordial adhesion of the people in the border slaveholding

States, it is only necessary to relieve them from the apprehension of perpetual interferences by Northern demagogues and fanatics with their local affairs. In several of those States not one fourth of the voters are slaveholders ; but they justly consider slavery an institution with which their more Northern neighbors have no business to interfere, and they resent such interferences as indignantly as the slaveholders themselves. Neither class have any interest to be subserved by the disruption of the Union, and no men would be more loyal to it, if satisfied that the reserved rights of their respective States will be sacredly respected.

It is a ̧. eat error to suppose that all the Northern men who voted for Lincoln and Hamlin have any disposition to interfere with the rights of the South. A large mass of them are Democrats, who were driven from their party by the acts of Southern disunionists, through whose insidious influence one obnoxious issue after another, culminating with the Lecompton Constitution, and the act relative to the admission of Kansas into the Union, was attempted to be incorporated into their creed. They are, as they always have been, the staunch friends of State rights. Another mass of those voters were from the old Whig party ; who, whatever may have been their errors in other respects, had no design or desire to interfere with Southern institutions. And it may be safely assumed that not one in twenty of those who voted the Republican ticket had the least conception that by so doing they were endangering the union of the States. How they now shrink back from the consequences of their own work, is shown by the result of the recent elections in Boston and surrounding towns ; and if such be the reaction in the very hot-bed of abolitionism, what must it be in the less excited portions of the North ! In short, Lincoln's election by a minority of the popular votes was the result of divisions artfully produced with a view to that result *by the Southern disunionists themselves ;* and now, for the purpose of carrying out their disorganizing schemes, they falsely assume that there is a settled hatred in the North toward the South, incompatible with the existence of the Union ! Woe to themselves as well as their country, if they shall succeed in inflaming the whole North with the hatred which burns in the bosoms of a Garrison and a Keitt, — one of whom calls our Constitution " *a league with hell* " because it protects slavery, and the other pronounces it " *accursed* " because it does not ! If these inculcators of popular hatred North and South shall succeed in their infernal work, how long will it be before the North and the South, whether in the Union or out of it, will precipitate themselves upon each other in a conflict more terrible than the pen of history has ever yet recorded ?

Lest this number should be too long, I postpone to another my remarks upon the specific remedies which the occasion suggests.

           AMOS KENDALL.

WASHINGTON, December 20, 1860.

P. S. — Since the foregoing was written, the following additional evidence of a decisive reaction in the North has come to hand : —

" BOSTON, *December* 18. — A strong address to the people of Massachusetts has been published, denouncing the unconstitutionality of the Personal Liberty Bill, and recommending its repeal. It is signed by thirty-five gentlemen, including Ex-Chief Justice Shaw, B. R. Curtis, late Judge of the U. S. Supreme Court, Ex-Governors Lincoln, Clifford, Washburn, Gardner, and other eminent citizens, representing nearly every county in the State."

SECESSION. — No. 11.

SOUTHERN UNION MEN MUST BE SATISFIED. — REPEAL OF LIBERTY LAWS. — AMENDMENTS OF FUGITIVE SLAVE LAW. — THE TERRITORIAL QUESTION, HOW SETTLED. BRECKINRIDGE, BELL, AND DOUGLAS CALLED UPON TO UNITE. — A DEMOCRATIC UNION PARTY. — NO WAR ON SOUTH CAROLINA, BUT THE DUTIES MUST BE PAID AND THE FORTS DEFENDED. — THE POLICY OF THE EXECUTIVE. — "THE FEDERAL UNION MUST BE PRESERVED."

TO THE PEOPLE OF THE NORTH AND SOUTH, — Obviously the first thing necessary to a peaceful solution of our present difficulties is to satisfy the conservative men of the South that there is no fixed determination in the North to deprive their property of the protection which is guaranteed by the Constitution. How is this to be done ? The first step toward it is a concerted effort of all the conservative elements of the North to repeal the so-called " liberty laws" wherever they have been enacted. The Republicans themselves admit them to be unconstitutional, and under ordinary circumstances it might be safely left to the judiciary to declare them void. But their passage and unrepealed existence are an evidence of hostility to the South which nothing but their repeal can effectually rebut.

As to the rendition of fugitives from labor, the following is the provision of the Constitution : —

" No person held to service or labor in one State, under the laws thereof, escaping into another, shall, in consequence of any law or regulation therein, be discharged from such service or labor, but shall be delivered up on claim of the party to whom such service or labor may be due."

It seems to me impossible to provide for the rendition of fugitives more effectually than is done in this provision as it now stands. The power of Congress to pass all laws necessary to effect the object is absolute ; and while the attempts of States to embarrass the execution of those laws are in a degree analogous to the secessionism of South Carolina, they leave all the citizens of such States subject to the laws and authorities of the United States in the full plenitude of their power. If, therefore, the existing laws are not adequate to the object, let them be amended. Let fine and imprisonment be imposed upon those who shall resist their execution, and if it be done with arms, let the guilty wretches be hanged as traitors.

The territorial question is of little practical importance. The Constitution was made for a country in which the slave question was already settled. By the ordinance of 1787, slavery had been excluded from all the territory north of the Ohio, while the country south of that river was left open to that institution. No serious question on that subject could ever have been raised but for the acquisition of territory outside of the original limits of the United States and outside of the provisions of the Constitution. It would have seemed but fair that the precedent already set should have been followed, and the new territory divided in like manner ; and, so far as related to Louisiana, it was attempted by the Missouri Compromise. The objection to that mode is, that to maintain the principle the line might have to be modified upon every new acquisition of territory.

There is another principle more general and just in its application, and more congenial with the philosophy of the case, which, if carried into a Constitutional provision, would settle the question forever in all past and future acquisitions. What reasonable objection can there be to an amendment of the Constitution somewhat in the following form ? " It shall be lawful for all citizens and residents of the United States migrating into any of the Territories thereof to carry with them all property and all persons held to service or labor under the laws of the States from which they emigrate, and said laws shall govern their rights of property and claims to service or labor aforesaid in said Territories, until the same shall be admitted into the Union, anything in the legislation of Congress or the territorial legislatures to the contrary notwithstanding."

Such a provision would be in harmony with the general plan of the Constitution, and would leave the people of each Territory free to settle the question permanently for themselves in framing their State constitution.

These three points seem to me all that is necessary to settle for the purpose of satisfying the conservative men of the South, and remove every plausible pretext for a disruption of the Union : —

1st. The repeal of the liberty laws, so called, of some of the Northern States.

2d. Such modifications of the Fugitive Slave Law as may be required to give it more efficiency, and at the same time render it, if possible, less obnoxious to Northern sentiment.

3d. A final settlement of the territorial slave question by an amendment of the Constitution.

But by what means shall these ends be brought about ? There are

three men whose enviable position enables them to give a turn to public opinion and political action which will rescue their country from the perils which surround it. Let Messrs. Bell, Breckinridge, and Douglas, throwing behind them all antipathies and all personal ambition, meet together on the platform of the Union, and by an united effort save their country. It is madness to quarrel about the future command of a sinking ship. Let their only emulation be which shall do the most to save it, and the crew will hereafter know how to reward him who may have been most active and devoted. It requires but an effort of these men to organize a DEMOCRATIC UNION PARTY which shall sweep over the country like an avalanche, burying abolitionism and disunionism beyond the hope of resurrection. It was the insidious arts of the disunionists, dividing and distracting the conservative vote of the country, driving multitudes into the Republican ranks, and keeping other multitudes from the polls, which secured victory to the Republicans in the late presidential election. There is the best evidence of which the nature of the case is susceptible, that a large proportion of the Republican party is thoroughly conservative, and is prepared, in concert with the conservatives of other parties, to concede to the South all that the Union men of that section really desire. What can resist a combination composed of these elements, united in a cause as holy as that which actuated Washington and his compatriots in 1788 ?

I do not speculate upon the course which may be pursued by the new administration after the 4th of March next, because it is still a matter of doubt. It seems to me that, as a matter of necessity, and I hope of choice, it must be conservative, but if it be not, it will be more powerless than any which has preceded it.

The course which any President of the United States, who regards his oath, must pursue in two important particulars, is pointed out by Mr. Buchanan in his last annual message.

He must collect the Federal revenues.

He must defend the forts and other property of the United States.

These duties he must perform, *any ordinances of secession to the contrary notwithstanding.* But it is not necessary for him to be the aggressor in any act of violence.

If a State chooses to withdraw her representation in Congress, let them go.

If the Federal judicial officers within a State resign, and none can be found to fill their places, it cannot be helped.

If the postmasters within a State resign, and none can be found to supply their places, or if they refuse to pay over their quarterly revenues, let the post-offices be discontinued.

But let not a ship enter her ports without paying the lawful duties to

the United States, nor leave them without a clearance from the Federal authorities.

Let the white population of South Carolina, about equal to one third of that of the city of New York, enjoy for a while the luxury of a direct tax to support an independent government with all its paraphernalia of an army and navy. It may be that a short experience would satisfy her people that the Union is not such an " accursed " thing as has been represented, and they may deem it best for themselves to resume their relations with the Federal government. But should she become restive under this state of things, and attempt by violence to " coerce " the United States into a surrender of their forts or their ships, the issue must be met, and " God protect the right."

" *The Federal Union must be preserved.*"

AMOS KENDALL.

WASHINGTON, December 28, 1860.

SECESSION. — No. 12.

RECKLESSNESS AND SELFISHNESS OF SOUTH CAROLINA — SHE RELEASES FROM ALLEGIANCE AND ABSOLVES FROM OATHS. — COURSE OF THE GENERAL GOVERNMENT.— A STRANGE SPECTACLE. — SHALL SOUTH CAROLINA BE ALLOWED TO RUIN THE COUNTRY ? — DISUNION THE KNELL OF SLAVERY AND OF FREEDOM. — SOUTH CAROLINA REPUDIATES ALL IDEA OF COMPROMISE. — DISUNIONISTS AS DANGEROUS AS ABOLITIONISTS. — A LETTER TO THE PRESIDENT. — THE UNION MAY BE SAVED. — CONCLUSION.

TO THE PEOPLE OF THE NORTH AND SOUTH, — South Carolina has adopted her ordinance of secession. A little State with a white population about equal to that of a second-rate city, embracing hardly seventy thousand adult males, with no tax by the general government on her soil or its products, drawing large sums from that government for the support of her custom-houses and postal facilities, enjoying a degree of prosperity never excelled, and suffering nothing herself from the grievances of which she complains, rushes madly into rebellion, and is seeking to involve in revolution thirty-three States and thirty millions of people ! She will take no advice, and listen to no counsel ; she spurns the remonstrances of those slaveholding States which really suffer from Northern aggressions ; she will not allow them to consult as to the means of their own safety ; she will admit of neither compromise nor delay ; but avowing her long-cherished desire to destroy the Federal Union, she declares her purpose to *compel* her sister States of the South, whom she cannot persuade, to follow her example.

She undertakes to release her citizens from their allegiance to the United States, and absolves her own public officers and judges, and the officers and judges of the United States within her borders, from their oaths to support the Constitution. She taunts and defies the govern-

ment she avows her purpose to destroy ; sets guard around its arsenal to prevent the removal of the arms and munitions which belong to it ; declares her intention to possess herself of the public forts, and her purpose to take them by violence should a man be sent to reinforce their feeble garrisons. She is collecting arms from every quarter, organizing military bands throughout her territory, and exciting her young men to brave the penalties of treason.

And what is the government of the United States doing to maintain its authority, collect its revenue, and defend its forts ? Is it true that our Executive, though it had months of warning, has taken no step to put the forts in a state of defence ? Is it true that it has been deterred from reinforcing them by threats of conspirators ? Is it true that cannon are now being mounted in one of them, at the expense of the United States, which contains not a soldier to use or defend them ? Is it true that there is an understanding between the Executive and the conspirators that the former shall not reinforce the forts, and in consideration thereof that the latter will not attack them while the present administration remains in power ? Has the commander of the handful of men occupying one of those forts, after being denied reinforcements, been instructed to surrender if attacked ?

If these things be so, the wealth of worlds cannot outweigh the awful responsibility our President has incurred. If they are not so, he owes it to himself and his country to make the truth known.

A strange spectacle our country presents to the world. Within a period of seventy years, under our incomparable Constitution, our States have increased from thirteen to thirty-three, our population from three millions to thirty, our country has expanded from the Mississippi River to the Pacific Ocean, and our wealth has accumulated with a rapidity heretofore fabulous. In the full enjoyment of peace and plenty, of every comfort and luxury which the heart of man could desire, we are suddenly alarmed by the cry of rebellion and revolution coming from a little State enjoying a higher degree of security and prosperity than almost any of her sisters. The alarm spreads over the whole extent of our broad country ; credit is destroyed ; the banks stop payment ; trade is paralyzed ; industry is prostrated ; want and destitution surround us ; anarchy is marching in upon us ; and the government, which should save us, seems paralyzed as by the wand of an enchanter.

All this is chargeable to the madness of a few politicians, who have already destroyed more property than all the lands and negroes of South Carolina are worth, and she is herself one of the greatest sufferers.

Shall this little State be permitted to complete, by the utter destruction of our government, the ruin she has so successfully begun ? The hopeless disruption of this Union would be the *knell of the black man's slavery and the white man's liberty.* It would be the tocsin of a war which, however delayed in its commencement, and from time to time intermitted in its progress, will cease only with the extinction of negro slavery in the South; while by its plunderings and taxes to support armies and navies, and minister to the cupidity and luxuries of military chieftains, it would reduce the white laboring man, North and South, to a condition compared with which that of the present slave is to be envied. There is no other property so much put in jeopardy by revolution as slaves. Look at St. Domingo, Mexico, and the Spanish Provinces of South America. In them all, slavery perished in revolution; while in Brazil and Cuba, which the revolutionary fires have never reached, it remains intact and unassailable. Why, but because it affords protection to negro slavery, do the ultra abolitionists denounce our Constitution "*as a league with hell*"? Why is it that *they* also would plunge into revolution to destroy it?

It cannot be too strongly impressed on the public mind, that the *avowed object of South Carolina is not a redress of Southern grievances, but the final and irretrievable destruction of the Union.* Every State and every man that joins or understandingly sustains her, is an opponent of all measures of redress, and unconditionally an enemy of the Union. There is not an intelligent man in the States of Virginia, Maryland, Kentucky, and Missouri, who does not know that the losses and dangers of those States would be incalculably increased by their joining South Carolina, and becoming the frontier of a Southern Confederacy. The disunionists of South Carolina, in their reckless selfishness, are practically the enemies of those States as truly as the raving fanatics of Massachusetts. She has already struck down the value of their property a hundred-fold more than all the abolitionism of the North, and the question comes home to every one of their citizens, *shall she be allowed to consummate the ruin she has so successfully begun?* Shall she "coerce" *them* to their destruction, or will they "coerce" *her* into a decent respect for the feelings, rights, and interests of her sister States?

If South Carolina were an independent nation, she would have no right so to use her liberty as seriously to injure the interests of other nations; much less, in the relations which she holds with her sister States, especially those in the South, has she a right to destroy their property and expose their institutions to new dangers.

Four years ago, alarmed at the current of political events, North and South, I took the liberty of addressing a letter, of which a copy is annexed, to the President of the United States. It is obvious that if the disunionists had then succeeded by their arts in causing the election of Fremont, the scenes now passing before us would then have been enacted.

The same threats of secession were made in case of Fremont's elec-

tion which preceded the election of Lincoln, and they were doubtless disappointed at Mr. Buchanan's success. They then induced him, by threats of opposition, to place the whole power of his administration at their disposition, and they used it to distract and destroy the Democratic party, which they considered the chief barrier to their designs. If, instead of surrendering himself into the hands of the conspirators against the Union, Mr. Buchanan had cut loose from them, and repelled the no less dangerous fanatics of the North, throwing himself upon the true lovers of the Union in the North and the South, the East and the West, the perils which now surround us might have been averted. That which might have been a preventive, must, if our country is to be saved, now be the remedy. It is the rally under one patriotic standard, of all true Union men, under whatever party flag they may have heretofore marched.

Let their motto be "*the Federal Union must be preserved,*" and let their first measures be, the removal of all just complaints on the part of the South by the repeal of the Northern liberty laws, and if need be, amendments of the Fugitive Slave Law and of the Constitution. Having thus given security to Southern institutions, let them say to South Carolina, "We cannot allow that all our agricultural and commercial interests shall be deranged, our property destroyed, and our political security endangered by the frowardness of a petty State, which is blind to her own interests, faithless to her own engagements, and reckless of the calamities she brings upon her neighbors." Talk not of governing her as a "conquered province," but tell her, in a voice of thunder, that she must lay down the weapons of her rebellion, and resuming her position of equality with her neighbors, no longer aspire to control them.

My task is done. Surely there is virtue and patriotism enough in the country to save it. To the men in active political life is committed the solemn duty of organizing the conservative elements, North and South, into one great party, and by its overwhelming power save the Union, and in so doing save the State institutions. Do not, I beseech you, through the want of concession on the one hand and firmness on the other, suffer our glorious Republic, which has been the world's wonder, to become the world's derision. Let it not be said that all wisdom, disinterestedness, patriotism, and energy lie buried with our Washingtons, our Jeffersons, and our Jacksons.

But if, through timidity or any less excusable causes, no antidote can be found, in a proper organization, for a paralyzed government and a crumbling confederacy, I can only, like one of a boat's crew going over the Falls of Niagara, fold my arms and submit to the common fate.

                    AMOS KENDALL.

WASHINGTON, December 28, 1860.

TO HON. J. D. CATON.

                 WASHINGTON, March 14, 1861.

HON. J. D. CATON :—

DEAR SIR, — I have just received your very complimentary letter of the 11th inst., for which I heartily thank you. If my hasty lucubrations shall aid in securing our country from the calamities which must sooner or later follow a hopeless disruption of the Union, I shall be amply rewarded.

You ask my opinion of the future. It is difficult to foresee results when so large a portion of our countrymen are no longer governed by duty or interest, but seem to have surrendered themselves to prejudice and passion. I am not without hope, however, that the storm will blow over, and that the Union may become stronger than ever. But it can be brought about only by moderation and wisdom in the administration of the government. The signs here are, that the present Cabinet understand their position. They will, I think, take special care to avoid an armed collision with the seceders, while they will probably attempt to collect the duties outside of their harbors, hoping that the inconveniences to which the people in the cotton States may be exposed, and the new taxes which may be imposed upon them, may produce a decided reaction. I do not think the administration contemplates any real concession, to pacify the border slaveholding States, and hence I look upon the result of their policy as extremely doubtful. Those States will probably hold a convention, and endeavor to agree upon conditions on which alone they will remain in the Union. If they should do so with great unanimity, their conditions must be acceded to, or all hope of a restoration of union and peace must be abandoned.

I have been a little surprised that Western men have said so little about the mouths of the Mississippi passing into the hands of a foreign power. The ordinance conceding its free navigation is a mockery. It simply concedes that vessels loaded with produce and merchandise may pass through the Confederacy on the river; but it makes no provision allowing the landing or transhipment of their cargoes. Your river boats cannot go to Europe, and ocean ships cannot ascend the Mississippi.

And how will your Western people like the idea of giving up the free trade of the Mississippi, and having their imports and their exports taxed on the rivers and railroads connecting them with the Confederate States?

If I were editing a newspaper in the West, I would make the country ring with these themes. I should take the ground, that the West ought not and would not submit to such a state of things; that we would remove every pretext of complaint touching slavery, and that the seceding States should then resume their position in the Union, peaceably if

they would, compulsorily if it must be so. And I think your editors and politicians can in no other way render so much service to the cause of the Union as by boldly assuming this ground, at the same time dwelling in detail on the injuries which the course of the cotton States must inflict on all the industrial and commercial interests of the West.

         With high respect, your obt. serv't.,

                    AMOS KENDALL.

OTTAWA, Ill.

NO WAR.

The seceders marched in armed bodies, and compelled the guards of the United States forts and arsenals to surrender them; *but it was not war.* With arms in their hands, they captured millions of dollars worth of cannon, small arms, and munitions of war belonging to the United States; *but it was not war.* They seized the ships of the United States; *but it was not war.* They seized the mints and the moneys of the United States, and applied them to their own use; *but it was not war.* They fired on an unarmed ship carrying supplies to a fortress of the United States; *but it was not war.* They are besieging two fortresses of the United States, having surrounded them with military works and cut off their supplies; *but it is not war.* But if the United States attempt to relieve their beleaguered garrison, or even send them provisions in an unarmed vessel, *it is war.* If they attempt to transport a cannon from one fort to another, or from a foundry to a fort, *it is war.* If they transfer a soldier from fort to fort, or from State to State, *it is war.* If they send out a ship to protect their loyal citizens, *it is war.* To talk of executing their laws, protecting their commerce, or collecting their revenue, *is war, — horrible war.*

Such are the inconsistencies of the seceders and their sympathizers! Is it not amazing that such stuff as this should operate on any sensible Union man in Virginia, or anywhere else, to distrust his own government, and thereby give countenance to the cause of secession, already stained as it is by treachery, perjury, robbery, and usurpation!

April 12, 1861.

TO SAMUEL MEDARY.

                 WASHINGTON, April 15, 1861.

SAMUEL MEDARY, ESQ. :—

DEAR SIR, — I received some days ago a copy of your paper containing General Jackson's proclamation against nullification, and the explanatory article in the "Globe." The two together show the true position of the Jackson Democracy of that day; alas, how different from the democracy with which the Southern mind has since been infected! how different also from the republicanism of this day.

My position is upon the old Jackson platform, intermediate between secessionism and republicanism; in one respect, however, with more affinity to the latter than the former. "The Federal Union must be preserved" is the first plank in my platform, and I may add, "peaceably if we can, or forcibly" *if we can*. In their unionism, therefore, I am with the Republicans; and if, as now stated, Mr. Lincoln proposed to withdraw the garrison of Fort Sumter, if allowed to retain possession by means of a corporal and two or three men, it appears to me he did all that could be expected of him to preserve the peace. He might, it seems to me, well doubt his constitutional right to give his voluntary consent to the surrender of the fort, or to omit any effort he could make to provision or defend it. A real "military necessity" is rather to be judged of by the officer in direct command than by the President, and may result from starvation or successful assault.

Knowing that the design of the leading seceders was to break up the Union *forever*, the talk about reconstruction being a *finesse* to toll certain States out of it, and secure the sympathy of the Northern Democracy, I am prepared to sustain the only measure which can by any possibility prevent the permanent division of the republic into hostile sections, exhausting each other by oft-recurring wars. And I am not without hope that the present breach may be healed without much bloodshed; but it can be done only by decisive measures, and presenting to the rebels an imposing front. . . . .

With high regard, yours truly,

AMOS KENDALL.

TO SIMON CAMERON, SECRETARY OF WAR.

KENDALL GREEN, April 17, 1861.

HON. SIMON CAMERON, *Secretary of War :* —

SIR, — Understanding that accommodations are wanted for troops destined for the defence of Washington city, I beg leave to tender for that purpose two houses owned by me, on lots adjoining the city, but little more than a mile from the capitol, on a ridge through which is the first deep cut on the railroad.

The government may fix its own terms, being responsible for any damage done to the houses and the adjacent property by the soldiers, or in consequence of their occupation.

I think other accommodations can be found in this quarter, and I would, if the public interest require it, give up my own residence for the uses of the government.

With high respect,

AMOS KENDALL.

TO WILLIAM H. SEWARD, SECRETARY OF STATE.

WASHINGTON, April 29, 1861.

HON. W. H. SEWARD, *Secretary of State :* —

MY DEAR SIR, — I am emboldened by the recollection of a friendly interview to which you invited me some time ago, to submit to you a few remarks upon the present aspect of public affairs. While I do not possess the means of information which belong to your position, I claim to have some skill in judging of the currents of popular opinion and the ends to which it may be directed.

The wanton attack upon Fort Sumter united all parties North and West in support of the government, and the massacre of the soldiers peacefully marching through Baltimore to the defence of the capital, has roused the people in those sections to a fury. "'Burn Baltimore, level it with the ground, exterminate the villains,' etc., etc., is the universal cry," says a gentleman from New York, who has contributed large sums of money and sent two sons to the defence of Washington.

A gentleman who has recently travelled from Washington to New York, by way of Frederick, Hagerstown, Chambersburg, Harrisburg, etc., after stating that all seemed quiet in Maryland, writes as follows : —

"The change after reaching the Pennsylvania line was striking. The whole country was in a blaze of wild excitement. In all the villages soldiers were parading the streets, preceded by fife and drum; cheers and hurrahs rent the air; flags waved from church steeples, across the streets, and from innumerable staffs; and all seemed carried away with one sentiment of patriotic enthusiasm. Here in New York the same spirit everywhere and *in all classes* prevails. Broadway is decked with flags from the Union Park to the Battery," etc., etc.

I need not multiply evidences that no people were ever more united and more determined to sustain their government and preserve their institutions than the people of the free States, from the far East to the far West, now are. The practical question is, how can this unity and enthusiasm be turned to a beneficial result by the government?

Not, I assume, by timid counsels and equivocal measures. It was a mistake, I think, to order the Pennsylvanians back from Cockeyville, and surrender to the mob that route to Washington. It will not do for the members or friends of the administration to talk of letting the seceding States "go in peace." And if, as reported this morning, an armistice for six months has been proposed, I think it is an awful if not an irretrievable blunder.

You must have observed in the New York papers doubts expressed as to the firmness and energy of the administration, produced, no doubt,

by the retrograde order to the Pennsylvania troops, and the indications that some of the cabinet despair of the Union. The letter, from which I have quoted above, proceeds to state what the writer hears. Says he, "It is said the government *must* prosecute the war with determined vigor, or Lincoln and his cabinet will be displaced to make room for some one who will. No vacillation, compromise, or delay will be tolerated. *Action* is the cry, and *that* they will have."

You may judge what effect the idea of an armistice will have upon the thousands upon thousands whose minds have already begun to distrust the administration. For the sake of the country, I most devoutly hope that the administration may be able to preserve the unity of Northern sentiment, and direct it, not to the sacking of cities, but to measures (as peaceful as circumstances will allow) calculated to bring back the erring States and their deluded people.

The attack upon Fort Sumter, and the threats of attack upon the capital, justify the concentration of a force here sufficient to overawe any army the South can bring against us. Davis's proclamation inviting privateers justifies the blockade of all the seceded ports. Let these two measures be enforced to the utmost. In addition to these measures, cut off as far as possible all supplies from the West, and beyond this *let the seceded States alone.*

.   .   .   .   .

Nothing will satisfy the Northern mind, in its present state, which seems to contemplate anything short of a restoration of the Union. It is only on that ground that the administration can sustain itself. The public mind North is not prepared to acquiesce in a severance of the Union, until it shall have put forth all its powers to prevent it.

Let the attempt be made. Let the administration put forth all its united energies to make it successful, and, if they can for two years cut off the commerce of the seceding States, the wants and the burdens of the people in those States will, I am confident, do the work of a conqueror.

Pardon me for troubling you with my lucubrations upon matters which you probably understand much better than I do, and believe me,

With great respect, your obedient servant,

AMOS KENDALL.

EXTRACT OF A LETTER TO WILLIAM STICKNEY.

WASHINGTON, April 30, 1861.

MY DEAR STICKNEY, — Washington is becoming a military camp. We have near twenty thousand troops in the city, and they are pouring in at the rate of two thousand a day. After the massacre at Baltimore, the government quietly directed the approaching bodies of troops to

land at Annapolis, and suddenly seized the engines and cars on this end of the railroad to Baltimore, and also those on the Annapolis road. There was no resistance, though a party of Baltimoreans came up to the junction for that purpose. When the New York Seventh and the Massachusetts men approached, they concluded that "discretion was the better part of valor," and retired. The Annapolis road had been broken in several places, but in twenty-four hours it was repaired, and now the cars run through from Washington to Annapolis.

Secessionism is completely cowed in this District and in Maryland, and it seems in a measure to be paralyzed on the other side of the Potomac. The universal uprising of the North has struck terror into the Virginia leaders.

Though all immediate danger here has ceased, I still think it prudent to take my family to the North. With forty thousand volunteer troops in and about Washington, it will not be an agreeable place of residence, especially for ladies. But there is no occasion for haste.

With love to all, as ever,

AMOS KENDALL.

In the autumn of 1861 Mr. Kendall with his household, then consisting of himself and wife, his oldest daughter by his second wife, Mrs. William Stickney, her husband and son, and his youngest daughter Marion, removed to Trenton, N. J., where they resided for a year.

His residence, Kendall Green, was little else than a military camp, — thousands of soldiers being encamped in its immediate neighborhood, — and it was in search of retirement that this temporary change was made.

While in Trenton, his then only surviving son John, a resident of Washington, died after a few weeks' sickness with the typhoid fever. He was taken sick about the middle of November, 1861. The attack was so light that it was not thought expedient to inform his parents of it for a whole week. Another week passed, when he requested that his father and mother should be sent for. They immediately repaired to Washington, and found him very low, but not beyond hope of recovery. During the last four days they were agitated with hopes and fears by the changing symptoms of the disease. On the 7th of December he quietly breathed his last.

In a letter written December 24th, 1861, to his afflicted daughter-in-law, Mr. Kendall said : —

Fac Simile of Amos Kendall's Handwriting.

Bridgeport July 11th 1861

My Dear Stickney

Your letter of the 9th inst. came to hand this morning.

If I live much longer I fear I shall have no memory at all. In writing a paragraph I seem to forget before I get to the end what I had said at the beginning; and it is unsafe to let any pass from under my hand without a careful revision.

This infirmity is sadly realized in reading my old journal. I find transactions recorded and names of acquaintances mentioned of which I have not and cannot recal the slightest trace in my memory. In other cases, the record and the memory of the same transactions, are essentially variant. My mind seems to be like a deguerreotype plate on which so many irregular impressions have been made that the original figures are buried up and the recent ones scarcely discernible. In writing of past events, therefore, I feel that I am in imminent danger of a departure from the truth whenever I have to rely on memory alone

I have been at a loss in what to invest the money I now have to spare, every thing is so uncertain; but I am now inclined to put it into the next government loan. The value of almost every thing else, depends on the government and hence its own stocks ought to be good property.

We are all in usual health and as for Mattie she enjoys herself so well, that she does little else.

Lest I should again forget the check, I will write it before I sign my name —————

There! the check is written and no mistake this time.

Wm Stickney Esq,
Washington

Affectionately
Amos Kendall

"I can scarcely realize that John is no more, but when I do, it is with entire resignation to the will of God. To you the blow is doubtless more severe; but the duty of resignation cannot be less. Both of us have still those around us whose happiness it is in our power to promote, and instead of wasting our days and distressing our friends by useless repining, let us rather resolve cheerfully to perform all our family and social duties. I am sure that John, if he be permitted still to love, will love you infinitely better if he sees you with smiling face and ready hand ministering to the comfort and pleasures of your father, mother, brothers, and friends, than if he beheld you sunk in desponding melancholy, useless to the dead and distressing to the living. I cannot but think that lasting mourning under afflictions is in the nature of repining against the God that sends them, and of rebellion against his will. It is, I think, a sin of an aggravated nature inconsistent with Christian sentiment, and almost as wicked as any other indulgence of our depraved nature. I do not censure outbursts of grief when calamities overtake us, and I should think the man or woman was to be shunned who could look on the death of a dear relative or friend without emotion. The sin lies in cherishing this grief, and sacrificing to it the duties we owe to ourselves and those around us. Is not he who kills himself with grief a suicide? Does not he who makes all around him unhappy by gloomy features and constant complainings become as much the guilty author of human misery as if he studied how to torture his fellow-men?

"All my household are engaged to-day in preparing a Christmas tree and other devices to interest the Sunday-school children on Christmas eve. I like this. How much better it is thus to make the little folks happy than to hide themselves in their chambers, clothed in weeds, bewailing the late act of God in taking to himself a son and a brother! Go thou and do likewise."

Writing subsequently to a friend on the 'death of his son, Mr. Kendall says:—

"I stand, as it were, an old tree in a broad field, with no young growth around me to occupy my place when I too shall be prostrated by the storms of heaven. Yet I am content. It is the will of God. I accept the teachings of the New Testament as far as I can understand them, and do not reject them wherein I do not. It teaches me to live a life of honesty, kindness, and charity towards my fellow-men, and of entire resignation to the will of my Maker. This I understand and endeavor to practise. But when I attempt to penetrate the mysteries of infinity and eternity, I find there is a limit to human thought which no mortal mind can penetrate. I cannot think of the infinite otherwise than as an extension of the finite, or of eternity otherwise than as time without end, yet as passing time. Thus is my mind walled in by the finite creations around me, beyond which all is dark and fathomless, into which imagination itself cannot penetrate without carrying with it the finite objects among which it dwells. I am content to live and die within this prison-house, without attempting to scale its narrow walls in the vain effort to grasp the infinite and understand the eternal, but not without hope that, in a future state of existence, my capacities will be so enlarged as to enable me, not to comprehend God as he is, but to approach him more nearly, enjoy his presence, and comprehend his ways with man."

CHAPTER XX.

THE following is extracted from a lecture given by Mr. Kendall before the Young Men's Christian Association at Trenton, in February, 1862.

GENERAL JACKSON AND THE PRESENT TIMES.

LADIES AND GENTLEMEN,— I am apprehensive that your attendance here this evening will subject you to serious disappointment. You see before you one whom his Maker never designed for an orator or a lecturer. A constitution always feeble, and a voice always weak, have been further enfeebled by the decay of nature and the infirmities of age, so that he can scarcely make himself heard throughout the hall which is before him. The desire to oblige the society for whose benefit this series of lectures was instituted, and to say something for his country, though it were with his dying breath, he hopes will be accepted by you as an excuse for any disappointment he may inflict upon you this evening.

We have indeed fallen on evil times. Under the protecting ægis of our Federal Constitution, our country had increased in population from three millions to thirty, in States from thirteen to thirty-four, and had expanded its territory to the capes of Florida, and from the Mississippi River to the Rio Grande and the Pacific Ocean. By our cotton we clothed half of the civilized world; by our bread-stuffs and provisions we fed the laboring millions in European manufactories; and California poured into the cup of our prosperity her long-hidden treasures. Lines of railroad and telegraph checkered the Atlantic States, seemingly destined to bind them in a closer union, and were preparing to leap across the deserts to the shores of the Pacific. The hand and the mind of man, freed from the apprehensions of danger and of care for the means of subsistence and comfort, were busy in the fields of mechanics and invention, illustrating the age and astounding the world with new achievements and discoveries. Each year brought us from the Old World emigrants enough to form a new State, who came to share in our wealth, our liberty, and our glory. Such a scene of active industry and increasing wealth, under the peaceful sway of liberty regulated by law, had never been witnessed on this earth.

All is now changed. Almost as suddenly as the fire of heaven fell upon Sodom, have the fires of war fallen upon this glorious scene, and daily is the smoke of battle and of burning habitations, instead of the incense of thanksgiving for these unparalleled blessings, ascending towards heaven; while desolation, want, and despair are spreading over large portions of our lately happy land. Surely a great crime has been committed,— a crime not only against our country, but against the brotherhood of man; a crime against high heaven itself; a crime never surpassed since the rebellion of the fallen angels.

Let us inquire into the causes of this calamity, look present dangers in the face, and consider our duties in relation to the future.

On the 13th day of April, 1829, being the birthday of Thomas Jefferson, a public dinner was gotten up at Washington by the extreme State rights school of politicians, of which John C. Calhoun was the leader, the immediate object of which was to embody a party for the purpose of making their chief President of the United States, as the the successor of General Jackson, while the ostensible purpose was merely to do honor to the memory of Thomas Jefferson and reaffirm adherence to his political principles. General Jackson was invited, and sympathizing with the professed objects of the meeting, he accepted the invitation. The usual routine of toasts and speeches was pursued, and State rights were the general theme. Quickness of perception and promptitude of action were characteristics of General Jackson. He saw in the extremes to which the doctrine of State rights was proclaimed, danger to the Constitution and the Union, and before he was called on for a toast he wrote one with a pencil and put it under his plate. It was given in these words, "The Federal Union: it must be preserved."

Is not this sentiment yours, as it is mine, now and forever? This was a heavy blow to the extreme State rights hydra, then just beginning to show its hissing heads; but the monster was not killed. Mr. Calhoun attempted to parry the blow by another toast to the Union, in which it was declared, that, "it can only be preserved by respecting the rights of the States, and distributing equally the benefits and burdens of the Union." Taken in connection with the fact that at that very time Mr. Calhoun was stoutly maintaining that "the benefits and burdens of the Union" were not equally distributed, and that the South was unjustly and unconstitutionally taxed for the benefit of the North, this toast was tantamount to a declaration that there was then just cause for breaking up the Union. Mr. Calhoun possessed a brilliant intellect; but it was meteoric and eccentric, seeing nothing in any light but its own. The sun of all human wisdom was darkness to him if encountered by the fitful radiance of his own conceptions. One of our most inconsistent statesmen, he earnestly insisted that he was entirely consistent. Mr. Benton said of him, that he seemed to have two sets of morals, one for private life which was very good, and another for public life which was very bad. Be that as it may, Mr. Calhoun aspired to be President of the United States, and he made State rights his hobby to carry him to the goal of his ambition. His ardent mind had reasoned itself into the belief that the cotton, rice, and sugar-planters of the South, whose products were not taxed by the United States at all, directly or indirectly, paid the major part of the duties on all imported merchandise ; and, therefore, that the tariff of that day was a tax upon the South for the benefit of the North, unequal, unjust, oppressive, and even unconstitutional ! He was right in the general position that the duties on imported merchandise, though paid by the consumer, are an ultimate charge on the profits of labor, constituting the income of the consumer, and that when levied for the purpose of enriching certain classes of the community, at the expense of all the rest, they are unjust. But he was not right in the position that the Southern planter had any more reason to complain or so much as the Northern farmer, mechanic, or professional man. He treated the question, however, as purely sectional, and attempted to rally the whole South in a consolidated party against the existing tariff. He was too impatient to wait or too wise to hope for a remedy for the assumed wrong, in time to meet the exigencies of his ambition, through the slow progress of public opinion, and imagined that he could hasten events by invoking the interposition of State authority. In the Virginia resolutions of 1798, he found a declaration of abstract principles, and in a passage from Mr. Jefferson's pen he found the word " nullification " as "the rightful remedy" for flagrant and persistent violations of the Constitution by the general government. Ignoring the fact that Virginia, in reaffirming her Resolutions, had declared in a report drawn by Mr. Madison, that the only mode of redress contemplated was through a change of public opinion, to be effected by discussion ; and though Mr. Jefferson had indicated no other process of " nullification," Mr. Calhoun's fertile mind proceeded to invent one. Assuming that the tariff laws were unconstitutional, and that the States, by virtue of their sovereignty have a right to decide whether the laws of the United States are constitutional or not, he proposed that South Carolina, through a convention, should declare the tariff laws void, and resist their execution in her ports. Accordingly his followers resorted to his newly invented process ; they assembled a State convention, which declared the tariff laws void ; and they proceeded to organize a military force to resist their execution. It is not supposed that they then expected a military issue with the government. With such a man as General Jackson at its head, such a deliberate purpose would have indicated a degree of madness to which their minds had not arrived. The

calculation doubtless was, that, as on a more recent occasion, other Southern States would follow the lead of South Carolina, and the combination would become so powerful and threatening, that Congress, to avoid the calamities of an impending civil war, would hasten to modify the obnoxious laws, when the leader of nullification would ride into the Presidency on the wave of victorious State rights. It may be that some even then contemplated disunion as the ultimate result, and it is said, though I know not on what authority, medals were struck inscribed with the words, " *John C. Calhoun, first President of the Southern Confederacy.*"

But a man who never knew fear or hesitation in the performance of a public or private duty was then President of the United States. Taking it for granted that the conspirators were in earnest, President Jackson sent troops and armed ships to the port of Charleston, removed the custom-house to Fort Moultrie, and compelled every vessel arriving to stop there and pay the duties. Through confidential agents, he organized the Union party in the State to the number of about nine thousand, of whom about seventeen hundred lived in the city of Charleston, all ready, upon the firing of the first gun, to rush to arms. By a patriotic proclamation he electrified the country, as it has never since been electrified until the rebel fire was opened upon Fort Sumter.

There was then, as more recently, a Union party opposed to coercion. A delegation of Union men from South Carolina visited Washington to dissuade President Jackson from using military force in the execution of the laws, lest it should lead to bloodshed and civil war. He quietly listened to what they had to say, and then he replied, " Gentlemen, there will be no bloodshed. I have in that drawer," pointing to a desk in the room, " the tender of one hundred and fifty thousand volunteers to aid me in the execution of the laws, and I have General Coffee now in this house to place at the head of a force to be called out in the West. When everything is ready, I shall join them myself. We shall cross the mountains into the upper part of South Carolina with a force, which, joined by the Union men of that State, will be so overwhelming as to render resistance hopeless. We will march through the State, seize the ringleaders, turn them over to the civil authorities, and come home. You need not fear any bloodshed, gentlemen," he repeated. This incident rests upon the authority of one of the delegation, confirmed by a letter from General Jackson himself, now in my possession.

To bring matters to an issue, a ship loaded with sugar attempted to enter Charleston harbor, claiming exemption from payment of the duties by virtue of the " nullification ordinance." She was compelled to stop at Fort Sumter. General Haynes, then Governor of South Carolina, issued a proclamation, and through General Hamilton, in command of

the army of South Carolina, proceeded to make military preparations for an attack on the fort. Civil war now seemed imminent. But no Southern State could then be found to follow the lead of South Carolina, and it soon became apparent that if she fired a gun in the cause of nullification, she would bring down upon herself the whole power of the Union, headed by a man whose name was a host. Congress clothed the President with almost dictatorial powers, and it became evident that nullification would be crushed at a blow. Mr. Calhoun, then in the Senate of the United States, saw his doom approaching. His whole scheme of ambition was a miserable failure, and if he went further, there was a tolerable certainty that his life would pay the forfeit. His haggard appearance and incoherent utterances showed the agony of his mind, and many thought he would soon become a fit subject for a lunatic asylum.

In this state of things, unfortunately, as I think, for the country, Mr. Clay interposed to rescue the necks of the leading nullifiers from the halter, by one of those compromises which distinguished his political life. Under his lead and influence, an act of Congress was passed providing for a reduction of the tariff duties, periodically, until the maximum should not exceed 20 per cent. President Jackson could not do otherwise than approve the act, though he did it with serious misgivings as to its ultimate consequences upon the future of the Union. And who can now doubt, that if the nullifiers had struck a blow, and a few of their leaders had been hanged for treason, the country would not now be under the necessity of putting forth all its resources and power for the suppression of a gigantic rebellion, gotten up and headed by the disciples of the nullification school !

The nullifiers claimed a victory, and not without some reason. The compromise involved no surrender of principles on their part, and they had influenced the government to make concessions by threats of violence. Glad, however, to escape the danger of meeting in rebellion the man who had little mercy for traitors to his country, they repealed their own ordinance of nullification, and betook themselves to other means for destroying the Union.

Nullification and secession are based on the same principle, and that is the absolute and unqualified sovereignty of the States. The difference is, that nullification claimed only to abrogate a specified law or laws of the United States, while secession claims a right by the same authority, to abrogate not only all the laws, but also the Constitution itself.

From the unfortunate compromise of 1833, we may date the commencement of the machinations which ended in the present rebellion. For this belief we have the evidence of some of the leaders in the South Carolina convention, which passed the ordinance of secession. Mr. Cal-

houn himself went home and announced that the slavery question would be thereafter the ground-work of division between the North and the South. Having signally failed in his effort to get up an effective sectional party on the tariff question, he resorted to the only subject, dangerous as it was, upon which the South could be consolidated in a party array against the North. In this effort he and his followers would have again signally failed, but for the aid they received from the North. That aid consisted not in sympathy, but in antipathy. I have reference to the Northern abolitionists. These men may be divided into two classes, one of which may be called *political abolitionists*, and the other *religious abolitionists*. The objects of these classes are very different, but they have alike, for years past, played into the hands of the Southern conspirators. The political abolitionists have no particular objections to slavery, but avail themselves of Northern hostility to the institution as means of gaining power. From them slavery never had anything to fear ; for, whatever language they used in stump speeches, they knew that the institution was constitutionally beyond their reach. The religious abolitionists are more sincere, and for that reason are much more dangerous. The political abolitionist has, when he comes to act, some regard for the Constitution and laws of his country ; but the religious abolitionist assumes to act under a " higher law," which nullifies all constitutions and laws which purport to sanction slavery. But both alike have, by their speeches and actions in their several States, enabled the Southern leaders to represent to their people that there was a settled majority of the Northern population determined to overleap the barriers of the Constitution, for the purpose of interfering with their local institutions, and setting their negroes free. And it must be confessed, that in the legislation of some of the Northern States, and in the conduct of some of their officers and people, there was evidence enough to give plausibility to the charge. Political abolitionism, now that it sees the temple on fire, has measurably ceased to play with this fire-brand, and would gladly extinguish the flames ; but religious abolitionism would see the temple of our liberty in ashes rather than it should protect the master and his slave.

This class of men seem utterly oblivious of the fact, that in relation to slavery and all domestic and local institutions, our States are as independent of each other as any two distant nations ; that we are one people and one nation only for the purposes specified in the Federal Constitution ; and that they have no more right to interfere with the institutions of the Southern States than with those of Cuba and Brazil. And having no rightful authority over the institution of slavery, they are no more responsible for its existence or abuses than they are for the peonage of Mexico or the serfdom of Russia. One would think, that seeing the terrible calamities which, by meddling with other people's affairs, they have aided the Southern conspirators in bringing upon the country, these men would desist from agitation and subside into quiet citizens, content with the peaceful enjoyment of their own rights under the institutions from which our country has derived all its prosperity and glory. But it seems that this pestilent political and religious heresy is not to be satisfied without a subversion of our present Constitution, and the establishment of a new one, purified in the crucible of their own fanaticism, no matter how many thousands of lives and millions of treasure are sacrificed in the process.

What further shall I say of Andrew Jackson? I may say of him, without disparagement to the men of this day, that had he been at the head of affairs for the last eighteen months, the rebellion would not have occurred, or if it had, the rebels would ere this have been driven into the Gulf of Mexico. Without ever courting popularity, he enjoyed the popular confidence in a higher degree than any other man of our country except George Washington. There was indeed a degree of enthusiasm in his popularity more fervid than in that of the Father of his country. They were in fact very different men. Washington was, in his temperament and actions, slow and cautious; Jackson was ardent and impetuous. His reasoning was like lightning, and his action like the thunderbolt. He never evaded danger or shrank from responsibility. He knew no fear, physically or morally. When he had made up his mind that it was his duty to do anything, he marched straightforward to his object, regardless alike of public opinion and personal consequences. Conscious of rectitude himself, he took it for granted that the country would sustain him. Yet, though he acted rapidly, he never acted rashly. The difference between him and other men was more in the rapidity of reasoning than in the prudence of action. Louis McLane said of him : "General Jackson is the most rapid reasoner I have ever met with. He jumps to a conclusion before I can start on my premises." If there ever was chivalry, it was found in him. He prized his honor above his life, and incurred danger for a friend as readily as for himself. As a husband, no man could be more faithful and devoted ; as a master, he was kind and indulgent ; and having no children or near relations of his own, he filled the office of a father to several of his wife's kindred. No man was ever more courteous in his manners, or more upright in his dealings, and it may surprise some to hear that a deep religious feeling pervaded his nature. The world was told that he was shockingly passionate and profane. It may surprise you to hear, that, although I was associated with him for nearly eight

years, most of the time as intimately perhaps as any one, not of his immediate household, I never saw him in a passion, or heard him utter a profane word. That he did sometimes, when excited, use the words, " By the Eternal," I do not doubt ; but he could hardly be said to "take the name of God in vain," for his oaths always meant something. He had no pride of opinion or of authorship. In his military campaigns he never submitted a question to a vote in a council of war. He asked the opinion of each member on the case presented, dismissed them, and they knew not what was to be done until his order was issued. He never took a vote in his Cabinet. Questions were submitted and discussed ; but, when it came to decision, " he took the responsibility." Nor was he so proud or self-conceited as to be above seeking information from any one whom he thought capable of giving it, and no President ever had a greater number or more faithful counsellors ; but, when it came to action, it was still, " I take the responsibility."

Time will not allow me to trace the history of General Jackson's life, and I must content myself with relating a few incidents and anecdotes, illustrative of his character, public and private.

Jackson was but a boy during the revolutionary war. At one period the Whigs and Tories in some parts of South Carolina hunted each other like wild beasts, and the only chance for safety was with parties in arms. No man dared to return to his own house, even for a night, without a strong guard. It was on such an occasion, that young Jackson went one night to assist in guarding a neighbor's house. He was acting as sentinel, and the rest of the party were in-doors. A strong party of Tories approached. After hailing them in vain, he fired upon them, and amidst whistling bullets ran into the house. A desperate fight ensued, which ended in the repulse of the Tories, though more than half of the Whigs were killed or wounded. General Jackson, in relating the incidents of those times, used to speak of a man named Wright, who, seeing the body of a friend murdered and horribly mutilated, swore that he would never spare a Tory, and he continued to hunt them until he had murdered upwards of twenty. " But," said the General, " he was never a happy man afterwards."

These shocking scenes have been renewed within the last year in some portions of Missouri ; but thanks to Providence and General Halleck they are at an end, and we hope forever.

Having been afterwards taken prisoner, the boy Jackson showed his spirit by refusing to black the boots of a British officer, in return for which he received a cut from the officer's sword, the scar of which he carried to his grave. Little did that officer think the proud boy he so abused was destined thirty odd years afterwards to humble the pride of the British arms at New Orleans.

The event which established Jackson's reputation in Tennessee was his duel with Dickinson. At the time of his advent at Nashville, there was in that place a club of profligate young lawyers, who had entered into an agreement not to bring suits against each other. The consequence was, that other citizens were without remedy when a lawyer was the debtor or offender. The aggrieved citizens went to the new-comer, who did not hesitate to take their cases. The conspirators found they were no longer to contract debts and commit outrages with impunity, unless this intruder were put out of the way. Their best shot was therefore put forward to insult and then shoot him in a duel. Jackson knew that he must kill or die. By the rules of this horrible game, either party may reserve his fire for a definite period after the word is given. Jackson reserved his fire, and Dickinson's ball cut a furrow across his breast nearly burying itself in its passage. Without the change of a muscle, Jackson buttoned up his coat, levelled his pistol, and Dickinson was a corpse, — being shot through the head. Jackson's friend, afterwards Judge White, did not know that he was wounded until they had ridden some miles from the field, when he observed blood at the top of Jackson's boot, where it had run down under his clothes from his breast. These particulars I had from Judge White himself. After that wonderful exhibition of nerve, nobody ventured to insult the young lawyer or doubted his courage.

When the war of 1812 with Great Britain broke out, Jackson was a general of Tennessee militia. The State authorized the enrolment of 5,000 volunteers for one year. General Jackson was ordered to New Orleans with a portion of this force, and had advanced as far as Natchez when he received an order from the War Department, at Washington, to suspend his march and discharge his men at that place, without any provision to take them home. The country between the Natchez settlement and Tennessee was then a wilderness, inhabited only by Indians and wild beasts, and to discharge men without money, provisions, or transportation under such circumstances, was so palpably unjust and oppressive that General Jackson did not hesitate to disobey the order. Believing that the object was to force his men to enlist in the regular army, he excluded all recruiting officers from his lines, and being refused transportation he seized it. His sick were placed in wagons, except one man, who was reported to be in a dying state. " Not a man who has breath in his body shall be left behind," said the General, and the insensible soldier was also lifted into a wagon. The train had proceeded some distance, and the General was riding beside the wagon, when the sick soldier opened his eyes and exclaimed, " Where am I?" " You are on the way to Tennessee," replied the General, " and will soon see your parents and friends." From that moment the man was convalescent.

Arriving in Tennessee, the General discharged his men, and reported his reasons for disobeying the order, and there the matter ended.

When the Creek war broke out, General Jackson was placed in command of the forces collected to put an end to it. At the battle of Tallahatchie an incident occurred, illustrative of the General's character, as well as that of the Indians. The battle was fought in an Indian village, and several women were among the slain. A male infant, unhurt, was found on the breast of its dead mother, and the soldiers brought it to the General. He sent for several squaws who had been taken prisoners and urged them to take charge of the child ; but they all declined, saying, " It has no father or mother, — kill it." He instructed his servant to scrape an empty sugar-barrel and make food for it, having no other means, and by the first conveyance sent the child to a friend in Huntsville. On his return from the war, he took the boy to the Hermitage, and raised him as kindly as if he had been his own son. But though raised entirely among the whites, all his tastes were Indian, and whenever any of the chiefs visited the Hermitage, he evinced the strongest desire to go with them on their departure. The poor fellow died of consumption before he became of age.

The Creek war produced many interesting incidents, showing the difficulties our hero had to encounter, and his courage and skill in surmounting them ; but I have not time to dwell upon them, and must hasten to New Orleans.

It was not the battle of the 8th of January which was the prime cause of saving the city of New Orleans, but that of the 23d of the preceding December. The enemy had avoided the forts built on the Mississippi for the defence of the city, by penetrating the swamp and reaching the river above them. Between the British troops which had reached the levee and the city there were no defences whatsoever, and General Jackson's force was neither in numbers or character competent to meet, in the open field, any considerable number of the Wellington veterans composing the British army. General Jackson's only hope was in concealing his own weakness and gaining time, and his lightning mind instantly suggested the most effectual method of attaining those ends. It was by a furious night attack on the portions of the British army which had landed, leading the enemy to suppose, in the darkness, that his force was much stronger than it really was, and thus deterring them from advancing on the city until he could prepare defences. The plan succeeded to admiration. The British were so roughly handled by their invisible foe, that they dared not advance until their whole army was landed. Jackson's force drew back out of sight, keeping out mounted videttes near the enemy, and fell resolutely to work erecting breastworks, extending from the river to the swamp. Thus it was, that by the time the British had recovered from their surprise, Jackson's force was protected by a formidable breastwork, and instead of encountering a small body of badly armed and ill-disciplined troops in the open field, they found that they would have to storm intrenchments defended by an increased and daily increasing army. The slaughter of the 8th of January, and the retreat of the British army, was the consummation of the measures inaugurated on the 23d of December.

But General Jackson's greatest victory at New Orleans was over himself. He found it necessary in the defence of the city to establish martial law, and supersede the civil authorities. A judge interfered and attempted to take a prisoner out of his hands. He ordered the judge to be arrested and sent beyond his lines. After peace was restored, the judge caused the General to be arrested, and fined him a thousand dollars for contempt of his court. Then was his triumph. The court-room was crowded with people who gave unmistakable indications of a disposition to mob the judge. The General mounted a bench and begged them, if they had regard for him, to respect the judicial authority and submit, as he did, to its decisions, whether right or wrong, as the only way of preserving peace and order in the community. The rising indignation of the populace was thus allayed; and having paid the fine, he left the court. The people on the outside took the horses out of a carriage, thrust the General into it, and, with shouts and yells, dragged it to his hotel.

How the General liked his ride is well illustrated by an incident. It happened that Mrs. Jackson was walking the street with General William O. Butler of Kentucky, and as the crowd of human horses passed, dragging her husband, she laughed immoderately. On being asked what amused her, she replied, " *This is the first time I ever saw Mr. Jackson* (as she always called him) *look as if he were ashamed of himself.*" This incident I learned from General Butler himself. A thousand dollars were raised by the people and sent to General Jackson to reimburse him; but he directed it to be distributed among the families of those who had fallen in the defence of the city. The reader of our country's history in future times cannot but be struck with the contrast between those times and the present. Then, in a case of extreme urgency, a General suspended the *habeas corpus* to prevent mutiny in his very camp, and in the presence of a powerful enemy; and though he atoned for the imputed violation of the law by paying promptly an unjust and vindictive fine, his country never showed its appreciation of the necessity of his act, and of his noble vindication of the judicial authority, by refunding the fine, until after his final retirement to private life. Now, the *habeas corpus* is daily disregarded without creating a sensation, not in camps only, but in cities and whole States, and the people murmur not, because, without knowing,

they take for granted that it is necessary to prevent conspiracy and suppress rebellion.

Time passed, and General Jackson became a candidate for the Presidency of the United States. In 1825 he was defeated by the coalition of the friends of Adams and Clay. The consequence was the union of all other parties upon him for the election in 1828. The contest was almost ferocious. General Jackson was charged with every folly and crime from cock-fighting to murder. Never before nor since did a candidate encounter such a storm of obloquy or abuse. The confidence of the people in General Jackson's integrity, disinterestedness, and devotion to his country prevailed, and placed him at the head of its government. The great mass 'of the people could sooner believe that other men perjured themselves than that Jackson had done wrong.

Take General Jackson all in all, had he not, as Mr. Jefferson said, " more of the Roman in him than any man living "? Yet the sternness of the Roman was blended with the gentler virtues of the Christian. " When shall we look upon his like again ?" There are many brave men at the head of our armies, candidates for glory and renown. Is there one of them who would not prefer the fame of a Washington or a Jackson to that of a Cæsar or of a Napoleon ? Not one. Like the exemplars they have before them, they will lay down their arms when the Constitution shall be re-established over every State, city, and hamlet of our country, becoming again peaceful citizens, and enabling us to fill whole albums with Washingtons and Jacksons, the pride of our own age and country, and the admiration of all times and nations. It is now our duty to give them our confidence and support, cheering them on in their glorious career, still shouting, until the stars shall re-echo it, " THE FEDERAL UNION ! *it must be preserved.*"

TO W. H. SEWARD.

TRENTON, N. J., January 26, 1862.

HON. W. H. SEWARD, *Secretary of State :* —

MY DEAR SIR, — I most heartily congratulate the President, yourself, and the country on the recent change in the head of the War Department. The equivocal position held by the late Secretary on the subject of slavery in connection with the war, and the extraordinary proclamations of some of his generals, will have cost this nation millions of money and thousands of lives.

The position of the President on this subject is the only judicious if not the only safe one, and I have been amazed and in some degree discouraged to find that any of the prominent men in the Cabinet have been allowed to hold a different language. The preservation of the

Union and the Constitution just as they are, should be held out at all times and everywhere as the only object of the war. If it be made a war for emancipation, it from that moment ceases to be on our side a legal and constitutional war, and we are set adrift on the billows of revolution. The two parties would become virtually two factions, neither of which would be contending for a government that is, but for such an one as they may desire to establish. They would stand on the same footing before foreign nations, who may with as much propriety recognize the independence of the one as the other.

I trust that under the new administration of the War Department the officers of the army and navy everywhere will be made to hold the same language on this subject; and the more thoroughly the privates of the army and the rebels themselves can be made to understand that the sole object of the war is the preservation of the Constitution pure and simple, the less protracted, expensive, and bloody it will probably be.

It seems to me the wildest abolitionist ought to be satisfied with the progress now being made. Though emancipation cannot lawfully be made the object of the war, it may be, and in fact every day *is, one of its results.* Nobody maintains that the slave of a traitor, finding his way into the Union lines or the free States, ought to be restored to him.

The master's right is forfeited by his rebellion. What in this respect is going on along the Southern coast ? About eight thousand negroes have been abandoned by their masters near Beaufort, and are now free. Should the slave-owners persist in their mad rebellion, the armies of the Union will advance into the interior of South Carolina, the masters will fly, and the slaves will be free. And what will be the end ? All the seacoast of South Carolina will be abandoned to the negroes, who will become a separate community under the protection of the United States. We already have the embryo of such a community around Port Royal, and its enlargement will be an incidental result of a long-continued war. A portion of the South will be abandoned to the negro, and slavery will cease to exist.

It has seemed to me that good might be done in the present condition of the country by discussing the slavery question in these aspects. Extreme men North might be quieted if shown that emancipation is in progress, by means most effectual and with all needful rapidity, and the slaveholders South might possibly be brought to their senses if made to comprehend that persistence in rebellion will assuredly end in the surrender of their plantations to their negroes.

If you think such a discussion would in any degree aid the government in its efforts to save the country, I am inclined to devote a portion of my time to such a purpose. A little labor with my pen is all I

can do for my country, and I would do nothing to embarrass its government.

With high respect, your obedient servant,
AMOS KENDALL.

The Administration having intimated to Mr. Kendall its desire that he would carry into effect the suggestion contained in the foregoing letter to Mr. Seward, he prepared and published a series of patriotic articles addressed to the President of the United States, which are omitted from this biography from want of space.

TO ALFRED T. GOODMAN.

TRENTON, June 10, 1862.

ALFRED T. GOODMAN, ESQ. :—

DEAR SIR, — Publications in the newspapers of this day are emphatically " like bread cast upon the waters." Few read them, and of that few a very small number pause to reflect upon them. We are all swept along, like drift upon a raging flood, by the torrents of argument and declamation which come pouring in from ten thousand sources, forgetting in the excitements of to-day the serious impressions of yesterday. It was in the hope that I might in some small degree aid in preventing general anarchy, by impressing upon the popular mind that there is a rock of safety in our Constitution, and that by planting themselves upon that rock they may defy the waves of tumultuous passion now beating against it, and see our beloved country again restored to unity and peace, that I took up my trembling pen. But whether the curse of reckless ambition in the South and the curse of blind fanaticism in the North, co-operating towards the same end, are not destined to subvert every vestige of a free government and place us under warring military despotisms, remains to be seen. Towards such a catastrophe we are manifestly tending; but there is yet *hope*, and while hope lasts *let us work.*

Yours truly,   AMOS KENDALL.

CLEVELAND, Ohio.

TO HENRY S. RANDALL.

TRENTON, N. J., June 10, 1862.

HENRY S. RANDALL, ESQ. :—

DEAR SIR, — Your letter of the 6th ultimo came duly to hand, and has remained unanswered only because matters of more immediate importance have pressed upon my attention.

I have never abandoned my purpose to finish the biography of General Jackson, commenced by me many years ago, and suspended for want of materials and means to procure them. Of Parton's life I have read but little, and that little with very unfavorable impressions. Its chief value is probable in the materials it embodies, though they are not in all cases reliable.

I never saw Mrs. Jackson, and know nothing of her character and habits otherwise than by report. But I do know that the old hero was enthusiastically attached to her, and I do not believe it was in his nature to love a vulgar woman. I saw myself evidences of the devotion he cherished for her memory, years after her death, which led me to believe that the hope he cherished of a happy immortality derived one of its dearest joys from the anticipated reunion with her whom he had so loved on earth.

From impressions derived from the conversations and acts of the General himself, and his family and friends, I believe Mrs. Jackson to have been one of the best and most pious women that ever lived, with as much refinement as could be expected in one raised upon the frontiers of civilization; and I look upon the stories which have been circulated about her, implying vulgarity of language and manners, as wicked caricatures, if not entirely false.

If I live to finish my biography of the General, I shall endeavor to do justice to one whose miniature, carried near his heart, was but an index to the love which dwelt within, during all the years of his eventful administration.

Yours very truly,

AMOS KENDALL.

CORTLAND VILLAGE, N. Y.

To John J. Crittenden, under date of February 18, 1863, he wrote:—

"What the country wants is a concert among loyal men of all parties, — I mean, men loyal to the Constitution and the country, — and this it must have, or God alone can save us.

"I am ready to labor to the last day of my life, if my labors can be made effective, without other reward than closing my eyes, for the last time, on a Constitution preserved and a Union restored; for in them alone can be found any sure guaranty of our country's happiness and glory."

W. D. WALLACH.

KENDALL GREEN, March 7, 1863.

W. D. WALLACH, Esq., *Editor of the Evening Star:*—

DEAR SIR, — With a reluctance amounting almost to loathing, I have undertaken to write a few more articles upon public affairs. The influence of my labors heretofore against secession has not been such as to encourage their renewal; and although I strongly disapprove the general

policy and many acts of the administration in the prosecution of the war, I would not knowingly do anything to lessen its power to suppress the rebellion. True, it has lessened its own power, and by its policy and acts has exposed the country to a new danger. My desire and object is to do what I can towards obviating that danger.

Loyal old Democrats say to me: " A few reckless or treacherous leaders seem to be rushing our young Democracy to their own and their country's ruin. You can speak to them from the age of Jackson; no man can charge you with having any aims of personal ambition to accomplish; perhaps they will listen to you." To those appeals I reluctantly yield, not without the conviction, however, that many of those who now rally under the name of Democrat would not be "convinced" though Andrew Jackson himself "rose from the dead."

Very respectfully, your obedient,

AMOS KENDALL.

TO HON. J. D. CATON.

WASHINGTON, April 17, 1863.

HON. J. D. CATON:—

MY DEAR SIR, — I read with great satisfaction the printed copy of your letter to Governor Seymour, of New York, which you kindly sent me, and do not doubt that it has had a happy influence in giving a more patriotic tone to the Democratic party. With distrust in my power to do any good, and an unwillingness to do or say anything which may lessen the power of the government to suppress the rebellion, I comply with your request, and place my views in relation to the policy and duty of the Democratic party at your disposition.

I concur with you in the opinion that President Lincoln has all along been desirous of using none but legitimate means for putting down the rebellion, and that his principal error has been in surrendering his better judgment to unsafe and designing counsellors.

I also concur with you in the opinion, that the success of the Democratic party in the elections of last fall was attributable, not to opposition to the war, but to the abuses and imbecility which attended its management. It was the beginning of a reaction which, if judiciously managed, would have relieved the President from the meshes in which he has become entangled, replaced the war on its original and only legitimate basis, preserved the Constitution and restored the Union.

Unfortunately for the Democratic party and the country, a few men who sympathized more with rebellion than with the Union, assumed the direction of this reaction, and endeavored to rush it into collision with the government, thus disarming the administration of all the power which its own mismanagement had left to maintain the integrity of the Union.

The consequences are seen in the result of the recent elections in New Hampshire, Rhode Island, and Connecticut. Thousands of intelligent men, disgusted with the management of the war and ready to join the Democratic party upon a patriotic platform, shrunk back from the precipice to which blind or traitorous leaders would hurry them, preferring the support of the administration, with all its abuses, to striking hands with the rebellion. Thus it is, that the next House of Representatives, instead of having a Democratic majority, has been thrown into the hands of the Republican party, and any reform in the management of the war has been rendered uncertain or indefinitely postponed.

I know that but few of the would-be Democratic leaders dare as yet to advocate giving up the Union, and acknowledging the Southern Confederacy. They only talk of an armistice with a view to ascertaining whether the Union cannot be restored by compromise. The great mass of the people have the sagacity to perceive that an armistice, under existing circumstances, could lead to but one kind of peace, and that involving a perpetual dissolution of the Union. Honest Union men who talk of an armistice seem to forget the facts of history and to be blind to passing events.

They seem to forget that the conspiracy which has culminated in rebellion originated more than thirty years ago, in the nullification doctrine of John C. Calhoun.

They seem to forget that the pretext then was not abolitionism in the North, but the alleged inequalities of the tariff.

They seem to forget the avowals of the South Carolina leaders, that a dissolution of the Union has been their aim and their study ever since.

They seem to forget, that having failed upon the tariff question, they next, as General Jackson predicted, seized upon the slavery question, and, by bandying abuse with Northern abolitionists, sought to create an inveterate hatred between the North and the South.

They seem to forget, that having broken up all other national parties, they sought to divide the national Democracy by proffering at their national conventions, as conditions of union, useless and obnoxious issues which they knew could not be sustained in the North.

They seem to forget, that the entire policy of the rebel leaders in Buchanan's Cabinet and in Congress was to disarm the general government, so that it should be unable to oppose the establishment of a Southern Confederacy with any prospect of success.

They seem to forget, that from the installation of the rebellion up to this hour, complete and eternal separation has been the avowed object of the rebel leaders, and they seem not to know that any suggestion from the North of negotiations for peace on any other basis, is met by those leaders and the Southern press with insult and defiance.

They seem to forget that the rebel leaders entered upon their criminal enterprise through perjury, fraud, and public robbery, and that their only chance for redeeming themselves in any degree from the deep infamy which their crimes deserve, is to be looked for only in the *éclat* which attends successful revolution and the establishment of a new empire.

Can any sane intelligent man believe that these proud and haughty men, conscious that they already deserve the infamy of the gallows, will ever give up the chance of gilding their crimes with success so long as they can keep an army in the field?

Let all such idle fancies be dismissed. They originate with semi-traitors, and are lures to betray the unwary into complication with treason. Every true Union man, whether Democrat or Republican, must make up his mind to the patent fact, that a restoration of the Union can be accomplished only by breaking the military power of the rebel leaders. There is not on earth a more ferocious military despotism than that which now grinds and starves the people of the rebel States, and it is not possible for them to bear it much longer. Whenever the rebel armies in the field are crushed, the leaders will disappear, and the great mass of the population will, if permitted, resume their position under the Constitution and the flag of the Union, from which they have been allured or driven by the arts and arms of those who now rule them with a rod of iron.

Our Union and Constitution cost a seven years' war. Are we so degenerate that rather than encounter a four years' war, we will surrender those precious legacies of our fathers and all the glorious hopes of our children? Rather let us encounter the dangers and privations of a war which shall end only with our lives.

"But," says the coward, the sympathizer with traitors, and their corrupt instruments, "the President has surrendered himself to a faction, has violated the Constitution and laws which it was his duty to maintain and enforce, and to sustain him in the prosecution of the war is to sanction all his usurpations."

I propose to discuss that proposition in another communication.

Yours very truly,

AMOS KENDALL.

OTTAWA, Illinois.

WASHINGTON, April 28, 1863.

HON. J. D. CATON:—

MY DEAR SIR, — In a former communication I conclusively showed, as I think, that all ideas of peace or an armistice with the rebel States, on any other basis than the independence of their Confederacy, are at present a delusion and a snare, and that their practical effect is to encourage the rebels and dishearten loyal men. Yet there is a class of men among us who delude themselves, or seek to delude others, with the idea, that peace and a restoration of the Union may be obtained by negotiation, and they recommend opposition to the prosecution of the war and an armistice for the purpose of trying the experiment. There are two classes of these men: one of them so very credulous and humane that they would have stopped to argue with Cain when in the act of knocking out his brother's brains; the other of men who have sympathized with the traitors from the outset, and now seek to secure their success by withholding from the government the means of carrying on the war, knowing full well that armistice is tantamount to an acknowledgment of Confederate independence, and that the government, looking upon it in that light, will not agree to any such measure, they seek to compel it by withholding men and money. In addition to the delusive cry of armistice and peace, they give as a reason for the course they recommend, the alleged fact that in their measures for putting down the rebellion the administration has violated the Constitution and laws. Let us admit, for the sake of argument, that this position is well founded, and then consider the conclusions which these men deduce from it. In this view, the Constitution and laws have two practical enemies: one of them seeking their entire subversion by force of arms; the other violating them in a resolute effort to preserve the life of the nation. What in such an emergency is the duty of the loyal citizen? Obviously the only means by which not only the Constitution but the nation itself can be saved from destruction is by repelling force by force. The only legitimate remedy for attacks on the Constitution by legislation and proclamation is by a change of rulers. The question for the consideration of the loyal citizen who disapproves the policy and management of the administration is, ought he to refuse to aid in defending his country and its Constitution against armed traitors, until they can be rescued from mismanagement or usurpation by incapable or treacherous public officers? Or,-instead of defending the Constitution against armed traitors, will he turn his arms against his own government, under pretence of correcting abuses, and thus insure the success of rebellion and the ruin 'of his country? Each of these attacks on our Constitution has its appropriate remedy, which the truly loyal citizen will know how to apply. The attack by arms, he will repel by arms; the attack by legislation and proclamations, he will endeavour to repel by a peaceful change of rulers through the independent exercise of the right of suffrage. Will he refuse to repel the attack by arms until he shall have repelled the attack by proclamation or legislation? The result might be that he would soon have neither Constitution, government, nor country to defend. Will he attempt to change the policy of his government by force? This would be destroying the Constitution under pre-text of defending it. It would be the inauguration of civil war in the North, and at once give success to the rebels. The Constitution knows no such process as force to effect a change of rulers or of public policy, and he who entertains any such projects is a traitor in his heart. Next to him in guilt is he who would encourage desertions, discourage enlistment, or in any way, whether treasonable or not, wilfully embarrass and weaken the government in the prosecution of the war. In its attempts to suppress the rebellion, if in nothing else, the administration is doing its sworn duty, and in performing it is entitled to the support of every patriotic citizen. A just people will excuse errors of judgment in the selection of means, provided they be honestly designed to accomplish the one great end. If they shall not be so designed, or shall be unnecessarily harsh and oppressive, let us charge them to an account to be settled at the great day of accounts after the suppression of the rebellion. Let us first defend our Constitution by conquering the armed rebels, and then vindicate its principles at the polls.

Obedience to a law is not necessarily an approval of the law. The good citizen will obey the law, however unjust it may be, and seek redress in the courts of justice or at the polls. The executive authority, to which the suppression of the rebellion has been intrusted, adopts a policy for that purpose which is obnoxious to the citizen, — shall the citizen refuse his aid in accomplishing the great end because he does not like the means?

Nothing can be clearer to my mind than the duty of all true Democrats under existing circumstances. It is to support the war with as much determination as if they heartily approved of its management, and at the same time give such a direction to their political action as may put an end to its mismanagement and abuses. Probably the salvation of their country, certainly the future fame and success of their party, depend on their taking and persevering in this patriotic course. Let us all adopt as our motto the sentiment of the invincible hero and incorruptible statesman, Andrew Jackson: —

"*The Federal Union:* IT MUST BE PRESERVED."

And let us add "SLAVERY OR NO SLAVERY." No true Northern man loves slavery for slavery's sake. The genuine patriot loves the Constitution and the Union more than he loves slavery or hates it. He would not give *them* up to save slavery or to abolish it. If one must perish, let slavery perish. Why should any loyal man sympathize with the rebel slave-holders for the loss of their slaves? They voluntarily put them in jeopardy by their rebellion; they are fast losing them by their obstinate persistence; they might now save what is left of them by submission to the Constitution and laws; but if they are determined never to submit,

who ought to regret to see the slave become an independent freeman upon the plantation of his master?

Let no one suppose from the contents of this letter that the policy or management of the administration in their attempts to suppress the rebellion is deemed by me unexceptionable; but I must write another letter to put myself right on that subject.

Yours very truly,

OTTAWA, Illinois.   AMOS KENDALL.

RESPONSIBILITIES OF POSTMASTERS.

To THE MORNING CHRONICLE: — My attention has been attracted to some comments on my official action when Postmaster-General, touching the circulation of printed matter through the mails, in one of your editorials this morning, and in a report of the present Postmaster-General. The principles involved in that action do not appear to be distinctly understood.

You say that "Under the strong appeals of the slaveholders and their Northern Democratic friends, and in utter defiance of the abolitionists of that day, the most drastic measures of prevention were enforced for a long period of time."

Now, if it be intended to mean that I, as Postmaster-General, enforced *any* "measures of prevention," it is an entire misapprehension. I did indeed express the opinion, that the United States had no rightful power to circulate through their mails and postmasters incendiary documents *prohibited by the laws of the States*, and I declined taking any measures to punish postmasters for refusing to be made instrumental in *violating those laws*. Of course, the abolitionists had as little regard for State laws then as they have for the Constitution of the United States now, and abused me most soundly; but I survived it.

Prima facie it is the legal duty of every postmaster to forward all newspapers placed in his office to be mailed, and, if he refuses to do so, he is liable in damages to the party aggrieved. The Postmaster-General cannot excuse him from the performance of that duty, nor shield him from damages if he refuses. The law prohibits postmasters and others from opening letters not addressed to them, under a heavy penalty. On one occasion the Washington postmaster came to me with a police officer, bringing a letter which they asked authority to open, believing it would lead to the detection of a criminal. My reply was, that I had no lawful power to open the letter myself or to authorize them to open it; but that knowing the motive, I would not punish the postmaster for opening it; but if he did so, he would expose himself to the penalty of the law from which I had no power to screen him. He opened the letter, and it fully verified his suspicions. Of course nobody complained of him.

So in reference to the circulation of incendiary newspapers and documents prohibited by the laws of the States. I had no rightful power to authorize the violation of those laws, or screen postmasters from punishment for so doing. I therefore practically left them in that, as in the first instance, to their legal responsibilities, with only this difference, that when called on I expressed the opinion that they were right. And the abolitionists thought so too; for they never ventured to sue the postmaster at New York for refusing to mail their documents to the South.

There is certainly a wide difference between my action and that of the present Postmaster-General, and it is a little singular that he first quotes me as a precedent, and afterwards repudiates the precedent altogether.

While I left the postmasters to forward the obnoxious papers or not, under their responsibility to the law, he peremptorily forbids their mailing them, without regard to the law. My *opinions* even justified them only in refusing to mail incendiary papers into States where their circulation was prohibited by law. The *orders* of the present Postmaster-General prohibit the mailing of certain obnoxious papers into any States, law or no law.

I do not write to censure the Postmaster-General, who, however, must look for full justification to an extreme political necessity not within the horizon of my limited vision. That there are papers claiming to be Democratic which ought to be suppressed, I have no doubt. Being now and forever a Democrat of the Jackson school, I have no affinity with those who, under that honored name, cry for peace by the sacrifice of the Union, and quite as little with those who seek to save the Union by the destruction of the Constitution. When the Democratic party becomes a secession party, and the Republican party becomes an abolition party, I shall seek for new political affinities, or remain *a party by myself*.

AMOS KENDALL.

February 19, 1863.

A CLERICAL REBUKE.

KENDALL GREEN, December 9, 1863.

REV. —— ——

SIR, — On the 4th instant you called on me with a letter from the Rev. Mr. H——, and asked for a subscription to aid you in completing a house of worship for the colored people.

To Mr. H.'s name was attached an apparent subscription of twenty dollars. Actuated by his recommendation and liberality, I gave you a check for thirty dollars.

I have since learned that Mr. H. did not attach any subscription to his name, and that another subscription of twenty dollars on your book is equally fictitious. You therefore came to me with *a lie in your hand,*

and thereby obtained my money. I fear you have studied the New Testament with little profit if you consider *forgery and falsehood* allowable means for raising money for any purpose whatsoever.

My first impulse on making this discovery was to advertise you as an impostor, seeking to raise money by false pretences; but in the charitable hope that in this matter you acted without due consideration of the moral turpitude of the transaction, and on being reminded of it, will at once abandon the use of such means to raise money, I content myself at present with writing this letter. How can you teach the observance of truth as a Christian duty to your flock, if you think it right to practice deception yourself? Of all men preachers should be most strict.

Very respectfully, your obt. serv't,

AMOS KENDALL.

Another series of articles on public affairs from Mr. Kendall's pen, signed "Andrew Jackson," was published in the "Evening Star" at this time. Their lofty patriotism and powerful arguments are shown in the following letter:—

CONSIDERATIONS WHY EVERY PATRIOT SHOULD SUSTAIN THE ADMINISTRATION IN THEIR ATTEMPTS TO SUPPRESS THE REBELLION.

To all Unconditional Union Men in the United States :—

The following considerations are conclusive in the mind of the writer, that it is the imperative duty of every true patriot to sustain the administration in their efforts to suppress the existing rebellion :—

1. Our country is at war, and the administration are the only constitutional organs by whom it can be carried on.

2. The object of the war on the part of the rebels is to break up the government and destroy the Union, now and forever, by the establishment of a Southern Confederacy. What would soon be the fate of the North if the administration be not sustained with men and money, may be conceived by imagining where the rebel armies of Lee and Bragg would now be had they been victorious at Antietam or Gettysburg, Murfreesboro' and Chattanooga? Not to support the administration with adequate means, is to give up our capital, Baltimore, Philadelphia, New York, Louisville, Cincinnati, Pittsburg, and the lake cities, to rebel occupancy, and the intermediate country to ravage and plunder by swarms of men more hungry than the locust of the African desert.

3. But it is alleged that the imbecility, bad policy, military jealousy, and political ambition of the administration and its adherents, have already sacrificed unnecessarily tens of thousands of Northern lives, and hundreds of millions of Northern money. What then? Shall we there-

fore submit to the rebels and give up forever the hope of handing down to our children the glorious legacy bequeathed to us by our fathers? Let us rather consider the imbecility, jealousy, and ambition of civil and military rulers in the same light as other obstacles to success, all to be overcome by sacrifices and perseverance.

4. But it is said the administration has made, and will make, an unconstitutional use of the means put at their disposition. That is a risk we must always encounter under any administration. But the possibility that they will not do their duty is no excuse for not doing our own. Give all the requisite means, and hold the administration to a strict responsibility for their proper application. Herein is the ground of a legitimate opposition, and it is already broad enough in all conscience.

5. If there were no principle which requires the patriot to furnish the Administration all the means they want for carrying on the war, partisan policy would dictate the same course. If furnished with abundant means as heretofore, the responsibility for failures will rest exclusively with themselves; but if they are restricted in means, they will cast the responsibility on those who may have denied them.

6. But there are those who would refuse to furnish the administration with the means of carrying on the war, because they think the Union cannot be restored by force, and would compel the government to resort to an armistice and negotiation. Many of these men are perfectly sincere; but they labor under a strange delusion. They seem to forget the origin, progress, and object of the conspiracy which in 1861 culminated in the great rebellion. That conspiracy was the growth of thirty years. Assiduously, during that period, have the leading conspirators inculcated their revolutionary dogmas on the Southern mind, and, by bandying insults with the abolitionists of the North, sought to produce implacable hatred between the two sections. They forced themselves, by threats of opposition, into the Cabinet of a weak President, and used their positions to disarm the government and lay the country prostrate before meditated insurrection. Their avowed object, from first to last, has not been a redress of grievances or further guarantees for their rights, but absolute and entire independence. They are proud and haughty men who have hazarded everything upon the chances of success, and had rather die than go down to posterity as unsuccessful traitors. They have set their hearts upon the establishment of a new empire, and will not give up the hope of gilding their crimes with the tinsel of victory so long as they can "set a squadron in the field." Every suggestion of compromise and peace on any other terms than the acknowledgment of their independence, has been, and will be, treated with scorn and derision. There is no alternative for this government, by whomsoever administered, but to deprive these men of power by defeating and dispersing the rebel armies.

Let that be done and the great mass of the Southern people will, if permitted, gladly return to their allegiance.

But were it otherwise, whence comes the cowardly or treacherous cry that the rebels cannot be conquered? When the war commenced, the men of the military age in the loyal States were as four to one compared with the white men of similar age in the seceded States. Now, the proportions, throwing into the loyal scale the whites and blacks capable of bearing arms in those portions of the seceded States occupied by the Union armies, are as five to one. The loss of one man to the rebels is equal to the loss of five to the loyalists; every drawn battle is virtually a Union victory; and every able-bodied rebel prisoner detained in custody, is equal to five soldiers added to the Union armies. There are already about forty thousand rebel prisoners in the North, and should not exchanges be resumed, there is ground to hope the day is not distant when half of the rebel army will be found in Northern prisons.

If, with this disparity of fighting men, the command of the sea, and an equal disparity in all the means and appliances of war, the North cannot, if need be, *subjugate* the people of the rebel States, we may as well admit their insolent claim to superiority and bow our necks to Southern domination.

It has seemed to me amazing that any Northern man, and *especially any Democrat*, can entertain the least sympathy for the perjured leaders of this inexcusable and bloody rebellion. They are rebels not only to their country and to mankind, but *doubly rebels to the Democratic party* which they betrayed and abandoned. Sympathy with them, by any loyal man, is a crime; but by a Democrat it is not only a crime, but a degradation. With what utter contempt must he be looked upon by these proud men! But let us not confound with the arch conspirators the mass of the Southern people who have been seduced or driven into rebellion. While we sustain our government in defeating and dispersing the rebel armies, let us be prepared then to demand that the popular masses shall be allowed to resume, *unconditionally*, their former position under the Constitution and laws of their country.

This leads me to consider the President's plan of restoration, which will form the subject of another letter.

January 21, 1864.   AMOS KENDALL.

On the 25th of June, 1864, Mr. Kendall was called to part with his second wife. In a letter to a friend of that date, he said :—

"But I feel it almost sacrilege to touch on any topic at this moment which does not relate to the dead. This morning, my second wife, with whom I have lived most happily for nearly forty years, took her departure for another world. She had been prostrate with that insidious disease, the

typhoid fever, near three weeks. Its fatal termination has been apprehended for some days, but not quite so soon. At ten o'clock last night she responded to my "Good night," and turned her head for a parting kiss, — and a *parting kiss it was*. When called to her bedside, soon after day this morning, she was insensible, and soon ceased to breathe. My mind flew back to the first kiss in contrast with the last, — the ecstacy of the one, and the sadness of the other. Such is life."

To another friend, under date of June 29th, he wrote :—

"My wife breathed her last on Saturday morning, and was buried on Sunday evening last. For several days we flattered ourselves with the belief that she was getting better; but typhoid symptoms then appeared, and she sank rapidly, but with little or no pain, and died as gently as a child goes to sleep. It is a terrible blow to me; but with God's help it will not unman me."

To his eldest daughter, residing in Minnesota, he wrote :—

"I had lost all hope, but did not think her end so near. I requested Mr. Fox, who sat up, to rouse me if there should be any serious change in the night. Soon after day he entered my room and said she was sinking fast. I found her insensible to voice or touch, passing away as gently as an infant falls to sleep, and she breathed her last without moving a muscle or giving any other sign of pain or suffering. And so placid were her features that one might say, *Death is beautiful.*

"It is to me an irreparable blow. But my remaining children are very kind to me, and for them I must live henceforth, until my Maker calls me home to meet the loved ones, and live in love and peace forever."

Writing to his daughter, now Mrs. Cutter, in the autumn of 1864, Mr. Kendall said :—

"Though my health is much as it has been for many years, I do not enjoy life as I did before your mother's death. Your sister Jeannie is as kind to me as a daughter can be, but no other relation can supply the place of a loving, ever-kind, and faithful wife. I wish all my daughters may make their husbands as good wives as your mother made me. We were very poor, and she was very happy. We became tolerably rich, and she was scarcely happier. We were in humble position, and yet there was sunshine at home; we were in high position, and our joys were scarcely brighter. Rich or poor, high or low, she encountered the vicissitudes of life with an equanimity seldom equalled, and perhaps never surpassed. The secret of all was in her own native good sense, aided perhaps by implicit confidence in her husband."

At the time of her death, Mrs. Kendall was an active, earnest, member of the E Street Baptist Church, in Washington, and the President of the sewing-circle connected with that church.

At a meeting of the circle, soon after her decease, the following resolution with others was adopted: —

"At a meeting of the managers of the Ladies' sewing-circle of the Calvary Baptist Church, held on the 23d day of August, 1864, the following preamble and resolutions were unanimously passed: —

"*Whereas*, It has pleased God by a mysterious Providence to call from her home, her friends, and her church, our beloved sister, Mrs. Amos Kendall, the President of this society; and

"*Whereas*, As her amiable disposition, her many moral excellencies, and her devotion to the cause of Christ, exhibited in her exalted life and consecration to his cause, have filled us with the highest admiration and regard, so that we deem it alike due to her memory, and to our own feelings to bear testimony to her worth;

"*Therefore, be it resolved*, 1st. That, while it is with deep emotion that we record her death, yet we rejoice that He who removed her from those she loved on earth, gave her the victory over death, and has raised her to the exalted companionship of angels, and the spirits of the just made perfect, and that she now lives in the immediate presence and glory of our Divine Redeemer. In this life she possessed and exhibited the entire galaxy of Christian excellencies: faith, virtue, knowledge, temperance, brotherly kindness, and love. The church of Christ was her home, and the prosperity of Zion her constant care and delight. Every enterprise for the welfare of the church found in her a ready and active assistant. Her influence, her personal service, and her munificent gifts fell together into the lap of the church. Among friends, bearing the dignity, kindness, and cordiality which a truly sanctified spirit bestows, the social circle in which she moved was exalted and blessed by her presence. As she was to the afflicted and bereaved a cordial sympathizer and benefactor, many beyond our circle will mourn the absence of her encouraging smile and conversation. Having been to the widow and fatherless a sister, a mother, and companion, many, as the coming winter sets in, will miss her benefactions, which were distributed often by another or an unknown hand."

For several years immediately preceding this affliction, Mr. Kendall's mind was much given to the subject of religion. It was always an agreeable topic of conversation as well as of correspondence; the Bible was his favorite study; and he often expressed great satisfaction in the thought that his wife, daughters, and sons-in-law were professing Christians.

The following letter to his former pastor best expresses his views on this subject: —

TRENTON, December 25, 1861.

REV. G. W. SAMSON: —

MY DEAR SIR, — Before I left Washington I received your kind letter of the 11th instant, in which you express a strong desire that I should make "an open profession of religion," which I have not until now found time to answer.

Years ago, when the same desire was expressed to me by another clergyman, who was intimate with me and my family, my reply was, " I am not hypocrite enough." To you in all sincerity I make the same answer.

I accept what I understand of Christianity as my rule of action; many of its mysteries I cannot say that I believe or disbelieve; and in all such cases " I am not hypocrite enough " to say before God and man that I believe them. I am content to say, in all that lies beyond the reach of finite mind, "God's will be done"; and few Christians, I am sure, are more ready to submit to that will with entire resignation.

About 1821 I might claim to have undergone the process of conversion. My wife was absent, and I had with a friend been attending an evening meeting. At its close I held a conversation with my friend, whose feelings sympathized with my own, and retiring to my chamber knelt in prayer. Suddenly a sensation of wonderful serenity pervaded my whole being, rendering me perfectly but quietly happy. It lasted several days; but gradually I became insensible to its influence. The whole thing was incomprehensible to me then, as it is now; it did not, that I am aware of, change my views in relation to morals or religion, and I should then have considered myself as unfit to join a church on the ordinary platform as I do now.

If this difficulty were removed, there is another which I should find as difficult to overcome. It is that there is so little *practical Christianity* among *professing Christians*. With few exceptions, their lives are no more exemplary than those of the great mass of their fellow-citizens out of the church. Their avarice is as grasping, their business subterfuges as deceptive, their pride as haughty, their envy as keen, their tongues as ungovernable, and their charities no more active. I do not urge this as an objection to Christianity; but it is a serious objection to churches under their present state and discipline. Unsuitable persons are too readily admitted, and unworthy persons too forbearingly retained. I have heard members of the church, with whom I am most familiar, relate transactions of other members for which, if I were a member, I should feel it my duty to institute proceedings for their expulsion. Nor have I reason to believe the members of that church to be worse than those of similar bodies in general.

Perhaps my standard of Christian morals and church discipline is too

high; but being what it is, I fear I should be a disturber of the peace in any of those bodies with which I might connect myself.

With these views I apprehend I shall die as I have lived, *a church by myself*.

With enduring regard, your friend,

AMOS KENDALL.

WASHINGTON, D. C.

In June, 1862, Mr. Kendall wrote to Rev. J. S. Kennard, his former pastor, in relation to matters connected with the Calvary Baptist Church, which had then been recently organized at Washington, and for whose benefit he had expressed the intention of making a liberal contribution: —

"What may be my own relations with the organization is as yet uncertain. I have heard unofficially that they have appointed me one of their trustees. If so, it has been done without consulting me and without communicating to me their regulations, if any have been adopted.

"My willingness to serve will depend entirely on the system which may be adopted for the management of the temporal affairs of the church.

"I am very anxious to see a *practical, working Christian church* at Washington, though I have no expectation of being anything more than an *outside* member of it. Your creeds require men to believe undoubtingly altogether too much, and make religion to consist more in *professions of faith* than in the active performance of Christian duties. I could become one of an organization of working Christians who should take the New Testament for their creed, and let me construe it for myself; but it would be most unreasonable in me to expect any body of men to modify their articles of faith for the purpose of accommodating them to my notions. Hence it is that I do not expect to become a member of any church, though I hope always to be a practical Christian.

"To me, however, men's speculative faith, if not inconsistent with positive duty, is of little consequence compared with practical Christianity, as inculcated by the precepts and example of Christ and his Apostles. Hence it is that I can consistently and cordially encourage and assist a religious society whose *practices* are in accordance with New Testament rules, though I may not be able to 'see eye to eye' with them in matters of faith. In the hope that the new organization may consist of practical Christians, whatever may be their Articles of Faith, I am disposed to aid them in their enterprise, not however without a distinct understanding of the rules by which they propose to be governed."

To his daughter, on the occasion of the baptism of her husband by a Baptist clergyman, an Episcopalian and Methodist minister

having administered the rite of baptism by immersion to candidates for membership in their respective churches on the same occasion, Mr. Kendall wrote: —

MY DEAR JEANNIE, — We received last evening your very interesting letter of the 3d instant. Your mother very much regrets that she could not be with you on Sunday evening. To me also it would have afforded much satisfaction, from the truly Christian spirit exhibited by the intermingling of different denominations. I am happy to see also the members of my family acquire that implicit faith which enables them with all sincerity to become members of a Christian church; for whatever is good among men is comprehended in the practical precepts taught in the New Testament. It is a matter of regret with me that I have never been able to command that degree of faith in the doctrines insisted upon by any sect of Christians which would justify me to myself in professing faith in its creed. Perhaps I am mistaken in the degree of faith required; perhaps the creeds are mistaken in requiring too much. Be that as it may, I have endeavored to live the life of a practical Christian, and feel as if I might belong to any Protestant sect if they would not require me to profess implicit faith in multifarious matters of a doctrinal nature which no finite mind can comprehend, and which, if it could, would make the man neither better nor worse. No man is more ready than I am to say " God's will be done," and to submit to that will without a murmur.

Your devoted father,

AMOS KENDALL.

MRS. WM. STICKNEY.

A TRUE PRACTICAL CHRISTIAN.

In February, 1865, Mr. Kendall wrote to a friend as follows: —

"As I understand it, the Christian system of religion is based on the fact that the human mind is incompetent to conceive the existence, or perhaps I should say the form, of any being or thing independent of matter. God himself was 'the unknown God' until made 'manifest in the flesh.' That manifestation gave man a material object of worship combining matter and spirit. To that material object, mysteriously spiritualized and transferred from earth to heaven, the Christian addresses his devotions. This incapacity of the human mind to conceive of the nature or form of spiritual beings independent of matter, undoubtedly gave origin to idolatry, and existence to 'gods many and lords many,' both in the fanciful theories of pagan mythology and in idol forms provided for human worshippers. Whether adoration is addressed to the sun, moon, fire, or any other thing or being, it was to something material in fact or in imagination. In this respect the Christian and the Pagan are alike.

" All or nearly all religions are also alike in recognizing the existence of God who governs the universe, of the depravity of man, of the necessity of a redeemer and intercessor with God; and some systems besides the Christian have attempted to supply this general want. No system except the Christian has succeeded.

" There appears to me to be two kinds of Christianity, which must be united into one to make a full grown Christian. I call one the *rational*, the other the *emotional*. The rational Christian is he who exercises his mind in studying out all that the human mind can grasp in the Christian system, and is content to receive the balance upon faith. The emotional Christian is he who scarcely thinks at all, whose religion is a matter of feeling, and develops itself only in prayers and enthusiastic demonstrations. One is of the *head ;* the other of the *heart.* Unite the two attributes in one person, and add a profusion of unselfish good works, and you have my ideal of a *true practical Christian.*"

On the 22nd of March, 1865, Mr. Kendall wrote to his pastor, T. R. Howlett : —

" I have been a pretty constant attendant at the prayer-meetings, but as yet have taken no part in them. You know something of my difficulties about joining the church. I have, however, so far overcome them some weeks since as to resolve on offering myself soon after your return. I perceive there is a strong desire that I should take that step, and I have determined, God willing, to announce my purpose to-morrow evening.

" O that you could be with us, but we know that your duties at present are at the bedside of your dear, dying wife. I can conceive of few situations more trying than yours at present. God give you grace to bear your trials with patience and resignation, and in his own good time restore you to your flock with increased energies to advance his kingdom."

To Rev. A. B. Earle, under date of March 31, 1865, he wrote : —

" The impulse which has decided me was in part a belief that I could do more good in the church than out of it, and in part that my position was in effect a standing argument with the world against Christianity. I felt that I was looked upon and spoken of as a good man, but not a Christian, involving the plain inference that to be a good man it is not necessary to be a Christian.

" But, my dear sir, I find it very hard to recover that blissful serenity

which once pervaded my whole nature. It seems impossible for me to approach God in prayer without trembling of heart and confusion of thought. I ask you to pray for me, and also to present my case for prayer to the Christian people among whom you are laboring."

TO THE REV. T. R. HOWLETT.

WASHINGTON, April 1, 1865.

REV. T. R. HOWLETT : —

MY VERY DEAR SIR, — My heart impels me to write you a few lines, in the nature of explanation. Last evening Mr. Olcott, his daughter Mina, Mrs. McKnew, and myself, related our Christian experiences, and were accepted by the Calvary Baptist Church. I believe every one of us, and I know that myself, would have preferred being baptized by you in preference to any other man. Of course, my first impulse was to await your return. But a little reflection satisfied me that such was not my duty. Your recent letters showed that the time of your return is entirely uncertain, and may be delayed for months. On the other hand, a revival was in progress ; it might be accelerated by the baptism of such as were ready, or checked by an unnecessary postponement, and if, as my family and friends thought, my example would have a happy effect, it seemed to me I could not furnish it too soon. Accordingly, when Mr. Kennard said to me, " I suppose you will wait Mr. Howlett's return," I replied, " No, I am ready to go into the water as soon as necessary arrangements can be made."

The ceremony will be performed by Mr. Kennard, God willing, in the E Street Baptist Church, after morning service to-morrow.

Remember me most kindly to Mrs. Howlett.

Your devoted friend,

AMOS KENDALL.

WINONA, Minn.

On Sunday, April 2, 1865, the ordinance of baptism was administered to the two ladies referred to in the preceding letter, and to Mr. Kendall.

The following account of the ceremony is taken from a Washington paper of the next day : —

" When the services at the E Street Baptist Church were concluded yesterday, according to previous arrangement the congregation of the Calvary Church with their fine choir entered, and were received by Rev. Dr. Gray and his church officers.

" Deep solemnity pervaded all present. A few moments elapsed, and then were seen advancing down the centre aisle the then officiating clergyman of the Calvary Church, Rev. J. S. Kennard, followed by two

ladies, each accompanied by a deacon, and then the venerable form of the Hon. Amos Kendall, with a time-honored officer of the church by his side.

" The minister, the two ladies, and Mr. Kendall were enrobed for the impressive services of immersion.

" The candidates took their seats in front of the pulpit, the choir singing, ' All hail the power of Jesus' name.' The hymn concluded, Mr. Kennard arose, and in most eloquent terms referred to his former relation with this church and people. Dr. Gray followed with a fervent prayer. Mr. Kennard then descended into the pool, where, amid deep solemnity, he received and baptized the two ladies. Mr. Kendall then rose, and in a firm step ascended the pulpit platform, then devoutly descended the steps leading into the pool.

" The older members here looked on with intense interest, for they remembered that but a few years since the devoted wife of the good man, two daughters, and one son-in-law had consecrated themselves freely to God in that identical spot, and they seemed to imagine his feelings as he too entered the pool. Mr. Kennard received Mr. Kendall, and put the usual- questions, to which he replied distinctly. The preacher then repeated these words : ' *Though for many years I have endeavored to live the life of an upright man, yet, by not attaching myself to the church, I feel that my life was a standing opposition to Christianity.*' These words are understood to have formed a part of Mr. Kendall's experience before the church. He was then baptized, and the services closed with prayer and benediction."

That immersion was the mode of baptism, as practised by the founder of the Christian religion and his apostles, Mr. Kendall never entertained a doubt.

Referring to this subject afterwards in a letter, he wrote : —

" The most interesting news I have to give you is the conversion of my grandson, Willie Stickney, and his baptism last Sabbath in Philadelphia, by Rev. J. S. Kennard, in the presence of his father and mother and myself. That the occasion was most interesting you may well imagine. And to me it is a great consolation to see all my surviving children devoting themselves to the service of the Redeemer. The only drawback is that some of them do not feel it their duty to follow his example and obey his commands in the matter of baptism ; but as their disobedience is not wilful, I trust it will be forgiven."

In the *new version* of the Bible he strongly deprecated the substitution of the word *immerse* for baptize, upon which he wrote the following characteristic article : —

IMMERSION NOT BAPTISM.

" The meaning of a word is the idea which it conveys. The English word BAPTIZE does not convey to the majority of those who hear and read it the idea of IMMERSION. But the idea of the Greek word BAPTIZO is IMMERSION. As BAPTIZE does not convey that idea, it is not a true and faithful translation. It is error, and displeases God.

" Does the Greek word BAPTIZO mean TO RAISE OUT OF THE WATER? No. It never had that meaning among the Greeks. The hundreds of quotations from Greek authors adduced in the books disprove any such supposition. None of the great scholars of Europe ever suggested it. The idea was never started till the question arose about revising the common version, and then opponents of revision inserted it.

" It is true that those who are IMMERSED on the profession of their faith, are *afterwards* raised out of the water. But the Greek word BAPTIZO does not mean TO RAISE OUT OF THE WATER."

I take issue with the learned gentleman and maintain that the Greek word *baptizo* does now, and has from the institution of baptism as a Christian rite, include the idea of *raising out of the water.* For the truth of this assertion, I appeal to the following testimony : —

1. The common sense of all those who have been baptized or have witnessed a baptism in font or river in the only true mode. Did any Baptist ever conceive that his baptism was complete until he was raised out of the water ? Did any spectator ever conceive that the ceremony was complete as soon as the subject was plunged under the water ? I am sure no one ever had that idea until it was recently invented to justify an abandonment of the name given by Christ and his apostles to this most solemn Christian rite.

2. The New Testament itself. What did Christ mean in this respect when he commanded his disciples to " go and teach all nations, *baptizing* them in the name of the Father and of the Son and of the Holy Ghost" ? Did he mean that they should plunge all nations under the water and *let them stay there ?* If that was the end of the rite, it was tantamount to a command *to drown* all nations ! If the idea of raising them out of the water is not embraced in the word baptize, or *baptizo,* then the administrator of the ordinance has complied with the command when he has put the subject under the water, and ought then to let go of him. He has, upon that hypothesis, no right to raise him out of the water ; for that is adding to the divinely prescribed ceremony, which he has no right to do.

The most minute description we have of the ceremony of baptism, in the New Testament, is in the case of Philip and the eunuch, Acts viii. 38, 39. " They went down into the water, both Philip and the eunuch ; and he baptized him. And when they were come up out of the water," etc.

CALVARY BAPTIST CHURCH, WASHINGTON, D. C.

Three acts are here described : First, going down into the water ; secondly, the baptizing ; thirdly, the coming up out of the water. Going down into the water was no part of the baptism, nor was coming up out of the water ; but the baptism was that which Philip did between the going down and the coming up. What was that ? He plunged the eunuch into and under the water and raised him up again, and this process is described by the word *baptize*. They did not come up out of the water while the eunuch was under the water, but after he was raised up out of the water. They went down and stood in the water ; Philip plunged him into the water and raised him up again *by one continuous movement*, which left them again standing in the water ; and *then*, the ceremony being completed, they came up out of the water. Every one who looks at a Baptist baptism may realize this scene by the evidence of his own senses. He may also realize that without the raising out of the water it would be a *drowning* instead of a *baptism*. Instead of being an incident like " clothing," and " numerous other attendant circumstances," it is *an essential part of the thing itself ;* so essential that without it *every baptism would be a murder.*

3. Much learning and labor have been wasted in hunting up passages in heathen authors to prove that the Greek word *baptizo*, as used by them, does not mean raising out of the water. What has all that to do with the subject ? The question is not what the word means in heathen authors, but what does it mean in the New Testament ? The word existed before the Christian rite of baptism was instituted. In adopting a name for the new rite, Christ and his Apostles selected this word as more analogous to the ceremony in its accepted meanings than any other in the Greek language. But to ascertain its meaning, in its new application, we must look to the new thing intended to be described by it, rather than to the old things to which heathen authors had previously applied it. If a new word, or any other old word of any other meaning in heathen authors, had been adopted, its true meaning, as descriptive of the new rite, could be ascertained only by reference to the rite itself. The rite does not derive its form or existence from its name ; but the name derives its meaning from the rite. Christ and his Apostles adopted the words *baptisma* and *baptizo* as the names of their new rite, and the process of administering it. They became equivalent to proper names, and the translators of our English Bible, not feeling authorized to alter them, or not being able to find equivalent English words, very properly retained the Greek, altered — not in meaning nor even in form — only so far as was necessary to conform them to the idioms of the English language. But our revisers have become more learned if not more wise. They have found an English equivalent for *baptizo* in the word *immersion ;* but as that literally means only *plunging into the water,* they are

obliged, in order to make it a true translation of *baptizo*, to *cut off one half of the sacred rite* and leave all poor Baptists under the water ? *Immerse* means simply to plunge into the water ; *baptize* means to plunge into the water and raise out of the water, and this is the only true Christian baptism, when done in the name of the Father, Son, and Holy Ghost.

4. Let us see how sundry passages of the New Testament would read with *baptizo* translated into simple Anglo-Saxon, meaning only to plunge under the water. Matthew iii. 13, 14, 16. " Then cometh Jesus from Galilee to Jordan unto John, *to be put under water* of him. But John forbad him, saying, I have need to be *put under the water* of thee, and comest thou to me ? . . . . And Jesus, when he was *put under the water*, went up straightway out of the water," etc. Matthew xx. 22, 23. " But Jesus answered and said, Ye know not what ye ask. Are ye able to drink of the cup that I shall drink of, or to be put under the water with the putting under the water that I am put under the water with ? They say unto him, We are able. And he saith unto them, Ye shall put under the water indeed of my cup, and be put under the water with the putting under the water that I am put under the water with," etc.

The Calvary Baptist Society, which Mr. Kendall had joined, was engaged in the erection of a new edifice, mainly by his aid. Referring to this subject and his own religious exercises, he wrote in a letter to Rev. J. S. Kennard, July 7, 1865 : —

" Our new church excites more admiration as its details are developed. But it will be very costly. My advances will be over $ 60,000 ; but all this I shall esteem as nothing if the church shall come up to my ideal of what a Christian church ought to be, and in " the beauty of holiness " far outshine the architectural beauties of their temple of worship. Of this I almost despair when I reflect upon my own imperfections. I find it hard to subdue my heart to the dispensation of Providence which has doomed me to a condition of comparative loneliness during the remaining period of my earthly existence. So smoothly had my life passed for many years that I took almost no note of time, and the death of a beloved wife first awoke me to the fact that I was *an old man*, — a fact I am more and more forced to realize when, looking around me, I find almost none left of the generation to which I belong, while those of succeeding generations, although they sympathize with me and perhaps love me as a son or a daughter may love, cannot reciprocate the love of that higher relation which binds two hearts in one. My children are as kind to me as children can be, and I believe love me as children ought to love a kind father ; but they cannot fill the void left by the death of

their sainted mother. I have sought relief by ' marrying the church,' and I hope to find in her that peace and happiness which cannot but flow from a cheerful acquiescence in the Divine will. Pray for me that it may be so ; for as yet it is *not* so."

The following is from a letter written July 12, 1865 : —

" I have a Bible class in our Sabbath-school, and the subject of our study and discussion during the last month was the Lord's Prayer. Many ideas in connection with that wonderful production, somewhat new to me, were elicited. One of the most impressive is the qualification for approaching the Throne of Grace, with any hope of being kindly received, implied in the petition, " *Forgive us our debts as we forgive our debtors.*" Who can utter this prayer in sincerity and at the same time cherish in his heart ill-will, enmity, or an unforgiving spirit towards any human being ? It is only as we *forgive* that we can ask *to be forgiven*, — not imaginary wrongs only, but real wrongs, however aggravated. What human wrong can be more aggravated than sin against God ? And how dare we ask forgiveness of him while we do not forgive those comparatively trifling wrongs which we may have received from our fellow-men ? It is an insult to our heavenly Father to ask forgiveness when we do not forgive. The very first thing we have to do to fit us to approach the throne of grace is to exercise that godlike virtue which we ask God to exercise for our benefit, and freely forgive every wrong which we may have received from our fellow-men. It is only *as we forgive* that we are entitled to ask forgiveness ; and if there be no forgiveness in our hearts, what do we pray for in this prayer but curses instead of blessings ? God's judgments are the only answers we have a right to expect to every petition coming up to him from unforgiving hearts."

On the 3d day of June, 1866, the new house of worship of the Calvary Baptist Church was dedicated to the service of God. The day was auspicious, and multitudes thronged the temple. For months this day had been looked forward to by Mr. Kendall with increasing interest. As chairman of the building committee, he applied his best energies to the work, watching its progress, supervising its details, scrutinizing the material, and devoting himself almost exclusively to the achievement of this enterprise, so dear to his heart. The cost greatly exceeded the original estimate, so that his own advances were not less than a hundred thousand dollars. Though so much pleasure had been anticipated by Mr. Kendall on this occasion, he was doomed to sad disappointment. He had been suffering severely with a bad cold for several weeks, and on

the morning of the dedication he had a fever and headache which continued during the day. He attended both services, and received with an almost fainting heart the congratulations of his friends.

Referring to these circumstances in a letter to a friend, he said : " We had anticipated too much worldly enjoyment on this occasion, and our heavenly Father has sent us this disappointment by way of rebuke."

As an active member of the church, laboring to build up its spiritual interests, Mr. Kendall was equally zealous. Constant in his attendance upon the meetings, public and devotional ; earnest in his exhortations to its members ; faithful in his duties as a teacher in the Sunday-school, where he seemed to forget his old age as his heart overflowed with love and sympathy for all its members ; visiting and ministering unto the sick ; liberal in his contributions ; — he had fully consecrated himself, his means, and his energies to the cause of his Divine Master.

His heart retained all the freshness and buoyancy of youth, though his almost snow-white hair, trembling hand, and feeble frame admonished him that the last of earth was near.

Although he never failed to attend any of the meetings of the church, unless prevented by sickness or other insuperable obstacle, the Sunday-school possessed for him peculiar attractions. He loved to be among the children, to be at their celebrations, and festivals, and picnics, and mingle in their sports.

Notwithstanding his familiarity with the Scriptures, his almost invariable rule was to devote from six to twelve hours' close study in preparing to go before his class. Commentaries he cared little for, but he compared scripture with scripture, examined critically the original Greek, studied the customs and habits of the ancients, and thus by diligent and patient investigation, prayer and meditation, he furnished himself for his Sunday-school labors. That his interest in this field of usefulness was not of recent origin, appears from the following letter, yellow with age, which was found among his papers : —

FRANKFORT, KY., September 17, 1829.

DEAR BROTHER, — This will be presented by Mr. Amos Kendall of this place, who has taken an active part in promoting a Sunday-school here, which is independent, and auxiliary to none. Mr. Kendall is anxious to obtain such information as may be productive of good to this school.

We therefore take pleasure in recommending him to your attention as a gentleman desirous of promoting the interests of religion, as one of the managers of the Sunday-school at this place, and as the editor of the "Argus of Western America," published here.

Yours, in the bonds of the gospel,

JOHN LITTLEJOHN.

B. T. CRANCH.

The custom which prevailed in most churches of taking up collections, Sabbath after Sabbath, was in the opinion of Mr. Kendall, simply an "abomination." The placing of boxes or other receptacles in the vestibule, for voluntary offerings from strangers and others, he approved and recommended; but the offering of bags or plates, with intent to solicit gifts during the service, he esteemed a wilful desecration of the Temple of God. He also regarded the incurring of debts by churches as not only detrimental to their usefulness, but positively immoral. His proposition to aid the Calvary Baptist Church was based upon certain conditions, designed to prevent these practices. The conditions set forth in his deed of gift to the church, and formally agreed to by that body, are as follows: —

"In trust, nevertheless, for the following uses and purposes, and subject to the conditions contained in the letter and agreement of the party of the first part, dated June 6, 1865, to the committee of said church, as follows: —

"1. As a place of public worship. For the accommodation of a Sabbath-school. For other religious business meetings of said society. For lectures, fairs, festivals, and exhibitions, all of a moral character, as means of raising money for religious and benevolent objects. For general meetings of Baptist associations and other religious assemblies. And it shall not be used for any other purpose whatsoever.

"2. The pastor of said church and congregation shall be elected, and may be dismissed, by the majority of the members of the church. All persons who do now, or shall hereafter, for a period of three consecutive months, contribute by pew-rents or otherwise towards the payment of church expenses, shall, so long as said contribution shall continue, be considered members of the congregation, entitled to the same vote as members of the church in the election of trustees, clerk, and treasurer, and in all matters pertaining to its temporalities. Provided, that individuals not thus qualified may at any time be admitted as members of the congregation by a majority of the church and congregation. Provided also, that a majority of all the members composing the church and

congregation, for good cause shown, may exclude any member of the congregation from all participation in its proceedings.

"3. No contributions shall be taken up on the Sabbath-day for the use of the church and congregation, in any respect whatsoever. Provided that this restriction shall not be construed so as to prevent the raising of money for such use, in any other mode, which may be adopted by said society or their trustees, nor to prevent occasional or stated collections, in the ordinary mode, for missionary, Sabbath-school, and other charitable purposes.

"4. Neither the church, nor the church and congregation, nor both united, shall contract or owe at any one time a debt or debts exceeding in the aggregate two thousand dollars.

"5. The office of pastor shall not be allowed to remain vacant at any one time for more than eighteen months.

"6. The church and congregation shall not suffer their board of trustees to become extinct by dissolution of their society or otherwise.

"7. They shall not suffer said lot and building to pass out of their own possession.

"8. If the said church and congregation shall hereafter allow said house to be used for any other purpose than those prescribed in the first foregoing conditions, or if they shall in any way disregard or violate any of the foregoing provisions, then, in that case, the title and property of said lot and church edifice shall be forfeited, and the property shall revert to me, or in case of my decease, to such of my heirs as shall be at the time of said revision, members of the Baptist church in good standing.

"9. But in case the said church and congregation shall not hereafter violate or disregard any of the conditions of the trust, then the said lot and building shall forever remain in trust, as aforesaid, for the uses of said church and congregation, and all claims by me or my heirs on account of any moneys expended therefor or thereon, heretofore or hereafter, shall be forever cancelled."

Several years' experience has vindicated the wisdom and propriety of these conditions, and though unusual in Baptist, or perhaps any other, churches, their influence has been most salutary.

The project of visiting foreign countries, especially the land of Palestine, had for some time occupied Mr. Kendall's mind. With the double motive of acquainting himself by actual observation with the lands of the Bible, that he might impart instruction to his Sunday-school class, and of improving his health, he sailed for Europe, in the *Scotia*, June 27, 1866, his daughter,

Mrs. William Stickney, her husband and son accompanying him. To many of his friends, this undertaking, in view of his great age — seventy-seven years — and his feeble health, seemed hazardous; while others, who knew him better, prophesied beneficial results from it.

The good ship, after a very rapid passage of eight days and three hours, landed her passengers at Queenstown on the evening of the 5th of July.

The nation's birth-day was celebrated on board ship with all due ceremony and enthusiasm. The morning was glorious. A fresh breeze from the northwest filled the canvas and sent the ship leaping at the rate of sixteen knots the hour. The passage had thus far been unprecedentedly short, and as we expected the next day to tread the soil of the Emerald Isle, all hearts were light and prepared to enter enthusiastically upon the celebration of the day.

The stars and stripes waved from the mast-head, and the national colors of Columbia and Albion in loving embrace decorated the cabin.

After dinner the company were called to order, and Mr. Kendall was chosen to preside. He came up from his state-room and said, with Neptune's permission, he would accept the honor, and endeavor to perform the duties of the place assigned him. He remained in the cabin but a few minutes, however, and again sought his state-room. Toasts, and speeches, and champagne, the latter liberally furnished by the Captain, enlivened the patriotic company for an hour; and, exhilarated by proud memories of the land we had left behind us, and pleasant anticipations of that we were approaching, the company separated, with three hearty cheers for Captain Judkins and his noble ship.

The following letter from Paris, written by Mr. Kendall to his pastor in Washington, tells the story of the travellers' adventures up to its date.

PARIS, August 25, 1866.

REV. T. R. HOWLETT: —

MY DEAR BROTHER, — Since we left the shores of America we have seen much to admire in the works of the great Creator and of his creature, man. The boundless ocean with its restless waves, the hills and lakes of Ireland and Scotland, the hills and dales of England, and the plains of France, lead the devout mind to the contemplation of the power and goodness of God, who has so diversified this beautiful world

as to prepare it not only to supply the wants, but also to gratify the tastes and minister to the pleasures of his earthly children. In the silent memorials of antiquity, and the rude Irish hut occupied by human beings in common with beasts and fowls, we are forced to contemplate the degradation to which man sunk himself by transgressing the laws of his nature; and in the ruined structures of barbaric ages we see him gradually redeeming himself by the aid of a Christianity not yet fully understood, and not at all appreciated in its most glorious attributes. It is quite remarkable that during the dark ages the religion of Christ was universally recognized, as attested by inscriptions upon tombs, palaces, and ruins still existing, when history informs us that at the same time its professors were strangers to all its loving precepts, and went forth to plunder and kill in the name of the Redeemer. And do we not still behold a remnant of the same infatuation even in our times, when Christian nations go to war with each other; each calling on God to aid them in the bloody strife?

Our first Sabbath on this side of the ocean was spent in the city of Cork, in Ireland. On inquiring for a Baptist church, we were told that there was now none in the city; that some years ago there was one in a flourishing condition, but their pastor left them in consequence of some difficulty; that they had never employed another; that their house of worship was dilapidated, and that now there were probably not ten Baptists in the city.

Our second Sabbath was spent in Dublin, where there are several Baptist churches. We attended service in "The Tabernacle"; a singular building for a church, having three galleries around three sides, with a pulpit projecting from the level of the second gallery. The service consisted of congregational singing led by the pastor, prayers, reading a chapter from the Bible with a running commentary thereon, and a repetition of the same course at night, but no regular sermon, — the whole being rather dull. The house would hold, I suppose, two thousand; but there were not five hundred in attendance.

Our third Sabbath was spent in Glasgow, Scotland, where there are several Baptist churches. We heard an excellent sermon from a young man named Medhurst. Observing the communion table set, we remained after the congregation was dismissed, and gladly accepted an invitation to participate; the pastor announcing that we were from Washington, in the United States. On the conclusion of the ceremony, the preacher and some of the elders clustered around us, and we had quite an agreeable conversation. On inquiring about their Sabbath-school, we were told that they had only a ragged school, to which the members of the church did not send their own children!

The difference between their service and ours is, that in theirs the invocation is omitted, the singing is altogether congregational, and the congregation is dismissed immediately after the close of the sermon.

Our fourth Sabbath was spent in Edinburgh. It was a wet day, and having no knowledge of the Baptist churches, Mr. Stickney went in the morning to hear Dr. Candlish, but was disappointed, and in the afternoon we all heard Dr. Lee, — both Presbyterians.

Our fifth Sabbath was also spent in Edinburgh, and having learned that there were several Baptist churches in the city, we sought them out. In the morning we heard a good sermon from a Mr. Watson, who stated in his discourse that he had been fifty years a preacher of the gospel, and twenty the pastor of that church. Here also we partook of the sacrament ; at its close were introduced to the pastor, and were treated very kindly. The service was like ours, with the omission of the invocation, and we were surprised to hear an organ and a choir.

In the afternoon we went to another Baptist church and heard a similar service, except that there was no organ, and the singing was altogether congregational. Here also the communion table was set, but we did not remain. The Scotch Baptists commune every Sabbath.

In general, no contributions are taken up by any denomination in Edinburgh during the services ; but they have conspicuous boxes in the vestibules of their churches, into which contributors drop their offerings unsolicited.

On inquiring about their Sabbath-schools, we were told they were suspended during the hot season, — a season so cold to us that we found it necessary for our comfort to have a fire in our parlor, every day after the first, during our stay in Edinburgh.

The Presbyterian is the predominant religious denomination in Scotland ; but it is divided into two classes, one the government church, supported by a general tax, the other "the Free Church," supported by voluntary contributions. But they are not the Presbyterians of John Knox's time. We visited Knox's house, and saw the window through which he preached to crowds in the streets. We saw pulpits, mere boxes of boards, still preserved, from which he addressed multitudes, standing in the old Catholic cathedrals. All is changed. The old cathedrals are now used as Presbyterian places of worship, having in some instances been divided by partitions into two or more apartments. We visited one in Edinburgh where three Presbyterian societies worship in separate apartments, each abundantly capacious, under the same old roof. In Knox's time they had no seats. Now the seats are generally straight-backed, uncushioned slips ; and they have no organs. On my asking one of our guides why they did not have organs, she replied she did not know, unless it was because the Catholics had them. This prejudice is gradually giving way to the enlightenment of our age, and we were told

they now began to have organs in cases where the societies unanimously desired it. But while these Presbyterian societies still maintain some of the prejudices of John Knox's time, they have become, perhaps, more exclusive than the Catholics or Episcopalians ever were. In some of their churches, a stranger cannot enter without a ticket previously procured. In most of them there are printed notices requesting strangers not to enter the audience room till after the first prayer. We were early at Dr. Lee's church, and, in addition to the placard notice, received a special warning ; but as it was raining, and there was no probability that the faithful would be out in numbers, a special dispensation was, after some delay, extended to us, and we were shown to seats before the commencement of the service.

These Presbyterians are also gradually falling into the formalism of the Episcopal service, having their printed prayers and lessons for each Sabbath in the month. We found in the slips of Dr. Lee's church a prayer-book compiled by himself, containing morning and evening lessons for every Sabbath in the year.

Desirous of witnessing the ceremonies and displays on the 15th instant, the birth-day of Napoleon I., we came to Paris direct from Edinburgh, without passing through London, and here we spent our sixth Sabbath in Europe. We attended divine service in the American chapel, and heard an ordinary sermon from a clergyman from Detroit. The services were of a mongrel character, half Episcopalian and half Presbyterian. The organ was played wretchedly, with long voluntaries of opera music between the stanzas, and the choir's voices, not strong at the best, were nearly drowned by its sound.

Our seventh Sabbath in Europe was spent in this city. I presume there is not a Baptist church in Paris, and if there were, its services would be little edifying to us who are so little conversant with the French language. We therefore spent most of the day in our rooms, not without soul-communion with our Christian brothers and sisters beyond the ocean. We have neither seen nor heard anything since we left home to make us think more lightly of our dearly beloved Calvary Baptist Church. On the contrary, we have seen much to attach us more strongly to its pastor, its choir, its prayer-meetings, general and special, its Sabbath-school, and to its members. So far as we can judge, it is far ahead of anything we have yet met with among the Baptists of Europe. More and more, as we become farther separated from it by distance and time, do we appreciate the charm of that harmony which has existed among its members from its first institution, and the more earnestly do we pray for its continuance. Love is the essence of Christianity, — love of God, love of Christ, love of the Church, love of its members, love of our neighbors, and, if we would "be perfect as God is perfect," even love for our

enemies. It is no part of the Christian to plead our natural infirmities and temperament as an excuse for a want of self-control and a failure in the performance of duties enjoined upon us by the word of God. The want of self-control is itself a sin, and if it be habitual in us, we have no right to consider ourselves Christians.

How often and how emphatically is love of the brethren inculcated by Christ and his Apostles as an essential characteristic of the true, Christian ! How emphatically does St. Paul warn the faithful against wrangling and excited discussions of any sort ! He knew and we know, that the spirit of love, as well of God as of man, flies from the bosom, whether of the church or of its members, which becomes agitated by angry discussions. Hence it is, that we are commanded to suffer wrong, whether of act or imputation, rather than expel the spirit of love from our hearts, and aid in expelling it from the bosom of the church.

Let us never forget these facts and these teachings in their application to ourselves individually, and to the Calvary Baptist Church as a body. It is the spirit of harmony and love which has made it what it is, and that spirit only can maintain and extend its usefulness. Let each member examine himself or herself, and with jealous care guard against the indulgence of those infirmities of temper, of ambition, of prejudice, of pride of opinion, which more or less cling around every human heart, and too often influence the words and actions of the best of men. To avoid, as far as may be, occasions calling into action these human infirmities, let us not indulge in useless discussions or bring into the church topics not connected with its duties or interests as a body. Our one great instrument for good is our church itself, composed of an united band of Christians. Around that, and the means of building it up, let us cluster with loving hearts and ready hands. There are many outside objects of benevolence, requiring the aid of such of us as have time or means to devote to them. Let all such be left to our individual sense of duty, lest by bringing them into the church they meet there differences of opinion, and cause excited discussions and angry feelings, chilling our Christian ardor and giving pain to pious hearts.

If these suggestions shall seem to be unnecessary and untimely, I have no excuse for making them other than an anxiety too strong to be repressed, that the Calvary Baptist Church may continue to be an example to the world of a band of professing Christians who live their religion, as well among themselves as in their intercourse, collectively and individually, with the world around them.

I am happy to say that my health has greatly improved, and that Mr. and Mrs. Stickney and Willie are in excellent health. We enjoy the glories of art with which we are surrounded, frequently dashed however, with the reflection that the labor of millions has been oppressively taxed

to bring them into existence, and that to a very great extent they are but monuments of human pride and ambition. But I have not time to follow out this train of thought now.

Within a week we expect to leave for Switzerland, and thence, after satisfying our curiosity, pass over into Northern Italy.

Please say to my brothers and sisters of the church that I should be much gratified to hear from them or any one of them, and that my address will for the present be Florence, Italy.

We shall now for a long time be among people whose language we do not understand, and with whose religion we do not sympathize. Pray for us that we may find a substitute for the privation in a closer communion in spirit with our God and Saviour, and with our unseen brothers and sisters of our beloved church.

Your friend,

AMOS KENDALL.

As it is impossible to give details of our trip, whose incidents would fill a volume, suffice it to say, that we visited the most interesting portions of Ireland, Scotland, and England, France, Switzerland, and Italy ; going from Naples to Alexandria, Cairo, the Red Sea, Joppa, Jerusalem, Dead Sea, Bethlehem, Samaria, Beyrout, Damascus, Cyprus, Rhodes, Smyrna, Ephesus, Athens, Constantinople, Pesth, Vienna, Munich, Prague, Dresden, Wittenberg, Berlin, Brunswick, Amsterdam, Antwerp, and Brussels ; again to Paris, thence to Lyons and the principal cities in the south of France, the Pyrenees, and back to Paris, London, and Liverpool, where we took passage on the Persia, and arrived in New York the 17th of October, 1867, after a passage of eleven days, and an absence from home of a little more than fifteen months.

During all our journeyings, which sometimes involved hardship and fatigue, Mr. Kendall proved equal to every emergency, and often referred to himself as the youngest of the party.

While the rest of us had assistance in climbing the steep and rocky sides of the crater of Vesuvius, Mr. Kendall disdained all offers of aid. The ball on St. Peter's at Rome, the head of the Bavarian statue at Munich, the tiresome ascent to Wartberg Castle, the *mer de glace*, excursions among the Alps and Pyrenees, the fatiguing journeys on horseback in Palestine, the sleeping in tents within view of Bedouin robbers, the daily visits to the Exposition in Paris, — none of these dangers or difficulties daunted him. With a light heart and buoyant spirits he entered into the full enjoyment of the tour; returning home with invigorated health, and laden with rich treasures of knowledge.

Soon after his arrival in Washington, the members of the church he so much loved gave him a cordial reception; congratulating him and themselves upon his safe return.

With unabated zeal he renewed his labors with them, striving by words and example to elevate the standard of Christian character, and exhorting the members to still greater fidelity in their duties.

A new calamity awaited him. Sunday morning, December 15, 1867, while the family at Kendall Green were preparing to go to Sunday-school, the pastor made his appearance, bringing the sad news that our beautiful temple of worship was in ruins; having been destroyed by fire during the night.

Joy was turned into mourning, but no murmur was heard. Mr. Kendall regarded the disaster as a chastisement for the overweening pride of the members of the church in their beautiful edifice.

In a letter to his former pastor, written a few days after the fire, Mr. Kendall said : —

"We are literally overwhelmed with public sympathy. Every principal Protestant church in the city — Baptist, Presbyterian, Methodist, and Lutheran, (the Episcopalian only excepted) — sent us messages of condolence with offers to share with us their places of worship, — most of them while the flames were still raging.

"Last evening our people assembled in the lecture room of Dr. Butler's church. They met in gloom, but separated in smiles. It would have done your heart good to see how a few words of cheer changed the aspect of this large assemblage. They resolved unanimously to restore their lost edifice with all practicable despatch; and, on adjournment, afforded another example of the difficulty our people have in separating when once they get together.

"Instead of a people met together to mourn over a great calamity, you might have taken them to be a joyous party met to celebrate the happy accomplishment of a glorious enterprise.

"Before this late calamity I began to feel that I would like to be at rest. Now I feel that my work on earth is not yet done, though a conscious gradual failing of my physical and mental powers admonishes me that what I would do I must do quickly."

The following is extracted from the account of the fire as given by the "Chronicle" of Monday, December 16th.

"The beautiful edifice which the members of the Society and others had viewed with a commendable pride is now in ruins, — the tower and walls, still graceful in their crumbling condition, alone remaining.

"The outside walls are coated with ice, while the branches of the surrounding trees glisten in their icy coverings. The dial of the clock remains intact, with the hands indicating half-past four.

"The fire is believed to have originated in the wood work adjoining the flues.

"The sexton, after getting the fires under good headway in the furnaces, left the building at one o'clock in the morning. About three o'clock the fire was discovered by a policeman, issuing from the windows and tower. The weather was intensely cold, and a driving snow-storm was prevailing."

Nothing was saved from the flames. The grand organ in the gallery, the pulpit furniture, Sunday-school organ, banners, library, — all were utterly destroyed.

The insurance of upwards of $ 50,000 was promptly paid, and the work of reconstruction energetically begun. In this, as in the former enterprise, Mr. Kendall was the leading spirit, though cordially sustained by the membership.

In a letter of May 5th, 1868, he wrote : —

"We are all in usual health; but I am made more sensible from day to day that my race on earth is nearly run. Not only is memory sadly impaired, but eyesight and hearing are gradually failing me. I would gladly live to finish some things undertaken and not yet completed, but whenever it is God's will, I am ready to go. Death has no terrors for me, not because of my fitness for heaven, but because of the mercy of God and the redeeming sacrifice of his Son.

"Our burnt church is rising from its ruins, and we hope to see it renewed in all its beauty within the present year."

In the autumn of 1868, Mr. Kendall, with his household, removed from Kendall Green to the city. In a letter of November 3d, of that year, he said : "We have left the country, and are now living in a rented house, until one building by Mr. Stickney shall be finished. I yielded to this change with reluctance, and chiefly because it will enable us better to serve the cause of religion in our church and Sabbath-school." Referring to his health in the same letter he continues : "My poor walking machine is wearing out by constant use and must soon tumble to pieces. Sometimes I feel as if I should like to be disembodied, that I might get rid

of the grossness which is inherent in flesh and blood, and love with a pure love, and worship with a pure devotion."

Notwithstanding his feebleness, Mr. Kendall relaxed none of his interest in the church and Sunday-school. A lesson in the latter, having for its subject the future condition of children, Mr. Kendall prepared and had printed the following views on the subject : —

LITTLE CHILDREN.

THEIR PLACE IN THE PLAN OF REDEMPTION.

In all ages of the Christian Church, the minds of its members have been much exercised in relation to the fate of little children who die before they are able to discriminate between right and wrong. It appears to me the whole difficulty has arisen from an imperfect view of the scope and beauty of the Christian system.

The following propositions appear to me to be clearly set forth in the New Testament : —

First. The redemption by Christ was as comprehensive in its spiritual effects as the sin of Adam, and perfectly parallel thereto.

Second. That young children are fit subjects for heaven.

In support of the first proposition, I quote the following passages of Scripture, namely : —

JOHN i. 29. "The next day John seeth Jesus coming unto him, and saith, Behold the Lamb of God, which taketh away the sin of the world."

JOHN iii. 17. "For God sent not his Son into the world to condemn the world; but that the world through him might be saved."

JOHN vi. 33. "For the bread of God is he that cometh down from heaven, and giveth life unto the world."

JOHN xii. 47. "And if any man hear my words, and believe not, I judge him not; for I came not to judge the world, but to save the world."

1 JOHN ii. 1, 2. "My little children, these things write I unto you, that ye sin not. And if any man sin, we have an advocate with the Father, Jesus Christ, the righteous; and he is the propitiation for our sins; and not for our's only, but also for the sins of the whole world."

1 JOHN iv. 14. "And we have seen and do testify that the Father sent the Son to be the Saviour of the world."

The word _world_, in all these passages, means _mankind_, — all the descendants of Adam; and lest some constructive limitation should be put upon the word, the Apostle John declares that the propitiation was not for the sins of believers only, but also for the sins of the _whole world_, — of the whole race of Adam, who were involved in the consequences of his transgression.

In direct confirmation of this view, I quote the following passages, namely : —

1 CORINTHIANS xv. 21, 22. "For since by man came death, by man came also the resurrection of the dead. For as in Adam all die, even so in Christ shall all be made alive."

ROMANS v. 18, 19. "Therefore as by the offence of one judgment came upon all men to condemnation; even so by the righteousness of one the free gift came upon all men unto justification of life. For as by one man's disobedience many were made sinners, so by the obedience of one shall many be made righteous."

The words _all_ in the eighteenth verse, and _many_ in the nineteenth, mean the same thing, inasmuch as Adam's disobedience involved _all_ men, and the phraseology in the latter instance was used to illustrate the idea that the effect of Christ's redemption is commensurate with the effect of Adam's disobedience.

That young children are fit subjects for heaven is proved by the following passages of Scripture, namely : —

MATTHEW xviii. 2 – 4, 10, 11. "And Jesus called a little child unto him, and set him in the midst of them, and said, Verily I say unto you, Except ye be converted, and become as little children, ye shall not enter into the kingdom of heaven. Whosoever therefore shall humble himself as this little child, the same is greatest in the kingdom of heaven. . . . . Take heed that ye despise not one of these little ones; for I say unto you, That in heaven their angels do always behold the face of my Father which is in heaven. For the Son of man is come to save that which was lost."

Then follows the parable of the lost sheep.

MARK x. 13 – 16. "And they brought young children to him, that he should touch them; and his disciples rebuked those that brought them. But when Jesus saw it, he was much displeased, and said unto them, Suffer the little children to come unto me, and forbid them not; for of such is the kingdom of God. Verily I say unto you, Whosoever shall not receive the kingdom of God as a little child, he shall not enter therein. And he took them up in his arms, put his hands upon them, and blessed them."

LUKE ix. 47, 48. "And Jesus perceiving the thought of their heart, took a child, and set him by him, and said unto them, Whosoever shall receive this child in my name receiveth me; and whosoever shall receive me, receiveth him that sent me; for he that is least among you all, the same shall be great."

LUKE xviii. 15 – 17. "And they brought unto him also infants, that he would touch them; but when his disciples saw it, they rebuked them. But Jesus called them unto him, and said, Suffer little children to come unto me, and forbid them not; for of such is the kingdom of God. Verily I say unto you, Whosoever shall not receive the kingdom of God as a little child shall in no wise enter therein."

I cannot read these passages of Scripture without the conviction that infants are fit subjects for heaven. Were it not so, is it credible that

Christ would have selected them as models for his adult followers? He does not tell his disciples that they must be more harmless, more innocent, or more holy, but simply "*as* little children," — "*as a little child* "; and in Luke ix. 48, he tells them that, "Whosoever shall receive *this* child"—the child sitting by him—"in my name receiveth me; and whosoever shall receive me receiveth him that sent me." And is it possible that a child fit to be the representative of Christ himself, is not fit for heaven?

But it may be asked how the children of sinful parents are made fit for heaven. I answer, by the mercy of God, through the atonement by Christ. Little children compose that *world* for which Christ died. Who is there of all the human race that has not been a child, — such a child as Jesus set beside him; such a child as he took in his arms and blessed; such a child as might have been a pattern of that innocent faith and humility necessary to enable adults to reach the kingdom of heaven? Thus did Christ redeem all the little children, and through them the whole world, from all the spiritual consequences of Adam's transgression. It is thus that, "as in Adam all die, so in Christ shall all be made alive." It is thus that, "as by the offence of one, judgment came upon all men to condemnation; even so by the righteousness of one, the free gift came upon all men unto justification of life."

If this view of the subject be correct, all children, through the re demption by Christ and the mercy of God, come into the world as sinless as Adam was when he came from the hands of the Creator. As with Adam, so it is with them; they are responsible and punishable for their own sins only. They are born within Christ's fold, and they stray from it only when they commit their first sin. Until they sin, they are of " the ninety and nine which went not astray." And if, having sinned, they sincerely repent and ask forgiveness, they are forgiven and restored to the fold, "not seven times only, but seventy times seven."

This view of the universality of redemption reconciles all difficulties in relation to the spiritual condition of infants and to the justice of God. That a good being should bring creatures into existence just to damn them to eternal misery, is a thought abhorrent to the human mind. How they could be saved from that fate was, and still is, a problem with those who consider infants responsible for Adam's transgression. An expedient to save them was thought to be found, soon after the Apostolic age, in baptism, not by sprinkling, but by immersion. It was believed that baptism literally and truly washed away all sin, and that baptized persons, old or young, were fit to enter heaven as soon as they came out of the water. So, to insure heaven to little children, if they should happen to die in infancy, the practice of baptizing them was introduced. Modern Protestants have discarded the idea that baptism washes away sin, or of

itself makes any change in the spiritual condition of the infant or the adult. In the adult it is esteemed, at least by Baptists, to be an act of obedience to the commands of Christ, and a rite of initiation into the visible Church. Other Protestant denominations, while rejecting the reason in which infant baptism originated, still profess to retain the practice, thus rendering the rite, to say the least of it, wholly unmeaning and useless.

Thank God, little children do not need baptism, or even repentance, to fit them for heaven. Washed by the blood of Christ from the taint of Adam's transgression, they are fit to be taken at once into the Saviour's arms and be forever blest. In the annunciation that "the seed of the woman shall bruise the serpent's head," our erring first parents were comforted by the assurance that the great enemy of their race had failed in his object, that provision had already been made to redeem their posterity from the spiritual death entailed by their sin, that every one of their descendants should be held responsible, not for the sins of his ancestors, one or many, but for his own sins only, committed after he became capable of discriminating between right and wrong.

See how, giving the most natural construction to the simple language of the Bible, the justice of God is vindicated; his character illustrated; the responsibilities of man defined; the difficulties in this subject, which have bewildered the human mind for ages, removed; the comprehensiveness of the atonement made plain; and the beauty of the Christian system of religion commended to the intelligent mind. But it does not follow that all men will be saved because all children are born redeemed. As God made the man, so Christ makes the infant, sinless, but prone to sin. As Adam fell, so may the infant when he becomes a man, or arrives at the age of moral responsibility. But in the language of St. John, if any of Christ's little children sin, they "have an advocate with the Father," who, upon repentance, is a propitiation for their sins, and upon his intercession they will be restored to the Saviour's fold.

How, then, should we treat little children in our Sabbath-schools? Shall we teach them that they are heirs of damnation for Adam's sin, and can reach heaven only by repentance for sins they never committed? Or shall we treat them as Christ did, take them to our arms, tell them that they are the redeemed lambs of his flock, and teach their expanding minds to look to him as their kind friend and Saviour, who has died that they might live, and who alone has redeemed them from the spiritual consequences of Adam's sin; and who alone can procure for them the pardon of their own sins, and secure for them a happy immortality in the world to come.

A TEACHER

In the Calvary Baptist Sunday-school, Washington, D. C.

In January, 1869, he wrote:—

"My own health is very feeble and my strength failing. My right eye and ear are almost useless, and my left failing. Every night I sleep soundly about three or four hours, when I wake up in much distress, and have no more sound sleep that night.

The doctors say the trouble is produced by imperfect digestion. It produces fever and headache, which pass away by breakfast time, and in general I feel pretty well until the next night. I apprehend my disease is incurable, being *old age*. We have weekly meetings at our house of the teachers of our Sabbath-school, which are very pleasant and instructive. One of them has been held this evening, since I commenced this letter. Our school is increasing in numbers and interest. The spirit of God seems to be among the scholars and also in the congregation. Five or six have professed Christ, and are ready to be buried in baptism, and we hope that the work has but just begun."

In February, 1869, he wrote:—

"There is little ground of hopefulness left for me in *this* life; and, though naturally cheerful, I cannot sometimes look back without sadness. How many relatives and associates have gone before me, and how few are left! My father and mother had twelve children. Parents and nine of the children are dead.

"My first marriage was into a family consisting of a father, mother, four sons, and three daughters. They are all dead. My second marriage was into a family consisting of a father, mother, two sons, and two daughters. They are all dead. I have had two wives, five sons, and nine daughters. The wives and the sons are all gone, and only four daughters are left. Of upwards of twenty men who held cabinet appointments under General Jackson and Mr. Van Buren, I am the only one left. I seem like one standing alone among the dead on the battle field of life, while generation after generation come marching before me. I too must soon lie among the dead around me, and the world will still march thoughtlessly onward.

"In spite of hope and faith, there is something sad in the thought that the past pleasures of life cannot be repeated or replaced, while before one is only that shadowy world opened to us by revelation. Material nature teaches only that we must die; that all is change; that life is produced and maintained by death, and death by life; that there is nothing fixed and eternal unless it be matter, in ever-changing forms, and the incomprehensible Mind which has imposed its laws. In that gospel which 'brought life and immortality to light,' and in that only, can be found a substitute for those earthly enjoyments which can return no more. And in its precepts are found those moral rules which,

if followed by rulers and people, would indeed produce 'peace on earth'; while discord, crime, and bloodshed, in nations and among nations, prevail just in a degree that those rules are violated or disregarded. This is a great truth which ought to be taught in every school and every college as well as the pulpit.

"The end with me cannot be far distant."

DONATION TO THE COLUMBIAN COLLEGE.

WASHINGTON, February 4, 1869.

To the Board of Trustees of the Columbian College:—

GENTLEMEN, — On behalf of the Calvary Baptist Church of the city of Washington, I tender you six thousand dollars to purchase a classical scholarship in your institution, upon the following conditions:—

First. That said church shall be entitled to perpetual representation in the election of the board of trustees of said college.

Secondly. That the trustees of public schools in the city of Washington in the District of Columbia, and their successors by whatever name they may be called, shall have the perpetual privilege of selecting from said schools one pupil annually to fill said scholarship; and the pupils so selected shall each be entitled to instruction in said college for the term of six years, free of charge for tuition, use of library and apparatus, or for any other privilege allowed to paying students of the same grade.

On receiving official notice of the acceptance of the foregoing proposition with the conditions annexed, by your board, I shall be prepared to pay to their order the proffered consideration of six thousand dollars.

With profound respect, your obedient servant,

AMOS KENDALL.

Mr. Kendall was not more jealous of his own honor than he was of the good name of General Jackson, and he never failed to repel with burning words the slightest imputation upon the character of the old hero, by whomsoever uttered. An article in the "National Intelligencer," containing a disparaging allusion to the General, was the occasion of the following:—

WASHINGTON, April 27, 1869.

EDITORS OF THE NATIONAL INTELLIGENCER:—Please discontinue your paper sent to my address at 443 11th Street.

I know of no more fitting way to express my indignation at your infamous attack upon the character of General Jackson in this day's issue. Can no degree of integrity, patriotism, and public service save the memory of the illustrious dead from the jackals of a licentious press?

Yours, etc.,

AMOS KENDALL.

Mr. Kendall was seldom idle. Reading or writing occupied his time indoors. The Bible was consulted and studied in these latter days of his life more than all other books together, and although he wrote with difficulty, his pen was always within reach, and his habit was to write out his ideas upon any subject that interested him, religious or political, for future reference and consideration.

A few days before leaving for the North, in 1869, he penned the following thoughts upon

MAN'S NATURE.

There is one God, and only one. Man was created by God. By means described or typified in the book of Genesis, human nature has become corrupt, so that the natural inclination of every human being born into the world is to violate the laws of God.

Obedience to the laws of God consists in a perfect morality and an entire submission to his will.

By reason of the corruption of man's nature, perfect morality and entire submission to God's will became practically impossible, and hence all mankind became sinners.

The mission of Christ had a two-fold object : First, to redeem all men from original sin, so that each should be responsible only for his own sins, and in this sense he died for all men. Secondly, to redeem every repentant sinner from the punishment due to sins actually committed by him. From these principles it results that all dying infants go to heaven, and adults are punished for their actual sins only.

Salvation is offered to all, not in mockery, but in sincerity and truth. The means by which all may obtain it are pointed out with equal clearness. It is optional with man to use those means or let them alone. God by his grace has given him power to will, and he is responsible for the use of that power.

God created the body of man, breathed into it the breath of life, surrounded it with an atmosphere capable of sustaining that life; gave it the power, by force of its own will, to rise from the earth or lie still, to continue to breathe or refuse to breathe, — to live or to die. So God has given man a soul; through his grace has diffused, as it were, an atmosphere around it, and endowed him with a perfect freedom of will to breathe it and live, or refuse to do so and die. As he has power to will a movement of his animal body, so he has power to control the action of his spirit. He can will to pray, just as he can will to walk. The power to do both is the gift of God. The will to do them is his own. Neither of them secures of itself any valuable result ; but both are only the means by which important results are brought about. "Ask,

and it shall be given you ; seek, and ye shall find ; knock, and it shall be opened unto you." God has given man power to will the asking, the seeking, and the knocking, as the means of receiving, of finding, and of being admitted ; and he has promised to give the good asked for and sought after, and an entrance into heaven in response to a proper use of those means. It is thus that "faith is the gift of God." It is thus that our heavenly Father "gives good things to them that ask him." He gives as the father gives bread to the child who asks for it. It is as free a gift as if bestowed without the asking.

God does not force his gifts, temporal or spiritual, on any one. He gives man physical powers, and leaves him at liberty to use them for good or for evil according to his own will. On the use he wills to make of those powers depends his temporal condition, whether in riches or in poverty, in honor or in infamy. He gives him the same freedom of will in spiritual matters, and in addition thereto lays down certain rules by the observance of which he may secure the favor of his Maker and everlasting happiness. He is not left to his own judgment as in temporal affairs ; but is told to *do this and live*, — to "believe and be baptized" ; to pray without ceasing ; to do good to his fellow-men ; to live in peace with all men ; to return good for evil ; not to resent injuries, etc., etc. Let him but observe these rules and he has the promise of God that he shall have abundant success in spiritual affairs, whatever may have been the result of following his own judgment in temporal matters.

On Sunday, July 11, 1869, the new church, having risen from its ashes, was rededicated in the presence of a vast congregation.

In his letter, dated July 31, 1869, to Henry Beard, the treasurer, proposing a donation of whatever sum was necessary to discharge all liabilities, Mr. Kendall wrote : —

"I enclose herein a check for $ 2,500, which I request you to place to the credit of the building fund, and I hold myself in readiness to meet any other demands actually incurred through the building committee. By thus relieving our society of all charge for the reconstruction of our house of worship, I hope to enable our brethren and sisters to enter upon the new career now opened to them with a more hopeful and determined spirit, — a spirit which shall stimulate them to make all needful sacrifices to maintain the efficient preaching of the gospel, and secure a more extended and salutary influence for our church. And while no further special grants must be expected from me, I am prepared to do my part in contributing the needful means to sustain the services of the sanctuary on a liberal and efficient scale.

"I expect to leave the city on Monday morning next, and be absent about three weeks. I hope the building committee will proceed at once to close up all unadjusted accounts, that all balances may be promptly paid.

Your brother in Christ,
AMOS KENDALL.

The advances by Mr. Kendall, on account of reconstruction, did not fall short of $15,000.

On Monday, the 2d of August, in company with his daughter, Mrs. Babcock, Mr. Kendall left for the North, hoping the change and travel would be beneficial. His rest at night had been much disturbed ; his food distressed him, and his nervous system was badly disordered.

He intended to visit his nephew, Andrew Kendall, in New York State, and if his health improved to go further East.

On the 6th of August he wrote the following letter, the last one the writer ever received from his pen : —

LEWIS, N. Y., August 6, 1869.

W. STICKNEY, ESQ. : —

MY DEAR SON, — We arrived here safely on Wednesday evening, having spent Monday night in New York, and Tuesday night at Whitehall. The journey this side of New York was far from pleasant, owing to delays and confusion on the railroads. The connections are such, that one cannot come from New York here in a day, without a night ride at one end of the line or the other. To get a trip down Lake Champlain by day, and avoid landing in the middle of the night, we remained over night at Whitehall, and leaving there at 11 A. M. on Wednesday, had a charming trip down the lake, and landed at an insignificant village called Westport, about 4 P. M. Thence we rode twelve miles in a primitive stage to a place called Elizabeth, and thence to this place, four miles, in a vehicle containing only ourselves, our trunks, the driver, and a small mail-bag. On our arrival we were kindly received by Mrs. Kendall, who informed us that her husband was down with his wagon at another landing waiting for us, and on casually hearing of our arrival he came home last evening.

Mrs. Guest remained with us all night in New York, and ticketed on Tuesday morning for Buffalo ; but through misinformation at Albany went on with us to Troy, whence we saw her start for Buffalo about 5 P. M., expecting to arrive next morning.

Andrew Kendall and his wife seem to be living very comfortably in a large new house, the finest in the place ; which, however, contains only

about half a dozen, — the village being nothing more than the centre of a country township.

It is quite cold here, and I took some cold yesterday, and had a bad night. I was well enough after breakfast this morning to take a ride, wrapped up in overcoat, shawl, and buffalo robe, and none too warm. If the weather does not improve, our stay here will be short.

Mallie joins me in love to brothers, sisters, nephew, and nieces, the Stickneys and the Foxes.

Affectionately, your father,
AMOS KENDALL.

WASHINGTON, D. C.

His cold so affected him, that he determined to return home. He arrived in Washington, Saturday, the 14th of August, greatly prostrated, and immediately took his bed. As his own household were making preparations to move to their new residence, Mr. Kendall went immediately to the house of his son-in-law, Mr. Fox.

Monday, the 16th, was his eightieth birthday. He was confined to his room, and a part of the time to his bed for three weeks, when he recovered sufficiently to join his household at their new residence. He was assisted from the carriage to his room in the second story, from which he never descended.

For three months he patiently but hopefully looked forward to the termination of his sufferings. The smallest quantity of food, and that of the most digestible character, caused him great distress. He remarked to the writer at this time, that but for the terrible sin of suicide he would abstain entirely from food, and thus hasten the end. His four daughters were constant and faithful in ministering to his comfort. His pastor, Rev. J. W. Parker, made frequent visits, which afforded him great consolation. He looked upon death as very near, but never expressed a regret. His only anxiety was in reference to the church, which was dearer to him than life. That the members would set a holy example, be faithful in all their duties, cultivate brotherly love, sustain their pastor, and by godly lives honor their Master, was the theme of his conversation and his constant prayer.

Events of his early and middle life were fresh in his mind. He alluded frequently to his relations with General Jackson, and regretted he had never completed the Life of that great man. In a letter to the writer in 1862, he said : —

"I have been reading Parton's Life of Jackson. It is a caricature of the noble old hero, and a libel upon his friends. It causes me to reproach myself for not finishing my work. I *must* do it with such means as I have. This is my seventy-third birthday; shall I ever see another? God only knows, and his will be done. I pray, however, that he will spare me and give me strength until I can do justice to my great and good friend, not mine only, but the friend of our country and our race."

A few nights before his death, Mr. Kendall about midnight sent for the writer, who was sitting in the library below. Approaching his bedside, I saw that he had some important communication to make. His mind was clear, his manner impressive, and his voice distinct, as he said: —

"I have sent for you, Mr. Stickney, because I want the public to know the reasons why I never finished the Life of Jackson. The first was my poverty. I was too poor to collect information from all over the country. Second, every person, *with one exception*, who had promised material for the work, disappointed me. I could only write what I knew from personal knowledge."

This was the message that he had to deliver; but now as ever the subject of Jackson was a fruitful and pleasing theme to dwell upon. He continued: —

"General Jackson was as gentle as a lamb. I was very intimate with him, and never saw him in a passion, or heard him use a profane word; but I do not doubt that when aggravated by some gross insult, he did sometimes suffer his passion to get the mastery over him, for he was a man of very strong passions. The honest old giant opposed the Bank of the United States from principle purely, not on account of some little quarrel with a branch bank in Virginia, as stated by Parton. This author has written a *caricature* of the old General, giving him occasionally a little praise for things that every one praised him for, but generally slurring it over afterwards."

When asked if he wrote much of General Jackson's messages, he replied, "No, the old hero wrote the most of his own messages. I wrote nearly all of those portions of his messages connected with the Indians."

During no period of his sickness was Mr. Kendall's mind so active, and his conversational powers so remarkable, as during the last few days of his life. For hours continuously, to several members of his family, children and grandchildren, to officers of the institutions he had been connected with, and of the church he had served, he poured forth a stream of calm, collected, earnest instruc-

tion, that seemed marvellous as the emanation of a mind just breaking loose from its prison. His statements as to the doctrinal difficulties of the Christian revelation were specially discriminating. As to the source of our knowledge of spiritual truth, he said: —

"Yes, it is by *faith* we see spiritual things. What is all our knowledge, after all, but belief in what we *see*, or *hear*, or *imagine*? True knowledge brings us back to our childhood; all we know begins in what we believe from the testimony of others. My personal faith in the whole body of religious truth is as clear and assured as is a child's confidence in what is told him."

Alluding to the nature of God, referred to as Father, Son, and Holy Spirit, he remarked: —

"We feel the difference when we are baptized into the three names, though we cannot *comprehend* or even *apprehend* it."

Of the future spiritual world he said: —

"You know I am no enthusiast, but I am just as sure that the other world is real in its joys and honors as I am that this world is real; besides, that is more substantial and enduring than this."

On the use of property he said: —

"I hold that children have no legitimate right to anything more than a living and an education, during minority, out of the property of a father; and that it is his duty to look at *all* the claims God has imposed on him, in his varied social relations, in disposing of his accumulations. Among these, the *first* is his duty to provide for his own household; but this is only *one* among many. I believe, too, that all experience shows it to be best for a man of property to make his donations to objects of charity during his lifetime, that there be no dispute and disappointment over his gifts after he is gone, and that he may personally superintend their appropriation."

For a few days before his death, Mr. Kendall talked almost incessantly. Like Joshua of old, he gathered his household about his bed, and in the most earnest manner exhorted them to be faithful in all their Christian and moral obligations.

"Read the Bible," he said, "take that as your guide instead of the institutes of men; take *that*; that is all I ask of any one. I cannot be satisfied to keep silent so long as I have the power to speak. Read the Book for yourself, each one of you, *each one of you*; because each one of you, whether parent or child, is responsible to God."

To his grandson, W. S. Stickney, he said: —

"You have been a good child; be faithful. Do all God enables you to in his cause, not only in the Calvary Baptist Church, but *everywhere*; for this religion is not confined to persons or individuals; but *whatever* your duty is, I hope you may ever be able to perform it. In the first place, comply with all your moral duties in the Old and New Testaments; fulfil your duties to your fellow-men; do not deceive them for any purpose, but go through life an honest man, as your grandfather has endeavored to do. What I would add to that is Christian faith; which is the only assurance we can have of any immortality at all. Be true. Be useful and honest with your fellow-men. Be true and faithful to your profession. Do all you can in every proper way to promote Christ's kingdom on earth while you live. Be honest, go straightforward. There is one point upon which you cannot deviate, whatever you have belongs to your creditors, if you get into debt, rather than yourself. First satisfy them, conceal nothing; be direct and honest. Be honest, first and last. No man can be a true Christian who is not in all his transactions truthful and honest. If we cannot get along according to the principles of the Bible, we cannot get along at all."

His message to the Deaf-Mute and Columbian Colleges was: —

"Tell the friends of the colleges that I have entire, *entire* confidence in the official management of these institutions, and in their future success and usefulness. I might have given more to them; but it was not right that I should take the work from others who are able, and will prove willing, to aid."

For two or three days before his death, that event was momentarily expected. But there was no dimness of his mental vision. As he approached nearer the heavenly world, his face was irradiated by new light, and his words glowed with almost divine inspiration.

"All that will be required of me is submission to the will of God, whatever it may be, that when this call comes, whether it be to-night or at any other time, I may be ready for it; relying not on myself or anything I have done, but upon the righteousness of Christ. There is my reliance for immortality; not upon anything I have done in any way, but simple faith in him and his sufferings and redemption, which without any merit of mine, may be applicable to me, and give me a title to immortality in the presence of God and all holy beings. I shall be glad that all my brethren in the church should know it is not anything I have done for them, or anything else, on which I place the

slightest reliance for the future; but it is faith in Christ and his redemption. That is the faith in which I die. I am willing to live as long as God wills it; but my own desire would be to die. If God wills that I should survive, his will be done; I do not pray for it, nor can I say I desire it; but his will be done.

"I would say to the Calvary Baptist Church, it is my strong desire they should all live in unity and brotherly love; that they all perform their duties to themselves and their God, so as to prove the sincerity of their faith; that they should be examples of *true Christian faith*; that they should be examples of that spirit which belongs to unselfishness, willing to sacrifice anything; that they would look upon what I have done not as a gift from me, but as a gift from God, — a sacred charge; that they would show their thankfulness to God for what has been done for them; that they will preserve the gift, and profit by it, by showing in some practical manner their gratitude to God; that the whole church are tenants of God, not of me; that they may show their gratitude, not by empty words, but by contributing of their means to keep up the worship of God in that sanctuary perpetually."

For some months Mr. Kendall had been deliberating upon the best method of endowing two mission-schools connected with the Calvary Baptist Church. Perceiving his end so near, he doubted if he would be spared long enough to carry out his designs, which he communicated fully to the writer. For one of those missions, now known as Kendall Chapel, he had previously purchased a lot of ground and had erected upon it a commodious building. The other mission-school was then held in a rented room poorly adapted for the purpose.

A deed was at once prepared conveying Kendall Chapel and seventeen thousand dollars in bonds to six trustees, with instructions to devote seven thousand dollars to the purchase of another lot, and the erection of a chapel thereon; reserving the remaining ten thousand dollars as a perpetual fund, the interest of which should be applied for the support of the two schools. This deed he carefully examined and duly executed. This gift increased his contributions, on account of the two mission Sunday-schools, to twenty-five thousand dollars.

The Sunday night preceding his death he expressed a desire to have the two hymns beginning, "Jesus, lover of my soul," and "On Christ the solid rock I stand," sung in the room below.

The day before his death he said in broken sentences: —

"I die in peace with all my fellow-men, and love to all those who are faithful to their profession. I rely upon that Saviour, that Redeemer who has been provided for those who sincerely repent of their sins in life. I rely entirely upon him. I have been a sinner up to the last moment. My thoughts have been sinful, but I rely wholly upon that Saviour and his sufferings. I thank God he has given me my mind in these last moments. Though my expressions are broken, my mind is clear."

When asked by Doctor Samson if he had any directions to give respecting his funeral services, he replied : —

"I leave all that to the discretion of my family. You know my own preference to avoid ostentation. If a public service in the church will do good, let it be there. If anything in my life and experience as a Christian can benefit others, let it be stated."

When asked if he had any choice as to who should take part in the services, he said : —

"I cannot choose. I love all Christ's ministers, and feel a special attachment to my three pastors. I wish you, however," addressing himself to Doctor Samson, "as having known me the longest and being familiar with all my views, to make a statement of my Christian experience."

Turning to his weeping children, he continued : —

"I thank God he has given me strength to say what I have. I thank God he has allowed me to have my mind clear. All my children are around me, ready to render any service, all affectionate and kind. I thank God for it."

Friday morning, November 12, he asked that the inside shutters of his room might be opened that he might see the rising sun, at the same time turning his face towards the window which faces the east, and placing his hand under his head. The sky was painted in gorgeous colors. He gazed intently for a few moments at the glorious picture, and then faintly whispering, "How beautiful, how beautiful," closed his eyes, and calmly, gently breathed his last. The golden bowl was broken, and the spirit returned to God who gave it.

Impressive funeral services, attended by a large concourse, including Sunday-school scholars, deaf-mute students, and others, were held at the Calvary Baptist Church, Sunday afternoon, the 14th November, conducted by Drs. Samson, Parker, and Sunder-

land, and Rev. Mr. Howlett; after which, Mr. Kendall's remains were buried in the Glenwood Cemetery.

Resolutions of sympathy and respect by the City Council of Washington, the Calvary Baptist Church, the Deaf and Dumb Institution, Columbian College, and other organizations, attest the warm affection in which Mr. Kendall was held by those who knew him best.

From among the many letters of sympathy from Mr. Kendall's surviving friends we select the following from Professor Morse, who bears cheerful testimony to the skill and energy of Mr. Kendall in the management of his telegraph interests, and acknowledges his great obligation to him for the pecuniary benefit derived from his invention.

FROM PROFESSOR SAMUEL F. B. MORSE.

NEW YORK, November 12, 1869.

MY DEAR SIR, — Although prepared by recent notices in the papers to expect the sad news which a telegram, this moment received, announces to me of the death of my excellent, long-tried friend, Mr. Kendall, I confess that the intelligence has come with a shock which has quite unnerved me. I feel the loss of a *father* rather than of a brother in age, for he was one in whom I confided as a father, so sure was I of affectionate and sound advice.

Very slowly recovering my strength from my long confinement with my broken limb, I have only been able to reach my winter home in the city, but not to leave the house except for a very short drive in the Park.

My heart, if not my body, is with you all on this mournful occasion. Were it possible, most gladly would I be with you to pay my sincere respect to his memory by attending the funeral solemnities, but my physical condition forbids. I need not tell you how deeply I feel this sad bereavement. I am truly and severely bereaved in the loss of such a friend; a friend, indeed, upon whose faithfulness and unswerving integrity I have ever reposed with perfect confidence, — a confidence which has never been betrayed, and a friend to whose energy and skill in the conduct of the agency which I had confided to him, I owe (under God) the comparative comfort which a kind Providence has permitted me to enjoy in my advanced age.

When your first telegram was received, announcing the serious illness of Mr. Kendall and the prospect of his not living many days, I was particularly struck with your expression in giving an account of his state of mind, that with an unclouded intellect he had a "*faith triumphant.*"

These words are full of consolation; all other words fall into insignificance before them. We mourn not then for him. He is forever free from the sorrows and sufferings that afflicted him here, and we cannot doubt he is happy in the bosom of that precious Saviour whom he loved and delighted to honor, — in whose footsteps he trod in all the walks of a large-hearted benevolence.

I beg you, my dear sir, to present to all the members of the afflicted family the sincere condolence and sympathy of all my family, and believe me,

With sincere esteem, your obedient servant,

SAMUEL F. B. MORSE.

WILLIAM STICKNEY, Esq., Washington, D. C.

His protracted, useful, and eventful life is ended. Who can doubt that he received the welcome greeting, "Well done!"

APPENDIX.

OFFICIAL PAPERS IN CASE OF STOCKTON AND STOKES.

THE following extract is from a deposition given by General Jackson himself, in the case of Stockton and Stokes against us, and included in a statement of the case prepared by Mr. Kendall : —

"Deponent, at this time, perceiving that Major Barry's health was sinking and could not endure the labor of the office, which was greatly increased by the numerous calls of Congress, through their committees, found it necessary to relieve him of his duties; and a sea voyage being suggested as the best means of preserving his valuable life, deponent proposed to send him minister to Spain. Major Barry accepted the proposition with kindness, but agreed to remain in the office until deponent could find a fit and competent individual to fill it. Deponent at once turned his thoughts to Amos Kendall, the defendant, who had displayed eminent talents under the able heads of the Navy Department, and had done much in clearing that branch of the public service of all its existing impurities, and restoring it to order and system. The proposition was made to him to accept the Post-Office Department, and he was made acquainted with the arrangement which had been made with Major Barry.

"Mr. Kendall, the defendant, stated that he did not desire the office. He said his health was not good; that the situation of the Post-Office Department was such as to require great labor in restoring it to order, and he well knew, from past experience, that the retrenchment which was necessary to bring its expenditures within its means, could not be effected without exposing the agent to censure and abuse; that the office he then held was the height of his ambition; that it was reduced to system, and that his labors in it were light compared to those which were required in the Post-Office Department. Deponent requested him to think of the subject more maturely; and, after an earnest expression of the hope that he would yield in this instance to his wishes, asked him to call again the next day. At the next interview, deponent again urged upon Mr. Kendall the acceptance of this office, and endeavored to meet his objections by assurances that he overrated the difficulties of the office, and that his talents and energy would be as successful there as they had been in the Fourth Auditor's Office. Finally, at deponent's request, but with great reluctance, he agreed to accept the office, when Major Barry was appointed minister to Spain, and the vacancy was filled by Mr. Kendall, the defendant.

Deponent adds, that the offer of this appointment to Mr. Kendall was spontaneous on his part, without any inducement from any quarter."

Again we appeal to the deposition of General Jackson, expressing his opinion of our administration, from May, 1835, to March, 1837, when his term of office expired. He says: —

"And this deponent further says, that, as far as the official acts of the defendant came to his knowledge, he acted with the greatest impartiality in all cases. Deponent believes that the defendant was incapable of being acted upon improperly, either by friendship on the one side, or enmity on the other; and that he was too honest to allow politics to interfere with the strict rules of justice in his decisions. Judging the tree by its fruit, deponent can safely say, that he never knew any public man who exhibited the qualities of integrity, independence, and impartiality in a higher degree than the defendant.

"Deponent here again repeats his conviction, founded on a long acquaintance with the character of the defendant, that he was incapable of being swerved from the performance of duty by any personal feeling, and that the scales of justice in his hands were never influenced by sordid or unworthy considerations."

On the 16th of February, Mr. Wright, from the Committee of Claims in the Senate, made the following report: —

"That, previous to the time of Mr. Kendall's holding the office of Postmaster-General, and during a part or the whole of that period, William B. Stokes, and others, were contractors for carrying the United States mails upon certain post-routes; that there came to be a difference between these contractors (usually known by the copartnership name of "Stockton and Stokes") and the Post-Office Department as to the amount due to them for their services as mail contractors; these differences arising, not upon the face of contracts subsisting, or which had been entered into between them and the Department, but principally, if not entirely, from claims presented by the contractors for "extra services," in the common parlance of these transactions; being claims for services alleged to have been rendered by them in carrying the mail above, beyond, and without the service which they had contracted to perform; and allegations on the part of the contractors, that such extra services had been performed under permissions or directions from the Department, with an express or implied promise of the compensation claimed. These claims and allegations were not admitted by Mr. Kendall, as the head of the Department; and payment of the claims was refused by him.

"These transactions, out of which the claims originated, were those which took place while the predecessor of Mr. Kendall was at the head of the Department, and not any contracts, or directions, or permissions, or promises, claimed to have been made or entered into by himself as the Postmaster-General.

"A claim was then interposed by them for the damages they alleged they had sustained by the delay; which, not being paid, they commenced a suit

against Mr. Kendall individually, before the courts of the District of Columbia, to recover the claim. A trial was had, and the contractors recovered a large verdict; the precise amount of which the committee have not, nor is it material that it should be given, inasmuch as the court before which the trial took place, upon a motion made on behalf of Mr. Kendall for the purpose, set aside that verdict, and granted a new trial.

"A second trial has been had before the same court, and a verdict of a second jury given in favor of the contractors, against Mr. Kendall, for the sum of $11,000; as the damages actually sustained by the contractors in consequence of the delay of payment complained of, caused by Mr. Kendall as Postmaster-General, — though the verdict and the judgment upon it is against Amos Kendall, as a private citizen, not against the Postmaster-General.

"Upon the judgment rendered upon this verdict, a writ of error was sued out by Mr. Kendall, and the cause thus carried before the Supreme Court of the United States, where it now is, without argument or decision, and with very little prospect, as the committee learn from the best inquiries they have been able to make, of being reached upon the calendar so as to be argued and decided at the present term of that court.

"The writ of error does not, as a matter of course, suspend proceedings upon the judgment and execution in the court below; and the only way in which it could be made to work that suspension was, for Mr. Kendall to give a bond, with sureties, for the absolute payment of the debt in case the judgment in error should be against him. This he has not felt at liberty to do, as he does not feel an assurance that he could indemnify such sureties in case that judgment should be against him, as the amount is large in proportion to any means he ever had, or now has, and for a consideration which gave him great labor and anxiety and care, and as is now presumptively shown, responsibility also, without adding one dollar, directly or indirectly, to his ability to pay such an amount.

"He has, therefore, while entertaining every confidence that the judgment in error, coming from a tribunal so elevated as the Supreme Court of the United States, will be in his favor, chosen rather to suffer in his personal liberty, so far as a confinement to the prison bounds of this city require, and in his property, so far as he has property within the reach of an execution issued upon the judgment given in the court below, rather than to involve friends in a liability of this singular character, and for this large amount.

"His choice in this respect has been followed by its legal consequences on the part of the contractors, the plaintiffs in the suit against him. An execution has been issued upon the judgment rendered in the court below, notwithstanding the writ of error, and the consequent uncertainty of the entire recovery, and his body has been arrested and imprisoned, and is now in prison within the limits of the liberty of the jail of this city, where it has remained for months, under the most perfect bond with sureties that it shall not move beyond those bounds without rendering the sureties positively liable for the payment of this whole judgment.

"This state of facts has, in the opinion of the committee, roused the public sense, and brought before the Senate the petitions which have been referred to them; and still were it simply this, and could the parties rest where they now

are, until a final decision of the court of last resort upon these strongly litigated and most important questions could be had, the committee would most cheerfully recommend to the Senate that no legislative step be taken to change the relations of the parties, or the interests in the questions involved.

"This has led them to examine the laws of this District under which Mr. Kendall is now in prison, and they find that, if within one year from the day of his confinement, the debt be not paid, or he be not discharged from his confinement as an insolvent debtor, under the laws of Congress applicable to such debtors within this District, it is, by an existing law, made the duty of the marshal, on the day that year shall expire, and notwithstanding his perfectly satisfactory bond and sureties to keep himself within the limits of the jail of this city and county, 'to recommit him to close jail and confinement, there to remain until the debt for which he is charged in execution shall be paid, or until he shall be discharged under the act of Congress for the relief of insolvent debtors within the District of Columbia.'

"Mr. Kendall was committed to the prison bounds upon the execution in favor of these contractors on the 4th day of October now last past, and the year permitted to him to remain a prisoner within these bounds, according to the present state of the law regulating imprisonment for debt within this District, will consequently expire on the 4th day of October next, after which day, unless the Supreme Court shall, by a decision upon the writ of error in his favor during the present term of that court, relieve him, or unless Congress shall interfere, or unless he shall actually pay the debt, or be driven through the process of insolvency, he must be committed 'to close jail and confinement,' and must there remain until he can be relieved in one of these modes.

"Were the demand upon which Mr. Kendall is now confined within the prison bounds, and is liable, after the expiration of one year of that confinement, to be locked up within the walls of the debtor's prison, a debt admitted by him to be justly due and owing, and not a matter resting yet in litigation, and a very novel if not a very doubtful claim, — were it a judgment of the courts, rendered and settled beyond the reach of appeal or review, — the question presented to the committee would be a very different one from that which his case in fact does present; and whatever might, in the opinion of the committee, be the claims of a debtor to relief in the supposed cases, they have felt called upon only to recommend a remedy for the evil and injustice now presented, leaving any further modification of these laws to future legislation.

"They believe the present state of the law regulating imprisonment for debt within this District wrong in principle, and most singularly in conflict with the spirit of the age upon this subject, as well as with the policy of modern legislation in this country.

"The present law intrusts the marking and laying out of the prison bounds within the district to the circuit court thereof; with power, from time to time, to 'renew, enlarge, or diminish the same.' The committee have added a section to their bill to prohibit any alteration of the prison bounds so as to affect that class of prisoners for which they are providing, by declaring that for them respectively those bounds shall be what they were at the times of their respective commitments. This they believe to be right in itself, and to be necessary

to render certain the relief they intend to extend to prisoners circumstanced as those are to be for whom the bill provides; nor do they see that any valid objection can exist against such a modification of this law, as it will leave all the parties in the situations they had themselves assumed, without invitations to make applications to the court, on the one side to enlarge, and on the other to restrict, the prison bounds.

"The committee adopt this mode of relief in the present case, because they think it just in itself, and because they believe it to be inexpedient and improper for Congress to legislate, in any way in reference to the judgment against Mr. Kendall, while the matter remains in the hands of the judiciary.

"The question raised as to his liability, under the circumstances, and the certificate of the jury as to his *bona fide* intentions faithfully to discharge his public duty, is a very delicate and important one, and it is difficult to measure the consequences which may follow from the establishment of this principle, if it shall be established. It may change very materially the relations between the government and its officers and agents and the citizens with and towards whom their responsible duties are to be discharged.

"The question behind that is not less delicate, and may not be less important to the public Treasury. If an officer of the United States, governed by the best intentions, mistakes his duty, by reason of which a citizen is damnified, and he is to be held by the courts liable for such damage in a civil action, prosecuted against him in his individual and private capacity, is the public Treasury to indemnify the officer? This is the question. Although seen to be an important one from its mere statement, reflection and examination will enlarge its influences, direct and consequential, upon the public interest and the administration of the affairs of the government.

"The committee believe that Congress could not now decide this question affirmatively, without imminent danger of influencing in fact the judicial settlement of the former one, — the liability of the officer himself under the circumstances; and it will certainly be early enough, so far as the unfortunate individual himself is concerned, to decide it negatively, after the exigency has risen to call for such action. It has been, therefore, the settled purpose of the committee not to consider either of these questions themselves, and not to recommend any action on the part of Congress which shall bring either of them before it for discussion or action.

"They respectfully ask leave to introduce the bill they have prepared, and recommend its passage.

"*Section 3 of 'An Act to amend the Laws within the District of Columbia.'*

"Sec. 3. And be it further enacted, That the benefit of the prison rules shall not be allowed to any debtor, hereafter taken or charged in execution within the said District, for more than one year from the date of the bond given by him or her for keeping within the said rules; after the expiration of which time, if the person so taken or charged in execution shall not be discharged by due course of law, it shall be the duty of the marshal or other officer, to whose custody such person was committed, to recommit him or her to close jail and confinement, there to remain until the debt for which he or she was taken or charged in execution be paid, or until he or she shall be discharged under the act of Congress for the relief of insolvent debtors within the District of Columbia.

" Section 16 of ' An act for the Relief of Insolvent Debtors within the District of Columbia.'

"Sec. 16. And be it further enacted, That the said court may cause to be marked and laid out, reasonable bounds of the prisons in the said District, to be recorded in the same court; and, from time to time, may renew, enlarge, or diminish the same. And every prisoner not committed for treason or felony, giving such security to keep within the said bounds, as any judge of the said court shall approve, shall have liberty to walk therein, out of the prison, for the preservation of his health; and keeping continually within the said bounds, shall be adjudged in law a true prisoner."

In the New York legislature, Mr. Wheeler, from Delaware county, introduced a resolution which was passed through the House of Representatives with only one or two dissenting voices, and through the Senate by yeas 17, nays 6, in the following form : —

"*Whereas,* Amos Kendall is now confined to the jail limits in the District of Columbia, on execution issued upon a judgment which was rendered against him in favor of William B. Stokes and others, for damages sustained by them in consequence of certain official acts of said Kendall; and whereas, the said acts complained of by said Stokes and others were performed by said Kendall, without any interest other than a desire faithfully to perform the duties of his office of Postmaster-General, and to protect the public interests committed to his charge, —

"*Resolved,* therefore, (if the Senate concur,) That our senators and representatives in Congress be requested to procure, if possible, at the present session of Congress, the passage of such a law as will entirely relieve Amos Kendall from all and every personal responsibility and damage in consequence of a certain judgment rendered against him in favor of William B. Stokes and others.

In the House of Representatives there was not opposition enough to elicit opinions, and little was said beyond a statement of facts by Mr. Wheeler.

In the Senate, it met with opposition from General Root and Mr. Dickinson, and was supported by Mr. Denniston, Mr. Faulkner, and Mr. Hunter. We have room only for short extracts from their remarks.

Mr. Denniston said : —

"Stockton and Stokes presented Mr. Kendall individually for damages, and obtained a judgment of $11,000 against him, for which he was now imprisoned, and, it was understood, unless relieved would soon be incarcerated. This, Mr. Denniston thought, was outrageous, that a public servant should thus suffer for having honestly endeavored to discharge his duty. The subject had been acted upon in the House of Representatives of the United States, and the committee

on claims — seven of whom were Whigs — had reported in favor of relieving Mr. Kendall, by liquidating the judgment. This showed that there was no party feeling on the subject."

Mr. Faulkner said : —

"Of Amos Kendall it was enough to say, that he was admitted by all parties to have been a faithful and vigilant public officer, and to have incurred this liability in the conscientious discharge of his duty."

Mr. Hunter said : —

"He had risen, however, at this time, and with regret, because he found his old friend opposing a resolution which was called for by justice, and demanded by national honor. Yes, sir, (said Mr. H.,) a servant of the republic has been deprived of his freedom, withheld from exercising his talents for the benefit of his family, — has been imprisoned, dishonored, — and why ? Because he fearlessly and faithfully performed the duties of his office. That man was Amos Kendall. He who assumed the duties of his office with unwillingness, because of his feeble health. Who was told by General Jackson, when he declined the appointment, that the condition of the Department occasioned him great anxiety; that there were many who could perform its duties, but "I know that you will." And he did bring order out of chaos; he made that prosperous which was unprosperous before. The whole transaction is disgraceful to the republic, — a blot on its escutcheon, almost without a parallel in the history of nations."

How shall we express our gratitude to the legislature of Maine ? Who would not suffer imprisonment a while for such perpetual testimony to his integrity, patriotism, and zeal in the public service as that body have spread upon the records of their State ? The first intimation we had that such a proceeding was in progress or was intended, was the reception of the following document from the Office of the Secretary of State, namely : —

"STATE OF MAINE.

" Resolved in Favor of Amos Kendall.

"*Resolved,* That while it is the duty of a free government to protect the people from injustice and oppression, it is also bound to sustain and defend its officers and agents in an honest, firm, and rigid discharge of their duties and trusts. That while all infringements of the laws should be visited with merited punishment, reparation of injuries incurred in the conscientious and impartial performance of their official functions should be prompt and complete.

"*Resolved,* That in the execution of his duties as Postmaster-General of the United States, the Honorable Amos Kendall evinced, not only talents of the highest order, but unswerving and unpurchasable integrity, exalted and disinterested patriotism, never tiring industry and zeal for the public weal, and eagle-eyed watchfulness of peculators and swindlers, which have never been

surpassed in the history of this government, and entitle him to the gratitude of the nation.

"*Resolved,* That in resisting what he deemed to be an unjust and exorbitant claim upon the Post-Office Department, for which he is now incarcerated within the jail limits of the city of Washington, Mr. Kendall acted with a single eye to the public good, and with a deep sense of an imperative duty as a public servant.

"*Resolved,* That the rank injustice of suffering a public servant, thus meritorious, to be placed in durance, not for any defalcation or misconduct, but on account of his fidelity to the government, is a stain upon the national honor, which, as far as it can be done by Congress, should be speedily erased.

"*Resolved,* That our Senators in Congress be instructed, and our Representatives requested, to exert all fair and honorable means to have the judgment on which the Honorable Amos Kendall is now imprisoned, for withholding his official sanction to the claim of Stockton and Stokes on the Post-Office Department, cancelled by the Treasurer of the United States, and also to have the said Kendall allowed and paid, from the public treasury, the costs and expenses incurred by him in defending the suit of said Stockton and Stokes against him, together with such further sum for his damages, by reason of said suit and imprisonment, as may be a full remuneration therefor.

"*Resolved,* That a copy of these resolutions be transmitted by the Governor to each of the Senators and Representatives in Congress from this State, and to the President of the Senate and Speaker of the House of Representatives of the United States.

"IN THE HOUSE OF REPRESENTATIVES, February 20, 1843.

"Read and passed.

"DAVID DUNN, *Speaker.*

"IN SENATE, February 21, 1843.

"Read and passed.

"EDWARD KAVANAGH, *President.*

"February 21, 1843.
"Approved.

"JOHN FAIRFIELD, *Governor.*"

THE END.